International Economic Transactions

Studies in Income and Wealth
Volume 55

National Bureau of Economic Research
Conference on Research in Income and Wealth

International Economic Transactions

Issues in Measurement and Empirical Research

Edited by **Peter Hooper and J. David Richardson**

The University of Chicago Press

Chicago and London

PETER HOOPER is assistant director of the Division of International
Finance, Board of Governors of the Federal Reserve System. J. DAVID
RICHARDSON is professor of economics at Syracuse University and a
research associate of the National Bureau of Economic Research.

The University of Chicago Press, Chicago 60637
The University of Chicago Press, Ltd., London

© 1991 by the National Bureau of Economic Research
All rights reserved. Published 1991
Printed in the United States of America
00 99 98 97 96 95 94 93 92 91   5 4 3 2 1

ISBN 0–226–35135–1

Library of Congress Cataloging-in-Publication Data

International economic transactions : issues in measurement and
  empirical research / edited by Peter Hooper and J. David Richardson.
      p.   cm. — (Studies in income and wealth; v. 55).
    Includes bibliographical references and index.
    1. International economic relations—Statistical methods.
  I. Hooper, Peter.   II. Richardson, J. David.   III. Series.
  HC106.3.C714   vol. 55
  [HF1359]
  330 s—dc20
  [337]   91-29567
                                                              CIP

⊗The paper used in this publication meets the minimum requirements of
the American National Standard for Information Sciences—Permanence
of Paper for Printed Library Materials, ANSI Z39.48–1984.

Contents

Prefatory Note

Preliminary versions of the papers and discussions contained in this volume were presented at two conferences, held in August 1988 in Cambridge, Massachusetts, and November 1989 in Washington, D.C. Funds for these conferences were provided to the National Bureau of Economic Research by the National Science Foundation through grant SES-8821944. Funding of the Conference on Research in Income and Wealth series is now provided by the Bureau of the Census, the Bureau of Economic Analysis, the Bureau of Labor Statistics, Statistics Canada, the Department of Energy, and the Statistics Division of the Internal Revenue Service. We are indebted to all of them for their support. We also thank Geoffrey Carliner and Charles R. Hulten for critical advice throughout the project, and the referees for critical advice on the final manuscript.

Executive Committee, November 1989

Charles Hulten, chair	Zvi Griliches, NBER
Ernst Berndt	representative
Geoffrey Carliner, NBER	Stanley Lebergott
representative	Robert Lipsey
Christopher Clague	Robert Parker
Irwin Diewert	Frank de Leeuw
Robert Gillingham	Marilyn Manser
Claudia Goldin	

Volume Editors' Acknowledgments

The financial support of the National Science Foundation, through the specific support of grant SES-8821944 for this particular conference, is gratefully acknowledged. Special thanks are due Robert Allison, Kirsten Foss Davis, and Ilana Hardesty of the NBER for considerable efforts with administrative arrangements. Finally, thanks are due to Ann Brown, also of the NBER, and to Julie McCarthy of the University of Chicago Press for invaluable assistance in the editorial process.

Introduction

Peter Hooper and J. David Richardson

The growing economic interdependence of the world economy, including the internationalization of markets for goods, services, financial assets, and factors of production, is creating increasing demand for the measurement and monitoring of economic influences across national boundaries. The international repercussions of sharp policy shifts and structural changes over the last two decades have rendered obsolete conventions of closed-economy measurement and assessment. Empirical research in open-economy economics has increased substantially in scope and magnitude over this period. In addition, fluctuating exchange rates, growing external imbalances, mounting U.S. net international indebtedness, and wide swings in financial markets across countries have stimulated international consultation and cooperation in the formulation of economic policies. These developments in research and policy analysis necessarily have depended increasingly on the monitoring and measurement of international transactions.

At the same time, concern is growing among professional economists in the research and policy communities (Juster 1988, Cole 1990, Lipsey 1990) that existing international economic data have not kept fully abreast of structural changes in the global economy and that they are in need of critical assessment, and in some cases significant overhaul. Federal budget support of data collection and maintenance has declined in real dollars over the past ten years. Methodological research and new ideas for measurement have borne the brunt of budget cutbacks. Lack of adequate data has inhibited empirical research of the highest quality in some areas of international economics, and ruling theoretical paradigms have not been tested sufficiently. While the same concern exists for economic measurement and research more generally (Miron and

Peter Hooper is assistant director of the Division of International Finance, Board of Governors of the Federal Reserve System. J. David Richardson is professor of economics at Syracuse University and a research associate of the National Bureau of Economic Research.

Romer 1990, Norwood 1990, Triplett 1990), the relative severity of the concern for international economics is generally acknowledged to be growing.

For these reasons, a conference was convened in November 1989, drawing together researchers, policy analysts, and statistical experts with proven commitments to measurement and empirical research in international economics. The objective of the conference, a preconference workshop, and this volume of proceedings is to publicize research that evaluates the scope and quality of existing data, explores the value of developing new or improved data, and more generally advances measurement, policy assessment, and knowledge of international transactions. In meeting this objective, the organizers tried to stimulate dialogue between the producers of the data and the users, so that each party would become better aware of the needs of and the constraints on the other party. The dialogue can be read in the words of the authors, discussants, and panelists presented in this volume.

Each author was asked to address an important research issue in international economics and to employ existing or constructed data in ways that revealed its advantages and inadequacies, with possible suggestions for enhancing the advantages and reducing the inadequacies. Given these objectives, papers were expected to differ naturally in methodological intensity, policy relevance and familiarity with the intricacies of measurement.

The papers and discussion presented in this volume are organized into the following five topic areas: merchandise trade flows, trade prices and price competitiveness, international transactions in services, foreign direct investment, and international comparisons of outputs and inputs. The volume concludes with the remarks of three distinguished panelists who were asked to draw summary observations from both the papers and the discussion at the conference.

In the remainder of this introduction we first summarize each paper and discussant's comments, stressing measurement issues that are raised and important conclusions that are drawn from the existing data. We then size up the project as a whole and identify possible issues for the future, drawing on the commentary of the concluding panel and discussion at the conference.

Part I   Merchandise Trade

The first paper dealing with merchandise trade is "Comparing International Trade Data and Product and National Characteristics Data for the Analysis of Trade Models," by Keith E. Maskus. Maskus illustrates the capabilities and problems of data used in estimating models of international trade and production of goods based on national factor endowments. He demonstrates the value of data improvements such as standardized concordances, mutually consistent price deflators for inputs, outputs, and trade, and breakdowns of sectoral labor inputs by occupational groups.

Using improved data, he compares indicators of productivity and technology across countries. International comparisons of labor productivity can differ significantly depending on whether outputs are translated into common currencies using nominal exchange rates or relative prices (PPPs), as Kravis and Lipsey document further in their own contribution to this volume. Comparisons based on nominal exchange rates suggest that for many industries there is little similarity in labor productivities among countries at different stages of development, whereas PPP-based comparisons suggest that labor productivities are similar across different stages of development, but can vary significantly across countries at the same stage of development. On balance, the technology comparisons across countries using PPPs provide some support for the familiar view that trade is caused by factor endowment differences across countries with access to similar technologies. Yet Maskus's regressions attempting to explain net trade by industry on this basis are not notably successful. Maskus concludes, inter alia, that measures of relative factor shares are not cyclically sensitive, whereas measures of factor productivity are, and he closes his paper with a helpful discussion of ways to improve the measures of determinants of competitive and comparative advantage.

Edward E. Leamer, in his discussion of the paper, emphasizes the dependence of analysis on the quality of measurement. At one level, this dependence is, of course, obvious. Leamer argues at a deeper level that to correct for econometric misspecification caused by measurement error in the data, it is necessary to know the specific properties of the measurement error. Since exact knowledge is unlikely, data collections ought to provide data analysts not only with estimated rates of measurement error, but with estimates of the sampling distribution of the estimated measurement error as well—the "standard errors of the standard errors," as he says, citing a paper stimulated by the conference (Leamer 1989).

Ellen E. Meade, in "Computers and the Trade Deficit: The Case of the Falling Prices," considers how the measurement, modeling, and forecasting of U.S. merchandise trade flows has been affected by new measures of computer prices. Meade begins by reviewing the hedonic (or quality adjusted) price index constructed by the Bureau of Economic Analysis (BEA) for domestic shipments of computers and its application to international trade. In doing so, she compares BEA's computer price index with price indexes for U.S. exports and imports of computers reported by the Bureau of Labor Statistics (BLS). Movements in aggregate U.S. trade quantities and prices (or deflators) differ significantly depending on which measure of computer prices is used. While the hedonic index is a step forward in the measurement of computer prices, the lack of distinction between imports, exports, and domestic shipments still represents a major drawback to the BEA data.

Meade also concludes that on BEA's measure, price and quantity movements in the computer sector have been sufficiently atypical that the sector probably should be isolated from the aggregate of other sectors when attempting to model and forecast trade. In empirical tests with a conventional model of U.S. trade flows, both in-sample and post-sample prediction of aggregate trade flows are improved when computers are treated separately. Most of this improvement stems from trade quantity equations, as key parameters in trade price equations appear to be insensitive to the inclusion of computers.

In his discussion of the paper, Richard D. Haas asks whether information gleaned from BLS data on the prices of imports and exports of computers might be used to adjust the domestic price series reported by BEA. He also suggests that in light of difficulties involved in estimating equations for trade in computers, improvements in modeling and forecasting trade in noncomputers could well be masked in the aggregate prediction results that are reported.

Bruce C. Walter, in "Quality Issues Affecting the Compilation of the U.S. Merchandise Trade Statistics," summarizes recent efforts by the Census Bureau and the Customs Service to improve the quality of U.S. trade data. The various efforts have included reducing lags (carryover) in the recording of monthly data, computerizing the editing and checking of data for consistency and measurement errors, auditing data collection operations at various ports, reconciling U.S. bilateral trade data with Canadian trade data (as well as data of other trading partners), calculating constant-dollar equivalents for monthly exports and imports, and developing the capacity to record data by business establishment, state of origin, destination, and intracorporate transactions. Some of these efforts have been funded by subscribers to the data, rather than out of general tax revenues. Among other findings, Walter reports that about 70,000 different establishments export each month, but that only 5 percent of them account for 40 percent of export value. Walter also discusses possible further improvements in the data and data collection efforts, including the need for further automation.

David J. Klock's comments on the paper question the need for the reporting of monthly trade data in real terms when scarce resources could be more profitably devoted elsewhere, although he does recognize the potential for more timely analysis of U.S. international competitiveness made possible by monthly volume and price data for trade. Klock also doubts that data reconciliation efforts with Europe and Japan would be as useful as those with Canada have been; a reconciliation effort with Mexico might offer greater potential.

Part II Trade Prices and Price Competitiveness

The first of two papers dealing primarily with trade prices and price competitiveness is "Price Trends in U.S. Trade: New Data, New Insights," by William Alterman. Alterman documents the ongoing development of true export and import price indexes at BLS. The coverage of merchandise trade prices has been virtually complete for imports since late 1982 and for exports since late 1983. Price indexes for selected categories of trade in services are being developed currently, with some country-of-origin indexes planned for 1992. Alterman illustrates how much the BLS price indexes for merchandise trade differ from the unit value indexes that they recently replaced in the National Income Accounts. For example, the BLS series is much more stable than the volatile unit value series. And its implications for trade volumes are quite different. Alterman calculates that the U.S. trade deficit in real terms (measured at 1985 prices) was running at an annual rate of just about $100 billion in mid-1989 when deflated by the BLS price indexes, compared with nearly $130 billion when deflated by unit value indexes.

Alterman uses the BLS price data to analyze the rate at which U.S. and foreign exporters "pass through" changes in exchange rates into the prices of U.S. exports and imports. He finds that rates of exchange-rate pass-through vary significantly across different commodity categories and that firms are more likely to raise the prices they charge (in terms of the currency of the country they are selling to) following a depreciation of their own currency than they are to lower their prices following an appreciation. He also finds that U.S. firms tend to pass through more of exchange-rate changes to their prices in foreign markets than foreign firms do to their prices in the U.S. market (consistent with the findings of Lipsey, Molinari, and Karvis, at least for the post-1985 period). Alterman also uses some data that became available as a byproduct of the BLS price collection effort to assess the currency invoicing of various categories of U.S. imports. He finds that an increasing proportion of U.S. imports is now priced in foreign currency—as much as half of imports of certain finished goods, particularly from Western Europe.

In his discussion of the paper, Richard C. Marston notes that Alterman's analysis serves not only to establish the superiority of the BLS price indexes, but also to indicate how misleading it may be to use historical unit values which were the only trade "prices" available until the early 1980s. With respect to Alterman's calculation of pass-through estimates, Marston questions the use of consumer prices as a proxy for costs in foreign countries. The insensitivity of consumer prices to movements in costs may have imparted a significant downward bias to the pass-through estimates. While data are limited for many countries, Marston would have preferred to see wholesale prices used in place of consumer prices wherever possible.

Robert E. Lipsey, Linda Molinari, and Irving B. Kravis in "Measures of Prices and Price Competitiveness in International Trade in Manufactured Goods," use disaggregated national price indexes for traded manufactures to construct indexes of export and domestic prices and indexes of price competitiveness for the United States, Germany, and Japan. Indexes of price competitiveness are constructed for each country with its own export weights vis-à-vis similarly weighted indexes for its major competitors, aggregated by their importance in world export markets. Price indexes are also constructed for total exports of developed countries and for the exports of developed countries to developing countries. These last indexes are adjusted for differential quality change, and domestic wholesale prices and hedonic price indexes are used to fill gaps where appropriate export price data are missing. To estimate prices that are missing entirely, the authors fit a regression equation with country-specific and commodity-specific dummy variables to a block of countries and commodities. In doing so, they use all available data to establish coefficients that can be used to form a "best-bet" prediction of the missing prices. This procedure eliminates a potentially important source of bias that arises in more conventional procedures, which use national prices indexes alone as proxies for the missing prices and disregard the availability of more closely related product prices in other countries.

The authors' painstaking construction of reliable price indexes pays off in some surprising observations. For example, over several periods during the past four decades, movements in both German and Japanese export prices relative to those of their major competitors tended to be more in line with those of the United States than had been thought previously. At the same time, the authors find very limited evidence for "pricing to market" (adjusting the margin between export prices and domestic prices to offset the effects of fluctuations in exchange rates). Except for the period after 1985 when German and Japanese export prices fell significantly relative to their domestic prices as their currencies were appreciating, only mild traces of such behavior have occurred since the 1950s.

Among other contributions, Lipsey, Molinari, and Kravis summarize correlations suggesting the frequency of supply shifts along relatively stable demand curves for major categories of trade in most manufactures (except semimanufactures, SITC 6), and they include tabular presentations of their raw export prices for other researchers to use.

Catherine L. Mann's discussion points out first how occasionally the "full-information" country/commodity dummy approach to correcting for missing values may cause measurement errors in recorded data to infect the proxies. Yet she also thinks that omission of typically low-cost Asian developing countries from the approach may impart systematic upward bias to the indexes that are constructed. Finally, she reminds the reader of the important potential divergences between indexes of international price competitiveness, which are the focus of this paper, and indexes of international cost competitiveness. Measures of relative international costs are of course rare and incomplete. However, the growing analytical literature on price-cost margins and how they respond optimally to exchange rates and other shocks, can be used to impute rough cost indexes from price indexes, and in any case can provide several alternative interpretations of any given price movement, each with a distinct policy implication.

Part III   Service Transactions

The first paper on international transactions in services is "Developing a Data System for International Sales of Services: Progress, Problems, and Prospects," by Bernard Ascher and Obie G. Whichard. Ascher and Whichard document the substantial improvements in statistics on international transactions in services that have been achieved over the past decade through the improvement of existing surveys, the introduction of new surveys, the increased use of gross recording methods, and the adoption of indirect estimation methods in areas where survey data are still not available. Such areas as financial, legal, medical, educational, and other professional and technical services, which a decade ago were largely uncovered, as well as services transactions with foreign affiliates, which were obscured by net recording, are now included and accounted for more than one-fourth of the measured total of U.S. trade in services of $175 billion in 1988.

Ascher and Whichard also stress the importance of improvements in measuring within-country or "establishment" transactions, between firms owned by residents of different countries and local purchasers. Measured establishment transactions by U.S. firms abroad and by foreign firms in the United States actually exceeded total U.S. cross-border transactions or trade in services in 1988. While the establishment transactions are not technically "international," they are closely related to issues in cross-border trade such as market access, reciprocity, and national treatment. They are also potentially a close substitute for cross-border trade, as discussed in the paper by Stekler and Stevens. Ascher and Whichard conclude with a review of the significant problems that remain in the measurement of international sales of services and the prospects for resolving some of these difficulties.

Samuel Pizer cautions against confusing statistics on international transactions in services, which are used in the balance of payments and national income accounts, with data on the transactions of affiliates established in foreign countries, which are an aspect of direct investment activities. Both types of data are important in their own contexts. He notes that the United States is ahead of most other countries in its coverage of trade in services and that it is the only country to date that has begun to collect data on the service sector establishments of multinational corporations.

Bernard M. Hoekman and Robert M. Stern, in "Evolving Patterns of Trade and Investment in Services," evaluate both international trade and direct investment in various services with data covering the past twenty-five years for a large number of countries. They find that developing countries are gaining world export shares in shipping, travel, passenger services, and other private services. Moreover, the services exports of the developing countries have been growing faster than merchandise exports for most of the past twenty-five years. Trade in financial and business services, however, remains a fairly stable and exclusive turf for developed countries. Similarly, until very recently most foreign direct investment (FDI) in services was between developed countries. Furthermore, FDI in services has been growing faster than FDI in manufacturing; because of higher trade barriers, it is larger relative to trade flows that FDI in manufacturing.

The tables in the Hoekman and Stern paper contain a wealth of country detail over five-year intervals, although the categories presented are rather aggregated, based on what is available in balance of payments accounts. The authors also make several recommendations for improvement in the data, relating to nomenclature, coverage, and presentation of detail on origin/destination, value/volume, and intrafirm versus arms length transactions. With respect to coverage, Hoekman and Stern document important but unsampled categories such as transborder data flows, health provision, and education.

Samuel Pizer commends the authors wryly for their heroic compilations and their attempt to test an important hypothesis. He believes that there is ample scope for more disaggregated and focused measurement of selected services but warns against using the very broad content of "services" to evaluate the role of service in development, citing cases in which the developing country was merely the locus for offshore finance. He also notes that studies of trade in services might be more reliably tied to data on domestic developments, with the foreign sector measured separately, or on surveys of direct foreign investors, rather than on the balance of payments data used by Hoekman and Stern.

Part IV   Foreign Direct Investment

The first of two papers on foreign direct investment is "Financial Flows versus Capital Spending: Alternative Measures of U.S.-Canadian Investment and Trade in the Analysis of Taxes," by Harry Grubert and John Mutti. They examine how much U.S.-affiliate investment activity in Canada, as measured either by balance of payments financial flows or by plant and equipment expenditures, is influenced by U.S. and Canadian tax policy. They also consider the extent to which real capital formation in the Canadian manufacturing sector is financed by U.S. direct investors. In addition to comparing real and financial investment data, their paper makes one of the few attempts in this volume to construct alternative measures of policy. One of their contributions is to show cases in which *average* effective tax rates, in addition to *marginal* effective tax rates, have empirical explanatory power. Another is to show the superior explanatory power of marginal tax rates when investors are assumed to require a real rate of return as much as double the normally assumed rate of 4 percent.

Grubert and Mutti find that taxes significantly influence real business fixed investment by U.S. affiliates, but not necessarily the financial measures of FDI. They also find that U.S. multinational firms account for a large share of the responsiveness of aggregate Canadian real manufacturing investment to tax rates. Capital formation by U.S. multinationals is estimated to be twice as sensitive to taxes as capital formation by other firms in Canada. U.S. merchandise exports to Canada also appear to be sensitive to tax incentives such as the U.S. provision for Foreign Sales Corporations.

Edward M. Graham reinterprets Grubert's and Mutti's distinction between a multinational's real capital formation and its FDI in a constructive, yet empirically undocumented, way. He hypothesizes that the two alternative investment measures are highly correlated for new investors in greenfield projects, but not otherwise, either for established investors or for takeovers or expansions of preexisting projects. Thus Graham is unsurprised that Grubert and Mutti find real capital formation in Canada more responsive to taxes than balance-of-payments FDI. Direct investors in Canada are established veterans. He hypothesizes that balance-of-payments FDI would be much more responsive to taxes (and other real fundamentals) in the case of impending first investments in new host countries—Eastern Europe perhaps—or formerly insular debtor countries.

Lois Stekler and Guy V. G. Stevens, in "The Adequacy of U.S. Direct Investment Data," review the history and current status of BEA's system for collecting direct investment data and assess various questions that have been raised in the profession about the coverage and accuracy of these data. They conclude that there seems little reason to doubt that BEA's surveys capture most direct investment transactions and that the basic data on direct investment income and capital flows are reasonably accurate, to the extent that they reflect the reporters' books. However, the accuracy of answers to survey questions pertaining to information that is not normally kept on the books of the reporters is likely to be much more variable. Moreover, late reporting, particularly by foreign-owned U.S. firms, periodically has resulted in large data revisions in the direct investment accounts.

Stekler and Stevens also review the problems associated with data on the U.S. net direct investment asset position and various efforts to estimate that position more accurately, as well as reasons for wide differences in apparent rates of return on direct investment holdings in the United States and abroad. They argue that surveys would be ineffective in trying to establish market values of direct investment holdings at home and abroad, and that scarce resources available for improvements in data in this area should be devoted to other efforts. One alternative they propose is to determine why the reported rate of return on foreign investments in the United States is so low.

The paper also assesses the adequacy of direct investment data for analyzing such questions as the implications of direct investment for merchandise trade, the welfare implications of direct investment, and the modeling and forecasting of direct investment transactions. The authors conclude that study of such empirical research issues would benefit significantly from a greater availability of data at the establishment level.

Betty L. Barker comments on the feasibility of implementing the recommendations for data enhancements that are made in the paper, and she discusses some of the improvements that are either planned or under way at BEA. Data on foreign investment in the United States at the establishment level will be published by BEA in mid-1992, as a result of legislation that has been passed giving BEA access to Census establishment data for foreign-owned U.S. companies. Obtaining accurate data on U.S. investment abroad at the establishment level will be more difficult, however. BEA is constructing market-value estimates of the U.S. direct investment position abroad and the foreign direct investment position in the United States, using indirect estimation methods rather than surveys; these estimates were published in the June 1991 *Survey of Current Business*. BEA has also obtained funding for 1991 and beyond to improve compliance with its surveys and to increase its research capabilities.

Part V   International Comparisons of Output and Inputs

The first of three papers dealing with international comparisons of outputs and inputs is Robert Z. Lawrence's "Issues in Measurement and International Comparison of Output Growth in Manufacturing." Lawrence addresses questions that have been raised by Lawrence Mishel and others about whether the relative international performance of U.S. output in manufacturing has been overstated in U.S. data as a result of improper weighting of computers and the use of domestic prices to deflate imported inputs, among other factors. Lawrence finds that while U.S. manufacturing and productivity growth was overstated during the early 1980s, this bias was largely reversed after 1985 when the downtrend in the relative price of imported inputs was reversed. He concludes that although BEA's data may somewhat overstate manufacturing output growth over the 1980s, manufacturing did not decline appreciably as a share of GNP.

Lawrence also documents a dramatic cross-industry dispersion of measured growth rates in both the United States and Japan, in which computers are an outlier on the high side. Since the rise in U.S. aggregate manufacturing output has been concentrated in only a few sectors, Lawrence notes that inference should be made with caution. A perferable approach might be to make comparisons at the industry level. However, two alternative sources of data on industry growth rates (GNP and industrial production) show very different patterns of cross-industry dispersion in both the United States and Japan. Lawrence argues that anomalies like this one and the mismeasurement of input prices would be greatly alleviated by more timely publication of input-output tables and by calculation of imported input price indexes with the same levels of disaggregation as the input-output tables.

Lawrence Mishel notes that in response to criticism of its manufacturing output data, BEA suspended publication of the data until it could be thoroughly revised. His estimates suggest that U.S. manufacturing output did decline significantly as a share of GNP during the 1980s, partly because, by his calculations, the shift in the relative prices of imported inputs after 1985 was not enough to reverse the bias that had accumulated earlier. Mishel also notes that little comfort can be taken in the fact that the Federal Reserve Board's industrial production series happens to have moved about in line with BEA's series on total manufacturing output, because the two series show such wide divergences at the industry level.

Barry Eichengreen presents a lucid review of the debate between Lawrence and Mishel, and he concludes that the data are still too fragile to pick a winner. It does seem clear that when computers are excluded, U.S. manufacturing output has weakened relative to activity elsewhere. However, Eichengreen argues that from the point of view of the international competitiveness of U.S. manufacturing as a whole, we probably should not be concerned about a decline in one sector (noncomputers) if it is offset by a rise in another (computers).

[Editors' note: In January 1991, BEA published revised estimates of U.S. manufacturing output after addressing some of the criticisms raised by Mishel and others. The revision resulted in a slightly slower rate of growth in manufacturing output during the 1980s. However, the revised estimates still show a moderate increase in the share of manufacturing in total output between the late 1970s and 1988. See De Leeuw, Mohr, and Parker (1991).]

John F. Helliwell and Alan Chung, in "Macroeconomic Convergence: International Transmission of Growth and Technical Progress," consider, among other issues, whether international transactions have influenced the convergence of technical progress among industrial countries. Using a measure of labor productivity as a proxy for technology in a sample of nineteen industrial countries, they find evidence of convergence in rates of growth of technology since 1960. Moreover, they attribute a portion of the explanatory power in their regressions to rapid growth in the ratio of trade to GDP, consistent with recent theoretical research that describes the potential for openness to enhance variety, productivity, and competitive performance in input markets. The authors also find evidence in some countries to suggest that technical progress is capital-embodied. Based on this finding and on the importance of openness effects, they conclude that the rates of generation and diffusion of technical progress are endogenous rather than exogenous, and hence can be influenced by a variety of factors affecting international linkages.

On measurement issues, in the spirit of work by Maskus and Kravis and Lipsey presented elsewhere in this volume, Helliwell and Chung test the use of both PPPs and nominal exchange rates to translate real outputs or productivities into common currency units. They find that the convergence results are strengthened when theoretically preferred PPPs are used. They also find that a narrow measure of capital, the private fixed stock of business capital, gives better results in explaining output than broader measures that include residential capital, public capital, or inventories.

Irving Kravis and Robert E. Lipsey, in "The International Comparison Program: Current Status and Problems," report on the history, purpose, and present status of the International Comparison Program (ICP), which is aimed at correcting for relative price differences across countries in the measurement of comparative levels of national output. They summarize the now-familiar finding that real incomes per person are much higher in low-income countries when sectoral outputs are valued at a set of "world prices" common to all countries (PPPs) than when simpler exchange-rate conversions are employed Less familiar is their finding that the Gerschenkron effect accounts for only about one-sixth of the 60 percent average difference between PPP and nominal exchange-rate conversions.

A significant innovation in this paper is the calculation of margins of error for the estimates of per capita income levels at world prices. Uncertainty in the estimates results from such factors as sampling error in the collection of price data, problems of quality comparison, and the presence of "comparison-resistant" expenditure categories, particularly among such services as health, education, and government. Uncertainty ranges are calculated by considering a plausible set of alternative methodologies for estimating comparative benchmark income levels. The results show margins of uncertainty on the order of 20 to 25 percent for lower-income countries and less than 10 percent for high income countries. These margins of uncertainty are considerably smaller than the deviations from benchmark estimates obtained by exchange-rate–based conversions. The authors challenge the widespread assumption that the conversions via the exchange rate are robust because, unlike the PPP-based conversions, they are not subject to variation depending on the methodological choices adopted for their calculation. The authors show that the results of exchange-rate conversions are, if anything, more sensitive to methodology than the PPP conversions. The authors end their paper with a number of suggestions for improving the methods of estimating comparative national performance and for extrapolating estimates to cover nonbenchmark countries.

Alan V. Deardorff emphasizes in his commentary the wide usefulness of the price and other measurements generated in the ICP. He also echoes Edward Leamer's plea for better integration of measurement with theory, pointing out the relevance to ICP calculations of the economic theory of index numbers and the econometric theory of missing data.

Deardorff closes his commentary with a speculation that the familiar ICP conclusion that developing-country prices are lower at prevailing exchange rates than comparable developed-country prices is incorrect. Since the lower developing-country prices apply to both tradable and nontradable goods, Deardorff hypothesizes that the apparent price differences might actually reflect real product differentiation by nations, with developing-country goods being typically lesser-quality varieties. If that were the case, the equally familiar ICP conclusion that real GDPs of developing countries are understated would be suspect—a product of neglecting generalized quality differences. This speculation assumes that the major effort of the ICP field work—to compare prices for goods of equal quality—ultimately failed to capture all quality differences. However, explanations for lower price levels in low-income countries on other grounds have been offered.

Concluding Observations

The concluding panelists, Robert E. Baldwin, Jack Bame, and Ralph C. Bryant, generally commended the timeliness of the efforts to blend perspectives on data and research in trade, services, and direct investment. They also underscored the overall thrust of the project, endorsing the desire to address both analytical and measurement needs and opportunities, with its concomitant interchange between data producers and users, between government, academic, and business professionals, and between specialists in international data and domestic data.

Bryant observed that data on international transactions are international public goods, and that international collaboration on the content of the conference would be highly desirable. Over time, Bryant remarked, both governments and analysts may want to support coordinated compilations of data by representative international organizations such as the World Bank. Bame documented some of the more successful of these efforts: the harmonized merchandise trade system, the drafting of the fifth edition of the IMF's *Balance of Payments Manual,* the U.N.'s revision of the System of National Accounts (SNA), and the work of the OECD and Eurostat on international services transactions.

Baldwin observed similarly that comparable trade, production, and input data are a *national* public good, and argued for better coordination across data-collection agencies to that end (see also Triplett 1990). Baldwin also observed that changing technologies and types of goods traded may make the idea of measuring at the "border" less relevant, and the idea of sampling firms in some randomly representative way the wave of the future. On this theme Baldwin and Bame cautioned that events may overtake principle, if and as border measurement is abolished within the European Community and possibly between Canada and the United States.

Bame observed, and Bryant seconded, the need for future consideration of data on international financial transactions. In principle, an entire volume could be devoted to this need. As Bryant detailed, the ideal might include "a breakdown of the balance sheets of financial institutions in all the important national jurisdictions, cross-classified by currency of denomination, residence of customer, and type of customer, . . . data on cross-border security transactions and the corresponding stock asset and liability positions, . . . substantial information about [off-balance-sheet items] as well, . . . [and] systematic international compilations of these data."

A number of points arose in general discussion. One was the value of researchers having confidential access to confidential data, recognizing the trade-off between such access and the willingness of private-sector actors to provide such data. Another was the need for monitoring agencies, such as corporate controllers' offices and the Office of Management and Budget, to be more sensitive to the benefits as well as burdens of data provision. Still another was the agenda's underrepresentation of some potentially important international transactions, such as financial capital movements, migration and remittances, and the meaning of large and volatile statistical discrepancies.

References

Cole, Rosanne. 1990. Reviving the Federal Statistical System: A View from Industry. *American Economic Review* 80 (May): 333–36.

De Leeuw, Frank, Michael Mohr, and Robert P. Parker. 1991. Gross Product by Industry, 1977–88: A Progress Report on Improving the Estimates. U.S. Department of Commerce Bureau of Economic Analysis, *Survey of Current Business* 71 (January): 23–37.

Juster, F. Thomas. 1988. The State of U.S. Economic Statistics: Current and Prospective Quality, Policy Needs, and Resources. Paper presented at the Fiftieth Anniversary Conference of the Conference on Research in Income and Wealth. Washington, D.C. May 12–14.

Leamer, Edward E. 1989. We Need Standard Errors of the Standard Errors of the Measurement Errors of Our Data. Typescript.

Lipsey, Robert E. 1990. Reviving the Federal Statistical System: International Aspects. *American Economic Review* 80 (May): 337–40.

Miron, Jeffrey A., and Christina D. Romer. 1990. Reviving the Federal Statistical System: The View from Academia. *American Economic Review* 80 (May): 329–32.

Norwood, Janet L. 1990. Distinguished Lecture on Economics in Government: Data Quality and Public Policy. *Journal of Economic Perspectives* 4 (Spring): 3–12.

Triplett, Jack E. 1990. Reviving the Federal Statistical System: A View from Within. *American Economic Review* 80 (May): 341–44.

I   Merchandise Trade

1   Comparing International Trade Data and Product and National Characteristics Data for the Analysis of Trade Models

Keith E. Maskus

1.1   Introduction

Empirical analysis of international trade models is a crude art. In part, this situation is due to the difficulty of articulating fully general trade theories that are amenable to rigorous testing with observable data. The empirical analyst is generally left making uncomfortable choices among functional forms, variable definition, and the like, in the hope of achieving a tolerable approximation of underlying economic relationships. The nature and validity of statistical inference in this context are often unclear (Leamer 1984).

A further difficulty, however, lies in the availability, quality, and comparability of international data needed to undertake trade analysis. This problem is literally huge. With the simultaneous existence of many countries and many competing trade theories (each theory with its suggested set of variables, aggregation levels, and so on), the researcher is faced with an enormous data-collection task in a comprehensive analysis. There is also the need to reconcile figures across the statistical reporting systems of countries or multilateral agencies. It is apparent that measurement problems and lack of full comparability across units (e.g., countries, industries, time) are likely to be endemic in empirical trade analysis.

This paper is focused on these data problems. Its main purpose is to illustrate several empirical hurdles that the researcher must surmount in assembling the data needed for a typical analytical project. In that regard, the paper resembles an extensive data appendix; the level of detail would in most studies be relegated to an uninformative page of supplementary text.

Keith E. Maskus is associate professor of economics at the University of Colorado, Boulder.

The author is grateful to Edward Leamer, J. David Richardson, and other conference participants for their comments.

The objective is to illustrate the major data-related problems facing the researcher in a particular area of trade analysis: models of production and trade inspired mainly by the factor-proportions theory. Because the thrust of the paper is on data issues, no attempt is made here to develop new analytical or econometric approaches to this branch of trade theory. Rather, I employ straightforward data analysis and descriptive devices to elucidate a variety of problems that surface in a typical research project: exchange-rate translation, adjustments for cyclicality, and measurement error.

The analysis begins in the next section with brief comments on developing an estimating framework from the factor-proportions model. That model predicts certain relationships among three types of economic variables across countries: technology, as embodied in factor intensities or factor productivities by industry; international trade; and factor endowments. Accordingly, in the subsequent three sections I consider data problems that emerge in separate forms of analysis found in the literature. I further use this tripartite split of empirical models to illustrate three significant data issues that surface in trade analysis. First, in section 1.3, I present indicators of technology similarity across 28 countries and 28 manufacturing industries in 1984, where these indicators are simply measures of factor productivity. The supplementary concern in this section is with the choice of market or purchasing-power-parity (PPP) exchange rates to translate factor productivities into a common currency. It happens that this choice makes a substantial difference in computing direct measures of labor productivity but does not fundamentally change international rankings of total factor productivity. Second, in section 1.4, I compute correlations between trade performance and factor intensities in each country across the set of manufacturing sectors. These correlations are taken mainly to be descriptive indicators of the input basis of international competitiveness. The supplementary consideration relates to the cyclicality of trade and intensity measures, which I examine with U.S. and Japanese data. The results suggest that factor shares are insensitive to cyclical influences, but that labor productivity varies over the business cycle. Third, in section 1.5, I estimate functions relating net exports in each industry to endowments across 38 countries, the model most closely suggested by the factor-proportions theory. Attention is paid there to the econometric issues of unequal error variances and measurement errors. The analysis suggests that inference in the trade-and-endowments model is sensitive to the existence of these problems.

I note here that the generic problems mentioned—exchange-rate measurement, cyclicality, and measurement errors—are neither exhaustive of potential difficulties nor unique to the models in which each is considered. Their empirical applications are limited here primarily to contain within reasonable bounds the volume of results to be reported. This study is highly data-intensive and yields a quantity of outcomes that likely will tax the patience of many readers. Further, the focus is on data problems, which I believe are adequately presented in the framework chosen.

1.2   Comments on Estimating Factor-Proportions Trade Models

To establish context for the data analysis, I begin with some comments on the state of the literature on empirical estimation of factor-proportions models (for recent reviews of this enormous literature see Deardorff 1984 and Leamer 1984). Interest centers on general variants of the model, with many goods, factors, and countries. The standard empirical framework has become that introduced by Leamer and Bowen (1981), based on Vanek's (1968) contribution.

Allow T_i to denote the vector of net exports across commodities for country i, A_i its matrix of total factor intensities, V_i its vector of endowments, s_i its share of world consumption, and V_w the vector of world factor endowments. Then equation system (1) follows immediately:

$$(1) \qquad T_i = A_i^{-1}(V_i - s_i V_w).$$

These equations state that commodity trade is a function of excess factor supplies, assuming the inverse matrix exists. This relationship depends not only on the distribution of endowments across countries, but also on different technologies and consumption patterns.

The Heckscher-Ohlin model places numerous restrictions on these relationships in order to focus strictly on factor endowments as sources of trade. Perhaps most significantly, it assumes that all countries have full access to all technological knowledge concerning production, resulting in the existence of identical production functions, which are themselves assumed to exhibit constant returns to scale. Moreover, countries are assumed to be sufficiently similar in their factor supplies that there emerges in general equilibrium a substantial overlap in the range of commodities produced. Under these conditions, factor prices are the same everywhere, and the country technology matrices all equal a common matrix, A. Under these and other assumptions, we can write the basic equations as

$$(2) \qquad T_i = A^{-1}(V_i - s_i V_w).$$

This system of equations is instructive in several regards. The Heckscher-Ohlin model consists of relationships among three variables: trade, factor intensities, and endowments. With respect to production techniques, general equilibrium under free trade is characterized by equal relative factor prices, factor intensities, and average and marginal factor productivities across countries. This prediction underlies the empirical comparisons made in the next section as simply and indirectly indicating differential technologies.

Further, the theory underlying equations (2) has inspired certain ad hoc empirical efforts to explain the structure of commodity or factor trade. First, many researchers have estimated the relationship between trade performance, such as scaled net exports, and factor intensities across industries within a country (Baldwin 1971, Branson and Monoyios 1977, Stern and Maskus 1981). It is clear from equations (2), however, that this technique provides no necessary inference on the structure of endowments or the validity of the theory. Moreover, the use of endogenous factor intensities as exogenous variables in regression analysis is questionable. Thus, such analysis is of descriptive value only, though it can be useful in that context. For example, cross-industry correlations can be informative measures of how differences in factor intensities are related to differences in trade performance, thereby serving as indicators of a particular definition of factor content. I perform in section 1.4 another such study on recent trade and production data across a set of 28 countries.

Second, other researchers have been inspired by the model to regress measures of net trade on factor endowments across countries within particular sectors (Leamer 1974 and 1984, Chenery and Syrquin 1975). This approach surely comes closer to the spirit of the Heckscher-Ohlin model, given the assumed exogeneity of factor supplies, but still admits no clear inference about the theory itself. Nonetheless, the results of such studies are informative estimates of the impacts of differences in endowments on trade. Again, I perform a similar analysis in section 1.5.

To be crassly empirical, I note that one sizable advantage of pursuing such ad hoc descriptive approaches is that the researcher is not constrained to satisfy the full requirements of the Heckscher-Ohlin model. The model, for example, is a proposition about trade across all commodities, rather than, say, across only manufactures, the typical focus of analysis and the one adopted here. Data availability for nonmanufactures is highly problematic, however, particularly for an analysis across countries. Data on trade in services are virtually absent. Thus, the researcher may proceed by considering subsets of goods (and factors and countries). However, it should be clear that statistical inference in such models is likely to be somewhat dubious.

This state of affairs is dissatisfying, though hardly unique to empirical international trade analysis. We can say relatively little about the empirical determinants of the pattern of trade in a rigorous way.[1] Yet we can say much about them in an informative way since we remain interested in examining suggested relationships in the data, even of an ad hoc nature.

It is in that spirit that I conduct the illustrative data analyses below. Again, the main point of this paper is to discuss practical data problems that emerge

---

1. Some analysts have performed fully articulated tests of the factor-proportions theory based on the factor-content version of equations (2) and independent measures of trade, intensities, and endowments (Bowen, Leamer, and Sveikauskas 1987, Brecher and Choudhri 1988, Maskus 1985). It is clear from these studies that the Heckscher-Ohlin theorem departs significantly from its exact quantitative predictions, which is hardly surprising given the extraordinary assumptions of the model. It is less clear how to interpret the severity of these departures; the consensus seems to be that factor endowments exert a positive and linear influence on the factor content of trade flows but that they hardly constitute the only important source of trade.

in the analysis of trade structure. This discussion takes place in the context of each approach in turn.

1.3 Factor Intensities, Factor Productivities, and Technology

As noted by Dollar, Wolff, and Baumol (1988), the factor-proportions model, or more accurately its cousin, the factor-price-equalization (FPE) theorem, implies numerous relationships that should be observable in comparative international production data in a free-trade equilibrium. The equalization of factor prices, in conjunction with identical constant-returns technologies, should result in identical factor intensities and factor productivities across nations within each tradable-goods industry. An interesting feature of this model is that labor productivity at the microeconomic level is unrelated to the aggregate capital-labor endowment, which plays a prominent role in macroeconomic explanations of productivity convergence (Baumol 1986, De Long 1988, Norsworthy and Malmquist 1983).

In the present context I focus on microeconomic labor, capital, and total-factor productivity in producing value added in 28 countries. The analysis is somewhat broader than that in Dollar, Wolff, and Baumol (1988), especially in terms of country coverage. That paper compared labor productivity in a set of 13 industrial countries across essentially the same set of manufacturing industries as those considered here. I add data on production and labor and capital inputs in 15 other countries, including several developing nations, in an attempt to examine technology indicators over varying levels of development.

Note that computations of international factor productivities do not constitute a rigorous test of the notion that technologies are linearly homogeneous and internationally common. For example, differences in productivities could be consistent with identical technologies if there exist impediments to trade or other influences that prevent FPE. Further, the FPE model presumes that factors are defined to be of homogeneous quality across countries, which presumption surely contradicts the facts in some degree. Finally, differences in observed productivities could simply result from measurement difficulties. Thus, computations of this sort are designed simply to investigate how prominently the predictions of the FPE model turn up in the data. If the FPE model appears consistent with the data, we might reasonably question the notion that technology differs markedly across countries.

1.3.1 Data Overview

For these purposes, data were assembled or constructed on value added, employment, and net capital stock (along with gross output and wages and salaries for later analysis) for the 28 3-digit industries of the International

Standard Industrial Classification (ISIC) in 28 countries for the year 1984. These data were taken from United Nations publications that attempt to present figures on industrial characteristics across countries on a consistent basis.[2] The countries and industries are given in table 1.1.

In studies of this sort, data-related problems of two general kinds emerge: the quality of the raw data themselves and conceptual difficulties in variable definition. Within the former problem we may consider international data availability and comparability, along with industry classification and aggregation.

The choice of countries was governed by the ability to assemble reasonably complete data sets from the U.N. volumes, along with a desire to include nations at different levels of industrialization or development. With 28 coun-

Table 1.1   Countries and Manufacturing Industries Used in Productivity Comparisons

Country	(Abbrev., n, Grade)	Industry	(ISIC Code, Abbrev., m, Grade)
Australia	(AU, 28, A)	Food products	(311/2, FD, 28, B)
Austria	(AS, 28, B)	Beverages	(313, BV, 27, B)
Canada	(CA, 28, A)	Tobacco	(314, TB, 26, D)
Chile	(CH, 28, C)	Textiles	(321, TX, 28, C)
Colombia	(CO, 28, C)	Wearing apparel	(322, AP, 28, C)
Cyprus	(CY, 24, C)	Leather and products	(323, LT, 28, B)
Denmark	(DE, 28, B)	Footwear	(324, FT, 28, C)
Ecuador	(EC, 28, B)	Wood products	(331, WO, 28, B)
Finland	(FI, 28, A)	Furniture and fixtures	(332, FU, 28, B)
West Germany	(GE, 24, C)	Paper and products	(341, PA, 28, B)
Greece	(GR, 28, C)	Printing and publishing	(342, PR, 28, C)
Indonesia	(IN, 25, D)	Industrial chemicals	(351, IC, 24, C)
Ireland	(IR, 24, C)	Other chemical products	(352, OC, 25, C)
Israel	(IS, 25, D)	Petroleum refineries	(353, PE, 21, D)
Italy	(IT, 21, C)	Petroleum and coal products	(354, PC, 20, D)
Japan	(JA, 27, A)	Rubber products	(355, RU, 28, B)
South Korea	(KO, 28, B)	Plastic products, nec	(356, PL 28, B)
New Zealand	(NZ, 26, C)	Pottery, china, etc.	(361, PT, 26, B)
Norway	(NO, 28, A)	Glass and products	(362, GL, 26, B)
Philippines	(PH, 28, C)	Nonmetal products, nec	(369, NM, 27, B)
Portugal	(PO, 27, B)	Iron and steel	(371, ST, 27, C)
Singapore	(SI, 24, C)	Nonferrous metals	(372, NF, 26, C)
Spain	(SP, 28, C)	Metal products	(381, MP, 28, B)
Sweden	(SW, 28, B)	Machinery, nec	(382, MA, 28, B)
Turkey	(TU, 28, C)	Electrical machinery	(383, EM, 28, B)
United Kingdom	(UK, 28, A)	Transport equipment	(384, TR, 28, C)
United States	(US, 28, A)	Professional goods	(385, PG, 27, B)
Venezuela	(VE, 28, C)	Other industries	(390, OT, 28, C)

Note: nec = not elsewhere classified; n = number of industry sectors per country; m = number of countries per industry sector; Grade = author's assessment of data reliability based on collection and reporting practices.

tries, 28 industries, and data on value added, employment, establishments, 15 years of gross investment and investment deflators (see below on construction of sectoral capital stocks), and two definitions of exchange rates, there are a maximum of 14,586 possible observations that could enter the analysis. As may be expected, however, some of these data were missing. My approach to missing data was twofold. If I believed that a reliable estimate of an unavailable figure could be generated from surrounding data (e.g., investment in a particular year from investment data in adjacent years or employment shares based on output weights), I made such an estimate. Otherwise, data were simply treated as missing. This approach resulted in 842 missing observations (5.8 percent of the maximum) and 1,004 constructed observations (6.9 percent of the maximum and 7.3 percent of the data used).

On this score, it seems that unavailable data do not pose a significant problem here. Note, however, that missing and estimated data are not evenly distributed across countries, sectors, and variables (full details on such data problems are available on request). Two comments may be made. First, the input variable with the most significant number of missing or constructed observations is past gross investment. This result is hardly surprising; data become increasingly thinner in the U.N. volumes as the researcher goes back in time. Particularly problematic countries in this regard include Greece, Indonesia, Israel, New Zealand, the Philippines, Spain, Turkey, and Venezuela. I constructed few other production variables, lending more confidence to the accuracy of the data beyond gross investment. Second, certain sectors are prone to have missing data because several countries combine them into aggregates, from which it is impossible to disentangle the contributions of subsectors. Data in other sectors simply are not reported by a few nations. These problems are most prevalent in industrial chemicals, other chemical products, petroleum refineries, and petroleum and coal products; the countries with the most limited sectoral data include Germany, Indonesia, Ireland, Italy, Singapore, and Cyprus.[3] A summary of this situation is provided in table 1.1.

The next issue is the international comparability of the data. The major purpose of the ISIC is to establish a consistent classification of industrial activity within which countries may report their production characteristics. Inevitably, however, there is some divergence in the country classifications from which the ISIC data are compiled. Interestingly in this regard, there is gener-

2. See United Nations, *Yearbook of Industrial Statistics,* vol. 1, *General Industrial Statistics,* various years (formerly *The Growth of World Industry,* vol. 1). Detailed output data are available in volumes 2 of these series.

3. In fact, Cyprus has several "zero" entries in its data, indicating the absence of industries, even at this level of aggregation (petroleum and coal products, iron and steel, nonferrous metals, and professional goods). This specialization is interesting from the standpoint of trade theory, but the empirical focus on intensities and productivities prevents meaningful use of the data. Hence, observations for these industries are considered missing.

ally less consistency between the ISIC and the classification systems of the developed countries than between the ISIC and those of the developing countries, because the former nations have long since established their own categorization procedures while the latter nations have developed theirs under the guidelines of the ISIC.[4]

A detailed reading of the country notes in the U.N. *Yearbook of Industrial Statistics* reveals that countries construct their measures of the input and output variables differently.[5] The meticulous reader is referred to that volume and to supplementary statistical publications.[6] To provide a flavor for the problem, I now list what might be considered the "standard" U.N. brief definition for each of the variables in question. In turn, table 1.2 lists my assessment of whether the variables may be considered overstatements or understatements in each country relative to these standards. For example, Indonesia includes in its estimates of wages and salaries employer contributions to national health and pension insurance programs, whereas the U.N. definition excludes these supplemental labor costs. Thus, Indonesia's wages are overstated, though by an unknown amount.

Gross output or value of shipments is a comprehensive measure of all explicit and implicit receipts of the industry, not simply sales of the principal output. It clearly is overly inclusive from the standpoint of the international economist's ideal definition of "final-goods output." Typically, output is in producer prices, including all indirect taxes but excluding subsidies.

Value added is gross output less the cost of materials and supplies consumed, electricity purchased, and contract and commission work done by others. Value added generally includes capital-consumption allowances and is typically measured in producer prices.

Employment is the number of wage earners and salaried employees averaged over the year (12 months or four quarters), excluding homeworkers, unpaid family workers, and working proprietors; including the latter categories results in *persons engaged.*

Wages and salaries include all payments in cash or in kind made to employees, including direct wages and salaries and other payments and allowances. Social insurance contributions and the like paid by the employer are excluded, though they could be included in a concept of total labor cost.

Gross fixed capital formation or gross investment includes the value of pur-

4. See United Nations, *Final Draft of the Revised International Standard Industrial Classification of All Economic Activities (ISIC);* Revision 3, ST/ESA/STAT/SER. M/4/Rev. 3/Add. 2, December 12, 1988.

5. Reference to official national statistical publications would likely reveal even more discrepancies, but this task lies beyond my patience and resources and that of most other researchers.

6. United Nations, *International Recommendations for Industrial Statistics,* ST/ESA/STAT/SER.M/48/Rev. 1, 1983, and United Nations, *Recommendations for the 1983 World Programme of Industrial Statistics,* ST/ESA/STAT/SER.M/71 (Parts 1 and 2), 1981.

Table 1.2   **Threshold Numbers of Persons Engaged per Establishment for Inclusion and Qualitative Indicators of Discrepancies in Variable Definition and Industrial Classification, by Country**

Country	Threshold Nos. of Persons	Gross Output	Value Added	Employment	Wages and Salaries	Gross Investment	Industrial Classification
AU	4	O	?	—	U	—	Minor
AS	20	—	—	O	O	O*	Medium
CA	1	—	—	—	—	—	Medium
CH	50	—	—	—	—	—	None
CO	10	—	—	U*	U*	O*	None
CY	1	O*	—	U	U	—	Medium
DE	6[a]	?	?	—	O	?	Minor
EC	10	U	U	—	—	O*	None
FI	5	U	U	—	—	—	None
GE	1[a]	O*	?	—	—	O*	Significant
GR	10	?	U	—	O	—	Minor
IN	20	—	U	—	O*	O*	Medium
IR	3	U*	U	?	U*	—	Medium
IS	5	U*	—	—	O	O*	Minor
IT	20[a]	U	U*	—	—	O*	Significant
JA	4	—	—	?	O	—	Minor
KO	5	—	—	O	—	O*	None
NZ	2–10	U*	?	?	—	—	Minor
NO	3–5	O*	—	—	—	O	Minor
PH	10	—	—	—	—	—	Minor
PO	1[b]	—	—	?	O	—	None
SI	10	U*	U	?	O*	O*	Minor
SP	1	U	U	—	O	—	Medium
SW	5	U	?	?	—	?	None
TU	25	O	—	—	—	O*	Minor
UK	1[a]	O	?	—	U*	—	Minor
US	1[a]	U	U	—	—	?	Minor
VE	5	U	—	—	—	—	None

Note: U = understated; O = overstated; * = potentially significantly misstated; ? = either direction of misstatement is possible. All comparisons are made with respect to "standard" U.N. definitions. Descriptors in final column refer to extent of difference of country classification scheme from ISIC.
[a]Estimated from data gathered from surveys at more aggregative levels.
[b]Selected industries only.

chases of new and used fixed assets, plus internal construction or improvements of fixed assets, less corresponding sales of assets. This definition does not include revaluation or depreciation of cumulated past investments.
Number of establishments indicates the quantity of units that, in principle, engage in predominantly one kind of activity at a single location under single ownership. The establishment is the basic reference unit for the ISIC

data. For purposes of comparison, I assume that the "standard" U.N. definition includes establishments with five or more persons engaged somehow in production at or for the site.

A glance at table 1.2 will demonstrate the qualitative variances in these definitions across countries. The most striking aspect of the table is that nations collect or estimate data for establishments of widely varying minimum sizes. This fact in itself generates concern over cross-country comparisons of inputs or outputs, since countries that exclude small establishments may be ignoring significant amounts of activity, perhaps by the cutting-edge new sectors. As it happens, however, in manufacturing this exclusion rarely eliminates more than 5–10 percent of employment and output.[7] However, it implies that international comparisons of, say, value added per establishment as measures of aggregate returns to scale are highly suspect.

The remaining entries in table 1.2 refer strictly to my qualitative assessments of differences in variable definitions, irrespective of the minimum threshold on size. The basic impression is of broad international consistency in most data groups, except for gross investment. The preponderance of overstatements in that category reflects the practice of about a third of these countries not to deduct asset sales from gross investment. These assessments should be kept in mind when considering the cross-country productivity comparisons listed below. Note, finally, that these judgments on data comparability are based solely on each country's definition, and presumed measurement, of the respective variables. It is not possible in this context to assess the inherent quality of the national data themselves. There are surely also substantive differences in internal data-collection methods (e.g., sampling versus full enumeration, mail versus in-person interviews, frequency of revisions) and subsequent data-manipulation techniques that influence the accuracy of the reported figures. This issue is not further considered here.[8]

Another issue worth brief discussion is industry definition or aggregation. Researchers working within the ISIC data-set on manufactures are constrained to using the 28 3-digit sectors, although a few countries report data on 9 additional 4-digit sectors. These categories are highly aggregative, and it might be preferable for the analyst to consult national statistical references in order to construct consistent definitions across countries of more detailed industry classifications—clearly a huge and complex task. The question of conceptually appropriate industry aggregation is complicated. In principle, we would like to know that subaggregates within a category are more alike in important ways than subaggregates are across categories. From the standpoint of the factor-proportions theory, inter alia, we would like factor intensities of sub-

---

7. See country notes in the *Yearbook of Industrial Statistics*.
8. We might expect that data quality is positively correlated with the level of development, which seems to be the case in the quality rankings in Summers and Heston (1984), but there is no written evidence to that effect in the U.N. publications.

aggregates within a sector to be identical, thereby defining an industry in those terms, and factor intensities across sectors to be as distinct as possible. There is no way to examine this question within the U.N. data-set across a broad sample of countries, although experimentation with available 4-digit detail suggests that within-aggregate intensities are marginally more similar than across-aggregate intensities. A related problem is that "enterprises" and "establishments," the main observational units in the ISIC data, undertake production in several activities that may be spread across different aggregate categories. The U.N., and presumably the statistical offices of the reporting countries, evidently take pains to allocate these activities appropriately, by principal sectors. Nonetheless, concern remains over the accuracy of the resulting industry classifications in this regard.

Beyond definition issues lies the fact that the cross-country distribution of inputs and outputs in each industry depends on sector-specific trade impediments or inducements. This problem is not easily quantified in any indirect context, and direct measures of the trade barriers and their economic impacts are scarce. I have incorporated a qualitative assessment of the severity of such barriers by sector (Nogues, Olechowski, and Winters 1986) into the rankings of the data quality discussed next.

The data problems discussed so far underlie the subjective grade I have assigned to each country and industry in table 1.1, which grades may be considered the sectoral analogues of the national data rankings in Summers and Heston (1984). These rankings are meant simply as warning markers to be kept in mind when considering the empirical results in the remainder of the paper.

The discussion so far has focused on difficulties in the reported data. There are also difficulties in matching measurement to theoretical concept. That is, even if the data were measured perfectly, the measured variables may not be completely appropriate for the estimation task. Consider, for example, the variables used here for the productivity comparisons. The output measure is value added, rather than gross output, for two reasons. First, it is not generally feasible to develop a measure of real use of materials and intermediates by constructing some price index of these inputs. Second, as noted earlier, gross output as given by the value of shipments is probably too inclusive a measure to serve as a clear indicator of production.

Using value added as output, however, carries the risk that different materials prices across countries will affect measured factor productivities. Equally troubling is that input productivity ideally should be measured as real output per unit of real input. The focus here, as in Dollar, Wolff, and Baumol (1988), is on the production of nominal value added. This usage is appropriate if the price of value added, an elusive concept, is equalized by trade and therefore serves simply as a scaling factor in comparative national outputs. Such equalization can be expected in the Heckscher-Ohlin model with free trade in outputs and intermediates, but the existence of such free trade is problematic, as noted earlier. A simple appeal to the Stolper-Samuelson theorem notes that output tariffs also will affect the international structure of factor productivity.

Two kinds of primary inputs are employed here. The first is simply employment by industry. Employment clearly does not fully capture the actual labor effort expended in production, and we might prefer a variable such as hours actually worked. The ISIC data-base provides data on hours worked by operatives (e.g., production workers plus clerical workers), but these data are not sufficiently inclusive of labor effort and are not available for enough countries to be useful. The International Labour Organisation[9] publishes data on average length of workweek across countries in some ISIC sectors; this data may be used with employment to construct an annual measure of total hours worked. The use of such measures here resulted in productivity computations that were nearly perfectly positively correlated with those simply using employment, so no additional information was provided. Hence, I report here results using employment only.

In my view, a more significant problem is that, ideally, one should find measures of labor inputs of identical quality both within and across countries. It is evident that laborers vary markedly with respect to education and skills and that the variance affects the measured productivity of the typical worker in each country. Attempting directly to adjust the data on an industry basis for this problem is virtually an impossible task, however.[10]

The second primary input is a constructed measure of real net capital stock by sector. These stocks are computed to avoid use of gross book value, which is a notoriously inconsistent concept across countries. One may approach this construction in a variety of ways, but in the context of the ISIC data I felt constrained to generate capital stocks based on accumulated and depreciated past investments. In particular, I assembled data on nominal gross fixed capital formation by industry for the 15-year period culminating in 1984. Net capital was computed as accumulated investment flows, assuming a 15-year asset life and a depreciation rate of 13.33 percent.[11] Annual investment figures were deflated by implicit capital deflators for each country (investment deflators by sector are unavailable) found in Summers and Heston (1988), which are based on PPP exchange rates for investment relative to the U.S. dollar. These deflators are expressed as indexes relative to the United States. Accordingly, a series of capital deflators (1984 = 1.0) for the United States[12] served as a basis for computing the country-specific investment-price indices, with 1984 as base year.

9. International Labour Organisation, *Yearbook of Labour Statistics*, various years.

10. See Clague (1991) for further discussion of the labor-quality issue and some efforts at adjustment.

11. For a few countries the investment series could not be extended backward the full 15 years, and so the depreciation factor was adjusted accordingly.

12. *Economic Report of the President* (Washington, D.C., 1989).

As with any measures of capital stock, this form of estimation is open to criticism. First, the use of 15-year investment flows forced me to push the data collection to periods well prior to 1984. As noted earlier, it seems that the U.N. data become thinner and less reliable the further back one examines them. There is the additional problem that classification schemes must be updated periodically to reflect changing economic activity. As it happened, the ISIC scheme was not varied during this period; all of the data here refer to ISIC Revision 2, which was adopted in 1968 and is only now being supplanted by Revision 3. However, individual countries effected changes in their classification systems over this period. The United States, for example, issued a major change in its Standard Industrial Classification in 1972, with subsequent revisions in 1977 and 1982. Where possible, I adjusted the investment data to reflect such changes, but otherwise I was forced to rely on the ISIC to report them consistently. In principle, of course, there should be consistency in each year because individual countries are supposed to report their data compatibly with the prevailing version of the ISIC. Second, and more fundamentally, the estimating procedure tends to overstate the capital stocks of countries that have experienced more recent investment growth relative to other countries, especially those with much larger initial stocks. That is, pre-1970 capital stocks are completely discounted here, which may not be fully sensible in mature economies and mature industries. Again, however, the informational requirements for assembling sectoral capital-stock estimates based on some vintage model are extraordinary. Third, the concept of capital itself is elusive in a world of changing relative prices (Leamer 1984). Finally, as with labor, there is the question of homogeneity of capital quality across nations, beyond simply the vintage issue. I cannot assess the severity of these problems with the given data. I simply note that the consistency with which the capital stocks have been computed should lend as much confidence as possible to their international comparability.

A final comment about the data is in order. The ISIC data are reported in the local currencies of each country, necessitating a conversion to dollars. As is well known, the choice of exchange rates for this purpose can have a substantial impact on measurements of productivity. Two cases are considered here. The first is simply the 1984 "market" exchange rate for each country's currency with the dollar.[13] It is likely that the value of the dollar was substantially in excess of many of its equilibrium bilateral values, however defined, in 1984. Thus, nominal value added outside the United States is presumably understated in dollars by conversion at these rates.[14] I therefore chose also to convert value data into dollars using the PPP rates for gross national product

13. See line *rf* in International Monetary Fund, *International Financial Statistics,* various years. I place the word "market" in quotation marks because for many countries this exchange rate is not determined in the foreign exchange markets.

14. Capital stocks would also be understated, but capital productivity, or value added per dollar of capital, would be unaffected by the choice of exchange rate.

listed in Summers and Heston (1988). Note, however, that PPP rates are not optimal for such comparisons because they are designed to equalize the local-currency value of a standardized basket of commodities with normalized international prices. Such equalization may bear little relationship to sectoral input productivity. In fact, the near hyperinflation that was experienced in the early 1980s in several of the countries in this study would argue for assigning substantially lower-than-market values to their currencies while the PPP rates generate substantially higher values for them. In turn, the PPP rates tend to overstate factor productivity in developing countries relative to the developed countries, as will be seen.

1.3.2 Comparisons of Factor Productivity

Armed with this lengthy list of caveats about the data, we turn now to the computations of factor productivity. To conserve space and to consider productivity at differing levels of industrialization, the 28 countries have been separated into three subgroups: a group of 12 industrialized nations (Australia, Austria, Canada, Denmark, Finland, West Germany, Italy, Japan, Norway, Sweden, the United Kingdom, and the United States); a group of 7 semi-industrialized nations (Greece, Ireland, New Zealand, Portugal, Spain, Cyprus, and Israel); and a group of 9 developing countries (Chile, Colombia, Ecuador, Indonesia, South Korea, Philippines, Singapore, Turkey, and Venezuela). Clearly, this classification is somewhat arbitrary, and complaints could be raised particularly about the placement of Korea and Singapore. The grouping seems instructive, however, and is maintained for the time being.

Measures of factor productivity and related variables are presented in table 1.3. For each industry and country group I note: average labor productivity, or value added per employee; average capital productivity, or value added per dollar of net capital stock; the average capital-labor ratio; and average value added per establishment. To examine dispersion of individual countries around these simple averages, I further list the coefficient of variation of each sample group in parentheses. These measures are computed using both market and PPP exchange rates, and this choice made a significant difference.

Considering first average labor productivity at market exchange rates, it is clear that in most sectors labor produced substantially higher value added in industrial countries (I group) than it did in semi-industrial countries (S group), while the latter laborers were marginally more productive than those in the developing countries (D group). Exceptions include most of those industries with unusually high capital-labor ratios (industrial chemicals, petroleum, petroleum and coal products, iron and steel, and nonferrous metal products) plus the other chemicals industry. In most of these cases labor productivity in Ds exceeded that in Ss, but still was below that of the industrial nations. In these industries the capital-labor ratios in the Ds were particularly high, perhaps reflecting more recent expansion of investment in that group. Note that the Is

Table 1.3   Simple Averages and Coefficients of Variation of Industry
                           Characteristics, 1984, at Market and PPP Exchange Rates for
                           Country Groups

Industry, Country		Value Added per Employee ($ thousands)		Value Added per Capital ($)	Capital per Employee ($ thousands)		Value Added per Establishment ($ millions)	
		Market	PPP	Market or PPP	Market	PPP	Market	PPP
311/2	I	30.8	34.5	1.7	19.2	22.1	1.9	2.2
FD		(.43)	(.36)	(.38)	(.24)	(.29)	(.56)	(.55)
	S	17.9	30.6	1.3	12.3	21.8	1.1	2.1
		(.38)	(.44)	(.23)	(.43)	(.58)	(1.09)	(1.48)
	D	13.2	26.9	1.1	14.3	28.5	1.0	2.4
		(.50)	(.51)	(.58)	(.64)	(.53)	(.96)	(1.08)
313	I	52.7	58.7	1.5	36.4	41.2	5.1	5.8
BV		(.36)	(.30)	(.29)	(.29)	(.27)	(.47)	(.45)
	S	27.0	48.2	1.3	19.7	35.4	2.0	3.6
		(.44)	(.46)	(.42)	(.60)	(.51)	(.85)	(1.00)
	D	27.7	57.4	1.7	20.5	41.5	3.9	8.7
		(.55)	(.45)	(.76)	(.51)	(.38)	(.68)	(.75)
314	I	138.8	162.8	4.6	26.8	30.4	35.5	40.9
TB		(1.04)	(1.11)	(.83)	(.57)	(.53)	(.73)	(.77)
	S	97.6	226.5	3.7	19.7	43.8	29.0	68.2
		(1.67)	(1.87)	(.66)	(1.14)	(1.37)	(1.78)	(1.94)
	D	91.1	200.5	7.8	21.2	41.7	29.4	66.4
		(1.49)	(1.71)	(1.32)	(1.02)	(1.11)	(1.52)	(1.65)
321	I	21.1	23.8	1.8	12.1	14.0	1.2	1.4
TX		(.25)	(.19)	(.28)	(.21)	(.26)	(.53)	(.55)
	S	11.3	19.1	1.5	7.7	13.0	0.8	1.7
		(.30)	(.33)	(.28)	(.42)	(.37)	(1.05)	(1.41)
	D	9.5	19.2	1.2	10.9	21.4	1.3	2.9
		(.58)	(.47)	(.91)	(.64)	(.35)	(.69)	(.76)
322	I	14.9	16.8	4.7	3.9	4.5	0.7	0.8
AP		(.27)	(.21)	(.66)	(.33)	(.40)	(.55)	(.50)
	S	8.4	14.5	3.0	2.8	5.1	0.4	0.8
		(.30)	(.43)	(.26)	(.32)	(.59)	(.95)	(1.25)
	D	6.2	13.0	2.8	2.7	5.7	0.5	1.1
		(.60)	(.63)	(.93)	(.52)	(.51)	(.70)	(.85)
323	I	19.8	22.4	2.9	7.7	9.0	0.7	0.8
LT		(.25)	(.21)	(.45)	(.31)	(.40)	(.53)	(.57)
	S	13.7	23.8	2.1	5.2	9.7	0.4	1.0
		(.36)	(.43)	(.08)	(.48)	(.59)	(1.38)	(1.65)
	D	8.6	18.3	1.7	5.8	12.4	0.5	1.2
		(.57)	(.61)	(.48)	(.57)	(.56)	(1.00)	(1.13)

(*continued*)

Table 1.3   (continued)

Industry, Country		Value Added per Employee ($ thousands)		Value Added per Capital ($)	Capital per Employee ($ thousands)		Value Added per Establishment ($ millions)	
		Market	PPP	Market or PPP	Market	PPP	Market	PPP
324	I	17.0	19.2	3.7	5.5	6.3	1.3	1.4
FT		(.25)	(.18)	(.57)	(.38)	(.38)	(.64)	(.60)
	S	10.8	17.5	3.2	3.3	6.2	0.6	1.1
		(.51)	(.37)	(.59)	(.48)	(.69)	(.88)	(1.20)
	D	6.2	12.7	1.5	4.9	10.2	0.5	1.1
		(.45)	(.43)	(.63)	(.57)	(.48)	(.90)	(1.03)
331	I	23.0	25.9	1.6	15.6	17.8	0.7	0.8
WO		(.24)	(.15)	(.39)	(.31)	(.30)	(.55)	(.54)
	S	12.1	20.9	1.4	7.5	13.2	0.4	0.9
		(.40)	(.34)	(.29)	(.40)	(.46)	(1.40)	(1.75)
	D	8.1	16.4	1.0	10.5	20.8	0.6	1.4
		(.52)	(.52)	(.76)	(.64)	(.47)	(.83)	(.95)
332	I	21.4	24.2	2.9	8.9	10.4	0.7	0.8
FU		(.22)	(.19)	(.59)	(.35)	(.39)	(.51)	(.50)
	S	9.4	15.2	2.0	4.3	7.5	0.2	0.4
		(.41)	(.30)	(.45)	(.26)	(.33)	(1.20)	(1.55)
	D	6.1	12.0	1.7	4.5	7.5	0.3	0.6
		(.52)	(.45)	(.82)	(.62)	(.52)	(.70)	(.85)
341	I	37.5	41.7	1.1	37.7	42.1	4.9	5.4
PA		(.34)	(.25)	(.32)	(.46)	(.42)	(.73)	(.68)
	S	27.2	52.6	1.1	26.5	53.6	3.5	7.9
		(.71)	(1.03)	(.45)	(.78)	(1.09)	(1.77)	(2.03)
	D	22.1	47.2	1.1	25.6	58.3	3.4	7.9
		(.90)	(1.06)	(.94)	(.78)	(.91)	(1.60)	(1.75)
342	I	30.4	34.2	2.7	11.9	13.7	1.2	1.5
PR		(.29)	(.23)	(.36)	(.29)	(.32)	(.47)	(.57)
	S	17.4	29.2	1.9	8.4	16.4	0.8	1.8
		(.47)	(.49)	(.30)	(.75)	(1.06)	(1.51)	(1.83)
	D	13.0	26.8	1.3	11.2	24.3	0.9	2.2
		(.49)	(.55)	(.60)	(.51)	(.58)	(1.20)	(1.32)
351	I	59.2	64.2	1.0	73.2	79.1	6.2	6.8
IC		(.44)	(.38)	(.28)	(.73)	(.68)	(.45)	(.41)
	S	26.2	52.2	0.9	32.6	64.4	2.4	5.1
		(.37)	(.53)	(.50)	(.30)	(.45)	(.71)	(.89)
	D	38.3	75.7	1.2	35.9	73.6	3.5	7.8
		(.82)	(.73)	(.73)	(.68)	(.57)	(.48)	(.63)
352	I	50.5	54.5	2.2	24.1	26.6	3.7	4.0
OC		(.56)	(.50)	(.41)	(.38)	(.36)	(.49)	(.45)

Table 1.3 (continued)

Industry, Country		Value Added per Employee ($ thousands)		Value Added per Capital ($)	Capital per Employee ($ thousands)		Value Added per Establishment ($ millions)	
		Market	PPP	Market or PPP	Market	PPP	Market	PPP
	S	19.6	37.1	1.8	8.8	16.2	1.5	3.2
		(.70)	(.80)	(.50)	(.36)	(.51)	(1.28)	(1.52)
	D	25.6	48.8	1.9	14.6	27.8	2.3	4.8
		(.73)	(.49)	(.47)	(.64)	(.54)	(.63)	(.71)
353 PE	I	123.0	136.0	0.9	158.6	173.9	44.7	49.1
		(.44)	(.43)	(.68)	(.55)	(.52)	(1.05)	(1.04)
	S	120.1	260.5	2.0	81.0	138.6	70.7	143.0
		(1.08)	(1.10)	(1.55)	(.72)	(.35)	(1.38)	(1.25)
	D	212.9	472.2	2.7	85.4	181.5	111.2	269.7
		(.73)	(.69)	(.78)	(.65)	(.54)	(.96)	(1.14)
354 PC	I	50.0	54.0	1.5	45.2	49.2	1.7	1.9
		(.46)	(.43)	(.50)	(.87)	(.84)	(.53)	(.49)
	S	22.1	40.4	1.4	14.6	30.3	0.8	1.8
		(.50)	(.53)	(.59)	(.48)	(.77)	(.73)	(.89)
	D	31.4	68.2	1.5	24.6	51.7	1.9	4.5
		(.65)	(.60)	(.59)	(1.01)	(.90)	(.89)	(1.15)
355 RU	I	28.1	31.4	1.6	17.6	20.0	3.9	4.5
		(.38)	(.30)	(.27)	(.32)	(.29)	(.74)	(.76)
	S	16.2	28.2	1.8	8.0	14.1	1.1	2.2
		(.34)	(.45)	(.44)	(.30)	(.24)	(.94)	(1.27)
	D	15.0	30.5	1.9	10.7	21.3	1.7	3.6
		(.73)	(.61)	(.86)	(.79)	(.63)	(.73)	(.67)
356 PL	I	26.6	30.0	1.7	16.5	19.0	1.2	1.4
		(.28)	(.21)	(.38)	(.21)	(.23)	(.53)	(.57)
	S	18.0	28.6	1.4	10.4	18.1	0.7	1.2
		(.60)	(.41)	(.25)	(.38)	(.32)	(.77)	(1.08)
	D	10.6	21.5	0.9	14.3	30.8	0.7	1.5
		(.49)	(.42)	(.59)	(.52)	(.63)	(.64)	(.73)
361 PT	I	22.2	24.4	2.3	12.7	13.9	2.0	2.3
		(.31)	(.24)	(.37)	(1.00)	(.95)	(.70)	(.70)
	S	11.8	19.4	1.6	8.1	13.8	0.8	1.6
		(.40)	(.28)	(.53)	(.57)	(.50)	(1.17)	(1.50)
	D	8.7	18.4	1.5	7.2	16.2	1.4	3.4
		(.63)	(.46)	(.77)	(.67)	(.57)	(.64)	(.74)
362 GL	I	34.4	37.5	1.5	25.3	27.8	3.1	3.4
		(.39)	(.31)	(.27)	(.62)	(.58)	(.61)	(.56)
	S	17.8	30.9	1.5	16.9	31.5	1.2	2.3
		(.37)	(.52)	(.63)	(.67)	(.87)	(.82)	(1.09)

(continued)

Table 1.3   (continued)

Industry, Country		Value Added per Employee ($ thousands)		Value Added per Capital ($)	Capital per Employee ($ thousands)		Value Added per Establishment ($ millions)	
		Market	PPP	Market or PPP	Market	PPP	Market	PPP
	D	15.5	34.0	1.0	20.8	46.5	2.1	5.3
		(.48)	(.41)	(.75)	(.75)	(.65)	(.50)	(.68)
369	I	35.7	39.6	1.3	29.3	32.6	1.2	1.4
NM		(.24)	(.20)	(.28)	(.20)	(.19)	(.35)	(.44)
	S	24.9	42.1	0.9	34.8	70.3	1.1	2.3
		(.49)	(.57)	(.64)	(1.04)	(1.35)	(1.45)	(1.83)
	D	16.7	33.9	0.8	31.2	72.1	1.3	2.9
		(.62)	(.68)	(.89)	(1.00)	(1.12)	(1.05)	(1.21)
371	I	33.9	37.7	1.0	42.3	47.1	7.6	8.6
ST		(.39)	(.31)	(.33)	(.88)	(.81)	(.69)	(.70)
	S	21.4	37.4	0.6	43.3	68.8	3.1	6.7
		(.46)	(.65)	(1.08)	(.79)	(1.63)	(1.42)	(1.64)
	D	26.4	57.1	0.9	40.8	80.4	6.4	15.8
		(.34)	(.42)	(.60)	(.61)	(.50)	(.88)	(1.11)
372	I	35.8	40.1	1.1	46.0	49.3	5.2	5.9
NF		(.34)	(.28)	(.43)	(.85)	(.75)	(.77)	(.76)
	S	43.9	87.8	1.2	27.2	51.4	11.3	27.4
		(1.05)	(1.42)	(.61)	(.66)	(.85)	(2.30)	(2.40)
	D	41.5	87.8	1.6	26.7	53.0	10.8	26.0
		(1.12)	(1.33)	(.60)	(.61)	(.72)	(2.22)	(2.35)
381	I	25.7	28.8	2.0	14.0	16.0	1.2	1.4
MP		(.32)	(.24)	(.35)	(.46)	(.43)	(.60)	(.69)
	S	16.0	26.0	1.6	8.0	14.2	0.6	1.1
		(.51)	(.38)	(.31)	(.26)	(.42)	(.98)	(1.24)
	D	10.9	21.9	1.3	10.4	20.4	0.7	1.5
		(.48)	(.36)	(.52)	(.63)	(.44)	(.63)	(.73)
382	I	29.4	33.0	2.2	16.6	18.6	1.9	2.2
MA		(.35)	(.27)	(.33)	(.87)	(.81)	(.71)	(.77)
	S	19.7	30.5	2.1	8.3	14.4	1.0	1.8
		(.87)	(.71)	(.47)	(.67)	(.60)	(1.10)	(1.20)
	D	10.3	20.3	1.1	10.7	20.7	0.8	1.9
		(.57)	(.36)	(.53)	(.63)	(.43)	(.82)	(.98)
383	I	29.2	32.7	2.1	15.3	17.3	3.6	4.1
EM		(.35)	(.27)	(.32)	(.50)	(.45)	(.61)	(.63)
	S	20.9	35.2	2.0	9.6	17.9	1.7	3.1
		(.47)	(.44)	(.26)	(.50)	(.73)	(.68)	(.77)
	D	14.5	30.1	1.4	11.8	25.3	2.1	4.5
		(.50)	(.51)	(.64)	(.46)	(.49)	(.57)	(.48)

Table 1.3   (continued)

Industry, Country		Value Added per Employee ($ thousands)		Value Added per Capital ($)	Capital per Employee ($ thousands)		Value Added per Establishment ($ millions)	
		Market	PPP	Market or PPP	Market	PPP	Market	PPP
384	I	31.0	34.5	1.6	22.1	25.0	6.6	7.7
TR		(.50)	(.43)	(.43)	(.68)	(.63)	(1.05)	(1.10)
	S	14.8	24.8	1.5	10.5	19.0	1.9	3.3
		(.49)	(.48)	(.59)	(.66)	(.74)	(.97)	(.82)
	D	13.3	27.0	1.0	15.0	31.7	1.6	3.5
		(.43)	(.37)	(.57)	(.44)	(.38)	(.51)	(.69)
385	I	30.0	33.7	2.3	14.6	16.8	1.8	2.1
PG		(.41)	(.34)	(.39)	(.54)	(.57)	(.67)	(.61)
	S	18.5	29.3	2.1	7.1	12.3	1.0	1.6
		(.68)	(.51)	(.43)	(.46)	(.38)	(1.10)	(.94)
	D	10.5	20.0	1.7	8.9	15.4	0.7	1.4
		(.69)	(.60)	(.76)	(.99)	(.73)	(.64)	(.50)
390	I	24.1	27.1	2.4	11.1	12.7	0.9	1.0
OT		(.31)	(.24)	(.38)	(.42)	(.43)	(.64)	(.72)
	S	12.2	19.8	1.8	6.4	12.0	0.3	0.6
		(.43)	(.27)	(.45)	(.44)	(.69)	(.72)	(.93)
	D	7.9	15.7	1.5	7.0	14.9	0.4	0.9
		(.57)	(.47)	(.81)	(.61)	(.67)	(.45)	(.59)

Note: Coefficients of variation are in parentheses. Country groups: I = industrialized group; S = semi-industrialized group; D = developing-country group.

have substantial measured labor-productivity advantages in the most labor-intensive goods (textiles, apparel, leather goods, and footwear).

Regarding capital productivity, or dollars of value added per dollar of net capital stock, if techniques of production are not equalized internationally, because of the existence of barriers to trade in goods and factors, we would expect highest capital productivity in Ds under the factor-proportions model, given the presumed scarcity of capital in those countries. As may be seen, there were a number of such cases in the 1984 data, but we generally observe a capital-productivity ranking across country groups similar to that for labor productivity, suggesting that the Is enjoyed some generalized advantage in production in manufactures.

Further, the Is exhibited the highest capital-labor ratios in all sectors except for nonmetal products and iron and steel. Capital-labor ratios were similar between the Ss and the Ds, suggesting that this country grouping provides little discrimination on that score. Similar comments apply to the ratios of value added per establishment, except for some highly capital-intensive sectors (petroleum, petroleum and coal products, iron and steel, and nonferrous metals), plus nonmetal products. Note again, however, that these latter computations are highly suspicious because of the different minimum sizes reported per establishment across countries.

Further perspective is provided by the coefficients of variation in each sample. These coefficients are generally markedly lower in the I group than in either of the other groups, indicating that within the Is there is relatively little dispersion in techniques. Thus, the factor-proportions model, with its notion of identical technologies, is borne out at least indirectly among these nations. However, there is much wider variation in techniques among the Ss and Ds, as many of the coefficients exceed unity. In conjunction with the sizable gap that typically exists between average techniques in these groups and those in the Is, I conclude from this information that there is relatively little similarity in productivities at different levels of development.

Clearly, however, this conclusion rests on the use of 1984 market exchange rates. Adopting PPP rates resulted in dramatic changes in measured labor productivity and capital-labor ratios across countries. The available PPP rates (Summers and Heston 1988) in 1984 suggested that the currencies for most of the Is were moderately undervalued relative to their PPP with the dollar. Thus, their use here resulted in slight increases in average labor productivities and capital-labor techniques for the Is. It also yielded reductions in the coefficients of variation on value added per employee by raising these figures for most countries relative to those for the United States and typically had the same effect on average capital-labor ratios. For the Ss and, especially, the Ds, on the other hand, PPP rates were typically far different from their (undervalued) market counterparts, and their use yielded large increases in measured value added and capital stocks in those countries.[15] In table 1.3 I show that this conversion typically doubled average labor productivities and capital-labor ratios in the Ds while raising those for the Ss on the order of 80 percent. This adjustment led to mean labor productivities that were much more similar across country groups and even resulted in higher figures for the Ds than for the Is in the most capital-intensive sectors (industrial chemicals, petroleum, petroleum and coal products, iron and steel, nonferrous metals), plus tobacco products and paper products. Moreover, the capital-labor ratios in the Ds became larger than those in the Is in 25 of the 28 sectors. Similar comments apply to the measures of value added per establishment. With these results, then, one might conclude that production techniques and direct factor productivities are generally similar across countries, in support of the factor-proportions model. Tempering this inference is the fact that use of PPP rates generated much larger adjustments for some Is and Ss than others, typically resulting in larger dispersion of techniques around their means.

15. The PPP exchange rates were those constructed for comparisons of GNP. However, in computing net capital stocks I used the country-specific investment deflators, which may be used to construct annual PPP rates for capital. These data may be found in Summers and Heston (1988).

To provide additional perspective on the structure of international productivity, I followed Dollar, Wolff, and Baumol (1988) in estimating translogarithmic production functions for each sector and for certain groups of industries (defined below) using both market and PPP exchange rates. The functions were estimated for each of the 28 sectors as follows:

(3) $\ln(VA/E) = C + a_1\ln(K/E) + a_2\ln E + a_3[\ln(K/E)]^2$, and

(4) $\ln(VA/E) = C + \Sigma c_j D_j + a_1\ln(K/E) + a_2\ln E + a_3[\ln(K/E)]^2$.

Here, VA represents dollar value added, E indicates employment, K is the constant-dollar capital stock, and the D_j's are country dummy variables. Estimation of equation (3) in each sector presumes the existence of an internationally common production function in which each country serves as an observation. Its main usefulness is that the coefficient a_2 provides a measure of returns to scale; if the coefficient significantly exceeds 0 there is evidence of scale economies. Scale economies are a clear alternative candidate to the simple factor-proportions model of production and trade, which makes their estimation interesting.

In equation (3), the constant term is an index of total factor productivity (TFP) in each industry, assumed identical across countries, after controlling for national differences in capital and labor. Given the results discussed above, however, it seems likely that TFP varies across countries. Accordingly, equation (4) introduces country dummies to estimate differences in TFP as a further check on the international efficiency of factor use. For this purpose, the 28 sectors were pooled into three industry groups in estimating equation (4) to provide sufficient observations for estimation. Roughly following Dollar and Wolff (1988), these groups were: light industries (AP, LT, FT, FU, PT, PG, OT); medium industries (FD, BV, TB, TX, WO, PA, PR, RU, PL, GL, MP); and heavy industries (IC, OC, PE, PC, NM, ST, NF, MA, EM, TR). As will be seen later, in table 1.8, the raw-labor intensity of these industries tends to decline as they move up this tripartite classification. However, I did no formal statistical testing of the acceptability of this grouping.

The individual industry regressions of equation (3) (run with and without dummies for Ss and Ds; the figures are available on request) performed reasonably well, generally explaining between 40 and 60 percent of the variation in log value added per employee. There was weak evidence of scale economies in 17 of the 28 industries, though this result was sensitive to the definition of the exchange rate and the inclusion of regional dummies.

Because this weakness could be due to the limited number of observations by sector, I repeated the regressions with the data pooled across the three industry groups. These regressions are reported in table 1.4 along with those including the country effects. The last set of equations exclude refined petroleum products and petroleum and coal products because these data seem particularly questionable. Note first that the equations with country effects per-

Table 1.4   **Translogarithmic Production-Function Estimates for Light, Medium, and Heavy Industries, 1984, with and without Country Effects, Using Market and PPP Exchange Rates**

Industry Group	Exchange Rate	Country Effect	Constant	K/E	E	$(K/E)^2$	R^2
Light	Market	No	0.90*	0.94*	0.11*	−0.09***	.40
	Market	Yes	3.05*	0.22**	−0.02	0.02	.92
	PPP	No	2.27*	0.18	0.05*	0.03	.15
	PPP	Yes	3.26*	0.06	−0.02	0.04	.75
Medium	Market	No	1.76*	0.18	0.01	0.10**	.33
	Market	Yes	4.46*	−0.38**	−0.15*	0.16*	.76
	PPP	No	4.08*	−0.84*	−0.01	0.20*	.19
	PPP	Yes	5.53*	−0.90*	−0.14*	0.21*	.62
Heavy	Market	No	1.50*	0.48**	0.05**	0.01	.34
	Market	Yes	3.46*	0.33	−0.09*	0.01	.60
	PPP	No	3.22*	−0.25	0.03	0.10*	.27
	PPP	Yes	4.53*	−0.30	−0.09**	0.09*	.51
Heavy (excluding PE & PC)	Market	No	1.44*	0.47**	0.09*	0.00	.35
	Market	Yes	3.31*	0.36**	−0.05	−0.01	.75
	PPP	No	2.79*	0.01	0.05*	0.05	.22
	PPP	Yes	3.45*	0.26	−0.04	0.01	.57

Note: *** = significantly different from 0 at 10% level; ** = same at 5% level; * = same at 1% level.

form substantially better than those without, as suggested by the adjusted coefficients of determination. The equations without country dummies suggest the existence of increasing returns in both light and heavy industries, but this result disappears when the country effects are included. The constant term rises when country terms are added because the benchmark country is the United States, which generally has the highest measured productivity levels. Again, many of the coefficients are sensitive to the choice of exchange rate.

The indexes of TFP that resulted from estimation of equation (4) are presented in table 1.5. These results suggest that nearly all countries had TFP levels significantly below those of the United States, with only Canadian, German, and Japanese TFP approaching them. Differences in TFP were least marked in the group of heavy industries, with Chile, Israel, Spain, and Venezuela among the Ss and Ds registering insignificant differences with the United States. In my view, these estimated differences in TFP are surprisingly large, though they diminish markedly with the use of PPP rates. If we accept them as accurate indicators, they leave the strong impression that the efficiency with which primary inputs are converted into value-added differs significantly across countries. Among the primary explanations that could be advanced for this finding are international differences in factor quality, man-

Table 1.5 National Indexes of Total Factor Productivity from Translog Production Functions with Country Effects, 1984, Using Market and PPP Exchange Rates, by Industry Group

Country	Light Industries		Medium Industries		Heavy Industries[a]		Heavy Industries[b]	
	Market	PPP	Market	PPP	Market	PPP	Market	PPP
US	100.0	100.0	100.0	100.0	100.0	100.0	100.0	100.0
AU	74.4**	67.9*	54.7*	45.1*	49.2**	44.8*	56.0**	52.2*
AS	36.7*	46.5*	34.9*	38.4*	32.0*	38.5*	34.6*	41.6*
CA	76.0**	77.6	66.6**	65.2**	68.5	69.7	73.0	75.6
CH	32.1	63.4*	31.7*	45.7*	41.7*	75.1	45.0*	86.5
CO	28.9*	54.8*	33.2*	52.6*	31.1*	53.2**	31.5*	57.4**
CY	23.9*	41.4*	15.0*	20.9*	12.1*	19.2*	13.9*	22.6*
DE	58.3*	67.8*	37.5*	38.8*	42.6*	48.9**	45.0*	51.9*
EC	18.3*	29.9*	11.6*	15.1*	20.6*	31.8*	24.1*	38.0*
FI	51.7*	57.9*	32.4*	32.9*	38.2*	42.1*	37.8*	40.6*
GE	57.8*	71.2**	60.9*	66.4**	58.0	67.8	54.4*	63.4**
GR	23.1*	36.4*	18.1*	24.5*	19.8*	29.6*	21.7*	33.9*
IN	7.5*	18.4*	6.5*	11.6*	12.5*	25.9*	12.8*	28.3*
IR	39.1*	52.1*	32.2*	35.9*	35.2*	44.5**	41.2*	52.3**
IS	60.8*	65.1*	38.1*	36.5*	62.5	60.1	66.2	75.9
IT	49.2*	68.4*	37.9*	44.8*	40.3*	52.0**	38.3*	50.3*
JA	64.3*	67.0*	64.8**	64.0**	61.8	61.4	65.6**	66.9**
KO	22.9*	37.8*	25.1*	32.7*	30.9*	44.0*	26.9*	41.2*
NO	44.1*	50.6*	33.9*	34.8*	39.1*	43.9*	44.5*	49.2*
NZ	41.2*	47.5*	28.2*	28.6*	14.1*	15.0*	25.6*	30.0*
PH	8.2*	17.2*	11.4*	22.5*	17.7*	35.0*	15.0*	32.2*
PO	18.2*	34.9*	15.7*	25.3*	16.0*	27.3*	14.8*	27.1*
SI	23.6*	27.4*	17.6*	19.1*	32.2*	37.8*	37.5*	42.7*
SP	41.1*	67.4*	38.6*	51.6*	44.3**	60.2	43.3*	66.4
SW	58.2*	61.6*	48.2*	45.8*	57.6**	58.6	54.0*	55.7**
TU	20.8*	46.9*	20.1*	37.4*	28.8*	58.0**	21.3*	46.7*
UK	53.0*	69.1*	55.3*	62.9*	53.9**	65.6	51.4*	65.4**
VE	51.9*	68.6*	49.8*	55.5*	54.7**	70.0	50.3*	66.6

Note: ** = difference significantly different from 0 at 5%; * = difference from U.S. estimate significantly different from 0 at 1%; [a]Estimated including sectors PE and PC; [b]Estimated excluding sectors PE and PC.

agement capability, public infrastructure, and technology.[16] I have emphasized the last factor in the approach to these productivity measures, but the analysis here is incapable of discriminating among these influences. On a more mundanc level, these differences in TFP might largely be due to the numerous data problems described earlier; that interpretation is more consistent with the tone of this paper. As Leamer notes in his comment, they could simply be the result of an underestimated U.S. capital stock under the 15-year accumulation procedure I applied.

1.4   Trade and Direct Factor Inputs

As noted earlier, a familiar descriptive approach to explaining trade structure is to relate cross-industry measures of trade performance to factor intensities. Such efforts attempt to characterize the input basis of international industry competitiveness in trade, though they do not follow rigorously from trade theory. For this purpose I report for each country simple correlations between industry net exports and factor shares, where the factors are defined as unskilled labor (U), human capital (H), physical capital (K), and materials and intermediate inputs (M).

1.4.1   Data Overview

With regard to data, I need to add consistent international measures of gross output, wages and salaries, and exports and imports to the data base. Output and wages, taken from the ISIC, were discussed in the previous section (see table 1.2). Incorporating trade data immediately raises the problem that production and trade figures are not reported on the same basis. The United Nations has developed a reporting system for trade, the Standard International Trade Classification (SITC) to accompany the ISIC. However, the systems are designed for distinct purposes and are not easily comparable at any level of aggregation.

Thus, the most vexing mechanical task for the researcher is to develop a concordance between the SITC and the ISIC. This problem exists in two dimensions. First, statistical classification systems must undergo periodic revision to reflect changing technologies, introduction of new products, and the like. This fact necessitates concordance building within each classification system over time if the analysis is of a time-series nature or if past observations are used to construct current data, as was done above to compute capital

---

16. On labor quality and management, see Clague (1991). From the standpoint of international data needs, one of the most glaring omissions is the near-absence of consistent information on industry employment of labor of distinctive skill levels. This absence forces the researcher to construct proxies of labor skills, as is done in the next section, or to rely on indirect and limited measures of skill, such as the occupation classification published by the International Labour Organisation.

stocks. The SITC is still reported under its second major revision[17] but a third revision was issued in 1988. Some countries still report their trade data on the basis of SITC Revision 1 (Chile is the only country included in this section of the paper that does so), providing another reason for a time-related concordance. The United Nations published such a concordance with Revision 2, but inevitably the changes were made at very disaggregated levels, imposing detective work and the need for making judgments on the researcher working at higher levels of aggregation.

The second dimension of the problem is simply the need to reconcile the SITC data to the ISIC basis. The United Nations recognized this need some years ago when it published a detailed concordance between the first revisions of both systems.[18] It is, therefore, possible to build a concordance between the second revisions of the ISIC and the SITC by using this source and the SITC mappings. Doing so carefully, however, is extremely tedious. At any level of disaggregation, some SITC categories will fit into two or more ISIC categories, requiring the development of an acceptable weighting system. The choice of the weights alone is not a straightforward question. Should they be based on shares of national or world trade, because of the SITC, or on shares of national or world output or capital stock, because of the ISIC? Should the weights change over time and across countries? Should there be separate weighting schemes for each bilateral trade flow? It is evident that the sheer volume of this task (recall that the U.N. concordances are at the 5-digit level of the SITC) would quickly overwhelm the resources of the researcher. This fact necessitates that some compromise concordance be developed that reflects the researcher's trade-offs between precision and tractability.[19]

In table 1.6 I present the crude concordance developed for the present work. The concordance is based on linkages between the 3-digit ISIC (28 sectors) and the 2-digit SITC (60 categories of relevance to manufactures). The weights are approximations, based roughly on contributions of trade in underlying 3-digit SITC categories to total 2-digit SITC trade in the United States in 1984.[20] These weights are applied to both the exports and imports of all countries, implying that the trade data employed below are measured with error beyond simple reporting and sampling error. It should be noted that the SITC trade data are reported in dollars at market exchange rates. Thus, the

17. United Nations, *Standard International Trade Classification*, Revision 2, ST/ESA/STAT/ SER.M/34/Rev. 2, 1974.

18. See United Nations, *Classification of Commodities by Industrial Origin: Links between the SITC and the ISIC*, ST/STAT/Ser.M/43/Rev. 1, 1967.

19. A great many such concordances have been developed by different researchers in the field, indicating that the continued introduction of new ones is an inefficient use of research time. It would certainly be useful for practitioners to agree on a standardized concordance and method for updating it.

20. I experimented with an alternative concordance with weights based on the joint trade of the United States, Japan, and Germany. It resulted in no qualitative differences in the analysis below and is not discussed further.

Table 1.6   **Concordance between the 3-Digit ISIC, Revision 2, and the 2-Digit SITC, Revision 2**

ISIC	Industry Abbrev.	SITC (weight)
311/2	FD	01(1.0), 02(.75), 03(.5), 04(.5), 05(.5), 06(1.0), 07(.5), 08(.75), 09(1.0), 21(.25), 22(.25), 29(.125), 41(1.0), 42(1.0), 43(.5), 59(.1)
313	BV	11(1.0)
314	TB	12(.5)
321	TX	26(.5), 65(1.0), 84(.1)
322	AP	84(.9)
323	LT	61(.75), 83(.9)
324	FT	61(.25), 85(1.0)
331	WO	24(.75), 63(.9)
332	FU	82(.8)
341	PA	25(1.0), 59(.1), 64(.9)
342	PR	64(.1), 89(.3)
351	IC	23(.1), 26(.1), 51(1.0), 52(1.0), 53(1.0), 56(1.0), 58(.5), 59(.33), 43(.1)
352	OC	53(.25), 54(.9), 55(1.0), 57(1.0), 59(.33)
353	PE	33(.5), 34(.1)
354	PC	32(.25), 33(.125), 34(.1)
355	RU	23(.5), 62(.9)
356	PL	58(.5), 82(.1), 89(.1)
361	PT	66(.125), 81(.05)
362	GL	66(.5), 81(.05)
369	NM	27(.125), 66(.375)
371	ST	67(.95), 69(.2)
372	NF	68(.95), 69(.1)
381	MP	67(.05), 68(.05), 69(.5), 71(.1), 73(.25), 74(.05), 81(.9)
382	MA	69(.1), 71(.4), 72(1.0), 73(.75), 74(.8), 75(1.0), 77(.125)
383	EM	76(1.0), 77(.875)
384	TR	71(.5), 74(.1), 78(1.0), 79(1.0), 89(.1)
385	PG	54(.1), 59(.05), 74(.05), 87(1.0)
390	OT	69(.1), 83(.1), 89(.4)

analysis below is restricted to inputs valued at market rates, and PPP rates are ignored.

For the 28 countries in the sample, the basic industry data-set thus consists of observations on exports and imports (filtered through the concordance presented in table 1.6), gross output, value added, employment (in thousands), and wages and salaries. All value figures are expressed in millions of U.S. dollars.

A final comment about data requirements is in order here. It is evident that accumulating detailed data involving countries, inputs, and trade quickly mushrooms into an enormous effort. However, time is an important additional dimension to incorporate into empirical research. The analyst must replicate the data search for every year under consideration. Moreover, if a time-series study is to be performed, the researcher must come to grips with the need for price deflators for all nominal values (wages, capital costs, output values, trade values, and the like). It is in this regard that international data are least accessible.

1.4.2   Trade and Factor Shares

For each country, net exports in each industry were scaled by the sum of gross output (at producer prices or factor values) across 27 countries (Venezuela was eliminated) as an approximation to world market size (Deardorff 1984 suggests such a scaling). For the purpose of computing unskilled-labor and human-capital shares, data on total compensation and employment were used to calculate an average wage in each industry. The minimum average wage across all industries was then taken to reflect the compensation of unskilled laborers. The unskilled labor share is then this minimum wage times employment as a proportion of gross output. The share of human capital is defined as the difference between each industry's wage and the minimum wage, multiplied by employment, divided by gross output:

$$(5) \qquad H_i = (\text{WAGE}_i - \text{MINWAGE}) \cdot E_i/Q_i.$$

Effectively, I assume the absence of human capital in the lowest-wage industry and standardize upon that industry. More direct measures of educational attainment by each industry's labor force would provide better indicators of skill distributions across industries, but such data are unavailable. The share of output paid to physical capital was taken to be nonwage value added as a proportion of output, under the assumption that value added comprises only payments to labor and capital. Ignoring land in this context is problematic and might be alleviated somewhat in a set of manufacturing industries by disaggregating capital into structures versus plant and equipment. To do so, however, one would need also data on appropriate depreciation factors and price deflators for capital types, plus some means of allocating residual value added. Finally, the materials share is simply cost of materials, as approximated by gross output less value added, as a proportion of output.

As discussed earlier, countries define their raw variables in the ISIC somewhat differently. Thus, the input shares computed here are not strictly comparable across countries because of further measurement problems. Nonetheless, it is of interest to compare the direct links between trade performance and factor shares in the various nations. Table 1.7 lists the simple correlations between scaled net exports and factor shares across all industries in each country. Thus, for example, Canadian manufactured net exports tended to be low in industries with high unskilled-labor (i.e., low-wage labor) and physical-capital shares but high in industries with high materials shares. In turn, though these correlations show nothing about the direction of dependence among the variables, they may be taken as indicators of the direct net factor content of trade. I also list the correlations of scaled net exports with scaled U.S. net exports to provide perspective on the similarity of each nation's trade pattern across industries to the U.S. trade pattern.

The figures in table 1.7 need little amplification, but a few comments are worth making. The trade patterns of some countries (Cyprus, Finland, New Zealand, and Turkey) are uncorrelated with any factor shares, suggesting essentially balanced net trade in all inputs. In contrast, some countries are distinctive in their relationships between factor shares and trade patterns, as evidenced by the positive correlations between net trade and low-wage labor for South Korea, the Philippines, Portugal, and Spain, and those between net trade and human capital for Germany, Japan, Sweden, and the United States. Indeed, these last four countries form a group in which the relationships between factor shares and trade patterns are highly similar, suggesting that they

Table 1.7   **Simple Correlations between Scaled Net Exports and Factor Shares by Country and between Scaled Net Exports and U.S. Scaled Net Exports, 1984, Using Market Exchange Rates**

Country	n	U	H	K	M	USNX
AU	28	−0.29	−0.48*	−0.15	0.38**	−0.65*
AS	28	0.19	0.23	0.14	−0.28	0.65*
CA	28	−0.53*	0.07	−0.31***	0.46**	−0.15
CH	28	−0.23	−0.18	0.24	−0.11	0.20
CO	28	0.21	−0.38**	−0.03	0.01	−0.37**
CY	24	0.14	−0.05	0.03	−0.07	−0.69*
DE	28	0.37**	0.26	0.06	−0.34***	0.78*
EC	28	−0.25	0.02	−0.07	0.17	−0.80*
FI	28	0.10	−0.01	−0.09	0.01	0.44**
GE	24	0.05	0.69*	0.24	−0.46**	0.73*
GR	28	0.28	−0.01	0.34***	−0.31***	0.53*
IN	25	0.07	−0.30	−0.22	0.25	0.07
IR	24	−0.56*	0.18	0.37***	−0.08	0.76*
IS	25	0.52*	−0.04	−0.25	−0.06	−0.27
IT	21	0.63*	−0.46**	0.16	−0.27	−0.90*
JA	27	0.22	0.41**	0.43**	−0.49*	0.79*
KO	28	0.46**	−0.21	0.02	−0.20	−0.04
NO	27	−0.34***	−0.02	−0.34***	0.24	−0.68*
NZ	26	0.12	−0.14	0.13	−0.12	0.37***
PH	28	0.45**	0.16	0.07	−0.32***	0.55*
PO	27	0.42**	−0.24	0.08	−0.18	−0.72*
SI	24	−0.19	−0.15	−0.16	0.26	0.22
SP	28	0.43**	0.15	0.00	−0.28	0.27
SW	28	−0.03	0.35***	0.20	−0.17	0.73*
TU	28	0.06	−0.07	−0.03	0.02	0.53*
UK	28	−0.48*	−0.01	0.02	0.21	−0.21
US	28	−0.15	0.38**	0.32***	−0.28	1.00*

Note: *** = significantly different from 0 at 10% level; ** = same at 5% level; * = same at 1% level. n = number of industry sectors. USNX = U.S. scaled net exports.

are mutual international competitors. Italy is a case unique among the industrial nations; it has a strong positive correlation of net trade with unskilled labor and a strong negative correlation with human capital. This distinctiveness is emphasized by the divergence in the U.S. and Italian trade patterns.

Perhaps the main conclusion to be drawn from this analysis is that the various computed correlations are generally weak, except those for the United States, Japan, Germany, and a few other isolated cases. These are precisely the three countries to which this model has been applied with some success in the literature (Stern and Maskus 1981, Urata 1983, Stern 1976). It therefore appears that this analysis of trade and intensities does not extend well to other countries. Note especially that for several developing countries (Chile, Ecuador, Indonesia, Singapore, and Turkey) there is no clear association of net exports with industries using greater amounts of unskilled labor, nor is there a clear association of net imports with industries using greater amounts of human capital; this result is contrary to what one might expect.

An important underlying empirical issue of interest is whether factor shares are sensitive to variations in the business cycle. If so, the researcher would need to exercise caution in the choice of years for analysis, while the traditional presumption that cross-section data reflect basically long-run influences would be challenged. In fact, one motivation for the choice of 1984 for the current paper is that it was a year of on-trend activity for many OECD countries.[21]

To examine the cyclicality issue, I assembled the production and input data for the United States and Japan in 1982, a trough year, and for the United States in 1978 and Japan in 1979, both peak years. I report in table 1.8 the average unskilled-labor and physical-capital shares for our three types of manufactures (light, medium, and heavy industries), on the possibility that cyclical influences may vary across these types (data for all industries are available on request). I also list figures for value added per laborer, expressed in 1980 prices for each country, to see if labor productivity is sensitive to the cycle.

From these data there appears to have been no cyclical effect on the levels of U.S. factor shares. Rather, the results are suggestive of secular declines in labor intensity and, perhaps, of secular increases in capital intensity in light and medium industries. In Japan, however, the lowest capital shares in each industry group were registered in 1982, the trough year, which is suggestive of cyclical impacts. Nonetheless, the differences are slight, and there seems little reason to discriminate among these years in computing factor shares for fear of cyclical distortions. Labor productivity, on the other hand, did seem to vary in both countries with the cycle, with 1982 seeing both the lowest average amounts and the highest relative variances of real value added per employee. I conclude that measured factor shares are likely to be relatively im-

21. See Organisation for Economic Cooperation and Development, *Main Economic Indicators*, various issues.

Table 1.8   **Average Unskilled-Labor and Capital Shares by Industry Group, Average Real Labor Productivity across all Industries, and Coefficients of Variation for the United States and Japan, Various Years, at Concurrent Market Exchange Rates**

Country	Year	(Cycle)	Light Industries U	Light Industries K	Medium Industries U	Medium Industries K	Heavy Industries U	Heavy Industries K
U.S.	1978	(Peak)	.193(.23)	.287(.20)	.104(.37)	.276(.22)	.072(.51)	.258(.33)
	1982	(Trough)	.184(.23)	.298(.19)	.103(.41)	.281(.30)	.075(.51)	.231(.47)
	1984	(Trend)	.174(.25)	.308(.22)	.095(.40)	.299(.32)	.066(.51)	.250(.44)
Japan	1979	(Peak)	.142(.39)	.241(.16)	.084(.27)	.260(.24)	.048(.59)	.246(.37)
	1982	(Trough)	.143(.40)	.233(.12)	.080(.32)	.247(.24)	.044(.59)	.225(.43)
	1984	(Trend)	.138(.44)	.238(.18)	.080(.33)	.254(.24)	.043(.58)	.233(.43)

Value Added per Employee, All Industries

Country	Year	(Cycle)	
U.S.	1978	(Peak)	50,594(.62)
	1982	(Trough)	48,329(.68)
	1984	(Trend)	54,268(.62)
Japan	1979	(Peak)	46,290(.80)
	1982	(Trough)	39,536(.91)
	1984	(Trend)	45,520(.79)

pervious to cyclical variations, but that computations of the levels of outputs and inputs are sensitive to them.

To conclude this section, I note that it is possible to expand the analysis to incorporate alternative ad hoc trade models, in which industries and countries may be combined in other arbitrary fashions to examine the influences of crude measures of scale economies, consumer-goods characteristics, and the like. Experimentation in those directions was largely unrewarding and is not further pursued here.

1.5 Trade and Factor Endowments

The discussion surrounding equation (2) earlier noted that the partial approach that comes closest to the true specification of the Heckscher-Ohlin model is a regression of net trade on excess factor endowments. Here, I regress net exports on the levels of factor endowments, which procedure may be considered, along with a relationship between GNP and endowments (not shown), to be the reduced form of equation system (2). Because factor intensities do not enter into this analysis, there is no need to develop data on input usage. This fact is a substantial advantage for this approach since it allows the direct use of SITC trade data, at the chosen levels of aggregation, in the equations without recourse to concordances. It also invites the inclusion of a greater number of countries in the analysis.

1.5.1 Data Overview

In table 1.9, I list the countries included in the analysis, along with an aggregation scheme of 2-digit SITC trade categories. There are 38 countries in the sample, again at all levels of development. The choice of countries was determined by the availability of appropriate endowment and trade data for 1984.

The international trade data, all based on SITC Revision 2, were taken from sources published by the OECD and the United Nations.[22] A few concerns about these figures should be raised. First, the SITC lists trade of all countries in current dollars, regardless of the currency of denomination of trade contracts. The trade transactions in local currencies are presumably translated into dollars at market exchange rates by the reporting countries, though there is little information in this regard. The existence of internationally traded goods argues for the use of market rates for conversion anyway, so perhaps this absence of information is unimportant. This fact allows me to convert endowment data in value terms to dollars at market rates also, without considering here any PPP conversions. Nonetheless, it would be interesting to know how accurate the dollar figures are, strictly on the basis of exchange-rate measurement. Second, it is not possible to tell how inclusive the trade data are for all countries. For example, countertrade has become prevalent in some of the developing countries in this sample, and it is not clear whether such trade is included and in what valuation. Third, there are some international discrepancies in the data because the United Nations allows countries to choose whether to report trade on a "special" or "general" (including entrepot-trade) basis and whether to value exports and imports on a c.i.f or f.o.b. basis. Some care has been taken here to account for reexports, but this task is not always straightforward. Fourth, import data tend to be more reliably collected in most countries than export data because they loom larger in the customs-revenue scheme. This problem seems especially acute in bilateral trade data, where one country's reported imports from a partner often exceed markedly the partner's reported exports, as is well known from the U.S.-Canadian reconciliation exercises.

Finally, there remains the fundamental question of aggregation. The SITC data are available at finely disaggregated levels. In principle, one could undertake to relate trade in each of these categories to factor supplies, but that task would be tedious for researcher and reader alike and would likely not be very

22. For OECD members, OECD, *Foreign Trade by Commodities, 1984*, vol. 1, *Exports*, and *Foreign Trade by Commodities, 1984*, vol. 2, *Imports* (Paris, 1986). For other countries, United Nations, *Commodity Trade Statistics, 1984*, ST/ESA/STAT/Ser.D, various issues. Countries that reported on the basis of Revision 1, necessitating adjustments to their trade figures, were Chile, Brazil, and Mexico.

Table 1.9   **Countries in the Analysis of Trade and Endowments and SITC Aggregation**

Country (Abbrev.)	Industry (Abbrev.; Included SITC Classes)
Argentina (AR)	Food, beverages, and tobacco (FDBV; SITC 00–09, 11–12)
Australia (AU)	Raw materials (MATE; SITC 21–23, 26–29, 41–43)
Austria (AS)	Petroleum and coal products (PECO; SITC 32–34)
Belgium (BE)	Chemicals (CHEM; SITC 51–59)
Brazil (BR)	Wood products (WOOD; SITC 24–25, 63–64)
Canada (CA)	Light industries (LITE; SITC 61, 65, 82–85, 87–89)
Chile (CH)	Machinery and transport equipment (MACH; SITC 71–79)
Colombia (CO)	
Cyprus (CY)	
Denmark (DE)	
Ecuador (EC)	
Egypt (EG)	
Finland (FI)	
France (FR)	
West Germany (GE)	
Greece (GR)	
India (ID)	
Indonesia (IN)	
Ireland (IR)	
Israel (IS)	
Italy (IT)	
Japan (JA)	
South Korea (KO)	
Malaysia (MA)	
Mexico (ME)	
Netherlands (NE)	
New Zealand (NZ)	
Norway (NO)	
Philippines (PH)	
Portugal (PO)	
Singapore (SI)	
Spain (SP)	
Sweden (SW)	
Switzerland (SZ)	
Thailand (TH)	
Turkey (TU)	
United Kingdom (UK)	
United States (US)	

instructive.[23] On the other hand, significant aggregation runs the risk of misidentifying trade flows that should be classified on an industry basis inspired by the factor-proportions model. I employed three aggregation levels for the present paper, though only the results of the last one are presented. These

23. Such detail would be useful for many other empirical purposes, such as studies of intra-industry trade, substitution elasticities in demand, and computations of unit values and quality indices.

levels were: first, the 57 separate 2-digit categories in SITC levels 0 through 8; second, the 28 three-digit ISIC-equivalent manufacturing industries identified earlier; and third, an aggregation of the 2-digit categories into the groups listed in table 1.9. This final grouping was arbitrary, relying on no statistical aggregation scheme such as that used in this context by Leamer (1984). My intent was to adopt a limited set of commodity aggregates that made some sense a priori as potentially having identifiable endowment-based sources of trade.

In defense of the trade data one can say that they are, in principle, collected on a reasonably consistent basis and reported in a standardized form. The situation is different for factor endowments, the measurement of which is, in any case, no simple task. First, we would like to have data on total potential supplies of inputs (e.g., proven reserves of minerals and energy), but we often must settle for factors actually in use. The latter variables clearly are endogenous to factor prices (as may be the former). Similarly, factor use may vary with the business cycle; it is unclear how to define capital endowment and labor force when there are multiple shifts, for example. Second, there is little likelihood that similar factor supplies across countries are of substantially equal quality. There is great variation in international definitions of labor types, for example. Further, a high-school graduate in one country may have far different skills on average than a high-school graduate in another country. Quality differences in capital, land, and minerals are also likely to be marked. And, finally, countries are likely to define various factors differently. For these reasons, we may expect significant errors of measurement to arise in computing endowments.

This study incorporates measures of seven factor endowments. The first two are LABORS, the sum of occupational categories 0/1 (professional, technical, and kindred workers) and 2 (administrative and managerial workers) as a measure of higher-skilled labor endowment, and LABORU, the sum of the other occupational categories (clerical and related workers, sales workers, service workers, agriculture, forestry, and fisheries workers, and laborers and production and related workers) as a measure of lower-skilled labor endowment (both measured in thousands).[24] The third endowment is CONG, an aggregate of the value (in millions of dollars) of production of coal, oil, and natural gas in metric ton equivalents.[25] The fourth factor is MIN, an aggregate of the value (in millions of dollars) of production of bauxite, primary aluminum, copper, iron ore, lead, manganese, nickel, potash, tin, and zinc in metric tons of mineral content.[26] As value aggregates of current output levels of heterogeneous

24. See International Labour Organisation, *Yearbook of Labour Statistics*, various years. These data are based on national surveys, which are often of sketchy temporal and sectoral coverage. Thus, a number of the observations on labor forces have been estimated; details are available on request.

25. See OECD, *Coal Information*, various issues and United Nations, *Energy Statistics Yearbook*, various issues.

26. See U.S. Bureau of Mines, *Minerals Yearbook*, various issues, for international production

commodities, CONG and MIN are conceptually quite weak as proxies for supplies of natural resources. Unfortunately, there appear to be no reasonable alternatives to this usage. The next two endowments are LAND1, the area of arable land and land under permanent crops or permanent pasture, and LAND2, the area of forests and woodland, both measured in thousands of hectares.[27] Again, this definition merges several presumably different forms of productive and nonproductive land (e.g., tropical land, temperate land, tundra) but is maintained for empirical tractability. Finally, the net capital stock, KSTOCK, is the accumulated, depreciated, and deflated series (15 years, 13.33 percent depreciation rate) of gross fixed capital formation in each country.[28] Data on gross national product in 1984 dollars were gathered as well.[29] Problems with international comparisons of GNP are well known.

1.5.2   Estimation Results

The estimation procedure follows that in Leamer (1984). In previous sections I examined problems that emerge in simple computations of variables for analysis, including exchange-rate valuation and cyclicality. Here, I focus on econometric problems that clearly affect inferences in the regressions of net trade on the levels of endowments. In particular, countries in the sample are of radically different sizes, suggesting the presence of heteroskedastic error variances. Further, measurement error is surely endemic in the endowments data described above, generating inconsistent least-squares estimators of the reduced-form coefficients.

The influence of heteroskedasticity is detailed in table 1.10. The first row in each pair of equations provides the coefficients from ordinary least-squares (OLS) estimation, where the net-exports variables were entered in thousands of dollars. Judging from the relatively high coefficients of determination, the endowments model explains variations in net exports rather well. The contributions of individual endowments to trade in the various sectors is evident from the coefficients and their significance levels. A high capital endowment, for example, is associated with high net trade in machinery, while a high endowment of arable land is a detriment to net exports in wood products. To account for the presence of heteroskedasticity, a simple procedure was followed in which the log of the squared residuals from each OLS equation was regressed on the log of each nation's GNP. The coefficients from these regressions, listed in the w column, were near unity except in the chemicals indus-

data, and International Monetary Fund, *International Financial Statistics*, various issues, for prices. Prices were taken here as the prevailing average price in the appropriate international commodity markets and were assumed to represent common international prices. No attempt was made to gather prices in individual countries.

27. See Food and Agricultural Organization, *Production Yearbook*, various years.

28. See Summers and Heston (1988) for investment deflators, and International Monetary Fund, *International Financial Statistics*, various years, for gross fixed capital formation (row 93e).

29. International Monetary Fund, *International Financial Statistics*, various years (row 99a).

Table 1.10   Ordinary Least-Squares (OLS) and Weighted Least-Squares (WLS) Regressions of Net Exports on Endowment Levels, 1984

Industry	Regressions	LABORS	LABORU	KSTOCK	LAND1	LAND2	CONG	MIN	R^2	w
FDBV	OLS	−106	−0.3	−4.9*	16**	11**	88**	−319	.69	.98
	WLS	−53	−4.7	−3.1	16**	12**	−12	−194	.40	
MATE	OLS	−384***	−0.6	−3.7*	9.3***	2.5	149*	100	.78	.96
	WLS	−312	5.0	−3.3	3.8	2.6	70***	460	.43	
PECO	OLS	−2753*	151*	−23*	−32***	2.1	313*	2136**	.93	.89
	WLS	−3228*	144*	−24*	−17***	5.0	633*	1101***	.79	
CHEM	OLS	519***	−27***	−0.2	−6.3	−2.8	−10	178	.40	.26
	WLS	461***	−27***	0.2	−4.4	−2.0	−11	54	.32	
WOOD	OLS	−470***	23***	−1.3	−23*	9.0**	48***	1167*	.63	.73
	WLS	−308	13	−0.9	−14**	10**	19	658**	.30	
LITE	OLS	814***	−4.2	1.1	4.7	4.4	−303*	−573	.79	1.12
	WLS	432	8.7	1.8	2.7	3.0	−151**	−510	.26	
HEAV	OLS	118	3.3	4.9*	−12***	6.5	−259*	717***	.85	.90
	WLS	−49	−2.1	4.5**	−4.7	6.0	−139*	341	.36	
MACH	OLS	−1705***	44	44*	−4.8	20	−764*	−841	.89	1.06
	WLS	−1461***	8.4	34*	5.4	14	−381*	−1349***	.59	

Note: *** = significantly different from 0 at 10% level; ** = same at 5% level; * = same at 1% level.

try, suggesting that error variances were proportional to GNP. These coefficients were used to develop inverse weights for the weighted least-squares (WLS) regressions in the second rows of each equation pair. In general, this adjustment tended to reduce the magnitudes and significance levels of the coefficients but did not alter their signs. It also reduced the explanatory power of the equations. Such results indicate the need for caution in using such equations for prediction or policy analysis.

This last conclusion is reinforced by consideration of measurement error in the data. Reverse regressions of each endowment on sectoral net exports and the remaining endowments were run, allowing for the existence of errors in each factor supply. Each equation was solved for the implied coefficients relating trade to endowments. If they are of the same sign, the minimum and maximum resulting coefficients provide a confidence interval for the true regression parameter (Leamer 1984, Kmenta 1986). If the bounds on this interval are close to the OLS estimates, we may infer the estimates to be reliable. If the sign changes between the minimum and maximum coefficients, however, the interval is unbounded and the regression parameters cannot be estimated reliably.

The ranges of estimates from the reverse regressions are reported in table 1.11. Forty-six of the 56 ranges cover both positive and negative numbers, indicating that the corresponding OLS coefficients cannot be confidently accepted. Seven of the remaining ten ranges are so wide that the OLS coefficients provide only qualitative indicators of a relationship and their use in, say, a forecasting model would be highly questionable. In only three cases (the negative effects of CAPITAL and LAND2 in CHEM trade and of LAND1 in WOOD trade) is there evidence of a reliably estimated parameter.

Thus, it appears that available data on factor supplies are either so poorly measured that they provide no evidence on the trade-and-endowments model, or, if measured adequately, cast doubt on the model. As noted earlier, it is the most appropriate indirect approach to the factor-proportions theory. One source of the difficulty is collinearity in the underlying true endowments, generating volatility in the trade estimates from measured proxies. The standard remedy is to place constraints on the error variances of the regression and the measured endowments in order to provide additional information (Leamer 1984), but the mismeasurements here appear to be so gross that such an approach would provide little benefit and is not further considered here. For present purposes, the point has been made that available endowments do not support precise estimation of the link between trade and factor stocks.

1.6   Concluding Remarks

It may be useful to conclude this paper with a "wish list" of steps that might be taken by data suppliers and data users to improve our ability to understand the relationships among trade, factor endowments, and factoral and sectoral

Table 1.11 Range of Coefficients from Reverse Regressions in the Endowment Model, 1985

Industry		LABORS	LABORU	KSTOCK	LAND1	LAND2	CONG	MIN
FDBV	max.	392307	1085	92	2718	1078	2575	537
	min.	-32697	-25381	-846	2.3	1.2	-32335	-103450
MATE	max.	110377	2533	12	775	167	1094	33333
	min.	-5780	-7246	-239	-467	-157	-9109	-29341
PECO	max.	-56	447	111	264	1887	1981	17544
	min.	-31887	-86	-37	-385	-72	211	-73566
CHEM	max.	42000	132	-0.2	52	-23	79	29412
	min.	519	-1016	-233	-429	-278	-3448	-866
WOOD	max.	4211	218	99	-13	54	490	4065
	min.	-4902	-88	-26	-72	-13	-116	-658
LITE	max.	57407	445	102	826	324	-21	657
	min.	-18060	-3711	-119	-15	-22	-5030	-36000
HEAV	max.	30303	2381	83	5.2	114	2744	10381
	min.	-35714	-1000	-91	-262	-90	-2576	-7857
MACH	max.	13214	1650	104	875	333	1287	153571
	min.	-26238	-313	-71	3571	-179	-1190	-62500

income distribution. The list might be useful in guiding future deliberations in this area.

First, there is a need for standardized concordances at higher levels of aggregation. With the advent of the Harmonized Commodity Description and Coding System and the issuance of the third revisions of the ISIC and SITC, detailed concordances will be available. I understand the reluctance of authorities to construct higher-level concordances, however, since doing so inevitably requires some arbitrariness. Thus, this may be an issue for data users to resolve.

Second, there is a pressing need for the development of international price deflators on a consistent basis for outputs, inputs, and trade. Such information would be of great use far beyond the kinds of models used here.

Third, available measures of sectoral labor requirements, such as the use of operatives versus other labor, are grossly deficient, while occupational detail for sectoral workers is limited. It would be useful to improve the information published on occupational employment, with a view to standardizing definitions of labor input and effort expended (e.g., hours worked). Similar comments would apply to different forms of capital input. Such standardization would ease concern over the differential-quality issue and make more meaningful the computation of factor prices. Of course, it will never be possible to measure inputs fully in quality-standardized units.

Fourth, it was demonstrated earlier that neither market exchange rates nor PPP rates serve effectively to compare inputs and productivity, and that measurements were very sensitive to the choice. The development of exchange rates for this purpose would aid in the understanding of international technology levels and in sorting out components of technology.

A final comment is in order here. International data are not collected on a basis suggested strictly by trade or microeconomic theory. This fact is unsurprising, given that economists are not the primary users of the data. Perhaps what is required is a greater effort by economists to settle on appropriate definitions themselves before expecting data authorities unilaterally to provide them on the preferred basis. An example might be the measurement of endowments. It is unsurprising that endowments are measured so poorly when we cannot agree on appropriate definitions for them, even in principle. Surely, however, the collection effort can be instructed by the specification of the most useful proxies a priori. Absent such efforts we will continue to construct approximations that are of questionable relevance to underlying variables.

References

Baldwin, R. E. 1971. Determinants of the Commodity Structure of U.S. Trade. *American Economic Review* 61:126–46.

Baumol, W. 1986. Productivity Growth, Convergence, and Welfare. *American Economic Review* 76:1072–85.

Bowen, H. P., E. E. Leamer, and L. Sveikauskas. 1987. Multicountry, Multifactor Tests of the Factor Abundance Theory. *American Economic Review* 77:791–809.

Branson, W. H., and N. Monoyios. 1977. Factor Inputs in U.S. Trade. *Journal of International Economics* 7:111–31.

Brecher, R. A., and E. U. Choudhri. 1988. The Factor Content of Consumption in Canada and the United States: A Two-Country Test of the Heckscher-Ohlin-Vanek Theorem. In *Empirical Methods for International Trade,* ed. R. C. Feenstra, 5–17. Cambridge, Mass.: MIT Press.

Chenery, H., and M. Syrquin. 1975. *Patterns of Development, 1950–1970.* New York: Oxford University Press for World Bank.

Clague, C. K. 1991. Relative Efficiency, Self-Containment, and Comparative Costs of Less Developed Countries. *Economic Development and Cultural Change* 39:507–30.

Deardorff, A. V. 1984. Testing Trade Theories and Predicting Trade Flows. In *Handbook of International Economics,* vol. 1, ed. R. Jones and P. B. Kenen, 467–517. Amsterdam: Elsevier Science Publishers.

De Long, J. B. 1988. Productivity Growth, Convergence, and Welfare: Comment. *American Economic Review* 78: 1138–54.

Dollar, D., and E. N. Wolff. 1988. Convergence of Industry Labor Productivity Among Advanced Economies, 1963–1982. *Review of Economics and Statistics* 70:549–58.

Dollar, D., E. N. Wolff, and W. J. Baumol. 1988. The Factor-Price Equalization Model and Industry Labor Productivity: An Empirical Test Across Countries. In *Empirical Methods for International Trade,* ed. R. C. Feenstra, 23–47. Cambridge, Mass.: MIT Press.

Kmenta, J. 1986. *Elements of Econometrics.* 2d ed. New York: Macmillan.

Leamer, E. E. 1974. The Commodity Composition of International Trade in Manufactures: An Empirical Analysis. *Oxford Economic Papers* 26:350–74.

———. 1984. *Sources of International Comparative Advantage.* Cambridge, Mass.: MIT Press.

Leamer, E. E., and H. P. Bowen. 1981. Cross-Section Tests of the Heckscher-Ohlin Theorem: Comment. *American Economic Review* 77:1040–43.

Maskus, K. E. 1985. A Test of the Heckscher-Ohlin-Vanek Theorem: The Leontief Commonplace. *Journal of International Economics* 9:201–12.

Nogues, J. J., A. Olechowski, and L. A. Winters. 1986. The Extent of Nontariff Barriers to Imports of Industrial Countries. World Bank Staff Working Paper no. 789. Washington, D.C.

Norsworthy, J., and D. Malmquist. 1983. Input Measurement and Productivity Growth in Japanese and U.S. Manufacturing. *American Economic Review* 73:947–67.

Stern, R. M. 1976. Some Evidence on the Factor Content of West Germany's Foreign Trade. *Journal of Political Economy* 84:131–41.

Stern, R. M., and K. E. Maskus. 1981. Determinants of the Structure of U.S. Foreign Trade. *Journal of International Economics* 11:207–24.

Summers, R., and A. Heston. 1984. Improved International Comparisons of Real Product and Its Composition, 1950–1980. *Review of Income and Wealth* 30:207–62.

———. 1988. A New Set of International Comparisons of Real Product and Price Levels Estimates for 130 Countries, 1950–1985. *Review of Income and Wealth* 34:1–25.

Urata, S. 1983. Factor Inputs and Japanese Manufacturing Trade. *The Review of Economics and Statistics* 65:678–84.
Vanek, J. 1968. The Factor Proportions Theory: The n-Factor Case. *Kyklos* 21:749–56.

Comment   Edward E. Leamer

This excellent paper is a fine way to start a conference on a subject that is sadly neglected by economists: the collection and dissemination of economic data. I can think of no other "scientific" discipline that pushes the division of labor so far that the activities of data collection and data analysis are performed by completely separate groups of individuals. This is not a healthy situation. Lacking training in data collection, the data analysts have very little appreciation of how inaccurate the data actually are. Though data analysts may "know" that there are imperfections in the data, they prefer to allocate their scarce time to other problems and to act as if the measurements were perfect. This creates a market for new data series but no market for improvements to existing series. Data collectors respond accordingly. I take the goal of this conference to be improved communication between users and collectors, which hopefully will improve both the use and the collection. I will make the point in this comment that there is still a lot of room for improvement in this communication.

Maskus's paper makes two contributions. He illustrates how the data are used to study the international structure of output and consumption. And he offers a comprehensive catalog of difficulties with the data. A point that I will make is that these two contributions are almost completely separate—just as are data collection and data analysis in our profession. What we need to do is to bridge the gap. More on this below. First I will comment on the problems with the data.

If you read Maskus's catalog of data problems it is hard to understand why we spend so much time on unit roots, cointegration, nonparametric tests for nonlinearities, and the like. Here is a list of problems that I have pulled out of Maskus's discussion:

(i) There are missing data. In one sample, 5.8 percent are missing, 6.9 percent are "constructed." Price data are often not available at all, and unit values are used instead.
(ii) The data are internationally noncomparable because methods of collection differ by countries.

Edward E. Leamer is Chauncey Medberry Professor of Management and professor of economics at the University of California, Los Angeles.

(a) Definitions differ.

   i. The form of compensation of inputs varies across countries. For example, retirement benefits, vacation pay, and health benefits can differ substantially.

   ii. The treatment of taxes on outputs and inputs varies.

   iii. The definition of employment varies across countries depending on factors such as hours worked or nature of contract with the firm.

   iv. Some countries value trade c.i.f., others f.o.b.

(b) Methods of sampling differ.

   i. Sampling frames differ (e.g., minimum establishment size).

   ii. Sampling methods differ (some use a census, others a stratified sample, etc.)

   iii. The questionnaire design differs (sometimes it is conducted by mail, sometimes by interview). The kind of people who provide the information varies.

(c) The data are sorted and processed differently. For example, multi-output establishments are disentangled differently.

(iii) The data are internationally noncomparable due to aggregation problems.

(a) Industrial aggregation combines industries with drastically different technologies. Apparent differences in productivities may be due to different industrial mixes.

(b) Capital aggregation combines vastly different equipment of vastly different vintages in different countries.

(c) Labor aggregation combines laborers with different skills. When education is used to sort workers, the resulting categories may be noncomparable because of vast differences in the meaning of a year of schooling.

(iv) Data are internationally noncomparable due to currency conversion problems, which are especially difficult in periods of extreme exchange-rate gyrations.

(v) There are substantial concordance problems since, for example, trade and production data are collected using different product classifications.

(vi) The classification systems change over time. ISIC Revision 2 was completed in 1968; Revision 3 is in process (SIC was revised in 1972, 1977, and 1982).

(vii) The treatment of re-exports can differ by country. This is an especially difficult problem when transactions occur entirely within a multinational firm.

(viii) Value-added data are internationally noncomparable if the prices of intermediate inputs differ. To express this differently, the value-added production function should depend on the prices of these intermediate inputs, as well as on the physical quantities of labor and capital.

Good heavens! That is quite a list. It leaves one wondering if these data are useful for anything. This concern is not put to rest by Maskus's report on how these data are used. First he apologizes for the lack of close connection between the theory and the data analyses. What this seems to imply is that more complete and more accurate data would not have a decisive impact, since the link between the theory and the data analysis is sufficiently weak that no "intellectual capital" is genuinely at risk when the data are examined. That should be the subject of another conference—improved communication between theorists and data analysts, who are almost as separated as data collectors and data analysts.

Concerns about the theory and the data notwithstanding, Maskus reports in table 1.5 a remarkable finding: total factor productivity is almost 50 percent higher in the United States than in any other country. I don't believe this, and neither does Maskus, who reports: "Among the primary explanations that could be advanced for this finding are international differences in factor quality, management capability, public infrastructure and technology. I have emphasized the last factor in the approach to these productivity measures, but the analysis here is incapable of discriminating among these influences." I would have looked elsewhere for the explanation. My guess is that the U.S. capital stocks are substantially underestimated because of the 15-year life that Maskus is forced by data limitations to assume. If you prefer, you may dismiss the finding by referring to other items on the list of data problems. But if that is your attitude, what can you learn from a data-set?

Now I want to make my most important point: *The methods that we use to analyze data need to make explicit reference to the possibility of measurement error, if we are going to learn anything from data that we suspect are subject to measurement error.* Otherwise we will merely use data to support our prior beliefs, dismissing contrary findings by referring to measurement errors. There is only one data analysis that explicitly refers to measurement errors in Maskus's paper, indeed in this whole collection of papers. Otherwise the data are analyzed as if they were free of error. For that reason, I think this conference has not been wholly successful in the creation of communication links between users and collectors.

The analysis to which I refer are the errors-in-variables bounds presented in table 1.11. If you are familiar with the traditionl discussion of errors-in-variables in econometrics, you probably have a mistaken viewpoint about the consequences of measurement errors. That literature deals with a bivariate problem in which measurement error of a certain kind causes "attenuation" of the estimates (downward bias). This leaves the impression that correcting for errors in variables can be done by enlarging the coefficients. This is a mistaken idea, first of all because attenuation in the bivariate case is associated with one special kind of measurement error. But more importantly, the attenuation result doesn't apply if more than one right-hand side variable is measured with error. Another theorem applies in the multivariate case.[1] A minimal set of

---

1. Reported in Steven Klepper and Edward E. Leamer, "Consistent Sets of Estimates for Regressions with All Variables Measured with Error," *Econometrica* 52 (1984):163–83.

estimates that in large samples will surely capture the true regression vector is found in three steps. First, one computes a set of regressions with each of the possible variables treated as the "left-hand" (dependent) variable. Then these estimated linear functions are reexpressed to have the same left-hand variable. If the signs of the coefficients are the same for each of these estimates, then the minimal set is the set of all weighted averages of these estimates, and in particular an errors-in-variable bound is the interval between the smallest and the largest coefficient. (Incidentally, this interval will include estimates that are both larger and smaller than the ordinary regression and in that sense the attenuation result does not apply in the multivariate setting.) On the other hand, if, as is the case of the results reported in table 1.11, there are *any* sign changes, then the minimal consistent set is unbounded and in that sense the data are informationless about individual coefficients. This occurs because the measurement error is treated by subtracting from the observed covariance matrix that part of the variability that is due to measurement errors. If the data are quite collinear already, removing a little of the observed variability can produce a perfectly collinear data set which cannot be used to produce estimates of individual coefficients.

I am afraid that the unboundedness result is most likely to occur with the kinds of multicollinear data-sets that we usually analyze. What that means is that in the absence of knowledge of the probable measurement errors, our data-sets are worthless for estimating regressions. Thus my point: We need to improve the communication from collectors to users of data. *The users need to be informed about the accuracy of the data.* They need standard errors of the measurement errors.

I know that this is asking a lot, but I think it is essential. Now I am going to ask for something much more, something that will seem mind boggling, greedy, and even absurd: *We need standard errors. But we also need standard errors of the standard errors.* Standard errors of the measurement errors are enough to correct econometric estimates for the biases that are associated with the use of mismeasured data. But in order to compute standard errors of these econometric estimates we need also to have standard errors of the standard errors. Expressed differently, if there are measurement errors in the data then econometric estimates are subject to both sampling error and misspecification error. If we knew the error rates in our data exactly, then we could correct perfectly the estimates, and we would be left with only sampling error. But we cannot know the error rates exactly, and we cannot eliminate altogether the misspecification uncertainty. In order to compute the probable amount of misspecification uncertainty, we will need some measure of the uncertainty in the error rate. Thus we need standard errors of the standard errors.[2]

To summarize, I speak to both data analysts and data collectors.

2. For further amplification, see the paper that this conference has stimulated, Edward E. Leamer, "We Need Standard Errors of the Standard Errors of the Measurement Errors of Our Data" (typescript, 1989).

To the data analysts I say: You need to make explicit reference to measurement errors when you analyze a data-set. This has two benefits. First, it will allow you to learn something from the data. Otherwise, whatever are your estimates, you will probably dismiss them as entirely due to measurement errors. Secondly, it will make you acutely aware of the need for more accurate data, and you may then communicate that to the data collectors.

To the data collectors, I say: To understand how the economy behaves, I need:

(a) more data

(b) more accurate data

(c) more accurate estimates of the accuracy of the data.

You surely overemphasize (a). You recognize (b). But please don't neglect (c). It is the real limiting factor right now.

2 Computers and the Trade Deficit
The Case of the Falling Prices

Ellen E. Meade

2.1 Introduction

Over the past two decades, technological advances in the computer industry have been enormous. During the 1970s, running a computer program involved a number of cumbersome tasks: typing out computer cards at a keypunch machine, submitting the job by processing the deck of cards through a card reader, and waiting for written output from a printer. Today, the same computer program can be run in a variety of ways, all of which are extremely simple, efficient, and affordable. And the reduction in the size of computers, from the gigantic mainframe to the portable personal computer, has made international trade in these goods more important. Today, we benefit not only from advances in the domestic computer market, but from technological gains in overseas markets as well.

For economists observing the rapid development in the computer market, a couple of important questions arise. First, how do we measure the advancement in the computer industry in a meaningful way? Ideally, we would like to measure a number of factors: for instance, the availability of new products, the apparent decline in the relative price of computer power, and the resultant increase in our productivity. Second, as computers become an increasingly important product in international markets, how can we best predict future developments? If we think that technological advances in the computer industry may be expected to continue as they have recently, then we want to treat

Ellen E. Meade is a staff economist in the Division of International Finance, Federal Reserve Board of Governors.

Thanks to NBER conference participants, Robert B. Kahn, David H. Howard, and William R. Melick for detailed comments and suggestions. Lucia Foster provided excellent research assistance and Virginia Carper provided graphics expertise. The views expressed in this paper are the author's and do not necessarily coincide with the views of the Federal Reserve Board or other members of its staff.

this industry separately when formulating predictions, because its behavior differs so much from other industries.

This paper addresses both of these questions. The proper measurement of prices of domestic computers has been the subject of a number of recent studies (including Cartwright 1986, Cole et al. 1986, Dulberger 1989, and Gordon 1989). The Bureau of Economic Analysis (BEA) has modified its traditional approach to price measurement with techniques to incorporate adjustment for quality change, in order to capture the developments in the computer market more comprehensively. A hedonic price index was developed to measure prices of domestic computing equipment; the same index is now being used to deflate exports and imports of computers as well. Section 2.2 gives a detailed discussion of the construction of the BEA index for computer prices and the potential problems involved in using a domestic index to deflate other categories of spending.

When the BEA index is used to deflate the value of traded computers, the quantity of exported and imported computers shows tremendous growth over the last decade. These data are reviewed in section 2.3. Empirical trade models have focused on aggregate historical relationships and have not accounted for developments in the computer industry separately. The paper examines the extent to which separate treatment of computers is warranted, by comparing a conventional trade model with a model that disaggregates exports and imports of computers from other trade flows. The models are outlined in section 2.4. The comparison of models in section 2.5 is based on parameter estimates as well as on the forecasting ability in and out of sample.

2.2   Measurement of Computer Prices

2.2.1   Limitations of the Traditional Matched-Model Approach

A traditional procedure for the measurement of prices is the "matched-model" approach. A matched-model index records the price for an identical product (produced by identical technology) across two different time periods.[1] Products that are available in the first period but discontinued in the second period, as well as new products that become available in the second period but are not produced in the first period, are excluded from the sample, since prices of these products are not available for both time periods. Generally, this does not present a problem for the construction of the index, if the price movements of the products included in the index accurately reflect the movement of prices omitted from the index. In order to form the price index across a number of

---

1. The formula for a price index (I) at time t, with a base period of $t - 1$ is:

$$I_{t,t-1} = \sum P_{i,t}Q_{i,t} / \sum P_{i,t-1}Q_{i,t}$$

where the index is constructed over i types of the product. $P_{i,t}$ represents the price of product i at time t. $Q_{i,t}$ is the quantity of i purchased at time t. The index is used to deflate current dollar figures (a Paasche index).

time periods, these adjacent-year matched-model indexes are linked together multiplicatively in a "chain" index.[2]

The discontinuation of outdated products and the introduction of new products may pose a problem for price measurement, however, if technological advancement in the industry is particularly rapid. This concept can best be explained by way of example: good x is produced in both the first and second periods; its price is sampled for the matched-model index. Good y, identical in characteristics to x but produced with a newer technology, is introduced in the second period. Because it is produced with a more efficient technology, good y is less expensive than good x. In the long run, both good x and good y should sell for the same price, since the products are identical. But in the short run, until equilibrium is established in the market, there will be a price differential. Since the matched-model index only includes the price of good x, it tends to overstate the level of prices. In some studies, this phenomenon is termed "technologically-induced disequilibrium," since it is the lack of instantaneous adjustment to a new equilibrium that causes the traditional matched-model index to misstate true price changes[3] (see Cole et al. 1986, Triplett 1986, and Dulberger 1989, for further discussion of the need for hedonic methods). Obviously, the more rapid is the technological advancement in an industry (implying frequent reductions in price and many new products), the greater is the concern about using the matched-model approach to capture price change.

2.2.2   The Hedonic Approach

Advances in the computer market since the early 1970s have generated incredible gains in efficiency and a broad array of newly available products. The concern about "technologically-induced disequilibrium" has prompted BEA to augment the traditional matched-model approach to the measurement of computer prices with techniques that adjust for improvement in quality. In essence, these techniques generate estimates for missing prices (in the above example, the price of product y in the first period), so that the matched-model index is formulated over a complete sample of prices. The method used to generate the missing prices is a hedonic regression that relates the behavior of product prices (the dependent variable) to a time dummy, important product characteristics, and a measure of technology (the explanatory variables).[4] A

---

2. Using the notation defined in footnote 1, the index for the entire period can be written as:

$$I_{0,t} = I_{0,1} \times I_{1,2} \times, \ldots, \times I_{t-1,t}.$$

3. The difference between the traditional matched-model index and an index that accounts for quality improvement is quite substantial for several components of computers. Cole et al. (1986) compare a matched-model index with three different hedonic indexes for four computer components (processors, disk drives, printers, and general purpose displays). For each component, the hedonic indexes declined twice as much or more on average than the matched-model index.

4. It is the time dummy that actually captures price movements, once characteristics and technology are controlled for.

number of authors have investigated the appropriate specification of hedonic regressions for computer processors and parts, including the choice of functional form, product characteristics included, and estimation restrictions (see Cole et al. 1986, Dulberger 1989, and Gordon 1989).

2.2.3 Product Coverage and Construction of the Hedonic Index

Underlying the hedonic approach is the assumption that the price of a product reflects the characteristics bundled in that product. If the hedonic regression adequately controls for changes in the embodied characteristics, then residual price change is the result of technological improvement. Implementation of hedonic techniques for computers requires an appropriate definition of both the product and the product characteristics. BEA defines the computer in terms of individual pieces of equipment and constructs price indexes for each component separately.[5] While the running of a job on a computer may require several pieces of computer equipment acting in sequence, the individual pieces possess different characteristics. Furthermore, although most computer purchases are of a system of components, only the individual prices are observed (and discounting is common for a system purchase). For these reasons, hedonic techniques are applied to the individual computer components rather than to the computer system as a whole. The components measured in the BEA index include computer processors, disk drives, printers, general purpose displays (terminals), and personal computers.[6]

In addition, adequate coverage of the characteristics that determine the value of each component is critical to the success of the hedonic technique. The IBM Corporation, in developing the hedonic regressions, selected the relevant characteristics for four of the components: for computer processors, speed of execution of a set of instructions and memory capacity; for disk drives, memory capacity and speed of transfer between the drive and the main memory; for printers, speed, resolution of print, and number of fonts available; and for terminals, screen capacity, resolution, number of screen colors, and number of programmable function keys.[7]

An augmented matched-model index is constructed for each of the four components, using predictions from the hedonic regressions to fill in missing prices. That is, the hedonic regression predicts what the price of the component would have been, given its characteristics and technology, if had it been

5. The initial research and development of the computer index was provided by the IBM Corporation and is documented in Cole et al. (1986). Since that time, BEA has altered the original index relatively little. BEA began using this adjusted matched-model index to deflate computer purchases in the GNP accounts in 1985 and has revised the historical data back to 1969 to incorporate this index.

6. Tape drives were covered in the index through 1983 but were excluded thereafter, reflecting their declining importance. Prices of tape drives are assumed to be represented by the average change in the prices of other components.

7. As Gordon (1989) points out, there are a number of critical attributes excluded from hedonic studies on computers. These are software maintenance, engineering support, and manufacturer's reputation—characteristics which are virtually impossible to measure.

available at a particular date. The price measure for personal computers does not involve hedonics; it is a traditional matched-model index covering price changes for IBM products and personal computers from several other manufacturers. The aggregate index for computers is a weighted average of the augmented matched-model indexes for computer processors, disk drives, printers, and displays, and the unaugmented matched-model index for personal computers. The weights used to construct the index are shares of each component in the shipments of domestic manufacturers.

2.2.4   Caveats

Several comments are in order regarding the construction and the usefulness of the BEA price index for computers. First, if the technological development in the personal computer market has been as rapid as in the market for other computer products, then the estimation of PC prices from a traditional matched-model index will bias the price upward.[8] Second, for all of the components in the BEA index, the data on prices were for list prices rather than for actual transactions prices. Discounting is a common practice in the computer industry, especially for the purchase of a system of components. To the extent that different components are discounted by different margins, this adds an additional source of bias.

Third, several recent studies have investigated the role of this computer price index in the measurement of productivity (see Baily and Gordon 1988 and Denison 1989). These studies consider whether the use of this computer deflator in the GNP accounts has biased measures of productivity and output and perhaps misattributed the gain in computer power (for the BEA opinion on this subject, see Young 1989). While this line of research is timely and important, it is beyond the scope of the study here.

Fourth, very few countries currently employ hedonic techniques for the measurement of computer prices. Based on the author's survey, only Canada and Australia use a hedonic price index. Both of these countries obtain the component price indexes from BEA, adjust for bilateral exchange-rate changes vis-à-vis the dollar, and use own-country weights to form the aggregate index. Japan measures prices of domestic and traded computers with a unit value index, derived from value and quantity data. While economists with the Economic Planning Agency in Japan acknowledge the need for hedonic techniques, they feel that these techniques are too complicated to pursue. The United Kingdom follows a traditional matched-model procedure.[9] Clearly, indicators of international price competitiveness may be biased by the lack of standardization in the measurement of computer prices.

A final concern involves the broad use of this computer price index in the

8. Another index for PC prices was described in Gordon (1987). Like the BEA index, the Gordon index was constructed as a traditional matched-model index.

9. These survey results are broadly consistent with those of an OECD survey of 13 member countries in 1985. At that time, only the United States and Canada employed hedonic techniques.

GNP accounts. The components in the index reflect prices for the domestic market, as well as exported and imported computers; the aggregate index is formed using weights in domestic shipments. While the index is a hybrid, it seems most appropriate for the deflation of the computer portion of producers' durable equipment. However, the price is also used to deflate exports and imports of computers.[10] Using this index to deflate exports and imports of computers will be unbiased only if: (i) export and import prices for the individual computer components are identical to domestic prices;[11] and (ii) the mix of each of the components in exports and imports is identical to that in domestic shipments.

To test the first of these two conditions, the research staff at IBM has gathered information on the prices of the individual components. These data reveal that, with the exception of printers, prices of domestic components do not differ systematically from the prices of traded components. Imported printers, however, exhibit systematic price differentials relative to domestic printers. This is because the United States has tended to produce and export system printers whose prices have fallen less rapidly than the prices of imported PC printers. Regarding the second condition, data for 1988 suggest that the component mix of exports is similar to that of domestic shipments. Imports, on the other hand, appear to have a lower share of computer processors and a higher share of printers and other peripheral equipment than found in domestic shipments.[12] Evidence on the above two conditions suggests: (i) that the domestic computer price index may be a relatively unbiased measure of the prices of exported computers, but be an inappropriate measure of the prices of imported computers; (ii) that if the prices of imported computer components and the mix of the components in imports were adequately measured, the prices of imported computers would likely be found to have fallen more rapidly than the prices of domestic and exported computers.

2.3   Computer Prices and International Trade

The BEA adjusted matched-model (or hedonic) index for computers used in the deflation of exports and imports is shown in figure 2.1 and table 2.1 below. According to this index, computer prices have declined more than 14

10. The price index is also used to deflate government expenditure on computers (federal as well as state and local). Currently, consumer purchases of computers are deflated using the matched-model index for PCs.

The domestic price index for office, computing, and accounting machinery (OCAM) is used to deflate exports and imports of business and office machines through 1984. From 1985 on, exports and imports of computers, peripherals, and parts are deflated using the computer index. The OCAM index is a composite of BEA's computer index, and the PPI for office and accounting machinery (excluding computers).

11. This bias will contaminate not only the deflation of traded computers, but the deflation of domestic purchases as well.

12. This is a preliminary finding of a project to construct component shares for exports and imports and then to use these shares to compute price indexes for computer exports and imports.

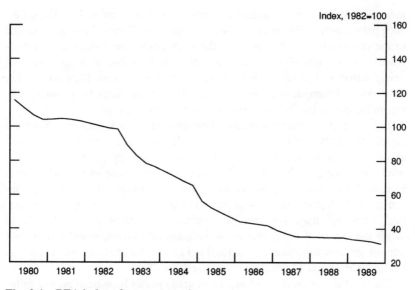

Index, 1982=100

Fig. 2.1   **BEA index of computer prices**

Table 2.1   **Measures of Computer Prices**

	BEA[a]		BLS—Export		BLS—Import	
	Level	Change[b]	Level	Change[b]	Level	Change[b]
1982:Q4	98.5	−4.6	n.a.		n.a.	
1983:Q4	76.4	−22.4	n.a.		n.a.	
1984:Q4	65.5	−14.3	102.4	n.a.	100.7	n.a.
1985:Q4	46.8	−28.5	99.1	−3.2	102.4	1.7
1986:Q4	41.7	−10.9	98.0	−1.1	104.1	1.7
1987:Q4	35.2	−15.6	95.0	−3.1	112.2	7.8
1988:Q4	34.8	−1.1	95.5	0.5	111.3	−0.8
1989:Q4	31.1	−10.6	93.6	−2.0	110.1	−1.1

[a]BEA uses the same price index to deflate exports and imports.
[b]Percentage change, computed on a Q4–Q4 basis.

percent per year on average since 1982 (fourth quarter to fourth quarter), and by the end of 1989 were almost 70 percent below their 1982 level.[13] These price movements differ markedly from the rate of price change in an alternative measure of computer prices constructed by the Bureau of Labor Statistics. The BLS index for the prices of exported computers has declined modestly since the end of 1984 (the data are not available prior to that time), while the

13. Measured from the beginning of the hedonic index in 1969 through 1988, the computer price declined almost 7 percent per year on average.

index of import prices has actually increased over the same period. The difference between the BEA price and the alternative BLS measures can be traced to the construction of the indexes; the BLS prices are traditional matched-model indexes, not adjusted to capture the effects of discontinued models or newly introduced products. It is interesting to note that the BLS price index for exports of computers differs significantly from the index for imports, calling into question the BEA practice of imposing identical prices.

The value of computers and related products in international trade has risen rapidly since the early years of this decade. As a share of nonagricultural exports, the value of computers had almost doubled by 1988 from its 1980 level (see table 2.2). The share of computers in the value of non-oil imports increased even more over this period, growing in excess of 400 percent. Because the BEA price index for computers has declined so much over this period, measured trade volumes have increased far more than trade values. While the shares of computers in the volumes of nonagricultural exports and non-oil imports were small to negligible in 1982, these shares had risen dramatically to 21 and 14 percent, respectively, by 1988.

The level and movement of aggregate trade prices have been greatly influenced by the BEA price deflator for computers. Two measures of non-oil import prices, the GNP implicit deflator and the fixed-weight price index, are shown in figure 2.2. The implicit deflator, which is a variable-quantity share-weighted index, has risen much less over the recent period than the fixed-weight index, owing to the increasing importance of computers in the variable-weight measure. Exclusion of computers from the implicit deflator (shown as the dotted line in fig. 2.2) results in a measure that moves quite similarly to the fixed-weight index. (Although not shown in fig. 2.2, a similar divergence between the implicit deflator and the fixed-weight price for nonagricultural exports develops over the same period.)

2.4 A Conventional Trade Model and Two Alternative Specifications

The changes in exports and imports of computers over the past decade or so may well have influenced our ability to explain and predict aggregate trade flows. Conventional empirical models of international trade generally de-

Table 2.2   **Computers as a Percentage Share of Merchandise Trade**

	1980	1982	1984	1986	1988
Value:					
Nonagricultural Exports	4.1	5.2	7.4	7.3	8.0
Non-Oil Imports	.9	1.4	3.0	3.3	4.5
Volume:					
Nonagricultural Exports	3.3	5.2	10.5	14.9	21.1
Non-Oil Imports	.8	1.4	4.2	7.2	14.2

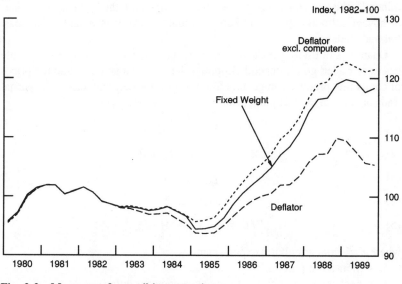

Fig. 2.2   Measures of non-oil import prices

scribe nonagricultural exports and non-oil imports, disaggregating agricultural exports and oil imports from other products. Agricultural exports and oil imports are modeled separately, owing to the relative importance of these products in trade combined with the "special" circumstances in these markets—government subsidies and trade restrictions for agriculture, and the influence of the OPEC cartel on the determination of oil prices and production.[14] Separate empirical treatment of exports and imports of computers may be warranted as well, given the construction of the price index, the rapid decline in that index, and the increasing importance of these products in trade. This section outlines a framework for evaluating this question by examining a conventional trade model and investigating whether simple modification of this model can account for recent developments, or whether computer trade should be disaggregated altogether.

The conventional trade model examined here is the part of the Helkie-Hooper (HH) model, a partial-equilibrium model of the U.S. current account used for analysis and forecasting by the staff of the Federal Reserve Board (see Helkie and Hooper 1988, Helkie and Stekler 1987, and Meade 1988).[15] The HH equations describe traded goods and services and capital flows; policy variables, as well as incomes, prices, and exchange rates, are predeter-

---

14. Oil exports and agricultural imports are not treated separately, however, because these products are relatively unimportant in overall trade.

15. The HH model is also used as the U.S. current account sector of the Federal Reserve Board Multicountry Model (see Edison, Marquez, and Tryon 1987).

mined.[16] The key equations for merchandise trade are the volumes and prices of nonagricultural exports and non-oil imports—the determinants of the partial trade balance.

Quantities of traded goods depend on real income and relative prices, while prices of traded goods depend on input prices, exchange rates, and the prices of competing products. In general, the form for the determinants of the partial trade balance in the HH model can be written as follows:

(1)
$$X = f[Y_f, (P_x \cdot E/P_f)]$$

(2)
$$M = f[Y, (TR \cdot P_m/P)]$$

(3)
$$P_x = f[P_w, (P_f/E)]$$

(4)
$$P_m = f[P_f, E, P_{cmd}]$$

(5)
$$PTB = X \cdot P_x - M \cdot P_m$$

where X = nonagricultural export quantity;
M = non-oil import quantity;
E = exchange rate (units of foreign currency per dollar);
$P(P_f)$ = domestic (foreign) prices;
P_w = producer price for nonagricultural exports;
$P_x (P_m)$ = implicit deflator for nonagricultural exports (non-oil imports);
P_{cmd} = price of non-oil commodities;
Y = U.S. real GNP;
Y_f = index of weighted average rest-of-world real GNP;
TR = index of tariff rates; and
PTB = partial trade balance.

In the HH model, several other variables augment the equations. A dummy variable to measure dock strikes appears in both trade volume equations (see Isard 1975). In the equation for non-oil import volume, a variable measuring capacity utilization abroad relative to capacity utilization in the United States captures cyclical variation (a cyclical measure in the export volume equation was dropped due to statistical insignificance). A relative secular supply variable (the ratio of measures of U.S. capital stock to foreign capital stock) appears in both trade volume equations as a proxy for supply-induced shifts in production (see Helkie and Hooper 1988, p. 20).

The HH formulation measures the prices of traded products with implicit deflators. As discussed above, price indexes in which the share of computers is variable have behaved quite differently over the recent period from indexes

16. A typical criticism of this partial-equilibrium framework is that different policies have different effects on incomes, prices, and exchange rates. In this sort of model, incomes, prices, and exchange rates are predetermined, and policy has no explicit role. Thus, a particular change in the predetermined variables has an identical effect on trade flows, regardless of the underlying policy. Essentially, the parameter estimates measure the responsiveness of trade flows to changes in predetermined variables, given the average mix of policies that generated the historical data.

in which the weight given to computers is fixed. Because of the rapidly changing role of computers between the estimation period and the postsample period, equations explaining the implicit deflator have predicted poorly out of sample. A proposed improvement to the conventional specification is to base the price equations on fixed-weight measures. In a modified HH formulation (termed the HHFW model), the behavioral price equations (3) and (4) are reestimated with fixed-weight price indexes in place of the deflators; bridge equations are then used to relate the fixed-weight price indexes to the implicit deflators, as follows:[17]

(3')
$$P_{Fx} = f[P_w, (P_f/E)]$$

(4')
$$P_{Fm} = f[P_f, E, P_{cmd}]$$

(6)
$$P_x = f[L1(P_x), \Delta P_{Fx}]$$

(7)
$$P_m = f[L1(P_m), \Delta P_{Fm}]$$

where P_{Fx} (P_{Fm}) = fixed-weight price index for nonagricultural exports (non-oil imports); and $L1(\cdot)$ defines the first-order lag operator. Equations (1), (2), and (5), which determine the quantity of nonagricultural exports, the quantity of non-oil imports, and the partial trade balance, respectively, remain unchanged.

A second, more fundamental, alternative to the original HH specification involves disaggregating computers from the other elements of the partial trade balance and determining trade in computers separately. In this formulation, equations (1), (2), (3), and (4) represent the volumes and prices of nonagricultural exports and non-oil imports excluding computers.[18] The computer (HHC) model is closed by adding three equations to determine the volume and price of computer exports and imports.[19] The initial specification tested for the quantity of computer exports and imports includes an income term, as well as two relative price measures. The first relative price term captures shifts in aggregate trade prices versus domestic prices; the second relative price term measures the shift of prices within nonagricultural exports and non-oil imports between computers and other products:

(8)
$$X_c = f[Y_f, (P_x \cdot E/P_f), RP_{xc}]$$

(9)
$$M_c = f[Y, (TR \cdot P_m/P), RP_{mc}]$$

where X_c = computer export quantity; M_c = computer import quantity; and RP_{xc} (RP_{mc}) = the price of computers relative to the implicit deflator for nonagricultural exports (non-oil imports) excluding computers.

17. It is still necessary to produce an estimate for the implicit deflator, as this measure is used to form the relative price term in equations (1) and (2) and to compute the partial trade balance in equation (5).

18. Thus, the endogenous variables, X, M, P_x, and P_m must be redefined to exclude computers.

19. Recall that the same price index is used to deflate the value of exports and imports. Thus, only one price equation is necessary.

The equation for computer prices differed from the other behavioral price equations. Because the BEA index for computer prices essentially tracks price conditions in the domestic market and is adjusted further to account for changes in quality, computer prices were modeled as a time series augmented by a linear trend term to capture technological progress:

(10) $$P_c = f[L1(P_c), \text{TREND}]$$

where P_c = implicit deflator for computer exports and imports; and TREND = linear time trend.

2.5 Empirical Results

The proper treatment of computers in empirical trade models is evaluated by the comparison of the original Helkie-Hooper (HH) model with the two alternative specifications—the fixed-weight aggregate model (HHFW) and the model with computers disaggregated (HHC). First, we examine key parameter estimates in the HH, HHFW, and HHC models. The parameters of particular interest include the income and relative price elasticities in the trade volume equations and the sensitivity of import prices to exchange rates (the "pass-through" coefficient). Second, we compare the forecasting ability of the components of the partial trade balance both in and out of sample using a summary error statistic (root mean square percent error). Finally, we examine the errors in the projection of the partial trade balance for each of the models.

2.5.1 Parameter Estimates

The structural equations of the three models were estimated in double-log functional form, using quarterly data through the end of 1986. Most of the equations were estimated beginning in 1970:Q1. However, the equation for export prices in all of the models was estimated beginning in 1973:Q1 due to limitations in the availability of data. In the HHC model, the equations for the volumes and price of computers were estimated beginning in 1978:Q1, since computers were relatively unimportant in international trade prior to this date. Tables 2.3 through 2.6 give the parameter estimates for the primary structural equations in each model.[20] Estimates for the computer sector of the HHC model are shown on table 2.7.

In general, parameter estimates in the equations for trade prices are fairly similar across models, despite the different measures for prices used as the dependent variable (see tables 2.3 and 2.4). While the dependent variable in the HH and the HHC specifications is an implicit deflator, the dependent variable in the HHC model more closely resembles the fixed-weight price in the

---

20. While the equations in the HH model are identical to those discussed by Helkie and Hooper (1988), the parameter estimates differ somewhat due to revisions to the historical data and the extension of the estimation range through the end of 1986.

Table 2.3   **Parameter Estimates for Export Price Equations, 1973:Q1–1986:Q4**

	Model		
	HH[a]	HHFW[b]	HHC[c]
Dependent variable	P_x	P_{FX}	P_{xnc}
Explanatory variables			
Intercept	.49	.93	.45
	(1.35)	(3.81)	(1.74)
U.S. producer price (P_w)	.89	.80	.90
	(11.69)	(15.59)	(16.63)
Foreign price[d] (P_f)	.05	.07	.08
	(0.68)	(1.59)	(1.46)
Exchange rate[d] (E)	− .05	− .07	−.08
	(0.68)	(1.59)	(1.46)
Summary statistics			
Rho	.83	.77	.80
	(23.81)	(11.00)	(18.68)
R^2	.99	.99	.99
S.E.R.	.011	.009	.010

Note: Equations are estimated in double-log form. *T*-statistics are in parentheses.
[a]Dependent variable is the implicit deflator for nonagricultural exports.
[b]Dependent variable is the fixed-weight price for nonagricultural exports. The bridge equation between the fixed-weight price and the deflator is

$$\text{Log}(P_x) = 0.03 + 0.99 \times \text{Log}(L1(P_x)) + 1.10 \times \Delta\text{Log}(P_{FX})$$

where $L1(\cdot)$ is the first-order lag operator; $R^2 = .99$; S.E.R. $= .005$; and all coefficients are highly significant. The estimation range is 1970:Q1–1986:Q4.
[c]Dependent variable is the deflator for nonagricultural exports excluding computers.
[d]4-quarter polynominal distributed lag.

HHFW model (see fig. 2.1). Because of this, it would not be surprising to find that the estimated parameters in the price equations of the HHC and HHFW models were more similar to each other than to the estimates of the HH model. This is not the case, however. On the whole, the key parameter estimates in the price equations are not terribly sensitive to the alternative price variables that are employed.

Domestic production costs are a significant determinant of U.S. export prices, but they are less than completely passed through in all three models. Price conditions in destination markets do not appear to influence export prices (contrary to the result in Helkie and Hooper 1988). Movements in foreign prices and exchange rates are the primary factors explaining the behavior of import prices, with some small adjustment for changes in the prices of non-oil commodities. The measure of foreign prices used in the models is a weighted average of consumer prices for the other G-10 and 8 developing countries. This variable acts as a proxy for the cost of production facing foreign suppliers. As discussed in Hooper and Mann (1989), while movements in foreign consumer prices and production costs were quite similar over the 1970s and early 1980s, a large divergence has emerged in recent years. This

Table 2.4   **Parameter Estimates for Import Price Equations, 1970:Q1–1986:Q4**

	Model		
	HH[a]	HHFW[b]	HHC[c]
Dependent variable	P_m	P_{Fm}	P_{mnc}
Explanatory variables			
Intercept	4.25	4.63	3.93
	(12.58)	(17.31)	(11.89)
Foreign price (P_f)	.84	.77	.85
	(20.85)	(24.15)	(21.63)
Exchange rate[d] (E)	− .89	− .81	− .84
	(12.42)	(14.45)	(11.97)
Commodity price[e] (P_{cmd})	.18	.08	.18
	(4.39)	(2.35)	(4.54)
Summary statistics			
Rho	.64	.56	.63
	(6.39)	(5.46)	(6.26)
R^2	.99	.99	.99
S.E.R.	.014	.013	.014

Note: Equations are estimated in double-log form. *T*-statistics are in parentheses.
[a]Dependent variable is the implicit deflator for non-oil imports.
[b]Dependent variable is the fixed-weight price for non-oil imports. The bridge equation between the fixed-weight price and the deflator is
$$\text{Log}(P_m) = 0.99 \times \text{Log}(L1(P_m)) + 1.12 \times \Delta\text{Log}(P_{Fm})$$
where $L1(\cdot)$ is the first-order lag operator; $R^2 = .99$; S.E.R. = .007; and all coefficients are highly significant. The estimation range is 1970:Q1–1986:Q4.
[c]Dependent variable is the deflator for non-oil imports excluding computers.
[d]8-quarter polynomial distributed lag.
[e]4-quarter polynomial distributed lag.

is an important point, to which we will return later in the discussion of simulation results.

Parameter estimates in the volume equations are more sensitive to the definition of the dependent variable. The volume equation for nonagricultural exports and non-oil imports is used in both the HH and HHFW models; in the HHC model, this same specification is used to explain trade volumes excluding computers. When computers are excluded from nonagricultural exports, the estimated sensitivity to changes in relative prices increases somewhat, and the estimated sensitivity to changes in foreign income is substantially reduced (see table 2.5). In addition, the effect of changes in relative secular supply becomes statistically insignificant. According to Helkie and Hooper, this variable has traditionally played an important role, measuring the effects of the introduction of new products that are not captured adequately in relative price movements. In the HH model, the relative secular supply variable has tended to reduce the discrepancy in income elasticities between the export and import volume equations. The tendency for the estimated income elasticity of U.S.

Table 2.5   **Parameter Estimates for Export Volume Equations, 1970:Q1–1986:Q4**

	Model	
	HH, HHFW[a]	HHC[b]
Dependent variable	X	X_{nc}
Explanatory variables		
Intercept	−4.85	4.12
	(7.47)	(5.01)
Foreign income (Y_f)	2.04	1.25
	(6.86)	(8.82)
Relative price[c]	−.86	−.99
	(7.57)	(9.46)
Relative supply (RSUP)[d]	1.12	1.20
	(2.25)	(0.20)
Dock strike	.83	.83
	(7.01)	(7.01)
Summary statistics		
Rho	.67	.68
	(7.11)	(7.75)
R^2	.99	.98
S.E.R.	.027	.027

Note: Equations are estimated in double-log form. *T*-statistics are in parentheses.
[a]Dependent variable is the volume of nonagricultural exports and is identical in models HH and HHFW.
[b]Dependent variable is the volume of nonagricultural exports excluding computers.
[c]The relative price in the HH and HHFW models is the nonagricultural export deflator relative to foreign consumer prices in dollar terms; in the HHC model, the relative price is the deflator for nonagricultural exports excluding computers relative to foreign prices in dollars. 8-quarter polynomial distributed lag.
[d]Ratio of the capital stock in the U.S. relative to foreign countries.

imports to exceed the income elasticity of U.S. exports (in the absence of adjustment for shifts in supply) is often referred to as the "Houthakker-Magee" result. For non-oil imports, the disaggregation of computers reduces the sensitivity of other imports to changes in relative prices and changes in relative secular supply (see table 2.6). The estimated sensitivity of imports to U.S. activity, however, is little changed across models. With the income elasticity of exports reduced and that of imports unchanged, the aforementioned discrepancy in income elasticities resurfaces in the HHC model.

In summary, there are several important points about the alternative model parameters. First, the estimates in the trade price equations are insensitive to the exclusion of computer prices from the implicit deflator (in the HH and HHC models). Second, the relative price elasticities in both trade volume equations are not very sensitive to the exclusion of computers and generally lie in the neighborhood of unity, whether or not computers are included.

Table 2.6   Parameter Estimates for Import Volume Equations,
                   1970:Q1–1986:Q4

	Model	
	HH, HHFW[a]	HHC[b]
Dependent variable	M	M_{nc}
Explanatory variables		
Intercept	.11	−1.49
	(4.21)	(.29)
U.S. Income (Y)	1.97	2.02
	(2.54)	(2.64)
Relative price[c]	−1.11	−1.02
	(9.81)	(8.90)
Relative supply (RSUP)[d]	−.90	−.74
	(2.14)	(1.83)
Relative capacity[e]	−1.28	−1.30
	(1.64)	(1.73)
Dock strike	.78	.79
	(4.24)	(4.26)
Summary statistics		
Rho	.48	.47
	(4.21)	(4.10)
R^2	.99	.99
S.E.R.	.031	.031

Note: Equations are estimated in double-log form. *T*-statistics are in parentheses.
[a]Dependent variable is the volume of non-oil imports and is identical in models HH and HHFW.
[b]Dependent variable is the volume of non-oil imports excluding computers.
[c]The relative price in the HH and HHFW models is the non-oil import deflator (adjusted for tariffs) relative to the U.S. GNP deflator; in the HHC model, the relative price is the deflator for non-oil imports excluding computers (adjusted for tariffs) relative to the GNP deflator. 8-quarter polynomial distributed lag.
[d]Ratio of the capital stock in the U.S. relative to foreign countries.
[e]Ratio of manufacturing capacity utilization in the other G-10 countries relative to U.S. capacity utilization.

Third, estimated income elasticities do appear to be quite sensitive to the treatment of computers, and the discrepancy between income elasticities of U.S. exports and imports (noted in other studies of U.S. trade) reemerges in the HHC formulation, despite the inclusion of the relative secular supply measure.

Table 2.7 gives the parameter estimates for the computer sector of the HHC model. Estimation of equation (10) indicates that computer export and import prices are determined primarily by the lagged value of prices, with a small but significant downward trend adjustment. The initial specification for the volume of computer exports postulated in equation (8) did not yield sensible empirical estimates. While the elasticity of computer exports with respect to foreign income was large and highly significant, neither relative price term

Table 2.7   Parameter Estimates for Computer Equations, 1978:Q1–1986:Q4, in HHC Model

BEA computer price (P_c)

$$\log(P_c) = .29 + .94 \times \log[(P_c)_{-1}] - .003 \times \text{TREND}$$
$$ (1.28)\ (21.50) (2.17)$$

$$R^2 = .99 \qquad \text{S.E.R.} = .028$$

Computer export volume (X_c)[a]

$$\log(X_c/PDE_{oca}) = -1.97 - 1.92 \times \log(Y_{-1}) + 4.04 \times \log(Y_F) - .42 \times \log(E)$$
$$\phantom{\log(X_c/PDE_{oca}) =} (0.51) \quad (2.31) (4.24) (2.89)$$

$$R^2 = .58 \qquad \text{S.E.R.} = .062 \qquad Rho = .35\ (2.08)$$

Computer import volume (M_c)[b]

$$\log(M_c) = 72.84 + 2.01 \times \log(Y - PDE_{oca}) + .36 \times \log(PDE_{oca}) - 19.90 \times \log(\text{RSUP}) - 2.93 \times \log(P_m/\text{CPI})$$
$$ (-2.93) \quad (2.43) (3.53) (10.31) (6.64)$$

$$R^2 = .99 \qquad \text{S.E.R.} = .044 \qquad Rho = .25\ (1.34)$$

Note: *T*-statistics are in parentheses. PDE_{oca} is investment spending on office, computing and accounting machinery in billions of 1982 dollars. CPI is the U.S. consumer price index.

[a] 4-quarter polynomial distributed lag on the exchange rate (E).

[b] 8-quarter polynomial distributed lag on the relative price (P_m/CPI). RSUP is the ratio of the capital stock in the U.S. relative to foreign countries.

was significantly different from zero. (When the homogeneity constraint on the relative price terms was relaxed, only the exchange rate entered the equation with a significant coefficient.) In addition, the relative secular supply variable was negatively correlated with computer exports, a result that runs counter to intuition. After considerable experimentation with alternative formulations, exports of computers were modeled as a ratio to domestic equipment spending on computers. This ratio responds positively to changes in foreign income and declines somewhat with an appreciation of the dollar. When U.S. income increases, domestic spending on computers rises relatively more than exports.

The estimated equation for the volume of computer imports is similar to the specification discussed in equation (9). All of the estimated parameters are statistically significant and of the expected sign (except for the price of computer imports relative to the price of other non-oil imports, which was dropped from the equation due to statistical insignificance). The activity variable was separated into two terms—real investment spending on office and computing machinery, and other real GNP—in order to allow for a differential response of computer imports to these two categories of income. While the estimated sensitivity of computer import volume to the relative secular supply variable and to the price of non-oil imports relative to domestic prices is of the expected sign, both elasticities are larger than expected.

In general, it was difficult to obtain sensible empirical estimates for the computer sector of the HHC model. The estimates are not particularly robust to changes in the range of estimation. Equations using time-series or error-correction techniques (instead of structural equations with a first-order autoregressive process) would likely do better at capturing the dynamics inherent in the data.

2.5.2   Simulation Performance

Simulation results for the estimation period and for the out-of-sample period (1987:Q1–1989:Q2) were produced for the three models. These results are presented in figures 2.3 through 2.7. In order to facilitate the comparison of results across models, the analysis is presented in terms of the components of the partial trade balance. Prediction errors for the HH model equal the difference between the individual equation forecast and the actual data. For the HHFW and HHC models, the prediction errors are an aggregate of individual equation errors. For example, in the HHFW model, the prediction error for the non-oil import deflator is obtained from both the error in the structural equation explaining fixed-weight prices and the translation equation for the deflator. In the HHC model, the procedure to obtain the import deflator is even more complicated, as computer prices are predicted separately. In sum, reported prediction errors for the various components of the partial trade balance shown in figures 2.3 through 2.7 are a mix of individual equation and

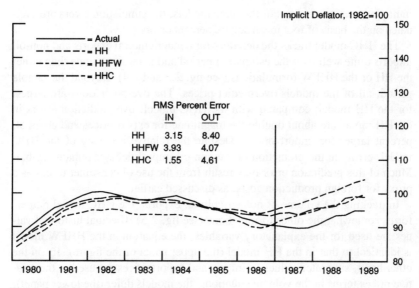

Fig. 2.3   Price of nonagricultural exports

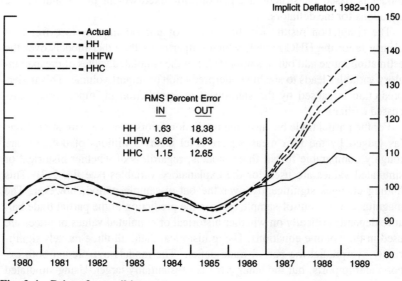

Fig. 2.4   Price of non-oil imports

multiple equation errors. For the three models, the simulation errors are evaluated on the basis of root mean square percent errors.[21]

The HHC model tracks the deflators for nonagricultural exports and non-oil imports quite well over the estimation period and is more accurate than either the HH or the HHFW formulations (see fig. 2.3 and 2.4). Beyond the sample period, all of the models overpredict prices. The overpredictions are largest for the HH model; compared with the HHC model, overprediction errors in the HH model are about double the magnitude for export prices and about 50 percent larger for import prices. Despite the relative accuracy of the HHC model, errors in the prediction of the non-oil import deflator remain sizable. Much of this prediction error may result from the use of consumer prices as a proxy for foreign production costs, as discussed earlier.

In tracking the volume of nonagricultural exports, the HHC model outperforms somewhat the other formulations (see fig. 2.5). If actual historical values are used for the explanatory variables, the equation in the HHFW model is identical to that in the HH model (the upper panel of the figure). If, on the other hand, simulated values of import and export prices are used in the relative prices terms in the volume equations, the models differ (the lower panel). This is because the prediction of export and import price deflators in the HH model involves structural equations, whereas the prediction in the HHFW model is based on structural equations for fixed-weight prices and bridge equations for the deflators.

The simulation results for the volume of non-oil imports (see fig. 2.6) clearly favor the HHC model, which outperforms the other models over the estimation range and out of sample. Use of the simulated values of the explanatory variables leads to sizable underprediction of import volume. This underprediction is caused by the significant overprediction of import prices discussed earlier.

For the partial trade balance, the prediction errors over the estimation range (as judged by the root mean square level error in billions of dollars), are roughly comparable for all three models, regardless of whether historical or simulated values are used for the explanatory variables (see fig. 2.7). This finding changes significantly over the out-of-sample period, however. The magnitude of the out-of-sample error in the prediction of the partial trade balance depends critically on whether historical or simulated values of prices are used in the volume equations. Using historical data, all three models significantly overpredict the partial trade deficit. The models overpredict both exports and imports, but the latter error is substantially larger. Using simulated values for the right-hand side variables not only reduces the prediction errors, but actually reverses their direction. The overprediction of import prices leads

21. RMS percent error is the root mean square error as a percentage of the sample mean of the variable. The in-sample errors are computed over the estimation range of the equation, or the intersection of the estimation ranges of the component equations. The out-sample errors are computed beginning in 1987 through the second quarter of 1989.

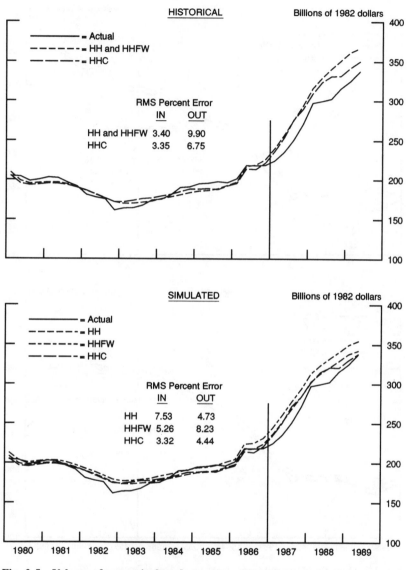

Fig. 2.5 Volume of nonagricultural exports

to an underprediction of import volumes, with the result that imports in value terms are predicted quite accurately. The HHC model tracks the partial trade balance relatively better than the other formulations.

To summarize, the simulation results indicate that the disaggregation of computers from the other components of the partial trade balance (as in the HHC model) tends to improve simulation performance both in and out of

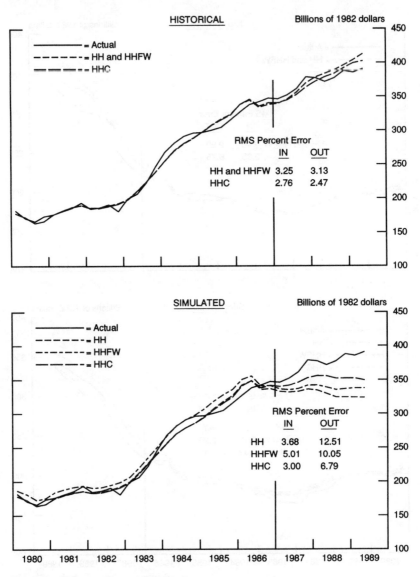

Fig. 2.6   Volume of non-oil imports

sample. Imports (both prices and volumes) are more difficult to predict than exports, however, regardless of the model used.

2.6   Conclusion

This paper has investigated two issues related to international trade in computers: measurement and prediction. In general, the approach adopted by

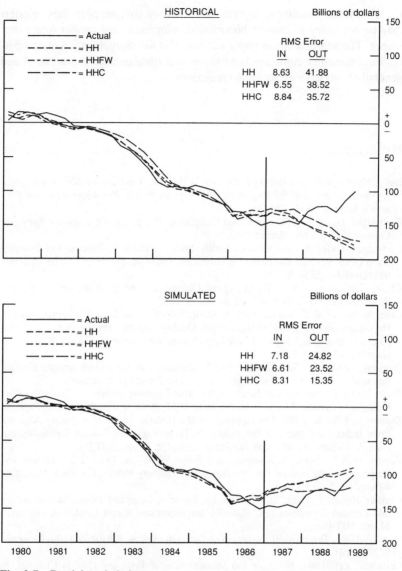

Fig. 2.7   Partial trade balance

BEA for the measurement of domestic computer prices is appropriate, given recent advances in technology. It may be inappropriate, however, to use this domestic price index for the deflation of international sales and purchases of computers. The development of separate price indexes for computer exports and imports is an important question for future research.

Further, the proper treatment of computers in empirical models of international trade is an open question. If the computer industry is sufficiently different from other industries, separate treatment of computers in these models may be necessary to capture historical developments and predict future outcomes. The analysis in this paper suggests that the disaggregation of computers from the other components of the partial trade balance is warranted and generally leads to more accurate predictions.

References

Baily, Martin Neil, and Robert J. Gordon. 1988. The Productivity Slowdown, Measurement Issues, and the Explosion of Computer Power. *Brookings Paper on Economic Activity* 2:347–420.

Cartwright, David W. 1986. Improved Deflation of Purchases of Computers. *Survey of Current Business* 66 (March):7–10.

Cartwright, David W., and Scott D. Smith. 1988. Deflators for Purchases of Computers in GNP: Revised and Extended Estimates, 1983–88. *Survey of Current Business* 68 (November):22–23.

Chow, Gregory C. 1967. Technological Change and the Demand for Computers. *American Economic Review* 57 (December): 1117–30.

Cole, Rosanne, Y. C. Chen, Joan A. Barquin-Stolleman, Ellen Dulberger, Nurhan Helvacian, and James H. Hodge. 1986. Quality-Adjusted Price Indexes for Computer Processors and Selected Peripheral Equipment. *Survey of Current Business* 66 (January):41–50.

Denison, Edward F. 1989. *Estimates of Productivity Change by Industry: An Evaluation and an Alternative.* Washington, D.C.: The Brookings Institution.

Dion, Richard, and Jocelyn Jacob. 1988. The Dynamic Effects of Exchange Rate Changes in Canada's Trade Balance, 1982–1987. Bank of Canada Working Paper.

Dulberger, Ellen R. 1989. The Application of a Hedonic Model to a Quality-Adjusted Price Index for Computer Processors. In *Technology and Capital Formation,* ed. Dale W. Jorgenson and Ralph Landau. Cambridge, Mass.: MIT Press.

Edison, Hali J., Jaime R. Marquez, and Ralph W. Tryon. 1987. The Structure and Properties of the Federal Reserve Board Multicountry Model. *Economic Modelling* 4 (April):115–315.

Gordon, Robert J. 1989. The Postwar Evolution of Computer Prices. In *Technology and Capital Formation,* ed. Dale W. Jorgenson and Ralph Landau. Cambridge, Mass.: MIT Press.

———. 1987. The Postwar Evolution of Computer Prices. NBER Working Paper no. 2227(April).

Griliches, Zvi. 1964. Notes on the Measurement of Price and Quality Changes. In *Models of Income Determination,* NBER Studies in Income and Wealth, vol. 28. Princeton, N.J.: Princeton University Press.

Helkie, William L., and Peter Hooper. 1988. The U.S. External Deficit in the 1980s: An Empirical Analysis. In *External Deficits and the Dollar: The Pit and the Pendulum,* ed. Ralph C. Bryant, Gerald Holtham, and Peter Hooper. Washington, D.C.: The Brookings Institution.

Helkie, William L., and Lois Stekler, 1987. Modeling Investment Income and Other Services in the U.S. International Transactions Accounts. International Finance Discussion Paper no. 319. Washington, D.C.: Federal Reserve Board.

Hooper, Peter, and Catherine L. Mann. 1989. Exchange Rate Pass-through in the

1980s: The Case of U.S. Imports of Manufactures. *Brookings Papers on Economic Activity* 1:297–337.

Isard, Peter. 1975. Dock-Strike Adjustment Factors for Major Categories of U.S. Imports and Exports, 1958–74. International Finance Discussion Paper no. 60. Washington, D.C.: Federal Reserve Board.

Meade, Ellen E. 1988. Exchange Rates, Adjustment, and the J-Curve. *Federal Reserve Bulletin* 74 (October):633–44.

Rosen, Sherwin. 1974. Hedonic Prices and Implicit Markets: Product Differentiation in Pure Competition. *Journal of Political Economy* 82 (January–February):34–49.

Triplett, Jack E. 1986. The Economic Interpretation of Hedonic Models. *Survey of Current Business* 66 (January):36–40.

———. 1989. Price and Technological Change in a Capital Good: A Survey of Research on Computers. In *Technology and Capital Formation,* ed. Dale W. Jorgenson and Ralph Landau. Cambridge, Mass.: MIT Press.

Young, Allan H. 1989. BEA's Measurement of Computer Output. *Survey of Current Business* 69 (July):108–15.

Comment   Richard D. Haas

This is a very good paper, one in which I find much to be in agreement with, and very little to take serious issue with. Nevertheless, I do have several comments to make. They are in three parts: those centering on data and specification; those dealing with estimation issues; and those focusing on the simulation results.

Data and Specification Issues

My first concern centers on the BEA hedonic index used. The advantages of correcting the series for quality improvements are amply demonstrated. But, as Meade notes, the drawback is that one price index is used for imports, exports, and domestic production of computers. The more conventionally measured—and less desirable—BLS data shows that these are not the same and, furthermore, are diverging over time, at least for imports and exports. This is a potential source bias in the derived volumes data in the model where computers are treated separately. My question then, is whether there may be a way to extract the information from the BLS import and export data to differentiate the hedonic import and export indexes.

With respect to the import price equations, Meade realizes that some measure of foreign costs or prices should be used, not the CPI; but this problem is not the focus of the paper, so I will not dwell on it.

Another concern is the use of the relative price term in the fixed-weight version of the Helkie-Hooper model—the HHFW model in the text. In a pre-

Richard D. Haas is an adviser at the Economic Research Department of the International Monetary Fund.

liminary version of the paper, I viewed this specification as conceptually preferable to the conventional Helkie-Hooper model, but inferior to a version of the model in which computers are modeled separately. Now, after reviewing the estimation results, I think the fixed-weight specification can be improved. If the problem is that variable-weight deflators convey the wrong information because they give increasing weight to computers, then the problem can be minimized, but not eliminated, by using a fixed-weight deflator where the weights are fixed at a point in time when computers constituted a small portion of trade. Meade does this in the price equations in the HHFW model, but continues to use the variable-weight deflator in the relative price terms in the volume equations. In commenting on an earlier version of the present paper, I suggested first taking the fixed-weight deflators and deriving new volume data and then using the fixed-weight deflators in the relative price terms. I now have doubts about the first recommendation, but continue to think I was right on the second. In other words, I would argue that we should use the better price series—the one in which bias has been minimized and the one that shows import prices increasing between 1985 and 1987 the way we all expected them to—to explain non-oil import volumes. Of course the fixed-weight deflators would not yield the proper partial trade balances; the bridge equations estimated in the paper would still be needed for that.

With regard to the bridge equations, they are both essentially first-difference log equations with coefficients greater than one on the fixed-weight term, something I have difficulty reconciling with the plots of the two series in figure 2.2. The export transformation equation has an additional trend term of 12 percent a year that would seem to compound the problem.

Estimation Issues

Turning to estimation issues, I believe that the export price equations probably should have been tested for homogeneity. It looks to me as if homogeneity would be accepted at conventional levels, and would improve the simulation characteristics of the model; a one-percent increase in the two explanatory variables, domestic costs and foreign prices, measured in dollars, would lead to a one-percent increase in export prices. Roughly similar data over approximately the same period led to an 86/14 split between the two variables when tested for (and accepted) in the IMF's World Trade Model.

The import price equations show an exchange pass-through of 85 percent. This represents the average effect over the estimation period, as the paper points out. Whether or not there will be full or zero pass-through, depends, I should think, on whether the exchange rate was moving in response to a real shock or a monetary shock. If the former, I would look for little pass-through; if the latter, 100 percent pass-through.

As for the volume equations, Meade seems concerned that the activity elasticity in the HHC model's nonagricultural export volume equation is too low—about one—relative to the activity elasticity in the non-oil import volume equation in the same model. I would reverse the concern and would worry about the high-income elasticity in the import equation. I would hope to find activity elasticities of about one in both equations, arguing that any other values imply undesirable steady state properties.

As for the separate computer sector in the HHC model, I sympathize, and I know that what we are presented with in the paper is the result of a lot of hard work with a very difficult data-set. But there are a couple of items worth mentioning. First, the price equation is an AR1 model; the specification precludes any exchange rate pass-through into import prices, in contrast to the rest of the model. Second, why should an increase in domestic expenditure on computers lead to an increase in exports and a decrease in imports of computers? I would have expected just the reverse. Third, why does the exchange rate enter the equation that explains the share of computer imports in the total? It already is included in the relative price term. And finally, in the import volume equation, why is the relative price term the ratio of the import deflator to the CPI? Wouldn't a better measure be the price of computers relative to the price of other imports?

An earlier version of the paper modeled the computer sector with traditional demand equations, with conventional price and activity variables. The activity elasticities seemed a little high, and I was concerned that rapid supply changes in the computer sector were a source of bias. I am pleased to see that supply variables in the spirit of the original Helkie-Hooper model have been tried and that this has been successful in the case of the computer import volume equation.

Simulation Results

Let me turn now to the simulation results. I must confess to a certain smugness here. In the preliminary summer conference, before the estimation and simulation of the alternative models, I likened my task to handicapping a horse race. To briefly recap, there are three models: HH, HHFW, and HHC. Think of them as an item for which Sears sells a good, better, and best model in its catalog. I argued then that the problem appeared to be one of painting the model with too wide a brush; that if significant qualitative differences in fact exist between computers and other traded commodities, then the best way to allow for that would be to model computers separately. And this is exactly what has happened, at least in three of the four equations. In the case of import volumes, the signals are mixed. On the basis of postsample prediction error, the HHC model performs worse than the alternative when actual right-hand-side variables are used, but somewhat better, at least in the longer run, when predicted right-hand-side values are used (see fig. 2.6).

As for the partial trade balances—the final aggregate—reported in figure 2.7, I would raise two questions. First, does the HHC model outperform the other on balance because of, or in spite of, the separate computer block? The estimated computer-price and volume equations are not as convincing as the other equations in the HHC model. Does its overall performance represent superior out-of-sample performance of the noncomputer equations that more than offsets the computer block, or are all equations contributing to the out-of-sample performance? Second, the dynamic simulations for the partial trade balance look much better than the static simulations; however, this is not true for all of the individual components. I find the increasing divergence of all of the simulated values from the actual values in the static simulation in figure 2.7 troublesome, and thus I take less comfort than I might in the apparently more accurate tracking shown in the dynamic simulations. (This is largely a result of the overprediction of the import-price equation being offset by a corresponding underprediction of import volumes in the dynamic simulations; there is no such offset to the overpredicted import prices in the static simulation, since historical prices were used to simulate import volumes but simulated prices were used to calculate the partial balance.)

My comments may sound more critical than I intended. Harry Johnson once wrote that for every economist willing to undertake difficult empirical work, there were four who were willing to explain what was wrong with it. I don't want to be thought of as part of the gang of four. This is a good paper. The really important point is that the paper correctly identifies a problem with the data that has important implications for how we view the economy, deals with the problem intelligently, and thereby improves our understanding of how merchandise trade balance is determined.

3 Quality Issues Affecting the Compilation of the U.S. Merchandise Trade Statistics

Bruce C. Walter

3.1 Introduction

After statistics on population, statistics on foreign trade are among the oldest sets of statistics continuously compiled by the United States government. The Treasury Department first compiled and published estimates of the balance of trade as far back as 1790. Statistics compiled from actual trade documents first became available in 1820. In recent years, however, with the dramatic increase of interest in the U.S. international trade position, the U.S. foreign trade statistics have come under critical scrutiny. The government has significantly increased its efforts to adapt the trade statistics program to the changing patterns of international trade and to produce the most accurate and timely statistics possible. To this end a number of significant changes and proposed changes have been undertaken in the ways in which the trade statistics are collected, compiled, and presented. In this paper I will discuss these changes and their impact on the quality of the trade statistics. I will also discuss other quality issues that have yet to be addressed and will offer some outlook for addressing them.

3.2 A Brief Overview of the Trade Statistics Program

In the United States, the Bureau of the Census is the agency responsible for processing, compiling, and publishing statistics on U.S. exports and imports of merchandise. These statistics, in the form of a monthly census or counting of individual merchandise shipments, do not include reports on trade in services or capital flows but cover only flows of merchandise.

Bruce C. Walter is assistant chief for methodology and quality assurance in the Foreign Trade Division of the U.S. Bureau of the Census.

The U.S. Customs Service also plays a vital role as the collection agent for the trade statistics. The Customs Service collects the basic documentation reflecting individual shipments of merchandise from exporters and importers at over 400 U.S. ports of exit and entry and transmits statistical information on these shipments to the Census Bureau on a daily basis. The Customs Service also checks the quality of the reporting by verifying the accuracy of certain statistical data.

The transmittal of data to the Census Bureau takes two forms: automated transmissions and mailings of paper documents. For import transactions, the Customs Service each month electronically transmits over 800,000 lines of data to the Census Bureau for processing. In addition, it mails 200,000 paper documents to the Census Bureau for data entry processing. For exports, U.S. exporters and freight forwarders transmit about 20 percent of total transactions directly to the Census Bureau in electronic or summary reports. Another 30 percent of export transactions are captured under an agreement with Canada that allows Canadian import data to be utilized for U.S. exports to Canada. The remaining 50 percent of export transactions are compiled by the Census Bureau from the approximately 500,000 export documents collected from exporters each month by the Customs Service.

No formal documentation is required for nontextile import transactions valued from $1 to $1,250 or for textile import shipments valued from $1 to $250. Export shipments valued from $1 to $2,500 require no documentation. The value of these low-value transactions is estimated by country of origin or destination, on the basis of historical relationships of low-value to total shipments established from independent studies.

The Census Bureau staff checks the data reported on documents for completeness. Incomplete documents are referred to Census Bureau commodity analysts for resolution or returned to the Customs Service or shippers for additional information. Following the review operation, all documents are microfilmed for record-keeping purposes.

The statistical data on the documents are then captured on electronic key-entry equipment. A number of validity checks are performed to minimize key-entry and reporting errors. Currently over 500,000 individual export records (each individual commodity line on a document represents a separate record) and about 250,000 import records are keyed each month.

Import and export data which are received via automated means are handled more directly. Upon receipt, the Census Bureau subjects automated data records to computer checks, which verify the completeness and accuracy of the data. If problems are uncovered, the Census Bureau immediately contacts the exporter or freight forwarder, or in the case of imports, the Customs Service, for resolution. The Census Bureau has worked with the Customs Service to incorporate many of its statistical edits into the Customs automated import system. This allows statistical editing to be performed as soon as an automated importer or broker enters information into the Customs system. After receipt and verification, the Census Bureau merges all directly submitted data with the Census keyed data for further screening by an extensive battery of Census computer edits. The computer edit screens are run on a weekly basis, and records intercepted during these edits are resolved for recycling into the following week's processing. Problems uncovered near the end of the monthly processing cycle, however, must be held for inclusion in the following month's cycle. These records generally account for less than one percent of value.

After completion of the processing cycle, the data are summarized monthly for release to the public. The public release, which is scheduled for about 45 days after the close of the subject month, begins with release of the overall import, export, and trade balance figures, followed closely by release of more than 100 separate reports in various arrangements.

3.3 Present Status

In recent years the volume of U.S. trade has expanded greatly, and the size of the U.S. trade deficit has become a major economic and political concern. In the 20-year period between 1969 and 1989, the value of imports plus exports has increased over 1000 percent, from $74 billion in 1969 to $837 billion in 1989, and from 8 to 16 percent of GNP. The trade balance during this period has changed from a surplus of $1.3 billion in 1969 to a deficit of $109 billion in 1989. As a result, interest in the Census Bureau's foreign trade statistics program has mushroomed, and the monthly trade balance has become one of the most publicized and scrutinized of the nation's economic indicators. In recent years release of the monthly trade statistics seems to have had a significant effect on the stock and bond markets.

It was natural for users to become concerned about the quality of the trade data, given increasing interest and the limited resources available for overseeing the production of the data. Problems with the timeliness of the import data and a growing undercount of U.S. exports to Canada cast doubts on the accuracy of the trade statistics. Even the U.S. Congress voiced its concern with the ability of the statistics to accurately measure the U.S. trade position. In the Omnibus Trade and Competitiveness Act of 1988, Congress specifically mandated that the monthly trade totals be expressed in constant dollars as well as current dollars, and that U.S. trade be expressed in terms of the International Harmonized System of commodity classification rather than the national classifications then in use.

With this increased scrutiny and criticism of the data, the Census Bureau has significantly increased its efforts to adapt the trade statistics program to the changing patterns of international trade and to produce more accurate and timely statistics. To this end it recently has introduced significant changes and has proposed more changes in the way in which the trade numbers are compiled and presented.

3.4   Recent Quality Improvements

Producing useful, high-quality trade statistics is complicated by the different requirements of the many users of the statistics. For national accounting and general economic policy purposes, it is important to have accurate aggregate estimates of exports and imports. To monitor trade policies and provide analyses to support trade negotiations or study trade markets, however, it is important to have accurate product and country detail, often for categories that cannot be determined in advance. For the purposes of this paper, I will look at recent quality improvement efforts on two levels: broad macroissues and microissues involving problems with the detail.

3.5   Macroissues

Since 1986, several major issues affecting the overall quality of the trade statistics have been identified, addressed, and resolved to varying degrees.

3.5.1   Timing

Timing problems occur when the statistics do not accurately reflect import or export transactions in the time period in which they occur. During the late 1970s and early 1980s, changes in the Customs Service's requirements for and handling of import documents, coupled with dramatic increases in import transactions, resulted in large numbers of documents being transmitted too late for the Census Bureau to process and include them in the proper month's statistics. The late documents were then carried over into a subsequent month's data. By late 1985, when the Census Bureau first recognized the extent of the problem, more than 50 percent of some months' import data represented "carryover." Equally as harmful to the quality of the statistics was the fact that carryover was volatile as well as large. In late 1985 and early 1986, carryover levels ranged from 30 percent to 55 percent. During the same time period, export carryover ranged between 8 and 14 percent. The Census Bureau was forced to discontinue seasonal adjustment of the foreign trade data because of the problems in determining true seasonality.

During the next two years, the Census Bureau and the Customs Service worked closely to change Customs collection and Census Bureau processing procedures to reduce the size of the carryover. By the end of 1987, these changes had allowed the Census Bureau to reduce carryover to about 20 percent.

Finally, with the March 1988 statistics, the Census Bureau announced that it would delay release of the trade statistics by two weeks to allow more time for receipt and processing of both the import and export documents. This delay, coupled with the earlier Census Bureau and Customs Service procedural changes, dropped the carryover level to under 5 percent. With recent advances in automated reporting of the statistics, the level has been further reduced to between 2 and 3 percent.

With the April 1988 statistics, the Census Bureau introduced two additional changes to further minimize the effect of carryover. First, it instituted a revision of prior-month trade totals to reallocate any remaining carryover to the proper statistical month. This revision further reduced carryover in the revised month to under 1 percent. Second, the Census Bureau reinstituted seasonal adjustment of the import and export totals at the overall level and for six broad end-use product categories.[1]

3.5.2 Undocumented Exports to Canada

Concern about missing export documentation has long been an issue. The Customs Service program for collecting and verifying export documents does not receive the same degree of attention and resources as the import program, since administration of tariffs and enforcement of trade agreements are major Customs mandates. Particularly along the extensive open U.S.-Canadian border with its heavy volume of trade, the undercount of exports became a major concern.

This concern was precipitated by a 1971 agreement between the Census Bureau and Statistics Canada to conduct an annual reconciliation of discrepancies in the trade data of the two countries and to reach a mutually agreed-upon estimate of the U.S.-Canada trade balance.

Over the next 17 years reconciliation studies showed discrepancies between U.S. exports and Canadian imports growing increasingly wider. In 1970 and 1971 the difference for northbound trade stood at $400 million, or about 4.5 percent. In 1978 the difference rose to $2.3 billion, just over 7 percent of northbound trade. By 1986, the discrepancy had skyrocketed to $11.5 billion, over 20 percent of trade. The 1986 reconciliation study also revealed that, as in previous years, the major contributor to the discrepancy was the nonreceipt of U.S. export documents, in an amount that was estimated in 1986 to be about $10.2 billion, or one in every five dollars of U.S. exports to Canada.

The extreme differences observed in the U.S.-Canada trade statistics during these reconciliation studies led officials from both countries to agree to a drastic plan of action.

In March 1987 the heads of the U.S. and Canadian customs and statistical agencies met in Washington to discuss ways of improving the accuracy of the trade statistics reported by the two countries. The agencies agreed that the best short-term solution was to share current import information and to use it to supplement undercounted export data.

---

1. Increased levels of seasonal adjustment are discussed in section 3.6.2.

These initial supplements for undocumented U.S. exports to Canada included adjustments to published totals for all months in 1987 and annual adjustments back to 1970. Each subsequent month's statistics (published prior to January 1990) included this adjustment. These adjustments, however, were applied only at the aggregate level. No estimates were made for detailed product levels.

The countries, as the result of discussions about long-term solutions to the problem, agreed in a July 1987 Memorandum of Understanding to a more complete solution to the problem. Each country would use the other country's import-detail data to compile its export statistics. As a result, both countries would substantially improve their export statistics while markedly reducing costs. In addition, the exchange would allow both countries to eliminate the requirement for export documents. In the United States this would result in the elimination of approximately 2.5 million export documents annually.

After two years of intensive work to align the two statistical systems, this proposal finally become reality with the release of January 1990 statistics, when both countries began full use of counterpart import data to compile their export statistics.

3.5.3 Export Port Audits

The estimates of undocumented exports to Canada have led to questions as to the extent to which exports to other countries might also be undercounted. In order to measure possible undercount, the Census Bureau began in late 1988 to conduct a series of export port audits.

In cooperation with the Customs Service, the Census Bureau selected a sample of ten major ports for audit. The ports included four airports, four vessel ports, and two Mexican border ports. The teams conducting the audits consisted of staff from the Census Bureau and the Customs Service Washington headquarters working with Customs officials in the local ports. Because of differences in the clearance procedures and documentation for the various methods of transport, different auditing techniques had to be developed for air, vessel, and overland ports. Audit teams detected nonfiling of export documents by conducting examinations of the merchandise and accompanying documentation before the exporting carrier left the country.

Joint Census Bureau-Customs Service audit teams used this "preshipment" approach to conduct two-week audits of export operations at Seattle-Tacoma, Miami, Los Angeles, and New York's Kennedy international airports. These four airports account for over 60 percent of the value of U.S. air exports.

The results of the airport audits, which were conducted over a five-month period ending in mid-May 1989, estimated undercoverage resulting from the failure of exporters or their agents to file the required export documents at $6.7 billion, or about 7.2 percent of the value of merchandise exported by air in 1988. The undercoverage ranged from an estimate of almost 10 percent at New York to about 1.5 percent at Seattle-Tacoma. However, the small number of flights sampled, generally around 30 to 40 at each airport, coupled with some difficulties in obtaining necessary documentation, makes it necessary to consider these numbers to be estimates rather than precise measurements.

The audits, designed primarily to measure nonfiling, also uncovered some indications of undervaluation of export shipments, especially in Miami. This undervaluation seemed limited to shipments destined for countries with particularly high tariff structures. Documentation accompanying export shipments is often used as proof of value in the importing country, so this finding makes intuitive sense. However, since the audit procedures were not designed to measure undervaluation, the auditors were unable to accurately quantify the effect on the value of total exports by air. The Census Bureau and the Customs Service are discussing the possibility of a future valuation audit involving examinations of exporters' books to determine actual selling prices.

The next planned step was to have been audits of export truck movements at the Mexican border crossings of Laredo and El Paso, Texas. These two crossings account for over 50 percent of the value of exports to Mexico. A Census Bureau team conducted a two-day pilot study of the two sites to determine how the audits could be conducted. However, because of resource limitations in the 1990 and 1991 budgets, the Census Bureau delayed plans to begin full-scale audits of the two ports.

In the interim, the Census Bureau has planned a small pilot study of vessel operations at the port of Baltimore to determine how best to conduct future vessel audits. In the future, when resources permit, the Census/Customs audit teams hope to conduct audits of vessel export operations at the ports of Baltimore, New York, Los Angeles, and Miami. These ports account for over 65 percent of exports by vessel.

3.5.4 Reconciliation Efforts with Other Countries

Since exports from one country are mirrored by imports in another and vice versa, reconciliations are an excellent tool for analyzing trade statistics and for judging their validity. The reconciliation process not only provides the tools to uncover macroproblems, such as undercounts or problems with valuation, but also provides insight into microproblems, such as commodity misclassification or problems with definitions.

In an effort to view more of the U.S. trade statistics from this perspective, the Census Bureau has begun reconciliation studies with four of its major trading partners: Japan, the European Economic Community, South Korea, and Mexico.

In an April 1989 meeting in Ottawa, Canada, representatives from the U.S. Census Bureau, Statistics Canada, and the Statistical Office of the European Communities agreed to a tripartite reconciliation of trade data between the EEC and North America. The agencies targeted early 1991 for completion of the reconciliation.

Representatives from the Census Bureau and the Customs Service met with

Japanese officials in Tokyo in July 1989 to lay groundwork for a reconciliation of Japanese and U.S. trade data. This meeting represented a significant breakthrough with the Japanese, who had spurned earlier attempts to initiate a reconciliation. After a series of meetings in Washington and Tokyo, preliminary reconciliation results were expected in late 1990.

In accordance with agreements reached with South Korean officials during meetings in Washington and Seoul, Customs Service and Census Bureau staff also are undertaking a reconciliation of U.S.-Korean trade data. No specific completion dates have been agreed on yet.

Finally, after a meeting with Mexican officials in April 1990, agreements were reached to undertake a reconciliation of U.S.-Mexican trade data.

Two major issues involved in all of these reconciliations were not part of the Canadian reconciliations. First, with Canada there was no complication in sorting out trade between the two reconciling countries caused by entrepôt or intermediary countries. Second, timing differences, which were not a factor with Canada, are considerable in the case of U.S. trade with Europe and the Far East.

For these reasons it is questionable whether an actual substitution of import data for export data is reasonable to expect as an end product of reconciliation efforts with the EEC, Japan, and South Korea, as it was with Canada.

3.5.5   Trade in Constant Dollars

Monthly trade data are traditionally valued in nominal (current) dollar amounts, with volumes expressed in various units of physical measure. A valid criticism, which was often leveled at the nominal trade statistics, is that these data reflect the effects of price and currency fluctuations and therefore cannot be used to measure changes in real trade flows.

The Census Bureau formerly produced what were termed "unit value indexes." These indexes simply calculated unit values based on the values and quantities or weights reported on the import and export documents. Because these indexes did not take into consideration changes in product mix or quality, they made poor indexes for converting nominal dollars to constant dollars, and so were discontinued.

The Census Bureau's sister agency in the Commerce Department, the Bureau of Economic Analysis (BEA), made quarterly adjustments to the trade statistics to create constant dollar trade totals for use in the national accounts. Most of the price indexes used by BEA to perform these adjustments were created from Bureau of Labor Statistics (BLS) quarterly surveys of import and export prices. These indexes, however, could not be applied to monthly trade data.

Out of concern with this absence of monthly constant-dollar trade statistics, Congress in the 1988 Omnibus Trade and Competitiveness Act instructed the director of the Census Bureau, in conjunction with the director of BEA and the commissioner of BLS, to study the feasibility of creating monthly constant-dollar trade statistics consistent with the BEA quarterly constant-dollar figures.

Even before passage of the trade bill, BLS, at the direction of the executive Office of Management and Budget (OMB), had begun to develop monthly price surveys of importers and exporters.[2] As a result, BLS released the first set of monthly trade indexes for six broad product categories in February 1989.

In the months after BLS first began producing monthly price indexes, the Census Bureau and BEA worked to devise ways to use the monthly indexes while ensuring consistency between the constant-dollar series produced by the two agencies.

Effective with the January 1990 statistics, the Census Bureau began compiling constant-dollar trade data. These data are produced for the same end-use product categories used in the national accounts, and with only minor exceptions are the same as the indexed data used in the national accounts.

3.6 Microissues

A very important segment of the users of foreign trade statistics is concerned with microlevel data. For example, one influential user of the detailed product level import statistics is the Office of the United States Trade Representative. It uses the data to monitor and administer the U.S. trade programs, many of which operate at detailed product and country levels under complex statistical formulae.

What has the Census Bureau done to address the quality of the detailed statistics? Here are some recent and proposed changes.

3.6.1 The International Harmonized System—A Common Product Classification

The passage of the Omnibus Trade and Competitiveness Act of 1988 empowered the United States to legally adopt the International Harmonized System (HS) for classification of merchandise in international trade. This classification system is the product of over 12 years of work by the Brussels-based Customs Cooperative Council, to which the Customs Service, Census Bureau, and International Trade Commission are the U.S. representatives. The system has a root 6-digit classification structure, providing for over 5,500 unique product classifications. Signatory countries must adopt the basic 6-digit structure but are free to add digits for national detail. The U.S. system has 10 digits and provides about 8,000 export and 13,000 import classifications.

The adoption of this system in January of 1989 brought the U.S. into line

---

2. These monthly surveys utilized a subsample of the BLS quarterly respondents.

with most other industrial nations, who had already instituted it. Over 70 nations are now using the system, including all major U.S. trading partners.

The adoption of the system has many benefits. First, it allows comparisons of U.S. trade statistics with foreign trading partner statistics on a level never before attainable, that is, at the 5,500 root classes adopted by all signatory countries. This is an immense aid in conducting reconciliations of detailed bilateral trade statistics with U.S. trading partners, discussed earlier. Also, the HS requires metric measures of weight and quantity. In the past most international transactions were conducted in metric measure, while the U.S. generally required English measure. Confusion often resulted.

Second, the system provides a widely used common classification system. For the first time it allows U.S. imports and exports to be reported on the same basis at a considerably detailed level. In addition, the Census Bureau has worked to align the Standard Industrial Classification (SIC) with the HS, allowing better comparisons of trade and production statistics. International statistical organizations such as the U.N. Statistical Office also are using the HS in structuring their international classification systems, such as the Standard International Trade Classification (SITC) and International Standard Industrial Classification (ISIC).

Finally, because U.S. shippers are using one system to trade internationally, the reporting of product classifications has been improving.

3.6.2   New Data Elements

In 1985 a rare opportunity allowed the Census Bureau to add new statistical data elements to the import and export documents simultaneously. Although resources did not exist at the time to compile statistics on the new information, the Census Bureau petitioned the Customs Service to add the new elements to the import entry documents, which it was in the process of revising. At the same time, the Census Bureau added new elements to the Export Declaration, a Commerce Department document, which was also being modified.

The new data elements were ones that had long been sought by U.S. data users: a unique identifier of the exporter or importer, the U.S. state of origin or destination of the shipment, and an indication of whether the transaction was between related parties (parent and subsidiary).

Although the Census Bureau was not successful in obtaining direct funding for the data elements, it was successful in getting sponsorship of some elements from other U.S. Government agencies and from interested private subscribers.

State and Regional Trade Data

For nearly two hundred years, trade data in the United States has dealt with flows of trade in terms of countries of destination or origin and U.S. Customs ports of exit or entrance. Only in recent years has there been general interest in data measuring the impact of foreign trade on the U.S. states that produce exports and consume imports. Global economic trends and their ramifications now touch all states and make it relevant to raise questions that few are concerned about in the past: What and how much does a state export or import? Where do these exports go or imports come from? How many exporters or importers are located in a state?

In an effort to address these questions, the Census Bureau produced with subscriber funding a set of three special reports for 1987 and 1988. These reports, available on tape, detail exports for the following:

(i) Nine geographic regions, with 4-digit SITC product detail and countries of destination.
(ii) The 50 states, with 2-digit SICs and countries of destination.
(iii) Total exports for each of the 50 states, showing port of exit and country of destination for each mode of transport.

Aside from the above, aggregate state export and import totals were made available for 1987 and 1988 in the regular Census Bureau foreign trade publication, the FT990, "Highlights of U.S. Imports and Exports"; and for 1989 and 1990, in the supplement to the monthly Commerce Department press release on U.S. merchandise trade.

Publication of import statistics by state, however, has been suspended pending improvements in the collection methodology. It appears that the reported states of destination quite often reflect importer or broker offices responsible for the account paperwork rather than the state for which the merchandise is actually destined. Large gateway states, such as New York and California, incorrectly receive credit for extremely large segments of imports. The wording on the Customs import document and the instructions for its preparation need to be reworked to prevent this bias.

The export origin data has some similar biases. Homogeneous nonmanufactured products, such as bulk grains and ores, are particularly troublesome. Since these commodities often come from various locations and are indistinguishable when mixed, the exporter is often unable to provide a true state of origin.

In order to improve the usefulness and reliability of the statistics, state export totals have been split into two categories, manufactured goods and nonmanufactured goods (including agricultural, mining, and other raw materials). It is expected that this distinction between manufactured and nonmanufactured products will yield a much more reliable picture for the manufactured products from a "point of origin" perspective.

Exporter Characteristics

The addition of a field on the revised export document for the exporter's Employer Identification Number (EIN) has provided the Census Bureau with the first opportunity to construct statistics on the characteristics of the exporting community. Simple questions, such as how many firms export, the frequency with which each exports, and the size of the average shipment, have long remained unanswered.

Using funding provided by BLS and the Commerce Department's International Trade Administration, the Census Bureau recently produced the first sets of statistics profiling the exporter community. For the first time, a count of active exporters (100,000 in any given month) is available, along with the frequency of shipments by these exporters and the dollar value of shipments. These data are only the beginning of statistics on the characteristics of exports.

The Census Bureau also is seeking to develop an "Exporter Data Base" (EDB) by using the exporter number to aid in linking commodity-export data available from the monthly trade statistics with business-establishment characteristics available from the Census Bureau quinquennial Economic Census. This link will open an important flow of data on U.S. firms and their production as related to exports.

Another and perhaps most significant use for the EDB is a mailing list to contact problem exporters. Until now, no complete automated exporter file has existed for informing exporters of general information about export reporting or for contacting specific exporters about problems with the data they have supplied.

Related Party Trade

Although the Census Bureau has received numbers of inquiries concerning the availability of data on trade between related and nonrelated firms, the Census Bureau has no resources with which to compile this information. A number of federal agencies, as well as some private data users, however, have expressed interest in this information, and we hope in the future to secure funding to compile some limited aggregate-level data.

Seasonal Adjustment of Detail Data

In January 1990, in order to align Census Bureau methods more closely with those used in the national accounts, product level adjustments were extended beyond the 6 broad end-use categories to the much more detailed 5-digit end-use level, with over 70 series adjusted.

In addition, the Census Bureau, since it has received repeated requests to extend seasonal adjustment to even more detailed levels of data, is working to extend seasonal adjustment to import and export totals at the country and world levels. If resources allow, we expect these new adjustments in 1991.

3.7   The Future

The Census Bureau's foreign trade statistics program has repeatedly been forced to do more with little or no increase in resources. Although the Census Bureau asked for $1.8 million in increased funding for the foreign trade statistics program in FY 1990, this funding increase was never approved. Funding requests were denied or substantially reduced in each of the previous six fiscal years.

In response, the Census Bureau is pursuing a number of initiatives which it thinks will not only reduce costs but maintain or improve the quality of the statistics.

3.7.1   Expanded Automated Collection

The Census Bureau views automated collection of data as having two major benefits in the current era of limited resources. First, it saves on processing costs by tapping automated sources which already exist in the trade community. Money saved by the automated collection can then be used elsewhere in the trade statistics program to increase quality and to improve or expand data products. Second, automation results in more accurate statistics, since the automated source data are generally more accurate than information currently captured from paper documents.

Over the last six years, the Customs Service has developed the Automated Commercial System (ACS), a giant computer telecommunications network designed to link all aspects of Customs activities (such as entry processing and cargo tracking) at all Customs ports throughout the United States.

Automated systems have progressed especially rapidly for imports. The Automated Broker Interface (ABI), which is part of ACS, provides electronic processing of import entry transactions for qualified computerized brokers and importers. Large-volume Customs brokers can submit information on import entries directly to the Customs Service via the ABI. These brokers receive priority handling and quick liquidation of their accounts from Customs. Brokers are now utilizing the ABI system at all major U.S. ports, and the system currently accounts for about 80 percent of all import transactions filed with Customs.

In 1983, the Census Bureau began working with Customs to develop a program to use ABI information for statistical purposes. The resulting system, the Census Interface, is a series of Census-developed programs residing in the Customs computers, which extract data from ABI, subject it to Census edits and validations, and prepare it for processing on Census computers.

In November 1987, after almost five years of development, testing, and quality checks, Census began extracting statistical data nationwide from the Customs system. At present about one million transactions monthly, or about 80 percent of all import transactions, are extracted from the Customs system. The Customs Service anticipates that by 1992, 90 percent of all imports will be processed through the ABI.

In addition, many of the Census Bureau's statistical edits have been programmed in the Customs Service system. Failures of the statistical edits require resolutions by importers or brokers before the data will be accepted by Customs. As a result, automated data arriving at the Census Bureau is more accurate and requires less additional processing.

The Census Bureau also collects about 50 percent of export data directly from automated exporters, brokers, and carriers through its own Automated Export Reporting Program (AERP) and from Statistics Canada via the U.S.-Canada data exchange.

The AERP Program has been slow to grow, with recent increases barely keeping ahead of expansions in trade. In an effort to increase the segment of export trade which is collected electronically, the Census Bureau has entered into discussions with the Customs Service about using the ACS to collect export data. Although initial resource outlays to create an export subsystem are substantial, the prospect of creating a national automated system for exporters and export brokers is very attractive.

3.7.2   Fees For Data Products

Recently the Census Bureau has been successful in initiating new data products for limited groups by having users provide the necessary resources, through direct user fees, subscriptions, or contracts.

Two major new data series, exports by state and exporter characteristics, have been launched in this manner. The Census Bureau will continue to seek user funding for new series, such as related-party trade.

3.7.3   Independent Review of the Current Statistical System

In an effort to better chart the future of the trade statistics program, the Census Bureau entered into a contract in 1988 with the Committee on National Statistics of the National Academy of Sciences for the establishment of a panel on foreign trade statistics, to conduct a study of the current system of collecting, processing, and reporting foreign trade statistics. The study, which is being jointly funded by the Census Bureau, the Customs Service and the Commerce Department's International Trade Administration and Bureau of Economic Analysis, is scheduled for completion in late 1991.

A distinguished panel, comprised of academic, business, and financial experts, began work on the study in June 1989. The panel is drawing on contacts with relevant federal agencies and private organizations in drafting its report and recommendations.

In conducting the study, the panel has been asked to consider the following issues:

(i) What trade data are needed? In particular, what domestic and foreign trade data are needed to assess our international economic position? What new uses can we expect for current and projected trade data? What new data products should be developed?

(ii) How should the data be obtained? Can a sample-based collection approach provide needed data? Should it replace or supplement existing systems?

(iii) How good are existing data? Are trade data adequate for their actual and intended uses? Will particular quality improvements help trade data users? Are data items collected but not fully utilized? What product changes might enhance data use? Could changes in schedule or sequence make trade data more useful?

(iv) How can the existing data system be improved? How can new technologies be applied to data collection and processing? What educational and other outreach methods might improve data collection or encourage better data use?

The Bureau expects this review to provoke independent thoughts and suggestions useful in planning and shaping the future of the trade statistics program.

References

Farrell, Michael G., and Anthony Radspieler. 1989. Census Bureau State-by-State Foreign Trade Data: Historical Perspectives; Current Situation; Future Outlook. U.S. Bureau of the Census. May 15. Washington, D.C.

General Accounting Office, Staff 1989. Merchandise Trade Statistics: Some Observations. Briefing Report to the chairman, Panel on Foreign Trade Statistics, Committee on National Statistics, National Academy of Sciences. April 17. Washington, D.C.

Puzzilla, Kathleen, J., Anthony Radspieler, and Bruce C. Walter. 1988. Changes in Foreign Trade Statistics at the Census Bureau. Paper presented to the Census Advisory Committee of the American Statistical Association. October 13. Washington, D.C. U.S. Bureau of the Census.

Waite, Charles A. 1988. Census Bureau Trade Data—Program Overview, Developments, and Directions. Briefing presented to the Washington Export Council. April 28. Washington, D.C. U.S. Bureau of the Census.

———. 1989. Perspectives and Issues—Merchandise Trade Data. Briefing presented to the Panel on Foreign Trade Statistics, Committee on National Statistics, National Academy of Sciences. June 9. Washington, D.C.

Comment   David J. Klock

The Walter paper is a useful status report. I am impressed with the scope of the efforts described in the paper to improve the quality of the basic monthly statistics on value of U.S. exports and imports, while at same time responding to a wide range of demands for more detail, especially given resource constraints. My remarks will focus on recent and potential improvements to the

David J. Klock is Director, Office of Balance of Payments Analysis, U.S. Treasury Department. Mention of the author's affiliation is for identification only. Nothing in this comment should be taken as reflecting official U.S. Government or Treasury Department policy.

aggregate-value or macro data discussed in the first half of the paper. I will touch on price/volume issues at the end of this comment.

The paper discusses three broad aspects of "quality"—accuracy,[1] timeliness, and availability of a range of underlying detail to meet needs of different audiences. The first two criteria are most relevant to the macro data.

Timeliness is a subjective criterion, and is in part the product of a tradeoff between promptness and accuracy. The specific instance discussed in the paper—accepting a delay in availability of data from four to six weeks, in exchange for a reduction in "carryover" by the substantial magnitudes indicated—seems to be a pretty good deal, especially since it allows for resumption of seasonal adjustment.[2] If seasonal adjustment can be extended to the geographic detail, so much the better. But at least two caveats might be entered. While availability of seasonally adjusted data is welcome, it would be very useful to have a little clearer indication as to what the criteria are for seasonal adjustment, and perhaps as to how stable the actual monthly seasonal factors are. Furthermore, six weeks clearly is close to the limit of what can be considered current data, given the time frame of some important consumers—policymakers, GNP estimators, and financial markets.

As regards accuracy, the paper points out a differential in the tightness of the collection net for exports as opposed to imports[3] and suggests several potentially valuable programs to improve export coverage, supplementing the Canadian reconciliation program.

But the Canadian example may be unique. I share Walter's skepticism concerning potential utility of a Canada-style reconciliation exercise with the EEC and Japan, in view of timing and entrepôt problems. Generally, it is interesting that work seems more advanced on checking exports to these countries; I would have thought Mexico, the trade situation with which is partly, though not entirely, analogous to that with Canada, might offer more potential.[4] The paper clearly brings out the importance of aggressively pursuing the

---

1. To reduce the danger of rediscovering the wheel, I took this opportunity to go back to Oskar Morgenstern's classic, *On the Accuracy of Economic Observations* (2d ed. Princeton, 1963).

2. This conclusion assumes that we can infer the degree to which the need for subsequent revisions has been reduced from the degree to which carryover has been reduced, i.e., that carryover was the dominant factor necessitating subsequent revision.

3. Inter alia, raw data are collected by Customs. As the paper makes clear, there is very close, continuous interaction between Customs and Census in the data collection effort. But compilation of trade data is not the sole or primary Customs mission, and it goes without saying that Customs also faces resource constraints. Morgenstern (p. 251) notes "some data that become available from Government agencies are a by-product of their administrative functions. This is frequently a strong reason to suspect the quality of data obtained in this manner."

4. As an aside on this issue, I would have thought export *over*valuation to Latin America would be at least as likely as the possible tendency toward *under*valuation noted in the paper, especially if U.S. export documents are used as proof of valuation in the importing country. Overinvoicing of imports and underinvoicing of exports are classic vehicles for capital flight. But perhaps the much-noted internationalization and liberalization of markets has made more direct and convenient channels available.

export audit program. Census's limited ability to do so is just one more example of how the budget imbroglio creates havoc with government priorities and decision making.

Walter notes that the 1988 Trade Act, whatever its other merits or defects, made several significant contributions to quality of the published trade data. Most economic analysis, at least that which goes beyond the "who struck John" level, requires data on prices and quantities. The 1988 Trade Act brought together the relevant players in the U.S. Government with a mandate to "conduct a study to determine the feasibility of publishing an index" of monthly trade volumes. I am not convinced of a crying need for monthly trade volume numbers, for several reasons.[5] The hope is that there might be enough commonality that the process of generating monthly volume (and perforce, price) data would contribute to resolution of some of the remaining problems with existing quarterly data as well. Clearly, improvement of the available *price* data is a top-priority quality issue,[6] for quarterly as well as monthly data. The Meade paper (ch. 2 in this volume) highlights what almost certainly is the most serious problem in this area. But this issue is much bigger than just deflation of the trade data. As is widely recognized, it gets into basic questions of measuring U.S. economic performance. Despite the inevitable resource constraints, hopefully the effort to develop monthly price series doesn't just carry over "best" existing methodology without at least another look.

5. They are likely to be inherently "noisy," even after seasonal adjustment; there is a danger that scarce resources will be diverted from maintenance and improvement of the existing quarterly series that most modelers and analysts use in their standard trade models; and this will be one more number for the markets to think they need to react to.

6. According to Morgenstern (p. 181), "A study of the accuracy of economic observations, however rudimentary, must deal at least briefly with the most basic economic and statistical variable of all, *price*" (italics in original).

II Trade Prices and Price Competitiveness

4   Price Trends in U.S. Trade
New Data, New Insights

William Alterman

4.1   Introduction

With the explosion of the U.S. trade deficit over the past decade and the issues which have become associated with it, substantial interest has focused on movements in the prices of U.S. exports and imports. These trends in prices have implications for U.S. international competitiveness, as well as for analysis of nominal and real trade flows, the effects of exchange-rate fluctuations, and the influence of developments abroad on domestic inflation. For several years analysts have had two separate series of data on U.S. trade prices to work with: the unit-value indexes constructed by the Bureau of the Census, and the import and export price indexes produced by the Bureau of Labor Statistics (BLS). Although the Census indexes are no longer being produced, a comparison of these two series is important, given the likelihood that unit-value series have been used and may continue to be used in certain instances (i.e., historical analysis, country-specific analysis). This paper begins by outlining the basic methodology and limitations of the unit-value series—limitations which led the Bureau of the Census in 1989 to discontinue publication of these series. It then addresses the BLS series, which were designed to overcome these limitations. The two series will then be compared, focusing on the period from March 1985, when the dollar was at its strongest, to June 1989, the last period for which comparable data were available. In addition to mak-

William Alterman is a supervisory economist in the Bureau of Labor Statistics of the U.S. Department of Labor.

The author would like to express his thanks to Peter Hooper, Richard Marston, Kim Zieschang, Ken Dalton, Jack Alterman, Katrina Reut, and the attendees at the preconference in Boston and the conference in Washington for their helpful comments. The author would also like to thank Michelle Vachris, Nick Peters, and Melissa Leonard for their help in constructing the tables and charts. The views expressed are those of the author and do not necessarily reflect the policies of BLS or the views of other BLS staff members.

ing some observations about this comparison, the paper also outlines the implications of using one series versus another for economic analysis, in particular how they affect the measurement of real trade flows and assessments of the impact of changes in exchange rates on the level of import and export prices. Some additional detailed analysis of the BLS data, using country of origin and currency of quotation, are also presented. Finally, the paper discusses some of the limitations of the BLS data as well as steps that are being taken in order to enhance the quality and utility of these numbers.

4.2 Methodology of Price Series

4.2.1 Bureau of the Census Unit-Value Indexes

For many years the unit-value indexes (UVIs), produced by the Bureau of the Census as a byproduct of the collection of U.S. trade data, were the only comprehensive source of information on price trends of goods in U.S. trade. Since companies engaged in U.S. trade are required to declare the value and quantity of a shipment of goods, it was a relatively straightforward process to construct price indexes using these data (by dividing the total value of goods in each specific category by the total quantity of goods in that category).

The basic data are supplied on export declarations and import entries filed with the U.S. Customs Service. All U.S. import or export merchandise shipments are represented in the index calculations with certain exceptions. U.S. goods returned, military equipment and parts, low-value shipments, and movies and exhibits are all excluded from the import index calculations. Military-type goods, low-value shipments, reexports, exposed film, repairs, and other special transactions are excluded from the export calculations.

The actual items included in the import and export indexes are based on a distinct nonrandom sample of commodities. The samples consist of those commodities having a significant value of trade each month for which reliable unit values can be drawn. Products that are only traded occasionally are excluded from the samples. Commodities that do not require a quantity to be reported (especially common in parts categories) are also excluded from the sample, unless a reliable proxy for quantity, such as shipping weight, is available. In addition, commodities which demonstrate erratic month-to-month changes, reflecting product mix changes rather than price changes, are not included in the sample.

The data used in the unit-value indexes reflect a customs value basis on imports (which excludes the cost of shipping, insurance, and duty), and an f.a.s. (free alongside ship at U.S. port) value for exports, which also excludes overseas shipping, insurance, and foreign duty. Until the recent decision to discontinue publication of these series, the indexes were released on a monthly, quarterly, and annual basis, usually several weeks after the trade values for that period were published. The series were constructed using a chained Fisher formula (which uses both base and current-period weights), because it was felt that this formula was appropriate in light of the constantly changing nature of foreign trade. Historical data have been calculated as far back as 1919.[1]

There are four general problems with the unit-value indexes. First, they reflect not only underlying price changes, but changes in product mix as well, even at the finest level of commodity detail. For example, if there is a market shift from cheap economy cars to expensive luxury cars, the unit value of the commodity (autos) will increase, even if all prices for individual products remain constant. Second, unit-value indexes do not account for shifts in the specification (i.e., quality), of an item. If, for instance, one month an automobile was imported without air-conditioning and the next month it was imported at a higher price but included air-conditioning, the unit-value index would reflect the full cost of the increase, even though the value of the basic good may not have increased. Third, not all data supplied to Customs can be used in the construction of these indexes, either because of unusable reported quantity figures or the heterogeneous nature of the products themselves. Overall, U.S. unit-value indexes were calculated for 56 percent of the value of imports and 46 percent of exports in 1985, the last year for which coverage data are available. In particular, in the finished goods area a large portion of the raw data must be excluded.[2] And finally, the Census data were only published at the one-digit end-use level of detail, making sectoral analysis difficult if not impossible.

The problems associated with unit-value indexes were a concern for some time. The 1961 report of the Price Statistics Review Committee of the National Bureau of Economic Research (also known as the Stigler Report), a comprehensive survey of U.S. government price data, reviewed the limitations of unit-value data, both in general terms and specifically in the case of the export and import unit-value series. A later report by an interagency committee, after comparing price and unit-value data, recommended that "specification-price data (such as those from the BLS Wholesale and Industrial Price Index Programs and other similarly constructed data) should be used more extensively as deflators in the absence of positive evidence of their unsuitabil-

---

1. For a more detailed methodology of the Census unit-value indexes, see U.S. Department of Commerce (1989).
2. More detailed coverage percentages based on 1985 trade values include:

	Imports	Exports
Foods, feeds, and beverages	59.9	91.7
Industrial supplies and materials	71.7	65.4
Capital goods	30.3	26.1
Automotive vehicles and parts	79.9	42.4
Consumer goods	37.0	40.5

ity in individual instances. This recommendation represents a change in order of preference from the present practice which provides for using unit values except where they seem unreasonable."[3]

Numerous other studies of unit-value indexes, in both the domestic and external sectors, have also provided evidence confirming their shortcomings. A list of such studies would include Kravis and Lipsey (1971), Holmes (1973), Murphy (1972), the first to compare BLS export price indexes with export unit values, Shiells (1987), which compared the BLS import-price indexes with import unit values, and Lichtenberg and Griliches (1989), which did a comparison of the Producer Price Index and domestic unit-value figures. In general, the various studies have found evidence of greater accuracy of transaction-price indexes compared with unit-value indexes.

Until 1989, a significant advantage of the Census unit-value data was that they were produced monthly. Since the Bureau of Economic Analysis of the U.S. Department of Commerce attempts to produce the quarterly foreign trade component of the GNP data by deflating each month individually, the unit-value series was taken as the most appropriate price deflator for product areas, such as grain and crude petroleum, which are highly volatile and therefore require monthly estimates.

Despite the discontinuation of the unit-value numbers, an analysis of this series and comparison with other series is important for several reasons. First, as a consequence of the relative newness of the BLS program, the unit-value figures, which go back seventy years, will continue to be the only source of data for long-term analysis (and have thus made up much of the BEA's historical price series). Second, while the now-preferred BLS indexes have been available for several years, a number of recent studies have used (either knowingly or otherwise) unit-value series in their analyses (e.g., Dornbusch 1987, Krugman 1987). Baldwin (1988), Froot and Klemperer (1989), and Kim (1990) appear to use the published BEA price-index values constructed from a combination of UVIs and BLS data. Third, since the original source data used in the construction of the Census unit-value indexes will still be available to the public, economists may still continue to construct their own series of unit-value indexes. See, for instance, Knetter (1989). Finally, given the limited number of major countries that produce import and export price indexes (U.S., Japan, and Germany), many international price comparisons must rely, at least in part, on unit value data.

4.2.2   BLS Import and Export Price Indexes

The BLS data were designed to overcome the basic limitations of the unit-value figures. Like the unit-value numbers, the BLS import and export price

---

3. The report (Interagency Committee on Measurement of Real Output, Subcommittee on Prices 1973) included two detailed studies in its appendixes which highlighted the limitations of unit values. A United Nations report (1981) also extensively reviewed the advantages and disadvantages of unit-value versus price indexes for external trade.

indexes are designed primarily to reflect price trends for the U.S. merchandise foreign trade sector. The BLS data, however, have the major advantage of being true price indexes, in that changes in the quality of an item are factored out of its price measures and the product mix is kept constant. Many of the concepts employed for these series, such as the use of a modified Laspeyres formula, are similar to those used in the BLS Consumer Price Index (CPI) and Producer Price Index (PPI).

The current program to collect import and export price data drew upon the seminal work of Kravis and Lipsey (1971) and dates back to the mid-1960s. In the late 1940s an earlier attempt by BLS to construct import and export price indexes survived only a few years. BLS now has export price indexes for selected commodity categories going as far back as 1966, and the Kravis and Lipsey study reports a limited number of export indexes covering the early 1960s. However, complete coverage was not attained until September 1982 for imports and September 1983 for exports.

The samples for the BLS indexes are drawn from a universe of all exporters and all importers (and their respective products) who filed Customs documents during a specified reference period (generally one year). The objective of the Bureau's sample design is to provide an unbiased measure of price change in each published index. A multistage survey design is employed to provide a sample of exporters and importers for general product categories, as well as for specific items which can be repriced over time. The survey design is responsive to the constraints of both cost and the burden on reporters. The cost constraints impose limits on the number of establishments selected in a sample, while the number of items priced in each establishment is controlled to limit respondent burden. Samples are overdrawn in order to allow for a certain amount of deterioration due to respondent refusals (like nearly all BLS data-collection efforts, the International Price Program is voluntary), discontinued products, products that for one reason or another are out-of-scope (e.g., misclassified or discontinued products), and products which are only traded irregularly. The sample covers approximately 90 percent of exports (excluding primarily commercial and military aircraft) and 95 percent of imports (excluding primarily works of art and small shipments).[4]

Price reporting by firms is initiated by a visit from a BLS representative. At the time of the visit the reporting requirements are explained verbally and in writing, and the selection of products for which the firm will report price information is made. The BLS has approximately 9,000 companies supplying data on roughly 23,000 items in the quarterly sample and approximately 2,000 companies and 4,000 products in the smaller monthly survey. In the overwhelming majority of cases, prices are collected directly from the exporter or importer, although in a few cases (e.g., crude petroleum and grain),

---

4. These items are excluded due to the difficulty in obtaining a consistent time series of prices for a comparable product (i.e., each item is unique.)

prices are obtained from secondary sources, such as the U.S. Department of Agriculture and Department of Energy. Normally, price data are collected by mail questionnaire; in some cases the information is collected by telephone. Generally, BLS is seeking the first transaction in the appropriate month, and the vast majority of prices in the surveys are from the first week of the reference month. Approximately 19,000 of the 23,000 products in the survey are only collected in March, June, September, and December. The other 4,000 products are repriced every month.

Accurate calculation of a price index requires that the collected price reflect the same item from period to period. To ensure this, the specifications for each product in the BLS survey include detailed physical and functional characteristics as well as the terms of the transaction (e.g., number of units bought or sold, class of buyer or seller). Any change in a product's specifications or terms of trade is appraised to ascertain its significance. If data clarification is required, the individual at the firm who is responsible for providing the price information is contacted by telephone. If the change is substantive, product substitution is made by an adjustment process (similar to the procedures used in the calculation of the CPI and PPI indexes) that ensures the index reflects only actual or "pure" prices changes and is not affected by quality changes.[5]

Approximately 15 percent of the import prices supplied by respondents are quoted in a foreign currency. These prices are converted into dollar prices by using the average exchange rate for the month immediately preceding the reference month.

The price basis used in the construction of the indexes varies and generally depends on industry practices. Products in the import price indexes are generally priced either c.i.f. U.S. port (which includes cost, insurance, and freight, but excludes duty), or f.o.b. foreign port (which is similar to a customs value basis and excludes insurance and freight). Exports are generally either f.o.b. factory (price at point of production) or f.a.s. (price at U.S. port). While ideally the basis for pricing the indexes would be consistent, at higher levels of aggregation an index may include product prices on different bases because different industries have differing pricing and shipping practices and procedures and are not able to supply price quotes consistent with another industry. In general, the only area where variations in price trends due to quotation basis may have an important impact is crude materials, for which transportation costs can be a significant portion of the delivered price.

Unlike the unit-value series, which use a Fisher index formula, the BLS

---

5. At present no special procedures, other than oversampling, are used for product areas, such as computers, that are subject to rapidly changing technology. Beginning in September 1989, however, as part of its producer price index series, the Bureau began publication of a limited set of computer indexes, which make use of a more sophisticated methodology. The methodology used in these experimental figures was reviewed in an article in the *Monthly Labor Review* (Sinclair and Catron 1990). Eventually, the Bureau intends to incorporate this new methodology into its import and export price indexes.

series use a Laspeyres formula. Conceivably the differences in index formula could have a substantial impact on index comparisons, particularly for indexes such as external price indexes, which use highly volatile trade flows for weights.[6] The BLS indexes are based on 1985 trade values for calculations from 1985 to the present and 1980 weights for all index values prior to 1985.

Since all reporting is voluntary and confidential, no index is published in such a way as to reveal the name, price, or price behavior of any respondent. No index is published when fewer than three companies provide data; for the vast majority of indexes there are considerably more. The index values are generally available four weeks after the end of the pricing month. Where possible, indexes have an index base of 1985 = 100.

BLS publishes indexes in three different classification structures: the Standard International Trade Classification (SITC) of the United Nations, Revision 2; the Standard Industrial Classification (SIC); and the BEA end-use classification. The multitude of publication structures is recognition of the fact that the data can be used in a variety of ways. The SITC structure is most useful for international comparisons, since a number of countries produce trade data using this classification system. SIC tables are appropriate for domestic industry analysis, as well as for comparisons with the BLS PPI series. The end-use classification (used in this analysis) is consistent with the structure of the U.S. National Income and Product Accounts. Within each series BLS also attempts to publish enough detail to allow micro and cross-sectional analysis. BLS currently publishes approximately 400 SITC series, 240 SIC series, and 275 end-use series. In general BLS attempts to publish all product categories that recorded either $500 million worth of exports or $700 million worth of imports in 1985. Indexes that represent areas of trade with smaller dollar values are incorporated into the calculation of higher-level indexes and may be published separately if coverage and user interest warrant. Prior to 1989 BLS collected data for only the third month of each quarter, for what is referred to as its *quarterly* index. Since January 1989, the Bureau has been calculating and publishing *monthly* indexes for selected categories for a subset of data from its quarterly survey. The monthly indexes are currently published only at the one-digit end-use level. The more comprehensive quarterly press release contains detailed information by SITC and end-use categories, as well as the foreign currency indexes. Indexes by SIC are available on request.[7]

4.3 Comparison of Price Trends

This section compares the recent historical index trends for the BLS indexes and the Census unit-value numbers. As no detailed data are published

---

6. For a general discussion of differences in index formulas, see Allen (1975).
7. For a more detailed methodology of the quarterly BLS import and export price indexes, see U.S. Department of Labor (1988).

by Census, comparisons are only made at the one-digit end-use level. In addition, since comprehensive BLS export and import indexes have only been published since 1983, the historical comparison must be limited. The period beginning March 1985 was chosen because this month was the point when the dollar reached its recent peak and began its downward slide. The comparison was made between the quarterly BLS series (which actually covers the last month of each quarter) and monthly unit-value figures for March, June, September, and December.

In comparing price trends of *imported* products, the BLS series, surprisingly, registered a consistently higher rate of increase between 1985 and 1989. Between March 1985 and June 1989 the BLS index rose 20.8 percent, while the equivalent unit-value index increased just 13.7 percent (see fig. 4.1). When petroleum imports are excluded, the comparable figures are 29.8 percent and 24.4 percent (see fig. 4.2). With the exception of motor vehicles, the major import components—foods, feeds, and beverages, industrial supplies and materials, capital goods, and consumer goods—all show larger increases in the BLS series than in the unit value series (see figs. 4.3–4.7). The most dramatic difference between the two series is found in the comparison for imported consumer goods. Between March 1985 and June 1989 the BLS series recorded a 30.7 percent increase, while the comparable unit-value series rose just 10.3 percent.

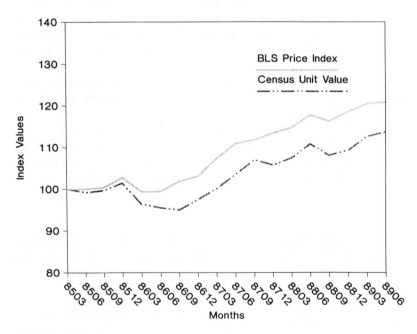

Fig. 4.1   All imports

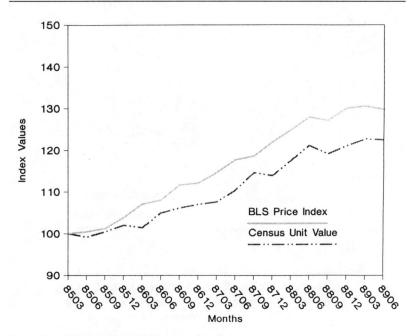

Fig. 4.2   All imports, excluding petroleum

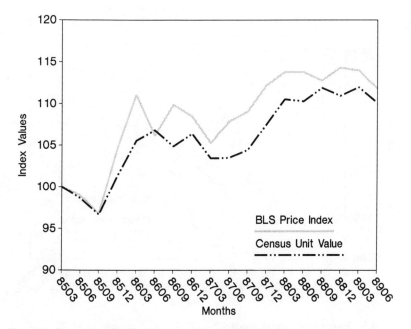

Fig. 4.3   Imports of foods, feeds, and beverages

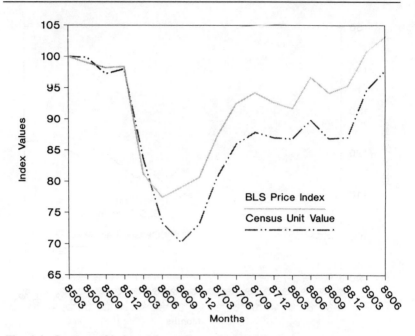

Fig. 4.4   Imports of industrial supplies and materials

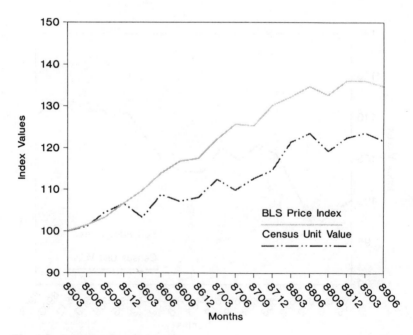

Fig. 4.5   Imports of capital goods

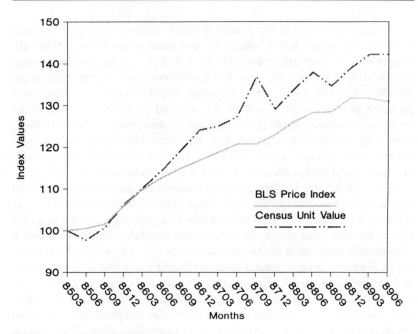

Fig. 4.6   Imports of motor vehicles

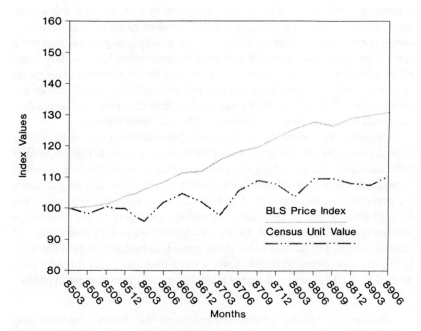

Fig. 4.7   Imports of consumer goods

The major exception to this pattern of larger increases in the BLS numbers is in the automotive sector, where the unit-value series shows a relatively steeper rise, 42.2 percent, compared with a 30.8 percent increase in the comparable BLS index (scc fig. 4.6). The automotive series, of course, is an especially interesting case. Since the motor vehicles category is a narrower grouping to begin with, it may be less affected by shifts over time in the weighting structure. There is considerable evidence that in the mid-1980s, there were significant quality increases associated with imported autos, arising from the voluntary export restraint agreement with the Japanese.[8] Such practices would lead to sharper increases in a unit-value series.

At first glance, the two price indexes measuring *exports* during this period appear more consistent (see fig. 4.8). From March 1985 to June 1989, export prices as measured by the BLS indexes rose 13.0 percent, compared to a 12.2 rise in the unit-value series. However, more detailed comparisons reflect a considerable variation in the two measures (see figs. 4.9–4.14). For exports, the BLS series registered greater increases during this period for foods, feeds, and beverages, industrial supplies and materials, and consumer goods. However, in the comparisons for capital goods and motor vehicles, the unit-value data reflected greater increases. Incidentally, earlier comparisons of the capital goods indexes for both exports and imports (from December 1979 to March 1985 for imports and from December 1978 to March 1985 for exports) also recorded a tendency to greater price increases in the unit-value figures.

One of the assumptions about unit-value series is that they would be most appropriate (and therefore most likely to match up with the BLS indexes) in those areas, such as raw materials, where product categories are relatively homogeneous, where there are relatively few quality changes over time for a specific product, and where the data used in constructing UVIs is most complete. The charts appear to bear this out, as data for both imports and exports of foods, feeds, and beverages and raw materials reflect relatively closer fits between the UVIs and the BLS price indexes than the charts for the finished categories of capital goods, consumer goods, and motor vehicles.

Delineating the source of the deviations between these two series can be difficult. For example, the tendency for the unit-value series to register smaller price increases, particularly for imports, appears to contradict one common assumption about unit-value indexes, which is that since they do not adjust for changes in an individual product's specification, they tend to overstate the level of price increases (assuming the average quality of traded products is increasing, as in the case of autos). As mentioned earlier, this pattern of smaller increases in the unit-value series could be a function of the differences in the two calculation formulas. Since a fixed-base Laspeyres formula, such as used by the BLS series, does not allow for substitution (changes in product

8. For an analysis of the response of Japanese automakers to the voluntary export restraints, see Feenstra (1988).

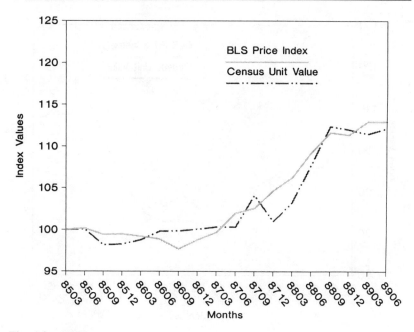

Fig. 4.8   All exports

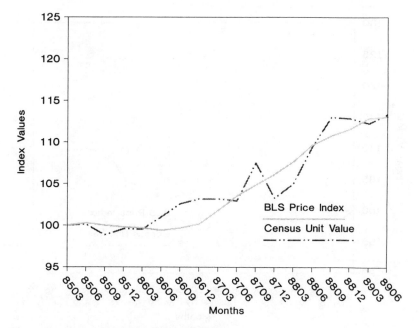

Fig. 4.9   All exports, excluding agriculture

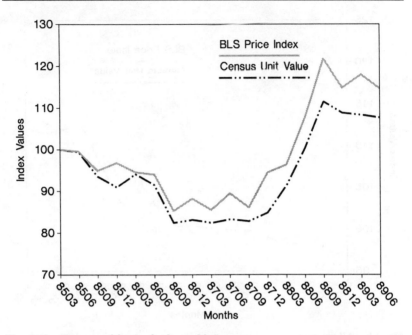

Fig. 4.10   Exports of foods, feeds, and beverages

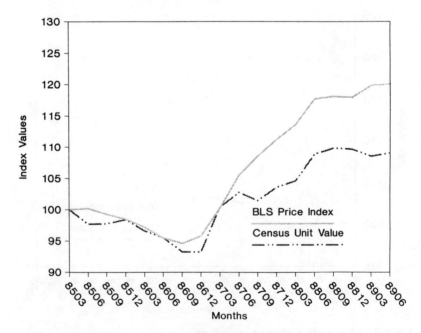

Fig. 4.11   Exports of industrial supplies and materials

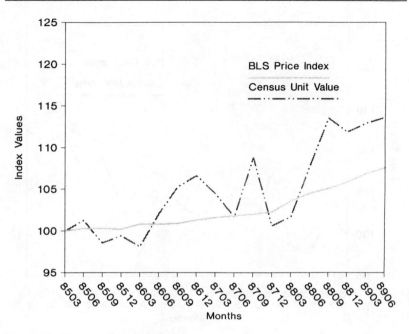

Fig. 4.12 Exports of capital goods

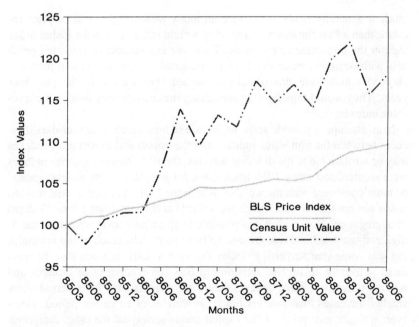

Fig. 4.13 Exports of motor vehicles

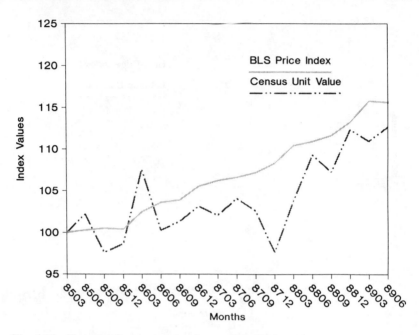

Fig. 4.14   **Exports of consumer goods**

mix), it generally tends to produce an index with a higher rate of price increase than a Paasche index or a moving-weight index such as the Fisher index used in the unit-value calculations. There are any number of imported products with declining price trends (e.g., personal computers and compact-disc players) which have dramatically expanded shipments over the past four years. They would thus have an increasing importance over time in the unit-value indexes.

In an attempt to provide some indication of how much, if any, of the differences between the unit-value indexes and the import and export price indexes may be attributable to the differing weights, the BLS transaction-price indexes were recalculated using 1988 trade flows for weights. These weights should be more consistent with the weights used in the UVIs. For operational reasons it was not possible to recalculate the weights at the very lowest level (7-digit) of aggregation. However, it was possible to apply new trade weights to the 5-digit end-use level and reaggregate up from there. The result of the reweighting was somewhat surprising. Index theory normally assumes that, because there is usually an inverse relationship between relative price changes and relative quantities, price indexes based on weights of a later period show smaller increases than indexes based on weights of an earlier period. However, with the exception of the capital goods series, all the other categories

Table 4.1   **Comparison of BLS Price Indexes and Census Unit Value Indexes;**
                           Percentage Changes from March 1985 to June 1989
                           (end-use categories)

	Exports			Imports		
	BLS Indexes			BLS Indexes		
	Unit-Value Indexes	1985 Weights	1988 Weights	Unit-Value Indexes	1985 Weights	1988 Weights
All Commodities	12.2	13.0	16.4	13.7	20.8	26.8
All Commodities						
excluding petroleum				24.4	29.8	31.4
excluding agriculture	13.4	13.1	14.9			
Foods, feeds, and bev-						
erages	7.7	14.7	25.5	10.5	11.8	16.6
Industrial supplies and						
materials	9.1	20.3	27.2	−2.1	3.1	14.8
Capital goods	13.6	7.6	6.9	21.7	34.8	32.9
Motor vehicles	18.1	9.7	9.9	42.2	30.8	31.1
Consumer goods	12.7	15.9	16.8	10.3	30.7	31.6

Sources: Bureau of Labor Statistics, Bureau of the Census.
Note: The experimental 1988 trade-weighted indexes were produced by attaching 1988 relative importance to 5-digit end-use indexes (constructed using 1985 relative importances). These indexes were then recalculated up to successively higher levels of aggregation using 1988 relative importances.

registered *larger* price increases when the indexes were recalculated using 1988 weights (as opposed to the calculations with 1985 weights). In general, changing the weights only served to exacerbate the differences in the overall trends during this particular period (see table 4.1).

Nonetheless, while the differences between these sets of indexes do not appear to be attributable to the weights used in their calculations, the sensitivity of import and export price indexes to their weight structure should be noted, as foreign trade flows do shift rapidly.[9] It was partially in recognition of this fact that BLS established a policy of reweighting the export-import price indexes every five years, (the CPI and PPI series are reweighted only every ten years). An illustrative example of the magnitude of this problem can be drawn from the petroleum component of the import price index. In 1980 petroleum represented one-third of U.S. imports. When the one-year change in the import price index from December 1985 to December 1986 was first published (using 1980 weights), the index *declined 8.7 percent.* However,

9. The weighting problem was also addressed in the NBER *Report on the Price Statistics of the Federal Government* (1961): "The fundamental problem of price index number construction—that of coping with a changing basket of goods—seldom appears in so exacerbated a form as in the case of price indexes for exports and imports. The patterns of consumption and production change but slowly compared to the rapid shifts that may occur in the commodity composition of imports and exports." Bear in mind that this was written back in 1961.

when the series was recalculated based on 1985 weights (petroleum represented only one-sixth of imports in 1985), the index covering the same twelve months *increased 0.3 percent.*

One final observation to be drawn from the graphs is that the BLS series has been relatively stable and consistent compared to the unit-value numbers. After removing the major volatile components (agriculture on exports, petroleum on imports), the BLS series are smoother than the unit-value series, particularly for exports, which tend to change both direction and magnitude frequently. This conclusion is supported by the simple analysis in table 4.2, which compares the unit-value indexes and the BLS indexes by the average of the absolute value of the quarterly percent changes, the standard deviation of the percentage changes, and the frequency of a change in the sign of the quarterly percentage changes. These limited findings are consistent with the more detailed results in some of the studies cited earlier.

4.4 Trade Flow Analysis

Currently, the most important use of export and import price indexes is to deflate the foreign trade component of the National Accounts. Although the actual methodology presently used at the Department of Commerce relies primarily upon the BLS indexes, an analysis of deflated trade data using the two different series is of considerable interest. In particular, most historical (that is prior to the early 1980s) inflation adjustments by BEA to trade data were done using primarily unit-value data. Thus long-term intertemporal comparisons of real trade flows may have been biased by the use of different indexes in making adjustments for inflation. In addition, some analysts have used, and may continue to use, unit-value indexes to construct country-specific estimates of inflation-adjusted trade flows, given that BLS does not currently produce import and export price indexes for specific countries.

Table 4.2   **Measures of Price Index and Unit Value Variability, Based on 1-Digit Components (3-month changes, March 1985 to June 1989)**

	Total		Exports		Imports	
	BLS Price Index	Census Unit-Value	BLS Price Index	Census Unit-Value	BLS Price Index	Census Unit-Value
Average of absolute percentage change	2.035	3.012	1.713	2.944	2.358	3.081
Standard deviation	2.533	3.826	1.982	3.730	2.623	3.734
Changes in direction of sign	45	86	22	46	23	40

Source: Bureau of Labor Statistics.
Note: The standard deviation values are a simple average of the standard deviation of the quarterly percentage changes within each of the 10 (5 import and 5 export) one-digit end-use categories over 17 quarters.

Table 4.3   **Estimates of Constant Dollar Trade Deficit (constant March 1985 dollars; annualized rates in billions of dollars)**

	Deflated by BLS Indexes	Deflated by Census Unit-Values
1985:		
March	99.3	99.3
June	117.5	117.9
September	119.1	116.9
December	134.2	133.8
1986:		
March	160.3	157.5
June	162.3	172.9
September	160.7	189.1
December	160.2	184.6
1987:		
March	140.3	166.0
June	135.6	155.5
September	139.6	161.0
December	139.5	156.3
1988:		
March	126.7	147.9
June	113.7	135.2
September	125.7	158.7
December	121.8	162.8
1989:		
March	98.0	127.4
June	98.8	128.4

Sources: Bureau of Labor Statistics, Bureau of the Census, Bureau of Economic Analysis.

Deflating recent trade data by these two series separately results in considerably different values (see table 4.3).[10] The annualized second-quarter 1989 "real" trade deficit, in terms of constant March 1985 dollars, would have been $128.4 billion if deflated by the unit-value series, but just $98.8 billion, 23 percent less, if adjusted for inflation by the BLS data. (The *nominal* trade deficit during the second quarter of 1989 was $108.9 billion.) Between 1985 and 1989 there is a $7.5 billion difference in the estimated annual growth in real net exports of goods, depending on which series is used. The BLS series produces a smaller inflation-adjusted trade deficit primarily because of the higher BLS import-price index, which results in a lower estimated quantity of imports. Also note that the month of greatest "real" trade deficit differs depending on which series is used. This point is critical given the keen interest

10. The actual deflation of the foreign-trade component of the National Income and Product Accounts is currently done (as of December 1989) based on 1982 constant dollars. For finished goods at least, deflators are applied at the most detailed level of data available, usually the 5-digit end-use class. This alleviates somewhat the problem of variation in indexes caused by the use of different weighting structures. For further details, see U.S. Department of Commerce, *Survey of Current Business* (1986).

in trying to establish when a trade deficit turns around (frequently referred to as the "J-curve" effect).

4.5 Analysis of the Price Effects of Exchange-Rate Changes

In order to expedite economic analysis for each 2-digit SITC import and export price index, BLS estimates a corresponding price index measured in foreign currency. These foreign-currency indexes are produced by multiplying the 2-digit SITC indexes in dollars by a trade-weighted index of the dollar's exchange rate in terms of 40 foreign currencies, whose weights are derived from U.S. bilateral trade-flow patterns in the base period 1985.[11] For example, the trade-weighted exchange-rate index for imports in the motor vehicle category are heavily weighted toward the currencies of Canada, Japan, and West Germany, who supply most U.S. automotive imports.

This information can be used in several ways. First, the exchange-rate index provides evidence as to which product categories may have been most affected by movements in the dollar's exchange rate. For instance, in the price index for professional and scientific equipment (for which Japanese and West German companies have been the major suppliers), the trade-weighted dollar fell 41.1 percent from March 1985 to December 1988. In contrast, the average dollar exchange rate relevant to imported apparel (which comes primarily from the so-called newly industrializing economies, or NIEs) fell only 16.5 percent over the same period. This provides important evidence on the question of why import prices of professional and scientific instruments rose twice as fast as import prices of apparel during this period.

Second, the data can be used to indicate what has happened to the price of U.S. exports and imports from the standpoint of the average foreign buyer or seller. On the export side, the foreign-currency index gives users an indication of how much cheaper U.S. goods have become as a result of the depreciation of the dollar, for example, from the standpoint of the average foreign buyer. The data indicate that between March 1985 and June 1989 the average price of all U.S. merchandise exports fell 15.0 percent in terms of foreign currency. Table 4.4 provides data comparing dollar indexes, exchange-rate indexes and average foreign-currency indexes for selected categories of U.S. exports and imports.

Third, these foreign-currency series and the associated exchange-rate indexes can provide an indication of how companies engaged in U.S. trade have reacted to the fluctuation of the dollar over the past decade. For example, they

11. The exchange rate series and foreign-currency series published in the regular quarterly press release are based on data for 40 countries. In addition, the Bureau also produces an experimental foreign-currency series which includes data for 63 countries and which has been deflated by foreign rates of inflation. This series set of countries was used in calculating the pass-through values in table 4.5. For further information on the methodology used in the construction of the foreign currency indexes, refer to Alterman, Goth, and Johnson (1987).

Table 4.4   Average Change in Prices of U.S. Exports and Imports, Denoted in Dollars and in Average Foreign Currency Terms, from March 1985 to June 1989 (selected SITC categories)

	Imports			Exports		
	Dollar Index	Exchange-Rate Index	Foreign-Currency Index	Dollar Index	Exchange-Rate Index	Foreign-Currency Index
All commodities	20.8	−27.8	−12.8	13.0	−24.8	−15.0
All commodities, excluding fuels	30.3	−29.7	−8.3	n.a.	n.a.	n.a.
Food	12.1	−18.3	−8.4	13.8	−30.0	−20.3
Crude materials, excluding fuels	42.6	−12.7	24.5	40.2	−32.5	−5.3
Chemicals	20.3	−29.7	−15.4	21.8	−25.2	−9.0
Intermediate manufactured products	36.4	−28.0	−1.8	22.7	−22.4	−4.7
Iron and steel	32.5	−34.6	−13.2	17.3	−18.7	−4.6
Machinery and transport equipment	31.8	−33.1	−11.8	7.6	−21.5	−15.5
Metalworking machinery	47.3	−38.7	−9.7	19.0	−22.1	−7.2
General industrial machinery	49.3	−33.8	−1.3	14.2	−19.8	−8.3
Office machinery	21.2	−35.0	−21.2	−6.5	−28.1	−32.8
Telecommunications equipment	13.0	−37.7	−29.7	7.2	−21.6	−16.0
Electrical machinery	32.0	−28.3	−5.5	6.3	−24.2	−19.3
Road vehicles and parts	32.1	−32.6	−11.0	8.9	−14.8	−7.3
Miscellaneous manufactured articles	29.6	−26.6	−4.8	13.6	−25.8	−15.7
Apparel	20.4	−16.3	0.7	n.a.	n.a.	n.a.
Professional and scientific instruments	47.9	−34.5	−3.1	20.0	−27.2	−12.6
Photographic apparatus, optical goods, watches, and clocks	31.7	−35.0	−14.3	−0.9	−27.9	−28.5

Source: Bureau of Labor Statistics.
Note: Foreign-currency indexes have been constructed by multiplying dollar indexes by trade-weighted exchange-rate indexes.

can be used to show to what extent foreign companies may, or may not, have "passed through" into higher dollar prices the changes caused by the exchange-rate fluctuation and to what extent they have absorbed the change, presumably either by lowering costs or lowering profit margins. While the literature on pass-through values is extensive, the availability of detailed product-category data permits considerably more detailed comparisons than would be possible using the more limited unit-value series.[12] The import pass-through values constructed for this paper incorporate dollar-exchange rates with the currencies of 63 countries and consumer prices in the same 63 foreign countries. The numbers attempt to estimate to what extent a change in the exchange rate times the selling country's CPI induces a change in the price faced by the buying country. The general formula used in construction of the pass-through values for importers is:

$$(1) \qquad MPT_i = \frac{\Delta\, PM_i^{\$}}{\Delta\, (ER_i \cdot CPI_i^*)}$$

where MPT = import pass-through rate; $PM^{\$}$ = U.S. import price in dollars; ER = exchange rate, in dollars per foreign currency (weighted average for 63 countries); CPI^* = foreign CPI in foreign currency (weighted average for 63 countries); i = pertains to the SITC group for which the index is calculated; and $\Delta\, (\,\ldots\,)$ = denotes the percentage change in the variable in parentheses over a specified period.

Pass-through figures can also be calculated for the export series. The formula used for export pass-through values is similar, except that exchange rates for four countries with extremely high rates of inflation were excluded:

$$(2) \qquad XPT_i = \frac{\Delta\, PM_{i^*}}{\Delta\left[\dfrac{1}{ER_i} \cdot CPI^{\$}\right]} = \frac{\Delta\left[\dfrac{1}{ER_i} \cdot PX_i^{\$}\right]}{\Delta\left[\dfrac{1}{ER_i} \cdot CPI^{\$}\right]}$$

where XPT = export pass-through rate; PM_i^* = foreign import price in local currency; $CPI^{\$}$ = U.S. CPI in dollars; $PX^{\$}$ = U.S. export price in dollars; ER = exchange rate, in dollars per foreign currency (weighted average for 59 countries), i = pertains to the SITC group for which the index is calculated, and $\Delta\, (\,\ldots\,)$ = denotes the percentage change in the variable in parentheses over a specified period. Note that in this model of pass-through, U.S. and foreign CPIs are being used as proxies for U.S. and foreign production costs.

The calculation of pass-through estimates was made for two periods (as shown in table 4.5): September 1980 to March 1985, a period of strong appreciation of the dollar; and March 1985 to December 1988, a period of dollar

---

12. For a recent review of the literature on pass-through rates see Hooper and Mann (1989).

Table 4.5   Pass-through Rates (Selected SITC Categories)

	September 1980 to March 1985 (dollar appreciating)		March 1985 to December 1988 (dollar depreciating)	
	Imports	Exports	Imports	Exports
All commodities	n.a.	n.a.	33.4	109.7
All commodities, excluding fuels	n.a.	n.a.	48.7	n.a.
Food	53.4	n.a.	39.3	102.8
Crude materials, excluding fuels	n.a.	n.a.	114.6	45.9
Chemicals	n.a.	n.a.	32.4	37.4
Intermediate manufactured goods	60.9	n.a.	57.4	49.6
Iron and steel	−7.8	n.a.	37.9	130.7
Machinery and transport equipment	n.a.	93.3	44.0	148.2
Metalworking machinery	99.0	98.9	55.8	80.8
General industrial machinery	n.a.	98.9	65.8	124.5
Office machinery	126.5	57.0	26.9	151.6
Telecommunications equipment	237.8	73.8	16.5	165.2
Electrical machinery	n.a.	76.3	59.6	133.2
Road vehicles and parts	n.a.	100.5	44.9	279.8
Miscellaneous manufactured articles	35.2	n.a.	52.9	107.2
Apparel	−176.0	n.a.	47.8	n.a.
Professional and scientific instruments	99.0	109.2	69.0	92.3
Photographic apparatus, optical goods, watches, and clocks	98.2	53.8	42.1	138.1

Source: Bureau of Labor Statistics.
Note: Exchange rates and price indexes used in these calculations have been inflation-adjusted. In general, consumer price indexes were used in adjustment process.

depreciation. In analyzing these data, one should bear in mind that CPIs are at best only very crude proxies for changes in the costs of inputs for individual sectors. Consequently, these pass-through estimates should not be used to assess changes in profit margins. Nonetheless, these data reveal several interesting patterns. For instance, they indicate that pass-through figures can vary significantly by product category; this finding is consistent with several earlier studies referenced in Hooper and Mann (1989, p. 2). For example, the pass-through figure from March 1985 to December 1988 for imported telecommunications equipment was 16.5 percent, while the figure for professional and scientific equipment was 69.0 percent. Together with the exchange-rate indexes, this information is useful in determining which product areas are most likely to incur significant price changes as a result of currency fluctuations.[13]

13. Of course, using the same CPI value as a proxy for costs in each industry would be a significant factor in the variation in pass-through, since some industries (especially in the high-tech area), have a tendency to lower costs.

Although the figures are somewhat sparse, the data indicate that for a given industry pass-through values are nearly always lower when the "home" currency is appreciating rather than depreciating. The data further indicate that pass-through values for foreign based industries (U.S. imports) tend to be lower than for corresponding U.S. industries (U.S. exports), particularly during periods of an appreciation of the home currency.

The finding that U.S. exporters to the world pass through more into the final selling price more of an exchange-rate change than foreign exporters to the U.S. do is consistent with earlier studies such as Mann (1986) and Moffett (1989). Two explanations come to mind. First, it is easier to pass along a depreciating currency, with the beneficial impact of lowering the selling price in foreign-currency terms without having to lower the home price, than it is to pass through an appreciating currency, with the negative impact of making goods more expensive in terms of the currency of the foreign buyer. Second, foreign companies may be less willing than U.S. companies to allow their selling prices (and presumably market share) to be affected by the vagaries of exchange-rate fluctuations. The results in table 4.5 seem to suggest that both factors may be at work.

Extreme care should be taken in analyzing pass-through rates for categories of raw and intermediate materials. Typically, volatile swings in prices in these categories reflect the influence of factors other than exchange rates. Prices for crude materials, for example, generally rose worldwide throughout the last half of the 1980s. This would account for the anomaly of the significantly higher pass-through rate during this period for crude materials for U.S. imports as compared to U.S. exports. Also note the inverse correlation between exchange rates and imported apparel prices during the early 1980s. One possible explanation is the introduction of apparel quotas in 1983, which presumably allowed for an increase in the price of imports, despite a favorable shift in the dollar's exchange rate.

Pass-through estimates based on the unit-value numbers would, of course, be different from those shown in table 4.5, because of the difference in price trends. For imports, the unit-value series would show a smaller rate of pass-through over the period of dollar depreciation, since the unit-value index was rising less rapidly than the BLS index. For imported capital goods, the pass-through figure using the BLS data would be roughly one-half, while using the unit-value data the corresponding figure would only be about one-third.[14] These differences have important implications for historical analysis of pass-through, since BEA only began to incorporate the BLS data into the construction of its price indexes in the early 1980s. The process was not completed until 1989, when BLS price data for the food and raw materials components

14. As of June 1990, the exchange-rate indexes are only available by SITC category. Consequently, no exact estimate of pass-through values can be constructed by end-use category at this time. However, the BLS plans to calculate exchange-rate indexes by end-use and SIC groups beginning in 1991.

were incorporated. Thus, virtually the entire historical data-base for the implicit price deflators and fixed-weight price indexes published by BEA as part of the quarterly GNP estimates uses a mix of BLS prices and Census unit values (as well as other data). Consequently, any study of historical pass-through values that uses price indexes associated with the National Income and Product Accounts, such as those cited in section 4.2, could show changes in "pass-through" behavior over time that to some degree may be merely statistical artifact.

Perhaps even more important to facilitating analysis of the effects of movements in exchange rates is the availability of the BLS data broken down by country and currency. Unlike the Census data, the BLS data are collected in whatever currency the company chooses to report in (usually the invoice currency). Since a significant portion of U.S. imports, approximately 15 percent, are invoiced in foreign currency, any fluctuation in exchange rates will have an immediate impact on the price data measured in dollars (as well as on nominal trade values in dollars). By looking at these patterns of currency invoicing, one can deduce which product areas are likely to show the greatest sensitivity of prices to exchange-rate changes. As shown in table 4.6, approximately one-half of the products in the category for professional and scientific equipment are priced in foreign currency, primarily the Japanese yen and the West German mark. Since BLS must convert these foreign-currency prices into dollar prices, the direct effect of exchange-rate movements on the import-price index is quite apparent. In contrast to finished goods, crude materials are priced primarily in dollars, and therefore in these sectors exchange-rate fluctuations generally have only indirect effects on dollar prices. The information on currency invoicing can be used to determine which suppliers, by country, have a tendency to price in their own currency and which tend to price in dollars. The data in table 4.7 indicate that companies located in Western Europe tend to price a higher portion of their U.S.-bound exports in their own currency than Japanese companies do. In turn, the Japanese tend to price a higher portion of their goods in yen than companies from the NIEs, such as South Korea and Taiwan, price in their currencies. There also appears to be a recent pattern of suppliers selling a higher percentage of goods to the U.S. in dollars. That this apparently was the case both when the dollar was appreciating (from September 1982 to March 1985) and when the dollar was falling (from March 1985 to June 1989) provides further evidence of the increasing unwillingness of foreigners to let fluctuations in the exchange rate dictate their selling price in the United States.

In the export-price indexes, with few exceptions, every product collected by the Bureau is quoted in dollars.[15]

---

15. Statistics on currency of invoicing are collected by a number of other countries. In general, they are consistent with the figures reported here. They do, however, indicate that some U.S. exports are being invoiced in a foreign currency. See Page (1981) for a breakout of invoicing currency for selected other countries.

Table 4.6   Percentage of U.S. Import Prices Quoted in Foreign Currency for Selected Product Categories (excluding petroleum)

	June 1989	March 1985	September 1982
Professional, scientific, and controlling instruments	48.7	52.2	51.5
Photographic apparatus, optical goods, watches, and clocks	42.7	39.6	43.3
Metalworking machinery	37.1	44.5	60.5
General industrial machinery	33.3	37.6	41.3
TOTAL WORLD	15.3	17.3	19.6
Intermediate manufactured goods	8.3	11.5	13.8
Apparel	6.5	6.4	7.8
Chemicals	5.9	6.7	4.2
Crude materials	0.6	2.7	1.4

Source: Bureau of Labor Statistics.
Note: These figures are simple averages; they would be somewhat different if they were trade-weighted.

Table 4.7   Percentage of U.S. Import Prices Quoted in Foreign Currency for Selected Country of Origin (excluding petroleum)

	June 1989	March 1985	September 1982
West Germany	52.2	54.4	57.9
Switzerland	48.5	52.7	54.2
United Kingdom	33.3	35.0	36.5
France	19.5	24.5	27.6
Sweden	18.7	28.9	18.9
Japan	18.2	19.1	22.3
Italy	17.2	13.3	11.9
TOTAL WORLD	15.3	17.3	19.6
Canada	9.1	8.3	9.4
Hong Kong	4.5	6.1	13.0
Taiwan	0.9	0.2	0.0
South Korea	0.0	0.0	0.0

Source: Bureau of Labor Statistics.
Note: These figures are simple averages; they would be somewhat different if they were trade-weighted.

4.6 Prospective Enhancements to the BLS International Price Indexes

In the mid-1980s, BLS undertook an extensive review of the International Price Program. The results of this review pointed to the desirability of further enhancements to the import and export price indexes in several areas. One enhancement concerned the development of monthly indexes, as discussed earlier. Others included the development of import-price indexes by country of origin, major revision in the sampling methodology, and modernization of the data-processing capabilities for the BLS International Price Program. Resources were made available in fiscal year 1989 to begin to address these areas over the next four years. In addition, work has been underway at BLS for several years to expand the coverage of price indexes to include international trade in services.

The demand for monthly indexes was associated primarily with a desire, particularly in the Reagan administration, to have the monthly merchandise trade data published on an inflation-adjusted basis. In addition, because of the short-term variability of U.S. import prices, it was felt that monthly import-price indexes would facilitate more accurate assessment of monthly fluctuations in the PPI and the CPI. In view of the critical need for this information, the Bureau developed and began publishing a limited number of monthly indexes at the beginning of 1989. By 1993 the BLS expects to begin publication of a complete set of monthly indexes. However, since budgetary constraints may require a reduction in the number of products priced monthly (compared to the current quarterly total), there may be some diminution in the number of series published.

Interest in the construction of indexes by country of origin was boosted in the mid-1980s by the uneven pattern of the dollar's fall against other currencies, as well as by the tendency of importers to shift from suppliers in one country to another. Country-of-origin indexes would, of course, greatly facilitate analysis of pass-through rates for U.S. imports. Although Census unit-value data at a very detailed level of commodity and country disaggregation have been used to construct country-of-origin indexes, those series tend to have the same problems as the published unit-value indexes. BLS is now in the process of addressing the methodological issues associated with country-of-origin indexes and plans to begin publication of a limited set of indexes by 1992.

Up until 1989, BLS's sampling methodology replenished each product area approximately once every three years. Beginning in 1990, however, the Bureau shifted to a two-year replenishment cycle. Under this approach a given company and product will be used in an index for four years, after which a new sample will be drawn (which may or may not include the same companies or products). More importantly, two samples will be drawn for each product area, one initiated in year 1, the other in year 3. The revision of the sampling system has been designed to serve three major purposes: to permit more rapid introduction of new products into the indexes, which is important given the highly volatile nature of external trade; to allow the entire sample to be replaced completely over a four-year rotation (currently there is not a systematic probability-based process of sample updating); and to enlarge individual samples enough to permit the index algorithm to use company information. Currently, data on value of trade by company is incorporated into the sample selection process but cannot be properly used in the actual price-index estimator due to the relatively small size of each sample. Instead, products in similar item categories are given equal weight, regardless of their relative importance in the category.

The automated data-processing system currently being used for the international price indexes is mainframe-based and dates back to the early 1970s. Although it has been modified several times, it has become increasingly inefficient over the years as the data-base has expanded and the need for faster turnaround has increased. The new system will make extensive use of the interactive processing capability of PCs, as well as wider and more effective use of optical scanning equipment. The new system will facilitate the production of additional outputs, reduce processing time, and enhance quality review procedures.

In order to accommodate the growth in the service sector, BLS has recently begun to construct price indexes for selected categories of services in international trade. Currently, BLS releases data for air-passenger fares, crude-oil tanker freight, and electricity. Where possible, the Bureau is attempting to construct two parallel series for each area of services. One will reflect a balance-of-payments definition: an individual in one country pays for a service provided by an individual in another country. The other will reflect a more inclusive definition of an international service: the service itself is of an international nature, regardless of who is the provider. For example, for export airline fares, one set of data (on a balance-of-payments basis) reflects only foreigners traveling on American carriers. Under the broader definition, the second set of numbers would also include data on U.S. citizens flying overseas on U.S. carriers. The Bureau plans to expand indexes in this area during the next several years, as resources permit.

Despite the current expansion of the BLS program, several issues still need to be addressed. For example, unlike the CPI or PPI, the import and export price indexes are not seasonally adjusted. There are several difficulties in constructing seasonal factors. First, since nearly all the historical data are available only on a quarterly basis, there are at present just four observations per year to work with. Second, on the import side, the extreme volatility of the exchange rate over the past five years has overwhelmed any cyclical trends. However, the Bureau will continue to do ongoing research on seasonal factors in an effort to determine if they should be published.

Another area which needs some additional research is the transfer-pricing policies of multinational corporations. With the growing role of these companies in international transactions (in 1987 38.2 percent of U.S. merchandise trade was intracompany[16]), there is concern that a rising proportion of items in the Bureau's sample do not represent "arm's length" transactions and are therefore unusable for the purposes of the indexes.[17] A related concern is how to handle items that are classified in tariff codes 806 and 807. These are items that are produced in the United States, shipped to other countries for further processing or assembly, and then shipped back to the United States for final sale or final assembly.

One difficult issue revolves around the appropriate exchange rate to use in converting from a foreign-currency price to a dollar price. The Bureau currently does not ask respondents what exchange-rate factor they use in making valuations. Instead, the Bureau uses an exchange-rate factor which represents an average for the month immediately preceding the pricing month. Although this appears to be a reasonable approach, it is not clear how closely this figure approximates the exchange-rate factor used in the valuation of the item.

Another important area BLS expects to review in the International Price Program is that of how the BLS series are used. This is a critical question, since how the data are used may have a significant bearing on what data will be collected and how the indexes will be constructed.[18] To date, these indexes have been designed primarily to be used as deflators for the National Accounts. For this purpose the data should reflect transaction prices (excluding duty) of commodities which cross the U.S. border in a particular period. However, a researcher studying the competitiveness of U.S. versus foreign merchandise might be more interested in the current market price of a good, regardless of the period in which it was shipped. (In fact, assessing competitiveness was the main intent of the price measures developed by Kravis and Lipsey, 1971). If one's interest is in evaluating the impact of import prices on domestic price levels, an appropriate price index might very well include any duty assessment. In addition, the appropriate weights to be used in the construction of price indexes could differ substantially, depending upon the use to which the indexes are to be put. For example, for a deflator the appropriate weights would be current-period variable U.S. trade flows; as a competitiveness measure some sort of world fixed weight may be necessary; and for domestic price analysis a Laspeyres fixed market basket consistent with PPI and

16. Data on the 1987 percentage of intrafirm trade were constructed from articles in the June and July 1989 issues of the *Survey of Current Business*. The percent of imports in intrafirm trade was 41.0 percent, while the figure on the export side was 33.8 percent. For a short discussion of the growing importance of multinational trade, see Little (1987). Many of the issues associated with transfer pricing are discussed in Rugman and Eden (1985).

17. If it is determined during the initiation process that the buyer and seller are affiliated and that the transaction price for the product selected does not mirror market trends, then the product will not be collected for repricing.

18. The NBER *Report on the Price Statistics of the Federal Government* (1961) did address the issue of multiple series, but noted: "While we recognize that for various purposes we would desire differently defined indexes, we suspect that the differences will not be so great as to warrant the calculation of more than one index number of export prices and one number of import prices."

CPI might be most desirable. Work on reviewing and possibly revising or modifying the conceptual foundation for the indexes commenced in 1991.

4.7 Conclusion

I hope I have established the importance of the BLS import and export price indexes, despite the need for further enhancements to them, and in particular their superiority compared with unit-value indexes. Despite the supposed similarity of unit-value indexes to these new series, I found significant differences over the past decade in their trends. In particular, prices in import categories as measured by the BLS indexes generally rose more rapidly than prices in the same categories as measured by UVIs. It is critical to realize that analysts may get different results in their studies depending on which source of data is being used, given that much of the historical information on external price trends for the U.S. is available only via unit-value figures.

I also used the BLS price indexes to estimate some pass-through values and concluded from the results that U.S. companies appear less willing to adjust their home-currency export price than foreign companies in the face of fluctuating exchange rates. Finally, I constructed some new data, which became available as a byproduct of the BLS data collection, on the percentage of U.S. imports invoiced in a foreign currency, both by country of origin and product area. I concluded that imports from Western Europe and imports of finished goods are more likely to be priced in a foreign currency. In some cases up to 50 percent of a category was priced in a foreign currency.

References

Allen, R. G. D. 1975. *Index Numbers in Theory and Practice*. Chicago: Aldine Publishing Company.

Alterman, William, John Goth, and Dave Johnson. 1987. BLS Publishes Average Exchange Rate and Foreign Currency Price Indexes. *Monthly Labor Review* 110(12):47–49.

Baldwin, Richard. 1988. Hysteresis in Import Prices: The Beachhead Effect. *American Economic Review* 78(3):773–85.

Dornbusch, Rudiger. 1987. Exchange Rates and Prices. *American Economic Review* 77(1):93–106.

Feenstra, Robert C. 1988. Quality Changes under Trade Restraints in Japanese Autos. *Quarterly Journal of Economics* 103(1):131–46.

Froot, Kenneth, and Paul Klemperer. 1989. Exchange Rate Pass-Through when Market Share Matters. *American Economic Review* 79(4):637–54.

Holmes, R. A. 1973. The Inadequacy of Unit Value Indexes as Proxies for Canadian Industrial Selling Prices. *Review of Income and Wealth* 19(3):271–77.

Hooper, Peter, and Catherine Mann. 1989. *Exchange Rate Pass Through in the 1980s:*

The Case of U.S. Imports of Manufactures. Paper presented at Brookings Panel on Economic Activity, 6–7 April 1989.

Interagency Committee on Measurement of Real Output, Subcommittee on Prices. 1973. Report on Criteria for Choice of Unit Values or Wholesale Prices in Deflators. Typescript (the Searle Committee Report). 17 June 1960. Reprinted with changes and a brief summary of the appendixes in *Review of Income and Wealth* 19(3): 253–66.

Kim, Yoonbai. 1990. Exchange Rates and Import Prices in the United States: A Varying-Parameter Estimation of Exchange-Rate Pass-Through. *Journal of Business and Statistics* 8(3):305–15.

Knetter, Michael. 1989. Price Discrimination by U.S. and German Exporters. *American Economic Review* 79(1):198–210.

Kravis, Irving B., and Robert Lipsey. 1971. *Price Competitiveness in World Trade.* New York: National Bureau of Economic Research.

Krugman, Paul. 1987. Pricing to Market when the Exchange Rate Changes. In *Real-Financial Linkages among Open Economies,* ed. S. W. Arndt and J. D. Richardson. Cambridge Mass.: MIT Press.

Lichtenberg, Frank R., and Zvi Griliches. 1989. Errors of Measurement in Output Deflators. *Journal of Business and Economic Statistics* 7(1):1–9.

Little, Jane Sneddon. 1987. Intra-Firm trade: An Update. *New England Economic Review* May/June:46–51.

Mann, Catherine L. 1986. Prices, Profit Margins, and Exchange Rates. *Federal Reserve Bulletin* 72(6):366–79.

Moffett, Michael H. 1989. The J-Curve Revisited: An Empirical Examination for the United States. *Journal of International Money and Finance* 8:425–44.

Murphy, Edward E. 1972. A Comparison of the Bureau of Labor Statistics' Indexes of Export Prices for Selected U.S. Products with Unit Value and Wholesale Price Indexes. American Statistical Association, *Proceedings of the Business and Economic Statistics Section* 69:462–67.

National Bureau of Economic Research, Price Statistics Review Committee. 1961. *Report on the Price Statistics of the Federal Government.* New York.

Page, S. A. B. 1981. The Choice of Invoicing Currency in Merchandise Trade. *National Institute Economic Review* 98(November):60–71.

Rugman, A. M., and L. Eden. 1985. *Multinationals and Transfer Pricing.* New York: St. Martins Press.

Shiells, C. R. 1987. Measurement Errors in Unit-Value Proxies for Import Prices. U.S. Department of Labor, Bureau of International Labor Affairs. Economic Discussion Paper no. 24 (December).

Sinclair, James, and Brian Catron. 1990. An Experimental Price Index for the Computer Industry. *Monthly Labor Review* 113(10): 16–24.

United Nations. 1981. Strategies for Price and Quantity Measurement in External Trade. Statistical Paper (series M) no. 69.

U.S. Department of Commerce, Bureau of the Census, Foreign Trade Division. 1989. U.S. Foreign Trade Indexes—Methodology. Typescript (May).

U.S. Department of Commerce, Bureau of Economic Analysis. 1986. *Survey of Current Business* 66(11):35–36.

U.S. Department of Labor, Bureau of Labor Statistics. 1988. *BLS Handbook of Methods.* Chapter 17, "International Price Indexes," pp. 138–47.

———. 1977. Estimating Price Trends of Industrial Countries' Exports to OPEC. BLS Bulletin no. 1969.

Whichard, Obie G. 1989. U.S. Multinational Companies: Operations in 1987. Bureau of Economic Analysis, *Survey of Current Business* 69(6):27–40.

Comment   Richard C. Marston

This paper compares the export and import price indexes developed over the past fifteen years by the Bureau of Labor Statistics with the unit-value indexes produced over a much longer period by the Department of Commerce. Since the unit-value indexes will be abolished shortly, the paper can be viewed in one of two ways. First, it is serving the valuable purpose of putting nails in the coffin of the unit-value indexes. Alterman has developed a clear case establishing why the BLS indexes are superior, and therefore why resources should be directed toward improving and extending them. But in addition, Alterman is helping to assess how misleading it may be to use unit-value indexes for past years. Since the BLS coverage is so spotty before 1980 and even before 1985, we have to use unit-value series to analyze the earlier period. So it is useful to emphasize how faulty the alternative unit-value series can be. Alterman's study thus is a valuable one; it should become a standard reference for research involving U.S. export and import prices.

I would like to add parenthetically that what puzzles me is why the U.S. government took so long to provide price indexes for exports and imports. The German and Japanese governments were years ahead of BLS in developing a full range of export-price indexes. Indeed, it wasn't until 1983 that BLS extended its coverage to all of manufacturing. Yet reports dating back to the early 1960s and academic research such as the 1971 study by Kravis and Lipsey presented clearcut cases for using genuine price indexes rather than unit-value series.[1]

Alterman uses data for the period from 1985 to 1989 to show how much difference there is between the two sets of price series. For most imports, the BLS series rises much more sharply than the unit-value series over this period. How important is the difference? Alterman shows that using the BLS series reduces the U.S. trade deficit in real terms for the second quarter of 1989 to $98.8 billion, rather than $128.4 billion if unit-value series are used to deflate trade in nominal terms.

Alterman investigates why the price series diverge so much. One reason may be that the BLS series uses base period weights, whereas the unit-value series uses Fisher-linked indexes. How important is the choice of weighting scheme? Does the fact that the BLS uses 1985 weights instead of current weights or Fisher-linked weights account for much of the deviation between the two series from 1985 to 1989? Alterman provides an answer to this question by reweighting the BLS series using 1988 rather than 1985 trade flows for weights. He finds that the 1988-weighted import series increase *more* than the 1985-weighted series. So the discrepancy between the BLS series and

Richard C. Marston is the James R. F. Guy Professor of Finance and Economics at the Wharton School of the University of Pennsylvania.

1. Irving B. Kravis and Robert E. Lipsey, *Price Competitiveness in World Trade*, Studies in International Economic Relations, no. 6 (University Microfilms).

unit-value series cannot be attributed to the use of base period weights in the former.

So what accounts for the greater rise in the BLS series? The answer to this question remains a puzzle. One possible way to approach the question would be to compare unit-value series for a few individual industries with specially constructed BLS series, using the *same* weighting scheme as in the unit-value series. In that case, the weighting scheme is common to both series, so we can assess the importance of using genuine price indexes rather than unit-value data. Using detailed industry-level data, it may be possible to determine the biases introduced in the unit-value series by neglecting changes in product composition.

Alterman uses the BLS series to examine pass-through behavior in the 1980s. During this decade, fluctuations of the dollar have had a greater impact on U.S. competitiveness than has any other factor. So it is important to be able to use export and import price series to determine the impact of exchange-rate changes on relative prices. Alterman provides estimates of pass-through rates for U.S. imports and exports across a number of commodity categories. The pass-through rates are defined as the ratio of the percentage change in the import or export prices to the percentage change in the exchange rate times the exporting country's consumer price index (as a proxy for production costs). The foreign-exchange rates and foreign consumer price indexes used are weighted averages constructed from data for 63 countries.

Because so many countries are included, it is necessary to use consumer price indexes as a proxy for costs. Consumer price indexes have obvious disadvantages for this purpose, since over half of the commodities included in the indexes are not even traded. But if Alterman had used wholesale price indexes for manufacturing or unit labor costs, the set of countries would have had to be narrowed considerably. Nevertheless, I would have preferred using the narrower indexes where available, and the consumer price indexes for other countries.

Alterman provides an interesting comparison between pass-through rates for U.S. imports and exports in table 4.5. The table shows that foreign exporters generally passed through a much smaller proportion of the dollar's recent depreciation than did American exporters. In the period from March 1985 to December 1988, the prices of American imports in dollars generally rose less than half as much as the change in the exchange rate, while many of the prices of American exports in foreign currency rose proportionately. Alterman suggests two reasons for the difference. First, both American and foreign firms may behave asymmetrically, passing through most of a depreciation of their currency, but passing through only a fraction of an appreciation. Second, American firms may pass through more than do foreign firms, regardless of the direction of the exchange-rate change.

Alterman looks for an asymmetric pattern of pass-throughs by comparing a period of dollar depreciation, September 1980 to March 1985, with a period of dollar appreciation, March 1985 to December 1988. In all ten import sectors for which price data are available for both periods, the pass-through rates are greater in the second period of dollar appreciation. But because the BLS series cover only about half of the sectors in the earlier period, the comparison between periods remains incomplete.

Using table 4.5, it is also possible to look for asymmetries between American and foreign behavior in periods when the exporter's currency appreciated. That is, pass-through rates for U.S. exports in the early 1980s, when the dollar appreciated, can be compared with pass-through rates for U.S. imports in the late 1980s, when foreign currencies appreciated. In all eight sectors for which BLS series are reported for the earlier period, the pass-through rates are larger for U.S. exports (for 1980–85) than for imports from foreign countries (for 1985–88). So differences in pass-through arise from two sources: differences in behavior in appreciations and depreciations and differences in behavior between U.S. and foreign firms.

One drawback of the pass-through effects that are estimated, however, is that they reflect two different influences on prices. Take the example of foreign exports to the United States. If foreign prices rise less than proportionately to the exchange rate, then this may be due to declines in *costs* abroad (that is, declines that are not adequately reflected in movements in consumer prices). In Japan, the costs of imported materials declined by one-half in yen terms, thus reducing Japanese costs of producing finished products, when the dollar appreciated after March 1985. Japanese consumer prices fell much less. But less than complete pass-throughs of foreign export prices may also be due to price discrimination or what has been called "pricing to market." Foreign firms may reduce their export prices in *their own currency* relative to the price of exportables sold in the firms' own market. In both cases, export prices in *dollars* rise less than proportionately to a depreciation of the dollar. But it would be useful to know the relative importance of each type of influence. As Alterman notes, consumer price indexes at best capture only part of the movement in costs within the exporter's country. Moreover, the behavior of costs may differ widely across sectors.

In the case of U.S. exports, we can study pricing to market directly by examining how export prices move *relative* to the domestic prices for the *same* products. My study of Japanese pricing to market shows one way to pursue such an investigation.[2] If such a price comparison is done at the sectoral level, the composition of the exports and domestic products will differ somewhat, but an examination of this ratio will still be instructive.

In the case of U.S. imports, it isn't possible to obtain national price series disaggregated by sector for each foreign country. It is important to note, however, that pass-through elasticities we see in table 4.5 may overstate the degree of pricing to market actually occurring. In any case, it is safe to say that the

2. Richard C. Marston, "Pricing to Market in Japanese Manufacturing," *Journal of International Economics* 29, no. 3/4 (November 1990):217–36.

inadequacy of foreign price data prevents us from fully understanding price behavior followed by foreign firms.

At the end of the paper, Alterman reports on several new price series being developed by BLS, including monthly rather than quarterly price indexes, indexes by country of origin, and indexes for some types of trade in services. Judging by the improvements in the BLS series that have already taken place and those that are planned for the future, we have moved far beyond the unit-value series of the past. All researchers on international trade should applaud BLS's efforts.

5 Measures of Prices and Price Competitiveness in International Trade in Manufactured Goods

Robert E. Lipsey, Linda Molinari, and Irving B. Kravis

5.1 Introduction

Our purpose in this paper is to explain the construction of a set of price indexes relating to international trade in manufactured goods. The indexes are intended to be free of some of the defects of existing measures and more suitable for the calculation of changes in quantities traded and for the analysis of the relationship between prices and quantities.

Measures of the prices of manufactured goods are a weak link in empirical studies of international trade. While most authors have accepted the existing indexes for primary products as reasonably accurate and representative, quite a few have been skeptical about the data for manufactured-goods prices. Their deficiencies affect studies of competitiveness, of real exchange rates, of income elasticities of demand, of price and substitution elasticities, of the terms of trade, and of the supply of exports.

The list of defects is a long one. For many countries, no price data are collected for exports and imports, and many studies of trade rely on indexes of export and import unit values, despite a long history of adverse appraisals of their accuracy, particularly for manufactured goods.[1] Not only are the unit

Robert E. Lipsey is professor of economics at Queens College and the Graduate Center, City University of New York, and a research associate of the National Bureau of Economic Research. Linda Molinari is technical support analyst, customer services, ISMD Division, LEGENT Corporation, Vienna, Virginia. Irving B. Kravis is university professor emeritus at the University of Pennsylvania and a research associate of the National Bureau of Economic Research.

The authors are indebted to Catherine Mann and J. David Richardson for many valuable comments and suggestions; to Osman Sari, assisted by Nisangul Ceran and Zhang Zhu, for price-collection and statistical work on the recent data; and to James Hayes and Rosa Schupbach for the preparation of the manuscript.

1. E.g., see NBER Price Statistics Review Committee (1961), Kravis and Lipsey (1971, 1974), and Murphy (1972).

values inaccurate as measures of the prices of individual products, but in each country they are combined with different weights and using different index-number formulas.

In the case of primary goods, quality changes were thought to be relatively small, and where they were not, prices based on narrow specifications were often available as a check on the data based on unit values. The introduction of new products was not thought to be a major problem. While there have been many large shifts in sources of supply for primary products, most scholars have been willing to accept that, for these goods at least, the "law of one price" worked well enough that a missing price observation could be safely filled in using the price of the same product from another country.

None of these reassurances can be applied to the prices of manufactured goods. It is possible that there is serious underrepresentation of new commodities, at least for part of their history. There have been suggestions that price indexes for manufactured goods suffered from upward bias due to the neglect of quality change. Export prices for automobiles, for example, might not take into account changes such as gains in horsepower, the shift to power brakes and steering, and antipollution devices. More important, perhaps, is the omission of many products from most countries' price indexes. Computers and computer accessories may be excluded completely, although they have become a major part of manufactured-goods trade. The fact that manufactured products from different countries are less substitutable for each other than primary products from different sources means that the omission of one country's prices for some manufactured products is much more likely to bias an index than the omission of one country's primary product prices.

An alternative to the unit-value indexes is the use of wholesale or producer-price indexes. These are collected with a much higher degree of quality control than is applied to the unit-value indexes, at least in some countries. However, the prices do not purport to apply to external trade. The difference in movement between domestic and export prices can be significant.[2] The producer-price indexes share a characteristic of the unit-value indexes: they are computed with different weighting, coverage, and index-number formulas in different countries. The methods of computation of both types of indexes differ greatly from one country to another because the indexes are computed by national statistical agencies for their own purposes, for which they may be quite satisfactory.

A further consequence of the dependence on price collection by individual countries is that it builds in an assumption about price behavior. The assumption is that prices of goods not covered by a country's price collection process

---

2. As is pointed out in the sources mentioned above, and in Kalter (1978), Kravis and Lipsey (1977a and 1977b, where these differences are interpreted as reflecting changes in export profit margins), Baldwin (1988), Dornbusch (1987), Krugman (1987), Mann (1986), Marston (1989), and Ohno (1989). The profit-margin interpretation and the literature on the related "pass-through" issue are reviewed in Mann (1986).

move identically with prices of covered commodities in the same general class or, if the whole class is uncovered, with the prices of commodities in general. It is implicitly assumed that price movements of the same product in other countries convey no information at all about the likely change in the missing prices. That is an odd choice of assumptions for a profession that often assumes the operation of purchasing power parity or the "law of one price." The practical implication can be imagined in the case of a comparison between a country that covers computer prices in its price index and a country that omits them and assumes they follow prices of other products.

In this paper, we construct a set of international price indexes for manufactured goods from 1953 to 1988.[3] Our indexes address these issues in several ways.

1. Weighting. We construct two types of indexes of manufactured goods prices. One is intended mainly for studies of competition in international trade. It is calculated for the United States and for the aggregate of many of its major competitors, using the export weights of the United States and weighting at a fine level of commodity detail, such as the 4-digit SITC. A similar calculation is performed for Germany and its competitors, using German export weights, and for Japan and its competitors, using Japanese export weights. Indexes of domestic prices with own-country export weights are also calculated for each of the three countries, to examine the possibility of divergences between export and domestic price movements and the implications for changing margins of profitability of export and domestic sales.

A second type of index, used, for example, in studying world trends in terms of trade, is a "world" index of manufactured-goods prices, using as weights aggregate developed-country exports or developed-country exports to developing countries. We also construct indexes for individual countries based on these two sets of weights.

For all of these types of indexes, we carry out the calculations using weights from a relatively early date, 1963, and from a later date, 1975.

2. Missing prices. In place of the assumption that prices for products not covered move in the same way as those covered in the same country, we use, in the aggregate indexes for all developed countries, a method that incorporates both country and commodity effects in estimating missing prices. The method is an adaptation of one developed by Summers (1973) for the estimation of country price levels. It involves fitting an equation to each block of country and commodity price change observations for a given year. The block is defined by the full list of commodities and countries in, say, a 2-digit SITC class. The equation contains dummy variables for both country and commod-

---

3. We define manufactures here as divisions 5 through 8 of the SITC Revision 1. The most serious omission for comparison with domestic industrial data is of manufactured foods, although there are also other minor omissions, some of which were rectified in Revision 2 of the SITC. We did not adopt them here because the indexes could not be recalculated to match the later classification without a major effort.

ity and therefore permits the data to determine the degree to which each influences the estimate of the missing price. The list of variables could be expanded to include, for example, a dummy variable for the use of a hedonic price index or a variable to represent the movement of the price in the preceding year.

3. Quality corrections. One reason for doubts as to the accuracy of price indexes for manufactured products is the suspicion that they do not take adequate account of changes in the quality of these goods and are biased upward on that account. There have been no studies that examine changes in quality specific to exports and imports, but there have been a fair number of studies of quality change, and of the correction of prices for quality change, by the use of hedonic price measures. We show the effect on the U.S. export price indexes of introducing the quality-adjusted price measures that have been calculated for a few commodities in the United States. We then also show the effect on world price indexes of introducing these quality adjustments, under several possible assumptions about the relation between quality change in the U.S. and quality change in other countries.

5.2 Methods and Sources

5.2.1. Sources of Detailed Price Data

The indexes are based on disaggregated export price data for countries for which they are available, with gaps filled by producer and wholesale price indexes and hedonic price indexes, where possible.

There are several basic ingredients for our indexes. The first are the international price indexes for metals, metal products, machinery, and transport equipment, for the United States, the United Kingdom, Germany, and Japan, covering 1953–1964, from Kravis and Lipsey (1971), with interpolations based on the other types of data, as explained for the case of Germany in Kravis and Lipsey (1972). The second are the official export price indexes produced by the United States, Germany, and Japan, the latter two fairly comprehensive, the first starting with the same coverage as the Kravis-Lipsey indexes and gradually increasing in coverage over time until they are now quite complete. The third element of our indexes is more fragmentary export price data published by the United Kingdom, Sweden, and the Netherlands, the last gradually increasing in scope over the years. The fourth type of data is producer price indexes or wholesale price indexes, or both, for each country mentioned above and also for France and Canada. The fifth type is hedonic price indexes for a few types of machinery and transport equipment in the United States. These are used in two ways. The first is in the data from Kravis and Lipsey (1971) mentioned above. The second is as a substitute for conventional price series, in a very rough attempt at adjustment for quality change, where we consider it appropriate and important.

The various sources of data, of course, overlap extensively in commodity coverage. It is therefore necessary to assign price series to the index by systems of priorities, determined by our view as to the appropriateness of each type of data as measures of export prices. In the world price series or those for developed-country exports to developing countries, the highest priority is given to series representing prices in international trade, first the Kravis-Lipsey series and then official export price series. The second priority is for producer or wholesale prices, and the third for the hedonic price indexes. Although we consider the hedonic price series more appropriate for our purposes than the conventional series, we have not given them priority because we wished to produce indexes from something close to conventional data. However, we have also calculated an alternative index in which hedonic price series are given priority, and we consider that to be the best estimate we can make of the movement of prices of manufactured goods.

In the export price indexes based on each country's own export weights, only export prices themselves are used in each own-country index. The indexes for competing countries give export prices the first priority, and producer or wholesale prices the second, but no hedonic price indexes are used because the hedonic price data are confined to the U.S. The results would depend too heavily on whether hedonic indexes were applied only to the U.S. or are assumed to reflect similar changes in quality in other countries' exports.

The domestic price indexes based on export weights use no export prices and are based entirely on producer or wholesale prices.

The precise sources of the price data are given in appendix A.

5.2.2   Weighting Schemes and Missing Price Observations

As was suggested in Kravis and Lipsey (1984), the selection of systems of weighting is second only to the selection of basic price data in determining the characteristics of the resulting price indexes. Several different methods have been used, implying different assumptions not only about the importance to be given to commodities but also, usually inadvertently, about the behavior of prices for which data are unavailable.

We can think of a set of worldwide weights representing the values of exports of each commodity (defined here as a 4-digit SITC subgroup) from each country (ω_{ij}), to be used in weighting price relatives showing changes over time in individual prices (P_{ij}). Table 5.1 shows the weights in the form of a country-by-commodity matrix.

The most common method for constructing price indexes for aggregates of countries, such as those used in models that call for "world" or "rest-of-world" prices of export goods or traded goods, is to use the published country-aggregate price indexes and to weight them together by some set of weights representing the importance of each country in world trade. The importance of each country might be measured by the value of trade or, in some cases, by

Table 5.1   **Commodity by Country Matrix of Weights**

			Country		
Commodity	1	2	3	. . . . m	Σ Countries
1	ω_{11}	ω_{12}	ω_{13}	. . . . ω_{1m}	ω_{1T}
2	ω_{21}	ω_{22}	ω_{23}	. . . . ω_{2m}	ω_{2T}
3	ω_{31}	ω_{32}	ω_{33}	. . . . ω_{3m}	ω_{3T}
.			.	. . . . .	.
n	ω_{n1}	ω_{n2}	ω_{n3}	. . . . ω_{nm}	ω_{nT}
Σ Commodities	ω_{T1}	ω_{T2}	ω_{T3}	. . . . ω_{Tm}	ω

$\omega_{11} + \omega_{12} \ldots \ldots + \omega_{33} \ldots + \omega_{nm} = \omega = 1.00$

weights derived from a model. In terms of the matrix above, these aggregate indexes are of the type

(1)
$$p = \sum_{j=1}^{m} \omega_{Tj} \sum_{i=1}^{n} \frac{\omega_{ij}}{\omega_{Tj}} p_{ij}$$

It is usually uncertain in these calculations, since they do not go behind published aggregates, what commodities are included with what commodity weights, and with what base years. It is likely that many of the country indexes lack proper representation of complex manufactured products. Given all these characteristics, it is not surprising if elasticities of substitution or price elasticities of demand are found to be low or if no significant relationships can be found.

In an effort to overcome some of these problems, we have at times calculated indexes for various countries in which the same set of commodity weights at the 4-digit SITC level was applied to each country's prices.[4] The differences between one country's aggregate price change and those of rival countries were then more clearly attributable to differences in price changes for the same products rather than to some mixture of these with differences in the coverage or weighting of products. In terms of the matrix above, these price indexes were of the form

(2)
$$p = \sum_{j=1}^{m} \omega_{Tj} \sum_{i=1}^{n} \omega_{iT} \, p_{ij}$$

Both of these types of indexes involve the same assumptions about the nature of the commodities priced at the most detailed level and about price relationships, since each involves filling in missing price observations using only data for the same country. The justification for starting with the calculation of

4. Kravis and Lipsey (1972, 1977a, 1977b, and 1982) and Bushe, Kravis, and Lipsey (1986).

country indexes is the assumption that missing prices tend to behave in a similar manner to the average of other prices in the same country for commodities in the same 3-digit, 2-digit, or 1-digit commodity class. These methods, therefore, ignore the behavior of other countries' prices for the same commodity; this is a difficult assumption to accept for anyone who believes price movements in different countries are correlated at all.

An alternative method of calculating world or other price indexes aggregated over countries would be

$$(3) \qquad p = \sum_{i=1}^{n} \omega_{iT} \sum_{j=1}^{m} \frac{\omega_{ij}}{\omega_{iT}} p_{ij}$$

in which a world price index for each commodity would be calculated first, and all these would then be aggregated across commodities using worldwide commodity trade weights. This procedure would come closer to acceptance of the law of one price than those outlined above, since it assumes that one country's price for a commodity tends to move with the average of other countries' prices for the same commodity. However, it therefore assumes that there is no country-specific effect on a price change. Thus, a currency revaluation is presumed to have no effect on the export price of the revaluing country in comparison to that of others. In our studies of international price behavior we have found this proposition to be contradicted frequently (e.g., Kravis and Lipsey, 1978).

A preliminary test of the two extreme assumptions, reported in Kravis and Lipsey (1984), was to compare the variance of price movements among countries at the 1-digit SITC level with the variance among 4-digit commodities within 1-digit commodity divisions within countries, using year-to-year price movements for the United States, Germany, and Japan. The variance among countries within 1-digit classes was larger than the variance among 4-digit commodities within a class within countries. The conclusion there was that "if either country alone or commodity alone had to be used as the criterion for assigning missing price observations, country would be a better choice." However, considerable further tests would be needed to make a definitive judgment on this issue.

5.2.3   Estimating Missing Prices by the Country-Product Dummy Method

Despite the range of sources from which we collected price data, it was not possible to collect prices for every item for every country for every year. In the earlier studies by Kravis and Lipsey, a procedure was adopted that is almost universal: setting some minimum level of coverage for a group of commodities and, if that level is achieved, using the average price change for covered commodities as an estimate of that for the whole group, assuming in effect that the prices of uncovered items move, on average, identically to those of covered items. We continue to use this method for the individual country price indexes based on own-country weights (appendix C).

Common though this procedure for estimating missing prices is, it discards some information about the missing category that is probably pertinent: the price change for the corresponding product in other countries. We have therefore used a different method for the developed-country price indexes. This method, referred to as the country-product dummy method, was developed by Robert Summers (1973) for use in estimating missing price levels for intercountry price comparisons in the United Nations International Comparison Project. Its purpose was to use information on both country influences and product influences on the price of a product to estimate each missing price. In its original version by Summers, it involved regressions for commodity groups using natural logs of the price levels as the dependent variable, and country and product dummies as the independent variables. There was a product dummy variable for every product in the group and a country dummy variable for every country but one, which was designated the base country. The coefficient of a country dummy term for country j in one of these equations represents the natural log of the ratio of the price level in this commodity group in country j to the price level in the base country. If we translate the equation into natural numbers, the price level for country j appears as an exponent in the equation.

We wished to estimate not only commodity-group price changes but also the price changes for each missing item. We created as dense a price matrix as possible at the 4-digit level as a first step, thereby permitting weighting and reweighting as our needs changed. We estimate the missing prices by using the commodity dummy coefficients in conjunction with the country dummy coefficients. Because there is no dummy for the base country, the commodity dummy coefficients are estimates of the prices for those commodities in the base country. To estimate a price missing in the base country's data, therefore, we used the exponent of the appropriate commodity dummy. For any other country, we multiplied the exponent of the coefficient for the product by that for the country, and we adjusted the "base" price for a commodity for the group price difference between the base country and the dummy country.

In running the regressions, we had two procedural problems to resolve. The first was to define the commodity groups within which we would run regressions. A group should be defined narrowly to make it as homogeneous as possible while still retaining sufficient degrees of freedom for a regression. The 2-digit SITC categories were the starting points, but some groups had too few SITC subdivisions and others had too few available observations. Therefore, in cases where the regression for a 2-digit group would have had less than 10 degrees of freedom, we pooled it with other small 2-digit groups in the same 1-digit division. The second problem was that data were so scarce for certain countries in various years and groups that we felt that the estimates for these countries would be statistically meaningless. Therefore, in any one regression, we included only countries for which we had price data for 3 or more commodities within the group, as well as those for which even a smaller number of items accounted for 30 percent of the group weight. The weights for commodities and groups were based on 1963 OECD exports. These procedures were applied on a yearly basis, so that while two groups may have been combined in an early year because neither one included a sufficient number of observations, they may have been treated separately in a later year if the number of available prices increased. Similarly, a country excluded in one year might be included in another if the coverage of its price data improved.

5.2.4   Aggregation of Detailed Price Indexes

Once we had run regressions for every 2-digit group and year for which it was feasible and the resulting price estimates were used to fill in any holes at the 4-digit level, the 4-digit price indexes were weighted up to the 3-digit level. Not every 3-digit group price index could be estimated by aggregation. If the price index for a 3-digit group was "missing" because there were not enough data at the 4-digit level, the index at the 3-digit level was estimated by the same regression procedure, where possible. After the 3-digit estimates were added, and the data were weighted up to the 2-digit level, regressions were run to estimate any missing 2-digit groups. In both cases, the weights used were 1963 OECD exports to the world.

After filling in as much data as needed, we created a master price file for each country that contained all the necessary data at every level. These are the files we used, weighted together using various weights, to create the various price indexes for total developed-country exports and developed-country exports to developing countries reported here.

5.3   Indexes of "World" Export Prices for Manufactures

5.3.1   Weighting and Country Coverage

We have calculated two aggregate price indexes for exports of manufactured goods by developed countries, differing in their weighting but not in the price series used. One is an index weighted by the value of all exports of manufactures by developed countries, including their exports to each other. The other is an index weighted by the value of exports by developed countries to developing countries. The former is relevant to issues such as the terms of trade between manufactures and primary products, and the latter is more relevant to discussions of the terms of trade between developed and developing countries.

Both of these indexes were constructed with two sets of weights: 1963 exports by all OECD countries and 1975 exports by the same countries. The developed market economies, a class almost equivalent to the OECD, accounted for 82 percent of the world's exports of manufactures in 1965, 84 percent in 1975, and 78 percent in 1985. Of the manufactured exports by developed market economies in 1985, those countries covered by our indexes (although not necessarily covered for all commodities) accounted for 77 percent or, in other words, about 60 percent of world exports of manufactures.[5]

5.3.2   Effects of Differences in Time Period Used for Weighting

Two time periods, 1963 and 1975, have been used to weight the price indexes for all developed-country exports and exports from developed countries to developing countries. If we compared the price movements between 1963 and 1975 derived from the two measures, it would be equivalent to the familiar comparison of Laspeyres and Paasche price indexes, with the index on the 1963 weight base the Laspeyres price index (or the one based on earlier weights) and the index on the 1975 weight base the Paasche price index. An increase in the 1963-based index relative to the 1975-based index would imply a negative covariance between prices and quantities, while a relative increase in the 1975-based index would imply a positive covariance. We could associate the negative covariance with a situation in which events were dominated by changes in supply, with demand relatively stable. The positive covariance implies a situation dominated by changes in demand, with supply relatively stable.[6]

The differences in the trend of prices produced by the shift in weight base from 1963 to 1975 are shown on Table 5.2. In every case, the index with a later weight base rose less than the one with an earlier base, implying the dominance of changes in supply and substitution in favor of products for which price increases were relatively small. The difference was larger in the index for all countries than in any of those for individual countries. That fact implies that in addition to substitution among commodities, there was also substitution among countries in favor of those with relatively declining prices, presumably those in which productivity and export supply were increasing most rapidly.

Despite the fact that there were wide divergences among the countries in the size of the increase in prices over the period as a whole, the effects on the price indexes of changing weights were fairly small, ranging only from 3 per-

---

5. Within the developed market economy groups, there were $217 billion of manufactures exports in 1985 by countries we did not cover. The largest omitted country was Italy, with $68 billion in exports, followed by Belgium/Luxembourg with $40 billion, and Switzerland with $32 billion. Other European countries, for which at least some detailed domestic producer or wholesale price data could probably be obtained with sufficient effort, were the sources of another $67 billion. Thus, Europe as a whole accounted for 95 percent of the manufactured exports of developed market economies that we did not cover.

Of the $265 billion in manufactures exports by other than developed market economies countries in 1985, 22 percent of the world total, over 60 percent were exports by developing countries, and the rest were from centrally planned economies. The $167 billion from developing countries were concentrated in Southeast Asian countries. More than 40 percent were from Hong Kong, South Korea, and Singapore. The concentration in Asia would be even higher if the figures included Taiwan, which was omitted from U.N. tabulations.

6. For a detailed discussion of the relationship to the covariances, see Lipsey (1963, pp. 85–90).

Table 5.2   **Export Price Index for All Manufactures, 1988 (1953 = 100)**

	OECD Export Weights of		
	1963	1975	1963/1975
All Developed Countries	430.3	409.9	105.0
United States	369.1	359.3	102.7
Germany	572.7	556.9	102.8
Japan	370.8	354.1	104.7

Source: Appendix tables 5B.1,5B.2, 5B.5, 5B.6, 5B.9, 5B.10, 5B.13, 5B.14.

Table 5.3   **Export Price Indexes for 1-Digit SITC Classes, 1988 (1953 = 100)**

	Index on 1963 Weights/Index on 1975 Weights:			
	SITC 5	SITC 6	SITC 7	SITC 8
All Countries	1.046	.993	1.109	1.031
United States	1.073	.980	1.034	1.037
Germany	1.072	1.003	1.045	1.049
Japan	1.044	1.031	1.024	1.040

Source: See note to table 5.2.

cent for the United States to 5 percent for Japan. That narrow range reflects the fact that the same weights are used for all the countries' indexes. In the case of the export price indexes based on own-country weights, shown in Appendix C, the differences are considerably larger, ranging from 3 percent for Germany to 9 percent for Japan and 11 percent for the United States. All the indexes show a larger price increase for the series using the earlier weight base, implying dominance by supply changes and substitution toward products falling in price, and there was apparently more substitution, or a wider range of price changes, within U.S. and Japanese exports than within German exports or those of all developed countries as a group.

The relationship between indexes based on the two sets of weights varied somewhat among commodity divisions. In most cases, the later weight base was associated with a smaller price increase, but there were some exceptions, as can be seen in table 5.3. The cases in which the earlier set of weights led to lower price index changes were in SITC 6, which consists mainly of semi-manufactures. In that group, for the United States, changes in prices and in quantities were positively correlated, implying the likelihood that the price changes were dominated by changes on the demand side rather than the supply side.

5.3.3   Export Prices to the World and to Developing Countries

Since the composition of exports to developing countries might be different from that of exports to other countries, it is conceivable that developing countries faced larger or smaller price increases than other buyers. That possibility is examined in table 5.4 for manufactured goods as a whole and for the four major categories of manufactures.

In most cases, exports to the world (and therefore exports to the developed world to a greater degree) increased more rapidly in price over the three and a half decades than exports to developing countries. That was the case for manufactured products as whole, for SITC divisions 6 and 8, and for the machinery indexes on 1963 weights. The largest differences, about 10 percent, were in SITC 8, a category in which the developing countries were themselves substantial exporters.

An earlier version of the price indexes for exports to developing countries was compared in Kravis and Lipsey (1984), to the U.N. unit-value index for manufactures that is customarily used for calculations of manufactured-goods prices and terms of trade. The conclusion was that prices of manufactured goods exported by developed countries to developing countries had risen much less than had been suggested by the unit-value indexes—something in the neighborhood of 75 percent over the period from 1953 to 1976, as compared with 140 percent for the unit-value index. About half of the difference stemmed from the corrections for quality change and the other half from some mixture of differences in the type of price data used (prices vs. unit values), in index-number formulas, and in country coverage. The different price measure for manufactured goods also implied, of course, a larger decline in the terms of trade of manufactured goods relative to primary products than had been shown by the unit-value indexes.

5.3.4 Adjustments for Quality Change

The proper treatment in a price index of changes in the quality of goods has been a controversial issue for many years. A considerable amount of work has been done, particularly by the application of hedonic methods, to adjust domestic price indexes for changes in quality that are supposedly not adequately accounted for, even in price indexes gathered with considerable attention to quality specifications. Most of this research has been directed to consumer

Table 5.4   **Export Price Index, 1988 (1953 = 100)**

	Exports to (1963 weights):		Exports to (1975 weights):	
	All Countries	Developing Countries	All Countries	Developing Countries
All Manufactures	430	415	410	400
SITC 5	349	368	334	344
SITC 6	421	408	424	415
SITC 7	459	443	414	421
SITC 8	426	387	413	377

Source: Appendix tables 5B.1–5B.4.

and producer capital goods, almost all of which are included in SITC 7 of our product range.

Almost no empirical attention has been given to the same issue in connection with prices in international trade, although speculations on the effects of omitting quality change have played a role in discussions of the long-run trends in the terms of trade (Haberler 1959, Viner 1953, p. 114). The only direct applications of hedonic methods to international trade prices that we are aware of, mainly for deriving price level comparisons, are in Kravis and Lipsey (1971). In a study of the terms of trade between manufactures and primary products, Kravis and Lipsey (1984) used hedonic indexes constructed for domestic prices to adjust indexes of export prices of manufactured goods; we follow similar procedures here.

There are many possible ways of using these domestic price adjustments for quality to correct international price indexes. Since these calculations have been performed only for domestic prices, it is necessary to assume that any adjustments in domestic prices are equally applicable to U.S. export prices. The hedonic price indexes are available only for the United States, and even for the United States, only for a few commodity groups. Therefore, the adjustments we make in the U.S. indexes are probably minimal, and those for the world can be considered to be no more than rough approximations that give some notion of the direction and range of conceivable quality corrections.

One possibility would be to assume that the adjustments apply only to the United States. If the quality-adjusted U.S. indexes are combined with conventional indexes for other countries, the result is a very conservative estimate of the effect of such adjustments on world or developed-country export price movements. That estimate of the quality change omitted from conventional measures, provided by the series described below as "adjusted for U.S. only," is conservative in several respects, all but one of which apply also to the series described as "adjusted for all countries." One is that it assumes that the upward bias in price indexes from this source affects only the U.S. data; this is an unlikely possibility. Another is that most of the hedonic price indexes end with 1983, and no adjustment can be made for later years in even those groups for which it was performed earlier. A third reason is that a number of price indexes that should be corrected for quality change were not, because appropriate indexes were not available. Finally, a fourth reason is that some quality adjustments are already incorporated into the "conventional" indexes for 1953–64 derived from Kravis and Lipsey (1971).

The procedure of correcting only U.S. prices is likely to leave an upward bias in a world price index. Ideally, we would like to have similar hedonic price measures for all countries. Failing that, we believe it is more appropriate to assume that any quality adjustment applied to, for example, U.S. computer and parts prices is equally applicable to the corresponding prices of other countries than it is to assume that the unmeasured quality change is confined to the United States. Also, on this assumption, if an otherwise empty cell for computer prices is filled in one country by a hedonic price index, it should be filled in the other countries by the same type of index. The assumption implied by that procedure is that the law of one price in time-to-time form, poor as we have found its predictions to be (Kravis and Lipsey 1978), still provides a better guess for these products than the assumption that, for example, computer prices in countries other than the U.S. move with all other prices in those countries. The indexes based on the assumption of identical price movements in all countries for products for which hedonic price indexes were used are described below as "adjusted for all countries."

This procedure of assuming identical price changes for a product in different countries is at variance with the method implied by our earlier conclusion that country influences, rather than commodity influences, were dominant in determining price changes. However, that conclusion reflected mainly the impact of exchange-rate changes and differences in inflation rates on price movements. The application of identical quality adjustments to a commodity in different countries reflects our judgment that radical changes in technology in an industry such as computers probably outweigh the country influences on price changes. That judgment is influenced partly by the fact that a substantial part of exports of machinery from countries outside the United States, especially in the computer industry, originates in subsidiaries of U.S. firms, and therefore embodies U.S. technological developments.

The effect of the quality adjustment applied to a few groups in SITC 7 (machinery and transport equipment) can be seen from the comparison in table 5.5. If the adjustment is performed only for the United States, the effect on the world export price index for manufactures is fairly small, only about .15 percent per year for manufactures as a whole and about .25 percent per year for SITC 7. If the corresponding quality adjustments are spread to other countries, the effect is multiplied. For manufactures as a whole, it is almost .5 percent per year, and for SITC 7 it reaches almost 1 percent per year.

The quality adjustments for manufactures as a whole would be larger for an

Table 5.5   **Ratio of 1988 to 1953 World Export Price of Manufactures, with and without Quality Adjustments (1975 weights)**

All Manufactures, OECD Export Weights	
Unadjusted	423.3
Adjusted for United States only	406.7
Adjusted for all countries	361.1
SITC 7, OECD Export Weights	
Unadjusted	427.7
Adjusted for United States only	389.0
Adjusted for all countries	310.9

Source: Appendix tables 5B.2 and 5B.19.

index based on U.S., or especially Japanese, export weights, because SITC 7 is more important in the exports of those countries than in those of developed countries as a group.

These adjustments are too gradual and not large enough to produce a different picture from the standard one of short-term fluctuations in the terms of trade between manufactures and primary products, or the terms of trade of individual countries. They are large enough, and sufficiently constant in direction, to give a very different story about long-term *trends* in prices and terms of trade.

5.4 Indexes of Export Prices, Export Price Competitiveness, and Corresponding Domestic Prices

The price indexes in appendix B for all developed-country exports of manufactures and for exports by developed countries to developing countries are constructed from indexes for individual countries that are all based on the same set of weights. However, these are weights that reflect the importance of products in world trade as a whole rather than in the trade of each country. To explain the exports of a single country, such as the United States, we consider an index based on that country's export weights more relevant. For this purpose, we have constructed price indexes for each country's exports that are based on the weight of each product in the country's exports. We have then constructed price indexes for competitors based on the same set of weights. Thus, for the United States, we have an export price index and a competitors' price index, both based on U.S. export weights. All of these are shown in appendix C.

For the individual country, the price index is a conventional export price measure. Unlike the indexes in appendix B, which use domestic prices where export prices are unavailable, these price indexes include only export price data. The index of competitors' prices is, in the case of the United States, weighted by the same U.S. export weights as the U.S. export price but includes both export price data and, where they are not available, domestic price data, as in the indexes of Appendix B. That procedure produces manufactured-goods price indexes for Germany, Japan, and other countries with U.S. export weights. To explain the exports of the United States itself, or its share vis-à-vis the rest of the world, we combine these competitors' price indexes on U.S. weights into a single rest-of-world price index. The weight for a competitor country in this index is the sum of the total manufactured exports of the country to destinations other than the United States (to represent the competition in world markets outside the competitor country and the United States) and total U.S. exports to the competitor country (to represent competition with U.S. exports in that country's home market).

The same procedure is followed to produce individual country and rest-of-world indexes for the exports of Germany and Japan.

One way to use these indexes is to ask what they show about the export price movements for each country relative to those of competitors. For example, if we separate the period into that preceding the Smithsonian agreements of 1971 and that from 1971 to the low point in the exchange value of the U.S. dollar in 1980, we find the estimates of changes in prices and relative prices shown in table 5.6.

Both U.S. and German export prices rose from 1953 to 1971 relative to those of other countries that sold the same export products. Japan's prices fell enormously relative to those of its competitors during the same period, with a decline of 25 percent in relative prices. From 1971 to 1980, the United States gained greatly on its competitors, with a fall of more than a third in relative prices. Japanese relative prices also fell during this period, although not as much as those of the United States, while German relative prices continued to increase.

The corresponding changes for the period of the rapidly rising exchange value of the dollar, which we can mark out as 1980 to 1985 in these annual average data, and the subsequent period of the declining dollar, are shown in table 5.7. The indexes show a large increase in relative U.S. prices during the five-year rise of the dollar and a sharp decrease during the next three years, with the net result being some increase over the eight years. The movements for Germany were the reverse of those for the United States, but involved a

Table 5.6   **Changes in Own and Competitors' Export Price Indexes, 1953–71 and 1971–80 (ratio × 100)**

	1971/1953			1980/1971		
	United States	Germany[a]	Japan	United States	Germany	Japan
Export Price Index	146.5	147.9	93.0	176.4	306.2	231.1
Competitors' Price Index	123.7	118.5	123.9	272.9	249.6	252.6
Ratio: Own/Competitors'	118.4	124.8	75.1	64.6	122.7	91.5

Source: Appendix tables 5C.4–5C.6.
[a]1971/1954.

Table 5.7   **Changes in Own and Competitors' Export Price Indexes, 1980–85 and 1985–88 (ratio × 100)**

	1985/1980			1988/1985		
	United States	Germany	Japan	United States	Germany	Japan
Export Price Index	125.5	74.2	94.9	110.1	172.3	150.2
Competitors' Price Index	82.1	94.6	87.8	160.5	140.3	146.6
Ratio: Own/Competitors'	152.9	78.4	108.1	68.6	122.8	102.5

Source: Appendix tables 5C.4–5C.6.

small overall decrease in relative prices. The changes for Japan were a relative price increase in 1980 to 1985, despite the rise in value of the U.S. dollar and an additional increase after that, quite small considering the sharp increase in the exchange value of the yen.

Perhaps the most surprising feature of these price measures is the apparent relative increase in German prices after 1985 without a corresponding reflection in German export shares. One possible reason for this seeming absence of response to price changes is that German exports gained from the growth and enlargement of the EEC. Another is that the omission of Italian and Belgian prices from our measures, along with poor coverage of French prices, particularly of machinery in the earlier years, may have caused these indexes for German competitors' prices to be biased upwards.

These relative price indexes are similar to those we have referred to elsewhere as indexes of price competitiveness (Kravis and Lipsey 1971), although the price competitiveness measures were based on OECD weights for the individual countries, as are those for individual countries in Appendix B. The relation between these measures and broader concepts of competitiveness, including "nonprice" aspects, was discussed in the earlier work. The "price competitiveness" measures were not intended to encompass all the economic influences on that broader concept, although the price measures must reflect some of the broad movements in relative productivity and costs that are part of changes in a country's competitiveness. We think of relative price changes, as we have measured them, as useful for reduced form trade equations. In more structural trade models, the export price changes become endogenous variables in supply equations.[7]

Even if these indexes have a more logical basis than the ones usually used to analyze trade, an obvious question is whether they produce any more reliable estimates of elasticities or better explanations of the flow of trade. An authoritative answer to that question could only come from attempts to use these measures in various types of trade equations and models of trade. We can report on a few experiments along these lines with earlier versions of the indexes[8]

In one of these experiments (Kravis and Lipsey 1974), we estimated elasticities of substitution between U.S. and German exports of metals, machinery, and transport equipment to third-country markets using, as alternative price measures, indexes of the type constructed here from export price data and indexes based entirely on domestic prices. We considered the test to be more favorable to the domestic price indexes than a comparison based on the usual published indexes because we reweighted the domestic prices by international trade weights to match the export price indexes.

7. Goldstein and Khan (1985). For an example using our price data, see Kravis, Lipsey, and Bushe (1980).
8. For some tests of U.S. import price data, comparing results based on BLS price data with those based on unit values, see Shiells (1987).

The results of the comparison were that the degree of explanation was between twice and three times as great in equations using the export price indexes and that the elasticity estimates were much higher. Furthermore, the response of relative exports was almost the same for a change in U.S. prices as for a change in German prices, while in the equation based on domestic prices, the elasticities were quite different.

A later version of these indexes covering machinery and transport equipment was used in Bushe, Kravis, and Lipsey (1986) to explain changes in U.S., German, and Japanese exports. It is difficult to compare the results with those of other studies because of differences in commodity coverage and time periods, but one conclusion was that the differences among countries in price elasticities were smaller than had been estimated using other price data. However, we could not be sure whether our use of more accurate price data or our confining the comparison to the same range of commodities was the explanation for the greater similarity of elasticity coefficients. Another conclusion was that lags in price effects on U.S. exports were much longer, extending out to four years, than those in most previously estimated export equations, so that "the United States might have to wait a long time for any relief from the effects of the high value of the dollar in the mid-1980s."

5.4.1 Margins on Export and Domestic Sales

We have also calculated domestic price indexes for exported manufactured goods for the United States, Germany, and Japan, using each country's export price weights (Appendix C). These data can be used to examine changes in the ratio of export to domestic prices for each country. If costs for domestically sold and exported goods changed identically, that ratio reflects the direction of change in gross profit margins in export sales as compared with domestic sales, and also, if domestic price movements are a good proxy for cost changes, the direction of change in export margins themselves. With the extreme volatility of exchange rates that has characterized the 1980s, and the observation that prices of Japanese goods in the United States have not risen in line with the depreciation of the dollar since 1985, there has been a renewal of interest in this issue with several studies of changes in the export/domestic price margin or "pricing to market" (Krugman 1987, Marston 1989, Mann 1986). However, as noted below, the phenomenon of pricing to market was evident to some degree in earlier periods, although not as dramatically as in the years since 1985.

On the whole, we would expect relative declines in export margins in periods when the exchange value of the currency is increasing or, more generally, when domestic prices are rising more rapidly than those of competitors. We would expect rising margins in periods of falling currency values or falling relative domestic prices.

The results for the United States from 1953 to 1980 do not give much support to these expectations. U.S. export prices hardly changed relative to domestic prices from 1953 to 1971, when U.S. prices were rising relatively, and they declined relative to export prices in 1971 to 1980 as U.S. prices fell with the depreciation of the dollar (see table 5.8).

The export/domestic price ratios for Germany and Japan did move in the expected direction during the period of mostly fixed exchange rates from 1953 to 1971. In the first period of changing exchange rates, 1971 to 1980, the German ratio was stable even as German relative prices increased, and the Japanese ratio fell even while Japanese prices were declining relative to those of competitors. That was a period in which Japan was under great pressure to expand exports to offset the rise in petroleum import costs.

The 1980 to 1985 period of great exchange-rate turbulence and rising exchange value of the dollar saw somewhat surprising changes in export/domestic price ratios. U.S. export prices rose relative to domestic prices despite a large increase in U.S. export prices relative to competitors. German export prices fell relative to domestic prices although German export prices were falling relative to those of other countries. And Japanese export prices hardly changed in comparison to domestic prices, while they were rising relative to foreign countries' prices.

The dollar depreciation in the following period was accompanied by a rise, as expected, in the export/domestic price ratio in the United States, but it was a small one. There were also the expected declines in export/domestic price ratios in both Germany and Japan, the German one quite small (see table 5.9).

Table 5.8   **Changes in Export and Domestic Prices of Export Goods, 1953–71 and 1971–80 (ratio × 100)**

	1971/1953			1980/1971		
	United States	Germany	Japan	United States	Germany	Japan
Export Price Index	146.5	147.9	93.0	176.4	306.2	231.1
Domestic Price Index	145.8	165.0	88.2	210.9	306.3	243.0
Ratio: Export/Domestic	100.5	89.6	105.4	83.6	100.0	95.1

Source: Appendix tables 5C.4–5C.6.

Table 5.9   **Changes in Export and Domestic Prices of Export Goods, 1980–85 and 1985–88 (ratio × 100)**

	1985/1980			1988/1985		
	United States	Germany	Japan	United States	Germany	Japan
Export Price Index	125.5	74.2	94.9	110.1	172.3	150.2
Domestic Price Index	120.2	79.5	95.5	107.7	174.3	175.2
Ratio: Export/Domestic	104.4	93.3	99.4	102.2	98.9	85.7

Source: Appendix tables 5C.4–5C.6.

The 14 percent fall in the export/domestic price ratio for Japan between 1985 and 1988 suggests that there must have been a very large decline in relative margins on exports.

A similar set of identically weighted export and domestic price indexes was used in Kravis and Lipsey (1977a, 1977b) to study separately the impact of exchange-rate changes and of differences in inflation rates between countries on ratios of export to domestic prices from the early 1950s through the mid-1970s. We interpreted changes in those ratios, as we do here, as evidence of changes in margins on export sales relative to those on domestic sales. U.S. export margins appeared to be sensitive to changes in the U.S. exchange rate with the deutsche mark and the yen and also to changes in relative inflation rates between the United States and the United Kingdom. German export margins were less well explained but responded to differences in inflation rates between Germany and the United States, the United Kingdom, Japan, and France. Japanese export margins, in the period of more stable exchange rates, responded more to European and U.S. business-cycle movements than to exchange rates, but in the 1970s began to respond to exchange-rate changes as well. The reactions to exchange rates and inflation rates could be summarized as a consistent response to changes in real exchange rates, over the whole period for the United States and Germany, and in the 1970s for Japan as well. The estimates covering all Japanese manufactures for what Marston (1989) refers to as PTM elasticities, are somewhat lower than his for individual products in the 1980s, but suggest that the phenomenon is not a new one.

5.4.2. Concluding Remarks

Aside from the indexes for 1953–64, which were drawn at least partially from our own data collection, all the indexes shown here were calculated from official, publicly available data. Therefore, aside from possible additions to the country coverage, further updating of the weighting, and a shift to a quarterly basis in place of the annual indexes presented here, most major improvements in the data would require action by the official agencies producing the data. An exception, open to outside scholars, might be an extension of the hedonic price calculations to countries other than the United States.

Among the improvements in the official data that would be useful would be extension of the coverage of price series in countries for which there are major gaps in the data. French data are among the poorest in this respect among the countries we cover. In addition, the calculation of export and import price indexes based on price data, rather than on unit-value data, is still confined to a small group of countries, although the recent attention to "pricing-to-market" and pass-through issues suggests that there is a great deal to be learned by having separate domestic and international price data.

There are, in addition, two other types of issues involving the quality of official price data that have not been extensively addressed, although both were discussed in Kravis and Lipsey (1971). One is the treatment of intracompany trade which, with the increase in the internationalization of firms and the increasing share in trade of the kinds of products in which international transactions tend to be internal to firms, is now a very large part of developed countries' trade. It is not clear to what degree the prices reported for such trade are artificial and to what degree they therefore distort export and import price measures. The principle suggested in Kravis and Lipsey (1971) was to use the price in the first arm's length sale in a country in preference to intracompany prices, where that is possible; we still believe that is the appropriate practice. For a U.S. export, for example, it would be the price at which the U.S. wholesale or retail trade affiliate in a country sold the product, rather than the price at which a U.S. manufacturer sold to its overseas subsidiary. And for a U.S. import it would be, for example, the price at which a Japanese car was sold to an unaffiliated buyer in the U.S., rather than the price at which the Japanese manufacturer "sold" it to its U.S. sales affiliate.

Another type of question is raised by the very small extent to which U.S. firms admit selling at different prices at home and abroad, in contrast to the large differences reported by foreign firms. While it is conceivable that the trading policies of U.S. companies are very different in this respect from those of companies based in other countries, it is also possible that since the export and domestic prices are collected by the same agency in rather similar ways, companies tend to report the same prices. For this reason, as well as others that have at times been suggested to price collection agencies, even for domestic price collection, it would be wise to collect prices not only from sellers, but also from purchasers.

Appendix A
Sources of Price Data

Export Prices

Aside from the data described in Kravis and Lipsey (1971 and 1974), the following sources were used. The German price data for earlier years appeared in Statistisches Bundesamt, *Preise, Löhne, Wirtschaftsrechnungen*, Reihe 1, Preise und Preisindizes für Aussenhandelsgüter. For later years, the source is *Preise*, Reihe 8, Preise und Preisindizes für die Ein- und Ausfuhr. A brief description is given in Angermann (1980) and in articles in *Wirtschaft und Statistik*, such as Rostin (1974). The Japanese export price data are published in the *Price Indexes Annual* (earlier the *Export and Import Price Indexes Annual*) of the Bank of Japan. The U.S. export price data are from releases of the U.S. Bureau of Labor Statistics entitled *U.S. Import and Export Price Indexes*. A brief description of these is given in *Comparisons of U.S., German, and Japanese Export Price Indexes*, BLS Bulletin no. 2046 (1980).

Export price data for other countries were more fragmentary. Two publications of the Central Bureau of Statistics of the Netherlands, *Maandstatistiek van de Binnenlandse Handel* and *Bijvoegsel Maandstatistiek van de Prijzen,* provided export price data with incomplete but increasing coverage.

For the United Kingdom, there are virtually no export price data outside the period covered by Kravis and Lipsey (1971). The exception is a set of export price indexes for products in SITC 7 for 1976 through 1979, part of an experimental program that was later discontinued.

Swedish export prices are reported in various issues of publications of the Central Bureau of Statistics, the most recent of which was "Prisindex i producent-och importled 1988" (1989). Some of the indexes are based on unit-value data, and we tried to avoid using these as far as possible, preferring the data on domestic prices mentioned below.

Domestic Prices

For Canada, wholesale price indexes are from tapes provided by Statistics Canada.

Domestic price data for the United States were price series at the most detailed level from a BLS wholesale price index tape. For the United Kingdom, some individual series were collected from publications of the Board of Trade and the Department of Trade and Industry. However, the United Kingdom did not publish individual series for most machinery or "engineering" groups for many years. For these, we used a set of indexes at the 2-digit SITC level calculated for us by the Board of Trade from detailed price data using OECD weights we supplied. For later years, we could not obtain these series and were obliged to use a similar set of 2-digit indexes calculated by the Department of Trade and Industry, based on U.K. export weights. For more recent periods, beginning in the 1970s, fairly detailed price indexes for machinery have been published in annual price articles such as "Wholesale Price Indices in 1981," in *British Business* (7 May 1982) and "Wholesale Prices in 1982," in *British Business* (6 May 1983).

The German domestic price indexes are individual series published in Statistisches Bundesamt, *Preise, Löhne, Wirtschaftsrechnungen,* Reihe 3, Preise und Preisindizes für industrielle Produkte, Index der Erzeugerpreise, and Reihe 8, Index der Grosshandelsverkaufspreise for earlier years; and in *Preise,* Reihe 2, Preise und Preisindizes für gewerbliche Produkte (Erzeugerpreise), and Reihe 6 for later years. The Japanese domestic price indexes are also individual series from the *Price Indexes Annual* and the *Wholesale Price Indexes Annual,* published by the Bank of Japan.

Swedish domestic producers price indexes are from the source listed above for export price indexes, but many more detailed indexes are available for domestic prices.

French prices through 1977 for a large number of products were kindly supplied on tape by Dr. Liliane Crouhy-Veyrac of the Department Economie,

Centre d'Enseignement Supérior des Affaires. These data were the basis for Crouhy-Veyrac, Crouhy, and Mélitz (1980). These data were supplemented by information from the *Bulletin Mensuel de Statistique de la France*, and the *Annuaire Statistique de la France*, all published by the Institut National de la Statistique et des Études Économiques (INSEE).

The other main set of data are the hedonic price indexes substituted for conventional price series in our calculation of the quality-adjusted price index. These indexes are originally from a number of sources, but most of them were collected in Gordon (1990). The exceptions are the price indexes for computers, from Cartwright (1986) and Cartwright and Smith (1988), and those for semiconductors, from Norsworthy and Jang (1990).

Appendix B
Indexes Based on Weights of OECD Exports to the World or to Developing Countries

Table 5B.1   Price Indexes For Manufactured Exports by Developed Countries: All Manufactures (SITC 5–8) and SITC Divisions, U.S. Dollars, 1963 Weights (annual averages, 1975 = 100)

Year	All Manufactures	SITC 5	SITC 6	SITC 7	SITC 8
1953	47.8	57.0	47.6	45.8	49.5
1954	47.4	57.4	46.5	45.7	49.1
1955	48.2	56.2	48.1	46.3	49.2
1956	49.5	55.5	50.1	47.9	49.8
1957	50.7	56.2	50.8	49.5	50.3
1958	50.3	55.8	48.7	50.0	50.4
1959	50.1	54.6	49.1	50.0	50.2
1960	50.3	54.4	49.5	50.0	50.7
1961	50.8	54.6	49.4	50.9	51.7
1962	50.4	53.0	48.3	51.0	52.3
1963	50.6	52.7	48.4	51.3	52.8
1964	51.4	52.4	50.0	51.9	53.6
1965	52.3	52.5	50.8	52.9	54.5
1966	53.4	52.7	52.2	54.1	56.0
1967	53.5	52.5	51.7	54.7	56.9
1968	53.0	50.9	51.6	54.1	56.8
1969	54.6	50.6	53.6	55.7	58.4
1970	58.0	52.7	57.3	59.6	61.4
1971	61.4	54.8	59.2	64.4	65.0
1972	66.7	58.3	64.6	70.0	71.3
1973	76.0	65.2	77.0	77.9	81.0
1974	89.6	86.3	94.4	87.2	90.9
1975	100.0	100.0	100.0	100.0	100.0
1976	102.3	100.2	103.9	102.3	101.3
1977	110.7	106.3	111.3	111.8	110.3
1978	125.7	117.6	124.9	128.7	126.6
1979	143.8	142.0	144.0	145.3	141.3
1980	161.5	165.2	161.8	162.3	157.9
1981	155.4	158.7	154.0	156.6	153.0
1982	151.4	152.9	146.8	155.2	148.6
1983	142.3	146.3	140.9	152.4	146.5
1984	142.4	141.6	136.8	147.0	141.4
1985	143.3	142.6	136.0	148.8	143.1
1986	171.6	166.4	159.5	180.1	178.6
1987	194.9	186.8	181.3	204.8	203.4
1988	212.6	207.0	205.8	218.1	216.6

Table 5B.2   Price Indexes For Manufactured Exports by Developed Countries:
All Manufactures (SITC 5–8) and SITC Divisions, U.S. Dollars, 1975
Weights (annual averages, 1975 = 100)

Year	All Manufactures	SITC 5	SITC 6	SITC 7	SITC 8
1953	49.4	58.9	46.8	49.5	49.2
1954	48.9	59.2	45.5	49.1	48.8
1955	49.3	57.6	46.9	49.4	48.8
1956	50.6	56.7	49.3	51.0	49.2
1957	51.8	57.1	50.1	52.8	49.7
1958	51.1	56.3	47.9	52.8	49.7
1959	50.8	54.9	48.1	52.4	49.5
1960	50.8	54.6	48.4	52.2	50.0
1961	51.2	54.6	48.4	52.8	51.1
1962	50.7	52.5	47.2	52.6	51.7
1963	50.6	52.0	47.1	52.5	52.1
1964	51.2	51.6	48.5	53.0	52.9
1965	51.9	51.6	49.1	53.8	53.9
1966	52.9	51.5	50.1	55.0	55.4
1967	53.1	51.2	49.8	55.6	56.3
1968	52.8	49.6	49.6	55.5	56.1
1969	54.2	49.2	51.6	57.1	57.7
1970	57.6	51.1	55.7	60.6	60.7
1971	61.0	53.1	57.6	65.2	64.4
1972	66.4	56.9	63.1	70.9	71.0
1973	76.2	64.9	76.1	79.2	81.1
1974	90.0	87.9	94.6	88.5	90.7
1975	100.0	100.0	100.0	100.0	100.0
1976	102.4	99.7	103.2	102.7	101.2
1977	110.3	105.3	110.4	111.1	110.4
1978	125.9	117.0	126.2	127.7	127.0
1979	142.7	142.9	144.6	141.3	141.8
1980	158.5	164.7	161.6	155.3	158.3
1981	152.5	155.4	152.7	151.6	150.4
1982	148.3	148.2	145.8	149.4	145.3
1983	144.6	141.7	139.2	147.7	142.2
1984	139.8	136.2	134.7	143.1	136.5
1985	140.4	136.6	133.8	144.4	138.0
1986	170.4	161.5	160.0	176.3	174.1
1987	193.1	183.6	181.4	199.3	199.1
1988	209.1	202.6	204.3	211.7	211.4

Table 5B.3 **Price Indexes For Manufactured Exports by Developed Countries: All Manufactures (SITC 5–8) and SITC Divisions, U.S. Dollars, 1963 Weights (annual averages, 1975 = 100)**

Year	All Manufactures	SITC 5	SITC 6	SITC 7	SITC 8
1953	50.6	57.9	50.1	48.1	55.6
1954	50.3	58.5	48.9	48.0	55.3
1955	50.9	57.3	50.2	48.6	55.4
1956	52.5	56.5	52.8	50.7	56.1
1957	54.0	57.6	53.7	52.7	56.6
1958	53.7	57.4	51.3	53.2	56.4
1959	53.6	56.2	51.7	53.4	56.2
1960	53.6	56.1	52.1	53.3	56.7
1961	53.9	56.2	51.9	54.0	57.3
1962	53.4	55.1	50.6	53.9	57.8
1963	53.4	54.9	50.6	54.1	58.1
1964	54.1	54.7	51.9	54.7	58.6
1965	54.9	55.2	52.5	55.6	59.5
1966	56.0	55.4	53.6	56.9	61.1
1967	56.2	55.3	53.3	57.6	61.9
1968	55.7	53.7	53.0	56.9	61.7
1969	57.1	53.4	54.9	58.5	63.4
1970	60.0	55.1	58.0	62.0	65.7
1971	63.3	57.3	60.0	66.4	68.5
1972	68.3	60.7	65.7	71.5	74.5
1973	76.2	67.0	77.1	78.0	82.5
1974	89.3	85.2	94.3	87.5	91.4
1975	100.0	100.0	100.0	100.0	100.0
1976	102.3	100.4	103.7	102.6	101.7
1977	110.8	106.8	111.8	111.8	110.2
1978	126.4	119.5	127.2	128.5	125.9
1979	143.0	141.5	143.5	144.3	140.1
1980	161.1	164.3	161.6	162.2	157.6
1981	159.7	162.3	158.7	161.1	157.5
1982	156.0	157.6	151.3	160.2	152.1
1983	152.4	151.6	145.7	158.1	150.3
1984	148.7	147.1	143.0	154.0	146.5
1985	150.4	149.4	142.8	156.4	149.3
1986	176.6	173.2	166.2	184.1	182.5
1987	196.8	191.9	184.9	205.4	204.8
1988	213.8	211.4	206.9	219.1	218.1

Table 5B.4   **Price Indexes For Manufactured Exports by Developed Countries to Developing Countries: All Manufactures (SITC 5–8) and SITC Divisions, U.S. Dollars, 1975 Weights (annual averages, 1975 = 100)**

Year	All Manufactures	SITC 5	SITC 6	SITC 7	SITC 8
1953	51.9	58.7	49.6	50.1	53.4
1954	51.3	59.1	47.6	49.9	52.9
1955	51.4	57.4	48.9	50.1	52.8
1956	53.5	56.2	53.5	52.1	53.1
1957	55.2	56.6	54.8	54.2	53.2
1958	53.8	55.3	50.4	54.1	53.0
1959	53.5	53.9	51.2	53.9	53.2
1960	53.5	53.8	51.3	53.7	53.8
1961	53.5	53.7	50.9	54.1	54.5
1962	52.7	51.8	49.2	53.8	54.9
1963	52.5	51.2	49.1	53.8	55.3
1964	53.0	51.3	50.0	54.1	55.9
1965	53.5	51.4	50.2	54.9	56.6
1966	54.3	51.2	50.9	56.1	57.8
1967	54.6	51.0	51.1	56.8	58.8
1968	54.9	50.1	51.2	57.5	59.8
1969	56.3	49.6	53.2	59.1	61.5
1970	59.0	50.7	56.7	62.3	63.9
1971	61.6	51.9	58.2	66.1	66.5
1972	66.8	55.2	63.9	71.6	72.7
1973	77.1	63.6	77.7	80.1	83.0
1974	91.4	85.5	97.9	89.4	92.9
1975	100.0	100.0	100.0	100.0	100.0
1976	103.2	100.3	105.0	103.8	102.7
1977	110.5	104.9	111.7	112.0	110.6
1978	127.2	115.8	130.6	127.8	126.9
1979	139.7	137.7	144.7	139.8	135.7
1980	151.8	156.4	159.0	151.3	147.0
1981	152.9	154.9	158.7	151.3	148.6
1982	149.0	148.4	151.8	149.2	144.0
1983	145.8	143.9	144.2	148.0	142.8
1984	142.5	140.0	141.9	144.4	139.5
1985	143.4	140.2	141.0	146.2	141.4
1986	169.9	159.8	160.9	176.9	173.0
1987	190.4	180.5	178.5	198.9	192.9
1988	208.9	199.9	207.4	212.8	205.2

Table 5B.5   Price Indexes For Manufactured Exports by Germany, U.S. Dollars,
                    1963 Weights of OECD Exports to World (annual averages,
                    1975 = 100)

Year	All Manufactures	SITC 5	SITC 6	SITC 7	SITC 8
1953	36.2	43.9	37.7	34.7	32.5
1954	35.4	43.4	36.6	33.9	32.1
1955	36.0	42.4	38.3	34.4	32.3
1956	36.4	41.6	38.8	34.9	32.6
1957	37.0	41.8	39.3	35.5	33.3
1958	37.1	42.4	38.9	35.7	33.5
1959	36.5	41.7	38.6	35.0	33.1
1960	36.7	41.0	39.3	35.1	33.5
1961	38.6	42.6	40.9	37.2	35.9
1962	39.3	42.1	41.0	38.3	37.3
1963	39.6	42.7	41.2	38.6	37.8
1964	40.2	42.3	42.7	38.8	38.6
1965	41.3	42.3	43.8	40.0	39.9
1966	42.1	42.5	44.7	40.9	41.2
1967	41.9	42.3	43.5	41.1	41.8
1968	41.6	41.1	43.3	40.9	41.7
1969	43.4	41.1	45.1	43.3	43.5
1970	49.1	45.7	51.2	49.0	48.8
1971	53.6	48.9	53.7	55.1	54.2
1972	60.2	53.8	59.5	62.4	62.5
1973	76.9	68.2	78.4	78.3	79.1
1974	90.8	92.4	96.1	87.6	89.0
1975	100.0	100.0	100.0	100.0	100.0
1976	101.3	98.6	101.8	101.8	101.0
1977	111.8	107.6	109.3	114.6	112.6
1978	130.7	123.5	127.0	135.0	132.7
1979	152.3	142.9	150.0	157.0	150.0
1980	164.0	158.0	162.6	166.9	162.8
1981	138.4	136.1	136.1	141.2	136.6
1982	134.8	129.2	132.8	138.2	132.9
1983	130.4	123.1	126.9	134.9	129.7
1984	120.8	114.2	118.7	124.4	119.1
1985	120.1	114.2	117.4	124.0	118.1
1986	162.0	151.1	151.0	172.5	163.7
1987	195.7	177.6	177.6	213.1	201.2
1988	207.7	185.4	195.2	222.2	209.5

Table 5B.6   **Price Indexes For Manufactured Exports by Germany, U.S. Dollars, 1975 Weights of OECD Exports to the World (annual averages, 1975 = 100)**

Year	All Manufactures	SITC 5	SITC 6	SITC 7	SITC 8
1953	36.7	46.0	37.1	35.6	33.4
1954	35.9	45.4	36.0	34.8	33.0
1955	36.4	44.4	37.4	35.3	33.0
1956	36.8	43.5	37.9	35.8	33.2
1957	37.3	43.6	38.5	36.3	34.0
1958	37.4	44.0	38.4	36.5	34.1
1959	36.8	43.2	38.0	35.7	33.7
1960	36.9	42.4	38.5	35.7	34.1
1961	38.7	43.8	40.0	37.7	36.4
1962	39.5	43.2	40.3	38.8	37.7
1963	39.7	43.5	40.4	39.0	38.2
1964	40.1	42.9	41.6	39.1	39.0
1965	41.0	42.8	42.5	40.3	40.3
1966	41.7	42.8	43.1	41.1	41.6
1967	41.6	42.6	42.0	41.3	42.1
1968	41.3	41.3	41.8	41.1	42.0
1969	43.1	41.1	43.7	43.3	43.8
1970	48.7	45.8	50.0	49.1	49.1
1971	53.5	48.8	52.7	55.3	54.5
1972	59.9	53.5	58.1	62.4	62.8
1973	76.2	67.8	76.5	78.2	79.4
1974	90.3	93.2	95.0	87.6	89.4
1975	100.0	100.0	100.0	100.0	100.0
1976	100.7	98.3	100.3	101.5	100.9
1977	110.9	106.7	106.7	113.8	112.5
1978	129.9	122.0	125.4	133.9	132.2
1979	151.4	142.4	147.5	156.3	149.2
1980	162.6	156.8	159.3	166.1	161.3
1981	137.4	134.2	134.4	140.4	135.0
1982	134.0	127.2	132.4	137.3	130.9
1983	129.4	121.2	125.6	134.0	127.5
1984	119.8	112.6	117.3	123.7	117.1
1985	119.2	112.4	116.3	123.3	116.3
1986	161.1	146.8	150.2	170.9	161.0
1987	194.1	172.8	175.5	209.9	197.3
1988	204.8	180.7	191.6	218.3	205.2

Table 5B.7   **Price Indexes For Manufactured Exports by Germany, U.S. Dollars, 1963 Weights of OECD Exports to Developing Countries (annual averages, 1975 = 100)**

Year	All Manufactures	SITC 5	SITC 6	SITC 7	SITC 8
1953	35.2	40.6	36.8	33.6	32.6
1954	34.4	40.3	35.7	32.8	32.2
1955	34.9	39.4	37.1	33.2	32.4
1956	35.4	38.6	37.5	33.9	32.9
1957	36.1	39.4	38.3	34.5	33.8
1958	36.4	40.7	38.3	34.8	33.9
1959	35.9	40.0	37.8	34.4	33.5
1960	36.1	39.3	38.5	34.6	33.9
1961	38.1	41.1	40.2	36.7	36.3
1962	38.9	41.3	40.6	37.7	37.7
1963	39.3	42.3	40.7	38.0	38.1
1964	39.7	42.1	41.7	38.3	38.8
1965	40.8	42.3	42.6	39.6	40.1
1966	41.5	42.6	43.3	40.4	41.4
1967	41.4	42.7	42.3	40.6	41.9
1968	41.0	41.7	41.9	40.4	41.8
1969	42.8	41.7	43.4	42.7	43.6
1970	48.5	46.4	49.5	48.6	49.1
1971	53.3	50.0	52.7	54.6	54.4
1972	60.0	55.5	58.5	61.9	62.8
1973	76.4	70.3	76.3	78.0	79.3
1974	89.7	90.7	93.3	87.4	89.0
1975	100.0	100.0	100.0	100.0	100.0
1976	100.8	98.7	100.0	101.9	101.0
1977	111.7	108.0	107.7	115.1	112.5
1978	130.9	124.9	125.7	135.8	132.5
1979	151.6	142.2	145.7	158.6	150.0
1980	162.5	155.7	155.9	168.9	163.1
1981	137.8	135.1	131.9	142.7	136.8
1982	134.6	128.1	130.3	139.8	133.1
1983	129.6	121.2	122.9	136.6	129.8
1984	119.9	111.3	114.5	126.0	119.7
1985	119.3	111.5	113.5	125.5	119.2
1986	162.2	148.6	148.1	174.8	165.3
1987	195.9	174.3	173.6	216.2	203.0
1988	206.3	181.6	187.1	225.7	211.1

Table 5B.8   **Price Indexes For Manufactured Exports by Germany, U.S. Dollars, 1963 Weights of OECD Exports to Developing Countries (annual averages, 1975 = 100)**

Year	All Manufactures	SITC 5	SITC 6	SITC 7	SITC 8
1953	35.7	44.0	36.3	34.3	32.5
1954	34.9	43.7	35.2	33.5	32.2
1955	35.4	42.8	36.5	34.0	32.4
1956	35.9	42.0	37.1	34.6	32.6
1957	36.5	42.3	37.9	35.2	33.2
1958	36.9	43.2	38.1	35.6	33.3
1959	36.3	42.5	37.6	35.0	32.9
1960	36.5	41.9	38.0	35.2	33.3
1961	38.4	43.5	39.5	37.2	35.7
1962	39.1	43.1	40.1	38.2	37.2
1963	39.4	43.7	40.1	38.4	37.7
1964	39.7	43.3	40.8	38.8	38.4
1965	40.7	43.3	41.6	39.9	39.8
1966	41.3	43.3	42.0	40.8	41.0
1967	41.2	43.2	40.8	41.0	41.6
1968	40.7	41.9	40.5	40.7	41.5
1969	42.6	41.8	42.5	43.0	43.2
1970	48.5	46.6	49.0	49.0	48.7
1971	53.3	50.1	51.9	54.9	54.2
1972	59.7	55.3	57.3	62.0	62.4
1973	75.9	69.5	75.4	77.8	78.9
1974	89.6	92.0	93.7	87.4	89.3
1975	100.0	100.0	100.0	100.0	100.0
1976	100.7	99.0	99.4	101.6	100.7
1977	111.1	108.0	104.7	114.6	111.8
1978	130.5	124.6	124.2	134.5	131.6
1979	153.0	143.2	144.2	159.7	148.9
1980	163.7	157.7	153.2	169.9	162.0
1981	138.6	135.8	130.2	143.6	134.6
1982	136.1	129.0	131.6	140.2	131.1
1983	130.3	123.2	120.7	136.6	128.2
1984	120.9	115.1	112.9	126.3	118.2
1985	120.4	114.2	112.9	125.6	117.6
1986	161.7	147.0	143.0	174.8	163.6
1987	195.0	173.3	164.9	216.2	200.9
1988	207.9	180.8	184.7	226.3	209.4

Table 5B.9   **Price Indexes For Manufactured Exports by Japan, U.S. Dollars, 1963 Weights of OECD Exports to the World (annual averages, 1975 = 100)**

Year	All Manufactures	SITC 5	SITC 6	SITC 7	SITC 8
1953	61.0	61.5	54.9	68.4	56.6
1954	58.6	61.5	50.7	66.9	55.1
1955	57.5	57.8	51.2	64.7	54.3
1956	60.3	57.3	56.9	67.1	53.9
1957	61.4	56.5	56.8	69.9	53.6
1958	56.6	52.5	49.2	66.2	52.9
1959	56.6	50.4	50.8	64.8	54.3
1960	56.4	50.3	50.9	63.7	56.1
1961	55.3	48.3	50.2	62.5	55.5
1962	54.0	45.7	48.2	61.7	56.0
1963	53.6	44.8	48.6	60.5	56.9
1964	54.2	45.9	49.5	60.4	58.0
1965	54.2	45.7	49.3	60.7	57.9
1966	54.2	43.4	49.9	61.1	57.4
1967	54.6	42.4	50.8	61.4	57.8
1968	55.2	42.8	51.4	62.1	58.6
1969	56.5	43.4	53.6	62.9	59.9
1970	58.1	43.0	56.1	64.3	62.2
1971	59.7	43.5	56.7	66.8	65.0
1972	65.7	47.0	63.4	73.1	72.3
1973	80.7	60.8	83.6	84.3	86.7
1974	99.0	92.3	106.3	96.5	97.6
1975	100.0	100.0	100.0	100.0	100.0
1976	103.2	100.8	107.1	101.1	102.9
1977	111.8	105.3	116.1	110.0	113.2
1978	135.8	120.0	142.1	135.1	138.0
1979	141.9	145.2	153.8	133.6	136.5
1980	151.3	167.1	171.3	136.0	141.2
1981	157.2	169.8	172.3	145.1	147.3
1982	143.8	149.8	156.3	134.8	134.6
1983	145.9	150.8	157.7	137.2	137.2
1984	146.6	148.7	159.4	137.8	138.8
1985	144.4	146.5	155.9	136.0	138.6
1986	181.2	178.3	189.9	173.1	184.4
1987	201.9	200.0	213.1	192.0	204.0
1988	226.9	230.0	249.1	210.2	220.7

Table 5B.10   **Price Indexes For Manufactured Exports by Japan, U.S. Dollars, 1975 Weights of OECD Exports to the World (annual averages, 1975 = 100)**

Year	All Manufactures	SITC 5	SITC 6	SITC 7	SITC 8
1953	62.3	63.7	55.3	69.2	56.7
1954	60.1	63.8	51.0	67.6	55.1
1955	58.8	59.6	51.8	65.5	54.3
1956	61.7	58.9	58.3	67.7	53.9
1957	62.8	58.1	58.6	70.3	53.6
1958	58.1	53.8	50.4	66.3	52.9
1959	57.9	51.6	52.1	65.0	54.4
1960	57.6	51.4	52.3	63.9	56.2
1961	56.3	49.0	51.4	62.5	55.5
1962	54.9	45.9	49.1	61.6	56.0
1963	54.1	44.6	49.0	60.2	56.8
1964	54.5	45.7	49.9	59.9	58.0
1965	54.5	45.3	49.7	60.2	58.0
1966	54.4	42.8	50.0	60.6	57.5
1967	54.7	42.0	51.1	60.8	57.8
1968	55.2	41.9	51.4	61.6	58.6
1969	56.3	42.3	53.4	62.4	60.2
1970	58.0	41.8	56.2	63.9	62.8
1971	59.9	42.2	57.1	66.7	65.7
1972	65.8	45.6	63.4	73.1	72.7
1973	80.2	60.2	82.7	84.1	87.6
1974	98.9	92.8	107.6	96.3	98.3
1975	100.0	100.0	100.0	100.0	100.0
1976	102.6	101.6	106.2	101.0	102.5
1977	110.6	105.4	114.6	109.4	112.5
1978	134.4	118.5	141.2	134.4	136.6
1979	140.3	147.5	153.2	132.3	135.1
1980	149.0	169.6	170.0	134.9	140.1
1981	155.8	171.8	172.9	144.4	146.0
1982	142.7	151.7	156.8	134.3	133.6
1983	144.1	152.3	156.8	136.4	135.7
1984	144.6	150.0	158.5	136.8	136.8
1985	142.4	147.2	155.1	135.1	136.3
1986	177.2	173.8	186.2	171.3	178.8
1987	197.3	198.3	207.6	189.9	197.0
1988	221.0	227.7	243.4	207.8	212.4

Table 5B.11   Price Indexes For Manufactured Exports by Japan, U.S. Dollars, 1963 Weights of OECD Exports to Developing Countries (annual averages, 1975 = 100)

Year	All Manufactures	SITC 5	SITC 6	SITC 7	SITC 8
1953	60.7	62.8	55.1	65.8	56.8
1954	58.5	61.9	51.1	64.3	55.2
1955	57.3	58.5	51.6	62.4	54.5
1956	60.2	58.0	56.9	65.1	54.4
1957	61.6	57.5	57.3	68.3	54.2
1958	57.3	53.9	50.1	65.0	53.2
1959	57.1	51.8	51.6	63.7	54.7
1960	56.9	51.6	51.8	62.9	56.3
1961	55.9	49.7	51.1	61.9	55.6
1962	54.7	47.7	49.0	61.2	56.3
1963	54.3	46.9	49.2	60.2	57.2
1964	54.8	48.1	50.0	60.1	58.5
1965	54.9	48.3	49.7	60.4	58.4
1966	54.7	46.1	49.8	60.8	57.7
1967	55.0	45.1	50.8	61.1	58.1
1968	55.5	45.3	51.2	61.8	58.8
1969	56.7	45.8	53.2	62.6	60.2
1970	58.2	45.3	55.6	63.9	62.6
1971	60.0	46.2	56.7	66.3	65.3
1972	66.0	50.2	63.5	72.5	72.6
1973	80.5	63.3	82.8	84.1	87.2
1974	98.0	91.0	104.7	96.4	97.5
1975	100.0	100.0	100.0	100.0	100.0
1976	102.8	99.9	106.4	101.3	103.1
1977	111.2	105.6	114.6	110.3	113.5
1978	135.7	124.3	140.4	135.5	138.8
1979	140.2	142.1	150.1	134.0	136.3
1980	148.9	160.5	165.8	136.7	141.9
1981	156.0	165.3	169.6	146.2	147.2
1982	142.9	145.1	155.2	135.7	134.2
1983	146.6	146.0	155.5	138.1	137.3
1984	145.0	144.3	157.4	138.3	138.7
1985	143.4	142.8	154.7	137.0	138.7
1986	181.3	180.1	188.6	175.4	184.6
1987	201.1	200.6	208.7	194.5	205.5
1988	225.8	227.9	243.2	213.9	224.0

Table 5B.12   Price Indexes For Manufactured Exports by Japan, U.S. Dollars, 1975 Weights of OECD Exports to Developing Countries (annual averages, 1975 = 100)

Year	All Manufactures	SITC 5	SITC 6	SITC 7	SITC 8
1953	60.4	63.2	54.7	64.5	56.3
1954	58.4	62.6	50.4	63.2	55.0
1955	57.4	59.3	51.5	61.5	54.5
1956	61.0	58.8	59.1	64.4	54.3
1957	62.9	57.9	60.1	67.9	54.0
1958	58.2	53.7	51.0	64.6	53.2
1959	57.8	51.5	52.7	63.3	54.5
1960	57.6	51.2	52.8	62.7	56.0
1961	56.4	48.8	51.8	61.7	55.9
1962	54.9	46.0	49.0	60.9	56.4
1963	54.2	44.8	49.0	59.8	57.1
1964	54.6	46.4	49.8	59.7	58.0
1965	54.7	46.4	49.5	60.0	58.1
1966	54.5	43.9	49.7	60.4	57.6
1967	54.8	42.8	50.8	60.7	57.9
1968	55.1	42.6	50.7	61.5	58.4
1969	56.2	42.8	52.7	62.3	59.9
1970	57.7	42.2	55.5	63.6	62.5
1971	59.4	42.4	56.5	66.1	65.1
1972	65.3	45.7	62.9	72.5	72.4
1973	79.4	59.3	81.5	84.2	86.4
1974	97.8	89.4	107.5	96.2	97.5
1975	100.0	100.0	100.0	100.0	100.0
1976	102.3	98.9	106.4	101.3	102.2
1977	110.3	102.3	114.5	110.1	111.8
1978	134.5	117.6	142.0	135.1	136.2
1979	139.1	141.0	153.2	132.5	133.9
1980	146.8	160.7	168.0	135.1	138.0
1981	155.0	164.8	174.1	145.2	142.6
1982	142.9	148.0	160.3	134.9	131.5
1983	143.9	149.0	156.3	137.9	134.2
1984	144.6	147.2	159.2	138.1	134.9
1985	142.3	143.4	155.8	136.5	135.0
1986	173.6	163.2	177.2	174.3	172.7
1987	192.6	187.0	193.8	193.6	186.2
1988	219.5	216.6	235.9	213.6	200.0

Table 5B.13   Price Indexes For Manufactured Exports by the United States, U.S. Dollars, 1963 Weights of OECD Exports to the World (annual averages, 1975 = 100)

Year	All Manufactures	SITC 5	SITC 6	SITC 7	SITC 8
1953	51.5	61.4	47.0	51.3	57.7
1954	52.0	62.9	47.1	52.0	57.7
1955	53.3	62.1	49.5	53.1	58.1
1956	55.6	60.8	51.9	56.1	59.8
1957	57.8	62.5	53.8	58.9	60.8
1958	58.2	61.7	53.6	60.2	61.6
1959	59.1	60.9	54.7	61.3	61.7
1960	59.4	61.6	55.2	61.4	62.2
1961	59.1	61.8	54.7	61.1	62.2
1962	58.9	60.3	54.7	61.0	62.4
1963	59.0	59.5	54.7	61.4	62.6
1964	59.3	58.7	55.5	61.9	62.5
1965	60.1	59.1	56.5	62.5	63.1
1966	61.1	59.5	57.7	63.5	65.0
1967	62.4	60.1	57.9	65.5	67.5
1968	63.9	59.3	59.7	67.2	70.7
1969	65.7	58.5	62.2	69.0	73.3
1970	68.1	59.9	64.9	71.7	74.7
1971	70.5	60.3	66.8	75.3	76.0
1972	72.4	60.5	69.7	77.2	77.4
1973	76.0	62.3	75.6	79.4	81.2
1974	89.2	79.7	92.5	88.9	92.9
1975	100.0	100.0	100.0	100.0	100.0
1976	105.4	104.4	106.0	105.6	104.3
1977	111.8	108.6	113.5	111.9	110.3
1978	119.5	111.8	121.8	120.9	116.2
1979	132.3	132.5	136.2	130.6	127.9
1980	146.8	152.3	149.5	144.3	142.6
1981	161.7	166.3	164.9	158.1	162.2
1982	168.5	173.1	165.2	168.9	170.3
1983	171.2	172.4	164.7	173.7	176.3
1984	176.2	177.4	170.3	178.6	179.6
1985	177.6	177.4	168.0	182.4	183.8
1986	179.3	177.2	167.4	185.6	188.3
1987	185.3	185.8	175.7	189.5	191.7
1988	197.5	209.9	193.7	195.2	199.4

Table 5B.14   Price Indexes For Manufactured Exports by the United States, U.S. Dollars, 1975 Weights of OECD Exports to the World (annual averages, 1975 = 100)

Year	All Manufactures	SITC 5	SITC 6	SITC 7	SITC 8
1953	52.3	65.5	45.9	52.3	58.3
1954	53.0	67.0	46.4	52.9	58.3
1955	54.1	65.9	48.6	54.1	58.5
1956	56.4	64.5	51.0	57.1	60.0
1957	58.8	66.4	53.3	59.9	61.1
1958	59.5	65.2	53.6	61.2	62.0
1959	60.3	64.0	54.6	62.4	62.4
1960	60.5	64.7	54.8	62.5	62.9
1961	60.1	64.6	54.2	62.0	62.9
1962	59.8	63.1	54.1	61.8	62.9
1963	59.8	61.8	54.1	62.0	63.0
1964	60.0	60.4	54.6	62.5	62.9
1965	60.5	60.6	55.4	63.0	63.5
1966	61.5	61.1	56.3	64.1	65.4
1967	62.9	61.7	56.7	66.0	68.1
1968	64.5	60.7	58.6	67.8	71.0
1969	66.2	59.8	60.8	69.7	73.6
1970	68.5	61.0	63.6	72.3	75.0
1971	71.1	61.3	66.0	76.0	76.3
1972	72.7	61.2	68.7	77.6	77.6
1973	75.6	62.7	73.3	79.6	81.2
1974	88.6	79.7	90.5	89.2	92.9
1975	100.0	100.0	100.0	100.0	100.0
1976	105.3	104.6	105.7	105.4	104.4
1977	111.4	108.5	113.1	111.4	110.2
1978	119.2	111.5	122.3	120.2	116.0
1979	131.6	133.9	136.4	129.3	127.1
1980	145.8	152.8	149.8	142.8	141.5
1981	160.7	166.9	166.0	156.5	159.3
1982	168.3	172.9	168.3	162.0	167.4
1983	170.8	172.4	167.0	171.8	172.4
1984	175.4	176.2	172.4	176.5	175.2
1985	176.8	174.9	169.9	180.2	178.5
1986	178.6	174.1	168.5	183.2	183.4
1987	183.9	184.5	176.0	186.9	186.5
1988	195.1	208.3	193.2	192.3	193.4

Table 5B.15   **Price Indexes For Manufactured Exports by the United States, U.S. Dollars, 1963 Weights of OECD Exports to Developing Countries (annual averages, 1975 = 100)**

Year	All Manufactures	SITC 5	SITC 6	SITC 7	SITC 8
1953	51.2	61.6	47.6	49.8	59.2
1954	51.8	63.3	47.9	50.2	59.3
1955	53.0	62.4	50.1	51.4	59.8
1956	55.2	60.8	52.6	54.5	61.4
1957	57.6	62.9	54.5	57.5	62.4
1958	58.4	62.7	54.7	58.9	62.9
1959	59.2	62.1	55.8	60.0	63.0
1960	59.4	62.8	56.3	59.9	63.5
1961	59.2	63.0	55.7	59.7	63.5
1962	59.0	61.9	55.7	59.5	63.6
1963	59.0	61.1	55.6	59.9	63.5
1964	59.3	60.4	56.2	60.3	63.4
1965	60.0	61.0	57.1	60.9	64.0
1966	61.0	61.7	58.0	62.2	65.8
1967	62.3	62.3	58.2	64.1	68.3
1968	63.8	61.8	60.1	65.8	71.2
1969	65.4	61.0	62.1	67.6	73.9
1970	67.8	62.2	64.4	70.6	75.1
1971	70.4	62.9	66.7	74.2	76.4
1972	72.3	63.1	69.8	76.1	77.9
1973	75.6	64.8	74.9	78.5	81.9
1974	88.6	80.3	92.1	88.3	92.9
1975	100.0	100.0	100.0	100.0	100.0
1976	105.5	104.4	105.7	105.9	104.6
1977	112.1	108.9	113.4	112.7	110.5
1978	120.1	113.8	121.7	121.8	116.0
1979	132.5	131.3	134.7	132.3	127.7
1980	147.5	149.3	149.4	146.6	143.3
1981	162.8	164.8	164.5	160.9	164.8
1982	170.6	173.2	167.3	171.8	171.6
1983	173.0	173.7	165.8	176.5	177.0
1984	177.7	178.1	171.3	181.1	180.2
1985	179.7	180.9	169.5	184.7	184.6
1986	181.2	181.3	168.4	187.8	189.4
1987	185.8	187.3	174.4	191.0	193.1
1988	196.6	206.4	189.8	196.9	201.1

Table 5B.16   **Price Indexes For Manufactured Exports by the United States, U.S. Dollars, 1975 Weights of OECD Exports to Developing Countries (annual averages, 1975 = 100)**

Year	All Manufactures	SITC 5	SITC 6	SITC 7	SITC 8
1953	50.7	62.7	44.7	50.7	57.1
1954	51.4	64.2	45.6	51.2	57.2
1955	52.5	63.4	47.7	52.3	57.7
1956	54.9	61.6	50.3	55.4	59.2
1957	57.4	63.4	52.9	58.3	60.3
1958	58.3	62.8	53.5	59.7	61.1
1959	59.1	62.0	54.4	60.9	61.2
1960	59.3	62.8	54.6	60.8	61.7
1961	58.9	62.8	54.0	60.5	61.7
1962	58.5	61.5	53.8	60.1	61.8
1963	58.5	60.3	53.8	60.4	61.8
1964	58.8	59.3	54.2	60.8	61.6
1965	59.4	59.7	54.8	61.5	62.2
1966	60.4	60.3	55.5	62.7	64.0
1967	61.8	61.0	55.9	64.6	66.9
1968	63.3	60.1	57.5	66.5	70.1
1969	64.9	58.9	59.7	68.5	73.0
1970	67.3	59.9	62.3	71.1	74.0
1971	70.0	60.4	65.1	74.5	75.1
1972	71.7	60.3	68.0	76.1	76.3
1973	74.6	62.0	72.2	78.7	80.1
1974	87.6	78.8	89.1	88.8	92.2
1975	100.0	100.0	100.0	100.0	100.0
1976	105.3	103.1	105.7	105.8	104.0
1977	111.7	107.3	113.3	112.4	109.4
1978	119.9	111.3	122.9	121.1	115.1
1979	132.0	130.4	135.7	131.2	127.0
1980	146.6	148.6	149.4	145.3	141.8
1981	162.0	163.4	165.3	159.7	164.4
1982	168.2	169.1	169.6	170.4	173.4
1983	169.3	168.3	163.5	175.3	179.5
1984	173.9	170.5	168.4	180.4	183.1
1985	176.0	171.8	166.4	184.8	186.9
1986	177.4	174.1	162.4	188.5	193.3
1987	182.4	185.2	168.7	192.2	197.8
1988	195.0	206.3	186.3	199.3	206.3

Table 5B.17   **Price Indexes For Manufactured Exports by the United States, with Quality Corrections for SITC 7 Using Hedonic Price Indexes, U.S. Dollars, 1963 and 1975 Weights of OECD Exports to the World (annual averages, 1975 = 100)**

Year	1963 Weights		1975 Weights	
	All Manufactures	SITC 7	All Manufactures	SITC 7
1953	59.5	71.1	59.9	68.5
1954	59.6	70.7	60.1	68.2
1955	60.8	71.3	61.2	69.2
1956	62.7	73.8	63.1	71.7
1957	64.7	76.1	65.3	74.0
1958	64.0	74.6	64.7	72.7
1959	64.0	73.8	64.8	72.3
1960	63.7	72.2	64.4	71.1
1961	63.2	71.3	63.9	70.3
1962	63.0	71.2	63.6	70.2
1963	62.7	70.7	63.2	69.6
1964	62.7	70.3	63.0	69.3
1965	62.8	69.2	63.0	68.6
1966	63.3	68.8	63.5	68.5
1967	64.1	69.6	64.5	69.5
1968	65.3	70.5	65.8	70.7
1969	66.8	71.6	67.1	71.8
1970	69.3	74.5	69.6	74.7
1971	71.2	77.1	71.8	77.7
1972	72.9	78.5	73.3	78.8
1973	76.3	80.2	75.8	80.2
1974	88.7	87.7	87.9	87.9
1975	100.0	100.0	100.0	100.0
1976	105.4	105.5	105.3	105.5
1977	110.9	109.7	110.3	109.3
1978	117.9	117.2	117.6	116.9
1979	128.7	122.7	128.0	122.2
1980	144.3	138.8	143.0	137.2
1981	158.8	151.6	157.3	149.8
1982	165.5	162.1	165.0	160.4
1983	166.9	164.2	166.6	163.1
1984	171.5	168.3	170.7	167.0
1985	172.5	171.0	171.8	170.2
1986	174.2	174.2	173.5	173.3
1987	179.4	176.9	178.5	176.3
1988	190.9	181.3	189.2	180.8

Table 5B.18   Price Indexes For Manufactured Exports by the United States, with Quality Corrections for SITC 7 Using Hedonic Price Indexes, U.S. Dollars, 1963 and 1975 Weights of OECD Exports to Developing Countries (annual averages, 1975 = 100)

Year	1963 Weights		1975 Weights	
	All Manufactures	SITC 7	All Manufactures	SITC 7
1953	58.0	64.5	57.6	64.8
1954	58.2	64.4	58.2	64.8
1955	59.1	64.7	59.0	65.3
1956	61.0	67.2	61.2	68.2
1957	63.2	70.0	63.6	70.7
1958	63.1	69.4	63.6	70.4
1959	63.2	69.2	63.5	69.9
1960	63.0	67.8	63.0	68.4
1961	62.5	67.2	62.4	67.6
1962	62.4	67.1	62.1	67.4
1963	62.0	66.5	61.6	66.7
1964	62.0	66.4	61.5	66.6
1965	61.7	65.0	61.3	65.7
1966	62.2	64.8	61.8	65.9
1967	63.1	66.0	62.7	66.9
1968	64.4	67.1	64.0	68.2
1969	65.9	68.9	65.4	69.9
1970	68.4	72.1	67.8	72.7
1971	70.6	74.8	70.1	75.3
1972	72.4	76.4	71.6	76.6
1973	75.7	78.9	74.4	78.7
1974	88.2	87.5	87.1	87.8
1975	100.0	100.0	100.0	100.0
1976	105.6	106.0	105.2	105.6
1977	111.4	111.0	110.8	110.6
1978	118.7	118.8	118.4	118.2
1979	129.2	125.5	128.8	125.0
1980	147.2	145.8	145.0	142.1
1981	162.2	159.3	159.8	155.4
1982	170.3	170.8	168.1	166.1
1983	171.6	173.3	168.1	168.9
1984	176.1	177.5	172.4	173.4
1985	177.9	180.8	174.3	177.3
1986	179.6	183.8	175.9	181.2
1987	183.8	186.5	181.2	184.6
1988	194.3	191.8	193.0	191.1

Notes to Tables 5B.17 and 5B.18

The hedonic price indexes for the commodities listed below were substituted for the conventional U.S. export or domestic price series used for the indexes covering SITC 7 and All Manufactures in tables 5B.13 through 5B.16. The hedonic indexes were also inserted in a few cases for which no conventional price indexes had been available, so that the commodity coverage in tables 5B.17 and 5B.18 is slightly higher than in the earlier tables.

SITC Group or Subgroup	Source	Period
711.1	Gordon (1990)	1953–83
711.5	Gordon (1990)	1953–83
712.5*	Gordon (1990)	1953–83
714.2	Cartwright and Smith (1988)	1983–88 (ave. of 3 qtrs.)
	Cartwright (1986)	1970–82
	Gordon (1990)	1953–69
719.1	Gordon (1990)	1953–83
719.4	Gordon (1990)	1953–83
722.1	Gordon (1990)	1953–83
724.9	Gordon (1990)	1953–83
725	Gordon (1990)	1953–83
729.3	Norsworthy and Jang (1990)	1968–86
732.1	Gordon (1990)	1953–83
734	Gordon (1990)	1953–83

*With wheel tractors weighted ⅙ and crawler tractors ⅚ in accordance with U.S. export weights.

Table 5B.19   **Price Indexes For Manufactured Exports by Developed Countries, with Quality Corrections for SITC 7 Using Hedonic Price Indexes, U.S. Dollars, 1975 Weights of OECD Exports to the World (annual averages, 1975 = 100)**

Year	All Manufactures		SITC 7	
	Adjusted for U.S. Only	Adjusted for All Countries	Adjusted for U.S. Only	Adjusted for All Countries
1953	51.0	57.6	53.5	67.2
1954	50.4	56.7	52.8	66.1
1955	50.7	57.0	53.0	66.2
1956	52.0	58.3	54.4	67.7
1957	53.1	59.4	56.0	69.2
1958	52.2	57.7	55.3	66.9
1959	51.7	56.9	54.6	65.4
1960	51.6	56.3	54.1	64.0
1961	52.0	56.5	54.6	64.1
1962	51.4	55.9	54.5	64.0
1963	51.3	55.6	54.3	63.3
1964	51.8	55.9	54.5	63.1
1965	52.4	56.1	55.1	62.7
1966	53.3	56.5	56.0	62.6
1967	53.4	56.4	56.4	62.5
1968	53.1	56.0	56.2	62.3
1969	54.4	57.2	57.5	63.3
1970	57.8	60.6	61.1	66.9
1971	61.1	63.4	65.5	70.5
1972	66.5	68.2	71.2	74.7
1973	76.2	76.8	79.3	80.6
1974	89.8	89.6	88.2	87.7
1975	100.0	100.0	100.0	100.0
1976	102.3	102.8	102.7	103.5
1977	109.9	109.1	110.5	109.1
1978	125.4	122.6	126.8	121.5
1979	141.7	136.5	139.2	129.7
1980	157.7	153.0	153.6	145.0
1981	151.7	150.1	149.7	146.6
1982	147.3	148.1	147.8	149.1
1983	143.4	144.5	145.5	147.6
1984	138.5	139.6	140.9	142.8
1985	139.0	139.9	142.1	143.7
1986	168.5	169.5	173.5	174.9
1987	191.1	192.0	196.1	197.2
1988	207.4	208.0	208.1	208.9

Notes to Table 5B.19

For the indexes labeled "Adjusted for U.S. Only," the U.S. indexes for SITC 7 from table 5B.17 are combined with the indexes for other countries, in the same way as for tables 5B.1 through 5B.4.

For the indexes labeled "Adjusted for All Countries," each U.S. hedonic price index was substituted for the conventional price index for that particular SITC subgroup or group at the 3- or (usually) 4-digit SITC level (or inserted where there was no conventional index) in the index for every country. The individual country indexes for all manufactures and the world indexes were then aggregated, as in earlier tables. To prevent the hedonic adjustment from affecting uncovered groups and subgroups, the substitution was performed by subtracting the unadjusted indexes from the SITC aggregate and adding back the adjusted indexes with the same weights. Where no unadjusted index existed for a group or subgroup, the subtraction was done assuming that the uncovered items had the same price index as SITC 7 as a whole.

Appendix C
Indexes Based on Export Weights of the United States, Germany, and Japan

Table 5C.1   **Price Indexes for Manufactured Exports by the United States and its Competitors, U.S. Dollars, U.S. Export Weights of 1963 (annual averages, 1975 = 100)**

Year	U.S. Price Indexes		Competitors' Price Index
	Export Prices	Domestic Prices	
1953	50.9	48.0	46.3
1954	51.5	48.6	45.8
1955	52.1	50.1	46.2
1956	54.9	52.4	47.2
1957	57.5	54.7	48.1
1958	58.5	55.5	47.8
1959	59.3	56.6	47.4
1960	60.2	57.0	47.5
1961	61.1	57.0	48.5
1962	61.6	57.1	48.1
1963	62.2	57.2	48.3
1964	63.1	57.6	49.1
1965	63.7	58.3	50.0
1966	64.8	60.1	51.2
1967	67.0	61.7	51.2
1968	69.0	63.6	50.2
1969	71.5	65.4	51.6
1970	73.3	68.1	55.3
1971	76.9	70.3	59.2
1972	79.1	72.0	65.5
1973	81.8	74.8	75.7
1974	90.0	87.5	88.8
1975	100.0	100.0	100.0
1976	106.1	105.6	101.6
1977	112.7	112.1	110.7
1978	118.5	119.9	127.8
1979	129.4	133.2	148.5
1980	143.3	148.6	167.8
1981	157.6	164.1	154.0
1982	169.3	169.5	147.3
1983	173.8	173.1	142.1
1984	178.4	177.6	134.4
1985	176.1	179.2	135.3
1986	181.6	179.9	170.3
1987	187.4	184.2	199.2
1988	198.3	194.9	218.8

Table 5C.2   Price Indexes for Manufactured Exports by Germany and its
Competitors, U.S. Dollars, German Export Weights of 1963
(annual averages, 1975 = 100)

| Year | German Price Indexes | | Competitors' Price Index |
	Export Prices	Domestic Prices	
1953	(36.0)	32.0	52.3
1954	35.1	31.2	52.3
1955	35.3	31.6	52.9
1956	35.9	32.3	54.9
1957	36.5	33.0	56.7
1958	36.3	33.3	56.4
1959	35.9	33.1	56.5
1960	36.4	33.5	56.4
1961	37.9	35.7	56.3
1962	38.4	37.2	55.6
1963	38.4	37.5	55.5
1964	39.3	38.1	56.2
1965	40.3	39.2	57.0
1966	41.1	40.3	58.2
1967	41.1	40.0	58.5
1968	40.7	39.9	57.5
1969	43.5	40.9	59.0
1970	48.6	47.2	61.6
1971	52.9	52.3	64.8
1972	59.1	59.0	69.6
1973	76.2	75.3	75.0
1974	91.3	89.2	88.2
1975	100.0	100.0	100.0
1976	101.1	100.8	102.2
1977	111.0	111.0	110.0
1978	130.3	130.6	124.8
1979	153.1	150.0	143.3
1980	163.4	161.5	164.2
1981	138.6	136.5	164.4
1982	135.4	134.0	161.3
1983	130.8	129.4	158.0
1984	121.4	119.5	154.4
1985	121.3	126.2	156.5
1986	164.4	171.5	180.8
1987	199.1	205.6	200.2
1988	209.9	217.2	219.5

Table 5C.3   **Indexes for Manufactured Exports by Japan and its Competitors, U.S. Dollars, Japanese Export Weights of 1963 (annual averages, 1975 = 100)**

Year	Japanese Price Indexes		Competitors' Price Index
	Export Prices	Domestic Prices	
1953	63.0	58.1	50.3
1954	59.6	54.9	50.0
1955	58.4	53.5	50.6
1956	61.4	57.4	51.5
1957	60.9	57.9	52.7
1958	55.0	53.8	52.5
1959	56.8	54.3	52.0
1960	57.2	54.6	52.0
1961	54.9	53.8	52.4
1962	53.2	52.8	51.7
1963	53.7	53.1	51.6
1964	54.5	53.3	52.3
1965	54.3	53.2	53.1
1966	53.8	53.4	54.1
1967	54.4	53.8	54.0
1968	55.1	54.2	53.4
1969	56.8	55.7	54.7
1970	58.6	58.3	58.2
1971	60.1	59.7	61.7
1972	65.9	67.4	67.1
1973	81.6	86.0	76.4
1974	100.0	101.4	90.2
1975	100.0	100.0	100.0
1976	102.8	105.9	101.4
1977	108.4	119.0	109.2
1978	130.3	153.9	123.6
1979	137.5	151.9	139.8
1980	147.6	159.4	157.3
1981	152.7	164.6	150.2
1982	140.6	145.5	147.4
1983	138.9	154.4	143.0
1984	139.8	155.8	137.6
1985	137.7	155.1	139.1
1986	168.0	212.7	165.2
1987	186.3	241.0	186.3
1988	210.1	272.1	200.6

Table 5C.4   **Price Indexes for Manufactured Exports by the United States and its Competitors, U.S. Dollars, U.S. Export Weights of 1975 (annual averages, 1975 = 100)**

Year	U.S. Price Indexes		Competitors' Price Index
	Export Prices	Domestic Prices	
1953	54.6	48.3	48.1
1954	55.3	48.9	47.5
1955	56.0	50.2	47.7
1956	59.0	52.6	48.7
1957	62.0	55.2	49.7
1958	63.0	56.2	49.1
1959	64.0	57.2	48.6
1960	65.0	57.6	48.6
1961	66.0	57.6	49.4
1962	66.2	57.6	48.8
1963	66.5	57.5	49.0
1964	67.1	57.8	49.6
1965	67.6	58.4	50.5
1966	68.9	60.0	51.6
1967	71.2	61.8	51.6
1968	73.1	63.6	51.0
1969	75.5	65.3	52.2
1970	76.6	67.9	55.7
1971	80.0	70.4	59.5
1972	81.6	72.0	65.9
1973	84.1	74.4	76.6
1974	92.1	86.5	89.0
1975	100.0	100.0	100.0
1976	106.2	105.6	101.7
1977	112.6	112.3	110.5
1978	117.3	120.4	127.8
1979	127.3	132.9	146.2
1980	141.1	148.5	162.4
1981	154.6	163.2	150.7
1982	165.4	169.7	144.1
1983	170.9	172.8	139.7
1984	175.7	176.9	132.5
1985	177.1	178.5	133.4
1986	179.5	179.2	169.4
1987	184.9	183.0	196.9
1988	194.9	192.2	214.1

Table 5C.5   **Price Indexes for Manufactured Exports by Germany and its Competitors, U.S. Dollars, German Export Weights of 1975 (annual averages, 1975 = 100)**

Year	German Price Indexes		Competitors' Price Index
	Export Prices	Domestic Prices	
1953	36.7	32.4	53.7
1954	35.9	31.7	53.6
1955	36.0	32.0	53.8
1956	36.5	32.7	55.8
1957	37.2	33.4	57.5
1958	37.0	33.6	56.6
1959	36.5	33.3	56.5
1960	36.9	33.7	56.4
1961	38.4	35.9	56.1
1962	38.8	37.3	55.0
1963	38.8	37.5	54.7
1964	39.7	38.2	55.5
1965	40.6	39.3	56.0
1966	41.3	40.2	57.1
1967	41.3	39.8	57.5
1968	40.7	39.8	57.1
1969	43.6	40.9	58.3
1970	48.7	47.2	60.7
1971	53.1	52.3	63.5
1972	59.1	58.9	68.7
1973	75.9	75.1	75.9
1974	91.1	89.1	89.7
1975	100.0	100.0	100.0
1976	101.0	100.5	103.1
1977	110.7	110.7	110.3
1978	130.0	130.2	125.1
1979	152.7	149.1	141.2
1980	162.6	160.2	158.5
1981	137.9	135.7	157.8
1982	135.0	133.4	155.4
1983	130.1	128.5	151.5
1984	120.8	119.0	147.7
1985	120.7	127.4	150.0
1986	163.2	173.9	175.2
1987	197.2	209.2	194.0
1988	208.0	222.0	210.4

Table 5C.6   **Price Indexes for Manufactured Exports by Japan and its Competitors, U.S. Dollars, Japanese Export Weights of 1975 (annual averages, 1975 = 100)**

Year	Japanese Price Indexes		Competitors' Price Index
	Export Prices	Domestic Prices	
1953	64.6	71.0	49.4
1954	60.2	67.6	49.1
1955	60.0	66.1	49.7
1956	64.5	70.7	50.8
1957	65.2	71.4	52.1
1958	57.3	66.3	52.1
1959	58.4	65.8	51.4
1960	58.4	64.9	51.0
1961	56.5	63.3	51.2
1962	54.7	61.5	50.6
1963	54.0	60.7	50.2
1964	54.8	60.3	50.7
1965	54.8	59.7	51.3
1966	54.4	59.6	52.3
1967	54.6	59.8	52.3
1968	54.9	59.1	51.9
1969	56.4	59.8	53.4
1970	58.3	61.3	57.3
1971	60.1	62.6	61.2
1972	65.6	69.5	66.4
1973	78.8	84.0	75.1
1974	100.5	99.9	88.8
1975	100.0	100.0	100.0
1976	99.4	104.2	101.4
1977	103.5	117.4	107.9
1978	125.3	151.5	122.6
1979	131.4	147.7	138.4
1980	138.9	152.1	154.4
1981	145.9	156.2	146.1
1982	134.1	137.3	144.0
1983	133.0	145.4	139.4
1984	134.2	146.7	134.0
1985	131.8	145.2	135.6
1986	157.8	199.4	163.4
1987	175.3	226.1	185.0
1988	197.9	254.4	198.8

References

Angermann, Oswald. 1980. External Terms of Trade of the Federal Republic of Germany Using Different Methods of Deflation. *Review of Income and Wealth,* series 26, no. 4, (December).

Baldwin, Richard E. 1988. Hysteresis in Import Prices: The Beachhead Effect. *American Economic Review* 78(4):773–85.

Bushe, Dennis M., Irving B. Kravis, and Robert E. Lipsey. 1986. Prices, Activity, and Machinery Exports: An Analysis Based on New Price Data. *Review of Economics and Statistics* 68(2):248–55.

Cartwright, David W. 1986. Improved Deflation of Purchases of Computers. *Survey of Current Business* 66(3).

Cartwright, David W., and Scott D. Smith, 1988. Deflators for Purchases of Computers in GNP: Revised and Extended Estimates, 1983–88. *Survey of Current Business* 68(11).

Crouhy-Veyrac, Liliane, Michel Crouhy, and Jacques Melitz. 1980. More about the Law of One Price. Institut National de la Statistique et des Sciences Economique, Série des documents de travail no. 8002 (March).

Dornbusch, Rudiger. 1987. Exchange Rates and Prices. *American Economic Review* 77(1):93–106.

Goldstein, Morris, and Mohsin S. Khan. 1985. Income and Price Effects in Foreign Trade. In *Handbook of International Economics,* ed. Ronald N. Jones and Peter B. Kenen, vol. 2, 1041–1105. Amsterdam: North-Holland.

Gordon, Robert J. 1990. *The Measurement of Durable Goods Prices.* Chicago: University of Chicago Press.

Haberler, Gottfried. 1959. *International Trade and Economic Development.* Fiftieth Anniversary Commemoration Lectures, National Bank of Egypt.

Kalter, Eliot R. J. 1978. The Effect of Exchange Rate Changes Upon International Price Discrimination. International Finance Discussion Papers no. 122. Board of Governors of the Federal Reserve System (August).

Kravis, Irving B., and Robert E. Lipsey. 1971. *Price Competitiveness in World Trade.* New York: National Bureau of Economic Research.

———. 1972. The Elasticity of Substitution as a Variable in World Trade. In *International Comparisons of Prices and Output,* ed. Donald J. Daly, Studies in Income and Wealth, vol. 37:369–98. New York: National Bureau of Economic Research.

———. 1974. Export Prices and Price Proxies. In *The Role of the Computer in Economic and Social Research in Latin America,* ed. Nancy D. Ruggles. New York: National Bureau of Economic Research.

———. 1977a. Export Prices and the Transmission of Inflation. *American Economic Review* 67(1):155–63.

———. 1977b. Export and Domestic Prices Under Inflation and Exchange Rate Movements. NBER Working Paper no. 176 (May).

———. 1978. Price Behavior in the Light of Balance of Payments Theories. *Journal of International Economics* (May).

———. 1982. Prices and Market Shares in the International Machinery Trade. *Review of Economics and Statistics* 64 (1): 110–16.

———. 1984. Prices and Terms of Trade for Developed Country Exports of Manufactured Goods. In *The Economics of Relative Prices,* ed. Bela Csikos-Nagy, Douglas Hague, and Graham Hall, 415–45. New York: St. Martin's Press.

Kravis, Irving B., Robert E. Lipsey, and Dennis Bushe. 1980. Prices and Market Share in International Machinery Trade. NBER Working Paper no. 521 (July).

Krugman, Paul. 1987. Pricing to Market when the Exchange Rate Changes. In *Real-*

Financial Linkages among Open Economies, ed. Sven W. Arndt and J. David Richardson, 49–70. Cambridge, Mass: MIT Press.

Lipsey, Robert E. 1963. *Price and Quantity Trends in Foreign Trade of the United States.* Princeton: Princeton University Press, for the NBER.

Mann, Catherine L. 1986. Prices, Profit Margins, and Exchange Rates. *Federal Reserve Bulletin* 72(6):366–79.

Marston, Richard. 1989. Pricing to Market in Japanese Manufacturing. NBER Working Paper no. 2905 (March).

Murphy, Edward E. 1972. A Comparison of the Bureau of Labor Statistics' Indexes of Export Prices for Selected U.S. Products with Unit Value and Wholesale Price Indexes. *1971 Proceedings of the Business and Economic Statistics Section,* American Statistical Association.

National Bureau of Economic Research, Price Statistics Review Committee. 1961. *Report on the Price Statistics of the Federal Government.* New York.

Norsworthy, J. R., and Show-Ling Jang. 1990. Cost Function Estimation of Quality Change Embodied in Inputs: The Use of Semiconductors in Computers and Telecommunications Equipment. Paper prepared for NBER Conference on Research in Income and Wealth, Workshop on Price Measurements and Their Uses. March 22–23. Washington, D.C.

Ohno, Kenichi. 1989. Export Pricing Behavior of Manufacturing: A U.S.-Japan Comparison. *International Monetary Fund Staff Papers* 36(3):550–79.

Rostin, W. 1974. Die Indices der Aussenhandelspreise auf Basis 1970. *Wirtschaft und Statistik* 6:387–94.

Shiells, Clinton R. (1987). Measurement Errors in Unit-Value Proxies for Import Prices. Economic Discussion Paper 24, Bureau of International Economic Affairs, U.S. Department of Labor.

Summers, Robert. 1973. International Price Comparisons based upon Incomplete Data. *Review of Income and Wealth,* series 19, no. 1 (March): 1–16.

Viner, Jacob. 1953. *International Trade and Economic Development.* Lectures delivered at the National University of Brazil. Oxford: Clarendon Press.

Comment   Catherine L. Mann

This paper constructs and analyzes new indexes for manufactured-goods prices. It starts by discussing the methodology behind the construction of the indexes, then addresses how our "view of the world" might be different using these indexes instead of others previously available. The questions are: Does the systematic aggregation of much micro data yield a macro index with a significantly different perspective? Should we "trust" it more than existing manufactured-goods indexes? My comments follow the two parts of the paper: comments first on methodology, and second on the analysis.

First though, as an occasional tiller of the hand-input data field, I can appreciate the amount of labor required to create these manufactures price indexes. It is a vast task to bring together for five countries price data at the 4-digit level

Catherine L. Mann is an economist at the Federal Reserve Board.

of the SITC. Beyond that, organizing the data into the indexes represents a computer effort of great scale and scope.

This paper starts with an excellent primer on index construction. All fledgling empirical economists should read it, before using the finished product or especially if they may someday create their own price indexes. Creating an aggregate international index from micro country data requires making decisions: how "micro" the data should be, how to weight the products, how to weight countries, how to handle "missing observations," which time period to use as a base. The strength of the methodology section of the paper is that it outlines at each juncture what decisions were made—no skeletons here.

The authors spend a good deal of time on the problem of "missing observations." There are three established ways to fill in missing observations: use cross-product variation within a country to infer the missing price of a product in that country; use cross-country variation in a product to infer that same price; use both cross-product and cross-country variation to fill in missing cells in the product-country matrix of price observations. The authors use the last method, called the country-product-dummy approach, pioneered by Summers for inferring missing cells in a international comparison of price levels.

Conceptually, the rationale for using the full set of information—about the relationship across countries within a product group and about the relationship within a country across products—is that using either relationship alone ignores some information. However, from an empirical standpoint, we cannot be so sure that using all the information yields a better estimate of the missing cell. This is because potential errors and biases are contained in the two relationships by themselves.

Consider an analogy from econometric techniques. Full information maximum likelihood estimation of a system of equations incorporates the variance/covariance matrix of the residuals into the estimation of the system of coefficients—all the information available in the system is used. However, a common concern in FIML estimation is misspecification or data measurement problems in any of the individual equations. If these are present, the econometric problems of this single equation will infect the estimation of the coefficients in all the other equations of the system through the variance/covariance matrix. In the CPD method, to complete the analogy, if data for country A is relatively more poorly measured or is misallocated to a particular product group, then using that country's cross-product information in the estimation of the missing cell for country B could yield a more biased estimate of that missing value than simply using the cross-product variation in country B alone. Country A's data problems infect country B's missing price estimates.

One way to examine whether this "infection" problem exists in these data is to compare estimates of the manufactured-goods index using the CPD method with estimates using the other two limited-information methods—cross-country variation and cross-product variation. The authors report on some previous work in this vein, but I would like to see direct comparisons using this data-set.

Continuing with a discussion of the methodology, let me consider the country coverage and the time-period base of the index. These two interact. I can understand, but nevertheless am troubled by, the limited coverage of the developing countries. And given the current interest in international competition, I would like to see the index created also for a time-period base of more recent vintage than 1975 and 1963. On the other hand, in 1963 and 1975 the role played by the developing countries was smaller, so the problem of underrepresentation perhaps is less relevant for the current set of estimates. But, for example, as of 1985 the developing countries accounted for 24 percent of total world exports, with "other Asia" (primarily the Asian NIEs) accounting for 13 percent of total world exports. Within certain of the 2-digit SITC groups, the share of the developing countries and of Asia is larger: in SITC 84 (clothing) developing countries accounted for 48 percent of total world exports, while "other Asia" accounted for 40 percent. If we think that the presence of lower-priced products from the developing countries puts downward pressure on product prices in the industrial countries, then failing to include the developing countries in the CPD calculations will upwardly bias the estimated manufactured-goods price.

It is of course difficult to find data of the appropriate frequency and length for the developing countries. I suggest using data for South Korea, since those data are compiled in a manner similar to Japanese data (good level of disaggregation, maybe computer-readable, and with English subtitles!). If Korean data do not go back far enough, I suggest trying to integrate them into the CPD methodology perhaps only for the last fifteen years. This would not be completely true to the CPD approach. But because the effect of the developing countries' trade on international prices of manufactured goods is probably only that recent, I would prefer to include those data for the recent years, even if they are absent for the early years of the sample.

The analysis section of the paper discusses the sensitivity of the final index to alternative decisions at key points in its construction, and what we might thereby infer about economic behavior. Let me emphasize and expand on certain of the comparisons made in the paper.

The authors examine what difference it makes whether the 1963 or the 1975 weights are used to aggregate products and countries. The evidence suggests that except for SITC 6 (semimanufactures) there has been a substitution toward the lower-priced products and toward countries producing lower-priced products. This also indicates supply response outweighing demand substitution. It is quite interesting that their results suggest a robust supply response. Most recent literature focuses on the lack of supply response, particularly in developing countries, because of an uncertain international environment and instabilities at home. Would updating the weights to 1985 and including developing countries reveal any differences in the data that are more in concert with ad hoc stories of today? Moreover, what could be unique about SITC 6 that yields the opposite result? Could it be that intrafirm trade is particularly important, or that quality changes have been different in this category?

In another analysis of their index, the authors compare measures of the terms of trade for developing countries using their index and the more commonly used unit-value index of manufactures exported from the industrial to the developing countries. Their index rose much less than did the unit-value index. This suggests that the terms of trade for developing countries worsened much less than heretofore thought. This terms-of-trade calculation is integral to policy recommendations and lending decisions of the multilateral institutions and underscores the importance of measurement.

There is one aspect of the paper that I think needs some additional thought. The paper purports to discuss competitiveness of different countries' manufactured products in international markets. Given the political state-of-play, one needs to be wary of providing ammunition without a warning label about usage and meaning. Specifically, the authors' price index may tell us whether there is a competitiveness problem in final goods, but does not pinpoint the source of the problem nor whether it represents a sustained deterioration or a self-correcting, shorter-term phenomenon. From a policy standpoint, these gaps are all-important. For example, short-run reductions in Japanese export prices may not be sustainable in the long run if the short-run change in competitiveness comes at the expense of profits. On the other hand, if costs change enough, say because of technology or outsourcing, the change in competitiveness as observed in the export price data could be permanent. Or (on the third hand), the Japanese producer may determine that a lower level of profits is required to remain a player in the international markets in the face of lower-priced competition from Korea.

The problem with using the relative price of exports as the definition of competitiveness is that it is not built up from costs. So we don't know whether changes in competitiveness (as revealed by movements in this ratio) result from changes in the exchange rate, changes in factor costs, changes in pricing strategies, or changes in cross-subsidization patterns between the various markets for the good (export and domestic markets). We should care about these different sources of changes in competitiveness because a policy reaction (whether warranted or not) should be different in each case, even if the consequence (reduced exports by the uncompetitively priced producer) is the same.

In their discussion of the relationship between movements in individual country indexes and movements in that country's weighted real exchange rate, the authors reveal some of the problems of interpreting events using only their manufacturers-prices data. They note that the United States lost competitiveness between 1980 and 1985, but do not explain this as caused by U.S. exporters maintaining dollar prices in the face of an appreciating dollar. They are surprised that between 1985 and 1987 Japanese relative export prices continued to fall despite the movement in the yen-dollar rate. Many researchers are not surprised by the comovement of exchange rates and Japanese export prices, pointing to changed costs, invoicing, strategic pricing, and cross-subsidization.

All in all, though, this paper represents a herculean task and is an excellent presentation. It also provides a data series that the rest of us will use as both the variable to be explained by more fundamental factors such as unit labor costs and productivity, or as an independent variable in the explanation of macro current account adjustment.

III Service Transactions

6 Developing a Data System for International Sales of Services

Progress, Problems, and Prospects

Bernard Ascher and Obie G. Whichard

Long before the advent of computers, television, or jet aircraft, "trade in services" was taking place regularly. Sea captains, explorers, engineers, tradespeople, money changers, travelers, couriers, and camel drivers engaged in a variety of international transactions involving such services as transportation, banking, construction, communications, and tourism. Most of these services were regarded as activities necessary to support trade in goods, rather than as parts of an integral business sector with distinct economic significance of its own.

Notwithstanding its lengthy history, trade in services has emerged only recently as a generic subject within international economics and as a concern of government policy makers and statisticians. The heightened interest in trade in services—and in its statistical measurement—has occurred in concert with the increase in the scope of services trade that has resulted from improvements in transportation, communication, and information-processing technologies, as well as from the general increase over time in the share of services in economic activity.

This paper describes recent U.S. government efforts—essentially, those made during the 1980s—to develop, expand, and improve a data system for international sales of services. It consists of six sections and an appendix. Section 6.1 provides background information on the context in which interest in services-trade statistics developed and on the data inadequacies that existed before steps to improve the statistics began to be implemented. Section 6.2

Bernard Ascher is director of Service Industry Affairs, Office of the United States Trade Representative, and chairman of the Interagency Task Force on Services Trade Data. Obie G. Whichard is chief, Research Branch, International Investment Division, Bureau of Economic Analysis, U.S. Department of Commerce.

The views expressed in this paper are those of the authors and not necessarily those of the U.S. government agencies with which they are affiliated.

examines and identifies the types of transactions to be covered and the information needed to measure and analyze international sales of services. Section 6.3 reports on the progress made to date in improving the data. Section 6.4 discusses a number of unresolved conceptual and technical problems that have received scrutiny within the United States or in international forums. Section 6.5 assesses the prospects for achieving further progress. Section 6.6 is the conclusion. The appendix gives a more detailed account of the improvements summarized in section 6.3.

6.1 Background and Introduction

It was not until the 1970s that the term "trade in services" began to appear in discussions of international trade among business and government groups. Led principally by insurance and other financial institutions, information-based companies, retailers, and travel organizations, various service businesses began to see a commonality of interest in dealing collectively with the U.S. government. At the same time, advancements in transportation, communications, and information-processing technologies made the internationalization of services virtually inevitable and helped accelerate the demand by U.S. service-producing industries for equal treatment with goods producers in trade promotion and trade liberalization initiatives. Through these efforts to attain government assistance, international trade became a rallying point for service industries. Trade considerations became a driving force behind the quest for better statistics on services generally, including indicators of both domestic and international activity.

6.1.1 Data Inadequacies

Data on trade in services are not as comprehensive, detailed, timely, or internationally comparable as data on trade in merchandise. Estimates of the value of U.S. international trade in services vary substantially, partly because of differing definitions of services trade and partly because of differing estimates of missing information. Although the dimensions of services trade are becoming more clearly defined as data improvements are made and as the subject receives more study, the findings of several studies conducted during the early to mid-1980s illustrate the uncertainty that existed at the time data improvement efforts were beginning to be made.

According to Economic Consulting Services (1981), in a study based on sixteen service industries with an important stake in international trade, the total value of U.S. services exports for the year 1980 was roughly $60 billion; this figure contrasts sharply with the figure then available through official statistics ($36 billion) (Krueger, 1981). A second study, by the U.S. International Trade Commission (1982), estimated foreign revenue generated by fourteen service industries operating overseas to be about $90 billion in 1980. A third study, by the U.S. Congress, Office of Technology Assessment (1986), estimated that services trade in 1983 ranged from $154 billion to $181 billion, consisting of $67–$84 billion in direct exports and $87–$97 billion in affiliate sales (excluding banking). A press release issued with the report (September 11, 1986) stated that "as much as half of U.S. service exports may escape the official statistics."

It is important to note that the primary sources of statistics on international services (balance of payments accounts and surveys of direct investment) were not designed to provide all of the information needed for trade policy purposes, nor were they designed to provide the kind of detail now being sought on services transactions. Although the U.S. data collection system on international transactions is among the best in the world, it does not provide information to suit all specific purposes. As the global economy has evolved and the role of international services has expanded, there is new and added need for more comprehensive and detailed information. Historically, worldwide collection of balance of payments statistics has focused on certain major categories of services, such as travel and transportation. Information on other services has tended to be fragmentary, with little uniformity among countries in the range of services covered.[1]

International comparability of data is hampered by both informational and presentational differences among countries. Few countries collect balance of payments data in the same detail as the United States, and no other country conducts regular surveys of services sold through direct investment enterprises. Where information does exist, use of a standardized format or classification system will facilitate comparability on an international level, as it has in the case of merchandise trade classified according to the Standard International Trade Classifications (SITC) system. Attempts to establish such a system for services trade are currently underway in international forums.

Before commenting further on the state of international services data in the period before data improvement efforts began (i.e., before the early 1980s), it is necessary to spell out in more detail the types of transactions that are to be covered.

6.2 Types of Services and Transactions to be Covered

Services have been defined in a variety of ways: *positively,* as intangible and invisible economic outputs; *residually,* as outputs other than those considered as goods; and *functionally,* as activities that bring about a change in the condition of a person or a good.[2] In most cases, the classification of an output is

---

1. Information on available balance of payments data on services in OECD countries is presented, with as much detail by type of service as could be assembled, in Organisation for Economic Cooperation and Development (1989).

2. The positive and residual definitions have been so widely used as to have attained almost a generic status, and cannot readily be attributed to specific persons. The functional definition was introduced by Hill (1977).

the same under each definition, and all of them would include services involved in international trade such as the following: banking, insurance, and other financial services; transportation; communications services; data-base and other information services; computer and data-processing services; management and consulting services; accounting, legal, and other professional services; advertising; franchising; tourism, lodging, recreation, and entertainment; and education and training.

Although differences of opinion remain, trade in services in the broadest sense incorporates all transactions that involve the movement of producers, consumers, knowledge, information, or legal instruments across borders, as well as movement of the services themselves. Trade in services differs from trade in goods in many respects. The export of goods almost always involves consumption or use in a country other than the one in which the goods were produced. The export of services, on the other hand, can involve consumption or use in the exporting country, the importing country, or even a third country. Production of services can take place in any of these locations as well.[3]

While technology makes it possible to deliver some services from remote locations, such as television broadcast of live sports or entertainment events or telefax transmission of architectural drawings, other services remain dependent upon on-the-spot performance, such as retail banking and insurance services or construction of buildings and bridges. To encompass these different means by which services are rendered internationally, the compilation of statistics on international sales of services must include information, not only on the cross-border transactions that are recorded in balance of payments accounts, but also on services performed or delivered through affiliates established within other countries (often termed "establishment transactions").

Cross-border transactions are transactions between residents and nonresidents. They are recorded in the nation's international transactions, or balance of payments, accounts. Examples of cross-border transactions include the movement from one country to another of: (i) passengers and cargo (transportation services); (ii) voice, video, and data (communication and information services); and (iii) intellectual property rights (patents; trademarks; franchises; distribution rights for books, records, films, and tapes; and broadcasting and recording rights).[4] Other forms of cross-border transactions are the travel-related services consumed by nonresident tourists,

---

3. The various possible combinations of places where production and consumption may occur are discussed in McCulloch (1987) and in Stern and Hoekman (1987). For discussions of the possibilities for production and consumption to occur at different locations—sometimes referred to as "disembodiment" of the service—see Bhagwati (1984) and Sauvant and Zimney (1985). Although many examples of disembodied services have been given, usually involving the use of communications technologies to transmit work products to the customer, available data for U.S. multinational companies show that a preponderance of sales of services is local (i.e., to customers in the same country as the parent or affiliate making the sale).

4. Payments and receipts for rights to use intellectual property may be considered a form of factor income, rather than nonfactor services. They sometimes are considered as services, however, and are included in this review of data needs for the sake of completeness.

students, and medical patients, and the services produced by business consultants, engineers, lawyers, and others visiting the country in which their clients are located.

Establishment transactions include sales of services (such as accounting, advertising, and insurance) through branches, subsidiaries, or other affiliates in another country. Sales by these entities in the countries in which they are located are not balance of payments transactions, because they are between residents of the same country. For the United Sates and many other countries, establishment transactions provide an important channel for delivering services internationally. In some cases, because of the nature of the service, such transactions may be the only practical means of performing services in, or delivering services to, foreign markets. For services such as banking and insurance, a local presence may be required by law to conduct business in a given country. The United States is currently the only country that regularly collects statistical information on establishment transactions. However, other countries have begun considering the collection of such information, as interest in services has grown and as the role of establishment transactions in the delivery of services to foreign markets has become more widely recognized.

Although the term "services" has historically been used in balance of payments presentations to refer to current account transactions other than merchandise trade and unilateral transfers, services are generally defined less broadly for purposes of trade policy or corporate planning. (Both the broad and the narrow definitions of services are included in the term "invisibles," which is composed of services in the broader sense and unilateral transfers; see Sapir 1982.) For these particular purposes, services generally are taken to exclude factor income—that is, returns to the factors of production of land, labor, and capital, such as returns on investments or wages of nonresident workers.[5]

In one sense, the focus of this paper is on this narrower definition of services, inasmuch as we do not consider factor income. In another sense, however, our focus is broader than the balance of payments accounts. We consider in addition to the traditional measure of "exports and imports" of services the sales of services abroad through foreign affiliates of U.S. companies and the sales of services in the United States through U.S. affiliates of foreign companies. For many purposes, including applications to trade policy or corporate planning and the measurement of international markets for services, it is more

---

5. A recent shift in usage toward the narrower definition can be noted. In the official U.S. balance of payments presentation, "services," which previously had been used in the broad sense, was more narrowly defined in June 1990 to exclude investment income. In January 1989 *The Service Economy*, a publication of the Coalition of Service Industries, began publishing a "True Services Balance," which was defined similarly but confined (as is this paper) to private services transactions (see Sinai 1988). However, inasmuch as both measures contain some flows of factor income, neither of them is in complete conformity with the narrow definition.

relevant to gauge the value of *sales* of services through foreign affiliates than the value of *earnings* derived from these affiliates.[6] In this regard, the use of sales revenue as the common denominator for measuring services transactions is parallel to the treatment of merchandise trade, whose statistics are based on the value of sales, not on the value of profits.

6.2.1   Specific Information Needed

Ideally, a statistical system for services should satisfy the need for a variety of data to quantify and analyze world markets for services. Such analysis requires information both on trade flows and on services activity within individual countries. The information should provide answers to the following basic groups of questions:

1. What types of services were sold in a given time period? This would include some detail on the specific type of service, such as the kind of insurance, training, or communication. A uniform classification system, applicable to all types of transactions, would be useful in this regard.
2. At what price, and in what quantity, was each type of service bought or sold? What was the total revenue involved in the transaction?
3. How was the service conveyed? Through what channels did the trade occur? To what extent were services delivered to, or obtained from, foreigners through cross-border transactions and to what extent through establishment transactions? In the case of the cross-border transactions, where was the service actually performed—in the country of the buyer, the country of the seller, or in a third country? Were the services sold in conjunction with the sale of goods or equipment?
4. What was the nationality of the seller? The buyer? And what was the relationship, if any, between the buyer and seller of the services? To what extent were the transactions between affiliated parties (e.g., between parent and affiliate or between affiliates of the same parent company) and to what extent were they between unaffiliated parties?

To facilitate further analysis of the significance of trade, an additional group of questions would seek information on market size:

5. What is the extent of domestic production and consumption of tradable services and, thus, what portion of production is exported and what is the market share of imports? What is the level of production and consumption of these services in other countries?

---

6. Investment earnings in the current account of the balance of payments include returns to investment in goods as well as services operations, in addition to income from portfolio investment and ownership of real estate. For these reasons, investment income in the balance of payments does not reflect the sales of services by U.S. affiliates abroad on the same basis as export sales of services by the parent companies in the United States. See Sapir (1982) and Stalson (1985).

The above questions provide criteria for judging the extent of improvement needed or attained in developing a data system with extensive detail on a wide variety of services provided internationally.

6.3 Progress

The basic approach to improving U.S. statistics has been a pragmatic one—building on or adapting existing sources of information, rather than creating a new system. Under this approach, services trade statistics are drawn primarily from two sources: the balance of payments accounts, which are compiled from survey data and a variety of other sources; and the data-base on the operations of direct investment enterprises, maintained by the Bureau of Economic Analysis of the U.S. Department of Commerce.

In general, these two sets of statistics correspond to the two broad groups of transactions identified in the previous section. Balance of payments statistics cover cross-border transactions (that is, transactions between residents and nonresidents). The statistics on direct investment include information on establishment transactions (i.e., sales by U.S.-owned affiliates in foreign countries and by foreign-owned affiliates in the United States); these are not balance of payments transactions.

6.3.1   Impetus for Data Improvement

The impetus for data improvement has stemmed both from an increased emphasis on services in U.S. trade policy and from a recognition that better information on services trade was needed for compiling the balance of payments and national income and product accounts.

By including services in the definition of "commerce," the Trade Act of 1974, for the first time, provided the President with authority to include services in trade negotiations. The Trade and Tariff Act of 1984 made this authority more explicit.[7] It also contained a number of other provisions dealing with services, including some pertaining to statistics. Specifically, it: (1) provided for the establishment of a services-industry development program, including various studies and reports; (2) called for a data-base to be established to help evaluate government policies and actions pertaining to services; (3) provided for mandatory reporting of trade in services; and (4) called for a benchmark survey of services transactions between U.S. persons and unaffiliated foreign persons. The Omnibus Trade and Competitiveness Act of 1988

---

7. The authority was utilized in September 1986, when services were formally placed on the agenda for the Uruguay Round multilateral negotiations being conducted in GATT. The *Economic Report of the President,* transmitted to the U.S. Congress in January 1987, took note of the possible link between these negotiations and the success of data-improvement efforts, stating that "developing better measures of activity in the services area could be an important by-product of the Uruguay Round trade negotiations."

extended and built upon these provisions. It provided, inter alia, for expansion of existing surveys to cover eight specified groups of services and for information on services to be included in a National Trade Data Bank to be established under the Act.[8]

Within the executive branch, an Interagency Task Force on Services Trade Data, chaired by the Office of the U.S. Trade Representative, was established in 1982 to review existing statistics and to examine specific needs of data users. Other functions of the task force are: to recommend data improvements; to coordinate the work of the various U.S. agencies with an interest in the data; to work with the private sector to develop needed information and to assess the feasibility, cost, and burden of collecting the data; to identify technical, legal, administrative, and financial problems arising from the data improvement program; and to recommend ways of resolving these problems. A number of private business groups and numerous individual firms have, at one time or another, been consulted in the development or evaluation of specific data-collection proposals.

6.3.2   Steps Taken

This section demonstrates the improvements in coverage of sales of services by presenting two tables, one containing information on cross-border transactions in 1979 (before the improvement effort began) and in 1988, and one presenting data on establishment transactions in 1988. (Data on establishment transactions are not available for 1979.[9]) A more comprehensive summary of recent steps to improve U.S. statistics on services trade appears in Appendix A.[10]

The improvements in coverage of cross-border transactions over the nine-year period spanned by table 6.1 are striking. At the beginning of the period, information on cross-border transactions was confined to travel, transportation, telecommunications, royalty and fee transactions with unaffiliated parties, construction and related services (available only for U.S. sales), reinsurance, and film rentals. Information on services transactions with affiliated parties was collected and recorded in the balance of payments accounts, but receipts and payments were netted for each type of direct investment (U.S. abroad and foreign in the United States), so that the data did not reveal the full two-way value of the transactions, as required by the format of the table.

---

8. The eight groups of services are: banking services; information services, including computer software services; brokerage services; transportation services; travel services; engineering services; construction services; and health services.

9. Information on the operations of foreign affiliates of U.S. companies and of U.S. affiliates of foreign companies had been collected for some time (see e.g., Pizer and Cutler 1957). However, as explained later in this section, the breakdown of sales needed to derive establishment transactions in services was not collected.

10. Appendix A updates and expands upon an earlier summary of improvements discussed in Ascher and Whichard (1987).

Information on most business, professional, and technical services was unavailable.

By 1988, estimates of the transactions with affiliated parties had begun to be made available on a gross basis, thus permitting the separate identification of U.S. sales and purchases. Information had also become available on transactions with unaffiliated foreigners in a variety of business, professional, and technical services, largely as a result of new Bureau of Economic Analysis surveys. Estimates of educational services, medical services, and (some) financial services had begun to be made using indirect methods.

Despite some missing elements, enough information is available to permit a meaningful total on cross-border transactions in services to be struck for 1988, whereas this could not be done for 1979. Measured U.S. sales of services to foreigners in 1988 were $95 billion, and U.S. purchases of services from foreigners were $80 billion. (If coverage had been the same as in 1979, the figures recorded would have been roughly $75 billion for sales and $69 billion for purchases.[11]) For both sales and purchases, travel and transportation accounted for the largest shares of the total.

For establishment transactions, sales of services to foreign persons by majority-owned affiliates of U.S. companies were $101 billion in 1988, while sales of services in the United States by U.S. affiliates of foreign companies were $107 billion (table 6.2).[12] Sales were largest for U.S. and foreign affiliates in finance (except banking), insurance, and real estate, and in "services."[13]

A number of data improvements during this period are not evident from the tables. For several services, data have improved in quality because of a change in the basis for reporting from voluntary to mandatory. Also, some surveys have been expanded to collect additional types of information, including surveys on insurance, construction, and intangible assets. Other improvements include expanded collection of information on domestic services activity by the Census Bureau, institution of an international price program by the Bureau

11. It should be emphasized that these figures are only rough calculations, intended to illustrate the order of magnitude of the data improvements. They were made by assuming that: (a) services transactions between affiliated parties would have been gauged using U.S. parents' net receipts from foreign affiliates (which appear in the U. S. balance of payments accounts under "exports") as the measure of U.S. sales and using U.S. affiliates' net payments to their foreign parents (which appear under "imports") as the measure of U.S. purchases; and (b) transactions between unaffiliated parties would have been measured as the sum for 1988 of items shown in table 6.1 for both years. A more precise estimate would require quantifying the effects of a variety of factors discussed elsewhere in this paper, such as the change in the basis for reporting on several surveys from voluntary to mandatory, changes in data sources, and changes in the scope of existing surveys.

12. See the note to table 6.2 for information on the comparability of the figures on sales of U.S. and foreign affiliates.

13. Here "services" corresponds to the Services division of the SIC. As indicated in the note to table 6.2, a broader group of industries is designated as services-producing for purposes of distributing sales between goods and services.

Table 6.1   U.S. Cross-Border Transactions in Services, 1979 and 1988 (millions of dollars)

	1979		1988	
	U.S. Sales	U.S. Purchases	U.S. Sales	U.S. Purchases
Total	n.a.	n.a.	95,480	80,017
With affiliated foreigners[a]	n.a.	n.a.	18,148	6,886
With foreign parents	n.a.	n.a.	3,266	3,539
Royalties and license fees	n.a.	n.a.	238	1,205
Other services	n.a.	n.a.	3,028	2,334
With foreign affiliates	n.a.	n.a.	14,882	3,347
Royalties and license fees	n.a.	n.a.	8,455	119
Other services	n.a.	n.a.	6,427	3,228
With unaffiliated foreigners	n.a.	n.a.	77,332	73,131
Royalties and license fees	1,204	309	2,522	1,086
Travel	8,441	9,413	28,935	33,098
Passenger fares	2,156	3,184	8,771	7,932
Other transportation	9,971	10,906	18,939	16,675
Freight	3,432	6,701	5,364	11,845
Port services	6,390	3,684	12,820	7,099
Other	149	521	755	732
Education	n.a.	n.a.	4,142	543
Financial services	n.a.	n.a.	3,831	1,656

Insurance	n.a.	n.a.	1,669	2,655
Primary insurance, net	n.a.	n.a.	1,500	561
Reinsurance, net	218	835	169	2,094
Telecommunications	1,101	1,244	2,203	4,577
Business, professional, and technical services	n.a.	n.a.	5,536	1,869
Accounting, auditing, and bookkeeping	n.a.	n.a.	37	31
Advertising	n.a.	n.a.	154	176
Computer and data-processing	n.a.	n.a.	1,255	107
Data-base and other information services	n.a.	n.a.	196	39
Engineering, architectural, construction, and mining (net)	1,054	n.a.	1,074	465
Installation, maintenance, and repair of equipment	n.a.	n.a.	1,289	618
Legal services	n.a.	n.a.	271	98
Management, consulting, and public relations	n.a.	n.a.	362	73
Medical services	n.a.	n.a.	541	n.a.
Research and development, commercial testing, and laboratory services	n.a.	n.a.	236	182
Other	n.a.	n.a.	121	80
Film rentals	284	63	784	40

Source: U.S. Department of Commerce, Bureau of Economic Analysis.

Note: n.a. = not available.

[a]Data on trade in services with affiliated foreigners were collected in 1979, but receipts and payments were netted for each type of direct investment (U.S. abroad and foreign in the United States), so that the two-way flow of trade could not be discerned. Because the net figures are shown in the U.S. balance of payments accounts, the sales and purchases figures shown here exceed exports and imports as recorded in those accounts.

Table 6.2   **U.S. Establishment Transactions in Services, by Industry, 1988**
                      (millions of dollars)

Industry of affiliate	Sales of services to foreign persons by foreign affiliates of U.S. companies	Sales of services to U.S. persons by U.S. affiliates of foreign companies
All industries	100,733	107,050
Petroleum	7,199	2,677
Manufacturing	11,440	5,493
Wholesale trade	11,341	1,580
Finance (except banking), insurance, and real estate	36,937	67,911
Finance, except banking	(D)	16,963
Insurance	20,673	39,967
Real estate	(D)	10,981
Services	27,702	16,471
Hotels and other lodging places	(D)	2,680
Business services	16,393	6,315
Motion pictures	3,388	(D)
Engineering and architectural services	2,612	1,383
Health services	684	(D)
Other services	(D)	3,484
Other industries	6,114	12,919
Transportation, communication, and public utilities	5,665	11,278
Other	449	1,641

Source: U.S. Department of Commerce, Bureau of Economic Analysis.

Note: D = suppressed to avoid disclosure of data of individual companies. Data for foreign affiliates cover only affiliates that are majority-owned by U.S. direct investors; data for U.S. affiliates cover all U.S. affiliates (i.e., all U.S. business enterprises owned 10 percent or more by a foreign direct investor). Data for foreign affiliates include, while data for U.S. affiliates exclude, investment income included in operating revenues of finance and insurance companies (see section 6.4 for discussion). The sales considered as sales of services in this table are those associated with the Services division of the SIC; and with finance (except banking), insurance, and real estate; agricultural, mining, and petroleum services; and transportion, communication, and public utilities. The exclusion for banking reflects the limitation of the data to nonbanks.

of Labor Statistics, and revision of classification systems. Information on these and other improvements is provided in Appendix A.

6.4 Problems

Most of the improvement efforts described in the preceding section can be characterized as pragmatic measures directed at closing gaps in coverage, expanding the amount of detail provided, or reorienting the data to facilitate use in a wider variety of applications. Progress is also needed in articulating and resolving a variety of conceptual and technical problems and in reaching a consensus on treatment of borderline cases.

This section discusses a number of problem areas and borderline cases. Several of them are being considered in connection with international exercises, including the development, under United Nations auspices, of the Central Product Classification, the revision of the United Nations System of National Accounts, the deliberations carried out over several years in a statistical working party of the Trade Committee of the Organisation for Economic Co-operation and Development, and the work done in anticipation of the eventual revision of the International Monetary Fund's *Balance of Payment Manual* (1977). Some of the other problems discussed here have been the subject of deliberations within the Interagency Task Force on Services Trade Data.

6.4.1 Separating Domestic and International Transactions

Sometimes it is difficult to distinguish cross-border transactions from establishment transactions. In the case of a service performed in the country of a foreign customer, for example, when should it be considered to have been provided by a U.S. person (a cross-border transaction) and when should it be considered to have been provided by a foreign affiliate of a U.S. person (an establishment transaction)? International guidelines are of only limited help in answering such questions. The IMF *Manual* (1977) provides guidance in the case of installation of equipment, where a one-year rule is applied: an affiliate is considered to exist only if the duration of the operations exceeds one year. This rule could be applied analogously to other services. In practice, the rule has not sufficed in every situation.[14] In view of these difficulties, the United States has established a number of supplementary criteria that focus on the nature of the operations rather than on their duration.[15] It has outlined them in various discussions and questionnaires at the international level, and other countries and international organizations have expressed an interest in them as a means of more fully articulating the definition of a resident enterprise for purposes of categorizing international transactions.

---

14. For example, a permanent establishment may be set up to install equipment or perform other services (such as construction) in the country in which it is located; it would not make sense to consider the services provided by such an establishment as cross-border simply because they involve installation of equipment (or construction) in periods of under one year. Also, in many cases companies may not be able to accurately forecast the duration of projects.

15. In the case of activity abroad by a U.S. entity, if the entity is incorporated abroad it is considered a foreign affiliate, resident in the country where the activity occurs. If it operates abroad but is not incorporated there, its status is determined after considering it in relation to several other criteria related to the nature of the foreign operations. Typically, an entity operating abroad is considered a foreign affiliate if it: pays foreign income taxes; has a substantial physical presence abroad (e.g., plant and equipment or employees); maintains records that would permit preparation of separate financial statements, including an income statement and balance sheet (not just a record of disbursements and receipts); and takes title to, and has receipts for, goods it sold or received funds for its own account for services it performed. If some or all of these criteria are not met, the entity probably cannot be construed, or accounted for, as a separate foreign business enterprise, and its transactions are attributed to the U.S. parent company. Analogous criteria are applied to determine the status of activities in the United States by a foreign entity.

6.4.2   Interpretation of Data on Establishment Transactions

Several problems in interpreting statistics on establishment transactions should be recognized. For example, some may view affiliates that have been acquired by foreigners as domestic entities, whose activities do not become international in character simply because of a change in ownership. Similarly, some long-established subsidiaries of foreign companies may be regarded as local companies, but are actually foreign-owned. Cases in which there are multiple owners with differing nationalities, such as international consortia and joint ventures, could similarly pose problems of interpretation, because sales are not prorated according to the nationalities of the various owners. Similar problems of interpretation may arise in comparisons of establishment transactions with cross-border transactions, since the two will normally differ with respect to the principal location of value added and the attribution of value added to the various factors of production in the countries involved in the transactions. Also, problems of duplication may arise where there are indirectly held affiliates whose sales could be included in the establishment transactions of both the country of the ultimate beneficial owner and the countries of intervening foreign parents in the ownership chain. Finally, no information on *purchases* of services by affiliates is available.

As indicated in the note to table 6.2, the data on U.S. and foreign affiliate sales are not strictly comparable: the data for foreign affiliates are restricted to affiliates that are majority-owned, whereas the data on U.S. affiliates cover all affiliates; also, the data for foreign affiliates include investment income of finance and insurance companies, whereas the data for U.S. affiliates exclude such income. (As explained in Appendix A, the latter comparability problem is being resolved.)

Although the U.S. statistics on establishment transactions are unique—to our knowledge no other country regularly collects such information—they are limited by a lack of information on the *type* of service. The only information collected is whether the sales are of goods or of services. The industry of the seller usually provides some guide to the type of service sold, but cases often arise involving sales outside a company's primary industry (for example, computer and data-processing services sold by a computer manufacturer, an aircraft manufacturer, or a bank).[16]

6.4.3   Uses of Data Limited by Balance of Payments Conventions

As noted earlier, balance of payments data are a primary source of information on international services transactions. However, such data cannot serve all specific purposes, and as new uses of the data have materialized, it has become clear that additional data are sometimes needed.

Transportation services provide a case in point. To gauge a country's market

16. For further discussion of the U.S. system of data on establishment trade in services, see Whichard (1987, 1988c).

for international transportation services, the balance of payments accounts are a ready source of information; indeed, transportation, as a necessary accompaniment of trade in goods, has among the lengthiest histories of coverage by such accounts. Partly because of balance of payments conventions, however, these accounts do not provide all the information needed for purposes of trade policy or market analysis.

In principle, the balance of payments should record transactions in transportation services, as in the case of other services, that are between residents of different countries. For transportation, this principle would be difficult or impossible to implement in its pure form, since it would require knowledge on a case-by-case basis of who owned goods at the time of shipment and who paid the freight. To circumvent these difficulties, the IMF, in its *Manual* (1977), recommends that a special convention be adopted for transportation. The convention—one of three presented in the *Manual*—uniformly values merchandise f.o.b. at the point of exportation and assumes that charges for shipment are, in effect, always paid by the importer, who in some ultimate sense does bear these charges, even if the payment is sometimes embodied in payments for imported merchandise, rather than made directly to a transportation company.

In the case of the United States, which follows the convention, exports (sales) of transportation services are recorded as U.S. carriers' receipts for carriage of U.S. exports, irrespective of whether the payments to these carriers were in actuality made by U.S. or foreign persons. Similarly, imports (purchases) of transportation services are recorded as foreign carriers' receipts for carriage of U.S. imports, irrespective of whether the payments were actually made by U.S. or foreign persons. These measures, while useful for compiling the balance of payments accounts and while having the virtue of allowing for the uniform valuation of merchandise, may be difficult to use or interpret for purposes requiring identification of the actual parties to contracts for transportation services. From the broader standpoint of data needed to support analyses in the maritime or aviation areas, the balance of payments information is inadequate, since such analyses may require information on the total value of transportation between a country and its trading partners.[17] In the case of the United States, a major step in meeting these broader needs would be for information on U.S. carriers' receipts for carriage of U.S. imports and on foreign carriers' receipts for carriage of U.S. exports to be devel-

17. The broader data needs could perhaps be met with balance of payments data if a different convention were followed. The alternative conventions for recording transportation transactions discussed in the IMF *Manual* provide for recording a wider range of transactions than does the recommended one, which was selected partly on grounds of practicality and partly because the additional information was not deemed to be of primary interest for balance of payments purposes. As we have noted elsewhere (Ascher and Whichard 1987), the alternative conventions can be characterized as "grossing up the transactions to include all those related to the international transportation of goods, and then providing offsetting entries for those assumed to be between residents of the same country."

oped. Although these are domestic transactions by balance of payments conventions, some of them are, in reality, international, and the availability of information on them as a supplement to the information now compiled for balance of payments purposes would enable the full two-way value of international transportation markets to be gauged.

6.4.4   Noninterest Income of Financial Institutions

Noninterest income of financial institutions is composed largely of fees and commissions for a variety of services, such as fiduciary activities, data processing, consulting, and payments and settlements services. Such income also includes some nonfee activities—namely, gains and losses from foreign exchange and from sales of assets. In addition, some of the data that are the most difficult to collect involve the newer financial and investment services, which are the areas of rapid growth and internationalization. For example, U.S. data on fees and commissions earned from underwriting and trading in government and private securities generally are sparse or lacking. The same can be said of fees earned on the newer financial instruments, such as swaps, options, and futures, fees earned for managing foreign customers' accounts, and fees associated with investment advice and the arrangement of mergers and acquisitions.

Some noninterest income of financial institutions consists of gains and losses on sales of assets.[18] According to current IMF guidelines and U.S. practice, such income should not be recorded in balance of payments accounts as service income since it does not correspond to the production of a service, but rather to a change in the value of existing assets. Trading gains of professional dealers (banks and money changers) should perhaps be an exception, however. Rather than an explicit fee, a differential between buying and selling rates is maintained to cover the costs of providing the service. Thus, the dealer's income would reflect both gains from foreign exchange trading and any explicit fees and commissions.[19]

6.4.5   Separating Services from Goods

It is not always easy to distinguish services from goods, especially when they are sold or provided jointly in a package.[20] The payments for leasing super-computers or other big ticket items, for example, may represent payments for a variety of elements, including depreciation, interest, taxes, insurance, technical services, and maintenance, that may represent payments for

18. This is true of noninterest income as reported by U.S. commercial banks on the Call Report (Consolidated Report of Condition and Income) to the Federal Financial Institutions Examination Council.

19. In the U.S. National Income and Product Accounts, a similar practice is already followed with respect to trading gains of securities dealers.

20. Similar problems may arise when a group of services is bundled. See Ascher and Whichard (1987).

services performed or for the use of goods. Under balance of payments guidelines, financial leasing (i.e., a lease arrangement that provides for the recovery of all, or substantially all, of the cost of the goods, together with carrying charges, and contemplates a transfer in title to the lessee upon expiration) is regarded as a means of payment for goods, whereas operational leasing is regarded as a service that makes possible the use of goods or equipment without ownership by the user. Goods sold with service contracts or extended warranties also incorporate services whose values generally are recorded as a part of the merchandise cost. The sale of sophisticated machinery frequently includes the cost of providing engineering assistance and maintenance to assure that the equipment is operating properly and the cost of training workers to operate the machinery. Another example of goods commingled with services is expenditures by tourists for goods such as souvenirs and gifts, which presently are included indistinguishably in the travel accounts of the U.S. balance of payments together with expenditures for services such as lodging, local transportation, and entertainment. Similarly, the value of transportation as reflected in data on port service expenditures includes the value of jet fuel in aircraft and diesel fuel in oceangoing vessels, neither of which can now be separately identified.

Construction is a special case because of its mixture of manufacturing and nonmanufacturing activities and also because its final product is tangible. Construction of bridges and buildings can be regarded wholly or partly as on-site manufacturing. Yet certain activities are separable from the physical construction process and can be performed at off-site or remote locations—the conception, design, and planning of the project, as well as the contracting, subcontracting, and procurement of materials, etc.

6.4.6 Services and Manufacturing

It has frequently been observed that whether a particular activity is associated with goods or services may depend on the organization of production. For example, customized production on a contract or fee basis for individual customers may be treated as a service, whereas the same activities performed in a factory setting would be treated as goods.[21] Similarly, an activity that is considered a service if performed as a separate activity by a specialized firm (such as an accounting or legal firm) will not be reflected as such if performed in-house by a goods producer. Bhagwati (1984) has observed that through a "splintering" process services functions may be spun off to such specialized firms with the result that, from the standpoint of final demand, the composition of output may be shifted statistically toward services without any ac-

---

21. The U.S. Standard Industrial Classification includes "establishments primarily engaged in customizing automobiles, trucks, and vans except on a factory basis" in services (Division I), but includes "establishments primarily engaged in customizing automobiles, trucks, and vans on a factory basis" in manufacturing (Division D).

tual change having occurred in the composition of activities that produce the output.

While it is generally accepted that this splintering process will occur in the case of specialized business services, there is less agreement where the activity spun off is more directly related to the process of producing goods. In some countries, for statistical purposes, certain intermediate production steps (e.g., cutting, sewing, dyeing, electroplating) are classified as services, particularly if they are performed on a contract or subcontract basis by an outside firm. In the United States these functions are treated as integral parts of manufacturing operations, and their values are recorded as goods.

Recently, similar issues have been discussed as they relate to "processing" (essentially, transactions in which value is added to goods not owned by the entity engaged in production) and to repair. Examples of processing range from activities such as bottling and packaging that have only a minor effect on the good being processed to factory-type assembly operations or offshore oil refining done on a contract or fee basis on parts, components, or materials owned by others. A variety of alternative treatments of processing as goods-producing or services-producing has been suggested.[22] The current U.S. practice, which to some extent is dictated by available methods of data collection, is to include goods for and after processing in merchandise trade on a gross basis; but other countries exclude goods for processing from merchandise and record the processor's fee as a service.[23]

Similar questions have been addressed with respect to repair. Repair is now treated uniformly as a service in U.S. balance of payments accounts. However, there have been proposals at the international level to record some types of repair as merchandise.[24]

22. For example, in the Central Product Classification (CPC), a provisionally adopted United Nations system for classifying goods and services, all processing would be considered a service. This is perhaps the most controversial feature of the CPC and one that has not found much support in the United States. Continuing with the example of oil refining, it may be of interest for some purposes to know how much of the amount that was refined in a given period was refined under contract for others. However, for analysis of the production of commodities, it is generally more useful to have all of the production of a given commodity classified in a single category.

A second treatment was tentatively agreed upon by an expert group of national income accountants and balance of payments compilers meeting under joint UN/IMF auspices in 1987 in connection with the revision of the System of National Accounts. The consensus of this group was that a distinction should be made between processing resulting in a major change or alteration in the goods being processed and processing not resulting in such a change or alteration. The former would be considered manufacturing, and the goods processed would be included on a gross basis in merchandise trade. In the latter case, the processing would be considered, and the processor's fee recorded, as a service. In practice, the two cases would be distinguished on the basis of differences between the classification of the processor's output and that of the goods received for processing.

23. In a recent survey of recording practices in member countries, the IMF found that about 60 percent of the countries from which responses were received recorded processing transactions in merchandise trade, while 40 percent recorded them in services.

24. The CPC would treat all repair as a service, whereas the UN/IMF expert group (referred to in footnote 22) agreed that repair should be divided into two categories—major and minor—

6.4.7   No-Charge Services

Certain services may be performed without charge and their cost absorbed in charges for other services or products. For example, charge-card companies provide a means of checking the creditworthiness of cardholders at the point of retail sale. This service to retailers is performed electronically, instantly, and even internationally. The automatic teller machine provides another example of services provided without explicit charge. Should the value of this service be imputed and reflected somehow in services statistics? An imputation is made in the National Income and Product Accounts of the United States for services performed without charge by financial intermediaries, including an imputation for international transactions. (The imputed charges of U.S. financial intermediaries for services provided to foreigners in 1988 was $7.0 billion, in comparison to the estimated $3.8 billion in explicit charges shown for financial services in table 6.1.) No similar imputation is now made in balance of payments accounts, but proposals to provide for one have been made in reviews of balance of payments accounting standards.

Many types of services may be performed free of charge within corporations (Vernon 1971–72). These may include intracorporate communications and various types of technical, management, and administrative services provided by headquarters to both domestic and foreign subsidiaries. Although U.S. data cover intracorporate services transactions, including allocated expenses, it is unlikely that the reporting system can capture the full range of services rendered, if for no other reason than that modern communications technologies make it possible for consultations between central administrative offices, research and development centers, engineering offices, and foreign subsidiaries to be conducted on an ongoing and informal basis. These informal services are vital to the operations of the multinational firm, yet there is no practical means for closely monitoring them. Even if they could be precisely identified, accurately valuing them would be extremely difficult because they are not purchased through market transactions.

6.4.8   New Services

Any statistical system must provide for coverage of new activities that may emerge in the future. Usually, provision is made for services (or products) not elsewhere specified. Although such categories are provided by almost every classification system, it is often difficult to assess the composition of data reported in them. Thus, it is important to revise classifications regularly, so that new services can be placed in more descriptive categories.

---

similar to the categories agreed to for processing. Repair of "investment goods"—e.g., overhaul of ocean vessels or commercial aircraft—would be included in merchandise trade, while repair of other goods, such as personal automobiles, would be treated as a service.

6.5   Prospects for Further Improvements

Evaluating prospects for achieving further improvements in statistics on trade in services involves answering several questions: What tasks remain to be accomplished? What obstacles stand in the way of accomplishing them? How likely is it that these obstacles can in fact be overcome? In other words, what is attainable?

Many of the needed data improvements appear to be attainable, given sufficient time and resources to compile the information. However, it is not possible to judge precisely what, in a practical sense, can be accomplished, inasmuch as unforeseen obstacles are likely to arise as the work progresses.

In surveying available information on U.S. international trade in services in relation to the criteria of the "ideal" data system outlined in section 6.3, it can be seen that while considerable progress has been made over several years, much work remains. Information on financial services needs to be improved, and statistics on transportation services need to be expanded beyond those provided for by balance of payments conventions. Prospects for improvements in both areas have been given new impetus by the 1988 Trade Act (see section 6.3). Also, price information needs to be developed for a wider variety of services. Statistics on establishment transactions disaggregated by type of service are needed, with a level of detail comparable to that of cross-border transactions. Data on local purchases of services by affiliates also are needed. If the data for merchandise trade, for which information on several thousand product categories is released monthly, are to be used as a standard, improvements in detail and frequency also are in order. Finally, more study of the concept of establishment transactions is needed, both to better relate the notion to established economic accounts and to provide additional insight into the proper use of existing data.

In the United States, three types of obstacles must be overcome before these or other tasks can be accomplished: budgetary, legal or administrative, and technical. Although the budgetary obstacles are probably the ones that in the current environment many would think of first, they may in fact be the least important. Funds are required to implement almost any of the remaining improvements, whether by instituting or expanding surveys or by utilizing existing information to make estimates. However, the amounts required for immediate needs are relatively small, and if a compelling need can be demonstrated they probably can be obtained.[25]

The major legal or administrative hurdle involves the Paperwork Reduction Act, under which information-collection proposals by government agencies are required to be approved by the Office of Management and Budget. The act's requirements are numerous. Their essence is that it must be demonstrated

---

25. As a point of reference, the annual survey of U.S. direct investment abroad and the benchmark and annual surveys of selected services transactions with unaffiliated foreigners together required augmenting BEA's budget by only about $1 million per year.

that the information has utility, can be provided by respondents without undue burden, and is not already available from existing sources. Agencies are given an information-collection budget under the act, and it is sometimes possible to expand one statistical program only by contracting another one, in order to remain within the parameters of the budget.

Despite the mandate of various trade laws, securing approval of a new survey may involve deliberations among statistical agencies, OMB, user agencies, and respondents. The process is time-consuming, but it is not impossible to obtain approval for new initiatives. The most recent experiences in securing approval for major new initiatives were with respect to the new annual survey of U.S. direct investment abroad (which was first conducted for 1983 and which also included many nonservices items) and the benchmark and annual surveys of selected services transactions with unaffiliated foreigners (first conducted for 1986). Both surveys were the subject of lengthy deliberations and both were ultimately approved. The benchmark survey of transactions with unaffiliated foreigners was initially disapproved, however, and a reduction in the scope of the survey and extensive consultations with the respondent community were necessary before it was cleared.

The major technical obstacles to data improvement concern recordkeeping systems of the businesses that must be the ultimate source of information. Some of the information needed on services trade is not now maintained by most companies in the ordinary course of business. For example, a company might not record transactions by country, or it might not maintain information by type of service, particularly for purchases.

When businesses cannot readily supply information needed by the government, three courses of action are possible: the companies can be required to develop a way to supply it (sometimes—following a one-time effort to establish mechanisms for tracking transactions—with a reduction in burden from the original estimate); exemption levels or other sampling techniques can be utilized to limit the burden; or the government can decide to do without the information. For surveys of international services transactions, the most common approach has been the use of exemption levels, which have made it possible to screen out of the reporting system very small companies or transactions that, while they may account for a significant portion of the universe in terms of *numbers*, do not have a significant impact upon its *value*.

It should be clear from the foregoing that the obstacles to improving data on services trade are not insurmountable, but neither are they trivial. A remaining task is to assess the prospects for overcoming them in some of the specific cases identified as needing further work.

For finance, the obstacles to data improvement are great, but the importance of the sector at least increases the chance that improvements will be forthcoming. The obstacles stem partly from conceptual problems peculiar to the sector. A major problem, alluded to earlier, lies in defining the boundaries between services, factor income, and capital gains. Business recordkeeping and government reporting systems that provide or require most items on a worldwide consolidated basis increase the difficulty of segregating the international transactions of multinational financial institutions or of disaggregating them by country, as is required for the analysis of trade in services. Finally, banks already have a heavy reporting load, and government agencies are reluctant to add to it. BEA and Federal Reserve staff have been consulting with major banks and other financial institutions in an effort to determine what information on financial services could be supplied and whether the best method of developing additional information is likely to involve additional survey work or intensification of efforts to produce estimates, or both.

In transportation, the major need is for information on transactions in international transportation that are not covered by balance of payments accounting conventions. As noted earlier, these transactions include U.S. carriers' receipts for carriage of U.S. imports and foreign carriers' receipts for carriage of U.S. exports. They also include similar transactions in passenger transportation, most of which is accounted for by air transport. The domestic carriers' receipts can be estimated using existing information available from the Census Bureau. Those of foreign carriers are not available from existing sources. It has been extremely difficult in the past to obtain reliable information from surveys of these carriers, and it would be difficult to obtain additional information from them. Probably the best that could be expected is that rough estimates might be made using indirect methods in conjunction with existing information.

Disaggregation of establishment transactions by type of service should probably be regarded as a long-term goal. Additional information cannot be obtained without imposing further burden on respondents, and the government would face added processing costs. One possible solution would be for the information by type of service to be requested only on benchmark surveys, which are conducted every five years. (A similar approach has been used with respect to data on U.S. merchandise trade reported on BEA's benchmark and annual surveys of direct investment; product detail is requested on benchmark surveys, but not on the annual surveys.)

Developing information on local purchases of services by affiliates is probably not feasible, particularly if the information requires a breakdown by type of service. Companies usually find purchases data difficult to report and do not ordinarily maintain their records in a way that would permit purchases to be reported by type of service. Insight into typical patterns of purchases might best be obtained through case studies of particular companies, rather than through surveys of large numbers of firms.

The frequency of reporting of statistics on services trade will probably never match that available for merchandise. Because services (unlike goods shipments) are not accompanied by customs documentation as transactions occur, statistics must be secured in other ways, mainly from periodic surveys of companies engaged in international transactions. In some cases, other types of information, such as might be provided by trade associations, is used instead.[26] Data on merchandise trade are compiled on a monthly basis through the use of customs documentation, but it is not realistic to expect surveys on services to be conducted with the same frequency. Most nonsurvey information is available no more frequently than annually. Thus, the best that can be expected is probably annual or, in some cases, quarterly data.

6.6 Conclusions

The efforts to improve U.S. statistics on trade in services during most of the last decade have resulted in a lengthy list of improvements: new surveys have been introduced and existing ones improved; transactions in some services have begun to be estimated using indirect methods; an international price program has been instituted; information on establishment transactions has been developed; and the legal basis for data collection has been improved. In the absence of these improvements, current estimates of both U.S. sales and purchases of services would be significant understatements.

In addition to providing a more accurate statistical profile of services trade, the data-improvement efforts have helped to focus attention on the manner in which business in services is conducted internationally. As a consequence, the concept of international trade in services is becoming better understood, and more detailed and pertinent information is becoming available. Although progress is relatively slow and statistics on trade in services are in their infancy, the conceptual framework is in place and should facilitate further progress.

The data-improvement efforts in the United States are being followed with interest by the rest of the world. Progress in this country will help spur other countries to develop better data on their own services trade.

Appendix A
Summary of Improvements

As summarized below, the improvements made to statistics on international services in recent years include not only the expansion in coverage evident in table 6.1, but also a number of other measures that have raised the quality of the data or provided types of information not reflected in the table.

---

26. In other countries, still other methods may be used, including compilations of foreign exchange requests by banks. The bank method is essentially unavailable in the United States, because of the absence of foreign exchange restrictions and the dollar's role as a key currency. A discussion of the various methods of data collection used worldwide can be found in International Monetary Fund, Working Party on the Statistical Discrepancy in World Current Account Balances (1987).

Mandatory authority for data collection. Mandatory authority for collecting data on trade in services was provided by the Trade and Tariff Act of 1984. The authority was provided by amending the International Investment Survey Act of 1976, which had provided authority to collect data on international investment, to include trade in services; the act was redesignated as the International Investment and Trade in Services Survey Act. A number of services surveys that had been voluntary were made mandatory under the amended act. As a result, the response rate to these surveys has increased, and the quality of the resulting statistics has improved. Because many firms have a policy of responding only to those requests for information for which a response is required by law, authority to require reporting has been essential to the success of new surveys.

Surveys of selected transactions with unaffiliated foreigners. One of the most pressing needs for improved statistics on services trade was in the area of miscellaneous cross-border transactions with unaffiliated foreigners. While transactions with affiliated foreigners had been collected for some time in surveys of direct investment, and specialized surveys of transactions with unaffiliated foreigners were conducted for a few services of longstanding importance, there was a variety of services (mainly business and professional services) for which no vehicle for collecting information existed. A benchmark survey of U.S. services transactions with unaffiliated foreigners for 1986 was conducted to close as many of the gaps in information as was practical to attempt in a single survey. In general, the services covered by the survey were those sold or purchased by businesses; thus, the survey did not cover such items as expenditures by individual students or medical patients. Also, the survey did not cover transportation, banking or other financial services.

The survey covered U.S. sales and purchases of eighteen types of services, most of which had not been reported previously.[27] An annual survey has been instituted to keep the results up to date between benchmark surveys, which are taken at five-year intervals. It covers the same eighteen services, but lacks certain detail that was collected on the benchmark survey.[28]

---

27. The services are: advertising; computer and data-processing services; data-base and other information services; telecommunications; research, development, and testing services; management, consulting, and public relations services; legal services; industrial engineering; industrial maintenance, repair, installation, and training; agricultural services; management of health-care facilities; accounting, auditing, and bookkeeping services; educational and training services; mailing, reproduction, and commercial art; personnel supply services; sports and performing arts; primary insurance (purchases only); and construction, engineering, architectural, and mining services (purchases only). Sales of the services marked as "purchases only" are collected in specialized surveys sent to firms that sell such services. The results of the benchmark survey are summarized in Whichard (1988a).

28. Specifically, the benchmark survey collected information on gross income of advertising agencies, as well as the gross billings measure that represents U. S. sales of advertising services, and three types of services in which policymakers and others have shown particular interest (telecommunications, computer and data-processing services, and data-base and other information

Development of information on establishment transactions. Initial efforts to identify data needs in the area of services trade were directed at cross-border transactions. However, it soon became obvious that for many services a more common channel of delivery was through establishment transactions. Unlike most countries, whose statistical systems were set up to provide information only on cross-border transactions, the United States also possessed, in the form of surveys that obtained financial and operating statistics for direct investment enterprises, a vehicle for collecting information on establishment transactions. Benchmark surveys, usually conducted once very five years, had existed for some time for both inward and outward direct investment. In 1977, an annual survey of U.S. affiliates of foreign companies was instituted. A similar survey was instituted in 1983 for U.S. parent companies and their foreign affiliates.[29]

Although financial and operating information was first provided on an annual basis for inward investment, surveys of outward investment were the first to focus particularly on services. They did so, beginning with the 1982 benchmark survey, by requesting that sales or gross operating revenues be disaggregated between sales of goods and sales of services. The latter were identified based on their association with specified industry groups (see note to table 6.2). For U.S. parents, sales of services were further disaggregated according to whether they were to a U.S. or a foreign person and whether the person was or was not a foreign affiliate of the U.S. parent. For majority-owned foreign affiliates, sales of services were disaggregated according to whether they were to persons in the country of the affiliate, to U.S. persons, or to persons in other countries. In each case, sales were further disaggregated between sales to affiliated persons (i.e., to the U.S. parent or its other foreign affiliates) and sales to unaffiliated persons.

Similar information began to be collected for U.S. affiliates of foreign firms beginning with the 1987 benchmark survey of foreign direct investment in the United States. However, as a result of the experience gained with the survey of U.S. direct investment abroad, an additional refinement was introduced to obtain a more precise measurement of services sold by finance and insurance companies. For such companies, income from investments is ordinarily included in operating revenues along with revenues from the performance of services. On the survey of U.S. direct investment abroad, this income had been included in sales of services because it had to be allocated to either goods or services and was related to activities in a service industry. In the 1987 sur-

---

services) were further subdivided on the benchmark survey. The annual survey only collects the billings measure for advertising and does not subdivide the other three services.

29. Financial and operating data had been collected for outward investment in earlier years, but there had been no annual survey for the years immediately preceding 1982. Balance of payments-type data on both inward and outward direct investment (i.e., on transactions between parents and affiliates) have been collected quarterly for many years.

vey of foreign direct investment in the United States, a separate category was provided for investment income included in gross operating revenues, in order to make the sales-of-services category more closely correspond to the performance of services. This change is being carried over to the surveys of U.S. direct investment abroad beginning with the 1989 benchmark survey.

Survey of foreign contract operations. Beginning in 1983, BEA's annual survey of foreign contract operations (which then mainly covered, and which has since been restricted to, construction, architectural, engineering, and mining services) was expanded to permit recording of transactions on a gross basis. In addition to data previously collected on net U.S. receipts, information is requested on gross income or operating revenues (the measure of U.S. sales comparable to that collected for other types of services), merchandise exports included in gross income, and foreign outlays or expenses.[30] In 1987, the survey was further expanded to include a question on new contracts awarded during the year.

Tourism and travel in-flight survey. In the fourth quarter of 1982, the U.S. Travel and Tourism Administration of the U.S. Department of Commerce instituted an in-flight survey of non-U.S. residents departing from the United States. Collection of information from U.S. residents began in January 1983. These surveys provide estimates of total expenditures, disaggregated by type of purchase, such as lodging, transportation, meals, entertainment, and gifts. Most of the resulting information is sold on a subscription basis, mainly to businesses and to tourism-promotion agencies of state, local, and foreign governments. The data have recently begun to be used in estimating the travel and passenger-fares accounts of the U.S. balance of payments. They replace data from a more limited BEA survey that was discontinued.

Greater use of gross recording methods. Historically, estimates of a number of services have been provided only on a net basis, and thus total sales and purchases have been obscured. Recently, gross estimates have begun to be made instead. One example of this, involving construction and related services, has already been noted. The other items involve services transactions between affiliated parties, including both royalties and license fees and other services. For a given type of direct investment (U.S. abroad or foreign in the United States), purchases (or U.S. payments) of services were netted against sales (receipts) before sample data were expanded to universe estimates, with

---

30. For construction, a large share of value added is typically accounted for by local factors of production (e.g., labor and materials). Information on payments to these factors is needed for balance of payments accounting purposes and for purposes of analyzing impacts on host-country economies. Although local outlays or expenses also occur in connection with other services involving travel by the producer to another country, they are less likely to be significant, and it is only in the survey of construction and related services that an attempt has been made to collect statistical information on them.

the result that only net sales or purchases were available. Because the modern multinational enterprise often contains specialized affiliates to perform specific functions for the entire global enterprise, services often flow not only from the parent to the affiliate, but also in the other direction. Consequently, the net figures did not provide a good guide to the two-way flow of trade.

Census of Service Industries. The 1982 Census of Service Industries was the first such census to include questions on sales to nonresidents. The questions appeared on forms for four industries: computer and data-processing services; management, consulting, and public relations services; equipment renting and leasing services; and engineering, architectural, and surveying services. In the 1987 census, the group of industries covered by these questions was expanded to include four additional industries: advertising, accounting, legal services, and research and development.

BLS International Price Program. The difficulties of developing price information for services are well known and stem in large measure from the difficulties in measuring services output.[31] Until recently, such price information as existed for traded services took the form of broad deflators used for national income accounting purposes and not intended, or able, to provide information on individual services.

In 1984, a special task force was formed in the Office of Prices and Living Conditions of the Bureau of Labor Statistics to explore the possibility of developing indexes for services applicable to producer prices and international trade. The initial attempts to construct indexes have mainly involved transportation, because of its importance in trade, the availability of data with which to construct sample frames, and the relative ease with which the service can be defined. (An index has also been developed for electricity.) Several quar-

---

31. Hill (1977, p. 315) summarizes the situation thusly:

There is little understanding about the nature of the physical units in which most services should be quantified, and consequently their prices are also vague and ill defined. Indeed, a price, perhaps the most fundamental concept in economics, is meaningless unless the physical unit to which it refers can be identified and specified. It is a sad reflection on the state of economics that there is so little perception of the physical characteristics of most services, that the outputs of major industries such as health and education are usually measured by their inputs, thereby making the measures useless for most analytic purposes.

Kenessey (1989, p. 3), however, has suggested that the difficulties in measuring services output may have been exaggerated:

The very size and diversity of the service sector make output measurement a complex task, but by no means an impossible one. Both the goods and services sectors contain unique activities that defy easy quantification. But the bulk of economic activity in most divisions of the SIC is comprised of mass produced or well standardized goods or services. The bulk of legal work after all, is not in leveraged buyouts, but in real estate closings, divorces, wills, and criminal litigations, which differ from case to case, but can be defined as items of output fairly closely. The same is true for large segments of medical services, banking, and several other services industries.

terly indexes are currently being published.[32] Additional transportation indexes, for liner freight, air freight, and port fees, are under development. Another service sector, communications, is under consideration as an area for future work.

Revision of classification systems. Rapid changes in technology in areas such as computer and communication services have made it difficult for classification systems to keep pace with the range of services traded. However, several developments relating to classification of services have recently occurred at the national and international levels. They include adding codes for services on survey forms and expanding or modifying classification systems.

One of the earliest developments occurred when, in revising industry codes for direct investment surveys in preparation for its 1982 benchmark survey of U.S. direct investment abroad, BEA added about a dozen new codes for services. When in 1987 the U.S. Standard Industrial Classification (SIC) was revised, particular attention was given to services. The new SIC provides specific codes for many types of services, such as on-line information retrieval services and computer-integrated systems design, that had hardly been thought of in 1972, when the previous version was released.[33] In preparation for the 1987 benchmark survey of foreign direct investment in the United States, BEA revised its industry coding system for international surveys to reflect the new SIC categories and again expanded the number of industry codes for services.[34] In 1987, BEA revised its survey on transactions in nonfinancial intangible assets to include detail on the type of asset involved; seven categories were provided, compared to the two that had existed previously.[35]

32. Four quarterly series of price indexes are published for international air-passenger fares. Two are for receipts of *U.S. carriers* from: foreign residents on international flights, computed on a balance of payments basis; and all passengers on international flights, regardless of nationality. These series have been published since the fourth quarter of 1986. Two additional series are for payments to *foreign carriers* from: U.S. residents on international flights, computed on a balance of payments basis; and all passengers on international flights, regardless of residency. These series have been published since the second quarter of 1988.

Two quarterly indexes are published for crude-oil tanker transportation: an import crude-oil tanker freight index, measuring changes in rates actually paid for foreign operators, computed on a balance of payments basis; and an inbound crude-oil tanker freight index, which tracks changes in tanker freight rates paid for all inbound crude-oil shipments regardless of nationality of vessel operator. These series have been published since the second quarter of 1987.

Regional subindexes are published for all of these series.

33. In the absence of specific codes, the newer activities were relegated to residual catchall categories or assigned on an ad hoc basis to whatever categories seemed most appropriate.

34. It is not always possible for BEA to translate increases in the number of codes into the provision of more detailed published data, both because of space constraints and, more fundamentally, because of the legal requirement to protect the confidentiality of company-specific data.

35. No comprehensive classification scheme could be found to provide guidance on the categories. Categories were provided for rights related to: industrial processes and products; books, records, audio tapes, etc.; trademarks; performances and events prerecorded on motion picture film and TV tape; and broadcast and recording of live performances and events. A sixth category covered business-format franchise fees. The remaining category was a residual under which transactions in any other intangible assets or rights could be reported.

On the international level, no product-based classification system has existed until very recently, when the Central Product Classification (CPC), prepared under United Nations auspices, was adopted on a provisional basis. Although certain aspects of the CPC are controversial (as reflected in its provisional status), it does represent an initial attempt to provide international standards for a product-based classification of services. The International Monetary Fund has been considering expanding its list of standard components of balance of payments accounts to include more services items. Discussions to date have used the CPC as a point of departure, although it will probably not be possible for balance of payments accounts to achieve complete consistency with the CPC.[36]

Medical services. In June 1987, estimates of U.S. medical services receipts were introduced into the U.S. balance of payments accounts. The estimates are for services performed at nonprofit and state and local government hospitals in the United States for foreigners who travel to the United States for treatment. The estimates did not require a new survey, but were made based on consultations with administrators of hospitals likely to provide services to foreigners (major medical centers, university hospitals, and hospitals in areas frequented by foreign tourists). Estimates of U.S. payments for medical services rendered abroad are not available, but these payments probably are much smaller than the receipts.

Educational services. In June 1989, estimates of U.S. receipts from foreign students in the United States and expenditures of U.S. students abroad were introduced into the U.S. balance of payments accounts. The estimates are made by BEA using information from the Institute for International Education and other sources. The first year covered by the estimates is 1981.

Primary insurance. Beginning with the survey for 1987, BEA revised a survey that had previously covered only international transactions in reinsurance to cover sales of primary insurance as well. (U.S. purchases of primary insurance appear on the benchmark and annual surveys of selected services transactions with unaffiliated foreigners.)

---

36. There are several reasons why complete consistency with the CPC is unlikely to be achieved. First, in comparison with worldwide production and consumption of services, international trade is skewed toward certain services that are more tradable than others. Thus, an hierarchy (e.g., based on numbers of digits) suitable for classification of services generally would, if applied to international trade, give too much prominence to some services, yet slight others. Second, the CPC categorizes items according to type of *product* (including services), but certain types of balance of payments transactions—government and travel, in particular—are categorized by type of *consumer.* Finally, agreement by balance of payments compilers on some of the more controversial aspects of the CPC, such as its treatment of manufacturing-type "processing" activities as a service (see discussion in section 6.4) may not be possible.

Domestic services. The availability of information on domestic services activity helps to place international trade data in context. A number of developments in this area have occurred in recent years. The Census Bureau has expanded its quinquennial economic censuses and its annual sample surveys to cover a greater number of services. The expansion responds to the growing interest in services and in some cases substitutes for statistical programs of other government agencies that were cut back or discontinued as a result of deregulation (Aanestad 1988). Also, the Federal Reserve has recently developed experimental output indexes for services, similar to its indexes of industrial production (Kenessey 1989). Leading, coincident, and composite indicators for the service sector have been developed privately, under the auspices of the Center for International Business Cycle Research at Columbia University (Moore and Layton 1988). These and other efforts to improve statistics on domestic services activity will help provide a more complete statistical depiction of that activity and be useful in drawing comparisons with statistics on international trade in services.

References

Aanestad, James M. 1988. Statistical Data on Services. In *United States Service Industries Handbook,* ed. Wray O. Candilis, 155–71. New York: Praeger Publishers.
Ascher, Bernard. 1988. Improvements in Trade Data on Services Gain Momentum. *The Service Economy* 2 (July):9–11.
———. 1989. Statistics on International Trade in Services: The Perspective of a Data User. Paper prepared for first meeting, Panel on Foreign Trade Statistics of the National Research Council Committee on National Statistics. Washington, D.C. June.
Ascher, Bernard, and Obie G. Whichard. 1987. Improving Services Trade Data. In *Emergence of the Service Economy,* ed. Orio Giarini, 255–81. Oxford: Pergamon Press.
Bhagwati, Jagdish. 1984. Splintering and Disembodiment of Services and Developing Nations. *The World Economy* 7(June):133–44.
Brock, William E. 1982. A Simple Plan for Negotiating on Trade in Services. *The World Economy* 5(November):229–40.
Cloney, Gordon J. II. 1983. A Review of Problems Relating to Trade Policy Use of Balance of Payments Data Describing Trade in Services. Discussion paper for the Working Party on Services of the International Chamber of Commerce. February.
Devons, Ely. 1961. World Trade in Invisibles. *Lloyds Bank Review,* n.s., 60 (April):37–50.
DiLullo, Anthony J., 1981. Service Transactions in the U.S. International Accounts, 1970–80. *Survey of Current Business* 61(November):29–46.
Economic Consulting Services, Inc. 1981. The International Operations of U.S. Service Industries: Current Data Collection and Analysis. Report prepared for the U.S. Departments of State and Commerce and the Office of the U.S. Trade Representative, Washington, D.C.
Economic Report of the President. 1987. Washington, D.C.: Government Printing Office.

Feketekuty, Geza. 1988. *International Trade in Services*. Washington, D.C.: Ballinger (American Enterprise Institute).

Hill, T. P. 1977. On Goods and Services. *Review of Income and Wealth* 23 (December):315–38.

International Monetary Fund. 1977. *Balance of Payments Manual*. 4th ed. Washington, D.C.

———. Working Party on the Statistical Discrepancy in World Current Account Balances. 1987. *Final Report*. Washington, D.C.

Kenessey, Zoltan E. 1989. The Development of a Monthly Service Output Index. *The Service Economy* 3(April):1–4.

Kravis, Irving B., and Robert E. Lipsey. 1988. Production and Trade in Services by U.S. Multinational Companies. National Bureau of Economic Research Working Paper no. 2615.

Krueger, Russell C. 1981. U.S. International Transactions, First Quarter 1981. *Survey of Current Business* 61 (June): 31–71.

Lederer, Evelyn Parrish, Walther Lederer, and Robert L. Sammons. 1982. International Services Transactions of the United States: Proposals for Improvement in Data Collection. Report prepared for the U.S. Departments of State and Commerce and the Office of the U.S. Trade Representative, Washington, D.C.

McCulloch, Rachel. 1987. International Competition in Services. National Bureau of Economic Research Working Paper no. 2235.

Moore, Geoffrey H., and Allan P. Layton. 1988. New Indicators for Service Sector Fill a Big Gap in U.S. Economic Information; Suggest Slowdown in Services Growth. *The Service Economy* 2 (July): 1–4.

Office of the U.S. Trade Representative. 1983. *U.S. National Study on Trade in Services*. Washington, D.C.: Government Printing Office.

Organisation for Economic Cooperation and Development. 1989. *OECD Countries' International Trade in Services, 1980–87*. Paris.

Pizer, Samuel, and Frederick Cutler. 1957. *U.S. Investments in the Latin American Economy*. Washington, D.C.: Government Printing Office.

Sapir, Andre. 1982. Trade in Services: Policy Issues for the Eighties. *Columbia Journal of World Business* (Fall):77–83.

Sauvant, Karl P., and Zbigniew Zimney. 1985. FDI and TNCs in Services. *CTC Reporter* 20 (Autumn): 24–28.

Shanahan, Eileen. 1985. Measuring the Service Economy. *New York Times*, October 27.

Shelp, Ronald K. 1981. *Beyond Industrialization: Ascendance of the Global Service Economy*. New York: Praeger Publishers.

Sinai, Allen. 1988. The Services Trade Balance: How Much is Really Services? *The Service Economy* 2 (July): 18–24.

Stalson, Helena. 1985. U.S. Trade Policy and International Service Transactions. In *Managing the Service Economy: Prospects and Problems,* ed. Robert P. Inman, 161–78. Cambridge: Cambridge University Press.

Stern, Robert M., and Bernard M. Hoekman. 1987. Issues and Data Needs for GATT Negotiations on Services. *The World Economy* 10(March):39–60.

United Nations, Statistical Office. 1968. *A System of National Accounts*. Studies in Methods, series F, no. 2, rev. 3.

U.S. Congress. House. Subcommittee on Commerce, Transportation, and Tourism of the Committee on Energy and Commerce. 1983. *Hearings on H.R.794, H.R.1571, H.R.2203, General trade policy.* Statements of Lionel H. Olmer, undersecretary for International Trade, Department of Commerce, Geza Feketekuty, Assistant U.S. Trade Representative for Policy Development and Services, Office of the U.S. Trade

Representative, and Bruce P. Malashevich, Vice President, Economic Consulting Services, Inc. Washington, D.C. 98th Cong., 1st sess. 66.

U.S. Congress, Office of Technology Assessment. 1986. *Trade in Services: Exports and Foreign Revenues—Special Report.* OTA-ITE-316. Washington, D.C.: Government Printing Office, September.

————. 1987. *International Competition in Services.* OTA-ITE-328. Washington, D.C.: Government Printing Office.

Vernon, Raymond. 1971–72. A Skeptic Looks at the Balance of Payments. *Foreign Policy* Winter:52–65.

Whichard, Obie G. 1984. U.S. International Trade and Investment in Services: Data Needs and Availability. U.S. Department of Commerce, Bureau of Economic Analysis Staff Paper no. 41.

————. 1987. U.S. Sales of Services to Foreigners. *Survey of Current Business* 67 (January):22–41.

————. 1988a. International Services: New Information on U.S. Transactions with Unaffiliated Foreigners. *Survey of Current Business* 68 (October):27–34.

————. 1988b. International Services Operations of U.S. Multinational Companies. In *United States Service Industry Handbook,* ed. Wray O. Candilis, 127–54. New York: Praeger Publishers.

————. 1988c. United States: Data on Sales of Services by TNCs. *CTC Reporter* 25 (Spring):56–59.

Comment   Samuel Pizer

Much of the discussion in this paper is concerned with the issues and requirements of GATT negotiations on services. This is separable from the issue of achieving better statistics for international transactions in services, as defined for use in the balance of payments accounts, and the two issues should not become confused. In particular, international *trade* in services has a specific meaning, and does not include sales by affiliates in other countries. The latter may be relevant for market analyses, however.

As noted in the paper, there has been a lot of progress recently in improving the coverage of services in the U.S. balance of payments accounts. Few other countries have gone much beyond the more or less standard items, and the accuracy of the available data certainly needs improvement. International agencies are heading toward a standard expanded list of services to be used in the balance of payments context. It will be less detailed, probably, than a list suitable for the System of National Accounts (SNA), primarily because the latter involve many services that are not significant in international trade. These lists tend to settle definition questions de facto.

Quite distinct from the balance of payments data are data on the transactions of affiliates established in foreign countries. There are some questions about the definition of "affiliate," but when the IMF definitions are followed

Samuel Pizer is a consultant at the International Monetary Fund and former adviser at the Federal Reserve Board.

the distinction between an international transaction and a transaction by an affiliate is clear in most cases. Where there are questions about residence they usually involve such activities as construction, transportation, offshore drilling, which are not often large in the scheme of things. In any case, for the balance of payments compiler, the net result for the international accounts is what counts most, rather than the distribution among particular items in the accounts.

Measurement of the sales or purchases of services by foreign affiliates is not to be confused with international transactions of the home country, as it sometimes is in critiques of the accuracy of balance of payments data. Only the United States has even made a beginning in collecting data on transactions of affiliates in foreign markets, and there is scant evidence of interest in other countries in monitoring the activities of foreign affiliates of their companies. However, with respect to inward investment, most countries are interested in the activities of foreign firms in their home market; but up to now this has referred mainly to the manufacturing sector and petroleum, not to most services. In this situation, negotiations will probably have to get along without these data—at least on a global scale.

Because many services cannot readily be traded between residents and nonresidents, they depend on the establishment of a permanent affiliate to reach the local market. For these types of services, the main issue seems to be freedom to form such establishments and to have them treated in the same way as other national enterprises. This is no different from the issues raised by international direct investment in general, and presumably the same set of principles is involved. On the other hand, these services have many quite distinct operational differences, and presumably these will require some specialized rule-making. Coming back to the theme of this conference, these considerations suggest that the development of global statistics is not a prerequisite for agreement on principles, and that, on the other hand, a great deal of specialized information may be necessary for negotiations affecting particular kinds of services. It may be that pushing for development of such data in the context of the balance of payments accounts is not the best procedure.

Another issue of interest in international services has been the apparent attempts by some countries to interfere with the free interchange of information, especially in the newer technological forms. At one level, this is an issue of principle: most would agree that such interference is wrong. At the level of measurement it might be useful to have more information on the value and volume of such information flows, as well as much more precise definitions of what such information consists of. That is, we need to know what is to be measured that is not already captured elsewhere in the international accounts (for example, intercompany payments for such services, or rentals paid for entertainment material or news transmissions are already entered into the accounts of most countries).

The paper identifies a number of well-known problem areas and borderline cases, and suggests some steps to be taken to achieve improvements. Fortunately, most of the special cases mentioned do not involve significant payments or receipts for most countries, and in some cases the issue will probably be dealt with as conventions are adopted by international statistical agencies. As to the suggested solutions of some of these data shortcomings, they may demand too much in the way of compliance by U.S. companies or of expenditures of scarce talent and money by the U.S. government. Even so, possibilities for improvement are far more realistic in the United States than in other countries, where resistance to questionnaires is even greater.

Under the prevailing conditions, it is remarkable that the U.S. data in this field have advanced to their present situation—which seems to be rather good coverage for purposes of the balance of payments accounts.

7   Evolving Patterns of Trade and Investment in Services

Bernard M. Hoekman and Robert M. Stern

7.1   Introduction

The purpose of our paper is to discuss and document the usefulness and limitations of existing data on international trade and investment in services. We concentrate especially on the conceptual and measurement issues involved in interpreting and trying to use the available data on international services transactions, and, in the process, identify gaps in the data that need attention.

We begin in section 7.2 with a discussion of the distinguishing characteristics of services, what is meant by trade and investment in services, and what economic theory has to say about how international services transactions may evolve through time. In section 7.3, we set forth a number of hypotheses concerning the evolution of international trade in goods and services and then examine and interpret the available data in the light of these hypotheses. Section 7.4 proceeds along the same lines in analyzing patterns of international investment in goods and services. We then discuss the reliability and accuracy of our main empirical findings regarding trade and investment in goods and services in section 7.5, calling attention to the limitations of existing data on

Bernard M. Hoekman is an economist in the Economic Research and Analysis Unit of the General Agreement on Tariffs and Trade (GATT), Geneva. Robert M. Stern is professor of economics and public policy in the Department of Economics and Institute of Public Policy Studies at The University of Michigan, Ann Arbor.

This paper is based in part on a background study prepared for the 1989 edition of *International Trade*, the annual report of the research department of the GATT Secretariat. Financial assistance was provided in part by a grant from the Ford Foundation to the Institute of Public Policy Studies at the University of Michigan for a program of research on trade policy. The authors are indebted to Patricia Crémoux for computational assistance and compilation of many of the tables, to Judith Jackson for editorial and typing assistance, and to Sam Pizer and other conference participants for comments. Helpful comments on an earlier version of the paper were also made by Alan V. Deardorff, James Levinsohn, and participants in the Research Seminar in International Economics at The University of Michigan. The views expressed in this paper are the authors' and should not be attributed to the GATT Secretariat.

international transactions in services. Section 7.6 turns to the type of improvements that are required for further analysis to be feasible. Some concluding remarks are made in section 7.7.

7.2 Conceptual and Measurement Issues

7.2.1 What is Meant by International Trade and Investment in Services?

We can say that international trade in goods or services occurs when there are cross-border transactions carried out between economic units (i.e., consumers, firms, governments) that reside in different countries. This is in contrast to production and sale of goods or services abroad that involves a change in residency from one country to another of certain assets or factors of production. While this distinction seems reasonably straightforward, in practice problems nonetheless arise when it comes to distinguishing cross-border trade from production by foreign-owned firms and separating international transactions in goods from international transactions in services.

Conventions play a large role in the distinction between trade and foreign production. Usually a one-year criterion is employed, in that factors are only considered to change their residence if they move abroad for longer than one year. However, this is not a uniform practice. Once firms are considered to have changed their residence, their sales are no longer registered in the home country's balance of payments.

Turning to the difference between goods and services, there is no generally accepted comprehensive definition of what constitutes a service. Despite efforts by national accounting experts in recent years to arrive at a definition, no acceptable definition has emerged. The general problem is that no one criterion suffices to distinguish goods from services.[1] One could take the view that from an economic perspective what really matters is that products are being produced and sold, and that efforts to break down products into goods and services thus may not be very meaningful. It is interesting to note in this connection that such a "product-based" approach is the one that has been taken by the economic statisticians in designing the new Central Product Classification (CPC) system; it focuses on the universe of products and makes no distinction between goods and services.[2] This reflects their considered judgment of the impracticality of measuring goods and services transactions separately.

The nature of technological change and corporate structure also undermines the practicality of distinguishing goods from services. Bhagwati (1984) has

---

1. See, for discussion, Drechsler and Hoffman (1988).
2. United Nations (1989). The CPC is a classification of products, as opposed to activities. It allows for much more detailed data to be collected as compared to an activity-based classification such as the International Standard Industrial Classification (ISIC). The CPC distinguishes over 600 service products, compared to only 130 activities in the most recently revised ISIC.

emphasized the ways in which the specialized activities of firms are "splintered" off—services from goods and goods from services. Thus, depending on the level of aggregation for recording transactions and particularly the time span involved, it may be quite difficult to distinguish goods from services and vice versa at the firm or industry level. This difficulty may become more pronounced, especially if services that previously were purchased at arm's length from other firms come to be subsumed within the firm.

The implication of the foregoing discussion is that there is unfortunately no airtight way of identifying and accounting for international transactions in services per se, and doing so may not be very useful. Whatever systems or classifications may be devised are bound to be somewhat arbitrary. It remains the case nonetheless that products with "service" characteristics are often considered to be of interest in their own right, and that certain conventions may be adopted in an effort to distinguish services from goods. In what follows we will take a "residual" approach, in that services will be considered to constitute categories 6–9 of the International Standard Industrial Classification (ISIC): wholesale and retail trade, hotels and restaurants; transport, storage, and communications; finance, real estate, and business services; and community, social, and personal services.

7.2.2 Characterizing International Transactions in Services

In Stern and Hoekman (1988a), we called attention to two distinguishing characteristics of services: production and consumption of services have to take place simultaneously, implying that services usually cannot be stored; and services tend to be intangible. We also noted that services can: be complementary to trade in goods; substitute for trade in goods; or be unrelated to goods. All of these characteristics have implications for how trade can occur.

Because of their intangibility and nonstorability, in order to become tradable services have to be applied to (embodied in) objects, information flow, or persons. Available means of "transportation" must then be employed to move the objects, information, or persons from one country to another (Feketekuty 1988, p. 28). Thus, for trade to occur, the means of transporting the services often have to be able and permitted to cross national frontiers. As a consequence, international transactions in services appear to be more complex conceptually than international transactions in goods.[3] Elsewhere, typologies have been developed characterizing the manner in which trade in services may occur. Usually these break down international transactions in services into three types: cross-border or separated trade analogous to trade in goods; demander-located services, which are transactions requiring the movement of the producer to the location of the demander; and provider-located services,

3. In particular, the issue of market access is much more important for services than for goods. In the sphere of merchandise trade, transportation up to the frontier may be enough to sell a good. In services this is often not sufficient, and either the means of transportation or the provider (factor) may need to be able to cross the border.

which are transactions implying movement of the consumer to the location of the provider (see Sampson and Snape 1985 and Stern and Hoekman 1987).

Such typologies are helpful in that they focus attention on the crucial role that technology plays in the tradability of services. Depending on the type of service, trade may or may not be technically feasible. To the extent that it is, there may be one or more avenues available to firms. These include trade in what Hirsch (1989) has called "service-intensive" goods, embodiment in cross-border information flows (separated services), and movement of provider or demander. We will have more to say on this topic below.

7.2.3 Possible Determinants of the Evolution of Trade and Investment in Services

In trying to understand the evolution of international transactions in services, it is helpful to begin by reviewing the factors that shape the role of services in a country's domestic economic structure.

Broadly speaking, the demand for both goods and services will depend upon the level and rate of increase of per capita real incomes and relative prices. The latter will be a function of changes in factor productivity (technological change), differential income elasticities, and changes in economic structure (urbanization, labor-force participation) and business practices. As services are often said to lag behind goods-producing sectors in terms of productivity improvement and to have income elasticities of demand greater than unity, one might expect that the share of spending on services (reflecting both final and intermediate demand) would rise with increases in per capita income.[4] It is noteworthy in this connection that the share of services in total output and employment especially tends to be higher in the industrialized countries as compared to the developing countries. This may be due in part to differences in the ways that services are measured in the industrialized and developing countries, in particular the difficulties of taking institutional and structural differences into account. But even if allowance is made for these intercountry variations, the importance of services appears to rise with levels of development and per capita incomes.

Table 7.1 records the percentage breakdown of gross domestic product (GDP) measured on a value-added basis in current prices for three major sectors—agriculture (including forestry and fishery), industry (mining, manufacturing, construction, and utilities), and services (wholesale and retail trade; hotels and restaurants; transport, storage, and communication; finance, real estate, and business services; and personal, social, and community services)—for the major industrialized and developing countries and other regions for 1965 and 1986. For convenience, when available, manufacturing is

---

4. As suggested originally by Baumol (1967) and Fuchs (1968). While the service sector as a whole tends to lag behind goods-producing sectors in terms of productivity growth, certain service activities have experienced very large increases in productivity. As Baumol (1985) has emphasized, there are both "stagnant" and "progressive" service activities.

also reported separately. It can be seen that most countries experienced an increase in the relative importance of services in total output.[5] In most industrialized countries the counterpart of this rise was a decline in the shares of agriculture and industry. In contrast, many developing countries experienced a simultaneous increase in the share of both industry and services. However, the trend in these countries is not uniform, and the share of services declined in a number of economies.

The relative importance of services in terms of employment can be seen in table 7.2 to have increased dramatically in the major industrialized and developing countries in the post-1950 period. In several of the industrialized countries, the share of services in total employment is currently greater than 60 percent. Reasons for the increases in the employment share of services include lagging productivity in services and structural changes such as increased participation rates of female labor, increased urbanization, technological changes, and increased specialization that have led to new service activities, expansion of part-time employment opportunities, and the growth of government services.[6] The relative importance of employment in services tends to be less in developing economies as compared to the industrialized countries.

Table 7.3 provides information on the average contribution of various service activities to GDP in the industrialized and the developing countries. Wholesale and retail trade, hotels, and restaurants tend to contribute most to total value added, followed by finance and business services, transport and communications, and social services. The major difference between developed and developing countries is the relative importance of agriculture and government.

A comparison of low and high income countries shows producer services (finance, insurance, real estate, professional services such as engineering, consulting, and accounting, as well as cleaning and maintenance) to be about three times more important in the high income countries (Park and Chan 1989). This holds for both services- and goods-producing sectors: the relative importance of producer service inputs is twice as large for distribution (transport and wholesale and retail trade), and three times as large for personal, social, and community services in high-income countries, as compared to low-income countries. Limited time-series evidence for specific countries supports the conclusion that producer services tend to become relatively more important over time. Green (1985) has demonstrated that arm's length expenditures on producer services as a proportion of the value of manufacturing

---

5. Data on regional and country groupings in this and subsequent tables are weighted averages of all the countries in a given group, not just those reported separately in the tables. In cases where country data were not reported or not available, the countries were given a zero weight in the groupings. This will of course tend to bias the weighted average downward, making it difficult to make comparisons among groupings and between years.

6. These issues have been analyzed at length in the literature. For a summary discussion, see Stern and Hoekman (1988b).

Table 7.1   Distribution of GDP (Valued Added) by Sector and Country or Region, 1965 and 1986

Country or Region	GDP (U.S. $ million) 1965	GDP (U.S. $ million) 1986	Agriculture (%) 1965	Agriculture (%) 1986	Industry (%) 1965	Industry (%) 1986	Manufacturing (%) 1965	Manufacturing (%) 1986	Services (%) 1965	Services (%) 1986
Industrialized Countries	1,373,360	10,451,880	5	3	40	35	29	NA	54	61
Australia	24,050	184,940	9	5	39	34	26	17	51	62
Austria	9,480	93,830	9	3	46	38	33	28	45	59
Canada	45,940	323,790	6	3	40	36	27	NA	53	61
European Community	455,220	3,354,430	7	4	44	38	NA	NA	49	59
Belgium	16,600	112,180	5	2	41	33	31	23	53	64
Denmark	8,940	68,820	8	6	36	28	23	20	55	66
France	99,660	724,200	8	4	39	34	28	NA	53	63
West Germany	114,790	891,990	4	2	53	40	40	32	43	58
Greece	5,270	35,210	24	17	26	29	16	18	49	54
Ireland	2,340	21,910	20	14	30	45	NA	NA	50	41
Italy	72,150	599,920	11	5	41	39	23	22	48	56
Netherlands	19,890	175,330	7	4	44	34	32	18	49	62
Portugal	3,740	27,480	24	10	37	40	NA	NA	39	51
Spain	23,320	229,100	15	6	36	37	NA	27	49	56
United Kingdom	88,520	468,290	3	2	46	43	34	26	51	55
Finland	7,540	62,370	16	8	37	37	23	25	47	55
Japan	91,110	1,955,650	9	3	43	41	32	30	48	56
New Zealand	5,640	26,630	14	11	31	33	NA	NA	55	56
Norway	NA	69,780	8	4	33	41	21	14	59	56
Sweden	19,610	114,470	6	3	40	35	28	24	53	62
Switzerland	13,920	135,050	NA	NA	NA	NA	NA	NA	53	62
United States	701,670	4,185,490	3	2	38	31	28	20	59	67

Developing Countries									
East/South Asia	348,960	30	19	31	36	20	NA	38	46
China	151,723	40	24	29	38	NA	NA	31	38
Hong Kong	65,590	39	31	38	46	30	34	23	23
India	2,150	2	0	40	29	24	21	58	71
South Korea	46,260	47	32	22	29	15	19	31	39
Singapore	3,000	38	12	25	42	18	30	37	45
Taiwan	970	3	1	24	38	15	27	73	62
Latin America	2,803	22	8	35	51	NA	NA	43	41
Argentina	87,240	17	11	34	38	NA	NA	49	51
Brazil	16,500	17	13	42	44	33	31	42	44
Chile	19,450	19	11	33	39	26	28	48	50
Mexico	5,940	9	6	40	39	24	21	52	56
Venezuela	20,160	14	9	31	37	21	26	54	52
Middle East/North Africa	8,290	7	9	41	44	NA	23	52	54
Egypt	18,980	18	10	40	29	NA	NA	43	46
Saudi Arabia	4,550	29	20	27	50	NA	NA	45	51
Other Europe	2,300	8	4	60	39	9	9	31	46
Turkey	18,820	27	15	35	39	NA	NA	37	46
Yugoslavia	7,660	34	18	25	36	16	25	41	46
Subsaharan Africa	11,160	23	12	42	42	NA	NA	35	46
Senegal	26,440	45	36	19	25	9	10	37	36
Tanzania	810	25	22	18	27	14	17	56	51
Zaire	790	46	59	14	10	8	6	40	31
Nigeria	3,140	21	29	26	36	16	NA	53	35
South Africa	4,190	53	41	19	29	7	8	29	30
	10,540	10	6	42	46	23	22	48	49

Source: World Bank, *World Development Report*, 1988.
Note: NA = not available.

Table 7.2   **Distribution of Employment by Sector and Country or Region, 1950–1980**

Country or Region	Agriculture (%) 1950	Agriculture (%) 1965	Agriculture (%) 1980	Industry (%) 1950	Industry (%) 1965	Industry (%) 1980	Services (%) 1950	Services (%) 1965	Services (%) 1980
Industrialized Countries	NA	14	7	NA	38	35	NA	48	58
Australia	16	10	7	39	38	32	45	52	61
Austria	34	19	9	36	45	41	30	36	50
Canada	20	10	5	36	33	29	44	57	65
European Community	29	17	9	38	42	38	34	41	53
Belgium	12	6	3	51	46	36	37	48	61
Denmark	26	14	7	34	37	32	41	49	61
France	31	18	9	35	39	35	34	43	56
West Germany	23	11	6	43	48	44	34	41	50
Greece	55	47	31	19	24	29	26	29	40
Ireland	40	31	19	25	28	34	35	48	48
Italy	44	25	12	31	42	41	25	34	48
Netherlands	18	9	6	36	41	32	46	51	63
Portugal	50	38	26	24	30	37	26	32	38
Spain	50	34	17	25	35	37	25	32	46
United Kingdom	6	3	3	50	47	38	45	50	59
Finland	35	24	12	35	35	35	30	41	53
Japan	49	26	11	24	32	34	28	42	55
New Zealand	19	13	11	35	36	33	47	51	56
Norway	26	16	8	37	37	29	37	48	62
Sweden	21	11	6	41	43	33	38	46	62
Switzerland	17	9	6	46	49	39	37	41	55
United States	12	5	4	37	35	31	51	60	66

Developing Countries									
	NA	70	62	NA	12	16	NA	18	22
East/South Asia	83	75	69	6	13	16	11	13	15
China	88	81	74	5	8	14	7	11	12
Hong Kong	12	6	2	56	27	38	32	41	47
India	78	73	70	8	12	13	14	15	17
South Korea	77	55	36	6	15	27	17	30	37
Singapore	8	6	2	20	27	38	71	68	61
Taiwan	56	46	20	17	22	42	27	31	38
Latin America	53	44	32	20	22	26	27	34	42
Argentina	25	18	13	32	34	34	43	48	53
Brazil	60	49	31	17	20	27	23	31	42
Chile	34	27	17	30	29	25	36	44	58
Mexico	60	50	37	17	22	29	23	29	35
Venezuela	43	30	16	21	24	28	36	47	56
Middle East/North Africa	55	63	47	16	14	20	29	23	33
Egypt	60	55	46	13	15	20	27	30	34
Saudia Arabia	76	68	48	9	11	14	15	21	37
Other Europe	82	68	49	9	16	22	9	15	28
Turkey	87	75	58	6	11	17	7	14	25
Yugoslavia	73	57	32	14	26	33	13	17	34
Subsaharan Africa	84	79	75	6	8	9	10	13	16
Senegal	85	83	81	5	6	9	10	11	13
Tanzania	87	92	86	4	3	5	9	6	10
Zaire	27	82	72	7	9	13	6	9	16
Nigeria	77	72	68	8	10	12	15	18	20
South Africa	34	32	17	29	30	35	37	39	49

Source: International Labour Organization
Note: NA = not available.

Table 7.3   Average Percentage Share in GDP (Total Value Added) by Activity, 1980–84

Activity	Developed Countries	Developing Countries
Goods-related		
Agriculture, forestry, and fishing	6	16
Mining	3	8
Manufacturing	24	21
Electricity, gas, water	3	2
Construction	7	6
Total Goods	43	53
Services		
Wholesale and retail trade, hotels and restaurants	15	17
Transport and communications	7	6
Finance, insurance, real estate, business services	14	10
Community, social, and personal services	7	7
Subtotal market services	43	40
Government	14	7
Total services	57	47

Source: Calculated from data reprinted in United Nations, National Accounts Yearbook, 1988.

output increased about 20 percent on average in West Germany, Italy, and the United Kingdom between 1975 and 1981. In the recent past, most service subsectors have been growing faster than manufacturing output in the United States, but this is the case especially for producer services such as telecommunications, brokerage, business, and miscellaneous professional services (Adams and Siwaraksa 1987; Duchin 1988).

Possible reasons for the growth of producer services include the increasing scope for arm's length sourcing due to innovations in information technology, as well as increasing specialization and product differentiation, driven in part by emerging economies of scale and scope and in part by demand for a larger variety and higher quality of services. It is often hypothesized that an important change in business practices has occurred involving firms shifting from in-house to arm's length sourcing of service inputs (also called unbundling or externalization). However, Kutscher (1988) demonstrates that unbundling has not taken place to any great extent in the United States, as the relative in-house employment of people engaged in producer service activities has remained constant or even increased. Thus, the increase in output and employment of business services apparently reflects increasing demand for these services, and not a shift in sourcing.

It can be expected that the various factors mentioned relating to a country's domestic economic structure will also operate internationally. As real per capita incomes rise, one would expect an increase over time in the share of services in international transactions. Thus, the presumption exists that both the level and the pattern of trade and investment in services will be in part a function of the level of economic development. In addition, familiar factors such as endowments, technologies, tastes, culture, and location will be important. Most trade theorists agree that the standard "toolbox" is applicable to trade in services (i.e., the principle of comparative advantage, predictions as to the factor content of trade).[7] The limited empirical evidence available supports the view that standard approaches can be fruitfully used to analyze trade in services (see, e.g., Sapir and Lutz 1980, 1981, Sagari 1988, and Langhammer 1989).

Government policies, of course, play an important role. The regulatory, trade, and investment policy regime of a country may encourage, deter, or change the mix between international transactions in goods and services (e.g., see Kaspar 1988, Noyelle and Dutka 1988, White 1988, and Yeats 1989). Many services require the physical proximity of the provider and recipient. This means that services provided by means of foreign direct investment and the international movement of workers and consumers may often be of considerable importance in comparison to services traded directly across international borders in a manner similar to trade in goods. Governments may require establishment (e.g., in the insurance sector), even though separated trade may be feasible. The opposite also occurs (e.g., retail banking) in that only cross-border trade is allowed, so in practice sales by foreign-owned firms are prohibited as these need to be established abroad.

The conclusion to be drawn is that the evolution of trade and investment in services will depend on differences in per capita incomes, variations in factor endowments, distances from markets, technology and technological gaps, the degree to which capital, labor, and demanders are mobile, government policies, and firm strategies (market structure). These are, of course, the same factors that shape trade in goods. But, trade in services is more complex because of the need to determine the tradability of services. Thus, analysis should also focus on the technological and regulatory considerations that determine the relative costs associated with alternative ways of providing services. Two questions then need to be answered: Is trade possible? If so, what means will be preferred? As noted above, options include temporary physical movement of either provider or recipient, embodiment in an information flow (phone calls, faxes, electronic data, and mail), and embodiment in a good.

7.2.4 Availability of Statistics

There are three main sources of available data relating to international transactions in services: the balance of payments; input-output tables; and industry- or sector-specific information collected by government agencies or the private sector. Current balance-of-payments (BOP) data are highly aggre-

---

7. There is not complete agreement, of course. Furthermore, while in principle standard theories remain valid, their application is made more difficult because there are multiple modes through which international transactions in services may occur.

gated, often inaccurate, difficult to compare across countries or time, only available on a value basis, and very rarely reported by origin and destination.[8] The classification of services found in BOP accounts is by type of activity and includes both nonfactor services (e.g., travel, transport, other private services) and what would be regarded as factor services in the national accounts (e.g., royalties and fees for intangible property, investment income, and labor income). The factor payments and receipts typically do not distinguish income from goods-related as opposed to services-related investment (production). Also workers' remittances are generally included under transfers in the BOP accounts, although they can be considered to be a component of factor services. BOP data are the only global source of services trade data currently available.

An alternative source of data on international transactions in services is national input-output (I-O) tables. These are especially useful in assessing the interindustry relations involving goods and services. However, depending on the country, I-O tables will employ different nomenclatures and have varying levels of aggregation and disaggregation, making cross-country comparisons difficult. More importantly, international transactions in services are often not clearly identified, making it difficult to determine how such transactions relate to domestic transactions. Furthermore, I-O data are rarely up to date and are often only available at five- or ten-year intervals. Large discrepancies exist between measures of trade in services based on I-O tables and the balance of payments (Hoekman 1988). For this reason we will not make use here of I-O data.

A third important source of data is surveys of foreign direct investment (FDI) by government agencies or financial flows monitored by central banks. However, these data are not often broken down geographically, may focus only on financial flows instead of sales by affiliates, and rarely identify services as separate activities. Finally, there are studies by official bodies, private organizations, and individuals that contain a great deal of information for a variety of services sectors. For example, data exist on construction contracts awarded, on trade in insurance, and on the largest firms in service sectors such as hotels and restaurants, accounting, and advertising. These data are very useful for sectoral studies, but less so for global analyses.

In line with the theme of this volume, the two sections that follow focus on what the available BOP and stock data on FDI in services can tell us. We discuss the reliability and accuracy of the data we use in section 7.5. To focus the discussion, some broad hypotheses or questions concerning the evolution of international trade and investment in goods and services are suggested in

8. For more detailed analyses of the deficiencies of data on international trade in services, see Ascher and Whichard (1987), U.S. Congress, Office of Technology Assessment (1986), Drechsler and Hoffman (1988), and Stern and Hoekman (1987). We will return to data issues in sections 7.5 and 7.6.

the next two sections. We then investigate the extent to which available data allow the analyst to answer.

7.3 Patterns of International Trade in Goods and Services

7.3.1 Hypotheses

1. *Shares*. The previous section indicated that there is reason to believe that the share of services in domestic transactions rises in response to increases in per capita income. Has a similar phenomenon occurred for international transactions in services? Have rates of change in output and trade in services been similar? Finally, have growth rates for trade in services been greater or smaller than for trade in goods?[9]

2. *Variety*. The variety of both intermediate and final services can be expected to increase, due especially to changes in demand and technology that allow increasing specialization to occur at the level of the firm in particular industries. Can such a development be observed in trade flows?

3. *Separated trade*. The relative importance of trade in separated services (i.e., taking place via telecommunications media as opposed to mobility or embodiment in goods) can then be expected to increase, and changes in the composition of services trade may reflect the increasing importance of technological developments. That is, given government policies, has trade in separated services grown faster than trade via the temporary mobility of providers and demanders?

4. *Comparative advantage*. Economic theory leads one to expect that, depending on patterns of comparative advantage, countries will specialize in the production of specific types of products. Are there any discernible trends to this effect for services?

5. *Producer services*. As per capita incomes rise, the relative importance of producer services can be expected to rise, while that of personal and distribution services declines. Can a similar phenomenon be observed in trade flows? Does this imply that trade in producer services will be mostly between developed nations? As developing economies grow, does the relative importance of developing regions in global trade in producer services rise?

---

9. The answers to the last two questions will depend in part on the respective income and price elasticities of demand and whether goods and services are complements or substitutes. While such information is not currently available, the answers may provide some indication of the relationship between goods and services.

7.3.2   Evidence and Analysis

Table 7.4 records average annual growth rates of sector contributions to GDP at constant prices for 1965–80 and 1980–86 for the major industrialized and developing countries. For most countries, growth rates of GDP dropped dramatically in the 1980–86 period, major exceptions including China and India. It is noteworthy that growth rates in agricultural output have recently risen substantially in both the industrialized and the developing regions. Indeed, in the European Community, Australia, and the Middle East/North Africa, agriculture was the most rapidly growing sector in the 1980–86 period.[10] This is in marked contrast to the 1965–80 period, when agriculture was the slowest growing sector in all regions. In general, growth rates of service sector output have not been significantly greater than growth in GDP.

Table 7.5 reports data on the nominal value of world exports of merchandise and "invisibles" for the period between 1970 and 1987. Invisibles comprise all the nonmerchandise components of the current account, while "private services" include travel, transport, and the private components of the IMF category "other goods, services, and income."[11] It can be seen that merchandise exports grew slightly faster than private services during the 1970s, whereas the opposite was the case in 1980–87. The relative importance of private services was more or less unchanged between 1970 and 1987. The largest changes were apparently recorded for investment income and account for the increase in the relative importance of invisibles in world trade. However, to a large extent these income flows are related to portfolio investment, not FDI. Furthermore, labor income flows and worker remittances are excluded. We will return to this topic in the next section.

Tables 7.6 and 7.7 focus respectively on the percentage shares of world exports and imports of merchandise and services for 1970 and 1987. They show that the share in world trade of merchandise held by the industrialized countries declined somewhat between 1970 and 1987, as did the share in total exports of private services. The share in world exports of maritime and air transport (shipment and passenger services) of these countries declined significantly, by about 10 percentage points, while shares in world exports of other transport, travel, and other private services (OPS) fell by approximately 5 percentage points. It is interesting to note that the decline in the shares in exports of service categories was larger than the decline in the share in world merchandise exports. The share of industrialized nations in world imports of

10. As was the case for the earlier tables, the weighted averages for country and regional groupings have a zero weight to countries for which data are not reported or not available.

11. The major categories employed by IMF are shipment (transport of freight, including insurance); passenger services (air fares); other transport (charters and port services); travel (expenditures and receipts associated with temporary stays of nonresidents); other goods, services, and income (labor and property income, as well as all other types of services). The last category includes both official and private transactions. For our purposes, the term "other private services" (OPS) will be used to denote the private component of this category, excluding labor and property income.

OPS remained virtually unchanged between 1970 and 1987. This fact supports the presumption that demand and supply of producer services are likely to be concentrated in high-income countries. The share in global imports of OPS by the dynamic Asian economies has doubled, in contrast to the much slower growth in the share of developing countries as a whole. Again, this is in line with the broad hypothesis noted above.

Many developing countries apparently experienced an increase in the relative importance of exports of private services after 1970, while the opposite was the case for most industrialized countries. This can be seen from table 7.8. Only 4 out of the 20 industrialized countries listed in table 7.8 saw an increase in the relative importance of private services, as compared to 18 out of 29 developing economies. This suggests that service exports grew faster than merchandise exports for many developing countries. This is, of course, the counterpart to the finding discussed above that the developing-country share in world exports of private services has increased.

Table 7.9 reports average annual growth rates of total exports and imports of merchandise and services for five-year intervals starting in 1967 for the major industrialized and developing countries. There are a number of interesting details. In the industrialized countries, exports of merchandise grew faster than exports of private services for all periods except 1977–82. In general, growth rates of exports and imports for the various categories tend to be quite similar. Developing countries demonstrate an opposite pattern. Thus, exports of services tended to grow faster than exports of merchandise, except during the 1972–77 period. For the period as a whole, services exports appear to have outperformed merchandise exports, while the opposite holds for developed countries.[12] Developing economies show a tendency for growth rates of service imports to exceed those of merchandise during 1967–82. During 1982–87, when growth rates were negative, this pattern persists, in that service imports fell faster than merchandise imports.

As is to be expected, regional and country experiences varied widely over time. Middle-income countries that export manufactures (such as Brazil, Ireland, Spain, and Yugoslavia) generally reported that imports of services grew faster than exports. Countries such as South Korea and Singapore started by having higher growth rates for exports of services than for imports, but reported the opposite for the 1982–87 period. The same is true for Asia as a whole. Latin American countries, in contrast, saw their imports of services grow faster than their exports from the late 1960s to the early 1980s. However, during the 1982–87 period growth rates of imports plummeted for most nations. Finally, it is noteworthy that the decreases in the growth rates of exports

---

12. Growth rates for the period 1967–87 are not reported, since the absence of data for many developing countries in 1967 implies that calculated growth rates would be inaccurate. It bears repeating that figures reported for country groupings will be biased due to nonreporting. This is especially the case for the 1967–72 period.

Table 7.4   Average Annual Percentage Growth Rates of Real GDP by Sector and Country or Region, 1965–80 and 1980–86

Country or Region	GDP 1965–80	GDP 1980–86	Agriculture 1965–80	Agriculture 1980–86	Industry 1965–80	Industry 1980–86	Manufacturing 1965–80	Manufacturing 1980–86	Services 1965–80	Services 1980–86
Industrialized Countries										
Australia	3.6	2.5	0.9	2.5	3.2	2.5	3.7	NA	3.6	2.6
Austria	4.0	3.1	2.6	6.1	2.9	2.0	1.2	NA	5.4	3.5
Canada	4.3	1.8	2.2	1.2	4.5	1.6	4.7	2.1	4.4	1.9
European Community	4.4	2.9	0.7	2.8	3.4	2.9	3.8	3.6	5.5	2.9
Belgium	3.6	1.5	1.4	2.7	4.4	0.8	NA	NA	3.9	2.0
Denmark	3.9	0.9	0.5	3.1	1.9	0.5	4.8	1.6	3.8	1.1
France	2.7	2.8	0.9	4.6	4.6	2.6	3.2	2.9	3.1	2.4
West Germany	4.4	1.3	0.8	2.8	2.9	0.6	5.3	NA	4.6	1.6
Greece	3.3	1.5	1.4	3.1	7.1	0.7	3.3	0.8	3.7	2.1
Ireland	5.6	1.5	2.3	0.3	NA	0.4	NA	0.2	6.2	2.5
Italy	5.1	0.7	NA	−6.2	4.2	−1.1	5.1	NA	NA	3.8
Netherlands	3.9	1.3	0.8	0.5	3.6	0.2	4.3	NA	4.1	2.1
Portugal	3.7	1.0	4.3	4.5	NA	0.5	NA	NA	4.0	1.9
Spain	5.5	1.4	3.0	0.1	5.8	1.4	6.7	0.3	4.6	1.7
United Kingdom	2.2	2.3	1.7	4.1	1.2	2.0	1.1	1.2	2.9	2.3
Finland	4.1	2.7	0.1	0.2	4.4	2.8	5.0	3.0	4.8	2.4
Japan	6.3	3.7	0.8	1.0	8.5	5.0	9.4	7.8	5.2	2.9
New Zealand	3.1	2.6	NA	2.1	NA	3.8	NA	NA	NA	2.0
Norway	4.4	3.5	−0.4	3.0	5.6	3.8	2.6	0.3	4.2	3.4
Sweden	2.8	2.0	−0.2	2.5	2.2	2.5	2.3	2.3	3.3	0.5
Switzerland	2.0	1.5	NA	NA	NA	NA	NA	NA	NA	NA
United States	2.8	3.1	1.1	3.1	1.9	3.2	2.7	4.0	3.4	3.0

Developing Countries	6.1	3.8	3.1	3.6	7.2	4.6	8.0	5.9	7.1	3.4
East/South Asia	5.6	6.8	3.1	4.5	7.7	8.2	NA	NA	6.0	6.9
China	6.4	10.5	3.0	7.9	10.0	12.5	9.5	12.6	7.0	9.4
Hong Kong	8.5	6.0	NA	NA	NA	NA	NA	NA	NA	NA
India	3.7	4.9	2.8	1.9	4.0	7.1	4.3	8.2	4.6	6.0
South Korea	9.5	8.2	3.0	5.6	16.5	10.2	18.7	9.8	9.3	7.2
Singapore	10.4	5.3	3.1	-3.5	12.2	4.4	13.3	2.2	9.7	6.1
Taiwan	13.1	6.8	NA	NA	NA	NA	NA	NA	NA	NA
Latin America	5.7	1.0	2.9	2.0	6.1	0.4	2.7	-0.4	6.3	1.4
Argentina	3.4	-0.8	1.4	2.3	3.3	-1.7	9.6	1.2	3.9	-0.8
Brazil	9.0	2.7	3.8	2.0	9.9	1.6	0.6	-0.2	10.0	3.8
Chile	1.9	0.0	1.6	3.1	0.8	0.7	7.4	0.0	2.7	-0.9
Mexico	6.5	0.4	3.2	2.1	7.6	-0.1	5.8	2.0	6.6	0.4
Venezuela	5.2	-0.9	3.9	2.3	3.4	-0.8	NA	NA	6.5	-1.2
Middle East/North Africa	6.7	1.3	4.5	5.2	7.6	-0.9	NA	NA	9.0	4.0
Egypt	6.7	4.7	2.8	1.9	7.0	6.3	8.1	6.1	9.5	4.4
Saudi Arabia	10.9	-3.4	4.1	10.3	11.6	-10.4	NA	NA	10.5	4.4
Other Europe	6.1	2.9	3.1	2.2	7.6	3.5	7.5	8.0	6.4	2.9
Turkey	6.3	4.9	3.2	3.1	7.2	6.4	NA	NA	7.6	4.7
Yugoslavia	6.0	1.2	3.1	1.4	7.8	1.1	8.5	0.3	5.5	1.4
Subsaharan Africa	5.6	0.0	1.6	1.2	9.4	-1.6	3.4	4.1	7.5	0.1
Senegal	2.1	3.2	1.4	2.3	4.8	4.0	5.6	-4.6	1.3	3.2
Tanzania	3.7	0.9	1.6	0.8	4.2	-4.5	NA	-0.7	6.9	2.9
Zaire	1.4	1.0	NA	1.7	NA	2.7	NA	1.0	NA	-0.7
Nigeria	8.0	-3.2	1.7	1.4	13.4	-5.1	14.6	-1.7	8.8	-4.0
South Africa	4.0	0.8	NA	-1.3	NA	-0.5	NA	NA	NA	2.4

Source: World Bank, *World Development Report,* 1988.
Note: NA = not available.

Table 7.5   World Exports of Merchandise and Invisibles, 1970–87

Category	Value (US $ billion) 1970	Value (US $ billion) 1987	Share in Total (%) 1970	Share in Total (%) 1987	Average Annual Change (%) 1970–79	Average Annual Change (%) 1980–87	Average Annual Change (%) 1970–87
Merchandise exports	269	2,194	71	67	20.5	2.5	13
Invisibles exports	115	1,099	29	33	21	5	14
of which:							
Private services	64	525	17	16	19	5	13
Investment income	26	415	7	13	25	6.5	17.5
Other official goods, services, and income	8	45	2	1	17	2	10.5
Unrequited transfers	12	114	3	4	22	4	14
Total	379	3,270	100	100	20.5	3	13

Source: IMF, *Balance of Payments Yearbook*, and national sources.
Notes: Figures have been rounded. Private services include labor and property income (about 5% of total).

experienced by many countries and regions in the post-1982 period were concentrated in merchandise rather than in private services. This suggests that the merchandise terms of trade may be considerably more volatile than the services terms of trade. Alternatively (or additionally), it may reflect increased competition in industrialized countries.

Tables 7.10 and 7.11 indicate respectively the average annual growth rates of exports and imports for various categories for 1967–87. Growth rates in general tended to be much lower during the 1977–87 period than during 1967–77. Industrialized countries' exports and imports of OPS were the fastest growing component of private services trade during 1967–77. While OPS continued to be the most dynamic component of exports during 1977–87, passenger services and travel became the fastest growing services on the import side. As far as the developing countries are concerned, no component dominated. During 1967–77, exports of OPS and passenger services grew fastest, as opposed to imports of other transport, followed by OPS. During 1977–87, passenger services and shipment were the most rapidly growing categories on the export side, while OPS was the fastest growing import. Again, country experiences varied widely. The growth rate of exports of OPS by South Korea and Singapore was very high during 1967–77, but fell below the developing-country average during 1977–87. Construction exports by South Korea fell dramatically during the 1980s. India, Taiwan, and Egypt substantially outperformed the developing-country average for exports of OPS.

Turning to imports of the developed countries, the largest import growth rates for OPS were registered by Ireland, Finland, Japan, and the United States. Developing economies reported a varied pattern of import growth rates. Growth rates of imports of all categories were substantial for Asian economies. Imports of OPS for most Asian countries (but not South Korea), as well as for Argentina, Chile, Mexico, Egypt, Turkey, and Yugoslavia, grew rapidly. However, rates of growth for these countries were not noticeably different from those of the more dynamic industrialized countries. Nevertheless, as mentioned above, imports of OPS were the fastest growing category for developing countries as a whole during 1977–87.

Great care must be taken when drawing conclusions based on the foregoing tables. As will be discussed in greater detail in section 7.5, data on trade in services are neither comprehensive nor very reliable. Thus, the following conclusions should be considered to be tentative.

What, then, are the answers suggested by the data for the questions noted at the beginning of this section?

1. *Shares*. There is a tendency among developing countries for the share of private services in total trade to increase. Thus, domestic trends appear to be reflected in international trade statistics. However, this is not the case for industrialized countries. If one compares growth rates of service sector output reported in table 7.4 with the growth rates of exports and imports, one can conclude that industrialized countries with higher-than-average service sector output growth are not necessarily the most dynamic traders of services. Developing countries on average experienced higher growth rates of services output than industrialized countries, and for much of the period under review developing-country growth rates of exports of private services tended to be higher than those of the industrialized nations. Developing countries with relatively high services output growth rates (including South Korea, Singapore, Brazil, Egypt, Saudi Arabia, and Turkey) tend to be high-growth exporters of services. No such pattern emerges on the import side.

2. *Variety*. No quantitative information is available with respect to the question of whether the variety of traded services has increased over time. The existing data are too highly aggregated.

3. *Separated trade*. The question of whether separated trade has become more important relative to trade via temporary mobility of provider or consumer also cannot be answered readily. BOP data are not broken down by mode of delivery. It is clear that travel data reflect a mix of provider- and consumer-mobility, whereas transport tends to comprise separated trade. The main problem is that OPS are a mix of the three major modes of delivery, and that the value of reported OPS for most industrialized countries is understated. One reason for this understatement is that virtually no information exists on the volume and value of transborder data flows. This issue will be discussed in the following section.

4. *Comparative advantage*. As for specialization, it is clear that on an aggregate

Table 7.6   Percentage Shares in World Exports of Merchandise and Services by Country or Region, 1970 and 1987

Country or Region	Merch. 1970	Merch. 1987	Ship. 1970	Ship. 1987	Travel 1970	Travel 1987	Pass. 1970	Pass. 1987	OT 1970	OT 1987	OPS 1970	OPS 1987	Total PS 1970	Total PS 1987	Prop. Inc. 1970	Prop. Inc. 1987	Lab. Inc. 1970	Lab. Inc. 1987
Industrialized Countries	81.1	77.9	92.8	81.2	82.7	78.2	91.3	81.2	83.3	78.4	86.9	84.6	87.7	81.6	99.6	99.4	83.5	76.5
Australia	1.7	1.2	0.4	0.6	0.6	1.2	4.5	3.2	4.3	2.0	1.1	0.3	1.3	1.0	0.3	0.7	1.1	1.5
Austria	1.0	1.2	0.6	1.6	0.7	0.6	NA	NA	0.1	0.2	1.6	2.7	2.1	2.8	0.2	0.3	NA	NA
Canada	6.2	4.5	2.0	0.8	6.4	3.0	NA	NA	1.9	0.6	4.4	2.7	3.5	2.0	NA	NA	NA	NA
European Community	41.8	41.7	54.6	46.8	46.6	43.8	57.2	42.7	39.3	42.6	56.3	53.1	50.9	47.5	26.5	36.8	78.7	66.3
Belgium	3.4	3.5	2.2	4.3	1.9	1.9	1.5	2.1	1.8	2.2	7.7	5.7	3.5	3.6	3.6	2.1	8.2	4.7
Denmark	1.3	1.2	2.4	2.9	1.7	1.4	0.2	0.3	2.8	1.6	1.6	1.5	1.7	1.5	NA	NA	NA	NA
France	6.7	6.4	8.9	10.2	7.3	7.4	NA	NA	NA	13.8	11.1	13.0	8.6	10.1	2.1	5.1	7.2	13.7
West Germany	12.8	12.7	9.9	7.0	7.3	4.8	13.5	10.4	5.7	5.5	6.7	9.8	7.9	7.9	3.9	6.3	20.6	25.6
Greece	0.2	0.3	0.2	0.2	1.1	1.4	NA	0.1	1.6	0.2	0.6	1.0	0.7	0.8	NA	NA	0.4	0.5
Ireland	0.4	0.7	NA	NA	1.0	0.5	0.7	0.8	0.5	0.9	0.1	0.2	0.5	0.4	NA	NA	NA	NA
Italy	4.9	5.3	5.5	8.1	9.0	7.6	11.1	4.6	3.9	1.4	6.5	5.1	7.4	6.2	3.6	10.5	35.6	15.7
Netherlands	4.0	4.0	5.8	5.6	2.4	1.7	6.7	4.5	10.0	8.5	4.6	4.2	4.9	4.1	3.0	4.1	6.8	3.9
Portugal	NA	0.4	NA	0.2	NA	1.3	NA	0.4	NA	0.7	NA	0.2	NA	0.6	NA	NA	NA	0.8
Spain	0.9	1.5	0.7	1.8	9.2	9.3	4.0	5.5	1.9	2.8	1.7	1.2	3.6	4.1	NA	0.2	NA	1.5
United Kingdom	7.2	5.9	18.9	6.1	5.7	6.4	18.5	14.0	11.0	5.5	15.7	11.2	12.1	8.2	10.3	8.5	NA	NA
Finland	0.9	0.9	1.1	0.8	0.7	0.5	0.3	1.2	0.6	0.8	0.4	0.7	0.7	0.7	NA	0.2	2.0	0.5
Japan	7.0	10.2	7.3	11.9	1.3	1.3	4.5	3.1	6.9	7.7	4.3	6.2	4.1	5.3	1.5	7.4	NA	1.6
New Zealand	0.5	0.3	0.8	0.3	0.2	0.6	NA	1.1	NA	0.6	0.2	0.2	0.3	0.4	NA	NA	NA	NA
Norway	0.9	1.0	12.5	6.3	0.9	0.8	NA	2.0	1.1	1.0	1.2	0.9	3.4	1.6	NA	0.4	NA	0.1
Sweden	2.5	2.0	3.8	3.0	0.8	1.3	3.8	2.5	2.7	1.7	2.2	1.6	2.1	1.7	0.5	1.7	NA	0.3

Region/Country																			
Switzerland	2.0	2.5	0.7	0.7	5.0	3.4	NA	4.7	NA	NA	5.1	3.7	2.8	2.7	NA	NA	NA	NA	4.3
United States	15.8	11.4	8.1	7.1	12.8	14.8	17.3	19.0	25.8	20.8	8.7	10.9	15.1	14.5	70.6	51.9	NA	NA	1.8
Developing Countries	18.3	21.6	6.2	18.0	16.9	21.3	8.7	17.9	16.7	21.7	11.3	14.7	12.4	18.3	0.4	0.6	NA	16.5	23.2
Asia	7.8	12.6	1.5	11.4	2.3	10.5	0.5	4.3	5.4	11.5	2.6	7.4	2.6	9.1	NA	NA	NA	2.0	14.2
China	0.9	1.6	NA	1.8	NA	1.1	NA	0.5	NA	0.5	NA	0.5	NA	0.9	NA	NA	NA	NA	0.3
Hong Kong	1.1	2.2	NA	1.3	2.1	2.1	NA	NA	0.6	4.8	NA	0.9	0.7	1.6	NA	NA	NA	NA	NA
India	0.7	0.5	0.6	0.8	0.2	0.8	NA	NA	0.9	0.3	0.6	0.7	0.4	0.6	NA	NA	NA	NA	NA
Singapore	0.5	1.2	0.1	1.3	0.4	1.3	NA	2.3	2.9	3.2	0.0	1.4	0.6	1.4	NA	NA	NA	NA	NA
South Korea	0.3	2.1	0.3	2.8	0.1	1.5	0.2	NA	0.2	0.4	0.4	1.8	0.3	1.6	NA	NA	NA	1.9	2.9
Taiwan	0.5	2.4	0.2	1.7	0.5	1.0	NA	NA	0.5	1.2	0.4	0.7	0.3	0.9	NA	NA	NA	NA	NA
Latin America	5.6	4.2	2.1	3.0	10.5	6.2	4.9	5.2	5.5	4.3	4.5	3.1	5.7	4.3	0.4	0.3	NA	11.1	3.7
Argentina	0.7	0.3	0.3	0.5	0.4	0.4	0.7	0.8	1.0	0.6	0.2	0.1	0.4	0.4	0.3	NA	NA	0.4	0.2
Brazil	1.0	1.2	0.7	1.2	0.2	NA	0.5	0.5	0.7	0.8	0.6	0.3	0.5	0.4	NA	NA	NA	0.5	NA
Chile	0.4	0.3	0.3	0.3	0.3	0.1	NA	0.3	0.2	0.2	NA	0.3	0.2	0.2	NA	NA	NA	NA	NA
Mexico	0.5	0.9	NA	NA	6.4	2.2	NA	NA	0.1	0.4	1.1	1.3	2.3	1.4	NA	NA	NA	7.2	2.4
Venezuela	1.0	0.5	0.2	0.2	0.3	0.2	NA	0.3	0.9	0.2	0.2	NA	0.3	0.1	NA	NA	NA	NA	NA
Middle East/ N. Africa	4.3	3.0	0.7	2.3	2.6	3.5	2.5	5.2	2.1	4.3	1.9	3.5	1.5	3.4	NA	NA	NA	NA	NA
Egypt	0.3	0.1	NA	NA	NA	0.4	NA	1.1	0.1	2.8	0.8	0.5	0.2	0.7	NA	NA	NA	NA	NA
Saudi Arabia	0.8	1.1	NA	NA	0.6	NA	NA	NA	1.5	0.1	NA	1.6	0.3	0.6	NA	NA	NA	NA	NA
Other Europe	0.8	1.0	NA	1.7	1.8	2.0	2.5	1.2	0.5	1.4	1.2	1.4	NA	1.5	NA	NA	NA	NA	NA
Turkey	0.2	0.5	NA	1.0	0.3	1.0	0.4	0.0	0.2	0.2	0.4	0.8	NA	0.7	NA	NA	NA	NA	NA
Yugoslavia	0.6	0.5	1.7	0.7	1.5	1.0	2.1	1.2	0.3	1.2	0.8	0.7	NA	0.8	NA	NA	NA	NA	NA
Subsaharan Africa	2.4	1.2	0.8	0.5	1.0	0.7	0.9	1.7	NA	0.7	1.3	0.5	1.2	0.7	NA	NA	NA	NA	NA

Source: IMF, *Balance of Payments Yearbook*, and national sources.

Notes: NA = not available; Merch. = merchandise; Ship. = shipment (i.e., freight and insurance on freight); Pass. = passenger services (primarily air fares); OT = other transport (mainly charters and port services); OPS = other private services); total PS = total private services (includes property income and labor income); Prop. Inc. = property income; Lab. Inc. = labor income.

Table 7.7　Percentage Shares in World Imports of Merchandise and Services by Country or Region, 1970 and 1987

Country or Region	Merch.		Ship.		Travel		Pass.		OT		OPS		Total PS		Prop. Inc		Lab. Inc.	
	1970	1987	1970	1987	1970	1987	1970	1987	1970	1987	1970	1987	1970	1987	1970	1987	1970	1987
Industrialized Countries	81.1	79.7	74.6	69.4	83.7	85.9	81.8	84.9	89.8	79.6	78.1	77.6	81.8	80.0	96.3	95.2	95.1	88.1
Australia	1.6	1.3	2.8	2.0	1.2	1.6	NA	3.4	3.8	1.1	1.1	0.8	2.1	1.5	5.3	2.9	1.3	1.3
Austria	1.4	1.5	0.6	1.1	1.7	3.6	NA	NA	0.1	0.2	1.8	1.6	1.1	1.8	1.5	1.2	NA	NA
Canada	5.4	4.1	2.6	1.1	7.7	4.3	NA	NA	2.0	0.6	8.0	4.7	4.7	2.9	NA	NA	NA	NA
European Community	42.7	40.5	43.4	40.7	40.6	41.7	34.3	35.3	46.0	41.5	46.8	43.4	47.7	42.7	61.9	57.9	75.0	58.6
Belgium	3.4	3.5	1.5	2.0	2.8	2.5	1.5	1.8	1.2	2.1	5.2	5.1	2.8	3.2	7.0	4.5	4.2	3.5
Denmark	1.6	1.2	1.5	1.2	1.5	1.8	NA	NA	1.8	2.7	0.7	1.0	1.2	1.4	NA	NA	NA	NA
France	6.9	6.8	9.5	8.8	6.3	5.4	NA	NA	NA	12.3	7.1	8.7	7.9	8.0	8.0	8.7	18.5	18.6
West Germany	11.2	9.5	10.1	7.1	15.8	14.9	13.5	12.3	7.1	5.6	13.9	12.6	12.1	12.0	13.6	13.5	39.4	28.9
Greece	0.6	0.5	0.4	0.6	0.3	0.4	0.4	0.4	0.3	0.2	0.4	0.2	0.4	0.3	NA	NA	1.0	0.4
Ireland	0.6	0.6	0.4	0.6	0.5	0.5	NA	NA	0.4	0.7	0.1	0.5	0.3	0.5	NA	NA	NA	NA
Italy	5.3	5.3	7.3	7.4	4.1	2.9	2.7	2.8	3.4	2.7	6.7	5.7	5.6	5.0	14.1	15.7	4.7	4.0
Netherlands	4.6	3.8	5.3	5.5	3.4	4.1	5.3	3.3	3.2	2.6	4.7	3.8	4.3	4.1	4.6	6.1	7.3	3.0
Portugal	NA	0.6	NA	1.0	NA	0.3	NA	NA	NA	0.3	NA	0.3	NA	0.4	NA	0.5	NA	0.1
Spain	1.7	2.1	1.7	1.8	0.8	1.2	1.1	1.4	0.9	2.0	1.4	1.7	1.2	1.6	3.3	2.1	NA	NA
United Kingdom	7.6	6.7	5.5	4.3	5.2	7.6	9.8	13.0	27.8	10.1	6.6	3.9	9.3	6.3	11.3	6.8	NA	NA
Finland	1.0	0.9	0.7	0.9	0.5	1.0	0.3	1.0	0.8	0.6	0.4	0.9	0.6	0.9	0.6	1.1	1.6	NA
Japan	5.9	5.9	9.1	8.0	1.8	6.9	5.7	12.7	11.6	13.3	8.2	11.6	7.1	9.8	16.4	21.1	NA	3.1
New Zealand	0.5	0.3	1.2	0.5	0.4	0.4	NA	1.0	NA	0.5	0.6	0.4	0.5	0.5	NA	NA	NA	NA
Norway	1.4	1.1	0.4	0.5	1.4	2.1	NA	NA	6.7	5.7	0.8	1.5	1.7	1.8	NA	1.1	NA	0.3
Sweden	2.5	1.8	1.8	0.7	2.7	2.4	1.8	2.0	5.1	2.2	2.5	2.2	2.6	2.0	1.8	2.5	1.0	0.9

Switzerland	2.5	2.8	0.8	1.4	2.4	2.8	NA	2.9	NA	0.1	1.6	1.1	1.5	2.2	NA	NA	16.2	19.7
United States	15.6	18.7	9.7	11.5	22.5	18.7	40.8	26.3	11.8	11.9	5.8	6.7	13.5	12.7	8.8	7.4	NA	4.1
Developing Countries	18.7	18.2	26.0	29.5	16.9	13.3	17.8	14.2	10.2	18.6	20.7	23.2	18.4	19.4	3.7	4.8	3.9	11.9
Asia	7.1	11.8	7.9	15.1	3.7	5.3	2.8	3.7	2.4	8.1	4.1	8.7	3.8	8.0	NA	NA	NA	NA
China	0.9	1.7	NA	1.4	NA	0.3	NA	NA	NA	0.8	NA	0.1	NA	0.5	NA	NA	NA	NA
Hong Kong	1.3	2.2	NA	1.5	0.4	1.6	1.6	1.8	0.5	0.4	NA	0.8	0.2	1.1	NA	NA	NA	NA
India	0.8	0.8	1.5	2.1	0.1	0.2	NA	NA	0.8	1.2	0.9	0.9	0.7	0.9	NA	NA	NA	NA
South Korea	0.7	1.8	0.8	0.9	NA	0.4	0.2	0.5	0.1	3.2	0.7	1.3	0.4	1.0	NA	0.3	NA	0.1
Singapore	0.9	1.4	0.9	2.0	NA	0.6	NA	NA	0.3	NA	0.3	1.4	0.3	0.9	NA	NA	NA	NA
Taiwan	0.5	1.5	0.7	1.7	0.1	1.0	NA	NA	1.6	2.4	0.6	2.0	0.4	1.7	NA	NA	NA	1.5
Latin America	5.7	3.3	8.0	4.7	9.4	4.2	10.5	5.0	5.0	6.5	7.5	3.6	7.4	4.3	3.4	3.5	2.2	0.1
Argentina	0.6	0.4	0.7	0.2	0.7	0.6	2.5	1.0	0.6	0.8	0.4	0.2	0.8	0.5	2.8	1.5	NA	NA
Brazil	1.0	0.7	0.9	0.7	0.9	0.2	1.0	0.4	1.7	2.5	1.2	0.8	1.0	0.7	NA	0.2	0.1	NA
Chile	0.3	0.2	0.4	0.2	0.5	0.2	0.7	0.5	0.5	0.5	0.3	0.3	0.4	0.3	NA	0.2	NA	NA
Mexico	0.9	0.6	0.7	0.6	4.3	1.6	1.8	0.8	NA	1.0	1.7	0.7	1.7	1.0	NA	1.0	NA	NA
Venezuela	0.7	0.4	1.1	0.9	0.8	0.3	0.6	0.2	0.5	0.4	0.9	0.3	0.8	0.4	NA	NA	NA	NA
Middle East/ N. Africa	2.5	3.1	4.8	6.6	2.5	3.1	1.1	2.9	NA	2.6	NA	6.7	3.6	4.7	NA	NA	NA	NA
Egypt	0.4	0.3	0.7	0.9	NA	0.1	NA	0.2	0.1	0.3	NA	0.9	0.3	0.5	NA	NA	NA	NA
Saudi Arabia	0.3	0.8	0.5	2.6	0.6	NA	NA	NA	0.2	NA	NA	4.9	0.3	1.7	NA	NA	NA	NA
Other Europe	1.3	1.1	1.7	1.6	0.9	0.4	NA	NA	1.5	1.9	0.8	2.6	1.1	1.4	NA	NA	NA	NA
Turkey	0.3	0.6	0.5	0.4	0.2	0.3	0.2	NA	0.1	0.4	0.2	0.3	0.3	0.3	NA	0.3	NA	NA
Yugoslavia	1.0	0.5	1.2	1.2	0.7	0.1	NA	NA	1.4	1.6	0.6	2.3	0.8	1.1	0.2	1.0	NA	NA
Subsaharan Africa	2.2	1.0	4.4	3.0	2.0	1.4	3.4	1.7	2.0	0.7	3.3	1.8	2.7	1.5	NA	NA	0.1	0.4

Source: IMF, *Balance of Payments Yearbook,* and national sources.
Note: For key to abbreviations, see note to table 7.6.

Table 7.8   **Ratio of Exports of Private Services to the Sum of Merchandise and Private Services Exports, Selected Countries, 1970 and 1987**

Country	1970	1987
Developed economies with a constant or declining share of private services		
Australia	16	16
Austria	32	36
Belgium/Luxembourg	20	20
France	23	28
Canada	12	10
Greece	42	44
West Germany	13	13
New Zealand	12	23
Denmark	25	23
Finland	16	16
Ireland	12	11
Italy	23	22
Japan	12	11
Netherlands	22	21
South Africa	24	11
Spain	48	39
Sweden	17	17
Switzerland	25	21
United Kingdom	28	25
United States	18	18
Developed economies with an increasing share of private services		
Austria	32	36
France	23	28
Greece	42	44
New Zealand	12	23
Developing economies with a constant or declining share of private services		
Algeria	8	6
Brazil[a]	10	7
Cameroon	18	17
Colombia	21	17
Iran[b]	6	2
Israel	38	29
South Korea	17	15
Mexico[c]	53	24
Nigeria	5	4
Taiwan	12	7
Venezuela	6	6
Developing economies with an increasing share of private services		
Chile	10	17
Ivory Coast	8	10
Egypt[d]	13	53
India[a]	13	23
Indonesia	1	5
Kenya	33	40
Malaysia	4	12
Morocco	26	32
Peru	15	16

Table 7.8   **(continued)**

Country	1970	1987
Philippines	14	32
Saudi Arabia	9	11
Senegal	25	27
Singapore	20	21
Sudan	9	35
Thailand	20	24
Tanzania[a]	20	23
Zaire	2	9
Zambia	1	5
World	20	20

Source: GATT (1989).
[a]1986 rather than 1987.
[b]1984 rather than 1987.
[c]When exports of maquiladoras are included, the share of private services in merchandise exports declined from 111 to 24 percent between 1970 and 1987.
[d]Exports of travel were not included in Egypt's reported exports of commercial services in 1970, resulting in a significant understatement of their value. In 1977, the first year for which travel was reported, exports of private services amounted to 77 percent of merchandise exports.

level this is reflected in this increasing developing-country shares in world exports of all categories of services. Private services have become relatively more important in their total trade. However, apparently several developed nations did become more specialized in certain types of services: OPS for Austria, France, West Germany, Japan, and the United States; travel for the United Kingdom and the United States; and shipment for Japan and Italy.

5. *Producer services.* There is some support for the hypothesis that trade in OPS will be an affair between industrialized nations. The highest share of these countries in world exports of services is in OPS. Although the share has dropped slightly, shares in world exports of other categories of services have fallen much more since 1970.

7.4   Patterns of International Investment in Goods and Services

7.4.1   Hypotheses

We have already noted that the provision or sale of a service frequently requires a physical proximity between provider and receiver. This implies that either establishment by the foreign provider in the consuming country or movement of the demander is required for provision to occur. Thus, either temporary or permanent factor movement may be necessary. Building again on the discussion in section 7.2, the following hypotheses suggest themselves:

1. *Services FDI concentration.* Given that the role of services tends to rise as per capita incomes increase, foreign direct investment in services will tend to

Table 7.9   Average Annual Percentage Growth Rates of Total Exports and Imports of Merchandise and Services by Country or Region, 1967–87 (current prices)

Country or Region	1967–72				1972–77				1977–82				1982–87			
	Merch.		Services		Merch.		Services		Merch.		Services		Merch.		Services	
	Ex.	Im.	Ex.	Im.	Ex.	Im.	Ex.	Im.	Ex.	Im.	Ex.	Im.	Ex.	Im.	Ex.	Im.
Industrialized Countries	14.7	14.7	13.9	14.6	19.6	21.1	17.8	17.5	10.1	9.9	10.6	10.4	8.3	8.2	7.7	8.7
Australia	13.1	5.1	12.8	11.6	16.0	23.2	14.1	20.0	9.5	13.9	13.6	10.5	5.1	2.7	5.2	2.0
Austria	16.4	16.9	21.0	17.8	20.4	22.2	21.3	27.6	9.6	6.8	11.5	8.0	11.5	10.9	9.1	12.8
Canada	13.9	12.9	5.5	13.7	15.5	16.1	12.3	15.5	10.3	6.7	10.2	6.9	6.8	9.9	7.1	8.4
European Community	15.6	14.9	14.6	16.1	19.7	20.6	18.9	17.5	9.3	9.6	9.4	10.2	9.6	8.0	8.2	8.3
Belgium	18.4	16.4	14.5	16.3	19.5	23.3	27.7	24.8	8.1	7.7	6.2	8.1	10.5	9.0	8.8	8.9
Denmark	11.7	10.1	12.5	9.4	18.1	21.6	18.5	20.0	9.4	5.3	5.5	9.1	10.4	8.6	7.9	10.0
France	18.3	17.8	19.5	22.5	18.8	21.0	24.5	20.0	8.4	10.7	9.6	10.2	8.8	6.8	7.1	7.0
West Germany	15.5	17.0	14.3	18.0	20.4	20.8	20.9	18.7	7.9	8.5	10.9	9.0	10.9	8.1	6.1	7.9
Greece	13.0	16.0	20.7	16.8	24.8	21.3	22.4	17.0	10.4	9.4	10.2	14.1	6.2	4.5	4.9	1.5
Ireland	13.3	12.9	3.1	8.5	21.8	20.9	16.2	22.4	13.4	12.5	10.6	13.2	14.4	7.3	10.9	12.9
Italy	16.4	16.3	9.8	10.6	19.4	19.5	15.2	13.0	10.2	12.7	10.2	10.7	9.8	7.3	10.6	12.7
Netherlands	18.2	15.6	21.9	23.9	20.7	21.5	19.6	20.5	8.7	6.9	8.0	9.7	7.5	7.8	6.8	8.4
Portugal	NA	NA	NA	NA	14.1	17.3	4.0	10.2	10.3	14.7	14.3	14.5	17.3	6.9	14.9	6.8
Spain	22.5	14.3	18.6	20.8	21.9	21.8	11.8	16.9	15.1	12.8	13.4	16.6	9.4	8.7	13.3	7.3
United Kingdom	10.2	9.6	12.2	10.8	18.7	18.5	14.1	11.1	11.8	9.4	8.7	11.7	6.1	9.6	8.3	7.7
Finland	14.0	13.4	18.0	13.4	21.7	19.1	20.5	21.3	6.0	12.0	13.6	12.9	14.9	6.9	4.9	12.6
Japan	22.3	16.0	23.1	17.2	23.1	26.6	22.6	21.5	11.7	14.0	13.1	14.1	10.3	1.4	5.9	8.5
New Zealand	14.6	10.7	28.5	15.6	10.6	16.4	20.9	16.6	10.4	12.0	9.9	12.3	6.4	3.9	12.4	5.1

Norway	13.5	9.8	10.1	9.0	22.6	25.0	12.9	26.4	14.1	3.0	9.3	8.0	3.7	7.5	1.2	5.8
Sweden	14.0	11.5	14.7	15.1	16.8	20.1	14.9	17.1	7.0	7.5	11.1	6.5	10.6	8.0	5.7	8.3
Switzerland	14.3	15.7	13.1	16.0	20.2	16.2	11.3	16.8	8.2	9.9	10.4	13.5	16.1	16.5	14.1	12.5
United States	10.0	15.7	9.8	10.3	19.6	22.2	14.5	12.3	11.8	10.3	14.8	9.8	3.4	10.6	6.2	11.3
Developing Countries	11.5	10.8	15.3	12.9	26.7	24.5	20.1	25.5	8.5	9.2	14.1	12.3	0.6	-1.0	3.0	-1.6
Asia	17.3	10.9	20.8	14.4	24.2	22.2	39.8	22.8	9.5	11.7	13.1	17.8	7.1	5.5	5.1	7.2
China	NA	NA	NA	NA	17.2	17.9	NA	NA	9.1	5.5	NA	NA	10.5	16.6	9.8	4.6
Hong Kong	NA	NA	NA	NA	19.1	18.5	NA	NA	12.4	13.1	5.5	NA	16.4	14.2	13.7	11.4
India	7.5	-1.8	4.8	0.9	21.5	18.3	33.0	19.2	8.1	21.5	18.1	22.6	4.3	3.9	2.4	3.9
South Korea	38.0	19.9	36.7	21.0	43.0	36.1	57.9	44.2	15.8	17.5	19.7	15.4	17.2	10.4	4.8	5.6
Singapore	14.0	18.2	40.7	31.3	30.6	25.5	24.4	21.4	20.8	21.9	25.8	23.1	7.0	2.6	-4.9	6.4
Taiwan	NA	NA	NA	NA	29.9	23.7	21.6	17.4	14.8	13.8	13.9	20.4	16.1	10.2	10.7	15.5
Latin America	9.1	11.0	13.4	13.5	23.6	23.5	17.3	18.9	13.0	11.1	11.0	15.2	-1.2	-3.8	2.5	-5.7
Argentina	5.8	11.7	7.4	3.7	23.8	17.6	24.2	12.3	6.1	5.0	14.5	18.5	-3.5	2.1	2.6	4.5
Brazil	19.0	23.8	23.0	24.1	24.8	23.5	21.9	21.9	11.1	10.0	10.9	12.8	5.3	-5.0	1.7	-5.6
Chile	-0.7	9.2	3.8	9.7	20.8	16.3	27.6	17.0	11.1	11.1	18.5	17.1	7.1	1.9	3.3	0.9
Mexico	8.3	8.2	13.9	17.9	21.8	16.6	11.0	7.5	35.8	20.6	7.1	21.2	-0.6	-3.2	7.3	-3.2
Venezuela	NA	10.2	7.1	11.5	24.8	35.6	24.4	35.2	11.3	5.9	15.0	15.2	-8.3	-7.3	-10.4	-19.6
Middle East/North Africa	14.5	14.8	14.0	14.8	43.8	39.3	28.0	40.7	6.7	8.9	10.1	13.5	-16.1	-10.6	0.6	-7.8
Egypt	6.4	6.1	-4.9	NA	19.4	28.1	38.5	NA	15.3	13.9	12.2	NA	-5.0	-0.8	5.2	NA
Saudi Arabia	20.8	14.2	23.1	16.8	59.5	65.1	42.1	69.5	12.9	18.6	19.0	27.6	-20.7	-12.4	-10.8	-11.4
Other Europe	11.9	14.9	21.4	19.6	17.3	27.3	14.4	21.4	18.7	7.7	19.5	17.8	5.8	3.4	3.7	1.9
Turkey	10.8	17.9	27.6	17.2	14.6	32.1	9.2	15.7	27.4	9.1	33.1	8.9	11.8	9.6	13.0	10.3
Yugoslavia	12.3	13.6	19.9	20.7	18.3	24.8	15.7	23.4	15.0	6.8	15.8	19.7	1.8	-1.9	-1.4	0.1
Subsaharan Africa	12.0	11.2	11.5	11.0	27.3	27.3	19.5	26.9	1.9	7.5	8.4	5.3	-5.9	-12.6	-7.1	-11.5

Source: IMF, *Balance of Payments Yearbook*, and national sources.
Note: NA = not available.

Table 7.10   Average Annual Percentage Growth Rates of Exports of Services and Other Invisibles by Contry or Region, 1967–77 and 1977–87

Country or Region	Ship.		Travel		OT		Pass.		OPS		Total PS		Prop. Inc.		Lab. Inc.		Inv. Inc.	
	67–77	77–87	67–77	77–87	67–77	77–87	67–77	77–87	67–77	77–87	67–77	77–87	67–77	77–87	67–77	77–87	67–77	77–87
Industrialized Countries	14.1	5.7	14.2	10.5	16.5	6.4	13.9	11.0	19.6	10.5	15.6	9.2	12.7	8.7	13.4	8.7	18.1	16.6
Australia	28.2	3.6	16.4	16.0	12.6	2.6	NA	14.5	9.8	11.4	13.5	9.3	9.7	23.9	26.4	9.5	14.6	18.0
Austria	22.2	10.5	19.8	9.0	21.5	10.6	NA	NA	25.6	13.3	21.2	10.3	20.4	8.3	NA	NA	29.4	20.0
Canada	7.5	0.4	4.5	9.6	11.9	−1.4	NA	NA	16.8	10.3	8.9	8.6	NA	NA	NA	NA	14.7	12.0
European Community	15.1	5.6	14.7	10.7	15.4	5.9	12.9	10.3	19.2	9.6	16.0	8.8	11.8	11.2	12.9	9.3	20.6	17.1
Belgium	21.1	7.7	17.0	9.8	18.4	5.5	NA	14.0	22.0	6.8	20.6	7.5	5.6	10.6	13.9	5.2	30.9	18.7
Denmark	16.6	5.2	15.4	9.0	NA	4.9	NA	8.6	NA	6.8	15.2	6.7	NA	NA	NA	NA	21.0	21.9
France	24.7	6.4	14.3	10.5	NA	8.5	NA	NA	NA	8.0	18.5	8.4	NA	12.2	NA	7.7	20.0	16.9
Germany	12.9	4.2	15.3	9.2	14.5	9.5	15.5	9.6	24.1	9.4	17.5	8.5	13.4	12.1	20.0	12.6	22.5	16.8
Greece	12.0	5.8	22.7	8.8	18.8	−14.0	1.6	23.3	27.0	14.4	21.6	7.5	NA	NA	34.8	6.2	29.3	3.7
Ireland	1.6	14.7	5.4	10.0	17.4	13.4	9.1	9.6	25.0	9.9	9.5	10.7	NA	NA	NA	NA	10.5	11.3
Italy	10.5	13.1	12.8	9.8	11.1	−0.1	9.2	7.2	NA	12.1	11.8	10.4	NA	14.8	7.9	8.3	15.0	16.8
Netherlands	51.4	5.5	13.4	9.3	NA	4.6	NA	8.5	NA	9.8	19.6	7.4	NA	12.0	NA	5.5	20.6	12.6
Portugal	NA	13.1	NA	18.0	NA	6.9	NA	12.3	NA	11.8	NA	14.6	NA	10.7	NA	16.6	NA	20.7
Spain	24.6	9.1	12.7	14.0	24.9	11.4	23.4	15.8	19.6	11.7	15.2	13.3	NA	3.5	NA	16.2	37.1	15.0
United Kingdom	8.3	−0.6	20.2	9.6	14.7	2.2	11.9	10.4	13.6	12.7	13.2	8.5	12.7	7.2	NA	NA	19.0	17.9
Finland	9.4	8.1	22.1	8.2	22.8	6.3	32.5	13.1	23.1	10.5	19.2	9.1	NA	22.7	15.6	4.9	25.9	27.7
Japan	23.7	6.7	16.7	17.4	21.7	3.0	NA	9.8	22.6	15.5	22.8	9.4	NA	19.9	NA	10.2	29.1	29.4

New Zealand	29.1	−8.7	22.8	19.6	NA	NA	NA	NA	NA	NA	14.7	14.7	24.7	11.1	NA	NA	12.5	12.9
Norway	8.0	3.4	16.8	10.0	16.2	8.4	NA	5.3	21.1	6.3	11.5	5.2	NA	3.5	NA	6.3	15.9	26.3
Sweden	4.6	10.8	15.1	16.4	14.3	6.9	15.4	8.1	24.8	4.5	14.8	8.4	25.0	14.4	31.3	−3.2	16.7	20.2
Switzerland	12.8	6.7	10.9	10.7	NA	NA	NA	8.8	NA	15.3	13.2	12.2	NA	NA	NA	4.9	22.2	19.1
United States	10.5	6.9	14.1	9.1	NA	9.7	NA	14.6	NA	14.4	12.8	10.4	NA	6.3	NA	3.2	14.9	12.4
Developing Countries	18.0	11.6	16.2	9.4	19.0	5.6	23.6	12.1	23.8	10.0	18.7	10.2	54.5	−4.2	18.1	11.3	30.9	10.0
Asia	23.9	25.4	21.5	16.2	18.8	6.2	13.1	16.3	26.4	16.3	22.5	11.0	10.3	20.3	16.2	16.6	24.5	25.7
China	NA	NA	NA	NA	NA	NA	NA	NA	NA	NA	NA	NA	NA	NA	NA	NA	NA	NA
Hong Kong	NA	NA	NA	NA	NA	NA	NA	NA	NA	NA	NA	NA	NA	NA	NA	NA	NA	NA
India	14.1	6.6	31.2	10.0	4.4	5.6	NA	NA	18.1	13.5	18.1	10.2	NA	NA	NA	NA	26.6	5.0
South Korea	39.3	19.4	36.9	19.5	47.5	5.3	43.0	19.9	54.2	6.4	46.9	12.1	NA	NA	11.4	15.6	55.9	10.2
Singapore	44.4	16.1	31.3	13.5	20.7	8.1	NA	NA	78.8	6.1	32.3	9.3	NA	NA	NA	NA	27.7	20.0
Taiwan	NA	30.6	NA	11.7	NA	13.4	NA	NA	NA	13.3	NA	14.2	NA	NA	NA	NA	NA	12.0
Latin America	22.5	6.5	11.2	6.9	12.9	3.3	23.6	11.6	22.6	7.3	15.3	6.7	53.1	−27.3	24.1	2.6	31.8	12.0
Argentina	17.0	7.5	16.3	11.2	10.9	6.3	22.6	8.2	17.4	7.0	15.5	6.7	21.5	0.2	NA	NA	25.5	5.0
Brazil	28.8	8.0	13.8	6.4	16.5	9.7	8.9	17.5	25.2	0.7	22.4	6.2	NA	−27.3	NA	−5.7	35.0	4.4
Chile	NA	5.5	6.1	8.7	−3.3	13.2	5.8	37.2	40.2	11.7	15.1	10.7	NA	NA	NA	NA	NA	25.6
Mexico	NA	NA	8.2	5.1	NA	9.6	NA	15.0	55.5	10.0	4.8	14.4	NA	NA	34.5	3.9	21.5	27.1
Venezuela	32.4	6.3	17.7	6.3	12.5	−5.7	NA	11.0	10.9	−13.3	15.4	1.5	NA	NA	NA	NA	38.1	6.1
Middle East/North Africa	12.7	6.8	22.1	2.8	27.0	−0.2	23.2	6.3	8.3	11.2	19.6	5.2	NA	13.4	15.1	7.8	38.9	9.3
Egypt	NA	NA	NA	0.1	NA	10.5	NA	12.7	7.2	16.5	14.8	8.6	NA	NA	NA	NA	5.8	29.3
Saudi Arabia	NA	NA	29.3	NA	34.8	−25.9	NA	NA	NA	NA	32.3	3.3	NA	NA	NA	NA	55.9	10.2
Other Europe	14.2	5.7	21.2	10.9	30.2	6.3	9.8	11.7	13.1	19.8	17.8	11.3	NA	NA	NA	NA	33.3	18.1
Turkey	27.4	21.2	31.8	21.8	27.7	−4.8	NA	NA	NA	NA	18.0	22.6	NA	NA	NA	NA	NA	58.6
Yugoslavia	13.0	−1.4	19.7	6.2	32.2	10.1	12.0	11.7	18.4	11.1	17.8	6.9	NA	NA	NA	NA	32.7	1.4
Subsaharan Africa	16.9	−2.3	15.8	5.6	16.6	−5.7	11.8	12.7	17.3	−3.4	15.8	−0.3	NA	−4.5	NA	7.5	17.6	−4.0

Source: IMF, Balance of Payments Yearbook, and national sources.

Note: For key to abbreviations, see note to table 7.6; Inv. Inc. = investment income.

Table 7.11   Average Annual Percentage Growth Rates of Imports of Services and Other Invisibles by Country or Region, 1967–87

Country or Region	Ship. 67–77	Ship. 77–87	Travel 67–77	Travel 77–87	OT 67–77	OT 77–87	Pass. 67–77	Pass. 77–87	OPS 67–77	OPS 77–87	Total PS 67–77	Total PS 77–87	Prop. Inc. 67–77	Prop. Inc. 77–87	Lab. Inc. 67–77	Lab. Inc. 77–87	Inv. Inc. 67–77	Inv. Inc. 77–87
Industrialized Countries	15.1	7.6	15.4	11.0	14.3	5.3	18.6	12.5	18.6	10.8	15.9	9.5	13.3	11.6	17.5	11.7	20.8	17.8
Australia	12.3	4.6	21.8	7.6	5.0	3.3	NA	5.7	18.6	8.8	15.7	6.2	11.5	7.7	26.4	9.5	14.1	15.5
Austria	22.0	9.0	25.4	10.2	22.8	9.1	NA	NA	18.1	11.3	22.6	10.4	17.9	7.7	NA	NA	28.3	17.6
Canada	15.5	1.5	15.4	11.1	5.5	0.7	NA	NA	14.8	10.5	14.6	7.6	NA	NA	NA	NA	14.1	11.5
European Community	16.4	7.6	16.7	10.8	11.4	5.2	15.8	12.6	18.7	9.8	16.4	9.3	12.9	11.1	17.6	11.3	23.9	17.1
Belgium	22.0	4.6	17.8	7.4	19.7	7.4	NA	11.3	21.4	10.4	20.5	8.5	8.8	12.7	23.8	8.8	30.3	19.9
Denmark	11.6	7.8	15.2	11.8	NA	8.1	NA	NA	NA	8.9	20.5	8.5	NA	NA	NA	NA	28.0	22.3
France	29.1	6.5	13.0	8.0	14.3	10.0	NA	NA	NA	9.9	18.9	8.6	NA	11.3	NA	12.5	28.4	18.6
West Germany	13.7	6.8	20.7	8.9	17.8	5.0	17.4	10.3	19.6	9.0	18.3	8.5	16.3	9.4	18.9	11.4	18.7	13.9
Greece	18.5	6.9	14.8	12.0	13.4	-0.8	16.7	11.7	16.1	6.6	16.9	7.6	NA	-1.8	17.4	3.4	17.5	21.4
Ireland	16.5	9.4	10.9	13.1	12.6	14.3	NA	NA	28.5	16.0	15.2	13.0	NA	NA	NA	NA	23.1	20.8
Italy	9.7	10.5	11.6	17.6	NA	4.8	12.8	15.6	NA	11.8	10.8	11.7	NA	13.4	5.9	16.3	21.4	18.3
Netherlands	21.3	6.9	20.0	10.1	NA	5.3	NA	7.5	NA	11.3	22.3	9.0	NA	12.0	NA	6.6	23.4	13.9
Portugal	NA	10.6	NA	11.2	NA	8.7	NA	0.3	NA	11.6	NA	10.6	NA	15.9	NA	-2.6	NA	18.7
Spain	13.0	10.2	18.3	13.9	31.0	10.6	28.9	16.3	20.3	11.7	18.8	11.8	7.8	11.3	9.5	14.4	26.1	14.8
United Kingdom	12.1	8.5	10.6	19.2	8.8	2.0	13.4	16.9	14.5	7.1	11.0	9.7	11.3	7.9	NA	NA	24.6	16.9
Finland	14.1	11.8	17.2	14.9	16.4	2.3	27.5	13.7	19.5	15.4	17.3	6.9	17.2	14.5	-8.4	2.9	25.9	15.1
Japan	8.8	11.2	30.5	17.5	26.1	1.9	NA	15.4	17.2	15.2	19.3	11.2	NA	14.5	NA	15.8	22.9	24.5
New Zealand	16.4	-2.3	20.3	10.3	NA	NA	NA	NA	12.3	9.6	16.1	8.6	NA	NA	NA	NA	17.9	16.0
Norway	17.3	7.9	18.6	11.7	12.0	5.7	NA	NA	31.6	3.9	17.3	6.9	NA	12.9	NA	16.4	21.9	13.6
Sweden	16.3	-2.7	15.8	11.7	13.0	0.8	21.5	11.1	19.4	10.3	16.1	7.4	14.9	13.0	15.4	14.1	30.3	19.5

Switzerland	16.1	13.1	14.1	14.6	NA	4.0	NA	12.2	NA	10.1	16.6	13.0	NA	NA	NA	14.5	21.5	32.3
United States	14.9	8.2	8.8	10.6	NA	9.2	NA	12.3	NA	14.5	11.4	10.5	10.1	NA	NA	5.2	17.9	19.4
Developing Countries																		
Asia	20.0	2.8	17.6	6.2	24.8	6.3	18.6	3.6	20.6	9.6	20.0	6.3	16.7	3.9	29.1	13.1	16.1	9.5
China	12.7	11.7	23.7	17.2	22.3	14.4	61.0	9.8	18.9	10.8	18.5	15.7	12.7	13.2	28.1	13.3	20.3	18.4
Hong Kong	NA	NA	NA	NA	NA	NA	NA	NA	NA	NA	NA	NA	NA	NA	NA	NA	NA	NA
India	NA	NA	NA	19.7	NA	NA	NA	5.6	NA	NA	NA	NA	NA	NA	NA	NA	NA	NA
South Korea	8.0	11.2	9.9	21.2	10.7	12.0	NA	NA	11.7	16.4	9.7	13.9	NA	NA	NA	NA	3.2	NA
Singapore	19.2	8.2	29.1	19.7	57.8	14.2	23.4	15.7	37.5	6.7	32.1	10.4	32.2	NA	NA	27.2	50.9	17.1
Taiwan	20.5	13.5	41.8	14.9	NA	NA	NA	NA	43.4	15.1	23.3	14.4	NA	NA	NA	NA	42.3	14.1
Latin America	NA	15.3	NA	18.8	NA	14.7	NA	NA	NA	23.0	NA	14.3	NA	NA	NA	NA	NA	NA
Argentina	13.4	1.7	13.0	5.2	32.9	5.7	12.7	6.1	16.4	6.7	15.4	4.8	3.1	20.1	NA	5.8	15.4	13.3
Brazil	9.0	-2.7	4.2	16.9	15.1	11.7	10.8	9.3	11.2	8.9	9.0	10.5	18.0	NA	NA	-5.7	15.5	18.3
Chile	14.0	4.4	16.7	2.3	66.7	3.5	22.4	-0.4	16.9	4.7	22.2	3.8	-13.1	NA	NA	NA	28.3	11.1
Mexico	4.6	3.0	17.8	5.5	39.9	5.4	6.1	16.0	8.7	20.1	13.0	8.6	7.8	NA	NA	NA	6.8	17.3
Venezuela	16.0	6.1	8.5	7.1	NA	24.3	8.1	-4.4	36.7	11.4	12.6	8.8	NA	NA	NA	NA	16.9	14.5
Middle East/North Africa	21.5	-1.9	26.1	-9.6	NA	2.4	3.3	-0.1	22.4	-2.2	22.7	-3.7	NA	NA	NA	NA	NA	14.9
North Africa	30.5	-2.8	26.8	0.9	25.9	0.6	21.4	-2.8	19.9	9.5	26.8	2.0	3.9	NA	41.1	12.1	14.3	-0.4
Egypt	18.0	6.3	21.9	-5.6	18.5	5.1	NA	5.8	26.8	9.3	21.9	6.8	NA	NA	NA	NA	21.0	12.0
Saudi Arabia	47.8	-2.4	32.9	NA	40.6	NA	NA	NA	34.7	24.7	40.7	6.3	NA	NA	NA	NA	21.0	-16.6
Other Europe	16.3	6.7	16.2	4.3	18.8	6.9	16.7	NA	29.3	13.1	20.6	9.5	NA	NA	NA	NA	17.6	19.4
Turkey	10.7	8.7	27.7	5.8	21.2	14.5	16.7	NA	11.7	16.2	16.4	9.6	NA	NA	NA	NA	17.9	16.0
Yugoslavia	18.7	6.1	5.8	-0.8	18.6	5.7	NA	NA	34.6	12.8	22.1	9.5	NA	NA	NA	NA	17.5	16.4
Subsaharan Africa	20.0	-3.1	14.6	-3.8	15.0	-6.1	8.1	-0.6	22.5	-5.3	19.3	-4.2	-5.2	NA	NA	21.5	17.0	4.8

Source: IMF, *Balance of Payments Yearbook*, and national sources.

Note: For key to abbreviations, see note to table 7.6; Inv Inc. = investment income.

be concentrated in markets with relatively high per capita incomes and relatively liberal foreign investment policies. Furthermore, the share of FDI in services will tend to increase as per capita incomes rise (given no change in government policies) and as FDI regulations are relaxed.

2. *Services FDI share.* As many services cannot be traded in a manner analogous to trade in goods, one might expect that FDI in services should, on average, be greater than FDI in manufacturing.

3. *Services FDI/services trade.* Because trade in goods is less constrained than trade in services, all other things equal, FDI in service activities will be more important relative to trade in services than relative to trade in merchandise (i.e., primary and manufactured products).

4. *Intrafirm services trade.* The relative importance of intrafirm trade in services will increase over time as technological advances allow disembodied (long-distance) provision to occur more cheaply. This can be expected to hold for any given level of FDI and will be strengthened to the extent that FDI increases over time.

7.4.2   Evidence and Analysis

Global data on FDI are unfortunately rather scanty, and to the extent that countries report data at all, it is usually at a high level of aggregation. The basis for FDI stock and flow figures varies widely, and statistics are usually not readily comparable across countries. It is important to recognize, moreover, that breakdowns of FDI between goods and services sectors are made by only a limited number of countries and that stock data are often biased due to the widespread use of historical cost valuation methods, the distorting effects of exchange-rate fluctuations, exclusion of retained earnings, the treatment of divestment, and measures that are drawn on commitments or approvals rather than actual investment flows.

Table 7.12 contains data on the book value of the stock of inward FDI in total and the portion in services for selected host countries for various years. FDI in services can be seen to vary between 25 percent and 50 percent of the total stock of FDI in most host countries. According to Sauvant and Zimny (1987, p. 30), as of the mid-1980s about 40 percent of the world stock of FDI and 50 percent of the annual new flow of FDI was in services. In countries that report data, FDI in services has almost invariably become more important over time. The rise in the relative importance of FDI in services occurs in both industrialized and developing countries, although the increase is more marked for the industrialized countries. Much of services FDI in developing countries appears to be either investment in offshore financial centers and tax havens or investment in flags of convenience. However, as noted in UNCTC (1988), even when the foregoing investments are excluded, the share of services in total FDI in developing countries has increased over time. All of this suggests that the increasing relative importance of services in terms of domestic production and employment that we noted in our earlier discussion appears to

Table 7.12   **Inward Stock of Foreign Direct Investment in Services, by Selected Host Countries, Various Years**

Country	Year	Value (billions)		Share of Services in total FDI (%)
		Total FDI	FDI in Services	
Industrialized Nations (national currency)				
Australia	1975	7.0	3.1	43
	1983	18.1	8.5	47
Austria	1975	33.5	17.1	52
	1981	46.0	20.5	44
Canada	1975	37.4	9.2	25
	1984	81.8	23.6	29
EEC				
Belgium	1970	113.8	11.1	10
	1981	238.8	41.3	17
Denmark[a]	1983	7.7	2.8	37
France[b]	1980	89.7	33.1	37
	1985	129.0	81.7	63
West Germany	1976	78.9	26.3	33
	1985	119.1	54.9	46
Italy	1974	5,449.0	1,723.0	32
	1985	31,769.0	11,752.0	40
Netherlands	1973	20.7	5.8	28
	1984	58.3	24.9	43
Portugal	1974	7.7	3.1	40
	1983	38.4	16.4	43
Spain	1975	142.8	31.2	22
	1984	1,097.8	339.2	31
United Kingdom	1971	5.6[c]	0.6[c]	11
	1984	38.5	13.3	35
Finland[d]	1975	0.9	0.7	76
	1986	4.6	1.9	46
Japan (U.S. $)	1975	1.5	0.3	18
	1986	7.0	2.0	29
United States	1974	26.5	11.5[c]	43
	1986	209.3	111.2	53
Latin America (U.S. $)				
Argentina[e]	1981	2.4	0.6	25
	1985	3.1	0.9	26
Bolivia[f]	1981	0.46	0.05	11
	1986	0.53	0.06	11
Brazil	1971	2.9	0.5	16
	1985	25.7	5.6	22
Chile	1973	0.4	0.1	27
	1983	2.0	0.7	33
Colombia[g]	1975	0.6	0.2	29
	1986	2.7	0.4	13
Ecuador[g]	1981	1.0	0.5	48
	1986	1.3	0.6	44
Mexico	1971	3.0	0.6	19
	1981	13.5	3.2	23

(*continued*)

Table 7.12   **(continued)**

Country	Year	Value (billions)		Share of Services in total FDI (%)
		Total FDI	FDI in Services	
Panama	1975	0.3	0.1	32
	1983	0.4	0.2	48
Peru	1978	0.8	0.2	25
	1986	1.4	0.4	30
Venezuela	1981	1.8	0.6	34
	1986	2.4	0.65	27
Asia (U.S. $)				
Hong Kong	1981	3.8	2.4	55
Indonesia[h]	1977	2.9	0.3	11
	1985	6.4	0.7	10
Malaysia[i]	1972	0.7	0.2	37
	1984	2.9	1.2	40
Philippines	1976	0.5	0.2	34
	1983	2.0	0.5	26
Singapore	1970	0.6	0.3	55
	1981	8.2	4.2	51
South Korea	1980	1.1	0.3	23
	1986	2.2	0.7	27
Sri Lanka[j]	1985	0.7	0.4	57
Taiwan	1986	5.9	1.4	23
Thailand[k]	1975	0.5	0.3	56
	1985	2.0	0.9	47
Africa (U.S. $)				
Egypt[l]	1979	7.0	4.0	57
	1984	14.9	6.7	45
Morocco	1975	0.2	0.1	48
	1982	0.7	0.4	54
Nigeria	1975	3.0	0.6	20
	1982	4.3	1.6	37
Zimbabwe	1982	1.9	0.7	34

Source: UNCTC (1988, pp. 378, 380–81).
Note: Shares were calculated before rounding of the stock data.
[a]Cumulative flows for 1974–83.
[b]Cumulative flows during 1975–80 and 1975–85.
[c]Excluding banking and insurance; services include agriculture and mining.
[d]Cumulative flows since 1967.
[e]Cumulative approved FDI since March 1977.
[f]Based on approvals.
[g]Excluding oil.
[h]Cumulative flows since 1977.
[i]Paid-up value of equity shares held by foreign residents in limited liability companies incorporated in Malaysia as of the end of 1972 and 1984, respectively.
[j]Cumulative flows since 1977 based on approvals.
[k]Cumulative flows since 1971.
[l]Cumulative flows 1974–79 and 1974–84 associated with projects established under the Investment and Free Zones Law.

have gone hand in hand with an increase in the relative importance of services in global flows of FDI.

Data on the sectoral composition of FDI in service activities are quite limited, as is evident from table 7.13. Where comparable sectoral data are available, it appears that FDI in wholesale and retail trade and financial services is especially important. However, most FDI in financial services apparently relates to offshore banking. There is reason to believe that maybe half of the stock of existing FDI in services reflects the establishment of service affiliates by firms whose primary activity is industrial (i.e., goods-related) in nature. In large part these investments appear to be directed toward financial and distribution-related activities and are intended to support parent-firm production and sales. Thus, much of the investment in finance and distribution is not independent. To illustrate this point further, according to the *CTC Reporter* (1987, p. 19), for West Germany service multinational enterprises (MNEs)

Table 7.13   **Composition of FDI in Services and Construction for Selected Host Countries (latest available year; in percentages)**

Country	Wholesale and Retail Trade	Finance and Insurance	Transport and Communications	Construction	Other Services
Industrialized Countries					
Canada	27.1	55.9	NSA	NSA	16.8
Belgium	35.1	NSA	NSA	NSA	64.9
France	30.3	55.5	1.2	NSA	8.7
West Germany	36.2	53.3	2.5	0.7	5.1
Italy	12.3	64.5	4.1	NSA	19.1
Netherlands	42.2	24.5	2.8	2.8	27.7
United Kingdom	24.1	43.3	1.5	1.5	1.5
Japan	43.7	35.2	2.9	2.9	15.4
United States	41.3	46.9	2.1	6.4	3.3
Latin America					
Brazil	17.7	65.9	NSA	NSA	16.2
Mexico	33.3	58.4	NSA	6.1	2.3
Peru	40.1	36.6	4.2	0.9	18.0
Asia					
Indonesia	44.9	NA	8.2	9.3	37.5
South Korea	NSA	12.7	4.0	18.9	64.4
Malaysia	17.2	64.3	NSA	2.0	16.5
Philippines	19.9	55.0	6.1	4.0	14.9
Singapore	32.1	57.8	6.6	2.6	0.7
Thailand	39.1	16.1	8.9	28.2	7.8
Taiwan	2.1	20.3	NSA	9.2	68.5
Africa					
Egypt	NSA	39.0	NSA	21.3	39.7
Nigeria	43.3	7.5	NA	46.4	NA

Source: UNCTC (1988), p. 593.
Note: NSA = not separately available; NA = not available.

controlled 29 percent of the total outward stock of FDI in 1984, while service affiliates represented 60 percent of the total number of affiliates and 45 percent of the total assets of all affiliates of German-based MNEs. The same phenomenon holds for the United States, where the figures were 55 percent and 68 percent respectively, given a share of services in the total stock of FDI of only 37 percent.

Some data pertaining to the distribution of total FDI by country or region of origin are contained in table 7.14. It is clear that Western Europe and the United States are the major sources of FDI, followed by Japan. Japan is important especially in the Asian region, as is reflected in its share of total FDI in Indonesia, South Korea, and Thailand. However, Japanese FDI has been of declining relative importance in the reported countries, reflecting in part increases in its share of FDI in industrialized nations. A weak tendency can be observed for Western Europe to become more important as a source of FDI. As one would expect, intraregional FDI is of some importance. Thus, Asian countries tend to invest in Australia, Indonesia, Japan, South Korea, and Thailand, while Latin American countries invest in Brazil, Colombia, Chile, Peru, and Venezuela.

While the data in table 7.14 do not permit a comprehensive breakdown by sector of FDI according to the country or region of origin, such information is available for outward stocks of FDI for a limited number of major industrialized countries and is presented in table 7.15. Two interesting facts emerge from this table. First, the share of FDI in services has tended to increase in most countries, but especially in industrialized ones. Second, most FDI is in developed nations. The implication is that FDI tends to be an intraindustrialized-nation affair. Also, the share of FDI in services, especially in the developed countries, has been increasing. Both of these observations are in accordance with the first hypothesis noted at the beginning of this section.

Table 7.12 indicates that inward FDI in services is less than half of total FDI in many countries. Data pertaining to the question of whether FDI in services tends to be higher than FDI in goods (i.e., manufacturing) are unfortunately not readily available as far as stocks of inward investment are concerned. Statistics on the sectoral breakdown of inward FDI reported in Stern and Hoekman (1988b, pp. 50–51) indicate that FDI in services is larger than FDI in manufacturing only for a number of the industrialized countries in the sample (Australia, New Zealand, and the United States). FDI in manufacturing was larger than FDI in services for all of the developing countries discussed.

Data reported in table 7.15 contradict this picture somewhat, as they show that as far as *outward* flows of FDI of major home countries are concerned, FDI in services in developing countries tends to be more important than FDI in manufacturing. However, in part this reflects a recent shift towards FDI in services; Table 7.15 also indicates that most of the major home countries reported the opposite in 1975. Of course, a general implication of the rising share of services in total FDI that one observes in the statistics is that FDI in primary and secondary activities will decline. It is interesting to observe, however, that while some source countries increased their FDI in primary activities, virtually all of them experienced a decline in the relative importance of FDI in manufacturing.

What can be said regarding the relative importance of trade versus FDI for services and merchandise, respectively? If ratios of FDI to trade for each of these two categories are calculated, one finds that ratios of FDI in nonservice activities to merchandise trade are usually lower than the comparable ratios for services. This is the case for many of the 39 countries included in table 7.12. In six, the latter ratio (not reported) is on average at least twice as large as the former. A corollary of this is that to the extent that ratios of stocks of FDI to trade are greater than one, this occurs for services, and not for merchandise.[13]

To be able to discuss the hypothesis that intrafirm trade in separated services will increase over time, data are required on the value and volume of transborder data flows (TDF). As noted in section 7.3, such data do not exist because of conceptual and technical measurement problems. Survey data, however, suggest that TDF have become increasingly important for many firms in the last decade and are expanding rapidly. Over 85 percent of multinationals in a sample survey conducted by Business International (1983) reported that they depended on TDF for at least one key aspect of their international operation. Important tasks for which TDF were used included financial management, marketing and distribution, and inventory control.

In conclusion, the data indicate that services-related FDI has been increasing in relative importance recently, mostly reflecting intraindustrialized-country flows. On average, it appears that FDI in services has been increasing relative to FDI in manufacturing. The available statistics also show that because merchandise trade flows are much larger, the ratio between merchandise exports and FDI in manufacturing is much higher than the ratio between exports of services and FDI in services.

7.5 Data Problems and Analytical Implications

While we have not dwelled on the reliability of the data discussed in the previous sections, we have noted that BOP statistics and stock data on FDI have a number of weaknesses. While we are of the opinion that many of the trends reported in the foregoing sections reflect "reality" as far as the direction of change is concerned for broad categories of services, comparisons across specific components of services must be made with the utmost caution. It thus

---

13. The ratio of FDI stock in services to trade in services was greater than one for ten of the countries included in table 7.12 (calculated for the most recent year).

Table 7.14   Book Value and Percentage Distribution of Inward Stock of FDI by Host Country and Country or Region of Origin

Host Country	Year	Total All Countries[a]	Percentage Distribution by Country or Region of Origin						
			Western Europe	Japan	U.S.	Other Developed Countries	Latin America	Asia	Less Developed Countries
Industrialized Countries									
Australia	1975	7,036	43.9	4.2	33.9	3.7	NA	NA	NA
	1984	20,274	35.3	10.0	36.7	2.8	NA	6.4	NA
Canada	1975	37,389	18.3	0.7	79.3	0.8	0.6	0.1	0.2
	1985	83,941	19.4	2.1	75.5	1.5	0.6	0.6	0.3
European Community									
West Germany	1976	63,531	52.7	2.2	40.9	0.9	1.1	0.2	0.9
	1985	88,256	48.8	6.0	38.6	1.6	1.6	0.4	1.4
Netherlands	1975	26,382	50.9	1.1	34.5	4.0	7.5	0.3	1.6
	1984	58,255	43.7	2.8	33.3	4.5	14.3	1.3	0.1
United Kingdom	1974	6,566	28.6	*	55.8	11.1	1.6	3.1	*
	1984	38,477	37.4	1.7	51.2	4.6	2.3	2.1	NA
Japan (U.S. $)	1975	1,500	21.1	—	60.0	2.5	0.7	0.9	1.9
	1986	7,007	23.4	—	48.6	1.8	NA	4.1	6.1
United States	1975	27,661	67.2	*	—	19.5	NA	1.2	NA
	1986	209,328	67.6	11.2	—	11.8	0.6	2.7	NA

Developing Countries

Brazil (U.S. $)	1975	7,305	11.5	32.8	6.3	6.6	0.2	5.8
	1985	25,664	9.3	31.4	5.9	6.9	0.6	3.0
Chile (U.S. $)	1985	7,613	0.8	66.8	10.4	5.3	NA	NA
Colombia (U.S. $)	1979	957	NA	53.0	3.4	17.2	1.2	NA
	1985	2,231	NA	64.1	2.8	9.7	1.8	NA
Indonesia (U.S. $)	1975	5,518	40.7	12.4	5.1	0.9	20.0	0.0
	1986	16,154	33.0	6.8	6.5	1.3	18.5	0.0
South Korea (U.S. $)	1976	675	64.8	20.2	1.5	5.4	0.6	0.6
	1985	1,829	47.5	32.1	1.1	2.2	2.4	1.3
Peru (U.S. $)	1977	791	2.2	44.7	4.2	14.3	0.1	0.4
	1985	10,359	26.7	16.6	3.0	0.5	24.0	0.2
Thailand	1975	3,714	41.6	14.5	0.5	0.9	23.0	2.2
	1985	10,359	26.7	16.6	3.0	0.5	24.0	0.2
Venezuela	1979	6,552	0.6	57.7	8.8	11.5	NA	3.5
	1985	11,075	3.1	54.1	5.9	10.0	NA	2.2

Source: UNCTC (1988).
Note: Total values in millions. Denomination is the national currency unless otherwise indicated.

Table 7.15   **Percentage Distribution and Book Value of Outward Stock of FDI by Home Country and Sector for the Industrialized and Developing Countries, 1975 and latest available year**

Home Country	Year	Industrialized Countries			Developing Countries			Total
		Pri.	Manuf.	Serv.	Pri.	Manuf.	Serv.	
Canada	1975	16.1	46.2	14.3	4.9	4.2	14.1	10,526
	1983	15.8	43.1	25.8	7.1	3.1	5.1	37,793
West Germany	1975	1.5	35.3	37.1	2.6	13.0	4.7	49,081
	1985	2.4	34.6	43.6	1.4	8.4	4.7	147,794
Japan	1975	10.9	8.8	26.5	17.2	23.6	13.0	15,942
	1986	4.0	12.8	37.1	8.9	13.8	23.4	10,970
Netherlands	1973	40.5	33.7	9.5	7.1	5.5	3.7	44,173
	1984	49.3	18.7	16.7	6.4	3.6	5.3	143,736
United Kingdom	1974	7.0	49.3	22.4	4.3	11.5	8.0	10,117
	1984	27.5	27.3	26.9	5.9	4.5	8.0	75,715
United States	1975	19.9	36.6	14.4	3.8	8.4	7.0	124,212
	1986	14.3	31.6	26.6	6.4	7.2	7.8	276,075

Source: UNCTC (1988).
Notes: Total values in millions of national currency with the exception of Japan, for which data are in U.S. dollars. Pri. = Primary (i.e., agriculture and mining).

seems fitting at this point to call attention to some of the most glaring data deficiencies that confront the analyst.

Because of their intangibility, data for trade in services are typically derived from central bank information on flows of foreign exchange or from periodic surveys of censuses of service industries. Banking data pertain to payments, not transactions, and thus this source can only give an incomplete picture of trade in services. Registered flows of foreign exchange often cover only part of a transaction, or, alternatively, may apply to a number of transactions. Only payments that are made via resident banks may be registered. Furthermore, some payments do not go through a financial intermediary. Finally, central bank cash-flow information sometimes is reported on a net basis and thus is useless in determining exports and imports.

Surveys of enterprises focus explicitly on transactions, not payments, so that in principle the foregoing problems do not arise. However, surveys lead to other potential problems. Imports by households and the government are sometimes not captured, nor are transactions made by firms that are not registered. Thus, it is crucial that an up-to-date registry of the universe of services providers be established.

In practice, services such as transport, insurance, and legal, financial, or professional services may in part be subsumed under the value of the goods to which they are related, or they may be misclassified, over- or underreported, or not reported at all. Most problems occur with respect to the reporting of

OPS. Overreporting may occur for categories such as merchanting (transactions of goods between residents and nonresidents where the goods stay in one country) and advertising. Some countries measure merchanting so as to include the value of the goods traded; others measure only the service component, that is, the trade margin.[14] Advertising is sometimes overreported, as a result of including establishment and operating costs. Misclassification may occur, as a result of reporting payments for services as payments for goods or factors, or vice versa. Also, labor and property incomes are often included indistinguishably in OPS. In part, these problems may be due to data-collection and reporting procedures.

This is certainly the case with respect to the registration of transactions between affiliates. The existence of differential tax rates, exchange restrictions, or investment performance requirements, and variations in the degree to which firms are forced to reinvest earnings lead to transfer-pricing strategies that bias reported trade figures. Separate statistics on transactions between affiliates do not exist on a global basis. This is regrettable, because it is likely that much of the trade that occurs between affiliates consists of intangibles. This is one reason to believe that total reported OPS is biased downward. Telecommunication and postal services are often the carrier (transportation technology) used to move services from the point of production to the point of consumption. The virtual nonexistence of data on the volume and value of services transported by these media constitutes another source of downward bias for OPS. Also, to the extent that trade data are reported, such data often are a function of accounting conventions and do not reflect actual payment flows.

Provider- and demander-located services appear only partially in the BOP, primarily under the heading of travel. Data for some services of this type, such as medical and educational services, are often not reported, even though the amounts may at times be substantial. For example, expenditures by nonresidents on U.S.-based health and education services in 1987 were estimated respectively at $518 million and $3,800 million (Ascher and Whichard, ch. 6 in this volume).

In the BOP, financial flows resulting from factor movements of some kind can be found under the following account headings: investment income; labor income not included elsewhere (n.i.e.); property income n.i.e.; worker remittances; and migrant transfers. The difference between remittances and labor income is that in the case of the former, the factor is considered to have changed residency. However, the one-year criterion for residency that is used in BOP statistics is rather arbitrary, and in practice it is often very difficult for statisticians to allocate financial flows to the two categories accurately. Indeed, the IMF tends to correct much of the data it receives. For example,

---

14. In the IMF statistics, merchanting is registered on a net basis. However, in national sources, merchanting is sometimes recorded on a gross basis.

about $5 billion of what countries reported as labor income in 1983 was re-classified as remittances (IMF 1987). In general, the five accounts noted above are unlikely to measure accurately payments accruing to domestic fac-tors. There may be some strategic reporting of income, for reasons mentioned above, involving transactions between affiliates. Also, what is reported as fac-tor income may at times be a flow associated with trade in a service. This is possible in those cases where demander-located services are provided via the physical movement of factors of production, since in practice it may often be difficult to distinguish factor inputs from service outputs.

By definition, services that are traded informally or in the underground economy are not recorded, nor are many services produced by firms whose primary activity is in the goods sector. In the latter case, which is likely to be more important, part of the value of trade in goods will actually be trade in services. Furthermore, nations differ substantially in terms of the composition of the aggregates reported to the IMF, as well as the methodologies employed to collect and estimate data.

Comparability across countries and time is also limited because coverage and methods of data collection may change (e.g., countries may improve the sectoral coverage of their data collection efforts). An example pertains to cur-rent U.S. collection of trade statistics for many service activities that had never been reported before (such as exports of health services). It is difficult to determine to what extent an increase in recorded trade in services for a specific time period is "real," and to what extent it may simply be an artifact of improvements in data-collection techniques.[15]

Another problem is that at virtually any level of aggregation, some nations may not report information on a certain item. For example, shipment exports are not reported by certain major ship-owning countries (e.g., Greece). Pas-senger services are often not reported separately by many countries but are included instead in travel or other transport. As already mentioned, this re-sults in biased figures when data are added across countries to arrive at re-gional totals, the total for developing countries, and so forth. Discrepancies also arise when comparing world imports for a category with world exports, which is another indicator of the nonreporting problem. For certain countries, publicly available statistics on trade in services do not appear to exist. While Eastern European countries and the USSR report merchandise trade statistics, there is no readily available source, with the exception of Poland, Hungary, and Romania for certain nonmerchandise items, for their nonmerchandise trade with each other and with the rest of the world.

The foregoing considerations suggest that it is very likely that the relative importance of services in the total trade of a nation will be underestimated. Research has indicated that in the early 1980s aggregate balance-of-payments

15. This may be the case, for example, in many of our tables where country data were reported for some but not all years.

data for the United States should have been anywhere from 40 percent to 100 percent higher than reported, depending on the definition of trade in services that is used (U.S. Congress, Office of Technology Assessment 1986). One implication is that calculations regarding the distribution of world trade across regions will be biased. Growth rates will, of course, also be biased, as will be conclusions regarding changes in the specialization of particular countries. However, we do not believe that the numerous data problems invalidate the trends that emerge. One of these trends is that the relative importance of services in the trade of developing countries has been increasing. The fact that there is a downward bias in the services statistics strengthens this conclusion. Also strengthening this conclusion are the possibly upward-biased growth rates of OPS, as the latter are primarily exported by industrialized countries. However, this bias could be a problem insofar as growth rates of OPS were compared to other categories of services or to merchandise.

As far as the statistics on FDI are concerned, to our knowledge there is no reason to believe that there are major differences between the accuracy of data pertaining to FDI in services and FDI in primary activities and industry. Some of the problems mentioned briefly in section 7.4—valuation based on historical cost, the distorting effects of exchange-rate fluctuations—affect all investment comparably, not just services. These problems should not bias our findings in section 7.4, as our main interest there is to compare services-related FDI with FDI in other sectors.

7.6   Data Needs and Priorities

There is obviously great scope for improvement of data on international trade and investment in services. Many of the questions (or hypotheses) suggested in our earlier discussion cannot be answered or investigated satisfactorily because the coverage of international transactions in services is inadequate. Thus, the absence of any data on the value and volume of transborder data flows and interaffiliate transactions in services makes it very difficult to determine what has been happening insofar as modes of delivery are concerned. It also makes it difficult to have confidence in any statement regarding the absolute and relative importance of services in world trade. We can say fairly confidently that even though the value of trade in services is currently underreported, in broad terms the trends suggested by existing data reflect actual developments. It is clear nonetheless that the current situation is less than satisfactory.

There are three groups of potential users of better data: policymakers, businesses, and analysts.[16] All three groups are likely to be interested in the same kind of improvements in the statistics. Arguably, what is needed is for data to

---

16. Policymakers include negotiators. For a review of data requirements from the point of view of negotiators in the Uruguay Round of multilateral trade negotiations, see Hoekman (1989).

be generated on a comparable country basis covering: the domestic production of services; trade in services on both a volume and a value basis by origin and destination; outward and inward FDI by sector and country; and the share of services production that is provided by firms and labor having ties to other countries. (The last should include only production by entities that have decided on longer-term establishment, because services provided via a short-term presence constitute trade.) It would also be desirable if: production and trade data could be reported on the basis of compatible nomenclatures; and the data on services could be linked with comparable data on goods.

Current BOP data are often not consistent with domestic statistics and classifications. It is difficult to relate trade data to the classifications used to report domestic data (such as the ISIC), so that one cannot relate trade to domestic production. This problem pertains to all the BOP service categories. For example, transport services in the BOP (i.e., shipment, passenger services, and other transportation) cannot be compared to domestic transportation data because part of traded transportation services is embodied in the value of traded goods.[17] Each item reported under the OPS heading consists of multiple items in the ISIC (or CPC), so that it often is not clear what the domestic counterpart of an item in the IMF category is. A related problem is that travel expenditures and receipts in the BOP are often not broken down by product or activity; very few countries currently do this.[18] Without this type of information it will always be very difficult to determine how trade in services via provider or consumer mobility has been evolving relative to separated trade.

In addition, information is needed on the existing government-imposed barriers and regulations that may impede trade in services or the right of establishment of foreign firms and the employment of foreign (nonimmigrant) labor. Much more information is required on what types of services are tradable in principle and what the relative costs are of alternative forms of trade for specific services. This type of information would allow the universe of services to be broken down into tradable and nontradable services (the latter requiring both long-term establishment abroad by the provider and the impossibility of movement of the consumer). It would help the analyst focus on

17. Currently, the IMF recommends that imports and exports be valued on a free-on-board (f.o.b.) basis. The implication of this is that there will be imputed imports (exports) of transportation (and other distribution) services if the invoice value of an import (export) transaction is greater (less than) the f.o.b. value. The use of the f.o.b. valuation convention for merchandise requires that gross flows of freight (shipment) services between countries be estimated. The convention recommended by the IMF is: to treat as credits all services performed by a country's residents on its exports once these have passed the border; and to treat as debits all services performed by nonresidents on a country's imports once these have been loaded on the carrier at the frontier of the country of export.

18. An exception is the United States, for which it was estimated that in 1984 visitors spent 26 percent of their total expenditures on lodging, 22 percent on gifts and other purchases, 21 percent on food and beverages, 16 percent on local transport, 9 percent on entertainment, and 6 percent on "other" items (OTA 1986). Note, incidentally, that these categories cannot be related unambiguously to ISIC categories.

substitution possibilities between alternative forms of trade. Thus, for some services the choice would be between embodiment in a good and separated trade, for others the choice would be between short-term or long-term mobility, and so forth.

All the foregoing data would provide information on the magnitude and composition of services in the international economy and permit a descriptive analysis of the stakes that particular countries and sectors have in the existing structure of trade and the foreign provision of services. It would become possible to analyze the effects of existing impediments on trade and (foreign) production of both goods and services, using either a partial or a general equilibrium computational framework. The object in either case would be to obtain estimates of the trade, employment, price, and welfare effects of existing restrictions and to determine how these effects would be altered if the restrictions were reduced or eliminated altogether. Since a foreign presence is essential in providing a wide variety of services, and in view of the substantial foreign production of goods as well, such analysis would need to take international factor mobility into account. This raises many new complexities, which to date have not been addressed systematically to any great extent in empirical work.[19]

However, budgets are limited, so that the question arises as to where the priorities should lie. A first priority is to improve the consistency and the comparability of the statistics. It would be a major improvement if data reported to and by IMF using its *existing* classification system were comparable across countries. In principle this could be achieved in a relatively short period of time and should not require a major outlay of financial resources.

Another short-run improvement that should be feasible is to inform the user of service statistics how "good" trade and investment data are, on both a sector and country basis. Obviously, some service figures will be reasonably accurate; statisticians may have a fair amount of confidence that the reported figure is within x percent of the "real" number. However, for other items the confidence in the number reported in the BOP should be much lower. Currently, there is no way for a user to determine this. Furthermore, wide discrepancies often exist between different sources. For example, travel exports for some countries as reported by the World Tourism Organization differ significantly from those reported by the IMF. In such a case, which figure should be considered to be more reliable?

From a longer perspective, the goal should be to improve on what is currently available. This would require the construction of a generally acceptable nomenclature for services allowing for a more detailed reporting of specific service activities or products. It should either be consistent with classification

19. It should be reemphasized that improved information is not of interest only to the analyst. Policymakers, such as negotiators involved in multilateral discussions, desire as much information as possible so as to be able to determine what the status quo is, and to be able to pursue tradeoffs and linkages.

systems used in the national accounts or be easily concorded. Fortuitously, in part thanks to the efforts of the Voorburg Group on Service Statistics, the basis for such a nomenclature is currently available in the form of the provisional CPC. The CPC has been used by the GATT Secretariat as the basis for a list of the universe of service products requested by negotiators. Work is ongoing in the EEC, OECD, UNSO, and IMF to develop a classification of international services transactions that is consistent with the CPC and the revised ISIC.

Given a nomenclature, data will have to be collected, preferably on an origin-and-destination basis. This will require more extensive use of sample survey techniques by many countries to augment central bank sources. Such procedures are probably the only way to obtain a good impression of the magnitude of intrafirm transactions, many professional services, and computer and communication services. Ideally, methodologies should be developed that allow trade data to be collected on a volume basis as well as a value basis. Currently, the absence of such data makes it very difficult to determine issues like the proportion of growth in a given year due to inflation and the role of changes in quality.

Developing countries will obviously face greater constraints, of both a technical and a financial nature, in attempting to improve their statistics. Three avenues, none of which is mutually exclusive, can be taken to deal with this problem. First, there could be assistance by industrialized nations and multilateral institutions. Second, as more disaggregated data become available from industrialized nations on an origin-and-destination basis, they will already provide an indication of developing-country trade. Third, datacollection efforts could be focused primarily on aggregates. Often there may be more interest in having an accurate picture of total trade rather than in having a detailed breakdown.

7.7 Conclusion

We have made an effort in this paper to identify and discuss important conceptual and measurement issues involving international transactions in services and to present and analyze available global data on services, to the extent feasible. Several hypotheses or questions were posed with regard to the evolution of trade and foreign direct investment in goods and services. While we are fairly confident in interpreting some of the changes that can be observed in the broad aggregates, more detailed analysis of services components unfortunately rests on a much shakier foundation.

There is obviously great scope for improving the accuracy and comparability of the existing data on services and for disaggregating the components, especially of OPS, which have been growing rapidly. However, because of resource constraints and especially because of the inherent difficulty of measuring many intangible services transactions, data improvements are bound to be slow in coming. In view of the fact that services have been given a prominent place on the Uruguay Round negotiating agenda, the need for better data has been underscored. Since interest in services issues in both domestic and international transactions is bound to grow, it will be important to maintain the momentum for national governments and international organizations to gather and report better and more detailed data on services.

References

Adams, F. Gerard, and S. Siwaraksa. 1987. A Disaggregated Study of the Service Sector. Fishman Davidson Center for Study of the Service Sector Discussion Paper no. 28. Philadelphia: University of Pennsylvania.

Ascher, Bernard, and Obie Whichard. 1987. Improving Services Trade Statistics. In *The Emerging Service Economy,* ed. O. Giarini. New York: Pergamon Press.

Baumol, William. 1967. Macroeconomics of Unbalanced Growth. *American Economic Review* 57: 415–24.

————. 1985. Productivity Policy and the Service Sector. In *Managing the Service Economy: Prospects and Problems,* ed. Robert P. Inman. New York: Cambridge University Press.

Bhagwati, Jagdish N. 1984. Splintering and Disembodiment of Services and Developing Nations. *The World Economy* 7:133–44.

————. 1987. Trade in Services and Developing Countries. In *The Emerging Service Economy,* ed. O. Giarini.

Business International. 1983. *Transborder Data Flow: Issues, Barriers, and Corporate Responses.* New York: Business International.

CTC Reporter. 1987. TNCs in Services and TDF. United Nations Centre on Transnational Corporations. New York. No. 23 (Spring): 18–21.

Drechsler, L., and H. Hoffmann. 1988. Conjectures on Services in the World Economy with Scanty Data. Department of International Economic and Social Affairs, Working Paper no. 10. New York: United Nations.

Duchin, Faye. 1988. Role of Services in the U.S. Economy. In *Technology in Services,* ed. J. Guile and J. B. Quinn. Washington, D.C.: National Academy Press.

Feketekuty, Geza. 1988. *International Trade in Services.* Cambridge: Ballinger.

Fuchs, Victor. 1968. *The Service Economy.* New York: Columbia University Press.

General Agreement on Tariffs and Trade (GATT). 1989. *International Trade, 1988– 89.* Vol. 1. Geneva: GATT.

Green, M. 1985. The Development of Market Services in the European Community, United States, and Japan. *European Community* (September).

Hirsch, Seev. 1989. Services and Service Intensity in International Trade. *Weltwirtschaftliches Archiv* 125:45–60.

Hoekman, Bernard M. 1988. The Uruguay Round of Multilateral Trade Negotiations: Investigating the Scope for Agreement. Ph.D. diss., University of Michigan, Ann Arbor.

————. 1989. Statistics on Services: User Needs Emerging from the Uruguay Round Negotiations on Services. Paper presented at the fourth meeting of the Voorburg Group on Service Statistics, October 2–5, Ottawa.

International Labour Organisation (ILO). 1986. *Economically Active Population: Estimates and Projections, 1950–2025.* Geneva: ILO.

International Monetary Fund (IMF). 1987. *World Current Account Discrepancy.* Washington, D.C.: IMF.

Kaspar, Daniel. 1988. *Deregulation and Globalization: Liberalizing International Trade in Air Services.* Cambridge: Ballinger.

Kutscher, Ronald. 1988. Growth of Services Employment in the United States. In *Technology in Services,* ed. J. Guile and J. B. Quinn. Washington, D.C.: National Academy Press.

Langhammer, Rolf J. 1989. North-South Trade in Services: Some Empirical Evidence. In *Services in World Economic Growth,* ed. Herbert Giersch. Kiel: Institut für Weltwirtschaft.

Noyelle, Thierry, and Anna Dutka. 1988. *International Trade in Business Services.* Cambridge, Mass.: Ballinger Press.

Park, Se-hark, and Kenneth Chan. 1989. A Cross Country Input-Output Analysis of Intersectoral Relationships between Manufacturing and Services. *World Development* 17: 199–212.

Sagari, Silvia. 1988. International Trade in Financial Services. World Bank, November. Typescript.

Sampson, Gary, and Richard Snape. 1985. Identifying the Issues in Trade in Services. *The World Economy* 8: 171–81.

Sapir, André, and Ernst Lutz. 1980. Trade in Non-Factor Services: Past Trends and Current Issues. World Bank Staff Working Paper no. 410. Washington, D.C.

———. 1981. Trade in Services: Economic Determinants and Development-Related Issues. World Bank Staff Working Paper no. 480. Washington, D.C.

Sauvant, Karl. 1987. *International Transactions in Services: The Politics of Transborder Data Flows.* Boulder, Col.: Westview Press.

Sauvant, Karl, and Zbigniew Zimny. 1987. Foreign Direct Investment in Services: The Neglected Dimension in International Service Negotiations. *World Competition* 31 (October): 27–55.

Stern, Robert M., and Bernard M. Hoekman. 1987. Analytical Issues and Data Needs for GATT Negotiations on Services. *The World Economy* 10: 39–60.

———. 1988a. Conceptual Issues Relating to Services in the International Economy. In *Trade and Investment in Services in the Asia-Pacific Region,* ed. Chung H. Lee and Seiji Naya. Boulder, Col.: Westview Press.

———. 1988b. The Service Sector in Economic Structure and International Transactions. In *Pacific Trade in Services,* ed. Leslie V. Castle and Christopher Findlay. Allen & Unwin Australia.

Transnational Data Communications Report. April 1987.

U.N. Center on Transnational Corporations (UNCTC). 1988. *Transnational Corporations in World Development: Trends and Prospects.* New York: United Nations.

U.N. Statistical Commission. 1989. *Report on the Twenty-fifth Session.* E/1989/21. New York: United Nations.

U.S. Congress, Office of Technology Assessment. 1986. *Trade in Services, Exports, and Foreign Revenues.* OTA-ITE-322. Washington, D.C.: Government Printing Office.

White, Lawrence. 1988. *International Trade in Ocean Shipping Services.* Cambridge, Mass.: Ballinger.

Yeats, Alexander. 1989. Maritime Transport. World Bank. Typescript.

Comment   Samuel Pizer

This paper is unusually broad in scope; it ranges from relatively philosophical questions about the definition and meaning of "services" to more mundane considerations of the quality and relevance of the data that are available. It is indeed thought-provoking to test whether various hypotheses about the evolution of the service sectors of different economies can be substantiated by reference to a wide array of statistical information assembled on a global scale. Like others, I have tried to set down a positive definition of "services," but there always seem to be exceptions. Pending an agreed-upon definition, however, the authorities are close to reaching agreement on a list of activities that should be covered in the service sector of the balance of payments accounts. These lists are fairly short—partly out of regard for the feelings of balance of payments compilers, but also because it seems sensible to organize the data for this purpose in terms of the main functional economic relationships among countries. These functional relationships, such as travel, shipping, or government, military, or economic programs, are measured as a blend of goods and services. This, of course, does not fit into the data cells that are considered to be necessary for analysis of the economies of the countries in which the payments occur. The gaps in the coverage of the data on international trade and services are also an indication of how recently an interest in some of the newer modes of international servicing has taken shape.

I have the greatest sympathy for researchers trying to educe significant trends and implications from the body of data on international trade and investment in services as it now exists. We certainly owe a debt to the authors of this paper for their heroic efforts in compiling the sweeping sets of statistics that underlie their thesis. To some extent we probably all have an ambivalent reaction to such statistical material. On the one hand, we would like to believe that it is good enough to sustain some line of argument that we are convinced is plausible. On the other hand, we are inclined to deplore the quality of the data and its failure to fit into the compartments necessary for our arguments. In the present instance, the authors believe they can find broad support for their propositions about patterns of trade and investment in services. I do not disagree with that judgment, provided it is limited to the observation that activities defined as services appear to have an increasing role in the economies of both developed and developing countries. I would be somewhat more cautious in making judgments about the significance of this development, especially as it applies to developing countries, and especially given the character of the services being measured for those countries. Another caveat, mentioned by the authors, is the need to refer to PPP-adjusted prices in comparing the relative shares of services between developed and developing countries.

Samuel Pizer is a consultant at the International Monetary Fund and former adviser at the Federal Reserve Board.

There is some consideration in the paper of hypotheses to be tested, mainly involving the link between the level and rate of growth of per capita income and the relative weight of service in the economy. It seems to me that the framework of this analysis is still very unsettled, and one of the reasons is the difficulty of deciding how and where to start measuring services in the economy. This is a well-known problem; perhaps the only measure reasonably invariant to structural shifts would be employment by occupation. While it is not within the purview of this paper to really tackle the problem, we should realize that it becomes particularly acute in comparing the economic structures of industrial and developing countries. Perhaps the term "industrial" is also becoming obsolete.

Turning to the statistical aspects of the paper under discussion, the sets of data that have been assembled are employed in a broad-brush manner as the basis for propositions about the growth of the service sector in international trade and investment and the development of economies in general. To do this, the data on services are sometimes combined, though the authors have also provided breakdowns by type of service whenever that is possible. My question is whether the constituent parts of the service sector—at least as they are summed up in data on international transactions or stocks of investment—add up to a functional whole. It seems to me that combining the data for the so-called service transactions produces a total that is not at all comparable to the result of combining all the data on exports or imports of goods. The latter yields consistent and comparable quantities that can be fitted into an analytical framework. The component parts fit along a spectrum of technical complexity and stages of production that can be compared across time or across countries. The component parts of the service sector (even if factor services are eliminated) do not fit along a spectrum in that way, though there are services that require advanced technology or training and others that require mainly a warm, sandy beach. Consequently, while there are types of services that can be analyzed comfortably in the standard framework of comparative advantage, I am not so sure that bundles of services can be dealt with in that way.

As noted in the paper, the problems of dealing with the service categories are made even more acute by the fact that, unlike goods, there are many kinds of services such as banking, commercial property, food services, and retail trade, that are important in home economies but cannot readily be traded between countries. In such cases the solution is often to establish locations abroad for delivering the services. Any analysis of international economic connections requires taking into account these offshore establishments. The same comment can be made about goods producers, but with the important difference that most goods producers have the alternatives of export or foreign production, while some producers of services have no practical exporting alternative. This may change as communication technology advances, with the interesting result that as the flow of information becomes swifter and deeper, the locus of production of either goods or services becomes increasingly detached from the locus of ownership or executive authority. Economies that are very poorly developed may well have foreign-owned enclaves of relatively high-technology goods or services. It will be difficult to know where to place these countries on the scale of development.

Much of what we see in the statistics as an upsurge in international service activity, or investment, in developing countries reflects the importance of a few developing countries as low-cost havens for financial, shipping, or insurance activities. Such developments should not be averaged across developing countries as a whole, nor should their economic significance for the populations of their host countries be exaggerated. In the paper under review, there are caveats about such interpretations of the data. Nevertheless, the picture conveyed of the rising share of service activities is certainly a key insight into the prospects of the evolution of international trade in the years ahead.

Without belaboring complaints about the available data in this field beyond the point already reached by the authors of the paper, a few additional observations on this aspect of the subject may be in order—particularly given that measurement issues are the central theme of this conference.

1. Much of the data used is drawn from the IMF yearbooks on balance of payments data. A few years ago the IMF commissioned a working party to study why the world balance on current account had a discrepancy of $75 billion (U.S.), including $79 billion in the service accounts in 1983. The working party recommended some steps to improve the situation, but by 1988 the total discrepancy was still $59 billion, and the discrepancy on services was $89 billion. If all the sectors of the current account—trade, services, and transfers—are added without regard to sign, the sum of discrepancies was $145 billion in 1983 and reached $200 billion by 1988. My point is not so much that the basic data are in difficulty, but to emphasize that remedial action is extremely difficult to achieve. Thus, one may be allowed a little skepticism in reaction to the statement in the paper: "It would be a major improvement if data reported to and by the IMF using its *existing* classification system were comparable across countries. In principle this could be achieved in a relatively short period of time and should not require a major outlay of financial resources."

2. On the other hand, there are grounds for optimism in the data for the OECD countries published in May 1989, which show extensive breakdown of service transactions, as well as in the new data now available in the U.S. balance of payments. It would seem that there is considerable momentum in measures to improve these data and their nomenclature, including a lively interest at IMF in this sector of the accounts—partly because it is in this sector that major discrepancies are found.

3. The authors comment that while there is a great deal of information for a

variety of service sectors, these data are not very useful for global analyses. My prejudice would run in the other direction. We know from the assembled data how dominant among the service sectors in international investment are two sectors, finance (including insurance) and wholesale and retail trade. We also know that some of the more abrupt shifts in imports or exports of goods and services are related to particular historical episodes (such as the debt crisis in Latin American countries), rather than to some change in the stage of development. This suggests that there may be quite a lot to be learned from somewhat narrower, yet global, studies, with rather more reference to historical circumstances.

4. With regard to the data on transportation and shipping, it is quite likely that much of the shift in the share of transactions from developed to less-developed countries represents the flagging-out of the major fleets to flag-of-convenience countries. This has little to do with the economic development of these countries, and is not a real shift in the center of economic interest of the owners or operators.

5. One of the relatively minor points noted in the paper is that as shown by table 7.11, Chile, Mexico, Egypt, and Yugoslavia had relatively fast growths of OPS (other private goods, services, and income) in the 1977–87 period. The issues here are that OPS is a quite vague category in the IMF's compilations and is often a catch-all category, and that, as the authors point out in their later discussion, there are difficulties with growth rates when it is not known how regular the data series may be. It may be too much to ask for the tables to contain absolute amounts as well as changes when the emphasis is on changes over time, but one must be very cautious in interpreting growth rates from an unknown base.

6. The data on inward FDI used in the paper were developed in a comprehensive study by the United Nations. They are not book values in all cases, but are derived in many cases from flow data or approvals. It is noted in the paper that these data are no worse than the data on FDI in other industries, and in any case the issue is the share of service industries in the total rather than an accurate absolute measure. There are several problems here. One is that it is indeed difficult to evaluate the significance of these figures, even if they were accurate, unless a great deal more is known about the characteristics of the investments. For instance, we see in table 7.12 that the share of services in total FDI is 57 percent for Sri Lanka, 47 percent for Thailand, 54 percent for Morocco, and 53 percent in the United States, but in the absence of information about the nature of the services it is difficult to know how to interpret these shares, or to know whether a rising share of services means a decline in some other sector has occurred. As to the stage-of-development question, in 1853 foreign investment in the United States was estimated at $1.2 billion, of which about 75 percent was in banks, railroads, and canals—but not necessarily as direct investment. In fact, it was probably normal for the initial direct

investments in developing countries to be in services—transportation, power, and communications—before these activities tended to be nationalized.

There is a more important point to be made. The relevant data for economic analysis are not the book values of these enterprises, or the capital and income flows connected with them, but rather the amounts that these enterprises contribute to production and incomes in the host countries. Unfortunately, only the United States at present compiles such data (after starting to do so about thirty years ago).

7. After a searching review of data shortcomings, the paper states, "Often there may be more interest in having an accurate picture of total trade rather than in having a detailed breakdown." This is an accurate reflection of the state of art in many countries, but it is not the interest that is lacking—it is a question of allocating scarce resources. It will always be a problem that some of the more interesting service accounts, such as information transmission, probably do not involve large cash outlays or receipts. Consequently, it may also be true, as stated in the paper, that the relative importance of service transactions will continue to be understated in the data on international trade.

8. One of the economic issues that is high on the agenda at present, and is referred to often in this paper, is bringing the international market for services into the Uruguay Round of trade negotiations. In that context, there is a demand for information on some types of international trade in services that have been neglected in the past—largely, I believe, because it has been assumed that they did not involve significant amounts. That may be changing now, but it is probably still the case that some of the services that can be enumerated are much less important quantitatively than others. If compilers have to concentrate on the most significant items, they need some guidance on the most fruitful targets. For instance, there is some emphasis in this paper on the need for better information on the value and volume of data transmitted electronically, but compilers cannot follow up on that suggestion unless they can recognize more concretely what it is that is now being missed and how to measure it.

The other dimension of the negotiation situation is the market activity of foreign affiliates. We have noted that little is known about this in the framework of the data collected on direct foreign investments, nor are the prospects bright for improving this situation in the foreseeable future. If progress is to be made, and I believe it is quite possible, it will probably come from surveys specifically tailored to particular kinds of services, or through collaboration with agencies collecting data primarily for use in domestic economic accounts. This would presumably yield information on the activities of foreign-owned enterprises in the home market more readily than information on activity in foreign markets.

I would like to recall that we are joined in an effort to promote the production of better data. It typically involves an exposé of the weaknesses of the data and may seem unnecessarily negative, but I believe it is best to proceed with as much insight as possible into the difficulties to be overcome and the economic issues to be addressed. Testing the data against a set of hypotheses, as is done in this paper, is certainly one of the most interesting and potentially fruitful methods of evaluating the adequacy of the information now available, and I look forward to further work, perhaps modified along the lines I have indicated.

IV   Foreign Direct Investment

8 Financial Flows versus Capital Spending
Alternative Measures of U.S.-Canadian Investment and Trade in the Analysis of Taxes

Harry Grubert and John Mutti

8.1 Introduction

The potential sensitivity of direct investment and trade flows to changes in tax rates in home and host countries often plays an important role in the evaluation of changes in tax policy. In U.S. discussions leading up to the Tax Reform Act of 1986, the fear was frequently expressed that the elimination of the investment tax credit and the reduction in accelerated depreciation would cause many U.S. companies to shift operations abroad. Canada was cited as one convenient, readily available location. As another example, in the 1970s Canada enacted a lower tax rate for manufacturing because of fears that the tax benefits granted to U.S. exports by the Domestic International Sales Corporation (DISC) provisions would adversely affect Canadian industry.

The purposes of this paper are to evaluate several alternative measures of direct investment, trade, and taxes, and to size up their interrelation in a U.S. and Canadian data sample. Almost all recent empirical analyses of the impact of tax policy on cross-border investments by multinational companies have focused on the financial flows used in the balance of payments accounts as a measure of investment (Hartman 1984 and 1985, Boskin and Gale 1987, Newlon 1987, Jun 1989, Slemrod 1990). These direct investment data represent new transfers to affiliates in the form of either debt or equity plus reinvested earnings abroad. But, as Guy Stevens (1972) suggested, the financial flow data are an inadequate starting point for a study of real investment deci-

Harry Grubert is an international economist in the Office of Tax Analysis, U.S. Treasury Department. John Mutti is professor of international economics at Grinnell College.

The authors would like to thank John Helliwell, the conference discussants, and participants in seminars at the NBER Summer Institute and at the Treasury Department for helpful comments. Jack Mintz, James Hines, and Jane Gravelle generously provided important data on taxes. David Belli of the U.S. Commerce Department gave very useful advice on the investment data. James Hodgson of Grinnell College rendered excellent research assistance.

sions and changes in the location of U.S. controlled production. Real spending by foreign affiliates on plant and equipment can be financed in several ways, including depreciation allowances, local borrowing, and reduced holding of financial assets, as well as transfers from the parent and reinvested earnings. Conversely, the foreign direct investment flow can finance increased holdings of financial assets and inventories as well as fixed capital.

One goal of this paper is to assess whether the two measures reported by the U.S. Commerce Department (real spending on plant and equipment by U.S. affiliates and foreign direct investment flows recorded in the balance of payments) give different indications of the importance of tax policy in influencing U.S.-controlled manufacturing in Canada. It is difficult to predict on a priori grounds whether financial flows or real spending will be more responsive to changes in U.S. and Canadian tax rates. On the one hand, it would appear that financial assets are more mobile than fixed capital assets and that financing decisions are very flexible, even with given investment plans. Higher statutory tax rates abroad may cause multinational corporations (MNCs) to shift their borrowing to their affiliates in countries where deductions are more valuable. However, it may also be true that factors such as exchange instability inhibit transfers from the parent, so that affiliates' fixed investment abroad may be highly responsive to local tax rates without any accompanying changes in financial inflows. Finally, any difference between financial flows and real spending may be purely a matter of timing. Funds may be transferred to the affiliate in the anticipation of capital expenditures, but the increased spending may not be observed for some time.

Real spending by U.S. affiliates in Canadian manufacturing is interesting in its own right and for how it compares with aggregate capital expenditures in Canadian manufacturing. Even in the absence of multinational corporations, increased U.S. corporate tax rates could lead to an outflow of portfolio investment and increased real spending abroad. Yet are MNCs vehicles for still greater capital mobility? The question is whether any response of total Canadian capital expenditures to U.S. and Canadian tax rates is attributable largely to the activities of U.S. MNCs.

The paper also considers the extent to which U.S.-Canadian trade patterns are influenced by changes in tax rates, including export incentives. Trade data are collected by both the U.S. and Canadian governments. In the 1980s, a discrepancy between Canadian measures of imports and U.S. measures of exports caused the U.S. government to begin using the Canadian figures. Another goal of this paper is to assess whether these different data series, and by implication efforts to measure trade flows more accurately, indicate a different role for tax policy in affecting trade. Alternatively, if data were more accurate, would analysts be able to determine the role of policy more clearly? Or is economic theory itself so imprecise that refinements in the trade data are not a critical step in helping sort out policy questions?

Still another empirical issue that emerges in the present study is the proper representation of tax policy. Recent analysis of domestic investment by public finance economists has focused on the marginal effective tax rate applicable to new capital spending. Such a measure is a constructed variable, dependent upon assumptions regarding the appropriate discount rate, inflationary expectations, and depreciation practices. In this study we test various assumptions to see if the ones commonly made are the most consistent with actual investment behavior.

The data comparisons in the paper are, therefore, of several types. In one type, such as in the comparison of the financial flow data and the real spending data, series which differ in concept are examined (although many studies have used direct investment as a proxy for capital expenditures). In a second type, exemplified by the U.S. and Canadian trade data, alternative measures of the same variables are tested. Yet another type is alternative measures of marginal effective tax rates, because the differences are due not to measurement error but to the different empirical assumptions made in constructing them.

The empirical results suggest that the role of taxes in the investment process is much clearer and more significant in the case of capital spending than in balance of payments flows. Effective tax rates based on assumptions typically made are not as successful in explaining investment as alternative measures. The effect of taxes on trade is less clearcut than the effect on investment. Finally, MNCs appear to be the major source of any tax-induced reallocation of investment between Canada and the United States.

8.2 The Alternative Data Sources and their Uses

Canada was chosen as the subject of the study in part because series on marginal effective tax rates can be adapted from other studies. In addition, the integration of the U.S. and Canadian economies may make it easier to identify the responsiveness of investment and production to changes in tax policy. Also, a long time series for U.S. investment in Canada can be assembled without disclosure problems. In the case of trade, Canadian statistics are a useful check on U.S. data. The analysis concentrates on manufacturing because investment in petroleum, mining, or agriculture may be subject to different forces and may be affected by very specific types of tax provisions.

8.2.1 Investment

The appropriate choice of the data series to be used depends on the issue at hand. As noted, expenditures on fixed investment are most relevant for considering shifts in the location of production and their impact on trade flows.[1] In contrast, the balance of payments direct investment data are useful in study-

---

1. After all, studies of domestic capital expenditure by U.S. corporations are not based on changes in the book value of their equity—which would be parallel to the balance of payment concept of foreign investment.

ing cross-border savings flows, the relationship between the capital and current account, and pressures on the exchange rate. For example, consider a large new investment project by a U.S. affiliate abroad that is financed entirely by local borrowing. It will eventually represent an important expansion of productive capacity abroad, but it may have very little current impact on the structure of the balance of payments or exchange rates.

These two measures of investment by U.S. affiliates in Canada, direct financial investment flows as reported in the balance of payments and fixed invest ment expenditures by majority-owned affiliates, are both published by the U.S. Commerce Department. After 1976, the definition of majority ownership changed from "50 percent or more ownership" to "greater than 50 percent," but this change seems to have had very little significance for Canadian investment.[2] While the plant-and-equipment series includes only investment by majority-owned affiliates, this difference from the financial flow series does not appear significant. The 1982 Commerce benchmark survey indicates that 93.5 percent of sales and 80.3 percent of capital expenditures by U.S. manufacturing affiliates in Canada are accounted for by majority-owned affiliates.

There are other coverage differences as well. For example, U.S. takeovers of Canadian companies would, in principle, be in the financial flow data if financed directly by the parent, but not in the investment-spending series (apart from the annual investment expenditures by the newly acquired affiliate). However, it is not clear that the failure to include takeover investments is a shortcoming from a conceptual point of view. Takeovers of existing Canadian operations may differ from investments increasing the capacity of affiliates in terms of their impact on technology and trade flows.

The foreign direct investment data itself are available in two forms. The version used in the analysis is the balance of payments capital outflow and is simply the sum of retained earnings plus equity and intercompany account flows. The other version is the change in the book value of the foreign direct investment position from the beginning of the year to the end of the year. These differ because of "valuation adjustments." For example, if a subsidiary is liquidated for more than its book value and the funds are repatriated, the decline in the direct investment position will reflect the original book value and not the larger capital outflow. Valuation adjustments are usually not large, but they are significant in some years.

Figure 8.1 displays the movements of gross plant and equipment spending by manufacturing affiliates (PPE) and the two versions of foreign direct in-

---

2. The major benchmark adjustment in both series in 1977 was dealt with by using dummy variables in the regressions. Data on a 1977 base were available through 1984. The data after 1984 on the new 1982 base were adjusted by using observations available on both bases for 1984. We chose to keep the data for 1982 through 1984 on the 1977 base in order to limit the number of years for which spliced data had to be used. Although data were available on both bases for two or more years when benchmarks were changed, no attempt was made to exploit the overlapping information for years other than 1984.

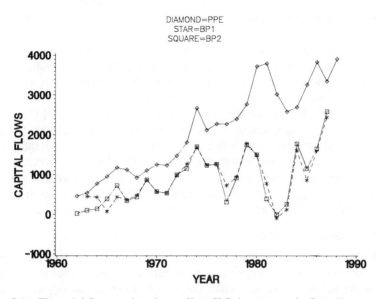

DIAMOND=PPE
STAR=BP1
SQUARE=BP2

Fig. 8.1   Financial flows and real spending; U.S. investment in Canadian manufacturing

vestment in manufacturing. BP1 refers to the change in the direct investment position, while BP2 is the total direct flow without valuation adjustments. It is evident that the real spending and financial flows frequently have behaved differently, particularly in the late 1970s and early 1980s. In fact, when each series is detrended, there is virtually no remaining correlation between them.

8.2.2   Manufacturing Imports and Exports

Two trade series are used. One is data on the value of trade by product category published in the *Bank of Canada Review*.[3] The product detail given made it possible to exclude manufactured products with a large resource content, such as forest products and nonferrous metals. It is one reason that total manufacturing import and export figures based on Canadian data may differ from the total manufacturing trade series derived from U.S. data.

The second series is based on various publications of the U.S. Commerce Department. Imports and exports from 1965 to 1980 were taken from *Overseas Business Reports*. For 1980 and subsequent years, *U.S. Foreign Trade Highlights* was used. The published data after 1979 have been adjusted for undocumented transactions over the Canadian border.[4] In addition, the defi-

3. In the 1966–87 period for which these data were available, there were occasional changes in some product categories. In all cases, however, there were several years in which the data were available on both bases. These overlapping data were used to splice the series together, with the accurate representation of the year-to-year rate of growth of trade as the objective.

4. Data were available for 1980 on both bases and could therefore be spliced together.

nition of manufacturing trade was expanded to include "category 9, other exports."

Figures 8.2. and 8.3 present U.S. manufacturing imports and exports, as derived from Canadian and U.S. published sources. The two alternative series on U.S. imports in figure 8.2, shown as Canadian exports (CNEX) and U.S. imports (USIM), are surprisingly close. Figure 8.3 confirms the year-by-year increase before 1980 of underreporting of U.S. exports by official U.S. data (USEX) compared to Canadian import data (CNIM). The published U.S. data for 1980 and later, which include the undocumented exports, were spliced to the earlier series. The gap between the Canadian and U.S. series would, therefore, be expected to continue because of the way we have constructed them. However, the gap does not seem to expand after 1980, so it appears that U.S. procedures have eliminated most of the inconsistency between the two series.

8.2.3   Effective Tax Rates

Marginal effective corporate tax rates for Canadian and U.S. manufacturing were derived from Hall-Jorgenson cost-of-capital estimates. The cost of capital is the annual pretax real return that a unit of capital has to earn for the discounted value of its net after-tax cash flows to just equal its initial price. The rate of return used to discount these real cash flows is the after-corporate-tax return required by investors in the corporate sector. The discounted real cash flow includes the gross earnings of the capital (net of the corporate tax rate on these earnings), plus the value of the depreciation deductions allowed for tax purposes and any investment grant or credit offered as an incentive by the government. Since the depreciation allowances are usually based on the historical cost of the capital, the discounted real value of these deductions depends on the expected inflation rate. Accordingly, the cost of capital (and the marginal effective tax rate derived from it) summarizes the various characteristics of the tax system, such as the statutory or nominal tax rate and depreciation allowances. However, it is necessary to make assumptions about the required real return and the nature of inflationary expectations.[5]

The effective tax rates for Canada are based on data provided by Jack Mintz and were used in Boadway, Bruce and Mintz (1987). In some cases, these basic data were revised after consulting Boadway and Kitchen (1980) and *the CCH Canadian Master Tax Guide*.[6]

The U.S. corporate effective tax rates were adapted from the data used by Auerbach and Hines (1988). In general an attempt was made to make assump-

---

5. A more detailed explanation of the derivation of effective tax rates is given in the Appendix.

6. Newlon (1987) computed Canadian effective tax rates from basically the same sources, and while his series is generally consistent with ours for earlier years, there appear to be unexplained disparities toward the end. (See fig. 8.4; NTAXCAN is Newlon's tax series.) In particular, Newlon has Canadian effective tax rates increasing sharply in 1981 and remaining high through 1985 (the last year in his sample). Neither our series nor the one developed by Boadway, Bruce, and Mintz shows such a large jump over this period. It is true that a half-year convention for tax depreciation was effective *after* 12 November 1981, but Newlon seems to exaggerate its effect.

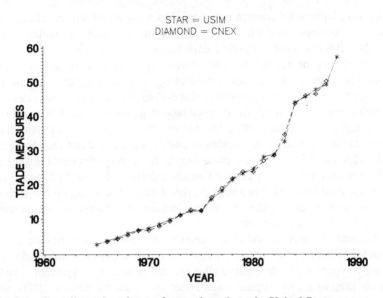

Fig. 8.2   Canadian sales of manufactured goods to the United States, measured by U.S. and Canadian sources

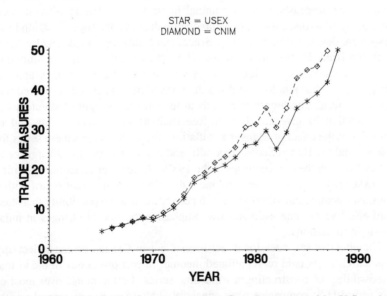

Fig. 8.3   U.S. sales of manufactured goods to Canada, measured by U.S. and Canadian sources

tions parallel to the Canadian estimates. Since the Auerbach and Hines data are only reported through 1986, information in Fullerton, Gillette, and Mackie (1987) was used to project effective tax rates after 1986.

In each case the effective tax rates refer to equity investment only. By introducing the statutory tax rate differential as an explanatory variable, an attempt is made to control for the possibility that differences in statutory tax rates and inflation rates make it relatively more advantageous to finance with debt in one country rather than another. In addition, there is no necessary connection between the location of an investment and the currency denomination of the debt with which it is financed. For example, the U.S. parent could finance its domestic investment with debt in Canadian dollars. Estimating effective tax rates for debt-financed investment is, therefore, not as straightforward as in the purely domestic context because it requires judgments on the currency denomination of the borrowing.

Alternative Canadian and U.S. marginal effective tax rate series were constructed based on differing assumptions on required rates of return and inflationary expectations. A required after-tax rate of return of 4 percent is commonly used (e.g., by Auerbach and Hines 1988, and by Newlon 1987), and we show it for Canada as TAXCAN4 in figure 8.4. Also, we calculated a set based on an 8 percent return, shown for Canada as TAXCAN8. In each case the required real rates of return are combined with expected inflation rates derived from ARIMA forecasts to form nominal interest rates. The nominal interest rates are used to discount future depreciation deductions. These inflation forecasts were developed by Boadway, Bruce, and Mintz for Canada and by Auerbach and Hines for the United States. The 8 percent rate-of-return assumption is in part motivated by Summers' (1986) finding that companies apply a higher rate of discount to cash flows than would be indicated by observed real rates of return. The higher rate tends to increase the weight of statutory tax rates relative to investment incentives such as investment credits and to smooth out the effect of changes in inflation. Figure 8.5 shows these series for Canada and the United States (TAXUS8), and it demonstrates the divergence in policy between the two countries in the 1980s. As another variation (identified as ITAXCAN in fig. 8.4), we combine a 4 percent required real return with a constant assumed rate of inflation of 6 percent, to test the possibility that standard effective tax rate estimates overemphasize the role of changes in inflationary expectations.

The effective tax rates for direct investment in Canada do not reflect any residual U.S. tax paid on repatriated income. In part this is due to the virtual impossibility of constructing a valid time series. Furthermore, over most of this period U.S. companies were apparently able to reduce or even eliminate the U.S. tax on Canadian income by using the "rhythm method" in timing their repatriations and real investments (or depreciation deductions) in Canada. They would repatriate in years in which their realized Canadian tax rate

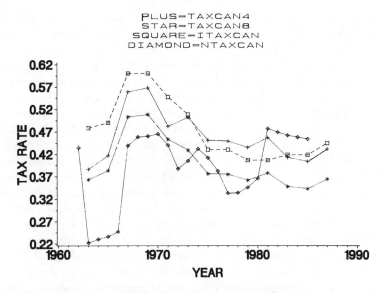

Fig. 8.4   Alternative measures of Canadian marginal effective tax rates

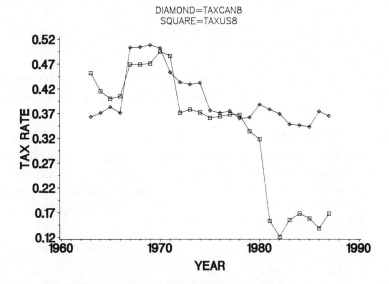

Fig. 8.5   U.S. versus Canadian marginal effective tax rates

was high so that they would earn higher credits against U.S. tax. (The Tax Reform Act of 1986 ended the benefits of these cyclic repatriation schemes.)[7]

In calculating effective tax rates relevant for investment decisions by U.S. MNCs, one issue that arises is the significance of the oligopolistic nature of MNC activities. Does the standard Hall-Jorgenson cost of capital calculation represent it adequately? Even if a corporation has market power for some reason, its marginal cost of capital is no more than the competitive return, because that is all it has to offer new shareholders or bondholders. In a purely domestic context, no adjustments appear necessary. If, however, an MNC is choosing between investment locations, the taxation of any monopoly rents becomes important. Consider the case in which the cost of capital (and therefore the marginal effective tax rate as usually measured) and marginal costs are the same in the two locations, but statutory rates differ. Shifting a dollar of capital from one country to the other (while continuing to supply the same market) will change the company's after-tax profits by the difference in the statutory tax rates times the average monopoly rent per unit of capital. This is a further reason for adding, as a variable, the difference in the statutory tax rates on manufacturing income. While the differential was never very great, the preference granted to Canadian manufacturing did create a gap of 8.0 percentage points for a time in the late 1970s.

In some of the trade regressions, the U.S. effective tax rate is adjusted to reflect the benefits, beginning in 1972, offered to export income by the Domestic International Sales Corporation (DISC) and subsequently by the Foreign Sales Corporation (FSC) provisions. The reduction in effective tax rates on exports attributable to the DISC-FSC rules is based either on deferral or exemption rates in the relevant statutes, or, when deferral rates could vary, the actual rates given in annual U.S. Treasury reports on the operation and effect of the DISC legislation.

8.2.4   Other Variables

Relative unit labor costs, adjusted for exchange rates, are used as one indicator of the cost of manufacturing in Canada relative to the United States.[8] Capacity utilization rates are used as an indicator of demand-side determinants. Unit labor costs and capacity utilization rates in manufacturing were obtained from *OECD Main Economic Indicators*.

---

7. A final reason for excluding the residual U.S. tax is the claim by Hartman (1985) that the residual U.S. tax is irrelevant for the choice of investment location if it is financed by an affiliate's retained earnings; the reason is that the tax has to be paid sooner or later. The analysis thus parallels the so-called "new view" of dividend taxation in the purely domestic context.

8. A conventional real exchange-rate measure could be used, but it might confound the role of taxes in costs. Because taxes are one of the costs that can be reflected in prices, some of the variations in real exchange rates could be attributable to tax changes. A real exchange-rate measure may play a role in determining foreign investment, apart from its effect on relative costs. For example, Froot and Stein (1989) have argued that the apparent increase in direct investment in the United States when the real value of the dollar is low results from the increased relative financial strength of foreign corporations.

8.3 Analysis of the Alternative Series

The investment equations used are designed to represent the choice of investment location by U.S. multinational corporations. Thus, they are not of the Jorgenson "neoclassical" type, in which output or sales are regarded as exogenous, because the amount of output or sales in a given location is part of the decision process.[9] Actual net rates of return earned in Canada by U.S. affiliates relative to U.S. returns are not included explicitly for several reasons. One is that, as Jun (1989) and others have pointed out, perturbations in rates of return are transmitted mechanically to measured direct investment, which is composed mainly of retained earnings. In addition, a reported profit in any location can itself be a function of the tax rate and may not be an accurate indicator of "true" profitability (e.g., Grubert and Mutti 1991).

In relating investment to tax and other variables over time, it is necessary to choose a proper scaling factor for investment because of potential heteroscedasticity problems when an unscaled dependent variable is used. Slemrod and Newlon each use host country GDP. For plant and equipment spending by U.S. affiliates in Canada, comparable investment spending in the United States seems a natural denominator. The ratio of Canadian to U.S. expenditures is expressed in real terms by first converting affiliate spending into Canadian dollars and then dividing spending in each country by the country's Gross National Expenditure deflator. The regression equation can then be interpreted as representing U.S. companies' choice between real investment in the United States or in Canada. One advantage of this formulation is that it controls for worldwide changes in capital costs, which would affect investment spending in both the United States and Canada. Financial flows are divided (scaled) by the total (internal and external) sources of funds of the U.S. nonfinancial corporate sector, as reported by the Federal Reserve Board. The variable therefore represents the share of the U.S. MNCs' funds (not including affiliates' third-party borrowing) that are allocated to Canada.

Tables 8.1 and 8.2 present results for balance of payments direct investment and capital expenditures respectively. The various cases correspond to different forms of the tax variables used, as well as to other changes in specification, such as whether the tax rates are lagged or not. (For example, "US METR 4% Return" refers to the U.S. marginal effective tax rate in manufacturing assuming a required real after-corporate-tax return of 4 percent.)[10] In most cases, a linear equation is used. In addition to U.S. and Canadian marginal tax rates, the independent variables include:

a. a dummy variable for the years after 1976, to reflect the 1977 benchmark adjustment;

---

9. For a discussion of various types of investment equations, see Feldstein (1982).

10. Durbin-Watson statistics are not separately reported because of space limitations. In no case were they of a level to suggest the need for correction for serial correlation.

Table 8.1   Comparison of Regressions Using Alternative Investment and Effective Tax Rate Measures. Dependent Variable: Balance of Payments Measure of Foreign Direct Investment, Divided by U.S. Flow of Funds (t-values in parenthesis)

Case	U.S. Tax	Canadian Tax	Dummy 1977	Time Trend	Canadian Capacity Utilization	Real Exchange Rate	Exchange Rate Uncertainty	Intercept	Adjusted R^2
US METR 4% Return / CN METR 4% Return	3.36 (.93)	3.98 (.54)	-4.53 (-3.15)	.30 (2.82)	.18 (2.01)			-16.17 (-2.01) / -17.57 (-2.50)	.57 / .60
US METR 8% Return / CN METR 8% Return	11.57 (1.83)	-4.09 (-.48)	-4.92 (-3.56)	.41 (3.51)	.19 (2.51)			-17.57 (-2.50)	.60
US 6% Inflation / CN METR 6% Inflation	16.18 (2.00)	-10.37 (1.38)	-5.69 (-4.11)	.44 (3.54)	.22 (3.01)			-18.69 (-2.60)	.61
US METR 4% Return / CN Newlon Tax	4.75 (1.33)	-3.66 (-.59)	-5.36 (-3.18)	.41 (2.64)	.17 (1.74)			-13.09 (1.64)	.57
US METR 4% Return, Total / CN METR 4% Return	13.00 (3.11)	-6.99 (-.98)	-4.77 (-3.97)	.40 (4.47)	.22 (3.42)			-18.72 (-3.06)	.70
US METR 4% Return, Total / CN METR 4% Return	17.08 (2.91)	-11.52 (-1.35)	-4.07 (2.59)	.44 (3.19)	.23 (3.36)	1.16 (.21)	-.30 (-1.19)	-20.02 (-2.30)	.69
US AVG TAX / CN AVG TAX	24.60 (3.38)	.47 (.03)	-3.95 (-2.75)	.23 (3.10)	.26 (3.52)			-18.43 (-2.92)	.71

Note: Time period is 1963–87, annual data (except for Newlon tax series terminated in 1985). METR = marginal effective tax rate; AVG = average effective tax rate after removing the influence of cyclical factors. Tax rates apply to manufacturing only, except where the total or economy-wide rate is noted.

b. a time trend, which indicates the impact of any difference in long-term growth in Canada compared to the United States;

c. the capacity utilization rate in Canadian manufacturing (in part intended as an indicator of the profitability of investing in Canada; for financial flows, there may be a more direct relationship if increased profits result in higher retained earnings);

d. a relative labor cost variable, equal to the ratio of U.S. to Canadian unit labor costs adjusted for exchanges rates; and   •

e. a measure of exchange-rate instability based on the squared changes in the previous three years, with the more recent years weighted more heavily. Companies may hedge exchange-rate uncertainty by engaging in more local borrowing in host-country currencies, reducing balance of payments flows.

The results for financial flows in table 8.1 reveal that the coefficient for U.S. effective tax rates is sometimes significant, although the Canadian rate generally is not; this result tends to cast doubt on the role of taxes. Tax rates tend to have more explanatory power when the U.S. economy-wide corporate rate, rather than the more noisy manufacturing-only rate, is used. The significance of taxes in determining financial flows is not increased when the tax rates are lagged.

Table 8.2 indicates that lagged effective tax rates *are* frequently significant in the capital spending regressions. This is particularly true when the effective tax rate based on an 8 percent required real return is used. In addition, we expect a reduction in Canadian tax rates to have at least as large an impact as an equivalent rise in U.S. tax rates, because the lower Canadian rate can attract investment from locations other than the United States and can lead to expansion in the total U.S.-Canadian market for the MNC's production.[11] The relative magnitudes of the Canadian and U.S. tax coefficients reported in table 8.2 for real capital spending generally support this view, whereas the effect seldom is observed in table 8.1 for financial flows. The lagged tax rates are also *highly* significant when stated as a differential to reduce the impact of multicollinearity. (In those cases only a coefficient for U.S. tax is given.) Table 8.2 also suggests that, while the *unlagged* form of the tax rates based on 4 and 8 percent rates of return are not significant, other variations of current tax rates are sometimes significant. However, these unlagged forms are gen-

11. Scholes and Wolfson (1989) claim that the rise in U.S. effective corporate tax rates as a result of the Tax Reform Act of 1986 actually increased foreign investment in the United States; foreign companies based in countries that grant a credit for foreign taxes could simply use the higher U.S. taxes to reduce their home-country tax liability. The ability to credit U.S. taxes gave them an advantage over domestic U.S. companies. This kind of effect could conceivably explain the insignificant or positive coefficient for Canadian taxes in some of the regressions, because the United States also grants a credit for foreign taxes. As noted earlier, however, before 1987 most U.S. companies in Canada were apparently able to eliminate any residual U.S. tax by using the "rhythm method." If that was the case, any increase in Canadian tax would not have caused an offsetting reduction in U.S. tax.

Table 8.2   Comparison of Regressions Using Alternative Investment and Effective Tax Rate Measures. Dependent Variable: Real Property, Plant and Equipment Expenditures of Affiliates, Divided by Real U.S. Expenditures for Plant and Equipment (*t*-values in parenthesis)

Case	U.S. Tax	Canadian Tax	Dummy 1977	Time Trend	Canadian Capacity Utilization	Real Exchange Rate	Exchange Rate Uncertainty	Intercept	Adjusted R^2
US METR 4% Return, Lagged	10.41	−17.16	−3.91	.21	−0.05			22.85	.49
CN METR 4% Return, Lagged	(2.64)	(−1.79)	(−2.20)	(1.52)	(−.53)			(2.20)	
US METR 4% Return, Lagged	10.05		−3.18	.18	−.03			17.54	.50
CN METR 4% Return, Lagged	(2.59)		(−2.08)	(1.35)	(−.28)			(2.19)	
US METR 8% Return, Lagged	20.75	−26.15	−4.74	.30	−.01			16.95	.52
CN METR 8% Return, Lagged	(2.86)	(−2.40)	(−2.68)	(1.96)	(−.07)			(1.87)	
US METR 8% Return, Lagged	23.92	−23.06	−2.60	.27	.03	−4.17	−.43	17.11	.52
CN METR 8% Return, Lagged	(2.43)	(−1.80)	(−1.01)	(1.14)	(.28)	(−.52)	(−1.31)	(1.52)	
US METR 8% Return, Lagged	23.78		−2.73	.27	.03	−4.05	−.42	17.50	.55
CN METR 8% Return, Lagged	(2.53)		(−1.30)	(1.18)	(.27)	(−.53)	(−1.44)	(1.75)	
US AVG Tax, Lagged	29.95	−17.86	−2.37	−0.02	0.21			−1.55	.50
CN AVG Tax, Lagged	(2.57)	(−0.87)	(−1.17)	(−0.16)	(1.90)			(0.16)	
US METR 4% Return, Lagged[a]	24.18	−44.88	−9.52	.84	−.57			89.29	.27
CN METR 4% Return, Lagged	(2.89)	(−2.22)	(−2.52)	(2.82)	(−2.65)			(4.07)	
US METR 8% Return, Lagged[a]	26.22	−43.10	−9.58	.68	−.38			70.55	.05
CN METR 8% Return, Lagged	(1.45)	(−1.59)	(−2.17)	(1.81)	(−1.68)			(3.12)	

								R^2
US METR 4% Return	.56 (.12)	1.40 (.14)	−2.72 (−1.44)	.02 (.11)	.09 (.75)		7.49 (.71)	.27
CN METR 4% Return	5.44 (.64)	−7.98 (−.70)	−3.21 (−1.72)	.08 (.51)	.08 (.78)		9.74 (1.03)	.28
US METR 8% Return								
CN METR 8% Return								
US METR 6% Inflation	−2.65 (−.25)	−13.17 (−1.34)	−3.92 (−2.17)	−.04 (−.22)	.11 (1.17)		14.84 (1.58)	.35
CN METR 6% Inflation								
US METR 4% Return, Total	11.55 (1.90)	−10.22 (−.98)	−2.91 (−1.67)	.14 (1.09)	.09 (.97)		7.46 (.84)	.38
CN METR 4% Return								
US METR 4% Return, Total	12.42 (2.56)	−16.30 (−2.35)	−4.64 (−2.58)	.37 (2.30)	.03 (.37)		11.15 (1.35)	.50
CN Newlon Tax								
US METR 4% Return, Total	10.13 (2.27)	−18.26 (−2.28)	−3.66 (−2.28)	.08 (.79)	.11 (1.33)		11.26 (1.40)	.49
CN METR 6% Inflation								
US METR 4% Return, Total	11.03 (1.95)	−15.96 (−1.71)	−1.53 (−.68)	.00 (−.01)	.14 (1.58)	−5.63 (−.71) / −.36 (−1.22)	15.55 (1.38)	.49
CN METR 6% Inflation								
US METR 4% Return, Total, Log	−.53 (−2.03)	.65 (1.92)	−.14 (−.55)	.00 (.08)	.34 (.24)	−.16 (−.22) / −.05 (−1.17)	3.03 (11.29)	.47
CN METR 6% Inflation, Log								
US METR 8% Return, Lagged, Log	−1.30 (−2.87)	1.08 (2.25)	−.11 (−.45)	.02 (.75)	.65 (.49)	−.36 (−.60) / −.07 (−1.60)	2.58 (7.93)	.56
CN METR 8% Return, Lagged, Log								

Note: Time period is 1963–87, annual data (except for Newlon tax series terminated in 1985). METR = marginal effective tax rate; AVG = average effective tax rate after removing the influence of cyclical factors. Dependent variable as noted, except in equations labelled with superscript a, where it is Canadian real plant and equipment expenditures in manufacturing divided by U.S. real plant and equipment expenditures. Tax rates apply to manufacturing only, except where the total or economy-wide rate is noted.

erally significant only when U.S. economy-wide tax rates are used, and they are conceptually less appealing than our basic rates for manufacturing.

In comparing the responsiveness of financial flows and real spending to tax changes, we are interested primarily in the absolute changes of investment spending in U.S. dollars. Does the increase of financial flows in response to changes in Canadian and U.S. tax rates greatly exceed any increase in real spending because of the mobility of financial capital? Alternatively, does the increase in financial flows represent only a small fraction of the increase in real spending because of other sources of finance such as local borrowing? The level of gross plant and equipment spending is always higher than direct investment flows because of the large base of gross investment necessary to replace depreciating capital. A comparison of elasticity measures is therefore not very helpful. Because different scaling factors are used for financial flows and capital spending, the coefficients have to be translated back into a comparable U.S. dollar basis.

Translating the coefficients in tables 8.1 and 8.2 into absolute changes in U.S. dollars suggests that not only is the effect of taxes more robust in explaining real capital spending, but the quantitative response to a given change in tax rates is also somewhat larger. For example if we take the typical coefficient of about -11.0 for Canadian tax rates in table 8.1 and -23.0 in table 8.2, and use the mean values of the appropriate denominator in the regression, we find that a reduction of Canadian tax rates of 10 percentage points increases capital spending (with a lag) by \$335 million and financial flows by \$265 million, a difference of about 20 percent.[12] While these are roughly comparable, they suggest that, if anything, capital spending is more responsive to tax rates than financial direct investment.

These results demonstrate that taxes can have a quantitatively large effect on cross-border investment. For example, the \$335 million increase in plant and equipment expenditures corresponds to a 15.7 percent increase in capital spending (using the mean value) in response to the 10 percentage point reduction in tax rates. Moreover, this represents a percentage increase in *gross* capital expenditures; the percentage increase in *net* investment is (at least in the short run) much larger.

Tables 8.1 and 8.2 indicate that financial flows and real investment also behave differently in other ways. One clear difference is the much greater significance of the Canadian capacity utilization rates in financial flows, presumably due to the effect of profitability on retained earnings, one of the components of direct investment. Financial flows also exhibit a much more consistent and significant rising trend.

A further difference is the role of real exchange rates (or relative labor

---

12. The mean value of the denominator in the balance of payments regressions in table 8.1 is 241.7. The comparable factor for capital spending, reflecting the combined effect of the deflators and the U.S. investment in the denominator, is 145.5.

costs). Foreign direct investment in Canadian manufacturing increases as the U.S. real exchange rate increases. This is consistent with the findings of Froot and Stein (1989) for direct investment in the United States. The coefficient is not significant, but it probably would be if direct investment were expressed in Canadian dollars to be consistent with Froot and Stein. In contrast, real spending by U.S. affiliates decreases with an increase in the U.S. real exchange rate, although the coefficient is again insignificant. Thus, the Froot and Stein result does not hold up for real capital expenditures and seems more related to the rearrangement of financial portfolios.

One area in which, surprisingly, a difference does not show up is the impact of exchange-rate instability. A comparison of results in tables 8.1 and 8.2 indicates that financial flows are discouraged by exchange-rate instability no more than is real investment.

The results in tables 8.1 and 8.2 for the various forms of the tax variables suggest that the standard assumptions made in constructing effective tax rates do not produce the most successful explanations of changes in investment. Tax rates based on a required real rate of return of 8 percent generally have much more explanatory power, with larger coefficients (and the expected sign), than rates based on the usual 4 percent assumption. Other alternatives seem frequently to perform better than the basic 4-percent-plus-ARIMA-forecast; for example, when a constant 6 percent expected rate of inflation is substituted. In view of these results, it appears that the standard assumptions used in constructing marginal effective tax rates should be reexamined. In addition, a required return of 8 percent leads to much different conclusions as to the effect of the Tax Reform Act of 1986 on corporate effective tax rates. Instead of an substantial increase in the effective corporate tax rate, there would have been virtually no change.[13]

Tables 8.1 and 8.2 also show that the *average* effective U.S. corporate tax rate performs very well in the regressions both for real spending and financial flows. This result is surprising in light of the research popularity of marginal effective tax rates. Average effective rates have some advantages over marginal effective rates, because the latter focus on only a few basic features of the tax system, such as depreciation allowances and investment credits and may overlook other provisions more difficult to model.[14] The average effective Canadian corporate tax rate is not significant, but the coefficient of the lagged

13. At a presentation of an earlier version of this paper, Jane Gravelle of the Congressional Research Service kindly offered to make her U.S. effective tax rate series available. The Gravelle series is much smoother than the Auerbach-Hines series. Nevertheless, the general pattern of the results tends to be confirmed when the Gravelle series is used, with real spending more responsive to tax rates than the financial flows. However, the significance of the Canadian tax rate is reduced.

14. The average effective tax rates we use have been cyclically corrected by using the residuals from a regression of the average rates on the country's capacity utilization rates. Otherwise, the observed average tax rate might spuriously reflect changes in the business cycle and not in tax policy, because the larger number of loss companies in a recession raises the measured average effective tax rate.

version does have the expected sign in the real spending regressions and is quantitatively almost as large as when marginal effective tax rates are used. The less significant role of the Canadian average tax rate is not surprising because, as with the U.S. average rate, it applies to all corporations and not just manufacturing. The Canadian tax incentives were targeted to manufacturing by means of a special statutory tax rate and highly accelerated deprecia tion if the equipment was used in manufacturing and processing.[15]

The regressions reported in tables 8.1 and 8.2 follow previous studies on the impact of taxes on foreign direct investment in relating the flow of new investment to the *level* of U.S. and foreign tax rates. However, if the relationship between desired stocks of capital and effective tax rates is the starting point for the analysis, the *change* in tax rates would be a determinant of the change in the stock of capital (i.e., the net investment component of gross investment). (The level of the tax rate would also have an effect on net investment because of the growth in the economy.) When the first differences of the tax variables were substituted in the equation for plant-and-equipment spending they were generally not significant and often had the wrong signs. In the financial flow equations, the first differences of the tax variables tended to have coefficients with the expected signs and were of borderline significance for some versions of the effective tax rate measures. However, a complete specification with both current and lagged taxes was not very successful because of the multicollinearity that arises from using several tax variables.

The differential between the U.S. and Canadian statutory tax rates was included as a variable in some of the investment regressions. As suggested above, it might be expected to play a role in the balance of payments equations because of the likelihood of greater local borrowing if the Canadian statutory tax rate is higher; real spending could be affected because of the benefits of locating monopoly rents in a low statutory tax rate country. Nevertheless, the statutory tax rate differential was not significant in either case.

A useful check on our conclusions regarding the relationship between financial flows to Canada and capital expenditure by Canadian affiliates is provided in table 8.3. Table 8.3 presents sources and uses of funds data for a sample of worldwide majority-owned manufacturing affiliates from 1966 to 1976.[16] (Nondisclosure problems made it impossible to construct data for Canada only.) The sum of the first two sources of funds correspond basically to foreign direct investment as reported in the balance of payments, although the second also includes a small number of transfers from affiliates other than the

---

15. The regressions in table 8.1 are all linear, not log-linear, in part to avoid the problem of negative values in the financial flow data. The log-linear regressions at the end of table 8.2 indicate that the coefficients of the tax variables are somewhat more significant statistically than in the comparable linear regressions. The tax elasticities (with the linear elasticity evaluated at the means) are very close. (In the log version, the tax variable is one minus the effective tax rate.)

16. It is unfortunate that after 1976 the Commerce Department no longer published annual data on the sources and uses of funds of affiliates abroad. Partial sources-and-uses data begin to be available again after 1982.

Table 8.3   Sources and Uses of Funds of a Sample of U.S. Affiliates in Manufacturing, 1966–76 (in millions of dollars)

	Sources						Uses		
	Internal					External			
Year	Retained Earnings	Parent and other Affiliates	Depreciation	Other	Total Internal	Total	Fixed Investment	Change in Inventories	Other (including financial assets)
1966	250	783	992	50	2,008	991	2,009	399	659
1967	464	453	1,165	41	2,123	514	2,121	8	508
1968	611	22	1,341	78	2,052	1,057	1,893	283	934
1969	908	204	1,458	174	2,744	1,431	2,175	776	1,224
1970	480	380	1,554	219	2,633	1,604	2,839	920	478
1971	773	404	1,849	225	3,251	1,386	3,114	611	912
1972	1,221	402	2,121	272	4,016	1,388	3,114	195	2,095
1973	1,937	431	2,481	345	5,194	3,467	3,892	2,343	2,426
1974	1,338	1,665	2,829	262	6,094	5,209	5,109	4,225	1,969
1975	1,394	846	2,945	449	5,674	−43	4,590	−430	1,431
1976	1,991	527	3,175	334	6,027	2,108	4,661	806	2,668

Source: "Sources and Uses of Funds of Majority-Owned Foreign Affiliates of U.S. Companies, 1973–76," Bureau of Economic Analysis Staff Paper (May 1976).

parent. The "other" internal source includes items such as proceeds from sales of assets. External sources include third-party borrowing by the affiliate.

As a result of the stability of depreciation allowances, fluctuations in internal sources of funds reflect mainly changes in foreign direct investment (indicated in the first two columns). Table 8.3 indicates that capital spending often tracks internal sources of funds but diverges significantly in some years, such as 1969 and 1972, when the increase in internal funds seems to be associated with increased financial assets. Overall, it appears that changes in inventories are the most volatile use of funds and are more closely linked to changes in external funding than to internal sources. On the whole, these data confirm our earlier finding that direct investment and capital spending are virtually uncorrelated apart from a trend and that they are affected by different forces.

One controversy in the analysis of MNCs is whether they contribute to more capital mobility and reallocation of investment than would occur simply because of portfolio adjustments. Even in the absence of direct investment, increased taxes on manufacturing companies in the United States could lower rates of return in the corporate sector and lead to an outflow of portfolio capital to other countries. The contribution of MNCs to capital mobility can be tested with regressions parallel to the affiliate spending equation in table 8.2, but with aggregate capital expenditures in Canadian manufacturing substituted for affiliate investment. The dependent variable would then become the ratio of total real capital expenditures in Canadian manufacturing to real investment in U.S. manufacturing.

The two equations marked with a superscript a in table 8.2 are based on this alternative dependent variable, and they suggest that MNCs are very significant contributors to the reallocation of capital between U.S. and Canadian manufacturing. The coefficients for U.S. tax rates in these linear regressions are virtually the same as in the comparable ones for U.S. affiliate investment only. The impact of U.S. tax rates on Canadian investment seems almost exclusively due to the decisions of U.S. multinational corporations. It is also interesting that the absolute size of the Canadian tax rate coefficient is much larger for total Canadian investment than for U.S. affiliates only; this may reflect the standard impact of taxes on investment in a purely domestic context. Even then, since total Canadian investment in manufacturing is on the average about three times the level of U.S. affiliate investment, investment by U.S. affiliates seems about twice as responsive to Canadian tax rates as other non-U.S.-controlled investment.

We now turn to the effect of taxes on trade. A standard formulation of Canadian demand for U.S. exports would express it as a function of economic activity in Canada (GDP), the price of U.S. goods expressed in Canadian dollars, and the price of Canadian goods. (The prices of other countries' products are generally ignored.) Determinants of U.S. and Canadian prices are substituted directly into this expression. Higher U.S. labor costs, a higher value of the U.S. dollar, and lower unit labor costs and activity in Canada contribute to lower U.S. exports.

Taxes can affect trade through several channels. One is by their impact on the investment and productive capacity of U.S. affiliates in Canada. Another route is the change in output sourcing for a given distribution of capital in the two countries. For example, if capacity is available in each country, the company may have an incentive to produce in the location with the lower statutory tax rate. (If capital is given, incentives such as investment credits that cause the discrepancy between effective and statutory tax rates are not relevant.) Finally, changes in corporate tax rates may change the comparative advantage of various industries because of differences in capital intensity and the extent of incorporation. This effect can operate even in the absence of capital flows or direct investment.

Table 8.4 provides results for (log-linear) regressions on U.S.-Canadian manufacturing trade that attempt to identify the role of taxes. Separate equations for U.S. exports to Canada and Canadian imports from the United States are given because of the measurement differences between them displayed in figure 8.3. Separate regressions for Canadian exports to the United States are not given because they are virtually identical to measured U.S. imports. The equations in table 8.4 are different from conventional trade equations in that the absence of available deflators for U.S.-Canadian manufacturing trade necessitates the use of nominal imports or exports on the left-hand side.[17]

In the regressions for U.S. exports, the tax coefficients have the expected signs; lower U.S. taxes increase U.S. exports and lower Canadian taxes reduce them. When the U.S. tax rate is adjusted for DISC and FSC benefits, the coefficient is larger compared to the unadjusted rate and is of borderline significance. The Canadian tax rate is also of borderline significance when the Canadian capacity utilization rate is added as a variable. When only one plus the percentage-point reduction in the tax rate on export income attributable to DISC is used as the U.S. tax variable, it is close to being significant. Furthermore, the coefficient suggests a potentially large effect. The .84 coefficient would imply an expansion of U.S. exports to Canada of about 14 percent at the beginning of the program when benefits were high, and would further imply that exports are now about 6 percent higher than they would be in the absence of FSC benefits.

The U.S. export and Canadian import equations yield roughly comparable estimates. Even though the Canadian trade data may be more accurate than U.S. data, economic relationships expected on theoretical grounds cannot be

---

17. That is another reason why the various components of the real exchange rate used in the investment part of the study (unit labor costs in each country and the nominal exchange rate) are entered separately. The unobserved deflators are presumably functions of these variables as well as the tax rates, but the deflators for U.S. exports are likely to depend on U.S. unit labor costs much more heavily than on the exchange rate or Canadian costs.

Table 8.4   U.S.-Canadian Trade Relationships

	DISC + U.S. Tax	DISC Only	Canadian Tax	Years	Real GDP of Importer	Exchange Rate	Exchange Rate Lagged	U.S. Unit Labor Cost	Canadian Unit Labor Cost	Canadian Capacity Utilized	Intercept	R^2	D-W
U.S. Exports													
	.13		-.14	-.05	3.45	-.27		-.66	.72		-15.86	.99	1.51
	(1.43)		(-.89)	(-2.20)	(7.45)	(-.94)		(1.49)	(1.92)		(6.43)		
	.15		-.14	-.04	3.31	-.16	-.25	-.73	.75		-14.93	.99	1.57
	(1.55)		(-.90)	(-1.82)	(6.46)	(-.47)	(-.71)	(-1.58)	(1.95)		(-5.28)		
	.15			-.04	3.30	-.16	-.26	-.76			-14.08	.99	1.59
	(2.00)			(-2.09)	(7.02)	(.52)	(-.83)	(-2.13)			(-6.30)		
		.84	-.11	-.04	2.94	-.16	-.22	-.69	.91		-13.88	.99	1.69
		(1.72)	(-.77)	(-1.60)	(5.35)	(-.51)	(-.65)	(-1.57)	(2.25)		(-4.73)		
	.14		-.22	-.04	2.92	-.46	-.18	-.22	.57	.53	-16.67	.99	1.62
	(1.52)		(-1.39)	(-1.68)	(5.30)	(-1.23)	(-.54)	(-.39)	(1.47)	(1.53)	(-5.69)		
Canadian Imports													
	.07		-.14	-.01	2.44	.37	-.49	-.33	.80		-12.54	.99	1.65
	(.59)		(-.68)	(-.20)	(3.95)	(.92)	(-1.17)	(-.59)	(1.73)		(-3.67)		
	.17			.02	2.24	.45	-.72	-.91			-9.67	.99	1.67
	(1.70)			(.63)	(3.52)	(1.10)	(-1.73)	(-1.90)			(-3.04)		
	.05		-.30	.01	1.40	-.36	-.32	1.00	.35	.53	-16.95	.99	2.16
	(.87)		(-2.63)	(.40)	(3.87)	(-1.50)	(-1.48)	(2.78)	(1.41)	(6.08)	(-8.89)		
U.S. Imports													
	-.08		-.56	.09	1.97	-.87	-.16	1.56	-1.32		-15.29	.99	2.05
	(-.61)		(2.65)	(2.03)	(1.99)	(-2.06)	(-.35)	(2.46)	(-2.75)		(-1.90)		
		-.74	-.55	.10	1.92	-.99	-.23	1.69	-1.59		-14.35	.99	2.12
		(1.26)	(-2.82)	(2.80)	(2.02)	(-2.36)	(-.55)	(2.79)	(-3.04)		(-1.86)		

Note: Time period is 1966–87. Tax variables based on 4 percent after-tax return in manufacturing.

identified any more precisely. Some differences do emerge when the Canadian capacity utilization rate is included. Canadian taxes are much more significant in the Canadian import series, but the signs of some of the other coefficients are unexpected.

In the U.S. import equation, the Canadian tax rate has an unexpected negative coefficient (in this log $1 - t$ version) and is highly significant. In other words, lower Canadian taxes decrease U.S. imports from Canada. A further disturbing aspect of the U.S. import equation is that, while the U.S. and Canadian unit labor costs are highly significant and have the expected signs, the sign of the coefficient for the price of U.S. dollars is negative and significant. This may be explained by the significant resource content of Canadian exports even in manufacturing. The Canadian exchange rate may be high during worldwide booms in which commodity prices and Canadian nominal exports are high.

To sum up the role of tax rates in U.S.-Canadian trade: there is suggestive evidence that U.S. tax incentives for exports increased exports to Canada. Nevertheless, it is difficult to make firm judgments on the overall role of taxes because the coefficients for some of the variables, such as Canadian taxes in the Canadian export equation, have signs contrary to expectations.

8.4 Summary and Conclusions

1. U.S. and Canadian marginal effective tax rates appear to have a more statistically significant, robust, and quantitatively large effect on real capital spending than on financial flows. The common assumption that financial assets are more mobile in response to tax rates does not seem to be borne out. Exchange rate instability also does not have a greater effect on financial flows than on real spending. Financial direct investment *is* strongly influenced by cyclical factors, which determine the amount of profits available for retention abroad.

2. Multinational corporations seem to be very important vehicles for the reallocation of capital between the United States and Canada. Any response of total investment in Canadian manufacturing to U.S. corporate tax rates is attributable exclusively to investment by U.S. affiliates. Investment by U.S. affiliates in Canada is also much more responsive to Canadian tax rates than is non-U.S.-controlled investment.

3. Marginal effective tax rates based on the standard assumptions with respect to required rates of return and inflationary expectations are not as successful in explaining changes in investment as rates based on alternative assumptions. In particular, much higher required rates of return than are usually assumed seem to be warranted. In some cases, average corporate tax rates even have more explanatory power than standard marginal effective rates.

4. The role of taxes in trade seems much less clear than it is in cross-border

investment. There is suggestive evidence that U.S. tax incentives for exports may have led to an expansion of U.S. exports to Canada.

Appendix
The Cost of Capital and Effective Tax Rates

The cost of capital services, c (the gross annual return a unit of capital must yield), is derived by equating the acquisition cost of a unit of capital, q, with the present value of the cash flows obtained by the capital. These cash flows are

$$\frac{c(1 - u)}{r + \delta} + qk + quZ$$

where u is the statutory corporate tax rate, r is the required real after-corporate-tax rate of return, δ is the exponential rate at which the capital good depreciates, k is the investment tax credit rate, and Z is the present value of depreciation allowances per dollar of investment. If depreciation allowances are in nominal terms based on historical costs, they have to be translated into real terms by discounting them with a nominal interest rate that is assumed to be the real rate, r, plus the expected rate of inflation. (We assume that the firm uses equity financing exclusively.) Equating q with the present value of the cash flows above and solving for c gives the familiar Hall-Jorgenson formula:

$$c = \frac{q(1 - k - uZ)}{(1 - u)}(r + \delta)$$

The marginal effective tax rate, t, is defined as the statutory tax rate that would yield the same cost of capital under a pure income tax with tax depreciation equal to real economic depreciation and no investment credit. Accordingly, it is the annual tax wedge (the difference between the gross cost of capital services c/q and $r + \delta$) divided by the pretax return net of economic depreciation, or

$$t = \frac{c/q - (r + \delta)}{c/q - \delta}$$

and can be computed using the above formula for c.[18]

---

18. See Auerbach (1983) for a detailed discussion of effective tax rate computations.

References

Auerbach, Alan, 1983. Corporate Taxation in the United States. *Brookings Papers on Economic Activity,* 451–505.

Auerbach, Alan, and James Hines, 1988. Investment Tax Incentives and Frequent Tax Reforms. *American Economic Review Papers and Proceedings,* 211–16.

Boadway, Robin, Neil Bruce, and Jack Mintz. 1987. *Taxes on Capital Income in Canada: Analysis and Policy.* Toronto: Canadian Tax Foundation.

Boadway, Robin, and Harry Kitchen. 1980. *Canadian Tax Policy.* Toronto: Canadian Tax Foundation.

Boskin, Michael, and William Gale. 1987. New Results on the Effects of Tax Policy on the International Location of Investment. In *The Effects of Taxation on Capital Accumulation,* ed. Martin Feldstein. Chicago: University of Chicago Press.

Feldstein, Martin. 1982. Inflation, Tax Rules, and Investment: Some Econometric Evidence. *Econometrica* 50:825–62.

Froot, Kenneth, and Jeremy Stein. 1989. Exchange Rates and Foreign Direct Investment: An Imperfect Capital Markets Approach. NBER Working Paper, no. 2914.

Fullerton, Don, Robert Gillette, and James Mackie. 1987. Investment Incentives Under the Tax Reform Act of 1986. In *Compendium of Tax Research.* Washington, D.C.: Office of Tax Analysis, Department of the Treasury.

Grubert, Harry, and John Mutti. 1991. Taxes, Tariffs and Transfer Pricing in Multinational Corporation Decision Making. *Review of Economics and Statistics* 73, no. 2.

Hartman, David. 1984. Tax Policy and Foreign Direct Investment in the United States. *National Tax Journal* 37:475–88.

———. 1985. Tax Policy and Foreign Direct Investment. *Journal of Public Economics* 26:107–21.

Jun, Joosung. 1989. U.S. Tax Policy and Direct Investment Abroad. NBER Working Paper no. 3049.

Newlon, Scott. 1987. Tax Policy and Multinational Firms' Financial Policy and Investment Decisions. Ph.D. diss., Princeton University.

Scholes, Myron, and Mark Wolfson, 1989. The Effect of Changes in Tax Laws on Corporate Reorganization Activity. Stanford Business School. Manuscript.

Slemrod, Joel. 1990. Tax Effects on Foreign Direct Investment in the United States. In *Taxation in the Global Economy,* ed. Assaf Razin and Joel Slemrod. Chicago: University of Chicago Press.

Stevens, Guy. 1972. Capital Mobility and the International Firm. In *International Mobility and Movement of Capital,* ed. Fritz Machlup et al. New York: National Bureau of Economic Research.

Summers, Lawrence. 1986. Investment Incentives and the Discounting of Depreciation Allowances. NBER Working Paper no. 1941.

Comment   Edward M. Graham

To my mind, the Grubert and Mutti paper is an excellent contribution, not so much to the literature on the effects of tax policy on foreign direct investment

Edward M. Graham is a senior research fellow at the Institute for International Economics, Washington, D.C.

(FDI) as to the debate on how best to measure FDI. This is not to say that the paper makes no contribution to the tax question. It does. It is simply to say that I find the latter contribution to be more interesting and more important.

FDI represents something other than an international transfer of physical or financial capital. The essence of FDI is that a firm domiciled in one nation acquires managerial control over a firm domiciled in some other nation. The most widely accepted explanation for the phenomenon is that the parent firm possesses some sort of asset—usually one of an intangible nature such as technology or some other form of "human capital"—that can be transferred to the controlled subsidiary so as to generate a rent. Quite a long literature has been developed in recent years centering around the hypothesis that for FDI to make sense there must also be an advantage to the firm associated with internalization of the asset. That is, the optimal strategy for utilization of the asset must be to "work" it inside the firm, rather than to license it for a fee to other firms.

A basic question then is how to measure FDI. The standard flow measure used in analytic work has been FDI on a balance of payments basis, a measure of financial flow between a parent firm and a controlled subsidiary. Different national authorities define this measure in slightly different ways, and thus there is a comparability problem when using data from different nations. In the United States, the relevant authority is the Bureau of Economic Analysis (BEA). BEA considers an FDI flow to be the sum of any increase (or decrease) in the equity investment (including retained earnings) of a parent in a foreign subsidiary (providing that the parent holds at least 10 percent of the voting stock of the subsidiary), plus any net change in the intrafirm debt position between such a parent and subsidiary.

This measure can be misleading in a number of ways with respect to the goal of detecting changes in a parent firm's directly controlled interests in a foreign country. (i) What is really a passive investment by a parent can sometimes be classified as a direct investment (e.g., the holding of a substantial block of Du Pont stock by Seagrams. This holding is classified by BEA as an FDI, but Seagrams has made a point of asserting that it neither now holds nor intends to try in the future to establish managerial control over Du Pont). (ii) A subsidiary can increase the level of its participation in the host-nation economy without this increase being reflected in an increased holding of equity or intrafirm debt by the parent firm in the subsidiary (e.g., the subsidiary expands its operations and finances its capital expenditures via local debt). (iii) The parent can increase its holding of equity or intrafirm debt in a subsidiary without the subsidiary actually increasing the scale of its business in the host nation (e.g., in the mid-1980s British Petroleum increased its share of the voting stock held in its U.S. subsidiary from something like 60 percent to 100 percent, thus creating a large FDI flow into the United States by the balance of payments measure, even though the subsidiary did not significantly alter the nature or scale of its participation in the U.S. economy).

But if balance of payments measure of FDI is not wholly satisfactory as a measure of FDI, what is? Grubert and Mutti suggest new plant-and-equipment expenditures (PPE) by foreign affiliates of U.S. firms, a data series that is also published by BEA for overseas affiliates of U.S. firms. The authors show that with respect to U.S. firms' activities in Canada, the balance of payments FDI flow measure is not highly correlated with the PPE measure, and that the latter is more responsive to changes in effective tax rates than the former.

For established subsidiaries, the first result is not really surprising. From the perspective of the subsidiary, PPE are uses of funds, whereas increases in equity held by parent or debt owed to the parent are sources of funds. Equity and intrafirm debt are but two means by which PPE can be financed. Elementary finance theory teaches that whether to make a capital investment and how to finance the investment should be treated as largely separate decisions by a firm. Thus, only to the extent that PPE is financed by subsidiaries by calling upon parent-firm resources would one expect it to be correlated with balance of payments FDI flows. The correlation would be relatively low if we restricted our attention to expansion of existing subsidiaries. A well-capitalized subsidiary could, for example, finance an expansion program by means of host-country borrowing. And, at least with respect to Canada, most PPE by local affiliates of U.S. firms are made by ones that have been long established there. This correlation would be greater, however, if we were to restrict our observations to the creation of new subsidiaries investing in greenfields projects. Presumably, the financing of such a new venture would include a substantial block of equity capital.

But then, which is the better of the two measures? The answer will depend entirely on the objective of the analysis. Again, if the objective is to measure the response of *existing* local affiliates under control of foreign firms to changes in domestic economic policy variables implemented by the host-nation government, then the PPE measure likely will be the more appropriate one. But if the objective is to measure the response of *new* FDI flowing into a nation (including takeovers of formerly domestically controlled firms by foreign investors) to changes in these variables, then use of the balance of payments measure is more likely to be warranted. Actually, as is detailed below, what one would really wish to use as a measure of such new FDI would be a disaggregated balance of payments measure, but this is not presently available.

Thus, my interpretation of the finding by Grubert and Mutti that PPE are more responsive to changes in Canadian effective tax rates than are balance of payment FDI flows is simply that changes in these rates affect the operations of the many established Canadian subsidiaries of U.S. firms much more than they affect the rate of creation of new such subsidiaries.

This interpretation must be tempered by consideration of the composition of the balance of payment flows. Balance of payment FDI flows do not correspond exactly with new subsidiary creation, nor are these flows wholly independent of PPE. BEA data do not at present allow disaggregation of new equity flows from parent to subsidiary into flows to new (greenfields) subsidiary creation, to takeovers of previously noncontrolled but existing firms, and to expansion of existing controlled subsidiaries. This disaggregation would be desirable for a thorough testing of my interpretation.

My major point here however is that the PPE and balance of payments measures of FDI activity really measure two quite different aspects of multinational firm activity. The contribution of Grubert and Mutti is to recognize that when one wishes to perform analysis of FDI to policy changes, one is dealing with a phenomenon (i.e., the behavior of multinational firms) that is both subtle and complex and cannot be adequately captured with one quantitative measure. Which of the two existing data series is appropriate for the analysis depends entirely upon what one is trying to do—with the caveat that neither of these series is likely to capture perfectly the exact behavior one wishes to know about. With respect to all econometric analysis of international economic transactions, of course, we live in a world of incomplete and imperfect information. But in the subworld of FDI, the existing data series tend to be more imperfect and incomplete than most.

9   The Adequacy of U.S. Direct Investment Data

Lois E. Stekler and Guy V. G. Stevens

9.1   Introduction

The term "adequacy" in the title implies a comparison with a set of standards. In the case of U.S. direct investment, are the data adequate to answer the questions that the profession and the public think it important to address? Since the questions deemed important may change, and indeed have changed over the years, an adequate data system must either change also or be extensive enough to be able to answer a variety of questions, some of which may only be dimly perceived at any given moment.

Direct investment is now a "hot" issue. New questions have claimed the attention not only of the economics profession, but also of the public at large. Alarmists have interpreted growing foreign direct investment in the United States as endangering our control of our own future, and, along with the accumulation of other net liabilities to foreigners, as implying a potentially crushing servicing burden on future generations. Ironically, these current concerns about direct investment in the United States are just the mirror image of the questions debated for many years in foreign countries with respect to U.S. investment abroad.

But there are more traditional questions that, in our minds, remain important for direct investment both in the United States and abroad. What are the net benefits and costs of direct investments in particular cases? What are the

Lois E. Stekler and Guy V. G. Stevens are staff economists in the Division of International Finance of the Federal Reserve Board.

This paper represents the views of the authors and should not be interpreted as reflecting those of the Board of Governors of the Federal Reserve System or other members of its staff. The authors are grateful for comments from a number of fellow economists: Michael Adler, Betty Barker, David Belli, Edward Graham, Peter Hooper, Ned Howenstine, Robert Lipsey, Ted Moran, Peggy Musgrave, Samuel Pizer, David Richardson, John Rutter, and Louis Wells. Jodi Garner, as usual, provided outstanding research assistance.

determinants of the flow of direct investment and the real assets and liabilities associated with it? And there is the perennial question: What is the relationship, if any, between trade and direct investment? We will try to evaluate the adequacy of the present U.S. data system with respect to these questions.

A wide range of data relating to the operations of direct investors is required to answer the questions posed above, certainly much more than accurate measures of the income and capital flows included in the balance-of-payments accounts or the stock, however defined, that measures the direct investor's stake in a particular country or industry. Unlike that of most countries, the U.S. system of direct investment statistics does provide a wide range of data, at least attempting to provide the information necessary to address many important questions. Although we will argue that the present system can and should be improved in important ways, we recognize that it has long stood as a model for other countries.

It is therefore disconcerting that an aspect of the recent public interest in direct investment in the United States has been a series of attacks on the adequacy of the data system itself—in contrast to debates about the use of specific variables to measure particular concepts. Most of these attacks, we believe, are wide of the mark; this is especially the case with respect to the criticisms questioning the coverage of the samples or the accuracy of the data collected.

Section 9.2 of this paper reviews the current Bureau of Economic Analysis (BEA) data-collection system and its history, including the definition of direct investment and general questions about data coverage and accuracy; a related question involves the adequacy of the system in delivering the data to its ultimate users. The following sections focus on a selection of issues that economists or policymakers might wish to address using the direct investment data; they also deal with the adequacy of BEA's data for that purpose. Section 9.3 considers the adequacy of the published direct investment position as a measure of U.S. wealth vis-à-vis foreigners and the accuracy of the direct investment payments data as an indicator of the servicing burden of growing foreign direct investment in the United States. Section 9.4 attempts to assess the trade implications of foreign direct investment in the United States. Section 9.5 examines our ability to measure the welfare impacts of direct investment, while Section 9.6 looks at data requirements for explaining and forecasting direct investment flows and activities. Section 9.7 reviews our major conclusions and recommendations.

9.2 The Present System

Most data systems dealing with direct investment activities were designed to be, and are today, balance-of-payments-oriented. On the current account side, they concentrate on the accurate measurement of direct investment receipts and payments—dividends, interest, and reinvested earnings. On the capital account side, they concentrate on the change in the ownership position (net worth) of enterprises controlled by direct investors—the sum of the changes in owners' equity, intercompany accounts, and reinvested earnings. Corresponding to this capital account flow is a net worth concept, denoted in the United States as the direct investment position, which is essentially the cumulation of previous capital flows.[1]

In the 1950s a small group of civil servants at what was then the Office of Business Economics (now BEA) had the inspiration to go beyond the balance-of-payments data in order "to evaluate the full effects of U.S. direct investments, both on our domestic economy and on the economies of foreign countries benefiting from this capital and advanced technology" (U.S. Department of Commerce 1960, p. III). Under the direction of Samuel Pizer and Frederick Cutler, a much more extensive system was instituted that included detailed balance-sheet and income-statement data, such as sales and plant and equipment expenditures, as well as data on employment, wages, and import and export flows. Over the years, there has been added to this core extensive information on parent-firm operations (for U.S., but not foreign, parents), details on R&D expenditures and research workers, and information on performance requirements.

The system today consists of periodic benchmark censuses of outward and inward direct investments covering the data mentioned above; quarterly reports for balance-of-payment flows; semiannual reports on capital expenditures of foreign affiliates abroad; and annual reports by both foreign direct investors in the United States and U.S. direct investors abroad, covering in somewhat abbreviated form the same areas as the benchmark surveys. In addition, reports are required for U.S. businesses taken over and newly established by foreigners.

9.2.1   Issues of Definition, Coverage, and Accuracy

In this subsection we will discuss issues that deal with the data system generally; in subsequent sections, subject-oriented in nature, we will bring up issues of coverage and accuracy as they relate to specific concepts or problems.

Definition of a Direct Investor

Conceptually, a direct investor, in contrast to a portfolio investor, participates significantly in the management of an enterprise, usually controlling it. Generally, it is assumed that different factors or variables motivate the actions of portfolio and direct investors; modern theories of direct investment tend to focus on "industrial organization" explanations,[2] while portfolio investment

---

1. BEA also adjusts the direct investment position for certain valuation changes, particularly for the difference between market price and book value for assets that are sold.

2. See Dunning (1988) for a survey.

is assumed to reflect mainly the flow of capital in response to return differentials across countries.

For the purposes of reporting requirements, BEA currently relies on an arbitrary percentage of equity ownership by a single foreigner—10 percent of the voting shares—to distinguish direct from portfolio investment.[3] In the past, it seemed of little importance where the percentage was set, for the aggregate magnitude of investments where the equity share was low, and control questionable, was small. In recent years, however, such investments seem to be occurring with increasing frequency. In addition, the inclusion in the totals for U.S. affiliates of foreign companies of certain companies with minority foreign ownership, and perhaps limited foreign participation in management, has given a misleading impression of the extent of foreign control of the U.S. economy. For example, foreign participation in the U.S. chemicals industry is inflated by the inclusion of Du Pont; Seagrams (Canada) has a minority but not controlling interest in the company.[4] Similarly, the minority and not controlling interests of Japanese financial institutions in Goldman-Sachs, Shearson-American Express, and Paine Webber inflate the size of Japanese-"controlled" assets in the United States.[5] On the outflow side there are also notable minority investments, including Ford's minority interest in Mazda and GM's stake in Isuzu.

We would suggest that BEA continue to use the 10-percent rule to determine reporting responsibility.[6] The direct investment reports provide a more reliable source of information on capital flows and investment income than the reporting systems for portfolio capital flows and the indirect estimation methods for portfolio investment income. However, serious thought should be given to alternative ways of aggregating and publishing the data. Given that the data are computerized, it should pose no problem to produce alternative measures of the stock of direct investment (and related measures, such as sales) based on different ownership-percentage cutoffs (e.g., at 10-percent intervals, from 10 percent and above, as is now the practice, to 50 percent and above). This flexibility would also facilitate comparisons of data with other

3. The reporting cutoff has not always been 10 percent; in the 1950 and 1957 censuses of direct investment abroad the cutoff was 25 percent, with some leeway allowed to include investments where control was well known even though the ownership percentage was less than 25 percent.

For practices in other countries and a proposal for moving countries to a common set of definitions, see OECD (1983).

4. See the May 1988 *Survey of Current Business,* page 63. U.S. affiliates of foreign companies account for about 30 percent of both assets and sales of all U.S. chemical manufacturers. All the assets and sales of Du Pont and Conoco are included in this figure.

5. See, for example, the *Washington Post* of June 28, 1989, asserting that Japan had become the largest direct investor in the United States in 1987, based upon the total assets of these financial companies (and not the prorated share of Japanese investors in these companies' assets).

6. However, this current criterion fails to include as direct investment certain U.S. investments in centrally planned economies or less-developed countries that are controlled by contract, rather than equity ownership. U.S. rules on foreign ownership of U.S. airlines may also encourage investments that would not trigger reporting requirements but could involve significant influence with minimal ownership of voting equity.

countries that use different ownership percentages as cutoffs.[7] Additional efforts by international organizations such as the IMF to harmonize definitions across countries are also necessary to facilitate international comparisons.

It would also be useful to divide affiliates into those controlled by foreign investors, those where foreigners have noncontrolling equity interests, and those that are joint ventures. Disaggregation along these lines would require judgment rather than a fixed cutoff by percentage of equity.

Coverage

Charges have been made in recent years that BEA's data on foreign direct investment in the United States seriously understate the growing foreign presence.[8] Thus, in recent Congressional testimony, Dr. Susan J. Tolchin, coauthor of *Buying into America* (1988), stated: "The U.S. is flying blind on foreign investment. No one knows the full extent of foreign investment, and some experts believe at least 50% of all foreign investment goes unreported. Lax reporting requirements, hidden ownerships, and other circumventions of the law—many of them already riddled with loopholes—have made it virtually impossible to keep track of the flood of foreign money" (Tolchin 1988).

After reviewing the evidence, we find nothing to support such extreme criticism. Occasionally these attacks have been based upon faulty comparisons of different measures of direct investment. Measures of the total assets of U.S. affiliates of foreigners differ substantially from measures of the amounts invested by foreigners to acquire or establish U.S. affiliates, and these amounts differ again from the direct investment capital flows and the cumulation of these capital flows into the international investment position. Moreover, some BEA data attribute investments to the country of residence of the ultimate owner, while other data are presented on the basis of residence of the direct owner. Perhaps BEA should make a greater effort to educate the public on the differences between various data series and the reasons for collecting data on different bases.

BEA data would understate the size of direct investment if a significant number of large investors failed to report. However, BEA devotes substantial resources to monitoring publicly available information for the names of new reporters. Undoubtedly some U.S. companies making direct investments abroad are missed, as are some foreign investments in the United States. This is more likely in the case of small investments or private transactions (SEC regulations require registration of purchases of 5 percent or more of the equity of publicly traded U.S. companies). If there are any problems, they are probably in real estate, where small investments are common. In addition, much

7. See Vukmanic, Czinkota, and Ricks (1985) for an excellent discussion of the direct investment definitions, practices, and inadequacies for other countries. Robert E. Lipsey's comment (1985) on that paper is very useful. See also OECD (1983).
8. See, for example, Congressional Economic Leadership Institute (1989, p. 33) or Tolchin (1988b).

foreign investment in U.S. real estate falls between the cracks of various reporting requirements; no direct investment reports are required on residential
real estate for personal use or on real estate investment through limited partnerships (since direct investment is defined as control of 10 percent of the
voting equity in a company).[9]

If additional funds were available, BEA could devote additional resources
to ferreting out direct investors who currently do not report. Since these are
likely to be small investors, they are unlikely to substantially alter the overall
picture of U.S. investment abroad or foreign investment in the United States.
Moreover, except for certain real estate transactions, as discussed above,
investors are already legally required to report; adding additional legal requirements to report would do nothing to improve coverage.

Accuracy

Despite the legal obligations to report, the accuracy of the responses to
BEA direct investment surveys depends primarily on voluntary compliance
with the law. Historically, BEA has not conducted detailed audits of the books
of direct investors, nor does it currently have the staff to do this. Since BEA
surveys are confidential and are not used for tax purposes, there is no obvious
incentive for firms to misrepresent data. However, firms pressed by competitive pressures to limit costs or firms recently acquired through takeovers may
not devote sufficient resources to ensure accurate reporting. Late reporting by
foreign investors in the United States has become a serious problem, producing, for example, large revisions in the data for the fourth quarter of 1988.
This problem, it must be said, has been exacerbated by the lack of concern
shown for the quality of economic data in the higher echelons of the executive
branch in recent years, particularly by the Office of Management and Budget.
Excessive attention by OMB to the laudable goal of reducing the "paperwork
burden," with very little attention to its traditional role of assuring statistical
quality, has been an invitation to a significant minority of businesses to resist
providing accurate and timely data.

The accuracy of data that firms provide is likely to be reasonably high for
information that home offices collect in any case for their own purposes, such
as parent and affiliate balance-sheet or income-statement data. However, it is
uncertain whether wholly-owned U.S. affiliates of foreigners report as instructed using U.S. generally accepted accounting practices rather than U.S.
tax or foreign accounting practices. In addition, firms more often may be lax
about the accuracy of data that they do not collect as a matter of course. A
case in point is the extremely low quality of data, mandated in the 1982 cen-

9. In theory, the Treasury International Capital S-reports currently include data on limited partnerships; in practice, only participations traded on exchanges are reported (aggregated with other
investments). Planned clarification of the TIC-S reporting instructions in July 1990 may help
some, but since many real estate partnerships are formed without the participation of current S-
form reporters, coverage is likely to continue to be inadequate.

sus, on investment incentives given by foreign governments to U.S.-owned subsidiaries abroad.[10] There also have been problems with the data on employment and employee compensation. Devoting additional BEA resources to monitoring the accuracy of direct investment reports would normally be the answer to such problems, but this, sad as it is to say, would probably not be worthwhile unless there is a political consensus to force the private sector to devote additional resources to eliminating inadequacies in statistical reports.

Some insight into the accuracy of U.S. data on direct investment might be gained by comparison with other countries. Unfortunately, since the United States is virtually the only country that collects and publishes extensive data on the operations of affiliates, the only comparisons possible are of balance-of-payments data on capital flows, receipts, and payments. And even here, many countries do not adhere to international standards established by the IMF. Only a few major countries collect information on reinvested earnings; treatment of short-term accounts receivable and payable differ; and the division between portfolio and direct investment is not uniformly set at 10 percent.

Comparisons of U.S. data on the direct investment position of Canada and Japan in the United States with data from these countries have been used to support the assertion that the U.S. data are inadequate. (See Congressional Economic Leadership Institute 1989, p. 33.) However, the United States and Canada regularly meet to reconcile international transactions data. Based upon these annual meetings, there is no evidence that Canadian direct investment in the United States is systematically underreported in the U.S. data (when common definitions are used). Moreover, the published Canadian and Japanese data on direct investment positions in the United States include investments made through third countries, while the U.S. data do not. For Canada, in particular, investments in the United States made through subsidiaries in the Netherlands are very large. In conclusion, international attempts to encourage common definitions probably should be supported. Until that is accomplished, efforts at bilateral reconciliation will remain very difficult.

The Delivery System: Confidentiality, Suppressed Data, and Access by Researchers

The necessary confidentiality of the underlying parent and affiliate reports has been a continuing problem in delivering the BEA data to its ultimate users. When consulting data presented by country and industry in published tables, one all too often finds a "D", indicating that the data point has been suppressed because the cell is, according to the statistical tests used by BEA, "dominated" by three or fewer firms.[11] This confidentiality problem also im-

10. See U.S. Department of Commerce (1985, appendix, p. 4 of form BE-10b, Report for Foreign Affiliate).
11. For an example, see Table III.T 3 of the 1982 census of direct investment abroad (U.S. Department of Commerce 1985, p. 347).

plies that it is frequently impossible to publish data at the disaggregated industry level. Users would be helped if data ranges could be substituted for the present "D"s.

Given the suppression problem and the additional fact that the existing time series for much operating data are short (e.g., sales), it is often tempting for researchers to try to work with the underlying, microeconomic affiliate data. For over twenty years BEA has cooperated with government and outside researchers, but because of the confidentiality problems and costs, research activity of this kind has been very limited.[12]

Because of the confidentiality requirement, the delivery system will probably always be bedeviled with problems. However, steps have been taken to improve the situation, and more could be taken. BEA has greatly expanded the range of data it now publishes in census tables and annual reports; some of the latter present a much richer set of data than appear in the *Survey of Current Business*. The aggregated data are also available on machine-readable diskettes.

The use of the microeconomic affiliate data, under proper confidentiality safeguards, has been encouraged by BEA through a program that has existed since the early 1970s. BEA personnel perform statistical work for outside researchers and, in some instances, researchers are permitted to be taken "in house" as consultants. Unfortunately, after an auspicious start, increasing responsibilities combined with tight budgets have made it very difficult for BEA personnel to participate in this program, even when outside researchers have the funds to pay for their services.

9.3   Measures of the U.S. Investment Position and Servicing Burden

According to BEA data, the United States shifted from a net positive international investment position of $141 billion at the end of 1981 to a negative position of $533 billion at the end of 1988. Concerns have been raised about the willingness of investors to continue to invest in the United States at current interest and exchange rates and about the servicing burden implied by this growing negative position. Because of these concerns, increasing attention has been focused on the accuracy of the data on the net international investment position and, in particular, on the use of book value in the measurement of the direct investment position. BEA estimates the market value of U.S. and foreign holdings of portfolio investments, but makes no attempt to estimate the market value of direct investments. However, in an inflationary environment, book value is likely to seriously underestimate the market value of old investments. Because foreign direct investment in the United States is, on average, more recent than U.S. direct investment abroad, the use of book value undoubtedly understates the net U.S. direct investment position.

---

12. However, some interesting work has come out of such cooperation: see, for example, Courtney and Leipziger (1975), Lipsey and Weiss (1984), Severn (1972), and Stevens (1969).

Historical cost is the accepted basis for company accounting records, so that, with few exceptions, book values are the only valuations readily available to companies required to report in BEA surveys. Moreover, most large affiliates of U.S. companies abroad and foreign companies in the United States are fully owned, so that direct assessment of market value through the prices of shares traded on public exchanges is not possible. Therefore, attempts to measure the current market value of direct investment must rely on indirect estimation methods, which undoubtedly are subject to large errors.

An estimate of the current value of direct investment is employed in the forecasting model of the U.S. current account used at the Federal Reserve Board (the "USIT model"). Direct investment receipts and payments, and implicitly the current value of direct investment assets, are assumed to increase with the general price level and vary in dollar terms with the weighted average exchange rate.[13] Under these assumptions, the value of U.S. direct investment abroad was about $750 billion at the end of 1988, while foreign direct investment in the United States was about $450 billion. (The book values were $327 billion and $329 billion respectively.)

Two recent papers have provided somewhat higher estimates than the USIT model for the net U.S. direct investment position at the end of 1987 (Eisner and Pieper 1988, Ulan and Dewald 1989). Both studies essentially use the methodology described above: starting with a base period, they inflate by subsequent price changes and add new investments. In contrast to the USIT model estimates, they start with an earlier base period, disaggregate by country (instead of using weighted averages), and do not use a general price index. Instead they produce two estimates, an estimate of market value using stock market prices and an estimate of replacement cost using implicit deflators for gross fixed capital formation.[14] In addition, Ulan and Dewald produce a third estimate based on the capitalization of direct investment income.[15]

At best, all of these estimates are crude approximations. Inflating earlier investments by some price index fails to take into account investment mistakes (e.g., the value of Volkswagen's closed U.S. plant is its resale value, not its replacement cost). Also, not all direct investment capital flows are used to finance plant and equipment expenditures; accurate replacement costs can only be calculated by examining the balance sheets of affiliates (not the direct investment position) and adjusting each component (e.g., plant, equipment, inventories, accounts receivable, etc.) to current value.[16] In addition, none of these approaches adjusts for the fact that depreciation charges may be inade-

13. See Stekler (1979). Starting at a base period, the investment position is inflated in each subsequent period by a price index (adjusted for exchange-rate changes in the case of investment abroad), and new investment is added to create an "adjusted" position series.

14. Stock market price increases reflect, in part, reinvested earnings. Eisner and Pieper adjust their stock indexes to exclude the effect of reinvested earnings in order to prevent double counting. (Reinvested earnings are also included in the capital flows data.) Ulan and Dewald do not.

15. The discount rate used was a three-year moving geometric average of the earning/price ratio for stocks in the Standard and Poor 500-stock index.

16. Walther Lederer has done some preliminary work along these lines.

quate to cover replacement costs when there have been substantial price or exchange-rate changes, or the fact that new capital, financed by depreciation charges, may be far more productive.

Ulan and Dewald's third (and much higher) estimate, based on capitalized earnings, appears to be rather implausible. For example, the estimated value of foreign direct investment in the United States at the end of 1987 is only $162 billion, compared with a book value of $262 billion. It is the case that several major investments by foreigners in the United States have not proved profitable (e.g., Volkswagen's auto production facilities, Midland Bank's investment in Crocker, and Campeau's retail store operations). However, it is hard to believe that foreign investments in the U.S. have lost, on average, 40 percent of their value in recent years.

In conclusion, the U.S. net direct investment position at the end of 1987 was probably closer to the $350 to $415 billion range estimated by the USIT model and by Eisner and Pieper than to the $36 billion published by BEA. Since direct investment inflows in 1988 were about $40 billion larger than outflows, the net position at the end of 1988 was probably about $300 to $400 billion.

While it is possible to make rough estimates of the market value of direct investment by the methods described above, each method has advantages and disadvantages, and no one method is clearly superior. The choice between them depends, in part, on the use envisaged for the data. For example, it would be circular to compare rates of return on U.S. direct investment abroad and foreign direct investment in the United States using a measure of direct investment assets derived by capitalizing earnings; the answer would be whatever you assumed in capitalizing earnings. In any case, BEA should continue to collect and publish numbers based on book value. In addition, BEA could explore alternative measures and indicate a range of estimates for value. However, given the shortage of resources available to BEA, and given the serious difficulties presented by the large cumulative statistical discrepancy in recent years, it is not clear that accurate measurement of the net investment position is possible, or that efforts to measure more precisely the market value of the direct investment position deserve high priority.

Under these circumstances, the value of publishing the overall U.S. net international investment position becomes questionable. Moreover, in assessing the creditworthiness of the United States, focus should probably be directed, not at the investment position, but at net investment income payments (see Stekler and Helkie 1989). In this context, the accuracy of the data on direct investment receipts and payments is crucial. Foreign direct investors in the United States appear to earn a very low rate of return on their investments, far below the rate earned by U.S. direct investors abroad, even when attempts are made to adjust the position to market value.[17] Whether this differential is

---

17. Using direct investment receipts and payments as reported in the balance-of-payments accounts and estimates of the value of the position from the USIT model, the real rate of return on

accurate (whether accounting conventions accurately measure economic returns) and whether it is likely to persist have important implications for future direct investment receipts and payments and for the size of the servicing burden associated with growing U.S. net international indebtedness.

Some differential might be expected on the grounds that a part of U.S. direct investment abroad is located in countries where political and economic risks are significant. Some differential might also be explained by the newness of foreign direct investment in the United States. Time might be required before new plants are fully operational, and accounting charges for amortization, depreciation, and interest might be larger in the early years of acquisitions. Investigation of the role of the factors in explaining the low reported rate of return would be useful.[18] Another part of the differential is probably the result of tax incentives which lead multinational firms to use transfer prices to shift reported profits to lower tax jurisdictions abroad (see Wheeler 1988). Although U.S. corporate tax rates were lowered recently relative to those of other industrial countries, they still remain above rates in various tax havens. The incentive to report profits abroad will probably persist, inflating reported receipts on U.S. direct investment abroad and depressing payments on foreign direct investment in the United States. Balancing this distortion of the direct investment accounts is the underreporting of exports of goods and services by U.S. corporations to their affiliates abroad and the overstatement of the imports of goods and services by the U.S. affiliates of foreign companies. These understatements of net credits on other current account items are likely to grow as direct investment in and out of the United States continues to expand, so increasing errors in the returns on direct investment are likely to continue to be offset by growing errors in the opposite direction in other current account items.[19]

9.4 Trade Balance Implications

Does the recent rapid increase in foreign direct investment in the United States indicate that the U.S. trade balance is likely to improve more rapidly than past experience (as measured by most econometric models) would indicate? Is the data collected by BEA adequate to answer this question?

Before addressing these questions, we want to acknowledge that our ap-

---

foreign direct investment in the United States in 1988 appeared to be about 4.5 percent, while the rate on U.S. direct investment abroad was 6.5 percent.

18. One way to investigate the role of newness in explaining low rates of return would require following individual affiliates and the change over time in their rates of return. This would require access to data that is not published.

19. This assumes that the cost used in calculating affiliates' profits is the same as the cost declared for customs purposes. In fact the IRS recently collected substantial back taxes from Toyota and Nissan on the grounds that their affiliates were overcharged for imported cars, understating profits. The IRS has ruled that if goods are subject to customs duties, firms may not charge their affiliates more for them than the amount declared for customs purposes.

proach is partial equilibrium. Obviously, in a general equilibrium context, any desired shift in capital inflows has implications for exchange rates, interest rates, inflation, GNP growth, and so on, and these implications will vary also depending on government policy reactions. In assessing the implications of direct investment for the trade balance, we focus only on the direct partial-equilibrium effects and do not attempt to consider the general equilibrium feedbacks on the trade balance. This partial equilibrium analysis would better be interpreted as indicating whether foreign direct investment in the United States is changing the U.S. industrial structure and comparative advantage, rather than as measuring the realized improvement in the trade balance. More-over, underlying this analysis is the assumption that there are imperfections in the markets for goods, capital, technology, and so forth, so that a billion dollars invested by Honda to build a car assembly plant in Ohio has a different implication for the U.S. trade balance than a billion dollars invested by Honda in U.S. Treasury securities.

Has foreign direct investment in the United States accelerated in recent years, so that trade equations estimated using past history are likely to err? Two alternative measures are shown in the top panel of figure 9.1: the direct investment position (the solid line) and the total assets of U.S. nonbank affiliates of foreigners (the dashed line). The bottom panel of the figure shows the direct investment position in constant (1964) prices.[20] By all these measures, the growth of foreign direct investment in the United States has been rapid throughout the 1970s and 1980s, although the absolute increases have obviously been much larger in recent years. Relative to the size of all U.S. businesses, value added by U.S. affiliates of foreigners increased between 1977 and 1981 and then remained level through 1987 (Lowe 1990). There is little evidence in these data to indicate that the trend in recent years has been a radical departure from the past, likely to invalidate trade relationships estimated over past years.

Has the industry composition of direct investment inflows shifted in recent years in ways that would be expected to have larger implications for merchandise trade? As shown on table 9.1, much foreign direct investment in the United States is in industries that are not directly involved in international trade: banking, finance, insurance, and real estate. In addition, acquisitions in retail trade, petroleum, or mining are not likely to result in the substitution of U.S. for foreign production on a significant scale. The merchandise sold at Bloomingdales is not likely to change significantly because the store is now owned by a Canadian company. Nor is the sale by Texaco of certain refining and distribution assets to oil-producing countries, or the purchase of stock from minority shareholders by Shell or BP, likely to reduce U.S. oil imports. Investment in wholesale trade is likely to be associated with increases,

---

20. This series was created by starting with the direct investment position at the end of 1964 and adding subsequent capital flows deflated by the CPI.

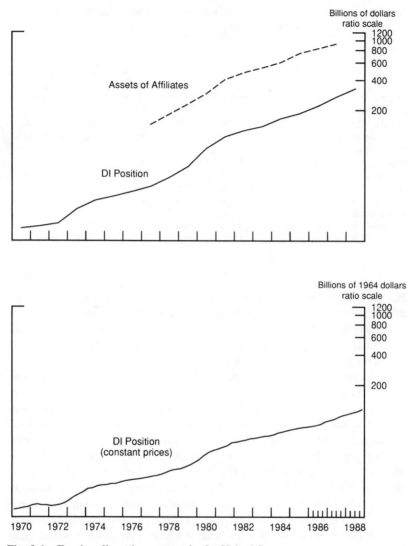

Fig. 9.1   Foreign direct investment in the United States

rather than with reductions, in U.S. imports. Much wholesale trade investment is in sales, distribution, and servicing facilities for imported goods. That leaves manufacturing, which accounts for only part of foreign direct investment in the United States, although its growth has accelerated in the last few years and has been faster than most other industries.

However, this analysis must be qualified because of the way affiliates' reports are consolidated and classified by BEA. All activities of a given subsid-

Table 9.1   Foreign Direct Investment Position in the United States by Industry
                   (billions of dollars)

	1981	1985	1988	Average Annual Percentage Change	
				1982–85	1986–88
All industries	109	185	328	14	21
Manufacturing	41	60	121	10	26
Wholesale and retail trade	21	36	65	14	22
Petroleum and mining	17	32	35	17	3
Banking, finance, and insurance[a]	15	27	40	16	14
Real estate	9	19	32	21	19
Other	6	11	36	16	48

Source: Survey of Current Business.
[a]The banking data are not strictly comparable with the data for other industries because changes in net debt of banks to foreign parents are generally not included in the direct investment accounts.

iary are consolidated and classified according to the primary activity of the affiliate. As a result, considerable investment by Japanese auto companies in manufacturing facilities in the United States is classified under wholesale trade; and plans by Bridgestone to expand Firestone's retail store network would probably appear under manufacturing.[21]

Replacing consolidate reporting on all direct investment surveys with reporting by establishment would involve a substantial duplication of effort. Census already collects extensive data by establishment, as part of annual surveys of manufacturing and the census of industry (every 5 years). BEA and Census are currently engaged in a pilot effort to use employment identification numbers for establishments reported to BEA, to identify establishments affiliated with foreigners in the Census data-base. We strongly support these efforts. Implementation would not only provide a more accurate picture of the role of foreign-owned establishments in U.S. manufacturing, but would greatly facilitate comparisons of foreign and domestic-owned operations. Legislation proposed in 1989 by Senator Murkowski (S.856) would allow BEA access to the survey reports of U.S. affiliates of foreign companies that are filed on a confidential basis with the Census. Since establishment data are necessary for many important purposes, we strongly urge that other issues

21. The 1980 and 1987 benchmark surveys did include some questions that shed light on these issues. Affiliates were asked to classify sales and employment (1987 only) by 3-digit industry codes. In addition, they were asked to give the value of land and other property, plants, and equipment used in manufacturing (including petroleum refining). In 1987, "wholesale trade" affiliates devoted more property, plants, and equipment to manufacturing motor vehicles and equipment ($4 billion) than did "manufacturing" affiliates ($3 billion).

raised by the proposed legislation be resolved so that it can be passed and implemented quickly.[22]

The rest of this section focuses exclusively on analyzing the impact on trade of foreign direct investment in U.S. manufacturing. There have been few studies of this subject, although there is a vast literature on the trade implications of U.S. direct investment abroad.[23] The typical investment considered in the theoretical literature is a "greenfield" investment (a new plant built abroad to supply foreign markets in place of exports of finished goods from the United States). Only a fraction of foreign direct investment in manufacturing industries in the United States fits this description. For purposes of analysis of trade impacts (and other issues as well) it would be useful if we could separate greenfield investment (e.g., Honda's building of an auto plant in Ohio) from mergers and acquisitions by firms in the same industry (e.g., Bridgestone's acquisition of Firestone) or acquisitions of firms in unrelated businesses (e.g., Seagram's investment in Du Pont). Mergers and acquisitions, particularly those motivated by the desire to diversify, are less likely than greenfield investments to have significant trade implications. Because BEA collects data on a consolidated basis, and because the same firm may establish some affiliates and acquire others, it is not now possible to classify reporters as representing greenfield investment. However, it might be possible (although perhaps costly) to make such distinctions using data at the establishment level.

Some light is shed on the relative importance of greenfield investment by BEA's Annual Survey of U.S. Business Enterprises Acquired or Established by Foreign Direct Investors (reported in the May *Survey of Current Business*). As indicated in table 9.2, the amounts invested in manufacturing through acquisitions and the total assets of the affiliates added through this method dwarf expenditures on new establishments in recent years. However, these data may be misleading. They provide no follow-up information on subsequent asset sales; acquisitions are frequently followed by spin-off of parts of the company acquired.[24] The new establishment data include expenditures only in the first year. It seems likely that greenfield investment plays only a small role in foreign direct investment in U.S. manufacturing, although we lack precise data to support this conclusion.

A related question is the relative importance of acquisitions versus plant and equipment expenditures in explaining the recent increases in the assets of

22. Legislation permitting BEA and Census to share data on direct investments was passed in 1990.

23. See Bergsten, Horst, and Moran (1978), for a review of this literature. More recent examples of the effects of U.S. investment abroad on trade include Lipsey and Weiss (1981, 1984) and Blomstrom, Lipsey, and Kulchycky (1988).

24. Information on assets sold by affiliates is available from a different BEA survey, although the data are not currently published. They do not distinguish between assets previously acquired through acquisition or new establishment.

Table 9.2   **Foreign Acquisitions and New Establishments in U.S. Manufacturing (billions of dollars)**

	Investment Outlays		Assets of Affiliates	
	Acquisitions	New Establishments	Acquired	Established
1981	7.8	.3	29.3	.4
1982	2.1	.2	4.6	.7
1983	3.0	.1	3.7	.2
1984	2.7	.4	5.7	.9
1985	11.7	.4	14.8	1.3
1986	16.1	.7	18.7	1.2
1987	18.9	.9	23.2	1.8
1988	29.7	1.8	35.4	3.6

foreign-owned manufacturing affiliates. Unfortunately, this question also cannot be answered with currently available data.[25]

One area of greenfield investment that has received considerable attention is Japanese investment in auto production in the United States. Case studies, such as the study of auto investment by GAO (1988), can be very useful in identifying analytic issues and data inadequacies. The GAO study did not use BEA data and focused primarily on the question of the direct impact on auto industry employment (ignoring macroeconomic determinants of employment). As the GAO study points out, assessment of the direct impact of Japanese car production in the United States on employment in the industry depends crucially on whether the cars produced in the United States displace imports from Japan or cars produced by U.S. or other foreign manufacturers. At one extreme, if it is assumed that car production in the U.S. by Japanese manufacturers is matched by reduced imports, then the improvement in the U.S. trade balance would equal the reduction in finished car imports less the value of imported parts used in Japanese car production in the United States. On the other hand, if production in the United States allows Japanese companies to increase their share of the market at the expense of U.S. producers, and if the import content of Japanese-brand cars is higher than the import content of U.S.-brand cars, investment by Japanese companies in production facilities in the United States could worsen the trade balance. The actual outcome is probably somewhere between these extremes.[26]

The presence of barriers to Japanese car imports increases the likelihood of the less favorable trade outcome. If the voluntary export restraints effectively constrained the market share of Japanese cars, then Japanese companies might

25. The benchmark survey asks firms to decompose the change in net property plant and equipment in 1987 and to provide data on new plant and equipment expenditures and depreciation. However, increases resulting from acquisitions are lumped into a category labeled "restatement." See U.S. Department of Commerce (1989), table D7.

26. The outcome would also depend on macroeconomic interactions.

build production facilities in the United States in order to increase their market share, even if production in Japan remained the cheaper way to supply the U.S. market. Under these circumstances, one would expect imports from Japan to remain at the quota level. Projections into the future would require assumptions about future price and exchange-rate developments. BEA currently collects some information on costs of production from U.S. affiliates, but none from foreign parents on their operations outside the United States. Such data would be very useful, but attempts to collect it might cause serious international frictions.

Another crucial question is the import content of Japanese- and U.S.-brand cars. Currently the import content of Japanese cars produced in the United States is estimated at about 40 to 50 percent, while the import content of U.S.-brand cars is about 10 percent. But, over time, many observers expect these percentages to converge as Japanese manufacturers increasingly use parts manufactured in the United States. These estimates of import content are based not on BEA data, but rather on auto industry sources. BEA does collect information on imports by U.S. affiliates, but consolidation of wholesale trade with manufacturing makes it impossible to use the data to calculate the import content of production.[27] For this purpose establishment data are needed. It would also be useful to have information on Japanese direct investment in the U.S. auto-parts industry. However, the industry breakdowns currently used by BEA do not provide information on an end-use basis.

In conclusion, case studies of greenfield investments can produce useful insights into likely effects on trade flows. However, it is very difficult to assess the relative importance of each case to the overall trade balance. What part of greenfield direct investment in the United States is in the auto industry? Are other greenfield investments clustered in protected industries? Does the import content of foreign-owned production in the United States tend to fall over time? These are all questions that could be answered if BEA data were available on an establishment level, and if greenfield investments could be separated from others.

We turn now to mergers and acquisitions. Their impact on trade could go in either direction. If acquisitions result in improved management, the application of more advanced technology, and modernization of plants and equipment, they could make production in the United States more competitive and tend to improve the trade balance. On the other hand, consolidation of the new company could result in the transfer of advanced technology to foreigners, the shift of production of some products abroad, or the use of the U.S.

---

27. The benchmark survey does ask for the value of imports from foreign parents and others that are for resale without further processing, assembly, or manufacture by the U.S. affiliate. By subtraction, one could obtain the value of imports that were used in production. However, it is not clear how to adjust the sales data to exclude the value of imported goods sold without further processing.

affiliate to distribute imports.[28] If foreign affiliates were identified in the Census of Manufacturers data, comparison of domestic establishments and foreign affiliates could provide information that would be useful in assessing these alternatives.

Another possibility is that the acquisition of 10 percent or more of a U.S. company's equity is essentially a portfolio investment and has no direct implications for trade. Seagram's investment in Du Pont would probably fall into this category. One piece of information that might be useful in distinguishing portfolio-type investments from others (apart from information on control, discussed earlier) is whether the parent is in the same industry as the affiliate. Currently BEA surveys do not provide information on what type of manufacturing a foreign parent is engaged in.

If foreign direct investments in the United States, whether greenfield investments or acquisitions, are likely to have a significant impact on U.S. trade, one would expect to observe increases in plant and equipment expenditures by these affiliates. New plant and equipment expenditures by manufacturing affiliates were level between 1981 and 1986, but increased by almost 25 percent in 1987 (the latest data available). In contrast, Census's survey of new plant and equipment expenditures in manufacturing for the U.S. economy as a whole indicated that they increased by only 2 percent in 1987. This quarterly Census survey of investment plans for U.S. companies in general could provide much more up-to-date information on recent investments and current plans of affiliates of foreign companies. This would be another reward of closer cooperation between BEA and Census.

9.5   The Impact of Direct Investment Operations on Economic Welfare

The analysis of the various effects of U.S. direct investment abroad has been a major preoccupation for many years.[29] The preoccupation has just recently been extended to direct investment in the United States.[30] However, since most empirical studies have dealt with U.S. direct investment abroad, our discussion of the effects of foreign investment in the United States will necessarily be limited.

The majority of the studies fall into two broad classes, with quite different uses of available data. The studies in the first class, which has by far the most

28. One of the reasons frequently cited in the literature on why U.S. direct investment abroad has had little negative impact on net U.S. exports is that U.S. firms setting up production facilities abroad also have expanded their distribution networks and have been better positioned to take advantage of market opportunities. Increasing market share outweighed the shift of some production abroad.

29. For comprehensive general surveys, see Caves (1982) and Reuber (1973). Musgrave (1975) is an outstanding and comprehensive investigation of the effect of U.S. direct investment abroad on the United States.

30. See, for example, Graham and Krugman (1989), Tolchin and Tolchin (1988), and for an interesting industry study, U.S. General Accounting Office (1988).

members, do not attempt a comprehensive evaluation of the impact of direct investment on economic welfare, but rather concentrate on specific tests of hypotheses concerned with the impact of particular factors. Methodologically, such studies usually compare the behavior of foreign-owned enterprises with a sample of other firms: local firms, domestic U.S. firms, or foreign subsidiaries in other countries.

The second class of studies, which has relatively few members, attempts to evaluate the *overall* impact of, usually, a single investment on economic welfare; invariably such studies proceed by applying cost-benefit analysis to the flows associated with a given direct investment project.

9.5.1 Tests of Particular Attributes of Direct Investment Enterprises

Most studies in this class have utilized one of two types of data: (1) data allowing the comparison of the operations of foreign subsidiaries with domestically-owned firms in a given country; and (2) data allowing the comparison of the operations of foreign subsidiaries in a number of different countries.

All studies using the first type of data involve detailed comparisons, often statistical, of firm operations at the level of the establishment. Occasionally, privately collected data are used (e.g., Wells 1973), but typically a national census of manufacturing is the source. Important questions examined are whether foreign affiliates are more efficient than their domestic counterparts, whether there are differences in the capital intensity of the production processes chosen, and whether foreign affiliates pay higher wages. A careful study at the establishment level (Lim 1977) confirmed the finding of other studies that, on the average, foreign subsidiaries pay higher wages than their domestic counterparts. For a given level of employment, this finding means a higher level of payments to domestic factors and higher economic welfare in the host economy. However, if the wage rate is higher than the true marginal cost of labor, the level of employment by the foreign subsidiary and, perhaps the capital/labor ratio, will be suboptimal. The evidence on efficiency and capital intensity was less clear. There was some evidence that in some countries foreign affiliates use more capital-intensive techniques (Wells 1973, for Indonesia), but other studies found no clear picture (Corbo and Havrylyshyn 1982, for Canada; Morley and Smith 1977, for Brazil).[31] In terms of productive efficiency, however, few if any studies could detect significant differences between the two classes of firms (Corbo and Havrylyshyn 1982, Vendrell-Alda 1978, Morley and Smith 1977).

Studies comparing the behavior of subsidiaries of multinational corporations have usually focused on the differences in behavior between subsidiaries in developed and developing countries. Two studies, in particular, should be

---

31. Morley and Smith seemed to find some tendency for foreign subsidiaries to be more capital intensive, although this was hard to detect because of what they viewed as deficient data on capital services (p. 275).

noted for their use of the BEA data to examine the question of the choice of technology and the efficiency of subsidiaries in developing countries (Courtney and Leipziger 1975; Lipsey, Kravis, and Roldan 1982). Both studies found strong evidence that subsidiaries respond to cost differentials by adopting more labor-intensive methods in developing countries. Lipsey, Kravis, and Roldan, in a very comprehensive investigation, arrived at this conclusion for both U.S. and Swedish-owned subsidiaries, comparing the labor intensity of production not only among subsidiaries, but also between subsidiaries and the parent firm.

The BEA data, collected at the enterprise level, may involve the aggregation of a number of establishments in a given country. Although the studies discussed above have shown that the analysis of the BEA data can lead to useful results, virtually all researchers advocate the collection and use of establishment-level data; these data minimize errors caused by the aggregation of different products and inputs that result from the aggregation of different establishments in a given country. Unfortunately, BEA has never required data at the establishment level, partly, perhaps, because the data system initially concerned itself only with balance-of-payments flows, where a natural unit of measurement is the country aggregate. We will argue below that the failure to require collection of data at the enterprise level is particularly regrettable since the requisite establishment data in most cases have already been collected by national authorities abroad, through national censuses of manufacturers (often modeled on the U.S. Census of Manufacturers). Hence, in most cases, no additional burden would be imposed on reporters by requiring data at the establishment level—data already reported to national authorities.[32]

9.5.2 Tests of the Overall Benefit-Cost Ratio of a Direct Investment

The ultimate goal of this second class of studies is the comprehensive evaluation of all the benefits and costs for a particular direct investment (or group of them), leading to an overall assessment of its desirability for a given economy. It is our goal to determine whether the existing BEA data, or any other data that BEA might feasibly collect, are sufficient to carry out the requisite benefit-cost analysis.

The typical calculation of the contribution of direct investment to the host or home country concentrates solely on its impact on the national income of the country in question. Other important welfare questions, such as the impact on the distribution of income, are set aside. The benefit-cost technique has

---

32. We understand the concern of our discussant, Betty Barker, with respect to the possible difficulties in interpreting data from different countries. However, since most of these censuses of manufacturing have been patterned after our own, there is much more consistency across countries than might initially be expected. On this issue, see Lipsey (1985).

These data for U.S.-owned subsidiaries reported at the establishment level to national authorities are, of course, the same data that were analyzed by Corbo and Havrylyshyn (1982), Morley and Smith (1977), and Lim (1977). Many other such studies are discussed in Caves (1982).

been applied to direct investment in rather convincing fashion by Lall and Streeten (1977) and Encarnation and Wells (1986). Given the data available, the ease of quantifying properly the appropriate benefits and costs depends importantly on whether the key product and input markets are perfect (i.e., on whether prices reflect societal marginal costs). If this is the case, the prices embedded in normally collected flows, such as sales and wage payments, can be used without modification; if not, adjusted or "shadow" prices must be used—estimates that are as close as possible to the societal marginal costs. Of course, most practical applications to direct investments in developing countries necessitate careful adjustment of or substitution for market prices. For the United States, probably fewer adjustments need to be made; but, we would argue, most of the interesting cases require some adjustments nevertheless.

The Perfect-Markets Case

The analysis of the costs and benefits of direct investment dates to Mac-Dougall's (1960) seminal article "The Benefits and Costs of Private Investment from Abroad." MacDougall analyzed primarily the perfect-markets case and treated direct investment as merely a transfer of real capital from a low-return home country to a high-return host country. Under such assumptions, as long as capital is paid its marginal product, the resulting national income of both host and home countries would be at least as high after the transfer, and probably higher. The capital stock that host country factors have to work with has increased, thus leading to increased returns, and owners of capital from the home country have improved their situation by shifting capital to a higher-yielding location.[33]

Can we measure these benefits in the classic case by using the available U.S. data on direct investments? In many situations we can. Given the perfect-markets assumption,[34] a traditional cost-benefit calculation using data provided in the Census of Direct Investments should lead to a sound empirical estimate of the gains to home and host factors. Rather than measures of *marginal* output, the Census of Direct Investments provides data on sales—total output times price. However, the marginal value created by the investment can be calculated from sales by subtracting the value lost from domestic production by bidding other factors away from domestic firms or importing factors from abroad. Assuming the prices of these factors represent their marginal value product, if we subtract off the value of payments to labor and other factors, what we have left is the direct investment's marginal output. This

---

33. Labor payments will generally be lower in the home country, but it can be shown that, given perfect markets and constant returns to scale, the gains to capital outweigh the losses to labor in the home country and that, therefore, national income increases.

34. And, probably, that of constant returns to scale, so that factor payments according to marginal productivity exhaust national income.

quantity is divided between taxes of various kinds and profits of the direct investor.[35] As noted above, these data have been available in census years since 1957.

Departures from the Classic Case

Unfortunately, we are frequently in a world in which prices depart from marginal costs or, in the case of product prices, from marginal benefits or utilities. As early as 1955, Pizer and Cutler made a start toward measuring costs and benefits of direct investment under nonclassic conditions (see U.S. Department of Commerce, Office of Business Economics 1957). Subsequent U.S. censuses of direct investment abroad and in the United States, which collected increasingly detailed data on the operating characteristics of affiliates, at least offer the possibility of making benefit-cost evaluations in the typical situation when markets are not perfect. Such situations, we might add, are not limited to developing countries. A good example is the analysis of the impact of foreign-owned automobile assembly and manufacturing plants in the United States, a market in which market prices for autos have been distorted by quotas on Japanese imports.[36]

A small but significant literature has developed since the work of Pizer and Cutler and MacDougall that has applied benefit-cost analysis to foreign investments in situations where one or more market prices are not proper shadow prices (i.e., are not equal to societal marginal costs). Important in this class are Encarnation and Wells (1986) and Lall and Streeten (1977). Both of these studies examine microeconomic data for specific foreign investment projects. For all such studies, where a particular observed price is distorted, the operating data for the foreign affiliates must be supplemented by estimates of shadow prices. In choosing shadow prices, both studies adopt the procedure advocated in the analysis by Little and Mirrlees (1974): where prices are distorted by tariff, quotas, or foreign-exchange controls, free-market prices should be used as the shadow price. An implicit assumption of this procedure is that free trade is a feasible alternative situation. A discussion of other approaches to certain shadow prices where free trade is not a feasible alternative, can be found in Lall and Streeten (1977) and Roemer and Stern (1975).

For concreteness, using the Little-Mirrlees framework, consider the calculation for a given year of the "net social income effect," Y:[37]

---

35. Implicit here is the assumption of constant returns to scale.

36. See the excellent study on the subject done by the U.S. General Accounting Office (1988).

37. Over the life of a given investment, the value of Y may vary over time; it may even be negative in some years (a likely possibility when the investment is starting up) and at times will involve payments for capital goods and construction. We agree with a discussant that to calculate the overall societal value of the investment, the analyst must use a social discount rate to calculate a net present (social) value. We also agree that the calculation of social discount rates and shadow prices is subject to substantial error and therefore warrants a sensitivity analysis of the results to changes in these variables.

(1) $Y = (X + S_d) - (C_r + R + D) - (C_t + C_{nt} + L_s + K_t)$

where X = the value of exports priced at free market prices; S_d = the free market value of domestic sales; C_r = the c.i.f. value of imported raw materials and other inputs; R = royalties and technical fees (after tax); D = after-tax profits and interest; C_t, C_{nt} = the shadow values of domestically produced tradable and nontradable inputs; L_s = the shadow value of scarce labor inputs; and K_t = the shadow value of local capital services. By using the identity linking sales and payments, the net social income effect, Y, can also be expressed as the sum of taxes and other payments to the government, payments above shadow wages to labor, and other payments above the relevant shadow prices to the local private sector.

Let us now consider whether present census data permit the calculation of the various entries listed in the above equation. Data in nominal dollars are reported for most of the categories appearing on both sides of the equality in equation (1). Possible exceptions deal with the raw materials categories. No direct figure for nonlabor inputs is collected in the present census, although it may be possible to construct one by eliminating wages and other items from the figure "cost of goods sold."

It is possible to get the proper data for imported inputs (C_r), at least for foreign affiliates in the United States (the total of imports in the category "goods intended for further processing, assembly, or manufacture"). For U.S. subsidiaries abroad, the fact that this break is available only for imports from the United States may be satisfactory, since this is the item that would be required to measure benefits to the United States.

The more difficult problem is to substitute shadow prices for the various prices embedded in the nominal flows reported in the census. Shadow prices in some countries are likely to deviate from actual prices, notably with respect to product prices, labor payments, energy prices, domestic financial costs, and anything going through the foreign-exchange market. Clearly the absence of separate price information for the firm's accounts is a hindrance; there is little or no breakdown of census flows into price and quantity components.[38] However, of the studies discussed in this section, only Encarnation and Wells had the luxury of such rich data. In lieu of the quantity-price breakdowns, what must be done is to estimate the percentage by which various prices are under- or over-valued and to apply the appropriate percentage-correction factor to the flow in question. At the micro and macro level this requires the further assumption that the observation in question deviates from the shadow price by the average percentage in the country or area. If we had at least some separate product-price information for the affiliates involved, we could then take account of affiliates whose observed prices deviate by more or less than

38. An exception is the labor sector, where the provision of real variables such as hours worked allows the calculation of at least rough wage rates.

the average deviation from the proper shadow price (assuming shadow prices are not firm- or affiliate-specific).

9.6   Explaining and Forecasting Direct Investment Flows and Activities

This section addresses the adequacy of data currently collected to test hypotheses about direct investor behavior. Understanding the role of various factors in explaining past developments is crucial to developing the ability to forecast. It is necessary to understand why firms launch investments across national boundaries, what factors influence the expansion of existing affiliates, and how these and other factors influence direct investment capital flows.

9.6.1   New Investments: Takeovers and Greenfield Investment

Research on the multinational firm has to a significant extent concentrated on the question of the determinants of new direct investments. (See, e.g., Hufbauer 1975, Caves 1982, and Dunning 1988, for good surveys.) The accepted theory emphasizes industry- and firm-specific advantages that for varying reasons are best exploited by foreign production and direct ownership, rather than by international trade or licensing. Thus, for example, whether a firm is a foreign investor or not is correlated with industry characteristics such as research and development and advertising intensity, and within a given industry, the size of the firm.[39]

Rarely are the BEA data alone sufficient to test hypotheses in this area, although in many cases these data are a necessary part of the data-set. Thus, Horst 1972a and Caves 1974 used as a dependent variable in their studies the ratio of sales of foreign subsidiaries to total industry sales; the numerator would require sales data for foreign subsidiaries as collected by BEA.[40] On the other hand, most of the independent variables are related to either industry characteristics or parent-firm data. Variables in the former category typically require data outside the BEA data-set, since the industry averages for the BEA sample alone are not likely to be indicative of the population as a whole; variables such as industry concentration ratios, R&D expenditures, and average plant size have been used in the studies mentioned above. For variables measuring the attributes of a parent firm that invests abroad, BEA's periodic censuses provide a data source of ever-increasing richness. However, when a study compares the characteristics of *noninvestors* to foreign investors, clearly data for the noninvestors must be gathered from separate sources.[41]

39. See Richard Caves's outstanding book, *Multinational Enterprise and Economic Analysis* (1982), for encyclopedic coverage of the issues discussed in this section and an evaluation of the evidence bearing on the related testable hypotheses. Of particular interest regarding the characteristics of foreign investors, see Caves's own article (1974) and Horst (1972b).

40. In the two studies noted, the authors used non-U.S. sources of data—from Canada and the United Kingdom.

41. Horst (1972b) continues to be an interesting study of this sort.

An additional level of data problems awaits researchers trying to explain the recent wave of takeovers and greenfield investments in the United States. One can assume, following the studies noted above, that much of the explanation depends on the characteristics of the investing parent firms; however, very little information is readily available on the foreign parents of subsidiaries in the United States. BEA collects virtually no data on the characteristics of the foreign parents of the U.S. subsidiaries that form its sample. BEA has an understandable reluctance to impose data requirements on foreign firms—the foreign parents—when such requirements might raise sensitive questions of international law. Some data on foreign parents might be filled in from public sources, but at present an important class of data has escaped BEA's data-collection system. Nevertheless, by using international data, data related only to the markets in the United States, and data on foreign parents from public and private sources, some interesting work has recently been completed. (See in particular, Ray 1989, Caves and Mehra 1986.)

9.6.2 The Expansion of Existing Subsidiaries

Most forecasting of direct investment variables—the balance-of-payments capital flow and, particularly, fixed investment expenditures—has been based on theoretical models developed to explain and predict the expansion of already-existing subsidiaries.[42] In such models, the factors discussed above that have determined the initial establishment of the subsidiary, such as the size and technical progressiveness of the parent, are assumed to no longer affect the expansion of the subsidiary. Rather, the dependent variables have been related to more traditional investment theories and data. To use plant and equipment expenditure as an example, ideas embodied in the flexible accelerator and neoclassic investment functions have been applied, sometimes with a twist, directly to the investment of foreign subsidiaries.[43] For fixed investment, such equations require measures of output and its growth and of the existing capital stock, and perhaps measures of the cost of capital and the costs of other inputs. Most of these variables are available in the balance-sheet and income-statement data supplied annually to BEA by the individual subsidiaries (both U.S.-owned subsidiaries abroad and foreign-owned subsidiaries in the United States). When an attempt is made to model the direct investment capital flow—a financial variable—in addition to the above variables, factors such as interest cost differentials and tax considerations presumably also come into play. Some of these additional factors may require data outside the BEA system.

---

42. See, e.g., Helkie and Stekler (1987) and the direct investment equations in Stevens et al. (1984); Stevens (1974) provides a survey of most of the issues and results discussed in this section.

43. Stevens and Lipsey (1988) found some evidence of an interdependence between parent-firm investment in the United States and the investment of foreign affiliates abroad. This interdependence implied a generalized investment function, where, in addition to the usual determinants mentioned in the text, investment in a given location is affected by variables specific to the others.

For aggregate equations that usually must be used for forecasting (e.g., Helkie and Stekler 1987), subsidiary output measures may be aggregated to appropriate country or area totals, or foreign or U.S. GNP may be substituted for the subsidiary aggregates. Although the specific explanatory or forecasting equations in these studies have been closely linked to the theory, it should be recalled that neither the theory nor the equations are really designed to explain takeovers and greenfield investments. Thus, in periods like the present one when this type of investment predominates, it should not be surprising if such equations do poorly.

9.7 Conclusions

BEA has for many years collected an impressive body of data on direct investment, designed to cast light on a wide variety of important issues. We have examined the adequacy of this data system for answering the important questions in four areas: the measurement of the U.S. investment position and servicing burden; the interaction between direct investment and the trade balance; the effects of direct investment on economic welfare; and the explanation and forecasting of direct investment flows and activities.

We find charges that BEA's data omit half of foreign direct investment in the United States wildly implausible. There may be many small investors who are unaware of reporting requirements and therefore fail to report, but it is unlikely that their omission changes any important feature of the overall picture. There seems little reason to doubt that BEA surveys include most direct investment and that the basic data on income and capital flows are in most cases accurate, in the sense that they accurately reflect the reporters' books.

On the other hand, the accuracy of answers supplied by the treasurer's offices of the reporters to survey questions requiring data that they would not normally collect for their own purposes is much more variable. Perhaps influenced by Washington's general preoccupation with reducing the paperwork burden and by OMB's abdication of its former responsibility for the assurance of data quality, firms seem increasingly less willing to go out of their way and to devote resources to provide accurate data. In our experience, this problem is not confined to the area of direct investment.

In the four subject areas we have explored, we have inevitably identified some important questions that cannot be answered with the existing data. The answers to some of these questions are in principle unobtainable by BEA, since the requisite data would have to come from outside the existing universe of direct investors. The prediction of greenfield investment by foreigners and the measurement of the impact of foreign affiliate production on imports may be two such questions.

However, we have also identified a number of ways in which we think the existing data system can be improved. Our specific recommendations include:

1. With respect to the definition of direct investment, it is our view that BEA should continue collecting data on the basis of the present 10-percent

rule. However, BEA should provide data on key variables (e.g., assets, sales, etc.) based on a range of ownership cutoffs, to call attention to the fact that currently published data using the 10-percent rule exaggerate the extent of foreign control of the U.S. economy. Some consideration should be given to efforts to distinguish affiliates with some foreign participation in management from those controlled by foreigners.

2. To facilitate comparisons and resolve inconsistencies, attention should be given to the harmonization of the definition of direct investment among different countries.

3. Given BEA's extremely tight resource constraints, the diversion of BEA resources to construct a market-based or replacement-cost value for the direct investment position should not be given high priority. Neither of these alternatives would provide a more accurate indicator of the future servicing burden implied by accumulating U.S. current-account deficits.

4. A much higher priority should be given to the question of why income reported on foreign direct investment in the United States is so low and whether these low returns are likely to persist.

5. Since, in our view, the direct investment data have been underutilized because of problems related to the confidentiality of the affiliate reports, we encourage BEA to reexamine its suppression rules for the published data and to pursue even more actively cooperative research projects with academic and government researchers.[44]

6. While recognizing that requiring data on the operations of the foreign parents of U.S. affiliates raises delicate questions of international law, we point out that insofar as affiliate production and investment decisions are related to parent operations, the United States is missing completely an important class of direct investment data. This is one of a number of areas where the provision of adequate data for any given country may depend upon international cooperation.

7. A recurring problem in the analysis of direct investment is the absence of data at the establishment level. Given that the U.S. affiliates of foreign companies report at the establishment level in the U.S. Census of Manufacturers, and that the foreign affiliates of U.S. companies report at the establishment level in similar surveys by many foreign governments, establishment-level data on production, investment, costs, prices, employment, and related areas could be provided without substantially increasing reporting burden.[45] These data are necessary to improve our knowledge in the following areas: the disaggregated industry composition of direct investment in the United States and abroad; the separation of greenfield from other investments; and the ac-

---

44. We note the similar conclusion reached by Vukmanic, Czinkota and Ricks (1985), Lipsey (1985), and Graham and Krugman (1989). It should also be noted that the statutory authority under which the direct investment data are now collected specifically envisages such cooperation with researchers.

45. See Lipsey (1985) for a similar view and details on how this step could be taken with little extra cost or reporting burden.

curate comparison of the behavior of foreign-owned and domestic firms with respect to, among other things, productivity and wage rates.

References

Bergsten, C. Fred, Thomas Horst, and Theodore H. Moran. 1978. *American Multinationals and American Interests.* Washington, D.C.: Brookings.

Blomstrom, Magnus, Robert E. Lipsey, and Ksenia Kulchycky. 1988. U.S. and Swedish Director Investment and Exports. In *Trade Policy Issues and Empirical Analysis,* ed. Robert E. Baldwin. Chicago: University of Chicago Press.

Caves, Richard E. 1974. Causes of Direct Investment: Foreign Firms' Shares in Canadian and United Kingdom Manufacturing Industries. *Review of Economics and Statistics* 56(August):279–93.

———. 1982. *Multinational Enterprise and Economic Analysis.* New York: Cambridge University Press.

Caves, Richard E., and Sanjeev K. Mehra. 1986. Entry of Foreign Multinationals into U.S. Manufacturing Industries. In *Competition in Global Industries,* ed. Michael E. Porter, Cambridge, Mass.: Harvard Business School Press.

Congressional Economic Leadership Institute. 1989. *American Assets.* Washington, D.C.

Corbo, Vittorio, and Oli Havrylyshyn. 1982. Production Technology Differences between Canadian-Owned and Foreign-Owned Firms Using Translog-Production Functions. NBER Working Paper no. 981. Cambridge, Mass., September.

Courtney, W. H., and D. M. Leipziger. 1975. Multinational Corporations in LDCs: The Choice of Technology. *Oxford Bulletin of Economic Statistics* 37(November):297–304.

Dunning, John H. 1988. The Theory of International Production. *International Trade Journal* 3, no. 1 (Fall):21–66.

Eisner, Robert, and Paul J. Pieper. 1988. The World's Greatest Debtor Nation? Paper presented to joint session of North American Economics and Finance Association and American Economic Association. New York.

Encarnation, Dennis J., and Louis T. Wells. 1986. Evaluating Foreign Investment. In *Investing in Development: New Roles for Private Capital?,* ed. Theodore H. Moran. New Brunswick, NJ: Transaction Books.

Glickman, Norman J., and Douglas P. Woodward. 1989. *The New Competitors.* New York: Basic Books.

Graham, Edward M., and Paul R. Krugman. 1989. *Foreign Direct Investment in the United States.* Washington, D.C.: Institute for International Economics.

Helkie, William, and Lois Stekler. 1987. Modeling Investment Income and Other Services In The U.S. International Transactions Accounts. International Finance Discussion Paper no. 319. Washington, D.C.: Board of Governors of the Federal Reserve System.

Horst, Thomas. 1972a. The Industrial Composition of U.S. Exports and Subsidiary Sales to the Canadian Market. *American Economic Review* 62(March):37–45.

———. 1972b. Firm and Industry Determinants of the Decision to Invest Abroad: An Empirical Study. *Review of Economics and Statistics* 54(August):258–66.

Hufbauer, G. C. 1975. The Multinational Corporation and Direct Investment. In *International Trade and Finance: Frontiers for Research,* ed. P. B. Kenen, 253–319. New York: Cambridge University Press.

Kindleberger, Charles P., and David B. Audretsch. 1983. *The Multinational Corporation in the 1980s.* Cambridge, Mass.: MIT Press.

Lall, S., and P. Streeten. 1977. *Foreign Investment, Transnationals and Developing Countries.* London: Macmillan.

Lim, D. 1977. Do Foreign Companies Pay Higher Wages than Their Local Counterparts in Malaysian Manufacturing? *Journal of Development Economics* 4(March):55–66.

Lipsey, Robert E. 1985. Comment. In *MNC's as Mutual Invaders: Intra-Industry Direct Foreign Investment,* ed. Asim Erdilek. London and Sydney: Croom Helm.

Lipsey, Robert E., Irving B. Kravis, and Romualdo A. Roldan. 1982. Do Multinational Firms Adapt Factor Proportions to Relative Factor Prices? In *Trade and Employment in Developing Countries,* ed. Anne O. Krieger. Vol. 2, *Factor Supplies and Substitution.* Chicago: University of Chicago Press.

Lipsey, Robert E., and Merle Yahr Weiss. 1981. Foreign Production and Exports in Manufacturing Industries. *The Review of Economics and Statistics* 63(November):488–94.

———. 1984. Foreign Production and Exports of Individual Firms. *Review of Economics and Statistics* 66(May):304–8.

Little, I. M. D., and James A. Mirrlees. 1974. *Project Appraisal and Planning for Development.* New York: Basic Books.

Lowe, Jeffrey J. 1990. Gross Product of U.S. Affiliates of Foreign Companies, 1977–1987. *Survey of Current Business* (June):45–53.

MacDougall, G. D. A. 1960. The Benefits and Costs of Private Investment from Abroad: A Theoretical Approach. *Economic Record* (March):13–35.

Morley, S. A., and G. W. Smith. 1977. The Choice of Technology: Multinational Firms in Brazil. *Economic Development and Cultural Change* 25(January):239–64.

Musgrave, Peggy B. 1975. Direct Investment Abroad and the Multinationals: Effects on the United States Economy. U. S. Congress, Senate. Subcommittee on Multinational Corporations of the Committee on Foreign Relations. 94th Cong., 1st sess. Washington, D.C.

Organisation for Economic Co-operation and Development (OECD). 1983. *Detailed Benchmark Definition of Foreign Direct Investment.* Paris.

Ray, Edward John. 1989. The Determinants of Foreign Direct Investment in the United States: 1979–1985. In *Trade Policies for International Competitiveness,* ed. Robert Feenstra. Chicago: University of Chicago Press.

Reuber, Grant L. 1973. *Private Foreign Investment in Development.* Oxford: Clarendon Press.

Roemer, Michael, and Joseph J. Stern. 1975. *The Appraisal of Development Projects.* New York: Praeger.

Rugman, Alan M. 1979. *International Diversification and the Multinational Enterprise.* Lexington, Mass.: Lexington Books.

Severn, Alan. 1972. Investment and Financial Behavior of American Direct Investors in Manufacturing. In *The International Mobility and Movement of Capital,* ed. F. Machlup, W. Salant, and L. Tarshis. New York: National Bureau of Economic Research.

Stekler, Lois. 1979. U.S. Direct Investment Receipts and Payments: Models and Projections. International Finance Discussion Paper no. 140. Washington, D.C.: Board of Governors of the Federal Reserve System.

———. 1989. Adequacy of International Transactions and Position Data for Policy Coordination. NBER Working Paper no. 2844. Cambridge, Mass., February.

Stekler, Lois, and William Helkie. 1989. Implications For Future Net Investment Payments Of Growing U.S. Net International Indebtedness. International Finance Discussion Paper no. 358. Washington, D.C.: Board of Governors of the Federal Reserve System.

Stevens, Guy V. G. 1969. Fixed Investment Expenditures of Foreign Manufacturing Affiliates of U.S. Firms: Theoretical Models and Empirical Evidence. *Yale Economic Essays* 8(Spring):137–200.

———. 1974. The Determinants of Investment. In *Economic Analysis and the Multinational Enterprise,* ed. J. H. Dunning, chap. 3. London: George Allen & Unwin.

Stevens, Guy V. G., Richard B. Berner, Peter B. Clark, Ernesto Hernandez-Cata, Howard J. Howe, and Sung Y. Kwack. 1984. *The U.S. Economy in an Interdependent World.* Washington, D.C.: Board of Governors of the Federal Reserve System.

Stevens, Guy V. G., and Robert E. Lipsey. 1988. Interactions Between Domestic and Foreign Investment. International Finance Discussion Paper no. 329. Washington, D.C.: Board of Governors of the Federal Reserve System.

Tolchin, Martin, and Susan Tolchin. 1988. *Buying Into America.* New York: Times Books.

Tolchin, Susan. 1988. Testimony before the Subcommittee on International Economic Policy and Trade of the Committee on Foreign Affairs, U.S. House of Representatives. September 22. Washington, D.C.

Ulan, Michael, and William G. Dewald. 1989. The U.S. Net International Investment Position: Misstated and Misunderstood. In *Dollars, Deficits, and Trade,* ed. James A. Dorn and William A. Niskanen. Norwell, Mass.: Kluwer, for the Cato Institute.

U.S. Department of Commerce, Bureau of Economic Analysis. 1985. *U.S. Direct Investment Abroad: 1982 Benchmark Survey Data.* Washington, D.C.

———. 1989. *Foreign Direct Investment in the United States: 1987 Benchmark Survey.* Washington, D.C.

U.S. Department of Commerce, Office of Business Economics. 1953. *Direct Private Foreign Investments of the United States.* Washington, D.C.

———. 1957. *U.S. Investments in the Latin American Economy.* Washington, D.C.

———. 1960. *U.S. Business Investments in Foreign Countries.* Washington, D.C.

U.S. General Accounting Office. 1988. *Foreign Investment: Growing Japanese Presence in the U.S. Auto Industry.* Washington, D.C.

Vendrell-Alda, J. L. M. 1978. *Comparing Foreign Subsidiaries and Domestic Firms: A Research Methodology Applied to Efficiency in Argentine Industry.* New York: Garland.

Vukmanic, Frank G., Michael R. Czinkota, and David A. Ricks. 1985. National and International Data Problems and Solutions in the Empirical Analysis of Intra-Industry Direct Foreign Investment. In *MNCs as Mutual Invaders: Intra-Industry Direct Foreign Investment,* ed. Asim Erdilek. London and Sydney: Croom Helm.

Wells, L. T. 1973. Economic Man and Engineering Man: Choice in a Low-Wage Country. *Public Policy* 21(Summer):319–42.

Wheeler, James E. 1988. An Academic Look at Transfer Pricing in a Global Economy. *Tax Notes.*

Comment   Betty L. Barker

This paper is a balanced presentation of both the uses and the limitations of the data collected by the Bureau of Economic Analysis (BEA) on U.S. direct investment abroad and foreign direct investment in the United States. After careful review, the authors conclude that BEA's basic data system is sound

Betty L. Barker is chief of the International Investment Division, Bureau of Economic Analysis, U.S. Department of Commerce.

and satisfies most of the needs of data users. However, they identify a number of data limitations. I agree with their conclusions. The question is the extent to which it is feasible to correct the limitations.

There are several constraints on BEA's ability to collect additional data. First is the requirement under the Paperwork Reduction Act to reduce the reporting burden of government surveys. Second, in some cases companies have indicated that the desired data are not available from their books and records and so cannot be reported. Third, in recent years budget and resource constraints have been a significant factor. Despite these constraints, BEA is working on improving its data in a number of areas.

My comments are focused on the feasibility of implementing the recommendations made in the paper. I will also discuss some of the data improvements BEA has made, is making, or plans to make.

The authors correctly point out that BEA's 10-percent ownership criterion for defining direct investment is somewhat arbitrary. It is, however, the percentage established by law at which an enterprise in one country is deemed to have sufficient influence over the management of an enterprise in another country that its interest is no longer purely passive. Stekler and Stevens recommend that BEA continue to collect its data using this 10-percent criterion, but that in publishing data, subjective criteria be used as well, in order to more closely approach a concept of "control." BEA believes that objective criteria are needed if the resulting data-set is to be consistently and clearly defined. Subjective criteria are difficult to apply consistently or to enforce in a large, complex data system such as ours. In addition, the use of subjective criteria would require the collection of more information (e.g., on the number of foreigners on the board of directors or in top management, or on how dispersed the remaining ownership interests are). Although BEA could consider collecting this information in future surveys, the basic definition of direct investment is unlikely to change.

Several shortcomings identified in the BEA data are the result of collecting data on an enterprise basis. On this basis, BEA obtains one report covering the fully consolidated U.S. business enterprise. Collection of data on an enterprise basis is necessary because this is the only basis on which financial-statement information and the information needed in compiling the U.S. balance-of-payments accounts are available. Also, for enterprises, consolidated reporting is the standard method of reporting for accounting purposes. Some of the consequences of collecting information only on an enterprise basis are: limited industry (and, for foreign direct investment in the United States, State by industry) detail; inability to compile separate data over time for U.S. affiliates that are newly established and for those that are acquired by foreign investors; and difficulty in disaggregating data for U.S. affiliates of foreign companies by percentage of ownership.

In the BEA data, each enterprise is classified in its primary industry (i.e., in the industry in which its sales are largest). This classification may obscure the industrial diversity of an enterprise that has activities in secondary industries. BEA has partly remedied this shortcoming by obtaining two data items, sales and employment, disaggregated by each industry in which an affiliate has sales. Thus, sales and the associated employment in secondary industries can be shown in those industries rather than all sales and employment being shown only in the affiliate's primary industry. It should be noted, however, that the resulting data on sales and employment disaggregated by industry of sales can only be shown at the (approximately) 3-digit SIC industry level at which the data are collected.

One way to obtain additional industry detail would be through collection of establishment- or plant-level data. The Census Bureau is already collecting establishment-level data for U.S. companies, but the data for the establishments of foreign-owned U.S. enterprises are not separately tabulated. If BEA and Census data could be linked, Census establishment data for BEA direct investment enterprises could be obtained without imposing any additional reporting burden on the business community. Legislation giving BEA access to the confidential establishment data collected by the Census Bureau and funding for the project to link BEA enterprise data and Census establishment data for foreign-owned U.S. companies have been obtained. Initial results of the link project are scheduled for publication in mid-1992.

Another consequence of collecting foreign direct investment data only on a consolidated enterprise basis is the inability to compile data separately over time for newly established and for acquired enterprises. An entity established in one year could in the next year acquire another enterprise that is merged or consolidated with the first entity. Thereafter, BEA receives one report for the consolidated enterprise and cannot show data separately for the part of the enterprise that was established and the part that was acquired. The linking of BEA enterprise and Census establishment data should facilitate the ability to track established and acquired U.S. affiliates separately over time.

Collecting data on a consolidated enterprise basis also makes it difficult to disaggregate the data for foreign-owned U.S. companies by percentage of ownership. In its surveys, BEA obtains the percentage of foreign ownership of the top U.S. parent in the consolidated enterprise, but not the percentage of ownership by a foreign person in each of the entities in the ownership chain below that top U.S. parent. Thus, arraying the data by percentage of foreign ownership of each of the entities in the consolidated enterprise is not possible. It is, however, possible to array the data by percentage of foreign ownership of the top U.S. parent of the enterprise. BEA published separate data for majority-owned and minority-owned U.S. affiliates of foreign companies on this basis for the first time in the July 1990 *Survey of Current Business*. We also plan to investigate how to refine the data further, as time and resources permit, to give data users a better idea of the extent of foreign ownership of U.S. businesses.

The authors indicate a need not only for establishment data for foreign-owned U.S. affiliates, but also for such data for U.S.-owned foreign affiliates. They recommend that BEA obtain from foreign affiliates any establishment data that these affiliates report to their host country governments. Although this idea deserves serious study, a number of problems may make implementation difficult. For example, establishment data are not available for all countries and, where available, are not consistent in concept and definition across countries. Also, the data may be reported in foreign currency units on forms that are in foreign languages. Compilation of comparable data across countries will therefore be extremely difficult. In addition, the collection of these data will impose a significant burden on U.S. parent companies, which must obtain the information from their foreign affiliates and forward it to BEA. It should also be noted that, in BEA's data, the foreign affiliates of U.S. companies tend to be less diversified, on average, than the U.S. affiliates of foreign companies, because BEA allows no consolidation of foreign affiliates across country or industry lines. Thus, the effect of consolidation on the data for foreign affiliates of U.S. companies is much less than that on the data for U.S. affiliates of foreign companies.

The authors recommend that BEA not place high priority on constructing market-value estimates of the direct investment position. Nevertheless, BEA has undertaken work in this area. Stekler and Stevens are correct in their assessment that survey methods are inappropriate for obtaining market values. Companies do not know the market value of investments made in the past, unless the investments have been sold or recently appraised. Even if appraised, the value can vary significantly depending on the purpose of the appraisal. Thus, indirect methods of estimating market values are necessary. BEA published current value estimates of the U.S. direct investment position abroad and foreign direct investment position in the United States, using indirect methods, in the May 1991 *Survey of Current Business*.

The authors recommend that BEA collect more data for foreign parent companies. However, the reach of BEA's legal authority to collect data stops at the U.S. border. BEA must collect the information from the foreign parent's U.S. affiliate rather than from the foreign parent itself. Collection of some additional detail is possible. It is unlikely, however, that U.S. affiliates will be able to obtain highly detailed information from their foreign parents to report to BEA.

As resources permit, BEA has made, is making, or planning to make, improvements in several areas not mentioned earlier. A layman's guide for data users that explains the differences in the various direct investment data series and how to use them correctly was published in the February 1990 *Survey of Current Business*. BEA has received funding for 1991 and beyond to increase its compliance efforts to improve the coverage of smaller investments, particularly in real estate, and to strengthen its ability to analyze the data collected and to respond to special requests for information on direct investment. In addition, BEA is continuing to explore ways to lessen the suppression problems in its published data and to publish the data on as timely a basis as possible.

V International Comparisons of Outputs and Inputs

10 Issues in Measurement and International Comparison of Output Growth in Manufacturing

Robert Z. Lawrence

10.1 Introduction

Estimates of manufacturing output are crucial for several issues of concern to policymakers. They are frequently used to draw inferences about the health of the U.S. industrial base and U.S. international competitiveness. Taken at face value, the official data suggest that U.S. manufacturing performance during the 1980s was reasonably good. These data show that:

1. Despite the emergence of a large trade deficit in the 1980s, manufacturing output has retained its share in real U.S. GNP. This conclusion suggests that fears of deindustrialization in the United States have been exaggerated. While U.S. manufacturing firms may have lost domestic market share and may have had relatively sluggish export growth in the first half of the 1980s, apparently the domestic demand for goods grew rapidly enough to enable them on the whole to expand production as rapidly as overall GNP.

2. Output per manhour in U.S. manufacturing grew at a 3.3 percent annual rate between 1979 and 1988. This pace is similar to the 3.2 percent growth rate recorded between 1960 and 1973 and suggests that U.S. manufacturing, unlike the service sector, successfully reversed the productivity slowdown of the 1970s. The performance of manufacturing suggests that U.S. policymakers concerned about aggregate productivity growth should pay much more attention to the service sector, where productivity growth rates have not recovered.

3. The 3.3 percent growth rate of output per manhour in U.S. manufacturing between 1979 and 1988 places the U.S. in the middle of the pack in man-

Robert Z. Lawrence is a senior fellow in the Economic Studies Program of The Brookings Institution.

The author is indebted to Sheryl Nowitz and Kash Mansori for research assistance, and to Lawrence Mishel and Barry Eichengreen for comments.

ufacturing productivity growth among industrial countries. This is a marked improvement compared to the 1960s and 1970s, when U.S. productivity growth in manufacturing was the slowest of the industrial nations. In particular, while U.S. output-per-manhour growth still lags that of Japan, in recent years this gap has narrowed. This evidence suggests that much of the earlier differences between the United States and the rest of the world reflected an inevitable catch-up phenomenon, rather than a fundamental flaw in U.S. performance.

4. When this productivity performance is combined with modest increases in compensation per manhour in U.S. manufacturing and the decline in the U.S. dollar, it shows there has been a marked improvement in relative unit labor costs since 1985. Indeed, purchasing power estimates suggest today that manufacturing unit labor costs are considerably lower in the United States than in any other major industrial country. Researchers relying on these data argue that with sufficient time, U.S. manufacturing will be highly competitive at current exchange rates (Hooper and Larin 1988).

10.1.1 Criticisms

The validity of the manufacturing output data, and thus of these inferences about the health of the U.S. manufacturing sector, has been called into question. In particular, questions have been raised about the accuracy of the Gross Product Originating (GPO) series, which is commonly used to measure output in the manufacturing sector. Lawrence Mishel has argued that the data overstate manufacturing growth on several counts.

1. *Alternative Measures.* Mishel argues that the GPO measure is inconsistent with alternative measures of manufacturing output (Mishel 1988, 1989). Mishel shows (1988, p. 25) that between 1982 and 1985, real gross output in manufacturing increased almost 10 percent less than GPO (24.5 percent versus 14.8 percent). He suggests this is suspicious. In the 1980s, U.S. manufacturers increasingly sourced components abroad. With less value added at home, he believes gross output measures should grow more rapidly than value-added measures. But the data suggest otherwise.

Mishel also finds support for the view that the value added is overstated from input-output (I-O) data. In particular, he points out that between 1977 and 1981 manufacturing output growth measured by the GPO series was nearly double the growth implied by the I-O data for these years. He suggests this outcome resulted from difficulties in assigning output to specific sectors during a period in which the sectoral composition of corporations were in a continual state of flux. Mishel argues that manufacturing value-added growth will have to be revised downwards if it is to track the benchmark from the I-O series.

Mishel is also critical of the major downward adjustments—"the fudge factors"—made by BEA to manufacturing output in 1972 and 1973 to make their estimates consistent with the rest of the GNP accounts. The official data indicate that, measured in 1982 dollars, in 1973 the share of manufacturing in GNP was 22.6 percent. Removing the downward adjustment would raise this share to over 24 percent in 1973. Mishel notes that without these adjustments manufacturing GPO would grow much more slowly between 1972 and 1979.

2. *Purchased materials and services.* The GNP input deflators for materials and services (except for crude petroleum) exclude import prices (Mishel 1988, p. 25). If import prices decline relative to domestic prices but domestic prices are used to deflate all inputs, the result is an understatement of the growth in inputs and thus an overstatement of the growth in value added. Since import prices declined relative to domestic prices between 1979 and 1985, according to BEA, which has accepted this point, this could reduce manufacturing growth, "perhaps by half a percentage point or more per year" (BEA 1988, pp. 132–33).

A related issue concerns the measurement of services inputs. Many believe manufacturing activities have increasingly been outsourced to the services sector. Mishel argues that prices of services used as manufacturing inputs are overstated because the deflators BEA uses for some service sector input into manufacturing fail to take account of productivity increases. This overstates service prices, understates service quantities and thus biases upward value added in manufacturing. The BEA estimates an overstatement of purchased services prices by one percent would lead to a 0.3 percent overstatement of manufacturing value-added growth in the 1975–85 period. (BEA 1988).

3. *Computer Prices.* Edward Denison (1989) has raised questions about the hedonic price measures for computers now used in the National Income and Product Accounts (NIPA). Denison advocates measuring capital goods output by labor inputs. He prefers picking up the impact of technology improvement in final goods output rather than in capital inputs, and he argues that the current practice leads to a significant overstatement of manufacturing output growth.[1] Denison estimates that the treatment of computers has raised the growth rate in manufacturing output per manhour by 1.02 percent annually between 1979 and 1986. Instead of the 3.48 percent annual growth in output per manhour actually recorded, without the extraordinary treatment of computers the rate would be 2.46 percent per year. Manufacturing output per manhour should be marked down accordingly.

A second issue, highlighted by Baily and Gordon (1988) relates to the index number problem which stems from using fixed base-period price weights for products like computers whose relative price has declined rapidly. They estimate that using current-year share weights for computers lowers the growth of output of producer's durable equipment between 1979 and 1987 from 2.64 to 2.20 percent. Mishel points out that the use of hedonic indexes

---

1. For a rejection of Denison's views, see *Survey of Current Business* (July 1989).

for inputs such as semiconductors would further lower estimates of computer output by raising input and import measures, although presumably hedonic measures would also raise estimates of semiconductor output growth.

10.1.2 Implications

Taken together, these criticisms raise doubts about the manufacturing output data. The problems they point to all suggest that U.S. manufacturing output growth has been overstated. Mishel estimates that taking account of the criticisms that are quantifiable leads to a downward revision in annual manufacturing value-added growth to 1.42 percent, rather than the official 1.94 percent, between 1973 and 1979, and to 0.91 percent rather than 2.04 percent annually, between 1979 and 1985 (Mishel 1989; p. 40).

These adjustments clearly could be important. Between 1980 and 1985, for example, accepting Mishel's estimates, the rise in U.S. unit labor costs would have been 7 percent more than estimated by Hooper and Larin (1988). Accordingly, the failure of the U.S. trade balance to respond to the incentives of allegedly lower U.S. unit labor costs would be less of a puzzle (Hooper 1988). Annual labor productivity growth in manufacturing between 1979 and 1985 would be 2.23 percent—a slower pace than in the period 1950 to 1973— compared with the official estimate of 3.38 percent.

It is noteworthy that while Mishel marks down the growth in labor productivity growth since 1973, his adjustments for the period 1985 to 1987 are minor. He would mark the output growth of manufacturing down by just 0.15 percent. Indeed, while the computer deflation issues remains, relative import prices were rising over this period, and thus the manufacturing output estimates are biased downwards rather than upwards. Between 1985 and 1988, output per manhour in U.S. manufacturing increased at an average annual rate of 3.7 percent. This suggests the labor productivity growth rates for manufacturing since 1985 *have* improved greatly over their performance between 1973 and 1979. *Between 1985 and 1988, the recovery in manufacturing labor productivity has been real.*[2]

In this paper, I will deal primarily with the objections to the measurement of manufacturing output that involve international issues, in particular the questions of outsourcing of imports and the deflation of imported inputs. I will argue that with the exception of the computer price deflation question, the case that manufacturing output growth has been seriously overstated has not been proved. I will show that even when chain-weighted prices are used to take care of the computer weighting problem, manufacturing output grew as rapidly as GNP in the 1980s. At the same time, however, I will argue that the manufacturing output estimates should be used with great caution and that

2. This does not mean, however, that aggregate U.S. productivity growth has fully recovered. Between 1985 and 1988, output per hour in the business sector grew 1.8 percent annually (a full percentage point below the pace between 1960 and 1973).

the estimates at even more disaggregated levels leave much to be desired. I will suggest that the data we have available are deficient in coverage and above all in their lack of timeliness. Major structural changes could take place in the United States, but not become fully apparent in the data for many years.

10.2 Alternative Measures

The Census, BEA, and input-output measures of nominal manufacturing value added are reported in table 10.1. Between 1972 and 1980 the Census measure grew more rapidly than the BEA measure. But since 1981 the relationship has reversed, and the GNP value-added measure has outpaced the Census measure. Mishel believes the GNP output numbers have become increasingly inaccurate because they are derived in part from data available only on an enterprise basis. He argues that the basis for assigning such data to particular sectors is outdated since it reflects classifications most recently revised in 1972 (Mishel 1988, p. 39).[3]

The critical feature of these data is that they all present a very similar picture of nominal value added in manufacturing. To be sure, the three different measures deviate in some years, and choosing these years as endpoints can exaggerate their differences. But over longer periods of time, their growth rates seem quite similar. As shown in table 10.1, between 1972 and 1977 and between 1977 and 1987 all three measures have similar growth rates. The differences arise between 1977 and 1980 when the Census measure grows more rapidly than the GNP measure and in 1981, 1985, and 1986 when the BEA measure grows more rapidly. But it is hard to see how differences in classification have led to a systematic overstatement in GNP value-added growth.[4]

Mishel found that between 1977 and 1981, the input-output data showed slower growth in manufacturing than the GNP. This is borne out by the calculations reported in table 10.1. However, as also reported in table 10.1, by 1983 the two series had converged. Accordingly, after 1977, the GNP series for value added matches the Census series in its growth through 1986 and the input-output series for growth through 1983. The shipments series in the Census and I-O data are virtually identical in 1977, 1981, and 1983.

In sum, this examination does not bear out the charge that the Census and I-O data suggest BEA has made serious classification errors.

Mishel is also concerned by the reported growth in the ratio of real value

3. The BEA and Census measures are conceptually different, since the Census data include purchased services. But Mishel argues the growth in purchased services is not a major reason behind the measured differences in the series growth after 1979. He points out that current-dollar service sector inputs accounted for only 9 percent of gross output in 1972 and have increased only slightly since then.

4. The Census cautions that the data after 1982 are not strictly comparable with the data prior to 1982 because prior to 1982, respondents were allowed to report their inventories using any generally accepted accounting method. See, for example, *Annual Survey of Manufactures* (1985).

Table 10.1   Alternative Measures of Nominal Manufacturing Output

Year	Value Added			Value Added (1977 = 100)			Ratios (1977 = 100)		Shipments	
	GNP	I-O	Census	GNP	I-O	Census	GNP/I-O	GNP/Census	I-O	Census
1987	854.00			1.84						
1986	820.00		1,035.00	1.76		1.77		1.00		2,280.00
1985	796.00		1,000.00	1.71		1.71		1.00		2,280.00
1984	767.00		983.00	1.65		1.68		0.98		2,253.00
1983	683.00	708.00	882.00	1.47	1.47	1.51	1.00	0.97	2 056.00	2,045.00
1982	635.00		824.00	1.37	1.34	1.41		0.97		1,960.00
1981	643.00	643.00	838.00	1.38	1.34	1.43	0.97	0.97	2,018.00	2,017.00
1980	581.00		774.00	1.25		1.32		0.94		1,853.00
1979	562.00		748.00	1.21		1.28		0.95		1,727.00
1977	465.00	481.00	585.00	1.00		1.00	1.00	1.00	1,359.00	1,358.00
1972	293.00		354.00	0.63		0.61		1.04		757.00

Sources: Bureau of Economic Analysis, *Survey of Current Business;* Bureau of Labor Statistics, input-output table diskettes; Bureau of the Census, *Annual Survey of Manufactures.*

added to shipments in the 1980s. He believes this growth is inconsistent with the widespread view of increased outsourcing. If producers now import products once made at home, Mishel argues this should be expected to raise the ratio of shipments to value added. However, in principle this is not correct. Shipments reflect both the value of imported inputs and the double counting of inputs shipped between domestic firms in partially finished form. Foreign outsourcing will raise the value of the former, but it will also reduce the value of the latter. If for example, General Motors makes auto parts in one plant and ships them to another for painting and to a third for final assembly, these parts will show up three times in the shipments data. If GM simply imports painted parts, the parts will show up only when embodied in the final product. Mishel implies that increased outsourcing should raise the ratio of shipments to value added. In fact, however, increased outsourcing has an ambiguous impact on the ratio of shipments to value added.

Mishel compares the real gross output growth rates with those of value added at a disaggregated level. He finds that between 1979 and 1986, the decline in the ratio of gross output to value added is widespread. It occurred in 15 industries accounting for 81.8 percent of gross output. But he also shows that the same phenomenon occurred in 15 industries accounting for 57.3 percent of output between 1973 and 1979. The data might be capturing a growing and widespread tendency to economize on inputs, rather than errors in input measures.

10.3 Deflation

When estimating real value added in manufacturing, BEA uses domestic producer prices (where available) to deflate manufacturing inputs. In fact of course, many inputs are actually imported. According to Mishel, the use of inappropriate deflators is another major reason for the overstatement of growth in the real GPO series.

But it is important to be careful about the years over which inadequate deflation presents a problem. According to BEA, the use of the inappropriate import deflators resulted in an overstatement of value-added growth in manufacturing of 0.5 percent per year between 1979 and 1985 (BEA 1988). During periods of dollar depreciation in the 1970s and after 1985, however, the bias was in the opposite direction. Indeed, between 1985 and 1988 almost all of the relative decline in import prices of the early 1980s was reversed. Moreover, according to BEA, "taking account of import prices would have little effect on manufacturing growth from 1972 to 1985, because prices of imported materials grew at about the same rate as prices of domestically produced materials" (BEA 1988, p. 132).

Mishel's study divides the period 1979 to 1985 in two. He finds that between 1979 and 1982 the series grew by similar amounts; constant dollar output measured by gross output declined by 11.1 percent, whereas the constant dollar GPO series declined 9.0 percent. It is in the recovery phase, between 1982 and 1985, that the two series differed; the gross output series rose only 14.8 percent, while the GPO series increases 24.5 percent. Thus, what he terms the value added intensity puzzle is essentially a feature of the subperiod 1982 to 1985, rather than of the period 1979 to 1985 as a whole. Indeed, this is precisely the timing one would expect if increased foreign sourcing is behind the puzzle, since it was during this period that imports grew especially strongly.

It seems reasonable to assume that imports of homogeneous primary commodities will have prices similar to domestically produced commodities. But this need not be the case with imported inputs of semifinished manufacturing components. Accordingly, the bias will stem mainly from the failure to use the correct deflators for imports that are classified as manufactured goods.

It should also be noted that domestic producer prices will miss the *first* use of an imported input in the production process, but will capture accurately the prices of products which embody imports. For example, if imported steel is used to make automobile axles, the prices of inputs into axles will be mismeasured, but when the axles are used to produce automobiles, their prices will be measured accurately.

To estimate how large a bias is introduced into the real value-added measures, a price series for imported inputs is required. The published price series that are readily available are reported in table 10.2. One series that by its name appears ideal for this purpose is the end-use, fixed-weight import price series for industrial supplies and materials. But it is unclear what domestic price series should be used. Between 1980 and 1987, the end-use import price series for imports of nonfuel industrial supplies rose 4 percent *more* than the producer price series for nonfuel crude materials, but it rose about 13 percent *less* than the producer price index for manufacturing materials and components.

Nonetheless, the comparison with the PPI for manufacturing materials suggests that most of the decline in relative import prices took place between 1980 and 1982 (and not during the subperiod 1982 to 1985, in which the value-added intensity puzzle appears. Between 1982 and 1987, the end-use import price series for nonfuel industrial supplies increased at the same rate as the PPI for manufacturing materials and components.[5]

Unfortunately, the concept of industrial supplies is not entirely appropriate for use in this context. The industrial supplies end-use category neglects the manufacturing inputs that are included in the end-use categories for capital

5. The end-use categories for *finished* goods present a similar picture. In 1987 the relative prices of imported consumer goods were back to their 1980 levels; relative imported automobile prices were about 10 percent above their 1980 levels, but relative imported capital goods prices remained 26 percent below their 1980 levels. The major declines in relative import prices appear to have taken place in 1981 and 1982. Even capital goods had returned to their 1982 relative levels by 1987. Of course, these categories may cover up rather large compositional differences.

Table 10.2   **Producer and Import Price Series**

Year	Producer Prices		Import Prices	Ratios	
	Manufacturing Materials & Components (1)	Nonfuel, Nonfood Crude Materials (2)	Nonfuel Industrial Supplies (3)	PPI Components (1)/(3)	PPI Crude (2)/(3)
1980	92	92	103	0.89	0.89
1981	99	110	104	0.95	1.06
1982	100	100	100	1.00	1.00
1983	101	99	95	1.06	1.04
1984	104	101	94	1.11	1.07
1985	103	94	87	1.18	1.08
1986	102	76	90	1.13	0.84
1987	105	89	104	1.01	0.86

Note: Import price series for fixed-weights end-use.

goods and automotive products. There are, therefore, no readily available import price aggregates that are suitable for the purpose at hand. Indeed, it would be extremely useful to a user of the import data if an import price series for manufacturing components was available.

Since there is no such series available, I have tried to construct one. However, even at the disaggregated 2-digit SIC code level, a complete set of import price data by industry is not available for the period under consideration. BLS has now completed the task of producing such data, but its coverage in the early 1980s was spotty.

Nonetheless I have tried to get a quantitative estimate of the problem by using the price series that are available. I have used the 1983 input-output table to obtain a system of weights for this purpose. I-O table 1 indicates the use of commodities by industries. By assuming that imports were used in the same proportions as domestic output, I can estimate the share of manufactured imports used as inputs in manufacturing.

Table 10.3 reports the ratios of domestic PPIs to import prices at several points in the 1980s. For June 1981, price data were available on industries accounting for 44 percent of 1983 manufacturing imported inputs. The weighted average of available PPI/import price ratios in 1981 was 16 percent below the 1985 levels. (That is, the weighted ratio had a value of 0.84 where 1985 = 1.0; in other words, relative import prices were 19 percent above their 1985 levels.) After rising to a peak in 1985, by the end of 1987 these relative prices had returned to their levels of June 1981. Over the period 1981 to 1987, therefore, the impact of these imported prices appears to have washed out. By 1987, relative PPIs in sectors accounting for 67 percent of all manufacturing inputs were 9 percent lower than in December 1982. PPIs in sectors

Table 10.3   Ratios of Industry Producer Price to Import Price Index (1985 = 1)

SIC Code	(1) RPPI June 1981	(2) RPPI Dec 1982	(3) RPPI Dec 1983	(4) RPPI Dec 1986	(5) RPPI Dec 1987	1987/1981 (5)/(1)	1987/1982 (4)/(1)	1987/1983 (4)/(2)
20	0.95	0.99	0.97	1.00	0.95	1.01	0.96	0.97
21	0.00	0.00	0.00	0.00	0.00	0.00	0.00	0.00
22	0.00	1.01	1.00	0.89	0.82	0.00	0.82	0.82
23	0.94	1.02	1.04	0.99	0.93	0.94	0.91	0.89
24	0.96	0.97	0.97	0.93	0.96	1.01	0.99	0.98
25	0.85	0.94	0.98	0.91	0.87	1.00	0.93	0.89
26	0.80	0.96	0.99	1.01	0.96	1.14	1.01	0.98
27	0.00	0.00	0.00	0.00	0.00	0.00	0.00	0.00
28	0.00	0.92	0.95	0.95	0.94	0.00	1.02	0.99
29	0.00	0.00	0.00	0.00	0.00	0.00	0.00	0.00
30	0.88	0.97	0.99	0.92	0.90	0.97	0.92	0.91
31	0.87	0.93	0.96	0.99	0.86	0.97	0.92	0.89
32	0.85	0.92	0.95	0.87	0.86	0.95	0.94	0.91
33	0.82	0.94	0.94	0.96	0.93	1.12	0.98	0.98
34	0.00	0.00	0.00	0.89	0.85	0.00	0.00	0.00
35	0.81	0.93	0.94	0.86	0.78	0.92	0.83	0.82
36	0.00	0.00	0.91	0.94	0.88	0.00	0.00	0.97
37	0.00	1.04	1.01	0.90	0.83	0.83	0.80	0.82
38	0.00	0.00	0.00	0.00	0.00	0.00	0.00	0.00
39	0.00	0.92	0.92	0.92	0.87	0.00	0.94	0.94
Weighted ratio	0.84	0.97	0.96	0.93	0.88	0.98	0.91	0.92
Percent of inputs covered	44	67	86	95	95	44	57	86

Source: Bureau of Labor Statistics.
Note: Weights of imported manufactured goods inputs derived using 1983 input-output table. RPPI = Ratio of domestic producer price index to import prices.

accounting for 86 percent of all levels were 8 percent lower than in December 1983.

Real value added is estimated by the double-deflation method. The series on outputs and inputs are deflated separately, and real value added is estimated from their difference. Using the 1983 I-O table, I estimate that imported manufactured inputs accounted for $79 billion of the total $1347 billion inputs into manufacturing. Manufacturing value added was $708 billion. Using an imports-input price index which was 10 percent too high would lead to an upward bias in estimated value added equal to $(.10 \times 79)/708$, or 1.1 percent. Between 1982 and 1985 relative import prices declined by 19 percent. Using the parameters discussed above suggests the bias to growth over this period would have been about 2.1 percent.

But in fact, the ratio of manufactured imports to shipments *increased* considerably between 1983 and 1986. Thus the 1983 value may underestimate the bias introduced to later years. I have used the shipments and import data for 1986 to estimate the value of imported manufacturing inputs that would be used in the 1983 output mix given the 1986 import-to-shipments ratios. This analysis indicates that given the rise in the ratio of imports to shipments between 1983 and 1986, the 1983 mix of products would have been produced using $108 billion of manufactured imports rather than $78 billion. This suggests that by 1986 a 10 percent import price bias would have resulted in a 1.5 percent overstatement of output. Given the 19 percent relative price increase, a bias of 2.9 percent in growth would have resulted.

These numbers are meant to be illustrative rather than accurate. They are based only on partial information about the price series. But they do suggest that the use of inappropriate deflators is unlikely to be the full explanation for the difference of almost 10 percent between the growth of the GPO and gross output series between 1982 and 1985. The data could be capturing reality rather than measurement error.

It should also be noted that most of the bias would have taken place in growth estimates between 1982 and 1983. By December 1982, relative import prices were only 3 percent above their 1985 levels. Thus, the downward bias in growth after 1982 would have been relatively minor. Moreover, by 1987 relative import prices had returned to their 1982 levels. Accordingly, inappropriate deflators are a minor factor in estimates for GPO growth between 1982 and 1987 measured in 1982 dollars.

In sum, this analysis does not suggest that major differences in price changes between domestic and imported products exerted an important downward bias on the manufacturing output measures between 1982 and 1987, and indeed, according to BEA itself, no bias was present over the period 1972 to 1985. The bias, may however, have been present in the early 1980s. The analysis also suggests that at most about 3 of the 10 percentage-point difference in growth between the GPO and gross-output series between 1982 and 1985 could be due to inappropriate import deflators.

BEA estimates that ignoring import prices biased the growth estimates of manufacturing output upward by 0.5 percent per year between 1979 and 1985. Assuming all of this took place between 1982 and 1985, it would amount to 3 percent—an estimate quite close to the one I have obtained. Even if we add in the additional 0.3 percent per year Mishel believes is attributable to the overstatement of services input prices (1989, p. 40), we could explain only about 4 percentage points of the value-added intensity puzzle.

10.3.1 Computers

Denison's objections to the procedures used to deflate computers raise fundamental issues.[6] His suggestions are appropriate for a measure which seeks to ensure that technological innovations appear in the residual rather than as inputs. However, from the standpoint of appraising sectoral productivity, it seems more appropriate to ensure that improvements in computers are ascribed to the sector producing them. The points made by Baily and Gordon (1988) about the weighting scheme used for measuring output is, however, relevant. The use of the 1982 implicit deflators leads to an overstatement of real manufacturing output growth after 1982.

Table 10.4 reports an estimate of manufacturing real output growth using a chain-weighting method for calculating growth. In each year, manufacturing output growth is calculated as the weighted average of growth in SIC 35, the 2-digit category which includes computers, and the growth in the rest of manufacturing, where the weights are the shares of each series in nominal manufacturing output in the previous year. This method indicates that between 1979 and 1987 manufacturing output increased by 18 percent, in contrast to the 20.4 percent rise in the NIPA accounts. Over the period 1979 to 1987, therefore, this effect reduced manufacturing growth by 0.26 percent per year. Almost all of the reduction took place between 1984 and 1987, the growth for which is overstated by an average of 0.53 percent per year.

The weighting scheme also affects estimates of overall GNP growth. Table 10.5 reports the growth in real GNP estimated by deflating the annual growth in nominal GNP by the chain-weighted deflator for GNP published by BEA. Between 1979 and 1987 this reduces the estimated GNP growth from 20.7 to 19.7 percent. Between 1979 and 1987 the share of the chain-weighted estimate of manufacturing growth in (chain-weighted) GNP declines by 1.1 percent. Specifically, taking account of the impact of the weighting of computers implies that instead of similar 21.8 percent shares of manufacturing in real GNP in 1979 and 1987, the share of manufacturing in GNP would (barely) decline from 21.8 to 21.5 percent.

---

6. For a more extensive discussion of the impact of computer deflation methods on trade flows, see the paper by Ellen Meade, chapter 2 in this volume.

Table 10.4   Percentage Growth Rates for Manufacturing

Year	Chain-Weighted Index (1)	In 1982 $ (2)	Difference (1) − (2)
1980	−4.51	−4.55	0.03
1981	1.63	1.61	0.02
1982	−6.15	−6.14	−0.01
1983	6.45	6.45	−0.00
1984	11.78	12.20	−0.42
1985	3.17	3.81	−0.64
1986	1.70	2.26	−0.56
1987	3.82	4.34	0.51
Annual average	2.24	2.50	−0.26
Total period growth	18.04	20.43	−2.38

Table 10.5   GNP/Manufacturing Ratios

Year	Chain-Weighted Technique			National Income Accounts Basis (1982 $)			Difference Ratio B − A
	GNP (1)	Manufacturing (2)	Ratio A (2)/(1)	GNP (3)	Manufacturing (4)	Ratio B (4)/(3)	
1979	1.000	1.000	1.000	1.000	1.000	1.000	0.000
1980	0.999	0.955	0.956	0.998	0.955	0.956	0.000
1981	1.020	0.970	0.951	1.018	0.970	0.953	0.002
1982	0.995	0.911	0.915	0.992	0.910	0.918	0.003
1983	1.029	0.969	0.942	1.027	0.969	0.943	0.001
1984	1.093	1.084	0.991	1.093	1.087	0.995	0.003
1985	1.126	1.118	0.993	1.134	1.129	0.996	0.003
1986	1.158	1.137	0.982	1.165	1.154	0.991	0.009
1987	1.197	1.180	0.988	1.207	1.204	0.988	0.011
Total period change			−0.014			−0.002	0.011

Note: Figures may not sum to zero due to rounding.

10.4   Other Measures

Mishel has examined alternative measure of manufacturing output to infer the accuracy of the manufacturing output measures. In fact, as reported in table 10.6, the most commonly used measures tell a consistent story. In particular, the Federal Reserve Board (FRB) Industrial Production Index for manufacturing, derived using different methods from the GNP output measure, provides a picture of manufacturing output which is remarkably similar to the GNP measure. Between 1979 and 1987 the FRB suggests output growth of 21 percent, an estimate virtually identical to the GNP measure. Similarly, those

Table 10.6   U.S. Manufacturing, 1979 to 1987

Year	Value-added Share in GDP[a]	Value Added	Industrial Production	Industrial Capacity	Gross Capital Stock	Net Capital Stock
1979	22.2	100	100	100	100	100
1980	21.2	95	97	104	104	104
1981	21.1	97	99	107	108	107
1982	20.4	91	92	110	111	109
1983	20.9	97	99	113	112	108
1984	21.9	109	110	116	115	109
1985	22.0	113	113	120	117	111
1986	21.8	115	116	123	119	112
1987	22.0	120	121	126	121	112

Sources: U.S. National Income Accounts; Federal Reserve Board; *Survey of Current Business.*
[a]Measured in 1982 dollars.

concerned about the manufacturing base can draw some comfort from the measures of the gross capital stock and industrial capacity, both of which have their own problems, but both of which indicate a rise in industrial capacity of over 20 percent. The net capital stock, which reflects the rapid depreciation of short-lived assets, is a less optimistic measure and the only indicator suggesting a sluggish expansion of the industrial base.

Finally, as reported in table 10.7, the national income accounts' measure of goods production, obtained from expenditure data, also shows a growth in the 1980s that has kept pace with GNP. This measure shows that goods value added accounted for 43.2 percent of GDP in 1979 and 44.3 percent in 1988.

10.4.1 Expenditure Measures

Measures of final demand expenditures have the virtue that they are not subject to sectoral allocation problems. When BEA estimates real consumption it measures purchases of products directly and can avoid the problems of allocating output by industry. In addition, the goods measure does not apply an inappropriate deflator to imported goods. The measure of goods in GNP is obtained by subtracting the deflated value of imported merchandise from real expenditures on consumption, investment, government spending, and exports. Accordingly, the goods measures offer a useful check on the consistency of the output data. Indeed, Edward Denison has argued that industry productivity measures should be supplemented by estimates that allocate inputs by sectors of final demand.

But the expenditure data do suffer from certain disadvantages if they are to be used to deduce U.S. manufacturing production. On the one hand, final expenditures on products classified as goods include not only value added in sectors such as agriculture, mining, and manufacturing, but also distribution margins and other service inputs embodied in goods. On the other hand, final expenditures on nongoods categories (e.g., construction and services) reflect

Table 10.7   **Goods Share in GDP**

Year	(1) GVA/GDP	(2) Margin	(3) Sales	(4) (2/3)
1960	43.9	13.6	48	28.4
1970	42.9	13.3	49.2	27.1
1979	43.2	14.4	52	27.7
1980	42.9	14.9	51	29.2
1981	43.3	15.1	51.4	29.3
1982	42.4	14.9	50.4	29.5
1983	42.3	15.2	51	29.8
1984	43.6	15.5	53.8	28.8
1985	43.4	15.2	53.6	28.3
1986	43.3	15.8	54.5	28.9
1987	43.5	16.1	55	29
1988	44.3			

Note: Sales = value added in goods plus merchandise imports in 1982 dollars; Margin = GVA minus value added in manufacturing, mining, and agriculture.

Table 10.8   **Sources of Goods Demand (derived from 1983 I-O table; in Billions of Dollars)**

	Goods-Producing Industries	Manufacturing
Value added	906.7	707.8
Due to nongoods end use	218	157.1
(2)/total nongoods end use	0.13	0.09
Due to goods end use	688.7	550.7
(4)/total goods final demand	0.54	0.43
Due to major nongoods end use	141.4	112.3
Share of major nongoods end use	0.65	0.71

Note: I-O sectors 11, 12, 65–68, 70–79 (i.e., construction and services besides trade). Major nongoods = construction (I-O 11 and 12), eating and drinking places (I-O 74) and health, educational, and social services and nonprofit organizations (I-O 77).

value added to services by the manufacturing and other goods-producing sectors. Final spending for construction, for example, reflects payments for building equipment and materials in addition to construction services. Similarly, final spending on health care reflects payments for the gold dentists use in fillings.

Nonetheless, the goods expenditure data corroborate the BEA value-added estimates, particularly for the 1981–86 period about which questions have been raised. As shown in table 10.8, goods output has matched GDP growth throughout the 1980s. Goods were actually a higher share of real GDP in 1982 dollars in 1988 (44.3 percent) than they were in 1980 (42.9 percent), 1979

(43.2 percent), or 1970 (42.9); the 1987 share was only slightly lower than the share in 1969 (43.9 percent).

In the light of the large trade deficit which emerged in this period, the rapid growth in goods output is a surprise. But it reflects the strength of the growth in final sales of goods. As reported in table 10.8, real goods sales, defined as goods value added plus merchandise imports, grew considerably more rapidly than real GDP. By 1987 the ratio of goods *sales* to GDP of .55 was almost 10 percent higher than in 1982. In 1987, real merchandise imports were equal to 11.5 percent of GDP in 1982 dollars, up from 7.4 percent in 1982.

Assume for the moment that none of the products of the goods-producing sectors (i.e., manufacturing, agriculture, and mining) are embodied in expenditures on services and construction. If value added in manufacturing production was overstated in the GNP accounts, but goods expenditures (and value added in mining and agriculture) were accurately measured, subtracting the GNP estimates of value added in the goods-producing sectors would yield too *low* a margin for distribution and other services embodied in final sales of goods. As reported in table 10.7, however, between 1982 and 1987 the margin computed in this fashion *increased* by 0.9 percent of GDP. One should of course expect some increase in the margin because it will include the distribution margins on imports. But even taking account of these goods by comparing the margin with sales rather than with output does not suggest that in 1987 the margin was suspiciously low. Thus the goods end-use data do not suggest a decline in the real share of manufacturing in value added over the 1980s.

But this analysis ignores the role of value added in the goods sector and embodied in final sales of nongoods (i.e., services and structures). If value added in the production of these goods grew at a different pace from value added in goods production elsewhere, this analysis could be seriously flawed.[7] To get a better handle on this issue I have used the 1983 input-output table to determine if this is in fact a problem. I-O table 5 for 1983 allows an estimate of goods production embodied in nongoods (i.e., services and construction) final domestic demand.

This computation requires taking account of imported inputs. I-O table 5 indicates the direct and indirect requirements by industry for each dollar of final demand. It does not, however, explicitly indicate the import content of these requirements. One plausible assumption is that purchases of imports of a product by an industry are proportional to the overall share of imports in total shipments of that product.

Using this assumption to adjust overall inputs for domestic inputs, I estimate that in 1983 the value of goods embodied in the final demand for services and construction was $218 billion (see table 10.8). This represented 12.6 percent of the overall value of nongoods final demand and 24 percent of the over-

7. I am indebted to Lawrence Mishel for pointing this out to me.

all value added in goods-producing industries. Subtracting $218 billion from total value added in goods-producing industries ($906.7 billion) implies that $688.7 billion, or 76 percent of the value added in goods-producing sectors, is embodied in the final demand for goods. In 1983, this represented 54 percent of final goods demand. A similar analysis indicates 22.2 percent of *manufacturing* value added is embodied in nongoods final demand and that *manufactured* goods account for just 43 percent of the value of final goods sales.

To use goods-output final sales data to infer performance in goods-producing sectors, it is necessary to assume that the relative influence of the services and construction sectors remained constant (the demand for goods due to nongoods final demand grew at a rate similar to the demand for goods due to goods final demand). This appears to have been the case. According to the input-output table, in 1983 three sectors (construction, food and drinking establishments, and health, education and nonprofits) accounted for about 65 percent of the overall demand for goods due to nongoods final demand (and 71 percent of the manufactured goods embodied in nongoods final demand). Between 1982 and 1986, real demand for construction, purchased meals and beverages, and health, education, and nonprofit services increased in all 5 percent *faster* than real GDP. It seems reasonable to assume, therefore, that the demand for *goods* embodied in sales by these sectors increased proportionately. Taking account of the role of goods embodied in services, therefore, *strengthens* the inference that goods production value added grew at least as rapidly as real GNP over this period.

For a precise estimate of the role of goods-value added in components of final demand, it is necessary to have I-O data that are up to date. Nonetheless, these back-of-the-envelope calculations using the 1983 I-O matrix and a few major final demand components suggest that BEA estimates of growth in real manufacturing value added are roughly consistent with the story provided by the expenditure data. And the story told by these data is that the ability of the United States to produce goods has grown as rapidly as its ability to produce services.

The data for final goods sales do not distinguish between value added to goods in manufacturing and value added in nongoods sectors. Thus the expenditure data are consistent with a shift of production activities from the manufacturing sector to the services sector.

10.5   Disaggregation

A related issue concerns the degree to which the data can be taken as representative of manufacturing performance in general. Most international comparisons are done for manufacturing sectors as a whole. These variables are often used to explain export and import prices and to predict trade and investment flows for manufacturing as a whole.

But if U.S. output growth has been confined, for example, to just one sector

Table 10.9   **Manufacturing Output Growth By Industry, 1979–86**

Industry	IP (1)	GNP Value Added (2)	IP − GNP (1) − (2)	Of which 1983/1979	Of which 1988/1983
Food and kindred	26.1	12.2	13.9	−0.12	14.02
Tobacco	−7.2	−30.3	23.1	6.9	16.2
Textile mills	4.6	8.8	−4.2	−6.48	2.28
Apparel	4.9	0.8	4.1	−4.07	8.17
Lumber	21.8	2.4	19.4	12.11	7.29
Furniture	28.9	10.2	18.7	10	8.7
Paper	23.2	15.8	7.4	2.23	5.17
Printing	42.8	12.5	30.3	8.91	21.39
Chemicals	18.5	15.8	2.7	−5.3	8
Petroleum and coal	−8.9	−8.6	−0.3	−0.58	0.28
Rubber and plastics	31.8	34.2	−2.4	−0.24	−2.16
Leather	−35.4	−29.4	−6	−2.13	−3.87
Stone, clay and glass	6.5	−5.1	11.6	4.57	7.03
Primary metals	−30.8	−31.2	0.4	7.28	−6.88
Fabricated metals	−1.2	3.3	−4.5	−7.57	3.07
Machinery, except electric	18.4	75.5	57.1	−7.2	−49.9
Electric and electronic equipment	31.8	33.3	−1.5	4.35	−5.85
Transportation equipment	17.9	8.4	9.5	1.36	8.14
Instruments	17.8	12	5.8	0.86	5.14
Miscellaneous	−0.9	13	−13.9	−8.62	−5.28

Sources: Data Resources Index, Bureau of Labor Statistics; Department of Commerce.
Note: IP = industrial production index.

of manufacturing (e.g., computers), does it make sense to use data on relative unit labor costs to draw conclusions for trade flows in general? Indeed, taking the U.S. GNP data at face value suggests that besides the nonelectrical-machinery sector (the sector that includes computers), U.S. manufacturing performance has been weak (see table 10.9, col. 2). Similarly, the dispersion in Japanese performance may be even higher than in the United States (see table 10.10). In particular, the electronics sector has dominated Japanese performance. Does it make sense then to draw inferences for Japanese trade flows and other aspects of manufacturing performance when the data actually reflect behavior in just a few sectors?

The comfort taken from the apparent consistency of the aggregate data quickly disappears when the components are examined in greater detail. Take, for example, the U.S. data on output growth by 2-digit SIC codes, as measured by the GNP accounts and by the industrial production index reported in table 10.9. While both measures suggest that manufacturing growth has been around 20 percent between 1979 and 1986, they locate this growth in very different sectors. These divergences have existed for a long time (Popkin

Table 10.10   Japanese Manufacturing Output, 1986 (1980 = 100)

Industry	Manufacturing Value Added	IP	Difference
Manufacturing Total	143.4	121.6	21.8
GNP Measure Greater:			
Chemicals	198.6	122	76.6
Machinery	226	154.2	71.8
Electric and electronic	299.3	227.9	71.4
Fabricated metals	150.6	97.7	52.9
Machinery, except electric	151.3	112.6	38.7
Transportation	130.7	104.8	25.9
Stone, clay and glass	113.9	92.1	21.8
Miscellaneous manufacturing	125	107.8	17.2
Paper	129.9	116.1	13.8
Textile mills	105.3	94.3	11
Primary metals	102.7	95.6	7.1
Instruments	155		
IP Measure Greater:			
Petroleum and coal	28.4	81.1	52.7
Food and kindred	87.5	103	15.5

Sources: National Income Accounts; Japan Statistical Yearbook 1987.
Note: IP = industrial production index.

1979, Gottsegen and Ziemer 1968). The GNP view suggests that the manufacturing performance is essentially a computer story; it reports nonelectric machinery growth at 75.5 percent over this six-year period.[8]

This suggests one should be very cautious in forecasting *aggregate* manufacturing trade and investment flows on the basis of these numbers. At a minimum these data should be adjusted to reflect their importance in trade flows rather than domestic production.

But the industrial-production (IP) data suggests manufacturing growth has been relatively diffused. Nonelectrical machinery IP grew by 18.4 percent, not much faster than the manufacturing aggregate. With the major exception of nonelectrical machinery, IP growth was considerably faster than GNP growth in most sectors. Remarkable differences for growth in the 1980s include the estimates for printing and publishing, with IP up 42.8 percent and GNP up just 12.5 percent, and those for tobacco and lumber.

10.5.1   The Role of Outsourcing

Is there a relationship between sectors which have high or increasing amounts of outsourcing and sectoral differences in growth as estimated by these different measures? If both measures are accurate, we might not be sur-

8. In the GNP data, manufacturing minus nonelectrical machinery grew by just 10.8 percent between 1980 and 1986. Nonelectrical machinery accounted for almost half of all manufacturing growth.

prised if, particularly in the short run, IP shows more rapid growth than GNP in sectors where the industry *increases* its degree of outsourcing. IP which measures physical output units will fail to take account of the lower value-added ratios. On the other hand, if the sector has a high *level* of outsourcing, IP will grow more slowly than GNP, if relative import price declines in inputs are ignored.

My proxy for levels of import dependence was derived using the 1983 input-output table, together with shipments and import data for 1986. As discussed above, purchases of imported inputs used by each 2-digit industry were estimated by assuming that the share of imported inputs of each commodity by each industry equals the share of imports in total output of each commodity. The variable LEV is equal to the ratio of estimated manufactured imported inputs to 1983 value added.

My measure of changes in sourcing is the growth in imports used by each industry if 1983 output had been produced using the share of imports in output of each commodity in 1986. The variable CHANGE is the ratio of the growth in estimated imported inputs to 1983 value added.

Table 10.11 reports the correlation between LEV and CHANGE, and the differences between growth in industrial production and in GNP by 2-digit industry over the years 1979–1986 and two subperiods (DIFF). If outsourcing is important, DIFF should be positively correlated with CHANGE. If deflation is important, DIFF should be negatively correlated with LEV and CHANGE.

The correlations are negative, but none are significant. Neither levels nor changes in the degree of outsourcing appear to provide an explanation for the differences between IP and GNP measures of growth. When these variables are regressed against DIFF neither is significant (*t*-ratios are around 0.2) and the R^2 is extremely low.

In sum it is not possible to find a simple explanation for the differences between the GNP and IP measures on the basis of the effects of levels or changes in foreign outsourcing. This result resembles that of Griliches and

Table 10.11   **Relationship of Differences in Growth of Industrial Production and Manufacturing GNP to Measures of Outsourcing**

	1983/1979	1986/1983	1986/1979	LEV	CHANGE
1983/1979	1				
1986/1983	0.275	1			
1986/1979	0.679	0.892	1		
LEV	−0.221	−0.342	−0.385	1	
CHANGE	−0.283	−0.309	−0.369	0.953	1

Sources: Data Resources Index; Department of Commerce.
Note: Values of R greater than .45 are significant at the 95% level. LEV = ratio of estimated use of manufacturing inputs to value added; CHANGE = ratio of estimated change in use of import manufacturing inputs to value added. Estimates of inputs derived using 1983 I-O table.

Siegel (1989). They concluded at a more disaggregated level that an industry's propensity to outsource was not related to its acceleration in productivity.

10.5.2   Comparison with Japan

Increasingly, industries in the United States are comparing their performance to that of Japanese industries (Gordon and Baily 1989). It is of interest therefore to consider if Japanese data present a more consistent picture of performance disaggregated by industry than the U.S. data do. Table 10.10 reports growth by 2-digit sector in Japan as reported in the GNP accounts and the Japanese industrial production data. The differences are striking. For the United States, at least for the aggregate the manufacturing GNP and IP indexes agree; in the Japanese data the growth story is orders of magnitude different. The overall rise in the GNP of 43.4 percent between 1980 and 1986 was over twice the 21.8 percent rise recorded in the industrial production index.

The similarity between the Japanese and United States data is in the degree to which growth has been concentrated in just a few sectors. Just as changes in U.S. manufacturing output growth have been influenced heavily by changes in the nonelectrical machinery sector, so changes in Japanese growth have been dominated by changes in electrical machinery. This suggests that the use of this aggregate data, weighted with domestic weights, may not be particularly useful when drawing implications about trade performance or international investment flows. Thus, for example, measures of manufacturing unit labor costs provide a very poor explanation for Japanese export prices. However, measures reweighting industry unit labor costs by export shares do much better (Lawrence 1979, pp. 101–212).

Those using the aggregate manufacturing to draw implications about trade, do so at their peril.

10.6   Conclusion

This analysis provides some comfort for those who use the aggregate data on manufacturing output. I have come to several conclusions. (1) The census and recent input-output data do not suggest that major systematic misclassifications led to an upward bias in the GPO output measures. (2) The inappropriate use of domestic deflators for imported inputs imparted an upward bias to growth of between 2 and 3 percent between 1982 and 1985, but by 1987 the bias had been almost completely reversed. (3) The goods output data, together with the expansion in expenditures by major goods-using sectors, suggest the GPO estimates for goods production are consistent with the more accurate expenditure data. (4) Some of the puzzling rise in value-added intensity in the early 1980s is due to the use of inappropriate deflators, but much of it could be a reflection of reality. On a priori grounds increased outsourcing could raise or lower the ratio of value added to shipments. (5) Finally, the

GNP, gross capital stock, and industrial production measures all tell the same story.

On the other hand, not all of the objections to the data can be laid to rest. In particular, the issues relating to the weighting of computer prices remain troublesome. Indeed there are reasons to believe that post-1982 growth *has* been overstated as a result of the weights used for computer prices (Young 1989a, 1989b). These weights bias upwards the post-1982 growth in both goods expenditure and manufacturing output. Using chain-weighted indexes suggests that between 1979 and 1987 the annual growth rates in manufacturing output should be lower by 0.26 percent.

The dramatic differences in the 2-digit industry output growth between the industrial production and NIPA measures do not inspire much confidence. I was unable here to find a simple explanation for the differences between these series on the basis of levels and changes in foreign outsourcing, so these troublesome differences remain. Such differences appear even larger in the data for Japan.

Edward Denison (1989) has questioned the validity of productivity analysis by industry. He argues that the allocation of output by industry is so difficult and unstable that industry productivity measures are unreliable. He advocates estimating productivity growth by allocating inputs to sectors of final demand. Nonetheless, policymakers are inevitably led to rely on these measures in making judgments about economic performance. The analysis here certainly lends support to Denison's view that disaggregated measures, particularly those below the one-digit SIC level, need to be taken with a large grain of salt.

The sectoral dispersion of growth appears relatively high. Those using these data to explain international flows should give serious thought to the degree to which the aggregate manufacturing data represent developments that are highly concentrated in a few sectors.

10.6.1 Mishel

While he raises numerous questions about the manufacturing data, Mishel (1989) concentrates on four effects which he quantifies to support his case that real manufacturing output growth has been severely overstated. What remains of these effects in the light of the analysis above?

1. The overstatement in growth due to the neglect of import prices is important in the early 1980s but, according to BEA, leaves growth between 1972 and 1985 unaffected. Since the dollar depreciated in 1971, growth between 1970 and 1985 is likely to be understated rather than overstated.

2. The fudge-factor adjustments are difficult to appraise. It does appear, however, that the BEA data conform with the industrial production and goods expenditure data. It should also be noted that these adjustments became necessary when the data were rebased to 1982. Measured in 1972 dollars, manufacturing growth in the 1970s was as rapid as GNP growth.

3. Mishel points out that the services purchased by the manufacturing sec-

tor have been overdeflated. He uses what he terms a "relatively arbitrary" estimate that this effect was one percent per year. Indeed, his estimate is totally arbitrary. In any case, this problem leads to an overstatement of growth in manufacturing but an understatement of the growth of services embodied in manufactured goods. It would have no impact on conclusions about what has happened to the ability of the United States to produce goods.

4. There remains the impact due to the weighting of computers. As demonstrated above, this effect is significant after 1984, but the argument remains valid that over the long run and over the 1980s, manufacturing has not declined as a share of GNP.

10.6.2 Data

There are two critical data problems faced by those trying to study these issues. The first is one of a lack of timeliness. The input-output tables present a unique set of matched nominal data for inputs, outputs, and trade, but there is an extremely long delay before these data are made available. This is a major hindrance, not only for analysts but also for those government agencies that estimate other data. In estimating purchased inputs to determine value added, for example, BEA assumes, in the absence of current dollar detail, that manufacturers continue to purchase inputs—both materials and services—in the same proportions as they did in the most recent comprehensive input-output table. This study utilized the most recent comprehensive input-output table available, based on the quinquennial census conducted in 1977. This table was published in 1984. The next benchmark table, based on the 1982 census, became available only in late 1989. The pattern of past delays suggests that this 1982 table will be used as a benchmark through 1994.

When the most recently available data for the United States were from 1977, some input-output data for Japan for 1987 were already readily available, and complete I-O tables for Japan were available for 1985. Indeed, the lag in producing the U.S. I-O table has become an obstacle to Japan's statistical work. The Japanese government is trying to construct an I-O table for a major portion of the world economy. It has been forced to purchase the (nonbenchmark) estimate of the I-O table for the United States for 1985 compiled by the University of Maryland, instead of waiting for the release of the official U.S. table for that year.

A second major problem is the absence of price series available at a level compatible with the I-O data. In the case of imports, this problem has been partially remedied recently with the new BLS price series. It would be useful if price aggregates were available that are more appropriate indicators of foreign sourcing than the end-use categories.

Finally, as international factors become increasingly important in the U.S. economy it is important that the data reflecting this activity be improved and that domestic measures take better account of international developments. Accordingly, even though over the period 1982 through 1987 as a whole, real manufacturing value-added growth measures have not been heavily affected by the inadequate input price measures currently used, the inadequacies in the data have led to serious distortions in other subperiods. BEA should deflate inputs by price series which include imported input prices.

References

Baily, Martin Neil, and Robert J. Gordon. 1988. The Productivity Slowdown, Measurement Issues, and the Explosion of Computer Power. *Brookings Papers on Economic Activity* 2: 347–431.

Bureau of Economic Analysis. U.S. Department of Commerce. 1988. Gross Product by Industry: Comments on Recent Criticism. *Survey of Current Business* 68: 132–33.

Denison, Edward F. 1989. *Estimates of Productivity Change By Industry: An Evaluation and an Alternative.* Washington, D.C.: The Brookings Institution.

Gordon, Robert J., and Martin Neil Baily. 1989. Measurement Issues and the Productivity Slowdown in Five Major Industrial Countries. Paper presented at the OECD, Paris.

Gottsegen, Jack J., and Richard C. Ziemer. 1968. Comparison of Federal Reserve and OBE Measures of Real Manufacturing Output, 1947–64. In *The Industrial Composition of Income and Product,* ed. John Kendrick. New York: National Bureau of Economic Research.

Griliches, Zvi, and Donald Siegel. 1989. Purchased Services; Outsourcing and Productivity in Manufacturing. Typescript.

Hooper, Peter. 1988. Exchange Rates and U.S. External Adjustment in the Short Run and the Long Run. Brookings Discussion Papers in International Economics no. 65.

Hooper, Peter, and Kathryn A. Larin. 1988. International Comparisons of Labor Costs in Manufacturing. Federal Reserve Board, International Finance Discussion Papers no. 330.

Lawrence, Robert Z. 1979. Toward a Better Understanding of Trade Balance Trends: The Cost-Price Puzzle. *Brookings Papers on Economic Activity* 1: 191–212.

Mishel, Lawrence. 1988. *Manufacturing Numbers: How Inaccurate Statistics Conceal U.S. Industrial Decline.* Washington, D.C.: Economic Policy Institute.

———. 1989. The Late Great Debate on Deindustrialization. *Challenge* (January/February): 35–43.

Popkin, Joel. 1979. Comparison of Industry Output Measures in Manufacturing. In *Measurement and Interpretation of Productivity,* 363–90. Washington, D.C.: National Academy of Sciences.

Young, Allan H. 1989a. Alternative Measures of Real GNP. *Survey of Current Business* (April): 27–34.

———. 1989b. BEA's Measurement of Computer Output. *Survey of Current Business* (July): 108–15.

Comment   Lawrence Mishel

I will limit my comments to the evaluation of the U.S. manufacturing output data, BEA's Gross Product Originating (GPO) Series. Of course, these data are essential to international competitiveness issues since they are used to measure: trends in U.S. manufacturing productivity and unit labor costs relative to our competitors; recent trends in U.S. manufacturing productivity relative to past performance; and the share of manufacturing in total U.S. output, an indicator of the shrinkage of our "industrial base."

My first comment is that Lawrence neglects to inform the reader that BEA has suspended publication of the GPO series pending a thorough revision. In July 1988 BEA responded to criticism of the GPO series, acknowledging that "the criticisms warrant careful attention," and providing their own estimates of the magnitudes of various measurement errors in the GPO series.[1] In June 1989 BEA suspended the series until it could be thoroughly revised (eventually back to 1972). As of December 1990, no new data have been released. Spokespersons for the Bureau of Labor Statistics, which uses the GPO series in its productivity series, have also indicated agreement with the criticisms.[2]

This history suggests two points. First, Lawrence may feel that GPO series reflects economic reality, but the two statistical agencies involved are quite skeptical of their own data. Second, given BEA's acknowledgement of measurement errors, the issue is not whether the GPO series is wrong; instead, the issues are the size of the measurement errors and whether a properly corrected GPO series will yield significantly different trends in manufacturing output and productivity growth. Lawrence, in a confusing logic, examines some measurement errors to see whether they explain the "value-added intensity puzzle" in one subperiod (1982–85), finds that they do not, and then concludes that the GPO series does not overstate the growth of manufacturing output enough to suggest that sector has declined as a share of GNP.[3]

Lawrence's analysis does not provide an evaluation of the GPO series. It is only a partial analysis covering selected time periods and measurement errors. Because Lawrence does not assess the cumulative effect of the measurement

Lawrence Mishel is the research director of the Economic Policy Institute, Washington, D.C.

1. Bureau of Economic Analysis, "Gross Product by Industry: Comments on Recent Criticism," *Survey of Current Business* 68 (1988):132–33. Criticism came from: Lawrence Mishel, *Manufacturing Numbers: How Inaccurate Statistics Conceal U.S. Industrial Decline* (Washington, D.C.: Economic Policy Institute, 1988); Edward F. Denison, *Estimates of Productivity Change by Industry: An Evaluation and an Alternative* (Washington, D.C.: The Brookings Institution, 1989); and U.S. Congress, Office of Technology Assessment, *Technology and the American Economic Transition: Choices for the Future* (Washington, D.C.: Government Printing Office, 1988).

2. See Bureau of Labor Statistics, Council on Competitiveness, "Manufacturing 'Comeback' Disputed," *Challenges* (March 1989).

3. For lack of space, I do not deal with Lawrence's doubts as to whether there is the "value-added intensity puzzle" I raised in Mishel (1988). It should be noted, however, that *all* measurement errors which lead to an overstatement of constant dollar value-added growth will contribute to an explanation of the puzzle.

errors his analysis is not disciplined so as to distinguish between "large" and "small" problems with the GPO series. My assessment of Lawrence's analysis will show that the measurement errors in the GPO series are so large that a properly corrected series will yield significantly different trends.

Table 10C.1 and the following analysis, drawn from my earlier assessment of the GPO series[4] provide a useful reference point.

How does Lawrence's analysis compare to mine? Let's start with the "import price bias," the problem arising when domestic price trends are used to track imported input prices. (When import prices rise more slowly than domestic prices, then inputs are understated and value added overstated.) Lawrence says a 10 percent import price bias results in a 1.5 percent overstatement of output and, consequently, that the 19 percent relative price increase between 1982 and 1985 overstated 1985 output by 2.9 percent. Data in Lawrence's table 10.2 allow us to extend this analysis to the 1980 to 1985 period, where a 32.6 percent import price bias implies a 4.9 percent output overstatement in 1985. My analysis (based on the BEA analysis) points to an 0.5 percent annual error, or a roughly 3 percent output overstatement over the 1979 and 1985 period. Lawrence's estimate for the 1982–85 period is thus equal to my estimate for the entire 1979–85 period. Extending his analysis to 1980–85 shows an estimated measurement error—the 4.9 percent overstatement—which is *larger* than my estimate (assuming no bias in 1979–80 based on the similar value of the dollar) and which is equivalent to saying that 4.9 percentage points, or more than a third, of the 13.4 percent manufacturing output growth in the GPO series between 1979 and 1985 is fictional.[5]

Now turn to computers. Lawrence calculates that one needs to reduce manufacturing output growth by 0.26 percent annually to correct for the misleading weighting scheme in the 1979–87 period. My correction was for an 0.3 percent per year error; there is not much difference on this point.

Lawrence in passing seems to accept the presence of a measurement error due to the overstatement of service input prices (see Denison 1989, BEA 1988, and Mishel 1989), which BEA suggests overstates manufacturing output growth by 0.3 percent annually.[6]

My evaluation of Lawrence's analysis is that he assesses the specific GPO measurement errors in the 1979–87 period to be as large or larger than I do. I

---

4. Lawrence Mishel, "The Late Great Debate on Deindustrialization," *Challenge* (January-February 1989): 35–43.

5. One reason it is larger may be that Lawrence, quite appropriately, accounts for both the rise in imports and the price bias, while BEA only examined the latter. Lawrence points out that BEA estimated the effect of the import bias over the 1972–85 period as inconsequential. Nevertheless, the measurement error clearly affects the timing of growth, improving trends in the 1970s relative to the 1980s.

6. Lawrence properly notes my "arbitrary" assignment of a one-percent overstatement of service input prices. My analysis simply repeats that of BEA. It can easily be argued that productivity growth in financial services and in other sectors selling to manufacturing has been understated by at least one percent.

Table 10C.1   Revisions to Output and Productivity Growth Rates (annual growth rates, %)

	1973–79	1979–85	1985–87
Published Data			
Value added (1982 $)	1.94	2.04	3.29
Hours	0.50	−1.30	−0.52
Labor productivity	1.43	3.38	3.84
Corrections			
Import prices	0.44	−0.50	0.35
Computer weighting	0.00	−0.30	−0.40
Service prices	−0.30	−0.30	−0.30
Adjustments	−0.70	−0.10	0.00
Corrected Estimates[a]			
Value added (1982 $)	1.42	0.91	3.14
Labor productivity	0.92	2.23	3.68

[a]Corrected estimates are not simply the difference between the published estimates and the individual corrections, because of the cumulative effect of corrections.

would therefore disagree with Lawrence's conclusion that his analysis "provides some comfort to those who use aggregate data on manufacturing output," especially for the years since 1979.

Any appraisal of the GPO data for the 1970s must center on the propriety of the fudge-factor adjustments made to the 1972 and 1973 data. These adjustments shifted output equal to 2 percent of GDP out of manufacturing and into other sectors, thereby raising output growth rates from that base period. The size of these adjustments is surprising, given that they were made for a benchmark year (1972) in the best-measured sector. I would only point out that BEA is reexamining the appropriateness of these adjustments.

Both of our analyses may overstate manufacturing output growth by not considering the possible upward bias in the measurement of nominal value-added growth (which leads to an understatement of nominal input growth and an overstatement of constant-dollar value-added growth). Lawrence dismisses this problem, saying Census and BEA nominal value added have had "similar" growth rates over the long period (1977–86). However, since Census value added includes purchased services, one would expect the Census measure to grow more rapidly, as it did in the 1972–79 period (according to table 10.1, 11.3 percent versus 91.8 percent). It is curious that when the GPO series increases at the same rate as the Census measure, as from 1977 to 1986, or much faster, as from 1979 to 1986 (45.9 percent versus 38.4 percent). Lawrence finds a "similar" growth rate by combining a period when the Census measure appropriately rises faster than the BEA measure and a period when the BEA measure inexplicably grows faster than the Census measure. It must be noted that a seemingly small difference in growth rates of nominal value added implies a significant difference in constant-dollar value-added growth.

The deviation between the Census and GPO nominal trends from 1979 to 1986 implies an annual difference of 0.45 percent in constant-dollar growth, an amount equal to one-fourth the reported growth.

Table 10.6 provides little comfort that the GPO series is correct. Lawrence's own analysis shows the vast disparity between the FRB industrial production (IP) indexes and BEA measures at a 2-digit level, so the fact that the aggregates move together is only serendipitous.[7] The FRB industrial capacity index adds no further independent information, since it is derived from the IP index and capacity utilization data. This leaves us with the gross and net growth of capital stock. I would argue that the net measure of capital is the better measure of the growth of our industrial base, and it grew only 60 percent as quickly as the GPO series. Lawrence should also consider the growth of gross output in this table; it is a measure of output that grew far less than the GPO measure.

What does all of this tell us about the critical international competitiveness indicators based on the GPO series? My "corrected" estimates of the GPO series and, I submit, Robert Lawrence's own analysis, suggest several conclusions. (1) Manufacturing productivity was better in the 1980s than in the 1970s, but significantly less so than previously believed. (2) U.S. manufacturing productivity growth was below average relative to other advanced countries during the 1980s. (3) Manufacturing's share of output declined by from 3 to 4 percentage points since 1973 (but mostly since 1979), indicating a shrinkage of our industrial base (called deindustrialization); more than half of the shrinkage of manufacturing employment is due to this deindustrialization (which has cost 3 to 4 million jobs), and not to relatively faster productivity growth.

Comment   Barry Eichengreen

The reader of Robert Lawrence's interesting paper and Lawrence Mishel's equally interesting response has the sense of observing a curiously choreographed boxing match. The two pugilists know one another well from prior encounters, it would appear. They circle one another warily. Many of the punches they throw fail to connect. To the crowd it is unclear whether their aim is off or whether they are really trying to set one another up for the ultimate sucker punch.

In this comment I put on my referee's striped shirt and step into the ring. I

---

7. It is worth noting that the annual growth rate of the IP series exceeded that of the GPO series by about 0.7 percent throughout the postwar period to 1973, and by 1 percent in the 1973–79 period.

Barry Eichengreen is professor of economics at the University of California at Berkeley and a research fellow of the National Bureau of Economic Research.

hope that proximity will enable me to ferret out the protagonists' true intentions. Hopefully there will be no stray punches to KO the referee.

Robert Lawrence has argued in a series of influential publications that the manufacturing sector of the U.S. economy is holding up relatively well. The share of manufacturing output in U.S. GDP has remained virtually unchanged over the past fifteen years. In contrast, Lawrence Mishel has argued in various publications on the subject that American manufacturing is in deep water. The standard statistics used to assess its competitive position, Mishel asserts, are seriously flawed. Appropriately corrected, they reveal an alarming downward trend in the share of manufacturing in national output.

According to the Commerce Department measure of value added upon which Lawrence relies, the manufacturing share of GDP has declined at most from 23 percent in 1973 to 22 percent in 1987. According to Mishel, these aggregates disguise the alarming fact that the share of noncomputer manufacturing in GDP has fallen from 20.4 percent to 18.0 percent over the period. Leaving aside computer production, Mishel warns, American manufacturing is shrinking before our eyes.

Should we be disturbed by this decline in the noncomputer manufacturing share of GDP? If we are shareholders or employees of other manufacturing industries, the answer is probably yes. If we are concerned, however, with the international competitiveness of U.S. manufacturing as a whole, the answer is probably no. Manufacturing competitiveness is renewed and maintained through structural shifts from sunset to sunrise industries. One can imagine similar calculations for the early twentieth century showing that the buoyancy of the manufacturing share of GDP was due largely to automobiles; we might have worried then about the competitiveness of other manufacturing, perhaps citing the declining wagon and buggy-whip trades as illustrations of the fate of American industry.

It is reassuring to learn from the paper that similar trends are evident also in some other countries whose manufacturing industries are rarely criticized for inadequate competitiveness. Lawrence shows that in Japan the contribution of electronics has been even more important than in the United States. Japanese textiles, primary metals, and food production are in decline. The broad similarities across countries in these patterns suggest that what we are observing is mainly the Schumpeterian process of creative destruction.

The more fundamental challenge to Lawrence's optimism is Mishel's next argument: that even including computer production, the share of manufacturing in U.S. GDP is in rapid decline, and that the phenomenon is disguised from the naive observer by flaws in the statistics. Value-added measures suggest more rapid growth of U.S. manufacturing output than do gross output measures. Such rapid growth of manufacturing is implausible, Mishel suggests, since there has been rapid growth of outsourcing in the 1980s. If all that Honda plants in the U.S. have been doing is assembling imported kits, then value added should be growing more slowly than gross output, not faster, as the official statistics show. Lawrence points out that gross output figures not only count foreign-sourced inputs but also double count shipments between U.S. plants. Outsourcing, while it creates one bias, eliminates another. Though this is a valid point in theory, we need more information about how much difference it makes in practice.

Another statistical problem concerns import prices. Since value added is constructed by subtracting inputs from gross output, accurate input price deflators are critical. The BEA input price series is derived from shipments by domestic facilities. When import prices are falling relative to domestic prices, as in the first half of the 1980s, the price of inputs will be overstated and their quantity understated. Estimates of output and productivity growth will overstate actual performance. The implication is that output and productivity grew more slowly than suggested by the official statistics before 1985, faster thereafter. Mishel eliminates a quarter of the growth of value added between 1979 and 1989 on these grounds and increases the growth rate by about 10 percent between 1985 and 1987.

Lawrence suggests that Mishel's adjustments are arbitrary. He shows that between 1982 and 1985 (the period during which value added grew more rapidly than gross output) the prices of imported industrial supplies fell by 18 percent when compared to the prices of manufacturing materials and components, but by only 8 percent when compared to the prices of domestic crude materials. The question is which comparison is appropriate. Compromising and assuming that domestic prices understate the fall in import prices by 10 percent and recognizing that imported inputs account for less than 10 percent of total inputs suggests that this bias can account for only a small share of the divergence between the value-added and gross-output measures of growth. Lawrence's own guess is that this bias accounts for 30 percent of the total divergence during the period.

Lawrence's data (table 10.3) suggest that the decline in the relative prices of industrial supplies was more than reversed after 1985. Mishel's data suggest that it was not. The dispute remains unresolved.

The Commerce Department itself adjusts its value-added data to make the components for manufacturing, services, and other sectors sum to aggregate output, which is derived separately and more reliably from expenditure data. These adjustments revise downward 1972–73 manufacturing output very dramatically, producing a much more rapid growth rate of output thereafter. Mishel argues that it is not valid to apportion any significant share of the discrepancy to manufacturing, since estimates for that sector are much more reliable than those for the rest of the economy. Input-output data, as he analyzes them, are more consistent with the preadjustment data. Mishel reverses half of the Commerce Department's adjustment and shows that this eliminates more than a third of the growth of U.S. manufacturing in the 1970s. For the 1980s, in contrast, the effect is minimal.

Lawrence also analyzes input-output data, demonstrating that it converges with other sources by the 1980s. He thus supports Mishel's conclusion that the Commerce Department adjustment has little impact on the estimated growth of U.S. manufacturing in the 1980s. This debate matters for how we view U.S. manufacturing's competitive performance in the 1970s, but not in the 1980s.

In the end, one comes away from this debate with the image of the protagonists as blowing soap bubbles at one another. The available statistics are simply too fragile to firmly support either view, or to do irreparable damage to either. If ever there was a debate that supported the case for further investment in statistical refinement, this is it.

11   Macroeconomic Convergence
International Transmission of Growth and Technical Progress

John F. Helliwell and Alan Chung

11.1   Introduction

Most studies of international transactions treat countries as essentially unaffected by trade, with their basic production technologies remaining unchanged by international contacts. However, there is a growing body of evidence that there is some international convergence of technical progress, especially among the industrial countries that have dominated world production and trade over the past thirty years. This paper attempts to evaluate the evidence, based on data for nineteen industrial countries over the period from 1960 to 1985. One important goal of the paper is to see whether the extent of convergence is altered by the degree to which countries have become more open to international trade. We will also assess the extent to which the cross-country evidence supports the hypothesis that there are increasing returns at the national level in the use of knowledge as a factor of production.[1]

A second aim, based on the conference focus, is to see to what extent the evidence of convergence depends on some key questions of measurement, including the exchange rates used to compare real output in different coun-

John F. Helliwell is professor of economics at the University of British Columbia and a research associate of the National Bureau of Economic Research. Alan Chung is at the Department of Economics, University of British Columbia.

Many helpful comments on earlier drafts were provided by Martin Baily, Barry Eichengreen, Peter Hooper, Irving Kravis, Robert Lawrence, Edward Leamer, Robert Lipsey, Catherine Mann, Samuel Pizer, David Richardson, and Guy Stevens. The authors are grateful for the continuing financial support of the Social Sciences and Humanities Research Council of Canada.

1. If this knowledge is domestically produced and owned, this implies that levels of per capita real income should diverge rather than converge as time passes, and that growth rates should "be increasing not only as a function of calendar time but also as a function of the level of development" (Romer 1986, p. 1012). If the external benefits of technical progress are available freely to all those in the national economy, as in the models developed by Romer and by Grossman and Helpman (1989b), then the appropriate scale variable is the level of aggregate total output rather than per capita output.

tries, the measurement and selection of the capital stocks to use in aggregate production functions, and alternative ways of representing embodied or disembodied technical progress.

This evidence on the international transmission of longer-term trends in technical progress will be based on a model in which the level of output is jointly determined by the underlying production structure and unexpected changes in demand and cost conditions. In a subsequent section dealing with shorter-term fluctuations of aggregate output, this framework will be compared with the production sector specification frequently used in real business cycle models of output determination, in which the level of output is based on a continuously binding production structure plus an autocorrelated series of technology shocks.

The three objectives listed above are each the focus of a separate section of the paper; following is a concluding section summarizing our results and two appendixes, the first describing the sources and construction of our alternative data series and the second describing our econometric specifications and test results in more detail.

11.2   What is the Evidence for International Convergence?

An important element in the international comparison of the levels and growth of per capita income and factor productivity has been the idea that growth rates, and perhaps levels, of productivity and real income, should converge over time.[2] To test this notion, it is first necessary to have internationally comparable measures of real income. In turn, data are required on purchasing power parities (PPP), in order to make income levels internationally comparable.[3] To extend the analysis to factor productivity, it is also necessary to have comparable data on real output, as well as on the inputs of capital and labor, if not also of natural resources. In this section we will make use of what we think to be the most comparable data for these purposes, and in the following section we will consider how the results might differ if alternative assumptions or data sources were used for some of the key variables.

The intuition behind the convergence hypothesis is that the ideas and techniques underlying economic progress are transportable across national bound-

2. Convergence has also been seen as one of the factors explaining some of the post-1973 slowdown of productivity growth in countries outside the United States, e.g., by Nordhaus (1982), Lindbeck (1983), Maddison (1987), Helliwell, Sturm, and Salou (1985), and Englander and Mittelstadt (1988). There is also international evidence of convergence at the industry level, as shown by Dollar and Wolff (1988).

3. This is true unless market exchange rates alter so as to maintain PPP in level form. Even then, estimates of PPP exchange rates would be required to assure that the exchange rates had indeed moved so as to maintain absolute PPP. In any event, Heston and Summers (1988) show that there are large and systematic departures of market exchange rates from their PPP values, such that market exchange rates consistently fall below PPP values for the poorer countries. Thus, international real income comparisons based on market exchange rates overstate the real income differentials between the rich and poor countries, as emphasized by Kravis and Lipsey (1984).

aries with increasing ease, so that nations starting out with lower levels of per capita income should be able to benefit not only from improvements in international best-practice technology, but also from the ability to close the gap between their previous methods and those used in the more advanced economies. Many qualifications are necessary:

1. The technologies of the richer countries may be relevant for relative factor prices and education levels existing in the richer countries, but not directly applicable to conditions existing in the poorer countries.[4]
2. The political and social systems of the poorer countries may not be ready or willing to accept the degree of international interdependence implied by the relatively unrestricted movement of technologies and production.[5]
3. The technologies themselves may be privately owned. Their importation might lead to higher levels of GDP per capita in the poorer country, but not of GNP per capita, if the rents attributable to the technologies accrue to foreign-owned firms.
4. Countries that may at one time have been in the vanguard of economic progress may for any number of reasons lose the desire or ability to design or keep up with productivity improvements.[6]

All of these qualifications suggest that the evidence for convergence is likely to be stronger among countries with reasonably comparable initial levels of income, which are open enough to international trade and investment that the necessary conditions for convergence are likely to be met. Evidence covering a hundred years of development of the currently rich countries shows considerable evidence of convergence (Maddison 1982, Baumol 1986). However, De Long (1988) emphasizes that there may be a sample-selection problem here and shows that the evidence for convergence is much weaker, and may even disappear, if the sample is increased to include some countries that were seen a hundred years ago to be promising candidates for continued economic growth.[7] Much larger samples of countries (which include many of the poorest countries) show weaker evidence of convergence over the past thirty

4. Rauch (1989) tests this idea by defining a "convergence club" of twenty countries that had illiteracy rates below 5 percent in 1960 and finds much stronger evidence of convergence than for much larger groups of countries. His proposed convergence club, based on 1960 literacy levels, differs from our sample of nineteen industrial countries in excluding Italy and Spain and adding three very small countries (Barbados, Iceland, and Luxembourg).

5. Following Ohkawa and Rosovsky (1973), Abramovitz (1986) refers to the factors influencing the ability of a society to benefit from catch-up or convergence as "social capability," which he roughly approximates by a measure of average years of schooling combined with consideration of the adaptability of the nation's political, commercial, industrial, and financial institutions. Psacharopoulos (1984) reviews various studies of the contribution of education to growth, most of which assume that the contribution is continuous and separable, and not part of the definition of the necessary conditions for a "take off" (Rostow 1978) for sustained catch-up growth.

6. These possibilities are emphasized by Abramovitz (1986) and De Long (1988).

7. See De Long (1988) and Baumol and Wolff (1988).

years.[8] For these much larger samples of countries, the necessary conditions for convergence are less likely to be met, and the data are not available to assess the extent to which productivity and income levels are simultaneously converging. To allow a clear focus on productivity comparisons, we restrict ourselves in this paper to a consideration of the growth experience of nineteen industrial countries for which reasonably comparable annual data are available for the period from 1960 through 1985, for PPP exchange rates, capital stocks, real output, and labor inputs. Even here, a number of difficult and sometimes arbitrary decisions have to be made to achieve completeness and comparability of data. We will return to these issues in the next section, after presenting our initial results on convergence among the nineteen industrial countries.

The primary sources of our data are the national accounts published by the OECD for the industrial countries, converted to common currency using PPP exchange rates for GDP.[9] The capital stock and employment data are also mainly from OECD sources, as described in appendix A. The primary measure of productivity used for the convergence tests is, for each country, a time series of real GDP attributable to each worker, derived by inverting a constant elasticity of substitution (CES) production function with common parameters, using a country-specific average real return to aggregate capital. International differences in average returns to capital thus pick up average returns to natural resources, education, market power, and other factors to the extent that they are not captured by differences in real wages.

The maintained hypothesis, in our base case, is that technical progress is labor-augmenting and follows a growth path that asymptotically approaches a path parallel to that of the United States. The United States is taken to be the base for the initial tests of the convergence hypothesis, since the PPP data show it to have the highest level and the smallest average rate of growth of capital-adjusted real output per employee over the sample period. We will consider later the implications that increasing internationalization might have for the definition of the source and rate of growth of technical progress seen from a global perspective. In order to separate cyclical movements in output per employee from longer-run improvements in factor productivity, the U.S. series used to define the convergence path is a smooth trend based on the average growth of the U.S. series over the sample period.[10]

8. E.g., those reported in Chenery, Robinson, and Syrquin (1986) and in section 2 of Helliwell and Chung (1988).

9. The data sources are described in more detail in appendix A. The PPP exchange rates are the 1985-base calculations (Blades and Roberts 1987), which are collaboratively produced by the national statistical agencies and based on the U.N. program described in Kravis, Heston, and Summers (1978) and in Kravis and Lipsey (1989), and on previous OECD efforts reported by Hill (1986).

10. The constant U.S. trend series is used to derive the technical progress indexes for the convergence models, as outlined in Appendix A. We also test several competing models of tech-

Following Gordon and Baily (1989), the algebraic form of the basic hypothesis of asymptotic convergence of country i's productivity growth rate to that of the United States is specified as follows:

(1) $$d\ln(\pi_{i,t}/\pi_{us,t}) = c_i + \alpha_i(\ln\pi_{us,t} - \ln\pi_{i,t-1})$$

where d is the first-difference operator; ln is the natural log; π_i is country i's productivity level; and α_i is the country-specific rate of convergence of country i's productivity level to that of the United States. The constant term c_i is equal to $-\alpha_i$ times the proportion by which, after the convergence process is complete, the U.S. productivity level in year t exceeds that in country i in the preceding year. Equation (1), as it stands, is not suitable for estimation, since the productivity indexes are not observed variables. For estimation purposes we use the time series for output attributable to each employee, calculated as described in appendix A, by inverting the production function and attributing a sample-average rate of return to the capital stock.[11] The logarithmic level form of the dependent variable is estimated, with the coefficient on the lagged dependent variable constrained to equal 1.0 on the right-hand side.[12] The initial estimation equations are thus:

(2) $$\ln(\pi_{m,i,t}/\pi_{m,us,t}) = \ln(\pi_{m,i,t-1}/\pi_{m,us,t-1}) + c_i$$
$$+ \alpha_i(\ln\pi_{m,us,t} - \ln\pi_{m,i,t-1}) + u_{i,t}$$

Where $\ln\pi_m$ is the log of measured output attributable per worker and the $u_{i,t}$ are disturbance terms.[13] These disturbances are assumed to have classical properties for individual countries, but the possibility of contemporaneous

---

nical progress against the maintained hypothesis of constant U.S. growth. These include a declining growth model which tests the possibility, emphasized by Nordhaus (1982), that there also has been a steady decline in the longer-run rate of technical progress in the United States, due to the depletion of natural resources and other factors that supported rapid growth in the early part of the sample period. We also test a popular form of this model in which longer-term productivity grows at a slower rate in and after 1974.

11. With a Cobb-Douglas production function, this series only differs by a constant term from the total-factor index of technology often referred to as the Solow residual, based on the influential analysis in Solow (1957).

12. The constraint of 1.0 on the lagged dependent variable implies that the estimates of coefficients and standard errors are not affected by the choice between the level or first difference of the logarithm of the measured productivity index as the dependent variable. Note that only the r-squares differ when the logarithmic level, rather than the logarithmic change, is used as the dependent variable in estimation.

13. The algebraic form used eliminates the effects of cyclical variance common to country i and the United States. Equation (2) differs from the form used in both an earlier version of this paper and in Helliwell and Chung (1988), where the logarithm of the measured productivity index was regressed on its lagged value and a constant-growth U.S. trend index, with the coefficients restricted to sum to one. The current form was chosen because the output equations using efficiency indexes derived using equation (2) fit somewhat better. The estimated catch-up coefficients are also slightly lower than with our previous specification. An alternative method of adjusting for estimation bias caused by the cyclical variance in the measured series for output attributable to labor, which also gives slower rates of convergence, is reported in table 3 of Helliwell, Sturm, Jarrett, and Salou (1986).

cross-country error covariance is allowed for by the use of the Zellner seemingly unrelated regression (SUR) estimator, which also facilitates the imposition and testing of coefficient restrictions across countries.

Table 11.1 shows the results of fitting equation (2) for each of the eighteen industrial countries (the United States is excluded). If there were no evidence of convergence, the log ratio ln $(\pi_{m,us,t}/\pi_{m,i,t-1})$ would have a zero coefficient, and the constant term would measure the difference between the longer-run trends of technical progress in country i and in the United States. The results appear to show strong evidence of convergence, with positive coefficients on the log ratio in all countries, with t-values above 2.0 in all but five countries and exceeding 3.0 in a third of them.[14] However, with coefficients ranging from .03 for Norway to .17 for Sweden, there appear to be substantial international differences in the rates at which the countries are converging. The constant terms suggest that for almost two-thirds of the countries, the estimated level of the asymptotic growth path for capital-adjusted labor productivity is not significantly different from that of the United States, while in the rest it remains below U.S. productivity.[15]

The convergence process implied by equation (2) involves relatively easy international transmission of technical progress, so that a good part of the early-1960s gap between U.S. and foreign productivity levels is closed by 1985. A rather different view of the external effects of technical progress is assumed by Romer (1986), in which there are external economies of technical progress available to other firms operating in the domestic economy, but not to firms operating in other countries. This implies an element of increasing returns at the national level (in terms of aggregate GDP, rather than, as sometimes inferred, in terms of GDP per capita). The largest economies would gain the most from the external economies and would hence have continuing

14. Despite the strong results, it is important to note that the success of the equations in explaining the trends in technical progress is not determined by the fit of the equations explaining measured productivity growth, because of the strong cyclical variance of measured productivity growth, but by the fit of the derived equations for output and factor demands.

15. The coefficient α_i in equation (2) is an estimate of the annual proportionate rate at which the existing gap between U.S. and country i productivity levels is closed. The coefficient α_i and constant term c_i can be combined to calculate the change in efficiency level for any country i in a given year. For example, Norway has a relatively low value of α_i (.0364) and a small negative constant term ($-.0093$). In 1990, its productivity change is calculated to be 1.51 percent and its productivity level to be 63 percent of that of the United States. Sweden has a much higher value for α_i (.1695) offset by a larger negative constant term ($-.1017$), which together give a 1990 productivity change of 0.74 percent and a level equal to 55 percent of that of the United States. The high catch-up coefficient implies that Swedish productivity levels initially rise then grow at U.S. rates, while remaining below U.S. levels. Thus by 1990, the Swedish productivity level is already near its final ratio to the U.S. value. For Sweden and others (e.g., Japan at 62 percent in 1990) whose productivity levels converge to levels lower than one would expect, restricting the constant term to zero (which implies that productivity levels for all countries will eventually converge to U.S. levels) would probably provide more plausible forecasts. Using this alternative model, Sweden's 1990 productivity level is calculated to have reached 64 percent of the U.S. level, while Japan's level is calculated to be 76 percent of the U.S. level.

Table 11.1   The Catch-up Model of Technical Progress

	$\ln(\pi_{mi-1}/\pi_{mus-1})$	$\ln(\pi_{mus}/\pi_{mi-1})$	Constant	SEE	R^2	Durbin-Watson
Japan	1.0000 (***)	0.1089 (5.95)	−0.0503 (3.21)	0.0362	0.9782	1.7087
West Germany	1.0000 (***)	0.0641 (2.87)	−0.0234 (1.55)	0.0282	0.9725	1.4658
France	1.0000 (***)	0.0778 (5.43)	−0.0248 (2.39)	0.0273	0.9851	1.2160
United Kingdom	1.0000 (***)	0.0607 (1.12)	−0.0379 (0.96)	0.0310	0.8769	1.7277
Italy	1.0000 (***)	0.1215 (5.54)	−0.0591 (3.57)	0.0375	0.9678	1.4089
Canada	1.0000 (***)	0.0739 (2.73)	−0.0134 (1.54)	0.0209	0.9550	0.8804
Australia	1.0000 (***)	0.0978 (1.81)	−0.0383 (1.50)	0.0288	0.8583	1.6486
Austria	1.0000 (***)	0.0798 (3.61)	−0.0431 (2.27)	0.0389	0.9640	1.5667
Belgium	1.0000 (***)	0.0607 (2.90)	−0.0137 (1.07)	0.0329	0.9687	1.7974
Denmark	1.0000 (***)	0.0679 (1.99)	−0.0346 (1.33)	0.0301	0.9388	2.3499
Finland	1.0000 (***)	0.0578 (2.36)	−0.0333 (1.37)	0.0407	0.9560	1.6772
Ireland	1.0000 (***)	0.0573 (1.93)	−0.0337 (1.08)	0.0463	0.9589	1.6982
Netherlands	1.0000 (***)	0.0577 (2.20)	−0.0045 (0.40)	0.0339	0.9619	1.4992
New Zealand	1.0000 (***)	0.1295 (2.47)	−0.0544 (2.66)	0.0391	0.6684	1.2372
Norway	1.0000 (***)	0.0364 (1.08)	−0.0093 (0.39)	0.0311	0.9474	1.9688
Spain	1.0000 (***)	0.0752 (4.93)	−0.0196 (1.57)	0.0315	0.9843	1.7462
Sweden	1.0000 (***)	0.1695 (3.21)	−0.1017 (2.91)	0.0385	0.7750	1.9567
Switzerland	1.0000 (***)	0.1337 (2.77)	−0.0431 (2.23)	0.0334	0.8197	1.8392

Note: The dependent variable for each non-U.S. country i is specified in logarithmic level form as $\ln(\pi_{mi}/\pi_{mus})$. The variable π_{mi} is the measured output attributable to labor for each country i, and π_{mus} is the U.S. measured value. The coefficient on the lagged dependent variable is constrained to equal 1.0, so that the logarithmic change in the dependent variable is estimated. The independent variable for each country is the logarithm of U.S. measured output attributable to labor divided by the lagged measured value for each country. See the section on specification in appendix B for a more complete description. Estimation was by Zellner's SUR estimation technique using sample 1961–85. The numbers in parentheses are absolute values of t-statistics, with *** denoting a constrained coefficient.

reductions in their relative costs. If the largest economy is also the one with the highest income per capita, as was the case in the 1960 to 1985 period being studied, then divergence might be expected, rather than the convergence we have modeled. It is possible to make a direct test of the importance of national returns to scale by adding to equation (2) the logarithm of a smoothed average of the ratio of each country's GDP to that of the United States. A coefficient value of $-.075$ ($t = -3.57$) is obtained when the variable is constrained to have the same coefficient across equations, suggesting that there are not technology-improving returns to scale at the national level. Thus, we feel more secure in continuing to model convergence based on the assumed international transfer of best-practice methods and techniques. We next turn to consider whether the pace of such transfer is related to some measure of relative openness.

Table 11.2 extends the basic convergence hypothesis by adding a variable representing the increase in each country's openness to foreign trade, as measured by the increase in its five-year moving average ratio of foreign trade to GDP. The cross-sectional hypothesis being tested here is that convergence is likely to be more rapid for countries that have increased their international linkages, with trade being used as an easily available proxy measure. The functional form used implies that it is proportionate changes in the trade share that affect the productivity level, and that the equilibrium efficiency level will be unaffected by the level of the equilibrium trade share.[16] The results reported in table 11.2 show that the openness variable attracts a significant positive constrained coefficient, with the coefficient value constrained to be the same for all countries to capture the cross-sectional effect. This supports the hypothesis that productivity growth has been faster in countries that have increased their openness to foreign trade. Subsidiary tests show that this effect is strongest in Europe and is weaker and sometimes perversely signed for countries outside Europe. The more restricted version embodied in Table 11.2 will be used for the further tests reported later.

Systematic tests of the two versions of the convergence model, as shown in tables 11.1 and 11.2, against alternative models are in tables 11.6 to 11.8. The two alternative models considered are the "constant" case (table 11.3) and the "break" case (table 11.4). The former involves the assumption that Harrod-neutral technical progress follows a constant rate in each country, while the rate differs among countries. In the "break" model, there are two separate rates of technical progress for each country, one applicable from 1960

16. Tests of an alternative functional form, where the efficiency level was influenced by the level of the trade share, as reported in Helliwell and Chung (1988), produced inferior results. Following a suggestion by Robert Lipsey, we have also tested a measure of openness based on the residuals from an equation that explains trade shares by country size and a trend, with the latter constrained to have the same coefficient for all countries. The resulting measure of residual openness attracted a positive but insignificant coefficient when added, along with the change in openness, to equation (2), and hence has not been used in our subsequent tests.

Table 11.2   The Effects of Globalization on the Catch-up Model

	$\ln (\pi_{mi-1}/\pi_{mus-1})$	$\ln (\pi_{mus}/\pi_{mi-1})$	DOPENA	Constant	SEE	R^2	Durbin-Watson
Japan	1.0000 (***)	0.0971 (4.49)	0.4971 (10.18)	−0.0521 (3.00)	0.0336	0.9751	1.7886
West Germany	1.0000 (***)	0.0527 (2.33)	0.4971 (10.18)	−0.0276 (1.89)	0.0252	0.9756	1.9740
France	1.0000 (***)	0.0755 (5.82)	0.4971 (10.18)	−0.0395 (4.35)	0.0223	0.9883	1.8298
United Kingdom	1.0000 (***)	0.0771 (1.49)	0.4971 (10.18)	−0.0547 (1.46)	0.0280	0.9016	1.9760
Italy	1.0000 (***)	0.0883 (3.76)	0.4971 (10.18)	−0.0523 (3.15)	0.0334	0.9682	1.6637
Canada	1.0000 (***)	0.0688 (2.19)	0.4971 (10.18)	−0.0215 (2.24)	0.0215	0.9488	0.9666
Australia	1.0000 (***)	0.1222 (2.05)	0.4971 (10.18)	−0.0516 (1.86)	0.0305	0.8285	1.6672
Austria	1.0000 (***)	0.0789 (3.66)	0.4971 (10.18)	−0.0535 (2.99)	0.0353	0.9668	1.8758
Belgium	1.0000 (***)	0.0430 (1.99)	0.4971 (10.18)	−0.0139 (1.12)	0.0300	0.9713	2.2481
Denmark	1.0000 (***)	0.0396 (1.08)	0.4971 (10.18)	−0.0232 (0.86)	0.0290	0.9367	2.4740
Finland	1.0000 (***)	0.0514 (1.98)	0.4971 (10.18)	−0.0326 (1.30)	0.0384	0.9577	1.8390
Ireland	1.0000 (***)	0.0577 (1.53)	0.4971 (10.18)	−0.0478 (1.24)	0.0498	0.9507	1.6097
Netherlands	1.0000 (***)	0.0392 (1.78)	0.4971 (10.18)	−0.0059 (0.64)	0.0279	0.9709	2.0922
New Zealand	1.0000 (***)	0.1230 (2.14)	0.4971 (10.18)	−0.0600 (2.63)	0.0388	0.6313	1.3045
Norway	1.0000 (***)	−0.0350 (1.06)	0.4971 (10.18)	0.0345 (1.53)	0.0299	0.9485	2.0673
Spain	1.0000 (***)	0.0336 (1.67)	0.4971 (10.18)	−0.0132 (0.87)	0.0335	0.9787	1.6343
Sweden	1.0000 (***)	0.1487 (2.54)	0.4971 (10.18)	−0.0951 (2.51)	0.0381	0.7440	2.0195
Switzerland	1.0000 (***)	0.1229 (2.63)	0.4971 (10.18)	−0.0492 (2.69)	0.0310	0.8343	2.0103

Note: This model is specified in the same way as the catch-up model in Table 11.1, but it includes the additional variable DOPENA. DOPENA is the annual change in "openness" defined as the log difference of current and lagged values of the five-year moving average of exports plus imports divided by GNP. See the section on specification in appendix B for a more complete description. Estimation was by Zellner's SUR estimation technique using sample 1963–85.

Table 11.3   **The Constant Model of Technical Progress**

	RTIME	Constant	SEE	R^2	Durbin-Watson
United States	0.0072	33.4020	0.0414	0.6331	0.3284
	(6.70)	(423.48)			
Japan	0.0408	30.2260	0.1078	0.8894	1.1356
	(14.46)	(147.11)			
West Germany	0.0295	31.1750	0.0462	0.9582	0.2292
	(24.41)	(354.14)			
France	0.0371	30.6200	0.0699	0.9408	0.0876
	(20.33)	(229.90)			
United King-dom	0.0170	31.9880	0.0376	0.9198	0.5007
	(17.27)	(445.85)			
Italy	0.0350	30.7230	0.0924	0.8896	0.1311
	(14.47)	(174.47)			
Canada	0.0193	32.2570	0.0445	0.9131	0.2151
	(16.53)	(379.93)			
Australia	0.0164	32.2880	0.0406	0.9024	0.4871
	(15.50)	(417.60)			
Austria	0.0338	30.010	0.0612	0.9451	0.1297
	(21.16)	(263.30)			
Belgium	0.0316	31.1250	0.0462	0.9634	0.2327
	(26.16)	(353.71)			
Denmark	0.0237	31.4890	0.0492	0.9287	0.3029
	(18.41)	(335.75)			
Finland	0.0327	30.6430	0.0459	0.9661	0.3588
	(27.24)	(350.52)			
Ireland	0.0367	30.2820	0.0505	0.9675	0.5218
	(27.82)	(314.71)			
Netherlands	0.0296	31.4430	0.0500	0.9516	0.2528
	(22.60)	(329.66)			
New Zealand	0.0018	33.4420	0.0524	0.0645	0.4934
	(1.34)	(334.86)			
Norway	0.0251	31.4520	0.0288	0.9770	0.6848
	(33.25)	(572.53)			
Spain	0.0423	30.1740	0.0670	0.9573	0.2139
	(24.16)	(236.40)			
Sweden	0.0174	32.0350	0.0482	0.8792	0.3070
	(13.75)	(348.41)			
Switzerland	0.0163	32.3790	0.0542	0.8361	0.1858
	(11.52)	(313.38)			

Note: The dependent variable is ln π_m, measured output attributable to labor. RTIME is an annual time trend equal to 60 in 1960, 61 in 1961. See the section on specification in appendix B for a more complete description. Estimation was by Zellner's SUR estimation technique using sample 1960–85.

Table 11.4   The "Break" Hypothesis

	RTIME	T74	Constant	SEE	R^2	Durbin-Watson
United States	0.0163	−0.0071	32.8140	0.0280	0.8318	0.6124
	(9.11)	(5.54)	(276.22)			
Japan	0.0657	−0.0196	28.6030	0.0675	0.9566	0.5292
	(15.25)	(6.35)	(99.92)			
West Germany	0.0362	−0.0053	30.7360	0.0402	0.9683	0.3431
	(14.13)	(2.89)	(180.36)			
France	0.0477	−0.0083	29.9300	0.0601	0.9563	0.2098
	(12.46)	(3.03)	(117.52)			
United Kingdom	0.0192	−0.0017	31.8430	0.0369	0.9230	0.5021
	(8.17)	(1.04)	(203.59)			
Italy	0.0515	−0.0130	29.6450	0.0736	0.9299	0.3602
	(10.97)	(3.87)	(94.98)			
Canada	0.0230	−0.0029	32.0150	0.0427	0.9200	0.2345
	(8.43)	(1.50)	(176.67)			
Australia	0.0247	−0.0065	31.7510	0.0295	0.9482	1.0096
	(13.10)	(4.80)	(253.52)			
Austria	0.0410	−0.0056	30.2360	0.0562	0.9536	0.2443
	(11.42)	(2.18)	(126.81)			
Belgium	0.0371	−0.0044	30.7620	0.0422	0.9694	0.3152
	(13.80)	(2.27)	(172.01)			
Denmark	0.0337	−0.0078	30.8400	0.0359	0.9620	0.7215
	(14.68)	(4.77)	(202.34)			
Finland	0.0390	−0.0049	30.2320	0.0406	0.9734	0.4968
	(15.03)	(2.67)	(175.42)			
Ireland	0.0346	0.0017	30.4220	0.0500	0.9682	0.5372
	(10.85)	(0.74)	(143.60)			
Netherlands	0.0352	−0.0044	31.0770	0.0463	0.9585	0.3985
	(11.92)	(2.09)	(158.30)			
New Zealand	0.0062	−0.0034	33.1610	0.0503	0.1366	0.6051
	(1.92)	(1.47)	(155.37)			
Norway	0.0262	−0.0009	31.3770	0.0286	0.9774	0.7505
	(14.39)	(0.69)	(259.13)			
Spain	0.0514	−0.0071	29.5820	0.0595	0.9663	0.3745
	(13.53)	(2.63)	(117.18)			
Sweden	0.0258	−0.0066	31.4840	0.0389	0.9215	0.7236
	(10.40)	(3.74)	(190.91)			
Switzerland	0.0287	−0.0097	31.5770	0.0348	0.9324	0.9470
	(12.90)	(6.08)	(213.86)			

Note: The dependent variable is ln π_m, measured output attributable to labor. RTIME is an annual time trend equal to 60 in 1960, 61 in 1961. T74 is a time trend equal to zero before 1974 and equal to 1 in 1974, 2 in 1975. See the section on specification in appendix B for a more complete description. Estimation was by Zellner's SUR estimation technique using sample 1960–85.

to 1973, and the second applicable thereafter, to embody the frequently noted post-1973 slowdown of output growth in the industrial countries (e.g., Bruno and Sachs 1985).[17] Before 1974, the average rate is shown as the coefficient on RTIME in table 11.4, while for 1974 and after, the rate is adjusted by the value of the coefficient on the auxiliary time trend T74. In each country, there was an apparent reduction in the average annual rate of technical progress after 1973, (with a t-value above 2.0 in all but five countries), by an amount averaging about 0.6 percentage points or roughly just under a fifth of the average pre-1974 rate of technical progress.

To provide a test of the productivity models estimated for the constant, break, and convergence cases, it is necessary to derive noncyclical indexes of technical progress for each of the models. The indexes can then be used comparably in equations that attempt to explain the actual movements of output in terms of the underlying production function (including the alternative derived series for technical progress) and other short-term demand and profitability factors possibly causing temporary departures from the normal productivity performance. As explained in appendix B, the technical progress indexes for the convergence models are calculated cumulatively, starting from a base chosen so that the calculated labor productivity index should equal the measured values on average, without any of the cyclical variance present in the measured values of the series for capital-adjusted output per employee.

The output equation used for the non-nested tests of the alternative indexes of technical progress is the factor utilization model, as described in Helliwell and Chung (1986). This approach treats the output decision of the representative firm as depending on its employed stocks of labor and capital (including explicit allowance for technical progress, based on whatever model of technical progress is being assumed), conditioned by unexpected sales, profitability, and inventory disequilibrium.[18] In this framework, the employed stocks of labor and capital, when combined with the index of technical progress in the synthetic production function, represent the expected level of demand to the extent that firms foresaw it as being sufficiently profitable and permanent to justify changes in investment and employment. Temporary and unexpected changes in demand and cost conditions are then accommodated partially by changes in the intensity of factor use[19] and partially by price changes. Inven-

17. A catch-up model was also subsequently tested which included, as an additional explanatory variable, a separate break term set equal to one from 1974, and to zero from 1960 to 1973. The break term was not significantly different from zero when constrained across equations, and hence we chose not to pursue this case further.

18. As shown in Helliwell (1986), this formulation is general enough to include the Lucas (1973), Barro (1978), and Keynesian output functions as nested hypotheses. The tests reported there showed that the more general formulation of the factor utilization approach rejected the more restricted models when fitted to data from each of the G-7 economies. Comparisons with the technology shock approach frequently used in real business models will be presented in section 11.4.

19. The use of buffering changes in factor utilization, with recognition that the usage of both labor and capital can be shifted back and forth between direct production and maintenance activi-

tories then act as a buffer for any residual excess demand or supply, to an extent that is influenced by the current discrepancy between the actual and normal ratios of inventory stocks to expected sales.

The output equation tests for the United States are reported in table 11.5, while those for all the industrial countries are reported in table 11.6.[20] For the United States, four competing models of technical progress are tested. These models are the constant productivity growth model, the constant growth model adjusted for the post-1974 productivity break, the constant growth model adjusted for the effects of increased openness, and a declining growth model.[21] Overall, the tests reject the break model, shown by the significant additional information provided by the competing models in the P test, and by the lower C-test coefficients for the break model when it is compared directly with each alternative model.[22] The C test indicates weak preference for the constant growth model over the model including the effects of increased openness, but it does not provide much guidance in choosing between the constant growth and declining growth models. The Godfrey tests do not support one particular model. For the convergence models reported in this paper, we therefore have chosen the constant model for the United States to derive the non-U.S. technical progress indexes.[23]

To summarize the output equation tests reported in table 11.6, the constant and break models of technical progress are very strongly rejected in favor of either of the convergence models.[24] Of the two convergence models, the

ties, is also starting to appear in real business cycle models, e.g., Greenwood, Hercowitz, and Huffman (1988).

20. Note that the parameter estimates for the output equations, assuming the convergence model for the non-U.S. countries and constant growth of technical progress for the United States, are shown in table 11.9.

21. The declining growth model uses a trend which declines by 30 percent over the 25-year sample period (as described in appendix B). The 30 percent declining growth model produced the output equation with the best fit when several alternative rates of decline were tested. Compared with the constant growth model, which has an efficiency index that grows at .73 percent per year throughout the sample, the 30 percent declining growth model produces a U.S. efficiency index that grows at an average rate of .81 percent for the period 1961–73, .67 percent for the period 1974–85, and .54 percent for the period 1985–2000.

22. Note that the P and C tests are described near the end of tables 11.5 and 11.6, and that the Godfrey test is described at the bottom of table 11.5.

23. Tests of convergence assuming a 30 percent declining growth model for the United States indicated that the output equations for the non-U.S. group of countries prefer the declining growth model. These new tests thus provide further support for one surprising feature of our earlier results: that most countries outside the United States show evidence of a convergence process that is projected to leave non-U.S. productivity levels below, and sometimes well below, those in the United States. Post-1985 data will help to show whether this is a continuing feature of the evidence or is due to the widespread recessions in the first half of the 1980s.

24. A declining growth model for all countries was later tested to examine whether there has been a steady decline in the longer-run rate of technical progress, as suggested by Nordhaus (1982). The 30 percent declining trend was used, as this trend was favored for the United States. The C tests of the non-U.S. output equations indicated that both convergence models were strongly preferred to the declining growth model, and that the declining growth model was preferred to the constant growth and "break" models. Thus for the current data sample, the non-U.S.

model without openness effects is preferred. This suggests that the openness effects are potentially important, but that the current specification does not quite capture them.[25]

Tables 11.7 and 11.8 extend the tests to include the derived investment and labor demand equations. These equations show much less power to discriminate among the different models of technical progress. In the case of the investment equations, for which the tests are reported in table 11.7, the F-statistics show that none of the four models can simultaneously reject all of the other three. As for the pattern among the models, the catch-up and break models are clearly the worst, and the constant model less clearly the best; the convergence model with openness effects falls in between. For the derived employment equations, the F-statistics show the catch-up model to be the least sufficient of the models, and the catch-up model with openness effects to be slightly better than the constant model, which is preferred to the break model. Although the statistical significance of these results is far less than for the comparison of the alternative output equations, they do tend to confirm the rejection of the break model, while qualifying the dominance of the convergence models over the model assuming constant technical progress.

Table 11.9 reports parameter estimates for the output equations of the industrial countries. Constant growth of technical progress is assumed for the United States and the convergence model is assumed for the non-U.S. countries. The results provide evidence that for the majority of countries, output is significantly affected by unexpected sales, profitability, and inventory disequilibrium.

11.3   Issues of Data and Measurement

In this section we emphasize issues of data and measurement, through the use of three sorts of sensitivity test. In section 11.3.1, we consider the consequences of using PPP rather than market exchange rates, while in section 11.3.2 we test the effects of adopting alternative measures of the aggregate

---

countries generally prefer some slowdown, as evidenced by the relatively good performance of the convergence and declining growth models. Although our current results show that the convergence models contain more information than the declining growth model, they also warrant further investigation, using models with possibly a broader range of targets for convergence, and estimating over a longer sample period.

25. A supplementary test of the output equations using the two convergence models was also done, and this showed the pure catch-up model to out-perform only slightly the model with openness effects. The investment and employment equations estimated under each model were used to derive predicted values for the factor demands. The predicted capital stock and employment series were then placed in the CES production function to calculate an alternative normal output (q_s) series for each country, and the output equations were reestimated as before. C tests of these new output equations showed that the catch-up model with openness effects was only marginally inferior to the pure catch-up model. These results thus illustrate the potential importance of the former model, given the superior fit of its estimated factor demands.

Table 11.5   **Non-nested Tests of U.S. Output Equations**

The following models of labor productivity were estimated and tested using non-nested tests of the U.S. output equations. H_0 denotes the maintained hypothesis, which is tested against the competing models. The output equations were estimated by two-stage least squares over the sample 1963–85 for all models. See appendix B for variable definitions.

Case 1: H_0: Constant case: $\ln \pi_m = a_1\text{RTIME} + c$
      H_1: Break case: $\ln \pi_m = a_1\text{RTIME} + a_2\text{T74} + c$
      H_2: Open case: $\ln \pi_m = a_1\text{RTIME} + a_2\text{DOPENA} + c$
      H_3: Decline Case: $\ln \pi_m = a_1\text{DECLINE} + c$

Case 2: H_0: Break	*Case 3:* H_0: Open	*Case 4:* H_0: Decline
H_1: Constant	H_1: Constant	H_1: Constant
H_2: Open	H_2: Break	H_2: Break
H_3: Decline	H_3: Decline	H_3: Open

(1) P Test

	t-statistics			
	Case 1	Case 2	Case 3	Case 4
H_1	.06278	2.5821*	1.07290	1.07720
H_2	.45623	2.3831*	.05634	.06300
H_3	.97296	2.5174*	.96835	.45631

Note: Because of collinearity between H_1 and H_2, each hypothesis was tested in separate regressions for case 2.
* = significance at the 95% level.

	F-statistics			
	Case 1	Case 2	Case 3	Case 4
$H_1 = H_2 = H_3 = 0$ (3,16) df	.43854		.67419	.55073
$H_1 = 0.0$ (1,16) df	.00394	6.66713* (1,18) df	1.15102	1.16027
$H_2 = 0.0$ (1,16) df	.20814	5.67904* (1,18) df	.00317	.00397
$H_3 = 0.0$ (1,16) df	.94665	6.33743* (1,18) df	.93769	.20822

* = rejection of the null hypothesis at 5% significance.

(2) C Test

	Coefficient	t-Ratio		Coefficient	t-Ratio
Case 1	.75144	2.71	Case 1	5.29500	1.04
Case 2	.24856	.90	Case 4	−4.29500	.84
Case 1	.83329	1.42	Case 2	.26871	.98
Case 3	.16671	.28	Case 4	.73129	2.66
Case 2	.37684	1.61	Case 3	.20768	.34
Case 3	.62316	2.66	Case 4	.79232	1.29

Table 11.5   **(continued)**

<table>
<tr><td colspan="5" align="center">(3) Godfrey Test</td></tr>
<tr><td></td><td>Case 1</td><td>Case 2</td><td>Case 3</td><td>Case 4</td></tr>
<tr><td>H_1</td><td>.4383</td><td>1.5259</td><td>.38028</td><td>.41335</td></tr>
<tr><td>H_2</td><td>1.5333</td><td>1.0676</td><td>.44562</td><td>.48691</td></tr>
<tr><td>H_3</td><td>.2668</td><td>1.4982</td><td>.56077</td><td>1.63110</td></tr>
</table>

Test Methods:

(1) P Test: Following Davidson and MacKinnon (1981), the following procedure was used. Given two alternative models,

$$H_0: Yt = ft(Xt, \beta) + e0t$$
$$H_1: Yt + gt(Zt, \gamma) + e1t,$$

the following artificial regression can be estimated for the P test:

$$Yt - fht = b\,Xt = \lambda\,(ght - fht)$$

where fht and ght denote the fitted values based on H_0 and H_1. The t ratio for λ is the P test. If it is significant H_0 is rejected, and if insignificant H_0 is not rejected. In cases 1 and 3 above, H_0 was tested against more than one alternative hypothesis at a time, with joint F-statistics reported to test whether H_1 and H_2 are zero.

(2) C Test: Again following Davidson and MacKinnon (1981), the C test involves estimating the following regression:

$$Yt = \alpha\,fht + (1 - \alpha)\,ght$$

where fht and ght are the fitted values of yt from the two competing models. If α is greater than $(1 - \alpha)$ and is significant, then fht is the dominating model.

(3) Godfrey Test: The statistics are derived using Godfrey's (1983) test of competing non-nested models estimated by an instrumental (IV) estimator (e.g., two-stage least squares). Let the two models be

$$H_0: Yt = ft(Xt, \beta) + e0t$$
$$H_1: Yt = gt(Zt, \gamma) + e1t$$

and let W be the set of exogenous variables included in the two-stage least squares estimation. We first estimate H_0 and H_1 by two-stage least squares and obtain the sample values of b and c (the two-stage least squares estimates of β and γ given W). We calculate the ordinary least squares predicted values Xht and Zht from the regression of X and Z on W. We then obtain the residual vector from the ordinary least squares regression of $Xht\,b$ on Zht and add it as an independent variable in the regression of the maintained hypothesis. The table reports the t-statistic for the variable. If it is significant, it indicates that H_1 adds significant explanatory power to H_0 and it implies the rejection of the null hypothesis against H_1.

capital stock in the specification of the aggregate technology. Finally, in section 11.3.3 we present some preliminary evidence with an alternative production model in which technical progress is embodied in capital via gross investment.

11.3.1   Exchange Rates and the Convergence of Productivity Levels

In the productivity comparisons of this paper, the OECD 1985-based PPP exchange rates for GDP are used to convert real values (in terms of national currencies at constant prices) into "international dollars." What difference would it make if market exchange rates were used instead? The answer to this question depends on the year chosen for the conversion base, since the departures of market exchange rates from PPP differ considerably from year to year. To test the impact of using market rather than PPP exchange rates, we can refit

Table 11.6   **Non-nested Tests of Output Equations for the Industrial Countries**

The following models of labor productivity were estimated and tested using non-nested tests of the output equations for the 19 industrial countries. For all non-break models, the constant case is used for the U.S. In the break base, the break model is used for U.S. and non-U.S. models, consistent with the hypothesis that the productivity slowdown was a feature of all the industrial countries. In the tests below, H_0 denotes the maintained hypothesis, which is tested against the competing models. The output equations were estimated by Zellner seemingly-unrelated regression technique with instrumental variables, using the sample period 1963–85 for all models.

Case 1: H_0: Pure catch-up case: dln (π_m/π_{mus}) $\quad = a_1\ln (\pi_{mus}/\pi_{m-1}) + a_2$
$\quad\quad$ H_1: Catch-up with openness: dln $(\pi_m/\pi_{mus}) = a_1\ln (\pi_{mus}/\pi_{m-1}) + a_2\text{DOPENA} + a_3$
$\quad\quad$ H_2: Constant case: ln π_m $\quad\quad\quad\quad = a_1\text{RTIME} + a_2$
$\quad\quad$ H_3: Break case: ln π_m $\quad\quad\quad\quad\quad = a_1\text{RTIME} + a_2\text{T74} + a_3$

Case 2: H_0: Catch-up/open	*Case 3:* H_0: Constant	*Case 4:* H_0: Break
$\quad\quad$ H_1: Pure Catch-up	$\quad\quad$ H_1: Catch-up	$\quad\quad$ H_1: Catch-up
$\quad\quad$ H_2: Constant	$\quad\quad$ H_2: Catch-up/open	$\quad\quad$ H_2: Catch-up/open
$\quad\quad$ H_3: Break	$\quad\quad$ H_3: Break	$\quad\quad$ H_3: Constant

(1) P Test

	t-statistics			
	Case 1	Case 2	Case 3	Case 4
H_1	2.66*	4.86*	4.96*	5.09*
H_2	.54	.66	2.38*	2.24*
H_3	.29	.58	.78	.45

* = significance at the 95% level.

	F-statistics			
	Case 1	Case 2	Case 3	Case 4
$H_1 = H_2 = H_3 = 0$ (3,430) df	3.08*	8.42*	77.79*	91.44*
$H_1 = 0.0$ (1,430) df	7.07*	23.58*	24.61*	25.86*
$H_2 = 0.0$ (1,430) df	.29	.43	5.64*	5.04*
$H_3 = 0.0$ (1,430) df	.08	.34	.60	.21

* = rejection of the null hypothesis at 5% significance.

(2) C Test

	Coefficient	*t*-Ratio		Coefficient	*t*-Ratio
Case 1	.70399	5.94	Case 2	.85986	13.80
Case 2	.29601	2.50	Case 3	.14014	2.25
Case 1	1.08540	15.04	Case 2	.86829	15.14
Case 3	−.08540	1.18	Case 4	.13171	2.30

Table 11.6   **(continued)**

		(2) C Test			
	Coefficient	t-Ratio		Coefficient	t-Ratio
Case 1	1.06690	16.31	Case 3	.80523	5.33
Case 4	−.06690	1.02	Case 4	.19477	1.29

Note: Case 1 = Pure catch-up; Case 2 = Catch-up with openness; Case 3 = Constant; Case 4 = Break.

Test Methods:

(1) *P* Test: Following Davidson and MacKinnon (1981), the following procedure was used. Given two alternative models,

$$H_0: Yit = fit\,(Xt, \beta) + e0it$$
$$H_1: Yit = git\,(Zt, \gamma) + e1it,$$

(where $i\,(= 1, m)$ indexes equations and $t\,(= 1, n)$ indexes observations), the following artificial regression can be estimated for the *P* test:

$$Yit - fhit = b\,Xit = \lambda\,(ghit - fhit)$$

where *fhit* and *ghit* denote the fitted values based on H_0 and H_1. The *t* ratio for λ is the *P* test. If it is significant H_0 is rejected, and if insignificant H_0 is not rejected. In the results above H_0 was tested against more than one alternative hypothesis at a time, with *F*-statistics reported to test whether H_1, H_2, and H_3 are zero.

(2) *C* Test: Again following Davidson and MacKinnon (1981), the *C* test involves estimating the following regression:

$$Yit = \alpha\,fhit + (1 - \alpha)\,ghit$$

where *fhit* and *ghit* are the fitted values of *yt* from the two competing models. If α is greater than $(1 - \alpha)$ and is significant, then *fit* is the dominating model.

the models using market exchange rates for conversion. Then we will be able to see how the conclusions would differ about the extent to which the convergence model predicts international convergence of income levels, both between the United States and the converging countries as a group, and among the eighteen non-U.S. countries.

Table 11.10 shows the results of tests of productivity level convergence using the PPP and market rates (for both 1980 and 1985) to convert the real incomes and capital stocks.[26] The top half of the table shows the results of tests of the basic convergence model of table 11.1, and the bottom half shows the same tests for the model of table 11.2, which includes the productivity effects of increasing trade shares. The Wald test results show that the use of market rather than PPP exchange rates makes the most difference when the specification constrains the convergence models to have the same asymptotic level of productivity in each country. In these cases, there is significantly more evidence of convergence when PPPs rather than 1980 or 1985 market exchange rates are used. It is encouraging, for both the data and the convergence hypothesis, that the theoretically preferable PPP data provide stronger evi-

---

26. Heston and Summers (1988, p. 471) note that PPPs for investment goods can be materially different from those for GDP; so we should in principle be using different PPPs for converting the real capital stocks into international dollars. Tests of this alternative have not yet been carried out.

Table 11.7   **Non-nested Tests of Investment Equations for the Industrial Countries**

The investment equations were estimated by Zellner Seemingly Unrelated Regression technique with instrumental variables, using the sample period 1963–85 for all models. The models of labor productivity are identical to those outlined in table 11.6.

(1) P Test

	t-statistics			
	Case 1	Case 2	Case 3	Case 4
H_1	2.63*	2.14*	2.62*	2.60*
H_2	3.89*	3.90*	3.89*	3.90*
H_3	1.24	1.24	1.24	1.21

* = significance at the 95% level.

	F-statistics			
	Case 1	Case 2	Case 3	Case 4
$H_1 = H_2 = H_3 = 0$ (4,430) df	9.35*	5.56*	9.36*	9.37*
$H_1 = 0.0$ (1,430) df	6.91*	4.59*	6.88*	6.78*
$H_2 = 0.0$ (1,430) df	15.14*	15.19*	15.17*	15.21*
$H_3 = 0.0$ (1,430) df	1.54	1.53	1.53	1.47

* = rejection of the null hypothesis at 5% significance.

(2) C Test

	Coefficient	t-Ratio		Coefficient	t-Ratio
Case 1	.15508	.66	Case 2	.34159	1.59
Case 2	.84492	3.61	Case 3	.65841	3.06
Case 1	−.45173	1.45	Case 2	.76096	3.64
Case 3	1.45173	4.67	Case 4	.23904	1.14
Case 1	.47991	1.96	Case 3	1.25870	4.45
Case 4	.52009	2.12	Case 4	−.25870	.91

Note: Case 1 = Pure catch-up; Case 2 = Catch-up with openness; Case 3 = Constant; Case 4 = Break

See note to table 11.6 for explanation of the test method used here.

Table 11.8   **Non-nested Tests of Employment Equations for the Industrial Countries**

The employment equations were estimated by Zellner Seemingly Unrelated Regression technique with instrument variables, using the sample period 1963–85 for all models. The models of labor productivity are identical to those outlined in table 11.6.

(1) P Test

	t-statistics			
	Case 1	Case 2	Case 3	Case 4
H_1	3.06*	1.86	1.77	1.79
H_2	1.85	1.85	3.06*	3.07*
H_3	.72	0.71	.74	1.85

* = significance at the 95% level.

	F-statistics			
	Case 1	Case 2	Case 3	Case 4
$H_1 = H_2 = H_3 = 0$ (3,432) df	7.95*	2.64*	3.78*	7.60*
$H_1 = 0.0$ (1,432) df	9.39*	3.48*	3.16*	3.20*
$H_2 = 0.0$ (1,432) df	3.42*	3.41*	9.39*	9.45*
$H_3 = 0.0$ (1,432) df	.52	.51	.55	3.41*

* = rejection of the null hypothesis at 5% significance.

(2) C Test

	Coefficient	t-Ratio		Coefficient	t-Ratio
Case 1	−.74296	1.84	Case 2	.50092	2.15
Case 2	1.74296	4.32	Case 3	.49908	2.14
Case 1	.16620	.79	Case 2	.76455	3.40
Case 3	.83380	3.97	Case 4	.23545	1.05
Case 1	.39331	1.83	Case 3	1.0697	3.23
Case 4	.60669	2.82	Case 4	−.0697	.21

Note: Case 1 = Pure catch-up; Case 2 = Catch-up with openness; Case 3 = Constant; Case 4 = Break

See note to table 11.6 for explanation of the test method used here.

Table 11.9   Output Equations for Industrial Countries (using Catch-up Model for non-U.S.)

	LNQS	LNCQ	LNSGAP	LNIGAP	SEE	R^2	Durbin-Watson
United States	1.0000	−0.1823	0.7039	0.0142	0.0085	0.9979	0.7797
	(***)	(11.93)	(19.32)	(4.42)			
Japan	1.0000	−0.0828	0.8035	0.0142	0.0075	0.9996	0.8851
	(***)	(8.27)	(32.69)	(4.42)			
West Germany	1.0000	−0.1097	0.6287	0.0142	0.0096	0.9978	1.1195
	(***)	(5.48)	(23.60)	(4.42)			
France	1.0000	−0.1764	0.8386	0.0142	0.0112	0.9981	0.6021
	(***)	(12.80)	(27.50)	(4.42)			
United Kingdom	1.0000	0.0170	0.4606	0.0142	0.0208	0.9758	0.5232
	(***)	(0.78)	(7.51)	(4.42)			
Italy	1.0000	−0.0171	0.9006	0.0142	0.0143	0.9964	0.3015
	(***)	(1.43)	(30.55)	(4.42)			
Canada	1.0000	−0.2793	0.6624	0.0142	0.0114	0.9985	0.6969
	(***)	(11.26)	(22.14)	(4.42)			
Australia	1.0000	−0.1316	1.1771	0.0142	0.0128	0.9972	1.0918
	(***)	(9.76)	(19.52)	(4.42)			
Austria	1.0000	−0.1009	0.6283	0.0142	0.0098	0.9984	0.6862
	(***)	(3.99)	(33.44)	(4.42)			
Belgium	1.0000	−0.0728	0.5889	0.0142	0.0087	0.9986	1.0531
	(***)	(4.66)	(26.65)	(4.42)			
Denmark	1.0000	−0.0877	0.4910	0.0142	0.0094	0.9968	1.1807
	(***)	(8.84)	(19.55)	(4.42)			
Finland	1.0000	0.0038	0.6342	0.0142	0.0133	0.9972	0.8017
	(***)	(0.27)	(18.57)	(4.42)			
Ireland	1.0000	0.0112	0.5677	0.0142	0.0288	0.9903	0.8485
	(***)	(0.26)	(9.99)	(4.42)			
Netherlands	1.0000	−0.0348	0.4984	0.0142	0.0102	0.9978	0.9815
	(***)	(2.26)	(29.36)	(4.42)			
New Zealand	1.0000	−0.0748	0.8826	0.0142	0.0155	0.9905	1.3872
	(***)	(5.45)	(28.10)	(4.42)			
Norway	1.0000	0.0074	0.2239	0.0142	0.0184	0.9954	0.8186
	(***)	(0.21)	(4.88)	(4.42)			
Spain	1.0000	−0.0155	0.5564	0.0142	0.0131	0.9978	0.6275
	(***)	(0.84)	(10.34)	(4.42)			
Sweden	1.0000	−0.0172	0.5554	0.0142	0.0108	0.9959	1.6575
	(***)	(1.04)	(15.11)	(4.42)			
Switzerland	1.0000	−0.2651	0.5239	0.0142	0.0219	0.9752	0.4475
	(***)	(5.23)	(10.28)	(4.42)			

Note: Sample 1963–85. Estimation method by Zellner's SUR estimation technique with instruments. The numbers in parentheses are absolute values of t-statistics, with *** denoting a constrained coefficient. LNQS is the logarithm of normal output, which is defined by the CES production function. LNCQ is the logarithm of the ratio of current unit cost relative to output price, which is an inverse measure of profitability. LNSGAP is the logarithm of the ratio of actual sales to normal sales. LNIGAP is the logarithm of the ratio of desired to lagged inventory stock.

Table 11.10   The Effects of using PPPs versus Market Exchange Rates

	Wald	χ^2
Tests of table 11.1 model using 1980 GDP PPPs:		
(a) Homogeneity of catch-up coefficients	59.64 (17df) vs.	28.0
(b) Constants = 0.0	52.94 (18df) vs.	28.9
(c) (a) + (b)	411.73 (35df) vs.	43.8
(d) Constants equal for non-U.S.	47.31 (17df) vs.	28.0
(e) (a) + (d)	400.60 (34df) vs.	43.8
Tests of table 11.1 model using 1980 market exchange rates:		
(a) Homogeneity of catch-up coefficients	59.64 (17df) vs.	28.0
(b) Constants = 0.0	120.17 (18df) vs.	28.9
(c) (a) + (b)	555.21 (35df) vs.	43.8
(d) Constants equal for non-U.S.	116.51 (17df) vs.	28.0
(e) (a) + (d)	510.87 (34df) vs.	43.8
Tests of table 11.1 model using 1985 market exchange rates:		
(a) Homogeneity of catch-up coefficients	59.64 (17df) vs.	28.0
(b) Constants = 0.0	130.07 (18df) vs.	28.9
(c) (a) + (b)	555.20 (35df) vs.	43.8
(d) Constants equal for non-U.S.	128.04 (17df) vs.	28.0
(e) (a) + (d)	511.48 (34df) vs.	43.8
Tests of table 11.2 model using 1980 GDP PPPs:		
(a) Homogeneity of catch-up coefficients	82.47 (17df) vs.	28.0
(b) Constants = 0.0	90.20 (18df) vs.	28.9
(c) (a) + (b)	221.60 (35df) vs.	43.8
(d) Constants equal for non-U.S.	63.92 (17df) vs.	28.0
(e) (a) + (d)	221.60 (34df) vs.	43.8
Tests of table 11.2 model using 1980 market exchange rates:		
(a) Homogeneity of catch-up coefficients	82.47 (17df) vs.	28.0
(b) Constants = 0.0	106.86 (18df) vs.	28.9
(c) (a) + (b)	267.63 (35df) vs.	43.8
(d) Constants equal for non-U.S.	106.55 (17df) vs.	28.0
(e) (a) + (d)	260.75 (34df) vs.	43.8
Tests of table 11.2 model using 1985 market exchange rates:		
(a) Homogeneity of catch-up coefficients	82.47 (17df) vs.	28.0
(b) Constants = 0.0	136.16 (18df) vs.	28.9
(c) (a) + (b)	267.82 (35df) vs.	43.8
(d) Constants equal for non-U.S.	121.29 (17df) vs.	28.0
(e) (a) + (d)	261.63 (34df) vs.	43.8

Note: The chi-square (χ^2) statistics in the above table are approximate.

dence in favor of the convergence hypothesis. This is true for both models assessed, and for comparisons including the United States as well as those among the converging countries other than the United States.[27]

11.3.2   Alternative Measures of the Aggregate Capital Stock

In this section we test the implications for the derived equations for the determination of aggregate output of using alternative measures of the capital stock. In the tests thus far, we have used the aggregate fixed capital stock, including business, housing, and government. In table 11.11 we show the output equations resulting if we instead employ the gross private stock of fixed capital (comprising business and housing). Table 11.12 shows the corresponding results using the stock of business fixed capital. As shown by the test comparisons in table 11.13, the results, in terms of the fit of the derived output equations, favor the use of the stock of business fixed capital over the other alternatives, and favor the private capital stock over the total stock.

The implied lower contribution of public and housing investment to subsequent levels of real GDP may reflect the nature of the data, as the GDP accounts do not take into direct account the value added by the public capital stock and the returns to the housing stock are heavily influenced by the assumptions about scrapping rates and the implied ownership return on the stock of owner-occupied housing.

We have also tested capital stock measures that include the stock of inventories along with one or more of the measures of the stock of fixed capital. As shown in table 11.14, for all three definitions of fixed capital, the models including inventories in the capital stock are inferior, in terms of the derived output equations, to the models based only on the fixed capital stocks.

11.3.3   Capital-Embodied Technical Progress

The models used thus far assume Harrod-neutral technical progress. The CES production function employed has a near-unitary elasticity of substitution between capital and labor, and hence there is little consequence, in terms of the variance of the synthetic output series, of attributing technical progress to labor rather than capital, so long as the progress accrues equally to new and existing capital. Potentially, it makes much more difference if one assumes that technical progress accrues only to the new vintages of capital and hence requires gross investment for its realization. Baily (1981) and others have suggested that the simultaneous post-1973 declines in both gross investment and observed productivity performance, in the aftermath of obsolescence-inducing increases in energy prices, indicate the likelihood of capital-

---

27. These results differ from those that appeared in an earlier version of this paper which did not adjust for the cyclical variance common to country i and the United States. In the earlier version, there appeared to be significantly more convergence of both rates of growth and levels when PPPs rather than 1985 exchange rates were used. The differences were also less marked when 1980 market exchange rates were used for comparison.

Table 11.11   **Output Equations for Industrial Countries (using Catch-up Model for non-U.S. and Gross Private Capital Stocks)**

	LNQS	LNCQ	LNSGAP	LNIGAP	SEE	R^2	Durbin-Watson
USA	1.0000	−0.2084	0.7028	0.0117	0.0086	0.9979	0.7737
	(***)	(12.28)	(19.61)	(3.68)			
Japan	1.0000	−0.0897	0.7992	0.0117	0.0074	0.9996	0.8912
	(***)	(8.75)	(32.25)	(3.68)			
West Germany	1.0000	−0.1419	0.6466	0.0117	0.0099	0.9976	1.0331
	(***)	(6.61)	(24.35)	(3.68)			
France	1.0000	−0.2057	0.8342	0.0117	0.0107	0.9983	0.6568
	(***)	(14.13)	(27.28)	(3.68)			
United Kingdom	1.0000	0.0099	0.5031	0.0117	0.0216	0.9740	0.4584
	(***)	(0.43)	(8.29)	(3.68)			
Italy	1.0000	−0.0265	0.9024	0.0117	0.0144	0.9963	0.3011
	(***)	(2.00)	(29.82)	(3.68)			
Canada	1.0000	−0.3378	0.6715	0.0117	0.0106	0.9987	0.7494
	(***)	(11.72)	(23.25)	(3.68)			
Australia	1.0000	−0.1477	1.2043	0.0117	0.0126	0.9973	1.1462
	(***)	(10.32)	(19.89)	(3.68)			
Austria	1.0000	−0.1366	0.6344	0.0117	0.0101	0.9983	0.6602
	(***)	(4.64)	(33.08)	(3.68)			
Belgium	1.0000	−0.0890	0.6024	0.0117	0.0087	0.9986	1.0673
	(***)	(5.33)	(27.37)	(3.68)			
Denmark	1.0000	−0.1075	0.5047	0.0117	0.0097	0.9966	1.1054
	(***)	(9.14)	(20.31)	(3.68)			
Finland	1.0000	−0.0080	0.6335	0.0117	0.0131	0.9973	0.8066
	(***)	(0.49)	(18.52)	(3.68)			
Ireland	1.0000	0.0140	0.5640	0.0117	0.0286	0.9904	0.8584
	(***)	(0.32)	(9.75)	(3.68)			
Netherlands	1.0000	−0.0465	0.5035	0.0117	0.0106	0.9976	0.9078
	(***)	(2.63)	(29.18)	(3.68)			
New Zealand	1.0000	−0.0797	0.8839	0.0117	0.0156	0.9903	1.3699
	(***)	(5.52)	(27.96)	(3.68)			
Norway	1.0000	−0.0300	0.2698	0.0117	0.0181	0.9956	0.8053
	(***)	(0.73)	(5.65)	(3.68)			
Spain	1.0000	−0.0244	0.5422	0.0117	0.0126	0.9979	0.6621
	(***)	(1.24)	(10.06)	(3.68)			
Sweden	1.0000	−0.0352	0.5672	0.0117	0.0107	0.9959	1.6315
	(***)	(1.93)	(15.78)	(3.68)			
Switzerland	1.0000	−0.3771	0.5780	0.0117	0.0213	0.9766	0.5057
	(***)	(6.40)	(11.66)	(3.68)			

Note: Sample 1963–85. Estimation by Zellner's SUR estimation technique with instruments. See table 11.9 for variables abbreviated in cols. 1–4.

Table 11.12   **Output Equations for Industrial Countries (using Catch-up Model for non-U.S. and Gross Business Capital Stocks)**

	LNQS	LNCQ	LNSGAP	LNIGAP	SEE	R^2	Durbin-Watson
USA	1.0000	−0.2533	0.7146	0.0095	0.0077	0.9983	0.7630
	(***)	(13.69)	(22.22)	(3.14)			
Japan	1.0000	−0.0870	0.7929	0.0095	0.0075	0.9996	0.8607
	(***)	(8.06)	(31.33)	(3.14)			
West Germany	1.0000	−0.1968	0.6466	0.0095	0.0095	0.9978	1.0025
	(***)	(8.32)	(26.37)	(3.14)			
France	1.0000	−0.2709	0.8088	0.0095	0.0093	0.9987	0.7524
	(***)	(16.80)	(29.66)	(3.14)			
United Kingdom	1.0000	−0.0153	0.5621	0.0095	0.0216	0.9739	0.4108
	(***)	(0.48)	(9.62)	(3.14)			
Italy	1.0000	−0.0497	0.8901	0.0095	0.0144	0.9963	0.3009
	(***)	(2.76)	(30.37)	(3.14)			
Canada	1.0000	−0.4741	0.6222	0.0095	0.0095	0.9990	0.9017
	(***)	(11.80)	(20.49)	(3.14)			
Australia	1.0000	−0.1873	1.2047	0.0095	0.0125	0.9973	1.1369
	(***)	(11.07)	(20.99)	(3.14)			
Austria	1.0000	−0.1788	0.6327	0.0095	0.0097	0.9985	0.6969
	(***)	(5.76)	(32.97)	(3.14)			
Belgium	1.0000	−0.0965	0.6048	0.0095	0.0083	0.9987	1.1159
	(***)	(4.81)	(27.11)	(3.14)			
Denmark	1.0000	−0.1202	0.5222	0.0095	0.0095	0.9967	1.0200
	(***)	(8.07)	(21.66)	(3.14)			
Finland	1.0000	−0.0137	0.6412	0.0095	0.0130	0.9973	0.8083
	(***)	(0.63)	(18.94)	(3.14)			
Ireland	1.0000	−0.0187	0.6078	0.0095	0.0286	0.9904	0.8425
	(***)	(0.32)	(10.94)	(3.14)			
Netherlands	1.0000	−0.0275	0.4960	0.0095	0.0106	0.9977	0.9144
	(***)	(1.32)	(28.70)	(3.14)			
New Zealand	1.0000	−0.0881	0.8849	0.0095	0.0157	0.9902	1.3596
	(***)	(5.79)	(28.42)	(3.14)			
Norway	1.0000	−0.1595	0.3876	0.0095	0.0178	0.9957	0.7522
	(***)	(3.04)	(7.22)	(3.14)			
Spain	1.0000	−0.0354	0.5723	0.0095	0.0119	0.9982	0.7211
	(***)	(1.35)	(10.70)	(3.14)			
Sweden	1.0000	−0.0608	0.5887	0.0095	0.0106	0.9960	1.5886
	(***)	(2.91)	(17.86)	(3.14)			
Switzerland	1.0000	−0.4938	0.7025	0.0095	0.0196	0.9803	0.6585
	(***)	(9.12)	(14.30)	(3.14)			

Note: Sample 1963–85. Estimation by Zellner's SUR estimation technique with instruments. See table 11.9 for variables abbreviated in cols. 1–4.

Table 11.13   **Non-nested Tests of Catch-up Models**

(1) Catch-up Output Model, table 11.9 (total capital)
(2) Catch-up Output Model, table 11.11 (private capital)
(3) Catch-up Output Model, table 11.12 (business capital)

		Coefficient	t-Ratio
C Test of output equations:			
Test A:	Model (1)	-0.1482	0.26
	Model (2)	1.1482	2.03*
Test B:	Model (1)	-0.1840	0.81
	Model (3)	1.1840	5.22*
Test C:	Model (2)	-0.6609	2.06*
	Model (3)	1.6609	5.17*

	t-Ratio		F-statistic (H $=$ 0.0)		
	H1	H2	H1, H2	H1	H2
P Test of output equations:					
H_0: Model (1), $H_1 =$ Model (2), $H_2 =$ Model (3)	3.92*	6.29*	22.10*	15.34*	39.63*
H_0: Model (2), $H_1 =$ Model (1), $H_2 =$ Model (3)	3.38*	6.24*	19.52*	11.42*	38.97*
H_0: Model (3), $H_1 =$ Model (1), $H_2 =$ Model (2)	3.41*	3.90*	7.89*	11.65*	15.22*

* $=$ significance at the 95% level for the "t" test and rejection of the null hypothesis at 5% level for the "F" test.

embodiment effects.[28] Previous efforts using data for the G-7 industrial countries to look for linkages between gross investment and productivity growth have not been encouraging.[29] We now have comparable data for a much larger sample of countries, so we can try again. To provide a simple comparison between our base case and a capital-embodied vintage model, we compare our constant and convergence cases with an alternative model based on the assumption that all technical progress inheres in new fixed investment. We estimate the rate of such technical progress in just the same way as was done

28. Baily emphasizes the reduction in capital services per measured unit of capital, because of increased obsolescence due to changes in energy prices and other changes in market opportunities and regulations. This implies that capital is not malleable ex post, and other things equal, that technical progress will be faster the higher the rate of gross investment, and hence the rate at which new techniques and current relative prices are embodied in the capital stock.

29. Some earlier attempts to test for these effects using data for the G-7 countries revealed no apparent link between gross investment rates and the growth of the capital-adjusted productivity measure used in this paper. See Helliwell, Sturm, Jarrett, and Salou (1986, pp. 91–95). However, cross-sectional evidence reviewed by Englander and Mittelstadt (1988), covering seventeen countries, suggests that capital accumulation may have more impact on productivity growth than would be consistent with Harrod-neutral technical progress.

Table 11.14   Non-nested Tests of Pure Catch-up Models (using alternative measures of gross capital stocks)

(1) Catch-up Output Model, table 11.9 (total capital)
(2) Catch-up Output Model (total capital with inventory stock)
(3) Catch-up Output Model, table 11.11 (private capital)
(4) Catch-up Output Model (private capital with inventory stock)
(5) Catch-up Output Model, table 11.12 (business capital)
(6) Catch-up Output Model (business capital with inventory stock)

C Test of Output Equations

	(1)	(2)	(3)	(4)	(5)	(6)
(1)	—	1.8939	−0.1482	0.2942	−0.1840	−0.1809
		(1.48)	(0.26)	(.44)	(0.81)	(0.68)
(2)	−0.8939	—	−0.0766	0.0086	−0.1060	−0.1494
	(0.70)		(0.17)	(0.01)	(0.51)	(0.60)
(3)	1.4818	1.0766	—	2.2409	−0.6610	−0.6185
	(2.03)	(2.41)		(2.12)	(2.06)	(1.61)
(4)	0.7058	0.9914	−1.2409	—	−0.4671	−0.6633
	(1.06)	(1.62)	(1.18)		(1.70)	(1.87)
(5)	1.1840	1.1060	1.6610	1.4671	—	2.3429
	(5.22)	(5.35)	(5.18)	(5.36)		(3.25)
(6)	1.1809	1.1494	1.6185	1.6633	−1.3429	—
	(4.44)	(4.63)	(4.21)	(4.68)	(1.86)	

F-statistic
(H1 = H2 = H3 = H4 = H5 = 0.0)

P Test of output equations:
HO: Model (1) (5,428df)   18.64 vs. 2.21
HO: Model (2) (5,428df)   19.05 vs. 2.21
HO: Model (3) (5,428df)   17.65 vs. 2.21
HO: Model (4) (5,428df)   18.38 vs. 2.21
HO: Model (5) (5,428df)   12.75 vs. 2.21
HO: Model (6) (5,428df)   14.26 vs. 2.21

in estimating the country-specific rates of Harrod-neutral technical progress in our constant case. Thus we calculate for each country the rate of investment-embodied technical progress that causes synthetic output from the production function to have the same rate of growth as actual output, averaged over the entire sample period. The estimated productivity equations for the capital-embodied model are reported in table 11.15.

When the derived output equations for the capital-embodied model (as shown in table 11.16) are compared with those of the basic convergence model (as reported in table 11.9), they show an overall preference for the convergence model, but there is an interesting pattern to the results. For ten European countries, including all of the original members of EEC, the convergence model is preferred, usually by a substantial margin. For the United States the two models have the same fit (there is, in any case, no convergence in the table 11.9 equation for the United States), and the comparisons are also rather close for New Zealand, Australia, Spain, and Sweden. For Norway and Japan, there is an apparent preference for the capital-embodiment hypothesis over the convergence hypothesis. In both countries, the largest growth of productivity was apparently linked to spurts of investment. For Norway, this is probably linked to the offshore oil developments, while for Japan it is more likely based on the addition of modern manufacturing capacity. By contrast, for the main EEC countries, the rapid growth of productivity appears to be more closely linked to the gradual integration of markets and less tied to variations in the rate of business investment.

The fact that the same pure vintage model of technical progress is for some countries preferred to the convergence model, and for most countries preferred to the model assuming Harrod-neutral technical progress at a constant rate, suggests that further research would be justified. In particular, it might be possible to generalize the capital embodiment hypothesis by adding some flexibility to the putty-clay assumption,[30] and to experiment with alternative ways of combining convergence with some degree of capital-embodiment.[31]

11.4. Modeling Business Cycles

Much recent analysis of business cycle fluctuations has made use of a neoclassical growth model with a production structure almost identical to that underlying the productivity analysis of this paper. Most of the real business cycle models surveyed by King, Plosser and Rebello (1988) use an aggregate Cobb-Douglas production function based on fixed capital and efficiency units of labor, with Harrod-neutral productivity growing at a constant expected annual rate. We also make use of the Harrod-neutral productivity assumption, and technical progress at a constant rate is one of the main alternatives we have assessed. In this section we attempt to compare the two approaches.

The main empirical applications of the real business cycle approach have involved the use of autocorrelated technology shocks to generate distributions

30. For example, in Helliwell, Sturm, Jarrett, and Salou (1986), a putty/semi-putty model for energy/capital substitution was developed, wherein an estimated fraction of the existing capital stock was able to be retrofitted to employ the same optimal energy/capital ratio being built into new investment.

31. Our tests of convergence models containing capital-embodiment effects have so far not produced strong embodiment results. The tests were done by adding the logarithm of the smoothed ratio of gross investment to gross domestic product, divided by the United States smoothed investment ratio to the basic catch-up model. When the embodiment variable was constrained to be the same across countries it had a positive (.0213) but insignificant coefficient ($t = 1.40$).

Table 11.15   The Capital-Embodied Model of Technical Progress

	RTIME	Constant	SEE	R^2	Durbin-Watson
United States	0.0194	126.8300	0.1116	0.6293	0.3312
	(6.64)	(596.31)			
Japan	0.1046	118.6800	0.2758	0.8899	0.1386
	(14.50)	(225.74)			
West Germany	0.0773	120.9800	0.1203	0.9587	0.2394
	(24.58)	(527.65)			
France	0.0982	119.4700	0.1845	0.9409	0.0882
	(20.34)	(339.70)			
Italy	0.0918	119.7900	0.2416	0.8903	0.1336
	(14.53)	(260.19)			
United Kingdom	0.0443	123.1300	0.0998	0.9172	0.5902
	(16.97)	(647.47)			
Canada	0.0515	123.7600	0.1200	0.9119	0.2163
	(16.40)	(541.22)			
Australia	0.0433	123.8900	0.1077	0.9008	0.4947
	(15.37)	(603.47)			
Austria	0.0881	119.7900	0.1586	0.9455	0.1340
	(21.24)	(396.32)			
Belgium	0.0833	120.8200	0.1212	0.9637	0.2402
	(26.29)	(523.24)			
Denmark	0.0627	121.7600	0.1298	0.9291	0.3083
	(18.46)	(491.97)			
Finland	0.0852	119.6100	0.1189	0.9666	0.3755
	(27.41)	(527.83)			
Ireland	0.0953	118.7100	0.1328	0.9666	0.5319
	(27.45)	(469.19)			
Netherlands	0.0786	121.6200	0.1322	0.9521	0.2594
	(22.74)	(482.57)			
New Zealand	0.0043	126.9800	0.1403	0.0506	0.4944
	(1.18)	(474.81)			
Norway	0.0662	121.6600	0.0759	0.9772	0.7040
	(33.37)	(841.30)			
Spain	0.1105	118.4000	0.1733	0.9581	0.2180
	(24.39)	(358.53)			
Sweden	0.0455	123.2300	0.1269	0.8787	0.3147
	(13.72)	(509.64)			
Switzerland	0.0432	124.1200	0.1449	0.8335	0.1889
	(11.41)	(449.39)			

Note: The dependent variable is ln π_m, measured output attributable to labor. RTIME is an annual time trend equal to 60 in 1960, 61 in 1961. See the section on specification in appendix B for a more complete description. Estimation was by Zellner's SUR estimation technique using sample 1960–85.

Table 11.16 **Output Equations for Industrial Countries (capital-embodied technical progress)**

	LNQS	LNCQ	LNSGAP	LNIGAP	SEE	R^2	Durbin-Watson
United States	1.0000	−0.1736	0.7176	0.0077	0.0085	0.9980	0.7876
	(***)	(13.58)	(24.23)	(1.95)			
Japan	1.0000	−0.1653	0.8621	0.0077	0.0070	0.9997	1.1251
	(***)	(14.50)	(49.82)	(1.95)			
Germany	1.0000	−0.3189	0.7525	0.0077	0.0199	0.9904	0.5244
	(***)	(12.45)	(15.37)	(1.95)			
France	1.0000	−0.2823	0.9381	0.0077	0.0145	0.9968	0.7504
	(***)	(15.84)	(23.12)	(1.95)			
Italy	1.0000	−0.0385	1.0526	0.0077	0.0154	0.9958	0.3175
	(***)	(2.67)	(36.77)	(1.95)			
United Kingdom	1.0000	−0.0577	0.5923	0.0077	0.0255	0.9636	0.2725
	(***)	(2.58)	(8.54)	(1.95)			
Canada	1.0000	−0.4089	0.6550	0.0077	0.0134	0.9979	0.7919
	(***)	(13.70)	(15.72)	(1.95)			
Australia	1.0000	−0.1142	1.3167	0.0077	0.0125	0.9973	1.3172
	(***)	(9.21)	(14.10)	(1.95)			
Austria	1.0000	−0.4514	0.6997	0.0077	0.0199	0.9935	0.5135
	(***)	(11.83)	(18.56)	(1.95)			
Belgium	1.0000	−0.2218	0.6346	0.0077	0.0119	0.9974	0.8781
	(***)	(16.44)	(22.80)	(1.95)			
Denmark	1.0000	−0.1299	0.6336	0.0077	0.0143	0.9927	0.7361
	(***)	(11.54)	(24.01)	(1.95)			
Finland	1.0000	−0.1014	0.6014	0.0077	0.0175	0.9951	0.4845
	(***)	(6.17)	(13.04)	(1.95)			
Ireland	1.0000	−0.1063	0.5865	0.0077	0.0309	0.9888	0.6745
	(***)	(2.82)	(8.66)	(1.95)			
Netherlands	1.0000	−0.2694	0.6173	0.0077	0.0230	0.9890	0.3747
	(***)	(10.18)	(20.35)	(1.95)			
New Zealand	1.0000	−0.0693	0.8537	0.0077	0.0152	0.9908	1.4148
	(***)	(5.27)	(22.06)	(1.95)			
Norway	1.0000	−0.1849	0.2579	0.0077	0.0150	0.9969	0.9998
	(***)	(5.94)	(5.46)	(1.95)			
Spain	1.0000	−0.1364	0.8391	0.0077	0.0131	0.9978	0.7713
	(***)	(8.14)	(21.81)	(1.95)			
Sweden	1.0000	−0.1329	0.5988	0.0077	0.0117	0.9952	1.2295
	(***)	(8.36)	(14.34)	(1.95)			
Switzerland	1.0000	−0.4773	0.6774	0.0077	0.0274	0.9614	0.4752
	(***)	(8.34)	(9.72)	(1.95)			

Note: Sample 1963–85. Estimation by Zellner's SUR estimation technique with instruments. See table 11.9 for variables abbreviated in cols. 1–4.

of key macroeconomic variables, with the aim of seeing to what extent these experimental distributions compare with those of actual data. Although it is theoretically possible to generate autocorrelated movements of output and investment in real business cycle models without autocorrelated technology shocks (e.g., Long and Plosser 1983), King, Plosser and Rebello show that if realistic assumptions are made about the longevity of capital it is necessary to have serially correlated technology shocks in order to generate realistic amounts of persistence in the simulated series for investment, output, and employment. The usual assumption made is that of first-order autocorrelation of the technology shocks,[32] and that is the form we shall consider here.

A modest generalization of the factor utilization model, using the constant technical progress assumption and adding some dynamic adjustment to the output equation, includes the output sector of the real business cycle model and the constant case of the factor utilization approach as nested special cases. This permits the encompassing principle (Mizon and Richard 1986) to be applied to see whether the general model can be reduced to either of the special cases without significant loss of information.

The generalization required is to add the lagged value of the utilization rate to the estimation of the output equation. Under the assumption of a serially correlated multiplicative technology shock, the previous period's factor utilization rate is the previous period's technology disturbance. It represents all the systematic information available, beyond the stocks of currently employed factors represented by the synthetic production function, to explain current output. If the production function with autocorrelated disturbances is a sufficient explanation of actual output, then the three additional variables reflecting current unexpected or temporary levels of demand, profitability, and inventories will add nothing to the explanation of current output. On the other hand, if the dynamics of the actual output decision are as specified in earlier sections, then the lagged dependent variable should not have a significant coefficient.[33]

Table 11.17 shows the results of estimating the more general hypothesis in the constant case, while table 11.18 shows the corresponding results for the catch-up case.[34] F-tests of the restricted hypotheses against the more general ones show that the restricted hypotheses are strongly rejected. This means that unexpected demand and cost conditions, with consequential changes in the rate of utilization of employed factors, are likely to be an important part of the cyclical movements in output, and that there are significant dynamics in

32. E.g., Kydland and Prescott (1982) and Hansen (1985).
33. Adding the lagged factor-utilization rate is equivalent to adding the lagged dependent variable under the maintained hypothesis that the log of synthetic output is constrained to have a unit coefficient in the equation for the log of output.
34. In both cases, the inventory gap coefficient is constrained to have the same value for all countries.

the response of output to these changes that are not captured by the contemporaneous versions of the output equation tested earlier in this paper.

11.5. Conclusions

Over the period since 1960, data for nineteen industrial countries show significant evidence of international convergence in the rates of growth of labor efficiency. The evidence is much less strong for eventual convergence of the asymptotic levels of real output attributable to each worker. However, there remain many international differences in natural resources, education levels, and other factors that would justify continuing differences in measured productivity levels.

There is also significant evidence that technical progress has been faster, other things being equal, for countries that have been increasing their openness to international trade. The results also suggest that more work needs to be done to develop better data and theory to explain the linkages between technology transfer and openness to trade and capital movements.

We also found some evidence that capital embodiment may contribute more to productivity growth than our previous research had suggested. Although we found convergence to be more important than embodiment effects, both effects appear to help in explaining international differences in the levels and rates of growth of productivity. When the two were combined in a single model, however, the embodiment effects were not strong.

Our results in favor of the convergence hypothesis should be regarded as provisional, especially as they involve joint tests within a specific model of output determination. Caution is especially appropriate because the tests based on the derived factor demand equations, while being much weaker in their preference rankings, are also less supportive of the convergence models.

Turning to questions of data, we found that the use of the theoretically preferable PPP exchange rates tended to strengthen the convergence results. This was clear when the PPP results were compared to results based on the use of either 1980 or 1985 market exchange rates, which differed markedly from PPP rates for many country pairs.

We also found that narrower measures of the capital stock (business fixed capital) appeared to determine output more closely than broader measures that included housing and public capital. Further research may help to suggest whether this result is due to greater measurement problems with the stocks of housing and public capital, to problems in measuring and attributing the real output effects of these forms of capital, or to lower marginal returns on these forms of investment. Adding inventories to fixed capital in the synthetic production function tended to worsen the fit of the derived output equations.

Finally, the constant and convergence versions of the factor utilization models estimated in earlier sections were compared to the output sector frequently used in real business cycle models, with both being nested in a more general

Table 11.17   Generalized Output Equation Incorporating Technology Shocks and Factor Utilization Variables (Using "Constant" Case)

	LN(QS)	LN(Q/QS)$_{-1}$	LNCQ	LNSGAP	LNIGAP	SEE	R^2	Durbin-H
United States	1.0000 (***)	0.2471 (5.13)	-0.1522 (9.21)	0.5210 (8.87)	0.0196 (4.55)	0.0079	0.9982	1.9890
Japan	1.0000 (***)	-0.0074 (0.18)	-0.1511 (12.40)	0.8808 (19.11)	0.0196 (4.55)	0.0072	0.9997	2.3285
West Germany	1.0000 (***)	0.7266 (10.03)	-0.2343 (9.27)	0.2555 (3.77)	0.0196 (4.55)	0.0130	0.9959	0.2654
France	1.0000 (***)	0.8038 (9.48)	-0.1167 (5.98)	0.2347 (2.47)	0.0196 (4.55)	0.0079	0.9991	2.5554
United Kingdom	1.0000 (***)	0.7698 (10.65)	-0.1068 (4.23)	0.3923 (4.06)	0.0196 (4.55)	0.0144	0.9884	-0.0429
Italy	1.0000 (***)	0.5837 (8.03)	-0.0606 (3.56)	0.4462 (5.22)	0.0196 (4.55)	0.0105	0.9981	0.7422
Canada	1.0000 (***)	0.5290 (7.76)	-0.3584 (11.35)	0.2786 (4.33)	0.0196 (4.55)	0.0100	0.9988	0.3281
Australia	1.0000 (***)	0.2128 (3.66)	-0.1062 (7.44)	1.0129 (11.94)	0.0196 (4.55)	0.0108	0.9980	0.2040
Austria	1.0000 (***)	0.9196 (14.31)	-0.1905 (5.72)	0.0433 (0.79)	0.0196 (4.55)	0.0111	0.9980	-0.1522
Belgium	1.0000 (***)	0.4556 (5.93)	-0.1557 (8.09)	0.3642 (7.03)	0.0196 (4.55)	0.0103	0.9980	0.1764
Denmark	1.0000 (***)	0.7556 (6.54)	-0.0733 (3.98)	0.1683 (2.23)	0.0196 (4.55)	0.0140	0.9930	-1.0259

Finland	1.0000 (***)	0.5718 (7.50)	−0.0975 (4.88)	0.2984 (4.55)	0.0196 (4.55)	0.0129	0.9973	0.5412
Ireland	1.0000 (***)	0.8490 (8.76)	−0.1171 (2.68)	0.1464 (1.56)	0.0196 (4.55)	0.0227	0.9939	−0.2673
Netherlands	1.0000 (***)	0.8361 (12.63)	−0.1879 (6.68)	0.1886 (4.37)	0.0196 (4.55)	0.0129	0.9966	−0.3399
New Zealand	1.0000 (***)	0.3250 (6.80)	−0.0421 (3.01)	0.6681 (14.96)	0.0196 (4.55)	0.0134	0.9929	−0.8706
Norway	1.0000 (***)	0.4643 (6.43)	−0.1589 (5.37)	0.2360 (4.93)	0.0196 (4.55)	0.0124	0.9979	0.1516
Spain	1.0000 (***)	0.5897 (6.17)	−0.1119 (5.52)	0.3537 (4.23)	0.0196 (4.55)	0.0107	0.9985	0.0262
Sweden	1.0000 (***)	0.3787 (4.19)	−0.1097 (5.59)	0.3601 (4.85)	0.0196 (4.55)	0.0109	0.9958	0.1932
Switzerland	1.0000 (***)	0.7067 (17.55)	−0.2539 (7.61)	0.2775 (7.07)	0.0196 (4.55)	0.0107	0.9940	−0.0310

Note: Sample 1963–85. Estimation by Zellner's SUR estimation technique with instruments. See table 11.9 for variables abbreviated in cols. 1 and 3–5. LN (Q/QS)$_{-1}$ is the logarithm of the lagged utilization rate, which is defined as the ratio of actual to normal output.

Nested Tests:

	Wald Statistic (19df):
LN(Q/QS)$_{-1}$ = 0.0	1457.4678 vs. 28.87
LNCQ = 0.0	835.3252 vs. 28.87
LNSGAP = 0.0	1229.7174 vs. 28.87
LNIGAP = 0.0	309.2629 vs. 28.87
LNCQ = LNSGAP = LNIGAP = 0.0	4970.1135 (57df) vs. 79.08

Table 11.18   Generalized Output Equation Incorporating Technology Shocks and Factor Utilization Variables (Using "Catch-up" Case)

	LN(QS)	LN(Q/QS)$_{-1}$	LNCQ	LNSGAP	LNIGAP	SEE	R^2	Durbin-H
United States	1.0000	0.2176	−0.1723	0.5691	0.0370	0.0078	0.9983	2.4005
	(***)	(4.21)	(10.02)	(8.81)	(9.82)			
Japan	1.0000	−0.1969	−0.0761	0.9572	0.0370	0.0076	0.9996	2.7124
	(***)	(3.83)	(6.75)	(21.00)	(9.82)			
West Germany	1.0000	0.2016	−0.1231	0.5495	0.0370	0.0095	0.9978	1.5421
	(***)	(2.72)	(5.74)	(10.70)	(9.82)			
France	1.0000	0.7960	−0.1257	0.4200	0.0370	0.0089	0.9988	3.1372
	(***)	(9.39)	(6.76)	(6.31)	(9.82)			
United Kingdom	1.0000	0.7213	−0.1002	0.3731	0.0370	0.0150	0.9874	0.7018
	(***)	(7.70)	(3.36)	(5.31)	(9.82)			
Italy	1.0000	0.5101	−0.0167	0.5920	0.0370	0.0101	0.9982	1.5232
	(***)	(7.78)	(1.02)	(10.52)	(9.82)			
Canada	1.0000	0.3697	−0.2907	0.4113	0.0370	0.0092	0.9990	1.3954
	(***)	(4.64)	(8.33)	(6.39)	(9.82)			
Australia	1.0000	0.2292	−0.1139	0.9748	0.0370	0.0111	0.9979	0.6887
	(***)	(3.32)	(6.68)	(11.56)	(9.82)			
Austria	1.0000	0.3159	−0.0443	0.4619	0.0370	0.0086	0.9988	1.7442
	(***)	(3.53)	(1.23)	(7.95)	(9.82)			
Belgium	1.0000	0.2200	−0.0683	0.4857	0.0370	0.0085	0.9986	1.0639
	(***)	(2.84)	(3.21)	(10.94)	(9.82)			
Denmark	1.0000	0.3813	−0.0726	0.3406	0.0370	0.0100	0.9964	0.0416
	(***)	(3.38)	(4.91)	(5.82)	(9.82)			

Finland	1.0000 (***)	0.2852 (4.64)	−0.0136 (0.84)	0.5327 (11.43)	0.0370 (9.82)	0.0112	0.9980	2.0879
Ireland	1.0000 (***)	0.7067 (7.54)	−0.0527 (1.09)	0.2598 (3.36)	0.0370 (9.82)	0.0220	0.9943	−0.2679
Netherlands	1.0000 (***)	0.3147 (4.93)	−0.0748 (3.47)	0.3834 (11.01)	0.0370 (9.82)	0.0097	0.9981	1.0165
New Zealand	1.0000 (***)	0.3602 (6.61)	−0.0515 (3.26)	0.6630 (12.44)	0.0370 (9.82)	0.0133	0.9931	−1.1015
Norway	1.0000 (***)	0.5333 (7.09)	−0.1049 (3.23)	0.2803 (5.55)	0.0370 (9.82)	0.0131	0.9977	0.4263
Spain	1.0000 (***)	0.5197 (5.33)	−0.0075 (0.25)	0.3693 (3.90)	0.0370 (9.82)	0.0103	0.9986	0.2635
Sweden	1.0000 (***)	0.2235 (2.52)	−0.0093 (0.47)	0.4482 (6.78)	0.0370 (9.82)	0.0104	0.9961	0.1744
Switzerland	1.0000 (***)	0.7019 (14.45)	−0.1740 (4.49)	0.2994 (7.95)	0.0370 (9.82)	0.0106	0.9942	0.3035

Note: Sample 1963–85. Estimation by Zellner's SUR estimation technique with instruments. See table 11.9 for variables abbreviated in cols. 1 and 3–5. LN (Q/QS)$_{-1}$ is the logarithm of the lagged utilization rate, which is defined as the ratio of actual to normal output.

Nested Tests:
LN(Q/QS)$_{-1}$ = 0.0
LNCQ = 0.0
LNSGAP = 0.0
LNIGAP = 0.0
LNCQ = LNSGAP = LNIGAP = 0.0

Wald Statistic (19df):
758.8765 vs. 28.87
327.6833 vs. 28.87
1790.4562 vs. 28.87
289.0660 vs. 28.87
2840.5842 (57df) vs. 79.08

model. The tests showed significant evidence that the more general model, including the demand and profitability effects of the factor utilization model, and the dynamics of the technology shock model, was to be preferred over either of the more restricted alternatives.[35]

Overall, the importance of the openness effects and the potential importance of capital-embodiment effects support the emphasis in the theoretical literature (Romer 1986, Grossman and Helpman 1989a) on the idea that the rates of generation and diffusion of technical progress are endogenous rather than exogenous variables, and are hence potentially affected by a variety of domestic and international policies.

A final general conclusion, supporting the focus on international data issues, is that the use of comparable data for a substantial number of countries has permitted far stronger tests and results than would be available from the analysis of time-series data for one or even several countries.

Appendix A
Data Sources

List of Variables and Parameters

Variables	Description
a	Real absorption, billion 1980 currency
c	Real personal consumption expenditures, billion 1980 currency
e_r	Exchange rate, U.S. dollar per domestic currency
g	Real government current and capital expenditures on goods and services, billion 1980 currency
i	Real total fixed investment, billion 1980 currency
ib	Real business fixed investment, billion 1980 currency
ip	Real private fixed investment, billion 1980 currency
i_{inv}	Real value of physical change in inventories, billion 1980 currency
k	Real total gross fixed capital stock, billion 1980 currency
kb	Real business gross fixed capital stock, billion 1980 currency
kp	Real private gross fixed capital stock, billion 1980 currency
k_{inv}	Real stock of inventories, billion 1980 currency
m	Real imports of goods and services, billion 1980 currency
N	Total employment, millions of persons

35. This is in line with the real business cycle research agenda proposed by Plosser (1989, pp. 70–71), who emphasized the need to study the source characteristics of the "technology shocks" and to undertake systematic comparisons of alternative approaches.

N_{pop}	Total population of labor force age, millions of persons
p_a	Implicit price of absorption, $1980 = 1.0$
p_{gdp}	GDP deflator, defined as ratio of nominal GDP to real GDP
p_k	Price of capital services
p_m	Price of imported goods and services, $1980 = 1.0$
p_q	Implicit price for gross domestic output, $1980 = 1.0$
p_x	Price of exports of goods and services, $1980 = 1.0$
q	Real gross output (at factor cost), billion 1980 currency
q_s	Real synthetic supply, billion 1980 currency
r	Average interest rate, annual percent
r_l	Average yield on government bonds, 10 years and over, percent
r_s	Average yield on government bonds, 1–3 years, percent
t	Time: $1960 = 1, 1961 = 2$, etc.
T_i	Total indirect taxes less subsidies, billion currency
W	Wage rate, thousands of dollars per year per employed person
x	Real exports of goods and services, billion 1980 currency
y	Real gross national product, billion 1980 currency
δ_2	Scrapping rate for capital stock (including housing)
Π	Labor productivity index for Harrod-neutral technical progress in CES function for q
ρ_r	Estimated parameter; real supply price of capital
τ	Estimated parameter; elasticity of substitution between labor and capital in the CES function
μ	Estimated parameter; distribution parameter in the CES function
ν	Estimated parameter; distribution parameter in the CES function

Note: Units exceptions to those specified above are for Japan and Italy. Currency data for these two are in trillions, demographic data are in billions, while wages remain in thousands.

Data Sources

Data for this study were taken from: IMF International Financial Statistics; OECD, *Flows and Stocks of Fixed Capital,* 1960–85; OECD Standardized National Accounts (SNA), vols. 1 and 2; OECD 1984, 1986, and 1987 INTER-LINK supply block tapes for G7 countries; and OECD 1987 INTERLINK supply block tape for the smaller OECD countries.

Most of the supply block data for this study can be derived from the OECD Standardized National Accounts (SNA) as indicated below. Square brackets indicate source and data mnemonic. Note that $ is used to denote domestic currency. Sample period: 1960–85.

YGDP = GDP in current $ billion [SNA GDP]

PGDP = GDP deflator (1980 = 1.00) [SNA GDPE/GDPEV]

I   = Private, housing, and government investment in 1980 $ billion [SNA GF]

IB   = Business investment = $I - IG - IH$

IG   = Government investment [SNA vol. 2 and OECD87 for smalls]

IH   = Housing investment [SNA vol. 2 and OECD87 for smalls]

IP   = Private investment = $I - IG$

A   = Absorption in 1980 $ billion [SNA PC + GF + GC]

PA   = Absorption deflator (1980 = 1.00) [SNA A/(PCV + GFV + GCV)]

C   = Private consumption in 1980 $ billion [SNA PC]

G   = Government expenditures in 1980 $ billion [SNA GC]

IINV = Change in inventories in 1980 $ billion [SNA STV]

TI   = Indirect taxes less subsidies in current $ billion [SNA ITX − SUB]

N   = Total employment, million of persons [OECD86, OECD87 ET]

W   = Average annual wage (thousands of $ per employed person per year) [OECD86, OECD87 (WSSE × EE + CGW)/(EG + EE)]

X   = Exports of goods and services in 1980 $ billion [SNA EXPV]

PX   = Price of exports (1980 = 1.00) [SNA EXP/EXPV]

ER   = Exchange rate [IFS]

RS   = Short-term nominal interest rate [Canadian Dept. of Finance and IFS 60]

RL   = Average yield of long-term government bonds (%) [Canadian Dept. of Finance and IFS 61]

R   = Average interest rate = $.5RS + .5(RL_{-1} + RL_{-2} + RL_{-3})/100/3$

XIY   = Total investment income receipts from abroad in current $ billion [SNA FIFW]

MIY   = Total investment income payments to foreigners in current $ billion [SNA FITW]

M   = Imports of goods and services in 1980 $ billion [SNA IMPV]

PM   = Price of imports (1980 = 1.00) [SNA IMP/IMPV]

NPOP = Total population (millions of persons) [IFS and SNA]

RSCR = Scrapping rate [OECD84 RSCRB and OECD87 for smalls]

KS   = Kick-off value for capital stock in 1980 $ billion (see below)

KINVS = Kick-off value for inventory levels in 1980 $ billion [for G7 OECD86 inventory stock, for smalls an aproximation of .06K (1960) was used]

Q   = $(YGDP - TI)/PGDP$ Real gross output

Y   = $YGDP/PGDP + XIY/PGDP - MIY/PGDP$ Real gross national product

The wage and employment data for both the G7 and small countries were derived from INTERLINK supply block data supplied by OECD.

Capital Stock Series

For the G-7 countries, *total* capital stocks were generated from base (1959) kick-off values (KS). For each year, the previous year's stock was added to new investment after allowing for some portion, which is scrapped off, i.e., $K_t = (1 - RSCR)k_{t-1} + I$. The KS data were taken from the OECD84 tape for the G-7 countries, and it is the kick-off value for the total gross stock series. In the case of Japan, however, data were available only from 1966; some extrapolation was done to get the 1960 total capital stock as the kick-off value. *Business* capital stocks were the KBV series from the OECD86 tape, rebased to 1980 $ where applicable. For Japan, data were available only from 1966; extrapolating backwards using the formula $KBV_t = (1 - RSCRB)KBV_{t-1} + IBV$ (RSCRB is business scrapping rate; IBV is business investment), the business capital stock was estimated for 1960–65. A business scrapping rate of 4.15% per year was assumed for the 1960–65 period, to approximate the rate of 4.197% in 1966, the first year when data were available. In the case of France, the business capital stock series was built up using a kick-off value of 2138.2 billion francs in 1960 and RSCRB from the OECD86 tape. This kick-off value is obtained from OECD, *Flows and Stocks of Fixed Capital. Private* capital stocks were generated the same way as total capital stocks, using a base (1960) kick-off value and business scrapping rate. As no data are readily available on private capital stocks, the kick-off stock is estimated based on the assumption that the 1960–69 average ratio of private investment to business investment applies to the stock ratio. For example, for the United States private investment was 165% of business investment in the 1960s. This ratio was applied to business capital stock of $2,251.6 billion in 1960 to get $3,722.2 billion as the kick-off value for private capital stock.

For the 12 smaller industrial countries, *business* capital stock data were readily available from the OECD87 supply block tape, with those for Austria, New Zealand, and Switzerland having to be rebased to 1980 $.

The OECD87 tape has data on government, business, and housing investments. These data were compared with corresponding data available from OECD SNA, vol. 2 and were updated and revised where necessary. The private investment series was then generated as the sum of business and housing investments (IPV = IBV + IHV). From this, the 1960s average ratio of private investment to business investment was applied to the stock ratio to derive the kick-off private capital stock in 1960, as in the case of the G-7 countries. The *private* capital stock series was then generated for each of the 12 smaller industrial countries, using the business scrapping rate to approximate the scrapping rate for private capital stock. (The RSCRB data were available from the OECD87 tape. For some countries, however, estimates had to be made for the earlier years, particularly 1960 and 1961.) In the same way, a government capital stock series was generated, which was then added to private capital stock to get the *total* capital stock series.

The inventory stock series was calculated using the equation KINV = KINV$_{-1}$ + IINV, with KINVS being the base kick-off value.

The 1980 GDP PPPs are obtained from the OECD *Annual National Accounts: Main Aggregates* computer tape (July 1988). They are available for the full sample of 19 countries examined in this paper. The values used are: United States 1.00; Japan 258.51; Canada 1.149; France 5.941; Germany 2.702; Italy 866.974; United Kingdom 0.517; Australia 1.042; Austria 16.626; Belgium 42.918; Denmark 8.517; Finland 5.022; Ireland 0.543; Netherlands 2.734; New Zealand 1.004; Norway 7.334; Spain 70.554; Sweden 6.888; Switzerland 2.449.

Table 11A.1   The Ratio of Market Exchange Rates to GDP PPPs

Country	1980	1985
United States	1.0000	1.0000
Japan	0.8771	1.0745
Canada	1.0176	1.1192
France	0.7113	1.2359
Germany	0.6727	1.1871
Italy	0.9879	1.4665
United Kingdom	0.8323	1.3719
Australia	0.8426	1.1548
Austria	0.7782	1.2464
Belgium	0.6814	1.3314
Denmark	0.6617	1.0812
Finland	0.7427	1.0382
Ireland	0.8969	1.3084
Netherlands	0.7271	1.3024
New Zealand	1.0229	1.4985
Norway	0.6734	0.9962
Spain	1.0162	1.7843
Sweden	0.6141	1.0557
Switzerland	0.6844	1.0166

Note: Market exchange rates are defined as domestic currency per U.S. dollar.

Table 11A.2 Capital/Output and GDP Per Capita Ratios (1960 and 1985)

Capital/Output Ratios (beginning and end of sample values)

Year	United States	Japan	Canada	France	Germany
1960	3.0347	1.8840	4.1617	4.7568	3.5406
1985	3.3563	3.9681	4.2062	4.2766	4.8882

Year	Italy	United Kingdom	Australia	Austria	Belgium
1960	3.7849	4.0276	3.2818	3.1809	3.3049
1985	4.1174	5.2576	3.9660	4.4477	3.7283

Year	Denmark	Finland	Ireland	Netherlands	New Zealand
1960	5.4335	4.6195	3.9028	3.6609	2.3222
1985	4.0901	5.2453	4.9717	4.3095	3.4696

Year	Norway	Spain	Sweden	Switzerland
1960	5.0479	3.3856	4.0842	3.9432
1985	5.0939	4.2115	4.6309	4.3347

GDP Per Capita (beginning and end of sample values)

Year	United States	Japan	Canada	France	Germany
1960	7.7728	2.3098	5.7863	4.1558	4.8670
1985	13.0052	9.2956	11.9753	8.9332	9.5511

Year	Italy	United Kingdom	Australia	Austria	Belgium
1960	3.3202	5.3185	5.3650	3.7339	3.9490
1985	7.1607	8.6127	9.8141	8.5101	8.4698

Year	Denmark	Finland	Ireland	Netherlands	New Zealand
1960	4.9574	3.8243	2.5642	4.9125	5.6987
1985	9.6846	9.0761	5.3365	8.9070	7.9725

Year	Norway	Spain	Sweden	Switzerland
1960	4.5277	2.4085	5.3356	7.2253
1985	11.0457	5.9864	9.9783	11.3867

Table 11A.3   Average Labor Share of GDP

Country	Average Share	Minimum	Maximum
United States	0.7919	0.5954	0.8957
Japan	0.7778	0.5232	0.9465
Germany	0.8060	0.6479	0.9140
France	0.8407	0.5952	0.9270
United Kingdom	0.8615	0.6339	0.9629
Italy	0.8970	0.6434	0.9749
Canada	0.8296	0.6253	0.9113
Australia	0.7841	0.4587	0.9241
Austria	0.8261	0.6485	0.9286
Belgium	0.8200	0.6282	0.9157
Denmark	0.8713	0.7268	0.9472
Finland	0.8856	0.7123	0.9677
Ireland	0.9173	0.7338	0.9809
Netherlands	0.8140	0.6472	0.9271
New Zealand	0.7781	0.2943	0.9446
Norway	0.8339	0.6347	0.9275
Spain	0.8741	0.5674	0.9748
Sweden	0.8463	0.6205	0.9432
Switzerland	0.7550	0.5805	0.8747

Note: Average share of labor is defined as the sample average of $gdp - p_k k)/gdp$, 1960–85.

Table 11A.4   Supply Price of Capital (Pr)

United States	7.0515	Canada	5.1707
Germany	4.6756	United Kingdom	4.1680
Austria	5.5411	Denmark	3.7215
Ireland	1.9759	New Zealand	11.4984
Spain	4.7292	Switzerland	6.7305
Japan	8.1297	France	3.8872
Italy	2.3127	Australia	8.5177
Belgium	6.4483	Finland	2.4184
Netherlands	6.0547	Norway	3.7659
Sweden	4.4788		

Appendix B
Specification

Modeling Labor Productivity

The CES two-factor production function which defines normal output q_s is:

(B1)
$$q_s = [\mu(\Pi N)^{(\tau-1)/\tau} + v k^{(\tau-1)/\tau}]^{\tau/(\tau-1)}.$$

The following will first discuss the procedure used to derive expression for the country-specific parameters v, μ, and Π. The final values of these parameters depend on the value of τ, the elasticity of substitution between labor and capital, which is determined iteratively. The iteration method used to calculate τ will be examined last.

(B1) can be rewritten by setting $q = q_s$ and by isolating the following expression for Π:

(B2)
$$\Pi = [(q^{(\tau-1)/\tau} - v k^{(\tau-1)/\tau})/(\mu N^{(\tau-1)/\tau}]^{\tau/(\tau-1)}.$$

(B2) is used to obtain an expression for the parameter v. First the optimum factor ratio is derived. The partial derivatives of (B1) with respect to labor and capital are calculated and set equal to the prices W and p_k. Assuming the factor ratio is optimal provides the following ratio:

(B3)
$$\Pi N^*/k^* = (p_k\Pi/w)^\tau(\mu/v)^\tau$$

where the price of capital services is:

$$p_k = (<\delta_2> + 0.01\ \rho_r)p_a,$$

and where

$$\rho_r = 100<1 - (WN + <\delta_2>\bar{k}p_a)/(qp_q)>/<(\bar{k}p_a)/(qp_q)>,$$

so that the ratio of factor costs to revenues is unity, on average (as $\langle x \rangle$ denotes the sample average of x).

(B2) is substituted into (B3). The parameter μ drops out and can be determined empirically when Π is normalized, as shown below. The parameter v is isolated in the substituted equation and sample averages are taken to provide the following expression:

(B4) $v = <(p_k/W)(q/N)^{(\tau-1)/\tau}>/[<(N/k)^{1/\tau}> + <(p_k/W)(k/N)^{(\tau-1)/\tau}>].$

Note that we normalize so that the sample average of the ratio of the factors raised to the $1/\tau$ power is equal to the average for optimum proportions.

The value of Π, the labor productivity index for Harrod-neutral technical progress, is derived by the following procedure. Output attributable to labor is defined by rewriting (B2):

(B5)
$$\mu\Pi^{(\tau-1)/\tau} = (q^{(\tau-1)/\tau} - v k^{(\tau-1)/\tau})/N^{(\tau-1)/\tau}.$$

In the constant growth model, the technical progress index is modeled to grow at a constant rate. The model is estimated by ordinary least squares by regressing the logarithm of the measured efficiency level, which is the logarithm of the value provided by (B5), referred to as ln π_{mi}, for country i, on an annual time index. Given the final value of τ, the fitted values ln π_i, can be estimated for each year. Using the latter, the value of μ is calculated by setting $\Pi_i = 1.0$ in 1980. Given that the value of μ is constant throughout the sample period, the labor efficiency index Π_i is defined simply as the exponent of ln $\hat{\pi}_i$ minus 1980 ln $\hat{\pi}_i$, which ensures it has a value of 1 in 1980.

In the second model, the growth of technical progress in the non-U.S. countries is assumed to converge to the U.S. rate of growth. This is modeled by regressing ln (π_{mi}/π_{mus}), where π_{mi} is the measured productivity index for country i and π_{mus} is the measured value for the U.S., on ln (π_{mus}/π_{mi-1}), with the coefficient on the lagged dependent variable constrained to equal 1.0 on the right-hand side of the equation. The fitted values ln $\hat{\pi}_i$ are then calculated by multiplying the estimated regression parameters by the right-hand side variables (the exception being the measured U.S. index, which is replaced by the smoothed U.S. constant trend series $\hat{\pi}_{us}$). The series $\hat{\pi}_i$ is then used to derive the noncyclical technical progress index Π_i, as was done for the constant case. In the third model, in order to allow for the effects of globalization on the model, we include the variable DOPENA along with the catch-up variables in the non-U.S. equations. DOPENA is the annual change in "openness," defined as the log difference of current and lagged values of the five-year moving average of exports plus imports divided by GNP. The values of the CES parameters are derived in a similar way to the constant case, using the fitted values of the catch-up case, ln $\hat{\pi}_i$. The fourth model tests the "break" hypothesis. The technical progress index is modeled with a constant time index, but includes an additional index starting in 1974. If the latter index is negative, there is some evidence for the hypothesis that there was general reduction in the underlying rate of productivity growth starting in 1974. The last model assumes declining growth and is modeled by regressing π_{mi} on a declining trend which straightforwardly replaces the single time trend for the constant case. The declining trend takes on values such that if the step from the first period to the second is 1.0, then the step from the next-to-last to the last period is only 0.7 (i.e., the rate of growth has declined by 30% over the 25-year sample).

Finally, an estimate of τ is needed to derive final values of the above parameters. The iterative procedure uses the expression for the optimum factor ratio, (B3). The log of this equation provides the following form that can be estimated:

(B6) $$\ln(\Pi N^*/k^*) = \tau \ln(\mu/\nu) + \tau \ln(p_k \Pi/W).$$

The coefficient of the inverse price ratio is τ. An arbitrary value of τ is used to define μ, ν, Π. (B6) is then estimated by ordinary least squares, and the estimated coefficient provides a new value of τ, which is used to redefine the other parameters in the next round. The process is repeated until the value of τ in (B6) converges. This value is used to obtain the final values of μ, ν, Π, and normal output, q_s. For our final estimates, a variant of (B6) was used in which the lagged capital-labor ratio was included along with cyclical demand and profitability variables (outlined in Helliwell and Chung 1986) as right-hand-side variables. The latter were included since the factor-share ratio has, in addition to its responsiveness to relative prices, a cyclical variance caused by the fact that labor adjusts more quickly than the capital stock to changes in desired output. The distributed lag response on the relative price term (which tends to produce a higher estimated equilibrium elasticity of substitution) also provides more reasonable elasticities across countries.

In the pooled estimation, we use an average of the country-specific τ and ν (with value of .99 for τ), thus providing common production function parameters. The econometric technique used to estimate the productivity equations is Zellner's seemingly unrelated regression technique, since there is significant evidence of cross-country correlation of the error terms. The systems of equations are estimated with the generalized least squares procedure, although the iterative procedure for the covariance matrix of residuals across equations is not used.

Output Investment and Employment

The following provides a brief description of the specification of the equations used in the non-nested tests reported in the tables.

The Output Equation

We follow the "factor utilization" approach outlined in Helliwell and Chung (1986). The rationale for explicitly modeling factor utilization rates lies in the observation that factors of production are quasi-fixed. That is, it is costly for firms to adjust the levels of inputs in response to short-run changes in demand and cost conditions. Consequently, temporary fluctuations in demand are met by varying the intensity of factor use—working the inputs harder or not as hard—or, in other words, by changing the factor utilization rates.

One difficulty with this approach is that factor utilization rates are not directly observable. In particular, we have no idea what constitutes a "normal" factor utilization rate. A simple way around the problem is to define the utilization rate as the ratio of actual to normal output and to form suitable proxies for the demand and cost conditions. When the proxy variables are at their normal values—the sample averages—then we have a normal rate of factor utilization.

The output equation thus has the following specification:

(B7) $\ln q = \ln q_s + \beta \ln sgap + \beta_1 \ln cq + \beta_2 \ln igap + e$

where *sgap* is the ratio of sales to normal sales, *igap* is the ratio of desired to lagged actual inventories, and *cq* is the ratio of current unit cost relative to output price (an inverse measure of profitability). Normal sales is defined as $<s/q_s> \times q_s$, and desired inventories is $<kinv - 1/q_s>q_s$, where *kinv* is inventory stock. The sample averages ensure that the means of *sgap*, *igap*, and *cq* are 1, which ensures "normal" utilization rates on average.

The Investment Equation

The equation explains fixed investment as a fraction of the corresponding capital stock, with the lagged ratio entering the equation to enrich the distributed lag response. Driving the investment equation is the gap between desired and the actual capital stock $(k^* - k)/k$. The desired k^* is derived as follows. First, define a level of output (q^*) which is the expected desired output for firms. We define $q^* = q_a (q/q - 2)$, where q_a is aggregate demand (output minus unintended change in inventories). The time horizon implicit in q^* is thus two years. Given our CES production function, the level of desired output is used in the long-run production function to determine the levels of capital and labor that would minimize costs if future relative prices were the same as those currently prevailing. Analytic expressions for k^* and N^* are thus easily obtained:

(B8) $$k^* = [v + \mu^\tau (\Pi p_k/wv)^{\tau-1}]^{\tau/(1-\tau)}q^*$$

and

(B9) $$N^* = (1/\Pi)[(q^{*(\tau-1)/\tau} - v\overset{*}{k}{}^{(\tau-1)/\tau})/\mu]^{\tau/(\tau-1)}$$

Lastly we include *cq*. This attempts to capture financial market conditions by defining profitability as the ratio of current unit operating costs to the current output price, where the numerator includes a rental charge of capital, which varies with the long-term nominal interest rate.

The Employment Equation

The employment equation describes a partial adjustment to the two-year forward-looking demand for labor (N^*). The employment equation follows a simple adaptive adjustment, with right-hand side variables, lagged and desired employment levels, constrained to sum to one.

References

Abramovitz, M. 1986. Catching up, Forging Ahead, and Falling Behind. *Journal of Economic History* 46:385–406.

Baily, M. N. 1981. Productivity and the Services of Capital and Labor. *Brookings Papers on Economic Activity* 1:1–50.

Barro, R. J. 1978. Unanticipated Money, Output and the Price Level in the United States. *Journal of Political Economy* 86:549–80.

Baumol, W. J. 1986. Productivity Growth, Convergence and Welfare: What the Long-Run Data Show. *American Economic Review* 76:1072–85.

Baumol, W. J., and E. N. Wolff. 1988. Productivity Growth, Convergence and Welfare: Reply. *American Economic Review* 78:1155–59.

Blades, D., and D. Roberts. 1987. A Note on the New OECD Benchmark Purchasing Power Parities for 1985. *OECD Economic Studies* 9:153–84.

Bruno, M., and J. Sachs. 1985. *Economics of Worldwide Stagflation*. Cambridge, Mass.: Harvard University Press.

Chenery, H., S. Robinson, and M. Syrquin. 1986. *Industrialization and Growth: A Comparative Study*. Washington, D.C.: Oxford University Press for the World Bank.

Davidson, R., and J. G. MacKinnon. 1981. Several Tests for Model Specification in the Presence of Alternative Hypotheses. *Econometrica* 49:781–94.

De Long, J. B. 1988. Productivity Growth, Convergence and Welfare: Comment. *American Economic Review* 78:1138–54.

Dollar, D., and E. Wolff. 1988. Convergence of Industry Labor Productivity among Advanced Economies, 1963–1982. *Review of Economics and Statistics* 70:549–58.

Englander, S., and A. Mittelstadt. 1988. Total Factor Productivity: Macroeconomic and Structural Aspects of the Slowdown. *OECD Economic Studies* 10:7–56.

Godfrey, L. G. 1983. Testing Non-nested Models after Estimation by Instrumental Variables or Least Squares. *Econometrica* 51:355–65.

Gordon, R. J., and M. Baily. 1989. Measurement Issues and the Productivity Slowdown in Five Major Industrial Countries. Paper presented at International Seminar on Science, Technology, and Economic Growth. June 6. Paris.

Greenwood, J., Z. Hercowitz, and G. W. Huffman. 1988. Investment, Capacity Utilization and the Real Business Cycle. *American Economic Review* 78:402–17.

Grossman, G. M., and E. Helpman. 1989a. Endogenous Product Cycles. NBER Working Paper no. 2913.

———. 1989b. Growth and Welfare in a Small Open Economy. NBER Working Paper no. 2970.

Hansen, G. D. 1985. Indivisible Labor and the Business Cycle. *Journal of Monetary Economics* 16:309–27.

Helliwell, J. F. 1986. Supply-side Macroeconomics. *Canadian Journal of Economics* 19:597–625.

Helliwell, J. F., and A. Chung. 1986. Aggregate Output with Variable Rates of Utilization of Employed Factors. *Journal of Econometrics* 33:285–310.

———. 1988. Aggregate Productivity and Growth in an International Comparative Setting. Paper prepared for the U.S. SSRC conference on International Productivity and Competitiveness. October. Stanford University, Palo Alto, California.

Helliwell, J. F., P. H. Sturm, P. Jarrett, and G. Salou. 1986. The Supply Side in the OECD's Macroeconomic Model. *OECD Economic Studies* 6:75–131.

Helliwell, J. F., P. H. Sturm, and G. Salou. 1985. International Comparison of the Sources of Productivity Slowdown, 1973–1982. *European Economic Review* 28:157–91.

Heston, A., and R. Summers. 1988. What Have We Learned about Prices and Quantities from International Comparisons: 1987. *American Economic Review* 78, no. 2:467–73.

Hill, T. P. 1986. International Price Levels and Purchasing Power Parities. *OECD Economic Studies* 6:133–59.

King, R. G., C. I. Plosser, and S. T. Rebello. 1988. Production, Growth and Business Cycles. *Journal of Monetary Economics* 21:195–232, 309–41.

Kravis, I. B., A. Heston, and R. Summers 1978. *The United Nations International Comparison Project: Phase II, International Comparisons of Real Product and Purchasing Power.* Baltimore: Johns Hopkins University.

Kravis, I. B., and R. E. Lipsey. 1984. The Diffusion of Economic Growth in the World Economy, 1950–80. In *International Comparisons of Productivity and Causes of the Slowdown*, ed. J. W. Kendrick. Cambridge. Ballinger.

————. 1989. The International Comparison Program: Current Status and Problems. Paper prepared for conference on International Economic Transactions. November. Washington, D.C.

Kydland, F., and E. Prescott. 1982. Time to Build and Aggregate Fluctuations. *Econometrica* 50:1345–70.

Lindbeck, A. 1983. The Recent Slowdown of Productivity Growth. *Economic Journal* 93:13–34.

Long, J. B., and C. I. Plosser. 1983. Real Business Cycles. *Journal of Political Economy* 91:39–69.

Lucas, R. E. 1973. Some International Evidence on Output-Inflation Tradeoffs. *American Economic Review* 63:326–34.

Maddison, A. 1982. *Phases of Capitalist Development.* Oxford: Oxford University Press.

————. 1987. Growth and Slowdown in Advanced Capitalist Economies: Techniques of Quantitative Measurement. *Journal of Economic Literature* 25:649–98.

Mizon, G. E., and J.-F. Richard. 1986. The Encompassing Principle and its Application to Non-Nested Hypotheses. *Econometrica* 54:657–78.

Nordhaus, W. D. 1982. Economic Policy in the Face of Declining Productivity Growth. *European Economic Review* 18:131–57.

Ohkawa, O., and H. Rosovsky. 1973. *Japanese Economic Growth: Trend Acceleration in the Twentieth Century.* Stanford.

Plosser, C. I. 1989. Understanding Real Business Cycles. *Journal of Economic Perspectives* 3:51–78.

Psacharopoulos, G. 1984. The Contribution of Education to Economic Growth: International Comparisons. In *International Comparisons of Productivity and Causes of the Slowdown*, ed. J. W. Kendrick. Cambridge: Ballinger.

Rauch, J. E. 1989. The Question of International Convergence of Per Capita Consumption: An Euler Equation Approach. NBER Summer Institute Paper (August).

Romer, P. M. 1986. Increasing Returns and Long-Run Growth. *Journal of Political Economy* 94:1002–37.

Rostow, W. W. 1978. *The World Economy: History and Prospect.* Austin: University of Texas Press.

Solow, R. M. 1957. Technical Change and the Aggregate Production Function. *Review of Economics and Statistics* 39:312–20.

12 The International Comparison Program

Current Status and Problems

Irving B. Kravis and Robert E. Lipsey

12.1 Introduction

A worldwide United Nations program to produce international comparisons of real GDP and its components and the purchasing power parities (PPPs) of currencies has been under way for twenty years.[1] In this paper we review the methodology of this work, the International Comparison Program (ICP) and describe its present status. (The effort was referred to as the International Comparison Project in its earlier stages.) We follow with discussion of the robustness of the results, some problems that have arisen in the extension and continuation of the ICP, and a look to its future.

The predominant method of meeting the need for comparative data on real GDP and related macrovariables is to convert own-currency value aggregates to a numeraire currency, usually the dollar, via exchange rates (as, for example, to obtain world expenditures on energy). Exchange-rate conversion is still the common practice, despite clear evidence that exchange rates fail to reflect the relative purchasing power of currencies, sometimes being off by a factor of 3 or more, even for output as a whole and still more for individual products.

Irving B. Kravis is university professor emeritus at the University of Pennsylvania and a research associate of the National Bureau of Economic Research. Robert E. Lipsey is professor of economics at Queens College and the Graduate Center, City University of New York, and a research associate of the National Bureau of Economic Research.

The authors are grateful for helpful comments by Alan V. Deardorff and Alan Heston, neither of whom is responsible for the views expressed here. The statistical work for this paper was done by David Robinson, and the manuscript was prepared by Maryellen Sykes.

1. PPP is defined here as the number of units of currency j required to purchase the same amount of goods as a unit of the numeraire currency can purchase.

12.2   An Outline of ICP Methods

The ICP comparisons relate to Gross Domestic Product (GDP) and its components as defined in the U.N. System of National Accounts (U.N. Statistical Office, 1968).[2] GDP is intended in concept to establish a production boundary marking off economic activity, which produces satisfaction-yielding goods and services, from other human activities. In this context, production is generally regarded as a measure of income, although there are circumstances in which it seems appropriate to distinguish between the two concepts.

The ICP approaches the international comparison of income through price comparisons for about 150 categories ("basic headings") of final expenditures on GDP.[3] Prices are usually compared for at least several specifications of goods in each category. Because the items priced in each country must be representative of the goods commonly found in the domestic market, a common list of price-compared goods in all countries is precluded. There are two ways in which category PPPs are calculated despite incomplete overlapping price comparisons for the included countries. In both, the missing prices are inferred from their relationship in all the other countries to prices of items that are available in the given country.[4]

The quantity comparisons for each basic heading are obtained by dividing the PPP into the expenditure ratio. That is, for a given basic heading,

$$\frac{Q_j}{Q_b} = \frac{E_j}{E_b} \div \frac{PPP_j}{PPP_j}$$

where j and b are countries, Qs are physical quantities and Es are expenditures in own currency.

---

2. See Kravis, Heston, and Summers (1982) for a fuller account of ICP methods. The methods have been summarized in a number of papers (see, e.g., Kravis 1984). The present outline is provided to enable readers not familiar with the methods to understand the discussions that follow.

3. In a few categories, quantities are compared, and the price comparisons are derived by dividing the quantity ratios into the expenditure ratios. Also, comparisons in some regions have been based on a more detailed breakdown and in others on a less detailed breakdown. The basic headings represent the most detailed breakdown of expenditures that it is possible to make for many countries. An effort has been also made to define them so that they include products that are alike with respect to price-determining influences. An approach which is more difficult to implement is to build up the GDP comparison in terms of the industries producing the output. See Paige and Bombach (1959) and Maddison and van Ark (1987).

4. The Country-Product Dummy (CPD) method does this through a regression in which the log price of an item is the dependent variable and the independent variables are two sets of dummy variables, one for the various countries and the other for the different specifications. The coefficient of the dummy variable for a given country represents the log of the PPP for the category in that country relative to the numeraire country. See Summers (1973) and Kravis, Heston, and Summers (1982). The other method of coping with differing price lists, offered independently by Elteto, Koves, and Szulc (hence, the "EKS" method), has been used in the European comparisons. The EKS index for a given pair of countries is the geometric mean of the direct Fisher indexes (weighted twice), and all the bridge-country Fisher indexes. (A bridge country is one that links together two countries through a comparison of each with the bridge country.) The CPD and EKS methods generally produce similar results (Krijnse-Locker 1982).

The PPPs and the quantity indexes for the basic headings derived by these methods are then aggregated to form PPPs and quantity indexes for summary headings (e.g., "meat," which includes fresh beef and five other basic headings), and for larger aggregates up to GDP. The method of aggregation involves the use of a set of average international prices (πs), one for each basic heading. Each average price (π_i) is calculated from the category PPP for each of the n countries weighted by the quantity share absorbed in that country. To make the PPPs of the different countries commensurate, each is divided by the overall PPP (i.e., the PPP for GDP) for the country. Thus,

$$(2) \qquad \pi_i = \sum \frac{PPP_{ij}}{PPP_j} \cdot w_{ij}$$

where i is one of m categories or basic headings, and w is country j's share in world consumption of category i.

The GDP PPP is the ratio of the country's GDP at own-currency prices to its GDP valued at international prices:

$$(3) \qquad PPP_j = \frac{\sum\limits^{m} PPP_{ij} Q_{ij}}{\sum\limits^{m} \pi_i Q_{ij}}$$

Thus the PPPs for GDP (or other aggregates) need the πs for their calculation, and the πs need the PPPs for their calculation. The solution, suggested by R. C. Geary and amplified by S. H. Khamis, is to rely on a set of equations in which all the PPPs and πs are simultaneously determined. To obtain GDP or other aggregates the quantity in each basic heading is multiplied by the international price, and the products obtained are summed over the appropriate headings.

A number of other index number formulas were considered. Geary-Khamis was selected both for its statistical properties and for its ready economic interpretation. The statistical properties include base country invariance,[5] transitivity,[6] and matrix consistency.[7] From an economic standpoint, the formula matches the underlying point of departure of the PPP comparisons—that there is a price level for each country which is an average of the different price levels of its GDP components. The use of cross-country averages of these relative prices to value the quantities in each country's GDP provides a common mea-

---

5. The base country serves merely as a numeraire. It makes no difference for the quantitative relationship among the countries which one serves as the numeraire.

6. For example, $I_{jik} = I_{jil} \div I_{kil}$ where I is an index of quantities or prices and j, k, and l are countries. This ensures that the relative positions of the countries will be unambiguous.

7. In a table with countries in the columns and categories in the rows, the entries show the correct relative quantities on any row and are additive in the columns to any desired aggregate such as consumption or GDP. This table is akin to the familiar national accounts time-to-time table showing final expenditures in constant prices.

suring rod for the GDPs of the included countries. This price-times-quantity-equals-expenditure feature of the Geary-Khamis formula fits well with national income accounting concepts.

A persistent finding in all phases of the International Comparison Program, which now covers eighty countries, is that the purchasing power of the currencies of low-income countries is much greater than that indicated by exchange rates. In 1980, for example, the price level of the developing countries of Asia included in the Phase 4 study (eight countries) was only half of that of the United States; for the developing countries of Central and South America, the price level was less than two-thirds that of the United States. This means that the real income per capita of the Asian countries was twice that suggested by exchange-rate conversions, and that of the Central and South American countries was half again as much as the exchange-rate conversions indicated. It is important to bear the size of these differences in mind when considering the margins of uncertainty that are attached to the ICP comparisons.

12.3 Robustness

Some errors in real income comparisons originate in the estimates of GDP and the national accounts of various countries. The accuracy and comprehensiveness of the accounts vary from one country to another. Countries without well-developed economic statistics can produce national accounts only with large margins of error. Also, some parts of the accounts, like the measurement of subsistence income or of depreciation, are particularly vulnerable to differences in treatment by the national statistical authorities of different countries. These uncertainties in the estimates of each country's national income pose the same problems for exchange-rate conversions as for PPP conversions. The seemingly unequivocal character of exchange-rate–based comparisons involves the conversion of these incomparable measures into equally incomparable estimates in the numeraire currency.

There are, however, other sources of uncertainty in the PPP conversions, and we try here to evaluate them.

12.3.1   Price Comparisons

There is first and most basically the problem of matching qualities in the price comparisons. The care taken to get these comparisons right varies from one phase of the ICP to another, and sometimes within a given phase from region to region or country to country. The comparisons involving the countries of the European Community (EC) meet these problems in a particularly thorough and careful way. The price comparisons involving the United States for the Phase 4 study were less than optimal because the decision of the United States to participate was taken late and prices collected for an earlier period had to be used (after adjustment to the reference date). It would be very difficult to measure the possible errors arising from incomparable qualities. The fact that so many individual prices of many items are compared (300 to 700 items per country) should help to reduce the sampling error. The fact that the price comparisons are distributed over the entire gamut of final products may diminish the likelihood of error from biased selection among types of goods. However, it is difficult to know what biases are introduced by the need for comparability of specifications among countries or the problem of "nonresponse" arising from the unavailability of data.

Sampling variability and errors in matching are also difficult to measure. An experiment reported in the Phase 1 study (Kravis, Kenessey, Heston, and Summers 1975, pp. 77f.) suggests that the sampling variability is generally in the 5 to 7 percent range at the 0.95 confidence level, with high-income countries at the lower end and low-income countries at the higher end, with one case of a sampling error of nearly 10 percent (see also Kravis, Heston, and Summers 1982, p. 97).

Variations in the results of the comparisons could also arise from differences in aggregation methods and from differences in the treatments of certain problem categories. Our method of assessing these uncertainties is the very crude one of examining the variations in results produced by the alternative methodologies using data of past comparisons (often those of 1975 because that was the most recent study offering much relevant material for this purpose).

12.3.2   Aggregation Methods

The use of the Geary-Khamis formula has not gone completely unchallenged (Isenman 1980, Drechsler 1988), despite a favorable verdict in an influential report by Peter Hill (1981), commissioned by the Statistical Office of the European Communities and the Economic Commission for Europe.

The main objection to the Geary-Khamis formula is that it produces the Gerschenkron effect (also referred to as Bortkiewicz's Law, or the own-price effect). Because the ICP prices are averages weighted by the quantities absorbed in each country, the world average price structure used in the ICP version of Geary-Khamis is heavily influenced by the United States and the other high-income countries. Given the usual negative correlation between quantities and prices, the real GDPs of the low-income countries will tend to be higher than if a set of prices more "characteristic" of them was used.

However, there is some evidence that the impact of different price regimes on Geary-Khamis estimates of real GDP is modest compared to the difference between PPP conversions and exchange-rate conversions. When the Geary-Khamis index for the Phase 3 countries was recalculated using equal weights for poor and rich countries in obtaining world average prices, the real GDPs per capita for the eight poorest countries (with real GDPs per capita 15 percent or less of the U.S. level) were smaller only by a range of 9 to 13 percent.

Exchange-rate–converted per capita GDPs were, by contrast, 60 percent lower on average than the PPP-converted figures, and one-third lower in the case of the smallest difference (Kravis 1984, p. 33).

The fact that objections are still raised to the Geary-Khamis formula leads us to report the difference that it would make if the chief alternative aggregation formula, the EKS, were used. The EKS is based on Fisher indexes, which are regarded favorably on the grounds of characteristicity.[8] The Fisher indexes are not transitive, and few would favor them for multilateral comparisons. The EKS (applied here to aggregate the PPPs for the basic headings) is transitive and minimizes the squared log deviations from the Fisher indexes. However, the EKS does not produce matrix consistency (its failure is in additivity; i.e., the sum of the basic headings does not produce the same GDP as the formula), and further transformations have been sought, but no widely acceptable one has been advanced.[9]

For the (nine) high-income countries in the Phase 3 study, the Geary-Khamis and EKS formulas produced nearly identical results, except for Japan, for which Geary-Khamis was 5 percent higher. The spread was larger for middle-income countries and greatest for low-income countries, averaging around 16 percent for the lowest fourth and reaching as high as 19 percent.[10]

12.3.3   Treatment of Problem Categories

For certain categories, there is little theoretical guidance for the choice between alternative methods.

In the first three phases of the ICP (1970, 1973, and 1975) the same team at the University of Pennsylvania, in close collaboration with the U.N. Statistical Office, produced the comparisons, and the differences in methods resulted from efforts to refine and improve the treatment of some difficult categories. In later phases of the ICP, the design and collection of the ICP was organized on a regional basis (more on regionalization presently), and differences arose even within a given phase.

Aside from regionalization, differences related mainly to the treatment of the net foreign balance and about a dozen "comparison-resistant" service categories for which domestic national accounts generally use input data to measure output.

---

8. Characteristicity is indeed promoted by the fact that half the weights in a Fisher index refer to the given country's own prices or quantities. However, the characteristicity on this account may be offset in the cases of partners with price or quantity structures that differ radically from those of the given country.

9. See Statistical Office of the European Communities; Organisation for Economic Cooperation and Development, U.N. Statistical Office 1989.

10. These calculations are based mainly on the thirty-four Phase 3 countries. An increase in the number of countries studied might turn up some larger differences.

Comparison-Resistant Services

The proportion of GDP spent on services ranges from less than 20 percent in low-income countries to 50 percent in high-income countries.[11] Services that lend themselves to price comparison make up more than half of the total. The others—the comparison-resistant services—are composed of the services produced by health care professionals, teachers, and government employees. They are "comparison-resistant" because it is difficult to find markets on which units of these service outputs are sold; consequently, there are cases in which no market price paid by final purchasers is available. In domestic national accounting, the absence of quantity indicators of output has been met by using changes in inputs as measures of changes in output, and a similar strategy has been followed in the ICP for the most part. In most but not all parts of the ICP, it was assumed that the productivity of workers with similar qualifications was the same in different countries. In the education sector, for example, it was assumed that a teacher in India with thirteen or fourteen years of education produced the same amount of output as a teacher in the United Kingdom with thirteen or fourteen years of education. Exceptions to this equal productivity assumption were made in Phase 3 and for the portion of Phase 4 comparisons involving Austria and the three eastern European countries.

Another difference in the treatment of comparison-resistant services was that allowances were made in phases 1, 2, and 3, but not in later phases, for capital inputs in the health and government service categories. The capital data for the adjustment were very rough, and it is understandable that the international organizations that produced phases 4 and 5 of the ICP abstained from their use. The result of omitting them, however, is surely an understatement of output in high-income countries, since both health services and government services must be much more capital-intensive in high-income countries than in low-income countries.

Still another difference in comparing these difficult services was the inclusion in Phase 3 of the number of students, in addition to the input of teachers and capital. The change may have been introduced with the idea of adding a measure of the output of education, but, because students' time is an input into the production of learning (learning itself being the output), the procedure of Phase 3 represents an enlargement of the coverage of inputs rather than a measurement of output. However, the procedure does not take foregone earnings into account or, in effect, treats foregone earnings per student as identical among countries. It therefore is likely to understate education input in high-income countries relative to low-income countries.

11. Based on thirty-four countries (Kravis, Heston, and Summers 1982, p. 194). In all of the phases, services in health and education provided at public expense are included in "consumption" rather than "government" so as to make the country-to-country comparisons of these aggregates invariant to the source of their financing.

How much difference do these variations in the treatment of comparison-resistant services make for the quantity comparisons for the sectors involved and for GDP? The answers are: not much for the developed countries, either at the sector level or for GDP; quite a lot for low-income countries at the sector level; and modest amounts for low-income countries at the GDP level.

What is probably a maximum estimate of the sensitivity of GDP to these variations is provided by doing the GDP comparison on the assumption that the PPPs for comparison-resistant services are the same as the PPPs for priced services. (Actually, in the Phase 3 report the PPPs for comparison-resistant services were as low as a third of those for priced services in the low-income countries, although near equality in the high-income countries.) This assumption would reduce the GDP for the lowest-income countries by approximately 15 percent, but would have little effect on the middle- and high-income countries.

The impact of different treatment of the comparison-resistant services is more realistically measured by examining the results of the Phase 3 changes in making comparisons for these services relative to those used in Phase 2. The main changes were the use of capital inputs in health and government services, an adjustment for productivity differences in health and education services, and the addition of the number of pupils as a quantity indicator in education. While the revised treatment has an enormous impact on estimates of the quantity of medical services for low-income countries, cutting them by 40 or 50 percent relative to the United States (Kravis, Heston, and Summers 1982, p. 161), the largest effect on GDP was to reduce it by 6 percent (in Kenya and India).

Another insight into the robustness of the estimates is provided by a recalculation of the results of phases 1, 3, and 4, using as nearly as possible the same methods in all three.[12] The methods were mainly those of Phase 4, the chief exception being that the fixity rule (see section 12.4) was not adhered to. The "standardized" results compare with the original benchmark results as shown in table 12.1.

The differences produced by the shift to alternative methods are quite small on average; ignoring signs, the mean difference varies from 4 percent to a little over 6 percent for the three benchmark surveys. The differences for individual countries in a few cases are as high as 17 percent, with an outlier at 25 percent (Malaysia, in 1970).

The Net Foreign Balance

The great preponderance of GDP is absorbed by domestic spending on consumption, capital formation, and government services, but there is often a net positive or negative balance between domestic absorption and production. There is no very clear way to account for the net foreign balance in making

---

12. Unpublished data kindly made available to us by professors Heston and Summers.

Table 12.1   **Standardized Benchmark Estimates of Real GDP Per Capita, Compared to Original Benchmark Estimates**

	Ratios: Standardized/Original					
	1970		1975		1980	
	All Countries	Lowest-Income Fourth	All Countries	Lowest-Income Fourth	All Countries	Lowest-Income Fourth
Number of countries	16	4	34	8	60	15
Range:						
Minimum	.75	.89	.87	.91	.81	.89
Maximum	1.04	.96	1.04	1.03	1.17	1.14
Mean Absolute						
Deviation from 1.0	.059	.061	.024	.031	.057	.061

comparisons of production or income. These claims are expressed in dollars or other currencies and have no obvious physical counterpart as do other components of final expenditures.

A simple method that has been favored by the EC and used in the more recent phases of the ICP, is simply to convert the net foreign balance to international dollars by use of the exchange rate. This method is not, however, symmetrical with that used for the other categories of final expenditures on GDP. For all of the other categories, an international price (π) is found by means of equation (2) above. A closer approximation to this method, involving the estimate of a π for the net foreign balance, was used in the first three phases of the ICP.[13]

The difference in the estimate of per capita GDP from these two ways of handling the category depends on the size and sign of the net foreign balance in each country and on the size of the π. In the Phase 3 study, the last in which a price was calculated, each country's net foreign balance converted to U.S. dollars at its exchange rate was multiplied by 1.28, the calculated π. Developing countries tended to have negative net foreign balances that year (1975); the largest was Zambia's, -19.5 percent of its GDP in its own currency. If the conversion to international dollars in the Phase 3 report had been at a price of $\$I = \$1.00$ instead of $\$I = \$1.28$, Zambia's per capita GDP relative to the United States would have been 4 percent higher (i.e., 10.7 percent of the U.S. instead of 10.3 percent). The conclusion is that different treatments of the net

13. For each country, the ratio of the exchange rate to its PPP as estimated from a preliminary Geary-Khamis calculation for GDP, excluding the net foreign balance, was used to form the international price. In this calculation the ratios for the different countries were weighted by the relative importance of each country in total GDP. The method of phases 4 and 5, in which the net foreign balance is not multiplied by an international price, is equivalent to taking that price as equal to one.

foreign balance are likely to have modest effects on comparative real GDP per capita, even if the surplus or deficit is very large.

12.3.6 Robustness Summary

The main concern that has been expressed about the benchmark results is that they exaggerate the relative real per capita GDPs of the low-income countries. Uncertainties may arise from measurement error, improper matching of qualities, sampling variability, and the treatment of problem categories. We do not attempt to measure either the errors common to exchange-rate and PPP comparisons or the effect of matching errors. We believe that the former are substantial for some countries and that the major thrust of ICP work to keep the latter small has been successful.

Sampling error cuts both ways, and we cannot tell whether the ICP estimate for a given country is too high or too low on this account. We cannot measure the margins of uncertainty arising from the problem categories in any rigorous way. What we can do is to use the sensitivity of the results of the earlier phases to different sources of error and uncertainty to get some rough approximations of the possible variation.

12.4   The Range of Uncertainty

There are two ways of drawing upon the materials we have presented to obtain some notion of the range of uncertainty in the benchmark results. In the "additive" approach we sum the crude allowance suggested above for sampling variability and for alternative methods. The worst case is that the true estimate will be approximately 10 to 15 percent lower than the benchmark estimate, the uncertainty consisting mainly of sampling variability. (This refers to those cases in which the sampling error makes the GDP too high.) The uncertainties for comparison-resistant services and for the net foreign balance work in offsetting directions to each other.

In the alternative "overall" approach, reliance is placed on the difference between the actual benchmark GDP estimates and those that would have been produced by a standardized set of methods applied as uniformly as possible to the data of the 1970, 1975, and 1980 phases. In this approach, errors or uncertainty arising from methodological factors may raise some estimates *above* the benchmark estimate. The worst case observed in table 12.1 suggests that the methodological factors could place the true per capita GDP 17 percent higher than the benchmark estimate. If sampling errors are in the same direction, the up-side margin could be approximately 25 percent.

We conclude that margins of uncertainty in the 20 to 25 percent range, plus and minus, are generous estimates of the outside limits of uncertainty in the benchmark estimates for low-income countries, originating from the factors we have examined. Error margins diminish as per capita income rises; for the high-income countries (two-thirds or more of U.S. per capita real GDP), they are around 7 percent, mainly sampling error.

These estimates do not include any allowance for differences owing to the use of different aggregation formulas. Our view is that the Geary-Khamis formula measures what we are seeking to measure from an economic standpoint. If that formula is regarded as merely one of a number of competing formulas, each attempting to answer a somewhat different question, the answer will depend on the formulation of the question.

By contrast with these uncertainties about the PPP conversions, exchange-rate conversions seem quite straightforward and free of methodological choices that are difficult to make. One need only, it would appear, take the exchange rate and divide it into the own-currency GDP.

But matters are not so simple. "The" exchange rate that is sought for this purpose is the annual average rate across all transactions, and it is often different from the regularly published "official" rate. When multiple rates apply to different transactions, or, more commonly, black market rates exist along with fully legal rates, then estimates of the average levels of the various rates may be subject to large margins of error, and the relative importance of the official rate and of other rates, necessary for a weighted average, may involve a large element of guesswork. The resultant uncertainty in the estimate of the average effective exchange rate has, of course, its mirror image in the estimate of real GDP that it is used to derive.

In addition, even the legal rates fluctuate erratically, while domestic prices and quantities tend to remain relatively stable. This combination produces erratic and implausible estimates of real GDP. One way of meeting this problem is to select an exchange rate for a past "equilibrium" year and to extrapolate it to the target year on the basis of relative rates of inflation in the given country and the numeraire country. An alternative is to use a moving average of recent exchange rates. The World Bank, whose *World Atlas* is the most widely cited source of international income comparisons, uses both of these methods, the former where the official rate seems to deviate from "equilibrium" by exceptionally large margins. The moving-average approach, applied to most countries, presently is based on the exchange rate for the target year averaged with exchange rates for adjacent years, adjusting the latter rates to the target year by relative rates of inflation.

The differences produced by these and other alternative exchange-rate methods are substantial. Ward (1989), for example, reports on the results of using two different three-year periods for averaging. One terminates in the target year, and thus is not centered on the target year; the other centers on the target year but is available only after a further year elapses. When these two methods were applied to 1987 data, three-year average rates centered on 1987 ranged from 54 percent to 127 percent of those centered on 1986. The mean absolute difference for the nine lowest-income countries was 20 percent. Thus this single source of different methodology produces differences in exchange-rate conversions that are larger than those encountered in the PPP-converted comparisons.

12.5 The Question of Regionalization

In accordance with long-held plans, beginning with Phase 4 (reference date 1980) the responsibility for worldwide comparisons was shifted completely to the U.N. Statistical Office (UNSO). At the same time, outside financial support dwindled, and the ability of UNSO to play a leading role in the comparisons diminished. Also, regional organizations, especially those in Europe, began to produce comparisons for their member countries. As a result, the 1980 comparisons for sixty countries were put together in seven sets of countries. In Europe, for example, the EC made up one block of twelve countries, and five more European countries were compared under the aegis of the Economic Commission for Europe (ECE), with Austria as the center country. Other European countries were added in a set of comparisons prepared by the Organisation for Economic Cooperation and Development (OECD). The UNSO took direct responsibility for seven Asian countries for which no regional organization formed a comparison group.

Thus, there were sets of regional comparisons, each based on its own average prices, and including some regions within regions (the EC within the OECD).[14] UNSO linked the regions together through "core country" comparisons. From one to three countries in each group served as core countries, providing prices that overlapped in all groups for each basic heading. For example, France and Spain were core countries for the EC and Kenya and Senegal for Africa. PPPs were estimated for the twenty core countries for each basic heading, using the United States as the numeraire country.[15] The other (noncore) countries were linked to the world comparisons through the core country or countries in their group. This produced a PPP for each basic heading which, with the expenditure data, provided the necessary inputs for a Geary-Khamis calculation for the sixty countries included in Phase 4.

This Geary-Khamis calculation would have provided the final result except for the insistence of the Statistical Office of the European Communities (Eurostat) on the "fixity" principle. Under this rule, the results of the intraregional comparisons produced by the different regional organizations are not to be altered when the regions are incorporated into the worldwide comparisons. That is, if Germany is 5 percent higher than France in real per capita income

14. The theoretical case for regionalization rests on grouping countries with similar price and quantity structures together. Geographical propinquity, while an obvious starting point in grouping countries, is not an adequate criterion. In the real world, the regionalization that is demanded is heavily influenced by political considerations; some "regional" groups cut across continental lines (OECD) and others subdivide continents (EC) (Kravis, Heston, and Summers 1982).

15. The CPD method was used.

in the EC calculation, the difference must be maintained when the EC countries are put into the context of OECD comparisons or worldwide comparisons. The strong support of the fixity principle by Eurostat was based on concern that the production of different relative standings for real GDP per capita for the different pairs of countries would create difficulties for the political and administrative uses of the ICP results.

To implement the fixity principle, UNSO used the results of the sixty-country Geary-Khamis calculation to obtain the total GDP for each region. These totals were then distributed among the member countries in each region in proportion to their shares indicated by the within-region comparisons. Each country's GDP was distributed to "condensed categories" (akin to the "summary" categories of phases 1–3) and twenty-three additional aggregations. This distribution was based on each country's distribution as produced by the intraregional comparison. This method of integrating the results of different regional comparisons (the "GDP consistency" method) has the virtue of comparability for the quantities of GDP at world prices (international dollars). However, it has the disadvantage that for a basic heading or condensed category, the sum of the entries for the countries in the region will not add up to the figure for the region as produced by the worldwide comparison. For these subdivisions of GDP, the results are not comparable for countries in different regions because they are based on regional rather than world prices. Very large distortions, some in excess of 100 percent, have been found in relative quantities for basic headings (Drechsler 1988). The alternative takes the worldwide quantity calculation for each basic heading or condensed category for each region and distributes it among the countries of the region in accordance with their shares in the results of the worldwide comparison (the "category-control-total" method). This method produces comparability for each subcomponent of GDP (food, etc.), but the components of GDP will not add up to the GDP total estimated directly at world prices.

The effect of the fixity rule has been somewhat mitigated by an agreement allowing international organizations to make available at their discretion the price, quantity, and expenditure data for the basic headings. These are not affected by the fixity rule. Thus, users are able to aggregate for themselves the phase 4 and 5 comparisons at worldwide average prices. Also the restrictions imposing fixity are to be lifted about three years after publication of the first regional results. Since Eurostat has put out its results well before UNSO, the delay for comparisons at worldwide prices imposed by adherence to the fixity rule restrictions may be closer to one year than three.

The fixity principle has serious disadvantages for the worldwide comparisons. It favors within-region comparisons to the detriment of comparisons between countries in different regions. The difficulty is that a different measuring rod (i.e., a different set of relative prices) is applied to different pairs of countries. Depending on the classification of countries into regions, the Germany-Japan comparison, for example, might depend on average prices based on EC, European, Asian, and world prices, while the Germany-France comparison might be based on European prices alone, and the Germany-United States, on European, North American, and world prices.

This is not to say that regional comparisons should not be made. Their advantage is that the average prices used to value the products of the member countries are likely to be more characteristic of each country than are world average prices. Regionalization thus diminishes the tendency for the estimates of real GDP per capita to be higher in countries with price structures very different from the one used for the valuation.[16] For some purposes even binary comparisons are appropriate. If, for example, a comparison of the real GDP of the Soviet Union and the United States is desired for strategic purposes, and no other country is concerned in this context, a binary comparison has strong appeal. If on the other hand, a comparison of France and Germany is desired for a reason related to the operation of the EC, a community-wide set of average prices would be more appropriate than either an average of French and German prices or average world prices, the latter including the price structures of such diverse countries as the United States and India. For general-purpose comparisons, however, the use of world average prices seems most appropriate. It seems sensible to have both regional and worldwide comparisons wherever there is a demand for regional comparisons. It should not be impossible to persuade EC officials and politicians that the EC comparisons are best for EC purposes even though another set exists.

12.6   Extensions to Nonbenchmark Countries

The benchmark comparisons made to date or planned have covered about half of the countries of the world, including all of the populous ones outside of the socialist bloc. The missing countries are almost all less-developed countries (LDCs) or socialist countries. For many analytical purposes, the covered countries are diverse enough to provide a sample of the distribution of real per capita GDPs in the countries of the world. For some purposes, however, it is important to have income estimates for all of the countries. In this context, benchmark estimates for upwards of fifty countries are missing. While the number of countries covered by the benchmark comparisons may expand, it is unlikely that all the countries will be covered in the near future. A number of ways have been suggested to prepare estimates of comparative real GDP per capita for missing countries by means that entail a smaller ex-

16. In fact, the fixity rule makes little difference in the relative per capita GDPs of the high-income countries, but can have notable effects on a few middle- and low-income countries. This statement is based on a comparison of the results for the sixty countries of Phase 4 (1980) published by UNSO and Eurostat, which embody fixity, and the estimate of GDP obtained by summing the international dollar values of the 151 basic headings available on a UNSO tape. None of the differences for the high-income countries exceeded 4.5 percent, while the difference was 5 to 10 percent for twelve other countries and over 10 percent for eight others (the largest difference was 21 percent).

penditure of resources (see Heston 1973). These various approaches are described and illustrated here.

The method closest to the benchmark studies, the "reduced information" approach, carries out price comparisons on the basis of a much smaller sample of specifications. The full set of the benchmark price comparisons, the rationale goes, contains some that are redundant; that is, their deletion would not alter the result (Ruggles 1977). The reduced information estimates would be based on the core of post-adjustment price comparisons that will yield approximately the same estimate as the benchmark comparisons.

Several other methods are still less costly, since they involve no field work at all. These methods, known as "short-cut comparisons," depend on an estimating equation using the data for the countries that have been included in benchmark studies to form a relationship between real GDP per capita and variables that are widely available for both benchmark and nonbenchmark countries. In some versions the independent variables are physical indicators such as steel consumption, and in others they are monetary in character, such as exchange-rate converted GDP, or prices used in adjusting cost-of-living allowances for personnel stationed in different countries. In all of these methods the estimate for each nonbenchmark country is obtained by plugging into the estimating equation the values of the independent variables for that country.

Equations based on benchmark countries that were developing countries did not yield predictions of benchmark results superior to those derived from equations based on all the countries; only the latter predictions are reported here. (Virtually all nonbenchmark countries were in the developing category.) The equations were used to estimate domestic absorption, and GDP was then obtained by adding the net foreign balance, which was converted to dollars via the exchange rate (see Summers and Heston 1984).

12.6.1 Reduced Information Estimates

The reduced information method, although considerably cheaper than the full benchmark survey method, still involves substantial cost and thus has been infrequently attempted. A major effort in this area was an experimental study of thirteen developing countries by Sultan Ahmad of the World Bank (Ahmad, 1988). Ahmad began by experimenting with ICP Phase 3 data to find out the minimum number of price comparisons which could satisfactorily explain the observed values of real GDP per capita in the benchmark countries. He identified a set of such price comparisons for 126 individual products in about 30 categories of GDP expenditures. Ahmad's subsequent estimates for the countries in his experiment, summarized in table 12.2, range from 68 percent of the benchmark estimate to 103 percent. The mean absolute deviation is around 10 percent. There is a tendency for the deviation from the benchmark to be smaller for the higher-income countries. In every case the reduced information estimate is closer to the ICP benchmark than is the

Table 12.2   Estimates of Per Capita GDP by Reduced Information Method Compared
                    with Benchmark Estimates, 1980 (U.S. = 100)

	Exchange Rate Converted (1)	Reduced Information (2)	Benchmark (3)	Ratio to Benchmark	
				Exchange Rate Converted (1) ÷ (3) (4)	Reduced Information (2) ÷ (3) (5)
Costa Rica	18.5	21.3	27.2	.68	.78
Dominican Republic	10.4	15.2	16.8	.62	.90
Guatemala	9.5	14.4	17.6	.54	.82
India	2.1	4.9	5.3	.40	.92
Indonesia	4.3	8.7	9.6	.45	.91
Kenya	3.7	5.4	6.0	.62	.90
Morocco	7.7	11.0	10.7	.72	1.03
Nigeria	8.7	6.9	7.5	1.16	.92
Panama	15.9	23.5	23.9	.67	.98
Senegal	4.6	4.9	7.2	.64	.68
Tanzania	2.2	3.0	3.2	.69	.94
Tunisia	11.9	16.9	16.9	.70	1.00
Zimbabwe	6.3	7.2	7.8	.81	.92
United States	100.0	100.0	100.0	1.00	1.00

Source: Ahmad (1988).

exchange-rate converted GDP. Ahmad finds his reduced information estimates also come closer to matching the benchmark estimates than short-cut
estimates produced by Summers and Heston (1988) using nominal GDP per
capita and openness as independent variables.

The experiment seems to support further exploration of reduced information methods. It should be investigated whether they work well for particularly small or poor countries for which benchmark studies cannot be readily
carried out or for which the costs would be too high.

12.6.2   Short-cut Methods: Physical Indicators

There is no very strong theory underlying the physical indicator approach,
although lurking in the background is the idea of Engel curves (that is, for
most goods, consumption is correlated with income).

In the physical indicator approach, the relationship between real GDP per
capita and each of a score or more of indicators is examined (see, e.g., Beckerman 1966, and U.N. Economic Commission for Europe 1980). One tactic
is to screen the indicators to identify those with high simple correlations with
real GDP per capita. Then alternative combinations of three or four of these
physical indicators with high simple correlations are correlated with real GDP
per capita to find the combination which yields the highest $\bar{R}^2$. (The multicollinearity among the indicators is so high that no more than a few variables add

to the degree of explanation.) An alternative tactic is to feed all the indicators for the set of benchmark countries into the computer and to allow the computer to perform a stepwise regression specifying a cut-off when added variables no longer reduce the unexplained variance by a stipulated amount. A disadvantage of the stepwise regression method is that the results are influenced by the order in which the variables are introduced into the regression.[17]

12.6.3   Short-cut Methods: Monetary Indicators

Another set of short-cut methods uses monetary indicators; that is, those relating to nominal or exchange-rate converted GDP. Additional variables may include openness, price isolation, money growth, and the trade balance (Kravis, Heston, and Summers 1978b, Kravis and Lipsey 1983, Clague 1986). Education and shares of minerals in GDP are sometimes included in this approach, as they are in the physical indicator method.

The systematic relationship found to exist between real PPP-converted GDP (r) and nominal (exchange-rate converted) GDP (n) provides the rationale for the monetary indicator approach. The coefficient in this relationship is not 1; prices are high in rich countries because services are relatively expensive. That is either because the rich countries' margin of superiority in productivity is lower in services than in goods, or because labor is expensive in rich countries and services are relatively labor-intensive, making services expensive (Kravis and Lipsey 1983, Bhagwati 1984). This circumstance, together with the fact that traded-goods prices tend to be closer to uniformity in different countries, creates higher price levels for GDP in rich countries. The consequence is that the ratio of r to n falls as n increases. Although the line of causation presumably runs from r to n, r is treated as a function of n for purposes of extrapolation.

12.6.4   Short-cut Methods: Price Indicators

Many multinational business enterprises and international organizations have employees stationed in different countries with different price levels and encounter the need to maintain a system of "post-adjustment" allowances to equalize the real incomes of personnel of equal status in the headquarters locations with those stationed elsewhere. This work often involves a rather elaborate system of price comparisons. The U.S. Department of State makes price comparisons for about 150 cities (U.S. Department of Labor 1981) and the United Nations for about 125 cities (U.N. 1980). Private organizations also

---

17. A further difficulty is that many indicators are not available for all of the countries in the benchmark sample. Indicators that have a large number of missing observations are dropped. For the remaining cases, it is possible to run separate regressions for the benchmark countries in which all of the indicators are present and for those in which all but one, all but two, or all but three are present. For each non benchmark country, per capita GDP is estimated from the equations with the largest number of independent variables available for that country. Thus, in this procedure the estimating equation used for real GDP per capita varies from one country to another.

produce comparisons for a large number of locations. These price comparisons may be treated as proxy PPPs in an estimating equation for the real domestic absorption of benchmark countries. Estimates for nonbenchmark countries may then be derived by inserting their comparative prices as shown in the post-adjustment data. The assumption underlying this approach is that the difference is the same everywhere between the national price level and the price level encountered by foreign personnel dwelling in the capital or another leading city for professional or business reasons. Experiments with alternative sources of post-adjustment price comparisons showed that they produced very similar results. For brevity and simplicity, we report here only on the results using the U.N. data.

12.6.5 A Comparison of the Results of the Short-cut Experiments

In table 12.3, some results of shortcut methods are presented; the shortcut estimates are expressed as ratios of the benchmark estimates. For comparative purposes, the exchange-rate conversions are also presented. Underlying equations appear in the appendix, table 12A.1.

Table 12.3   Predictions of LDCs 1980 Real GDP Per Capita by Various Short-Cut Methods

| Set of Countries upon which Regressions Are Based | Estimates Produced for Developing Countries in the Opposite Set as Ratios to Benchmark Estimates | | |
| | Range | | Mean Absolute Deviation |
	Maximum	Minimum	
I. *Physical Indicators*			
Odd-numbered	1.811	.313	.213
Even-numbered	1.771	.737	.183
II. *Price Indicators*			
Odd-numbered	1.335	.714	.145
Even-numbered	1.459	.682	.102
III. *Monetary Indicators*			
Odd-numbered	1.516	.698	.164
Even-numbered	1.574	.571	.142
IV. *Exchange Rate Converted*			
Odd-numbered	1.291	.279	.294
Even-numbered	1.323	.223	.318

Source: See appendix table 12A.1.
Note: The phase 4 countries were arrayed according to increasing real GDP per capita as measured in the benchmark study and were divided into two sets (odd- and even-numbered countries). For the countries in each set, a regression equation was estimated with per capita domestic absorption as the dependent variable and the various indicators in I, II, and III as the independent variables. (In some equations, data were not available for all countries.) Each equation was then used to "predict" the 1980 real GDP per capita (adding the net foreign balance) for the developing countries in the opposite set. The "predictions" are compared with the benchmark estimates in the three columns of the table. The figures in IV are exchange-rate–converted per capita GDPs.

The basic procedure was to array the developing countries in the 1980 (Phase 4) comparisons in order of PPP-converted per capita GDP, and to use each half of the sample (odd ranks and even ranks) to predict a 1980 estimate for the countries in the other half. In this very preliminary comparison of methods, the price indicator approach appears to produce marginally better results than the monetary approach, and both are better than the physical indicators. The price indicator method has the advantage over the monetary approach that it is not dependent on exchange-rates and related prices. Its predictions are on the average within 12 percent of the benchmark estimates, although the range is from predictions 46 percent above the benchmark to predictions as much as 32 percent below.

All the short-cut estimates clearly outperform the exchange-rate conversions; the latter are characterized by mean deviations of 30 percent and understatements of relative GDPs by more than 70 percent.

12.7   Extensions to Other Years

The availability of benchmark studies for quinquennial years leaves open the question of estimates for the in-between years. Not every benchmark country participates in every benchmark year, and the need for extrapolating the available benchmark estimates to other years, benchmark and nonbenchmark, arises in these cases too.

A rough and ready extrapolation is possible of the benchmark-year estimate for real GDP per capita relative to that of the numeraire country. The benchmark-year real GDP per capita for the country and the numeraire country are simply multiplied by the ratio of extrapolation-year to benchmark-year real per capita GDP from national data. An alternative procedure is to extrapolate the PPP of the given country and divide the result into the extrapolation-year current price GDP per capita; the resulting estimate in dollars may be put in index-number form by dividing by the per capita GDP of the United States in current (extrapolation-year) dollars.

The disadvantage of these simple procedures is that the growth rate in the given country's GDP between the benchmark year and the extrapolation year is measured using the relative prices of that country, whereas the growth rate of the numeraire country GDP is measured using its (different) relative prices.

At the other extreme, one can envision extrapolating each price from the benchmark year to the extrapolation year, recalculating the PPPs for the basic headings, and using these PPPs in conjunction with the extrapolation-year expenditure breakdown, to produce a Geary-Khamis calculation. This would be very close to producing a new benchmark study. If the PPP for each basic heading rather than each price were extrapolated, differences among countries' price structures would still have an impact, but it would be confined to the influences within the basic headings. For combining the basic headings, the average price structure would be used. The extrapolations can be made to obtain the comparisons in either current-year or benchmark-year international prices.

A question that remains is the time span over which extrapolations can be made without introducing very substantial differences from benchmark estimates. The implicit assumption in the scheme for quinquennial estimates is that a five-year period is not too long. As experience in benchmark comparisons accumulates it will be possible to determine whether this or a longer interval is feasible.

An alternative being followed by the EC is to do benchmark comparisons segment by segment over a three- or five-year cycle. Benchmark-type comparisons might be made for food in one year, other consumer nondurables the next year, and so forth. Extrapolated values would be filled in for those components not covered in the pricing of that year. This has the merit of integrating ICP data with the price and quantity indexes and national-accounts work of the participating countries. It is relevant to observe here that the work on the ICP by many developing countries has proved valuable in strengthening their domestic statistical systems. The disadvantage of complete comparisons at five-year or longer intervals is that institutional memories are short. Studies made five years apart may require a great deal of learning all over again. Continuity might help domestic statistical work as well as international comparisons.

A set of international comparisons of real per capita products and of price levels for over 130 countries annually from 1950 to 1988 has been offered by Robert Summers and Alan Heston (1985, 1991). Using the breakdown of total GDP per capita into consumption, government, capital formation, and the net foreign balance, they extrapolate benchmark-year comparisons backwards and forwards to other years in order to derive estimates in current prices of each year, as well as in 1980 international prices.[18] They show breakdowns for consumption, investment, and government both in current prices and 1980 prices and also in the price level for each of these components. (Price level is the PPP divided by the exchange rate.) The data for 1980 are printed out in a table, and data for all years are made available in the form of diskettes.[19]

A problem of consistency arises in the Summers-Heston effort for countries for which there have been two or more benchmark comparisons. Consistency requires that:

$$\frac{y_{t+5}}{y_t \cdot g} = 1$$

---

18. For some users of these comparisons, presentation of the original benchmark data in the tables would also have been valuable. The omission of own-country growth rates is not a disadvantage, because they can be readily computed from widely available summaries of the national-accounts data of different countries (e.g., IMF, *International Financial Statistics*).

19. For an analysis based on a different concept of world prices, see Bhagwati and Hansen (1973).

where y_t is the per capita GDP (in current international prices) of a given country relative to the numeraire country in the year t (say 1975); $y_t +_5$ is the same for a benchmark five years later (1980); and g is the growth rate of the given country relative to that of the numeraire country between t and $t+5$, as obtained from national-accounts data.

Summers and Heston achieved consistency by an ingenious method that first measures the deviation from consistency and then decomposes it into the amounts attributable to y_t, y_{t+5}, and g. On this basis an adjustment factor is derived for each of the three elements.

The reconciliations alter some of the benchmark estimates to a notable degree; the largest decline in a 1980 benchmark is about 8 percent, and the largest increase about 9 percent. On average, however, the ups and downs virtually cancel out.

A limitation of these calculations—unavoidable without a great deal of work with each country's national accounts that would often require data not in the public domain—is that g is based on a mixture of domestic and international prices. The reason is that for practical reasons (the unavailability of price indexes) the extrapolation of y_t in 1980 has to be done, not for 150 benchmark components, or even for 35 summary categories, but for a breakdown of GDP into only four major subdivisions. For consumption, for example, the extrapolation is based on each country's own GDP consumption deflator, embodying the country's own prices and weights for the goods and services that make up its consumption total. More generally, each of the four major subdivisions receives an international price relative to the other three. But the extrapolation necessary to prepare the inputs of PPPs of the Geary-Khamis aggregation is carried out with a purely domestic index. Furthermore, not only is g affected by the intermingling of domestic and international prices, but so are the adjustments made to the benchmark estimates. Estimates for the later benchmark years are extrapolated backward to measure the inconsistency from the earlier benchmark year, and the earlier year estimates are extrapolated forward to obtain a second equally meritorious measure of the inconsistency. Then an average of the two is taken. This process introduces ambiguities about the date of the price structure that is being applied.

Even if this problem were to be corrected, the massaging of the benchmark comparisons and of the growth rates to make them consistent with one another further diminishes the transparency of the prices that are used to evaluate the quantities. The price structures of the benchmark year and of the domestic deflators—representing different things—are meshed together.

For some users, the advantage of having consistency between time-to-time and place-to-place data compensates for the ambiguity in what is being measured. For others, growth rates based on international prices may be so attractive that they are willing to overlook the limited role that international prices actually play in the calculations.

Our view is that the best general-purpose estimates of growth rates are those derived directly from the national accounts—from domestic price deflators of the countries. They have relatively clear conceptual underpinning. (They are, to be sure, made less comparable from country to country by the use of different base years.) Similarly, we think that the best estimates of real GDP per capita levels are those produced by the benchmark studies, unaltered by modifications based on a mixture of domestic and international prices.

Having said this, we add that Summers and Heston have produced the most comprehensive set of PPP-based estimates that exists; their "consistentized" data cover almost all countries and thirty-five years. As noted, their data are aimed at uses requiring consistent estimates of levels and of changes in output.

12.7.1   Growth Rates

The usual way of calculating growth rates is to take the changes in the real GDP of each country as measured using its own market basket and its own base-year prices. Thus, the growth rate of a given country measures the change in a basket of goods that is different from the basket measured by the growth rate of the numeraire country; also different (price) weights are assigned to overlapping goods in the two countries. Such comparisons answer the question, "How much change has there been over the period in the quantity of the base (current) bundle of goods produced in country 1, compared to the change in the quantity of the different base (current) bundle produced in country 2?" Such growth rates have the merit of dealing with a basket of goods that reflects the preferences of purchasers of final product in one of the years being compared. (In the language of the ICP, they have the desirable property of characteristicity.) They have the drawback that an equal growth in two countries in the quantity of a given good may be counted as contributing more to aggregate growth in one country than in another.

Comparisons of growth rates based on international prices of a given year answer the question, "How much change has there been over the period of the total quantity of goods absorbed in country 1, compared to the change in the total quantity of goods absorbed in country 2, recognizing that the list of goods may be different in each situation, but valuing the goods at the same set of world average prices?" Such growth rates have the merit of treating a given increase in a given good as making the same contribution to growth in both countries. They have the drawback that the prices used may be very dissimilar from the prices of one or both of the situations.

The choice between the two approaches depends on the use to be made of the growth rates. If the purposes are closely related to welfare considerations, own-price growth rates are preferable because they are more closely related to the choices confronting the purchasers of final product in each country. If, on the other hand, the purposes are related to production, it may be argued that international price growth rates are preferable. It can be claimed that the international average prices are more closely related to world opportunity costs;

for the world as a whole, the international prices show the rates of transformation of different goods.

12.8 Future ICP Work

Phase 6 (reference date 1990) is encountering difficulties because a number of the binary comparisons which were to be used to link regions appear to be languishing. There is a great danger that Phase 6 will be a series of regional comparisons without enough links to produce systematic worldwide comparisons. A way should be found that does not require large resources to revive the prospects for worldwide comparisons.

One possibility is to modify the comparison strategy from a core-country approach to a core-commodity approach. The U.N. Statistical Office would develop a core-commodity list consisting of items found in most if not all regions (e.g., eggs, sandals). Countries would be asked to provide prices for as many as possible of the core items. In addition, each country would price items that were specific to its own region. Between the two lists of specifications, there would be an adequate number to make possible price comparisons for each basic heading. The price comparisons between the regions would be based on the common core. It would not be necessary for every country to price every core commodity. The price comparisons between countries within a region would be based on a combination of core commodities and commodities found mainly or only in the region.[20]

As already suggested, a consequence of the reliance on regions to organize much of the data in phases 4 and 5 has been the emergence of some differences in methods, although the broad strategy of the ICP and most of its detailed methods were adhered to.

The differences are greater than they would have been had UNSO the resources to coordinate the work of the different regions. The differences will grow larger unless UNSO takes a more extensive role. U.N. experts on consumer goods pricing, capital goods, and construction should attend at least one of the planning meetings of every regional group. The UNSO experts could encourage the regions to include some specifications that could be matched in other regions and to provide UNSO with data to enable it to do the worldwide comparisons by a standard set of methods. Continuing efforts should be made to reach a world consensus on the problem points, but as long as the regions supply UNSO with the standard data-set, they should be free to use differing methods in their own regional comparisons.

---

20. CPDs could be calculated for each region and used to fill in missing prices in the regional set. Then a second-stage CPD could be calculated, covering all included countries, each with a complete set of the prices used in its region. The PPPs derived from the second-stage CPD could be the inputs for a Geary-Khamis calculation for all the countries. Thus, advantage would be taken of the similarity of price structures within regions to cope with the missing-price problem, but the desired properties of multilateral comparisons would be retained. A single set of international prices would be used to value each country's quantities (income).

Another important role that a U.N. presence at planning meetings might fill is to discourage any tendency to influence the results by manipulating the inputs. An objective outside presence in the course of data collection and processing might further diminish this possibility.

In addition to the benchmark work, there is a need for more research into methods of extending the benchmark estimates to nonbenchmark countries.

12.9   Conclusion

A system of international comparisons of income and of the purchasing power of currencies is now in place, covering most countries and currencies for the period 1950–85. Estimates, which are on an annual basis and include breakdowns for consumption, capital formation, and government, rest on a relatively small number of benchmark comparisons. The latter include nearly eighty countries, some for single years (the earliest of which is 1970) and others for as many as five years (the latest of which is 1985). The benchmark estimates are based primarily on price comparisons, which have been produced by a worldwide cooperative effort involving many countries and international governmental agencies.

The income comparisons relate to GDP as defined in the U.N. System of National Accounts. They are derived by applying a set of world average prices to the quantities composing each country's national absorption of final goods (and net claims against foreigners). Given this approach, the benchmark results are not very sensitive to plausible alternative treatments of certain methodological issues, to the resolution of which theory gives little guidance. ("Plausible" alternatives include those seriously considered or adopted by UNSO, Eurostat, ECE, or OECD.)

We conclude that margins of approximately 20 to 25 percent are generous estimates of the outside limits of uncertainty in the benchmark estimates for low-income countries originating from the factors we have examined. The margins narrow as per capita income rises; for high-income countries, they may be around 7 percent.

If the Geary-Khamis formula is not regarded as uniquely suitable for the comparisons, the results will be further affected by the formulation of the question to be answered and the appropriate aggregation formula.

Even if these estimates of the range of uncertainty prove too small, they have to be weighed against the errors involved in the use of exchange-rate conversions, the only alternative to conversions via PPPs. For the very poorest countries the PPP conversions yield estimates of per capita GDP that are more than three times the exchange-rate converted figure; for the group of developing countries the average ratio is over two times. The exchange-rate converted figures are farther from the lowest PPP-converted estimates of real GDP per capita that emerge from the considerations concerning uncertainties.

The uncertainties of PPP conversions are inherent in international comparisons. They can be reduced by the investment of further resources, especially by extending benchmark estimates to more countries (particularly low-income ones) or years. Time may bring further consensus on methodological questions and narrow the uncertainty range. But it is unrealistic to expect that real product estimates will ever have the illusory certainty of exchange-rate converted estimates. Exchange rates, however, can be justified as converters only if they reflect the relative purchasing power of currencies better than the ICP PPPs do. The current literature on exchange-rate determination, with its stress on capital movements and expectations, and the recent volatility of exchange rates accompanied by relatively sluggish movements of domestic prices, make clear the inadequacy of exchange rates as PPPs. Users of real GDP comparisons can either delude themselves with unequivocal but wrong—often far wrong—and biased estimates of real GDP based on exchange rates, or accept the fact that the closest we can come to comparative GDPs involves uncertainties about the exact figures.

The future of ICP estimates appears assured in Europe, particularly in the EC. In other regions, prospects vary, but as of mid-1990 the outlook for systematic worldwide comparisons for Phase 6 (1990) does not look bright. It will take a renewed impetus, which in the circumstances can only be provided by UNSO and the World Bank, to establish an ICP with comprehensive coverage on an ongoing basis.

There has been an international effort, stretching over the better part of the half-century, to develop comparability in the national accounts of the various countries (i.e., the SNA). It would be ironic to lose the momentum that has been gained with great effort toward the final step in establishing comparability—the translation of own-currency GDPs into comparable measures of real income.

Appendix

Table 12A.1   Equations Used to Generate Predictions Summarized in Table 12.3

I. *Physical Indicators*

A. DA_{pc} = .763 + .193 (calorie intake p.c.) + 1 .698 (life expectancy)
    (0.36)   (1.56)   (2.82)

               + .225 (energy consumption p.c.) − .429 (% of labor force in agriculture)
               (2.95)   (3.90)

$$\bar{R}^2 = .95$$

B. DA_{pc} = − 3.899 + .543 (calorie intake p.c.) + .201 (secondary school)
    (1.42)   (1.74)   (2.43)

               + 1.501 (life expectancy) + .194 (energy consumption p.c.)
                (3.21)   (3.67)

               − .237 (% of labor force in agriculture)
                (4.17)

$$\bar{R}^2 = .97$$

II. *Price Indicators*

A. DA_{pc} = 2.18 + .744 (DA_{UN}) − .221 (D_A)
    (8.46) (23.16)   (2.44)

$$\bar{R}^2 = .97$$

B. DA_{pc} = 2.448 + .742 (DA_{UN}) − .397 (D_A)
    (11.25) (27.02)   (5.44)

$$\bar{R}^2 = .98$$

III. *Monetary Indicators*

A. DA_{pc} = 1.305 + .691 (n) − .036 (openness) − .442 (D_A)
    (9.79) (21.17)   (0 .54)   (4.64)

$$\bar{R}^2 = .97$$

B. DA_{pc} = 1.641 + .620 (n) + .129 (openness) − .649 (D_A)
    (12.75) (19.61)   (1 .61)   (6.93)

$$\bar{R}^2 = .97$$

Notes: The predictions for developing-country real GDP per capita that are generated by these equations are summarized in table 12.3. The regressions are based on all the Phase 4 countries and are in log form; *t*-statistics are in parentheses. A = equations for odd-numbered countries; B = equations for even-numbered countries. The variables are on a per capita basis where appropriate (e.g., energy consumption, domestic absorption, etc.): DA_{pc} = domestic absorption in international prices, from benchmark studies; DA_{UN} = own currency domestic absorption ÷ PPP from U.N. post-adjustment data; D_A = dummy variable with value of 1 for African countries; O for others; n = exchange-rate–converted GDP per capita; openness = exports plus imports/GDP. The prediction of real GDP per capita was obtained for each country by adding the net foreign balance to the estimate of DA_{pc} produced by the equation. *t*-ratios are in parentheses.

References

Ahmad, Sultan. 1988. International Real Income Comparisons with Reduced Information. In *World Comparisons of Incomes, Prices, and Product,* ed. J. Salazar-Carrillo and D. S. Prasada Rao. North Holland: Elsevier Science Publishers.

Beckerman, Wilfred. 1966. *International Comparisons of Real Incomes.* Paris: Development Center, Organisation for Economic Cooperation and Development.

Bhagwati, Jagdish N. 1984. Why Are Services Cheaper in Poor Countries? *Economic Journal* 94(374): 279–86.

Bhagwati, Jagdish N., and Bent Hansen. 1973. Should Growth Rates be Evaluated at International Prices? In *Development and Planning,* ed. J. Bhagwati and Richard S. Eckaus.

Clague, Christopher. 1986. Short Cut Estimates of Real Income. *Review of Income and Wealth* (September): 313–31.

Drechsler, Laszlo. 1988. The Regionalization of and Other Recent Developments in the U.N. International Comparison Project. In *World Comparisons of Incomes, Prices, and Product,* ed. J. Salazar-Carillo and D. S. Prasada Rao. North Holland: Elsevier Science Publishers.

Gilbert, Milton, and Irving B. Kravis. 1954. *An International Comparison of National Products and the Purchasing Power of Currencies: A Study of the United States, the United Kingdom, France, Germany, and Italy.* Paris: Organisation for European Economic Cooperation.

Heston, Alan W. 1973. A Comparison of Some Short-Cut Methods of Estimating Real Product Per Capita. *Review of Income and Wealth* 19(1): 79–104.

Hill, T. Peter. 1977. On Goods and Services. *Review of Income and Wealth* 23(4): 315–38.

———. 1981. Multilateral Measurements of Purchasing Power and Real GDP. Report prepared for the Statistical Office of the European Communities and the Economic Commission for Europe. Luxembourg.

Intersecretariat Working Group on the International Comparison Programme. 1989. Report of the Meeting of the Intersecretariat Working Group on the International Comparison Programme (ICP). July. New York.

Isenman, Paul. 1980. Inter-Country Comparisons of "Real" (PPP) Incomes: Revised Estimates and Unresolved Questions. *World Development* 8(1).

Kravis, Irving B. 1984. Comparative Studies of National Incomes and Prices. *Journal of Economic Literature* 22 (March).

Kravis, Irving B., Alan W. Heston, and Robert Summers. 1978a. *International Comparisons of Real Product and Purchasing Power.* Baltimore: Johns Hopkins University Press.

———. 1978b. Real GDP Per Capita for More Than One Hundred Countries. *Economic Journal* 88(350): 215–42.

———. 1982. *World Product and Income: International Comparisons of Real Gross Product.* Baltimore: Johns Hopkins University Press.

Kravis, Irving B., Zoltan Kenessey, Alan W. Heston and Robert Summers. 1975. *A System of International Comparisons of Gross Product and Purchasing Power,* Baltimore: Johns Hopkins University Press.

Kravis, Irving B., and Robert E. Lipsey. 1983. Toward an Explanation of National Price Levels. Princeton Studies in International Finance, no. 52 (November).

Krijnse-Locker, Hugo. 1984. On the Estimation of Purchasing Power Parities on the Basic Heading Level. *Review of Income and Wealth* 30(2): 135–52.

Maddison, Angus, and Bart van Ark. 1987. The International Comparison of Real Output, Purchasing Power, and Labor Productivity in Manufacturing Industries: A

Pilot Study for Brazil, Mexico and the USA for 1975. Institute for Economic Research, Faculty of Economics, University of Groningen. Typescript.

Paige, D., and G. Bombach. 1959. *A Comparison of National Output and Productivity of the United Kingdom and the United States*. Paris: Organisation for European Economic Cooperation.

Ruggles, Richard. 1977. *The Wholesale Price Index—Review and Evaluation*. Report of Council on Wage and Price Stability (June). Washington, D.C.

Statistical Office of the European Communities. 1977. *Comparisons in Real Values of the Aggregates of ESA, 1975*. Luxembourg: European Economic Communities.

Statistical Office of the European Communities, Organisation for Economic Cooperation and Development, United Nations Statistical Office, *Expert Group on ICP Methodology*, June 14–16, 1989) Paris; and *Report of the Expert Group on ICP Methodology*, (June 6–10, 1988) Luxembourg.

Summers, Robert. 1973. International Comparisons Based upon Incomplete Data. *Review of Income and Wealth* 19(1): 1–16.

Summers, Robert, and Alan W. Heston. 1984. Improved International Comparisons of Real Product and Its Composition, 1950–80. *Review of Income and Wealth* series 30, no. 2 (June): 207–62.

————. 1988. A New Set of International Comparisons of Real Product and Price Levels: Estimates for 130 Countries, 1950–1985. *Review of Income and Wealth* (series 34, (March): 1–25.

————. 1991. The Penn World Tables (Mark V): An Expanded Set of International Comparisons, 1950–88. *Quarterly Journal of Economics* (May): 327–68.

Summers, Robert, Irving B. Kravis, and Alan W. Heston. 1980. International Comparisons of Real Product and Its Composition, 1950–77. *Review of Income and Wealth* 26(1): 19–66.

United Nations. *Monthly Bulletin of Statistics*, 1975 (August), 1980 (September).

U.N. Economic Commission for Europe. 1980. *Economic Bulletin for Europe* 31(2)

U.N. Statistical Office. 1968. *A System of National Accounts*. Studies in Methods, series F, no. 2, rev. 3.

U.S. Department of Labor. 1981. United States Department of State Indexes of Living and Costs Abroad and Quarters Allowances. Report 646 (April).

Ward, Michael. 1985. *Purchasing Power Parities and Real Expenditures in the OECD*. Paris: OECD.

————. 1989. The Reliability of Estimates of Per Capita Income. Paper prepared for conference of the International Association for Research in Income and Wealth. August 20–26.

Comment   Alan V. Deardorff

What a pleasure it has been to read this paper. I have had a passing awareness of the International Comparison Program, of course, for many years. But I have never had occasion to make direct use of the ICP data, as many others here have, and I therefore never came to learn in detail how it had all been put together. This paper does a fine job of introducing the ICP, and I would have

Alan V. Deardorff is professor of economics and public policy at the University of Michigan.

learned a great deal from it for that reason alone. The full picture of the project can be seen in the various reports, mainly by Kravis, Heston, and Summers, that are referred to in the paper. I will comment mostly on the current work dealing with robustness.

One of the unintended messages of the paper, of course, is that the ICP has entailed a huge amount of painstaking work, over many years and by many individuals and agencies. I can't imagine anyone voluntarily getting into such a project knowing in advance how much work it would be and the difficulties and complications that would arise. Were it not for the fact that the authors have been involved in other projects as well that are of daunting size and complexity, I would have assumed that they did it unintentionally. However, since this is their second paper in this conference reporting on such work, I have to conclude that they are economists of exceptional courage, or perhaps masochism.

But I must be careful, or I will give the impression that this is a paper that requires an equal dose of courage or masochism to read. That is not the case at all. The massively detailed body of data that the ICP has produced over the years is very much behind the scene here. The paper itself, based on the various Kravis, Heston, and Summers reports, is a wonderfully careful and thoughtful discussion of the methodological issues that have come up along the way. It is clear that over the years the authors have confronted numerous problems with the data and its interpretation, as well as conceptual problems as to how to make valid international comparisons. They share with us here what these problems have been and how they have been resolved.

Finally, and this is the unique contribution of the Kravis and Lipsey paper presented today, they have been able in a surprising number of cases to quantify the limits of error that may have been introduced by the choices they have made or been forced to make. In a conference that deals with the limitations of available data, the paper is a prototype of how these limitations should be acknowledged and evaluated in assessing the results that are based upon those data. We would all do well to follow their example in this regard, though few of us will have two decades of research on a single topic to draw upon.

This conference has dealt primarily with issues of data, and seems therefore to be concerned primarily with empirical issues rather than theoretical ones. Yet the thoughtful approach of this paper shows, I think, that the very inadequacies of the data provide a need for more careful theoretical research as well. The ICP staff has shown wisdom and ingenuity in dealing with these inadequacies, without apparently much guidance from the theoretical literature. Those who follow will do well simply to follow their example, but it would be useful if these issues could be dealt with in more general terms, so that empirical research using inadequate data could in the future be guided by general principles rather than have to develop solutions to problems as they arise, as Kravis and Lipsey have done here. I would therefore like to enter a plea for both economic and econometric theorists to devote more of their theoretical attention to the problems of inadequate data and the appropriate methods for dealing with them.

Edward Leamer, in his comments on Keith Maskus's paper, gives us a list of many of the problems that arise with data, especially in the international context. It is fascinating to see how many of these problems have come up in the International Comparison Program and been dealt with there.

Consider first the problem of missing data. The ICP is plagued by missing data at the most basic level, since many products are not produced in common across all countries. Yet prices of these goods must nonetheless be compared across countries. In their other paper on prices, Kravis and Lipsey mentioned the Country-Product Dummy (CPD) method of constructing missing prices. This method was actually developed by Robert Summers specifically for use in the ICP.

The ICP produces a full comparison of prices and real outputs only for selected years and countries. This leaves as missing data the values for the intervening years and excluded countries. The ICP has used a variety of methods that are detailed in the paper for filling in these missing values. Like the CPD method for constructing missing prices, these methods also are based on regressions of known values on various explanatory variables that are somewhat ad hoc but nonetheless seem to do a decent job of predicting the missing values.

What I would like to see is a more general treatment of this problem of missing data. I understand that the econometrics literature has dealt with how best to perform estimation when there are missing observations, but this literature is directed at perfecting the estimation, not at replacing the missing observations themselves. Yet it strikes me that there must be some general guidance that could be provided on this issue, and that very likely such an analysis would lead one to perform very much the sorts of calculations that Kravis and Lipsey have in the ICP.

My point is not that this kind of analysis is necessarily needed for the ICP; it has done a more-than-adequate job of dealing with these issues. Rather, there are many areas of empirical international economics (and no doubt of empirical economics more generally) where missing data are a recurring problem, and a systematic methodology for filling them in would be very useful. I know, for example, that in the work Robert Stern and I do with computational general equilibrium models, missing data are a constant source of difficulty.

Edward Leamer also listed the problems caused for international data by exchange-rate gyrations and the more general issue of noncomparability across countries of international data. These, of course, are precisely the problems that the ICP has dealt with all along. Most of us are content to use the most readily available data, perhaps acknowledging its deficiencies, perhaps not. Kravis and Lipsey and their coauthors have confronted these problems head-on and have sought to correct them—with remarkable success!

Here, incidentally, the problem is not one of missing data, or even necessarily of bad data. Rather, it is that the data one seeks in some sense *cannot* exist. There is no uniquely correct meaning that attaches to the concept of real GDP, given that countries differ as they do in the assortments of goods and services that they produce and in the prices at which they produce them. The problems are familiar index-number problems, and so today are not a very hot topic in economic theory. Yet the contortions that have been endured in dealing with them in the ICP indicate to me that the conceptual problems have not all been solved. The ICP relies on something called the Geary-Khamis method of aggregation, for example, and Kravis and Lipsey make a compelling case in its favor in terms of various plausible and apparently desirable properties that it possesses. Yet I would have thought that this kind of problem could be addressed from a theoretical standpoint that, though perhaps not conclusive, could nonetheless shed light on what is and is not being measured.

I'll conclude with a question for the authors that may not be fair, since it deals with something that was not in the paper. One of the most important findings of the ICP is that developing-country GDPs are routinely underestimated by converting at nominal exchange rates. This means that the nominal values of LDC currencies are typically quite a bit below their PPP levels. This finding intrigued me because I thought I had understood LDC currencies to be typically overvalued, not undervalued. If the findings were true, it would merely underscore the well-known inadequacy of PPP as a guide to equilibrium exchange rates. Yet the authors told me that they doubted that it *was* true. Indeed, they said that, though not reported in this paper, the ICP has found that even traded-goods prices in LDCs are lower at prevailing exchange rates than comparable prices in developed countries, and that the result for real GDPs is therefore not just a reflection of exceptionally cheap nontraded goods, as I had supposed.

Now this surprises me a great deal. For whether or not LDC exchange rates are overvalued, it is certainly the case that most LDCs have high barriers to trade, both tariffs and nontariff barriers, and it is my impression that they also have frequent subsidies to exports as well. Both of these will lead to the prices of imported and exported goods being higher within the LDCs than on world markets. If indeed the prices of domestically produced tradable goods for domestic absorption are lower in these countries than abroad, then it must surely suggest another source of noncomparability.

In computable general equilibrium (CGE) modeling we routinely find that traded goods must be modeled as imperfect substitutes for apparently comparable traded goods from abroad. Otherwise it is impossible to replicate the data on the amounts and price-responsiveness of trade. I had supposed that this imperfect substitutability, which is usually modeled via the Armington assumption of goods that are differentiated by country of origin, was forced upon us by our levels of aggregation. But if the ICP finds such price discrepancies even at the very disaggregated level where they do their price comparisons, then I wonder if in fact the goods produced in LDCs are not after all rather imperfect substitutes for their developed-country counterparts.

If so, and if this by any chance means that the LDC products are of lower quality overall than other goods, then the conclusion that LDC real GDPs are understated may be suspect.

Concluding Observations

Robert E. Baldwin
Jack Bame
Ralph C. Bryant

Robert E. Baldwin

In my comments, I should like to focus on a few issues of measuring international transactions; in particular, on measuring U.S. merchandise trade and on relating the data collected to other domestic and international economic variables. First, I want to emphasize the importance of collecting accurate and timely trade figures and of being able to integrate these figures with other economic and social data. Next, I will comment on the manner in which trade data are collected, as well as the frequency and detail with which they are assembled. This leads into a discussion of the comparability of trade data with other economic and social data needed for understanding the operation of the world trading system. Finally, I will briefly consider foreign trade data needs in the future and the best methods of collecting the information.

There is increasing interest on the part of both government officials and private business leaders in ways the United States can best maintain a strong competitive position in the international market for goods and services. This interest has led to all sorts of proposals for improving the U.S. competitive position, ranging from extensive government intervention in shaping the nature of production to a completely "hands-off" role for the government.

One important reason for the disparity in views as to how best to promote international competitiveness based on real comparative advantage rather than on artificial factors such as continuing government subsidies, is that we do not understand the sources of comparative advantage very well, to say nothing of their measures. For many years, international economists emphasized the role

Robert E. Baldwin is the Hilldale Professor of Economics at the University of Wisconsin-Madison and a Research Associate of the National Bureau of Economic Research.

of relative endowments of productive factors, such as capital, skilled and unskilled labor, and natural resources, in relation to the technological production
requirements for these factors, as the main basis of a country's long-run international competitive position. Empirical testing of the factor-proportions hypothesis, using the imperfect data that are available, has clearly demonstrated,
as Leamer points out, that "the main currents of international trade are well
understood in terms of a remarkably limited list of resources."[1] However, the
testing has also shown that the relationships are by no means exact ones, in
the sense that holds in a rigorous Heckscher-Ohlin model.[2]

While many investigators have suggested that there are numerous other factors shaping comparative advantage, such as increasing returns, differences in
technology, and market imperfections, especially in manufacturing, both the
inability to quantify the importance of these factors and the lack of adequate
theories explaining how they influence comparative advantage have hampered
efforts to gain a better understanding of the forces influencing a country's
international competitive position. Fortunately, there has been a breakthrough
at the theoretical level in recent years in better understanding how increasing
returns in manufacturing production can arise and how these can affect patterns of trade. What is now needed, and is already underway to some extent,
are careful investigations that can cast light on how important increasing returns are empirically in shaping comparative advantage. In other words, if we
are to understand better how increasing returns and other factors influence
international competitiveness, we need not only theoretical models that put
forth reasonable relationships between these factors and competitiveness, but
good data that will enable investigators to determine the importance of these
relationships in the real world. It is only with the understanding that comes
from the interaction between theorizing and empirical testing that one can
begin to formulate public policies that can better contribute to a country's
competitive ability.

Unfortunately for public and private officials and for researchers interested
in better understanding the forces shaping international competitiveness, the
data on foreign trade has been collected for purposes quite different from the
testing of various theories and the formulating of policies relating to international competitiveness. The main motivation for collecting import data has
been, of course, to be sure that the government collects the duty revenues
levied on imports. U.S. law requires the collection of import data on a
monthly basis by tariff item. Collection of detailed export data seems to be
legally required only quarterly; but aggregate exports and imports must be
reported monthly.

As the paper by Bruce Walter points out, there have been impressive im-

1. Edward E. Leamer, *Sources of International Comparative Advantage* (Cambridge, Mass:
MIT Press, 1984).
2. Harry P. Bowen, Edward E. Leamer, and Lea Sveikauskas, "Multicountry, Multifactor Test
of the Factor Abundance Theory," *American Economic Review* 77.5 (1987): 791–809.

provements in the quality of U.S. trade data in recent years. While increasing the degree of automation on the part of traders, exchanging data among countries, and other efforts on the part of Census and Customs are operating to improve the quality of trade data, there are some developments working in the opposite direction. As tariffs continue to fall to minimal levels for most traded goods and the trend toward new and expanded free trade areas accelerates, the incentive for collecting accurate trade data, especially on the import side, is weakened. One wonders, for example, whether the quality of U.S.-Canada trade statistics will deteriorate as tariffs are removed on most items. The most striking example of this problem is in the European Community, where border controls are being abolished. Intra-EC trade will only be reported on a voluntary basis, after this has taken place. If U.S. experience with exports is any indication, the data obtained under this method is likely to be of very poor quality.

Contemplation of this problem, along with the severe budgetary constraints under which collectors of trade data are operating and the growing importance of other types of international transactions, suggests that we should ask whether we need the level of detail and the frequency with which data on merchandise trade are currently being reported. Few people are likely to argue with the value of monthly data on the value of total exports and imports and of major commodity-group exports and imports, although the volatility of the data suggests that they must be interpreted cautiously. But one wonders about the value of processing import data for the 14,000 import items under the Harmonized System by country of origin and customs district. The Panel on Foreign Trade Statistics is about to conduct a survey to find out how the data is used, but, on the surface, it is hard to imagine how data in such detail and frequency can be very useful to either the government or the private sector. No other economic data are reported in such detail and so frequently. Obviously, there may be some instances where very detailed data on a monthly basis are very valuable to businesses or the government, but it would seem that a special effort could be made to collect these data without collecting all the other levels of detail now available. In such cases, consideration should be given to requiring the users of the data to bear the costs of the data collection.

One suggestion that seems to have merit is to apply sampling procedures to collect monthly data on total trade and its broad components and to provide the commodity and country detail now made available on a monthly basis only on a quarterly basis. Such an approach would require a change in the law, but in view of the current budgetary tightness, it might be welcomed by the executive branch as well as by Congress. Even if the current system is retained, the use of sampling to obtain figures on total trade would greatly shorten the present six-week delay in reporting monthly figures.

Trade data by themselves may be of interest to some data consumers, but these data are not very useful for analyzing economic trends and relationships unless they are related to other economic and social data. For example, to help assess an industry's international competitive performance, it is necessary to present trade data in constant dollars and relate them to such variables as domestic output, world output, and world exports of the product. However, the dispersion of authority for collecting and integrating economic and social data, coupled with the lack of an integrated governmental view of the purposes for which data-bases are collected and related to each other, has meant that the level of detail and frequency at which various sets of U.S. economic information can be related to each other varies enormously. For example, the 10,500 7-digit import items in the old U.S. tariff schedule are grouped into about 2,500 5-digit SIC product sectors. Price deflators are available only at a much more aggregative level and, until recently, only on a quarterly basis. Production data at the 4-digit SIC level is available only on an annual basis. Input-output tables are available only every five years, and there usually is a long delay before they are published; they also have the drawback that the imports consumed by each industry are not available.

Not only are U.S. trade and related data collected by several different agencies and classified differently by these agencies, but no agency seems to have the responsibility for trying to bring the data together on a comparable basis. Furthermore, the various collecting agencies generally do not publish time series of their data. Occasionally, some agency such as the International Trade Commission or the Labor Department will pull available data together into a data-base covering a number of years and make it available to a private researcher, but usually it is up to the private researcher to construct the needed data-set or to buy it from a private firm. Those within the government have access to the computerized data-set of government data, termed COMPRO, but the various bodies of data in this set do not appear to be integrated very well. When it comes to trying to collect comparable data on an international basis, the problems are much worse, as the paper by Keith Maskus shows.

Thus, if we are to be able to understand better the various forces that shape international competitiveness and to make better policy decisions, we should begin by doing a much better job of integrating the data we already collect. Simply allocating differently the funds already available could bring about a significant improvement in the data system.

The last issue I want to consider briefly is how organizational and technological developments over the next few decades will affect the type of international transactions on which we want statistics and the optimal ways of collecting the data. One trend that is continuing, at what seems to be an accelerating pace, is the internationalization of business. More and more major producers of traded goods are jointly owned by citizens of several countries, produce a wide variety of goods and services, conduct their business in many different countries, and produce their final products with components made in several countries. The statistics on exports and imports, as now collected, do not convey much of the information policymakers and researchers wish to know about these businesses. For example, they would like to know the types, values, and sources of the various manufactured components that enter into the final value of exported and imported goods. In addition, they would like information on the foreign activities of companies controlled by U.S. citizens and domestic activities of foreign controlled companies that do not enter into the balance of payments statistics. Data are also needed on the international movements of people and technology, as well as capital, that occur in connection with the business activities of these firms.

The continuing technological improvements in electronics, telecommunications, and transportation are another development that is beginning to have profound effects on the way international transactions are conducted. These changes are further blurring the distinction between goods and services. They have already significantly increased the international mobility of financial capital, and by enabling certain types of services that flow from goods and individuals to be transferred across borders electronically, are likely to have a major impact on the way traditional international trade is conducted.

The above and other developments suggest that more and more of the information about international transactions desired by business officials, public policymakers, and researchers will have to be collected directly from firms and other economic actors. Collecting data as goods and services cross international borders is not only becoming increasingly difficult but a smaller part of the information that is desired. Consequently, shifting toward the collection of trade data by sampling techniques like those used to collect information on most other economic variables should be seriously considered. The complete enumeration of trade in goods might be reserved for those goods where the revenues from import duties are high or where quantitative import controls or national security considerations make a complete monitoring of trade necessary. Such an approach would provide the opportunity to collect more of the type of data needed for good policy making in the 1990s, to better integrate trade data and other related economic and social information, and probably to reduce present data collection costs.

Jack Bame

It has been a pleasure to participate in a conference concerned with international issues and with measurement and empirical issues. All too many "experts," both here in Washington and in academia, don't want to be burdened by data considerations or by empirical work, which are viewed as too dull and too difficult, respectively. This aversion is particularly evident when these "burdens" might not support preconceived notions or particular ideologies. So, taking my cue from a Canadian report of a few years back, *two* cheers for

Jack Bame is Consultant, Statistics Department, International Monetary Fund.

us. I have several comments on what was and was not covered here in the past two days.

First, in reference to a comment that Ed Leamer made at the August preconference meeting—he suggested that data providers color-code data in red, amber, and green, according to their "quality"—I would respond that perhaps the same might apply to research papers. In any event, it might be more productive for data users and readers of research papers to delve into the data involved and designate color codes for the data and research conclusions, respectively.

Second, it became quite apparent, from the first paper presented on through the conference, that much work remains to be done in the area of harmonizing, improving, and refining international data so that consistent comparisons can be made over time. Researchers carry the responsibility to utilize whatever data is available intelligently and innovatively (some of the best researchers are represented in this volume and have done so). One caveat: we can't expect too much too soon. Priorities must be established by both national and international data providers and users, hopefully reflecting a happy compromise between the two groups.

We must also keep in mind the fact that different sectors of the user community have quite different time horizons. For the foreign-exchange trader, thirty minutes to one hour can be long-term; *instant* data are the necessary ingredient for operations. Researchers, on the other hand, often require long and consistent time series; even ten years can be "short-term." The time horizon of policymakers lies in between the two extremes, often within the time span of whatever election cycle is involved. They provide or administer the appropriations for data providers.

Measurement problems in several specific areas are noted time and again in the papers in this volume and in work in progress that is alluded to. High on the list are computer prices (and the lack of reliable import price indexes), international services (where much has been and is being done to improve the data, especially in the United States), linkage of inputs and outputs, international classification, exchange-rate conversion (where virtually all acknowledged a huge debt to Lipsey, Kravis, Summers, et al.), and, notably, price deflators for exports and imports (which in some cases may be so questionable that current totals may be more "real" than deflated totals).

I note a lack of attention in this project—and at too many other conferences—to nondirect investment financial capital flows, emanating from what I consider to be an artificial divorce between international economic and financial transactions. Measurement and empirical research issues are discussed in depth for merchandise trade, international services, and direct investment income, capital flows, and stocks. The importance accorded current-account balance of payments components and, in the capital account, only direct investment, is in sharp contrast to the virtual nonrecognition of other financial flows and stocks, together with serious problems concerning the measurement of those items. These flows often are the dominant factor driving exchange rates and their volatility in global markets. There is an interplay between current- and capital-account developments, but the days when financial flows were considered to be merely "accommodating" to current account developments are long since gone.

In a more positive vein, I would spotlight ongoing international cooperative efforts to achieve improved data concordance and harmonization on a number of fronts. The significance of these efforts should not be ignored, especially in light of the need for better international data comparability noted in a number of the papers presented here. Together with national experts, leading international agencies, including the United Nations Statistical Office, World Bank, International Monetary Fund, Organisation for Economic Cooperation and Development, and Eurostat, have achieved substantial progress toward standardization of international services components; toward the first revision in the U.N. System of National Accounts (SNA) since 1968; and toward increased harmonization between national accounts and balance of payments accounts concepts and practices. A new harmonized system of merchandise trade statistics already is in place. Finally, preparations for a fifth edition of the IMF balance of payments manual are underway (the fourth edition was published in 1977), with one of the major objectives being to achieve increased concordance with the new SNA.

Unfortunately, along with this progress, new problems have arisen and will continue to complicate international transactions measurement issues. I will mention just two areas of concern here: merchandise trade and financial flows. First, the abolition of customs frontiers in Western Europe in 1992, although certainly a most positive development for trade, poses a question as to how trade statistics will be collected. Evidently, this problem was not addressed early on in the complicated negotiations leading to the single 1992 customs area, but hopefully it is being dealt with now. Should customs procedures at some time in the future be abolished at the U.S.-Canadian border, I am confident that, even if the United States is remiss in anticipating data collection problems, Statistics Canada will be there!

Second, as for international financial flows, the emergence of new players, innovations, and instruments—with new acronyms added to the international financial vocabulary almost daily—creates actual and potential data collection and measurement problems. Increased use of off-balance sheet vehicles and of asset securitization, together with the tailoring of securities to meet specialized needs of investors, complicates the world of reporting forms that were designed for a few basic types of securities. Some specialized financial instruments also may lead to potential reporting difficulties involving the separation of income and capital flows in recording international transactions. Nonetheless, at least some problems can be mitigated by modifications in existing reporting forms, and many new instruments can be integrated into existing or somewhat modified methodological frameworks.

As a concluding comment, I believe that this conference (and the precon-ference, where there were a few lively exchanges of ideas that resulted in enhancements to several papers) has made an important contribution to a bet-ter understanding of measurement and empirical issues in international trans-actions. The participation of those who provide data and those who use it should contribute to a more rational agenda and a better setting of priorities to help direct efforts towards improvements in data that are needed by respon-sible policymakers and researchers. And as a final suggestion, I believe that there may be significant benefits for all from increased participation by economists and others from the business community at conferences such as this one.

Ralph C. Bryant

The two days of this conference have been for me—and I suspect for almost all the participants—a productive exchange of ideas. I have attended many conferences where the fare has been tantamount to several light souffles. I departed from those occasions feeling undernourished, even though the souffles had an undeniable elegance and I had admired the prestidigitation of the chefs. At such conferences, I often found myself doubting that the papers were addressing the untidy and inelegant world as it actually exists. In con-trast, this conference has been a full-scale banquet. We have had numerous appetizers and several main courses—including the roast beef and potatoes and Brussels sprouts, and even the Yorkshire pudding. The fare has been meaty. It has suggested many valuable avenues for future research and policy analysis.

There has not been a stability condition, a vector autoregression, a unit root, or a cointegration test in sight. Nor have we greatly missed such discus-sions. I do not mean, of course, that the most advanced techniques of theory and econometrics should play no role in the analysis of the topics under study here. Rather, I interpret the bulk of the work presented at this conference as an effort to analyze the data preconditions that must be satisfied before such advanced techniques can be fruitfully applied.

The banquet has not been faultless. There appear to have been a few slip-ups in the kitchen; for my taste the Brussel sprouts were a bit overcooked, and the service for one or two of the courses was on the sluggish side. Nonethe-less, all told it has been a satisfying and nourishing repast.

Perhaps the biggest problem is the concluding panel. At the end of a fine meal, the organizers are supposed to hand around the vintage port. I fear that today you have a decided anticlimax: the appropriate metaphor may be tired

Ralph C. Bryant is a senior fellow in economic studies at The Brookings Institution.

wine (whine?) that has been open too long. Or, should we say, just a small bowl of nuts?

To be serious: the volume resulting from this conference will be a highly useful one for international economists who care about the quality of statistical data and who wish to use them for careful empirical research and policy analysis. Richard Marston remarked that economists working with the data for trade prices and costs should be forced to read the Alterman paper, especially the appendix. Other discussants made similarly favorable comments about the papers they were discussing. I feel inclined to make an analogous statement about most of the papers prepared for the conference: empirical researchers in international economics should treat the papers as required reading.

I take my hat off to the organizers for successfully arranging the conference. They deserve more than the usual credit, because it is so difficult to generate attention for these data issues. It is not popular in the economics profession to do the hard work of carefully focusing on empirical data. One sometimes hears economists maligned with the familiar slur: "An economist is someone who likes to work with numbers but doesn't have enough personality to be an accountant." But as economists, we know that such a slur is altogether inappropriate. As Richard Haas (quoting Harry Johnson) has reminded us, an economist [in these times] is someone who does *not* like to work with numbers but who is quite willing to stand up and explain what is wrong with the research of someone else who has *tried* to work with the numbers!

In his comments yesterday, Edward Leamer argued that there was a tendency in the economics profession to identify data deficiencies as a problem, perhaps even to use the data problems as an excuse, but then to carry on as before. These economists are like the preacher described by Ken Arrow, who comes to the portion of his sermon that turns on a subtle theological point. Instead of dealing with the point, he tells the congregation, "Brethren, here there is a great difficulty; let us face it firmly and pass on!" Leamer does not like that kind of bypassing. He wants to encourage a tradition in econometric work that emphasizes issues of data accuracy and that makes the data deficiencies condition the econometric procedures. His view resonates with me. To be sure, it smacks a bit of the counsel of perfection. We cannot obtain the standard error of the standard errors, as he wants us to do, until we have obtained the standard errors themselves. Nonetheless, for all of us, I believe, there is much food for thought in the theme that Leamer is emphasizing.

The portfolio capital account of the balance of payments has not received much attention in the discussion at this conference.[1] Because of that oversight, I want to put on the record here an obvious point: for the study of a

---

1. We cannot fault the organizers for this deficiency; they were not successful when trying to commission a paper on the subject.

variety of analytical questions in international economics, one needs to have much better data on the portfolio capital account than we actually have.

In principle, one would like to have a breakdown of the balance sheets of financial institutions in all the important national jurisdictions, cross-classified by currency of denomination, residence of customer, and type of customer. One certainly would need better data on cross-border security trans-actions and the corresponding stock asset and liability positions. Because off–balance sheet items are becoming increasingly important, one would need substantial information about them as well. Further, one needs systematic international compilations of these data.

The actual status falls very far short of what is desirable in principle. For many countries, significant parts of the requisite data are not collected at all. Some of the data collected by governments are not published. The statistical definitions used by countries are sometimes noncomparable (e.g., what is a "bank"?). These problems are analogous to the noncomparabilities across countries in computer price indexes mentioned in Ellen Meade's paper. The international institutions in the 1970s and 1980s have provided more compre-hensive compilations of financial data (e.g., the Bank for International Settle-ments and the International Monetary Fund for the banking data, and the World Bank for data on external debt). Even so, "concordance" problems re-main; users of the international-institution data confront many difficulties in trying to use these compilations in conjunction with the national statistical sources.[2] When we focus on international data problems and construct wish lists for improvements, therefore, let us not neglect the portfolio capital ac-count and the stocks of cross-border and cross-currency financial assets and liabilities.

Another data problem has received little discussion here. While not first-order in nature, this problem is a significant second-order issue. The govern-ment of the United States and other governments to an even greater degree possess some useful data that are not made publicly available for analysis and research. Because these data have already been assembled, no further collec-tion and processing costs would be incurred if they were made available. In several such cases, I believe, the benefits would substantially exceed the costs if the data could be made available to the public, or at least on request to those wishing to use them. The examples that come most readily to mind are three: release of further details about cross-border direct investments, so that re-searchers can incorporate these data into their work; publication of some clas-sifications in the international banking statistics that are not now made avail-able; and release of the actual daily data on exchange-market intervention conducted by monetary authorities. Sometimes (though not always!) there are

---

2. These concordance problems are analogous to the difficulties with the trade and trade-price data emphasized by Keith Maskus and Bob Lipsey.

manifest difficulties about confidentiality of the data, such as with exchange-market intervention. Yet confidentiality concerns are often exaggerated. And with such data, delayed release may be possible (e.g., with intervention data, release with a one- or two-year lag). Where confidentiality is a legitimate constraint but inhibits important research, the onus should be on governments and central banks to carry out the research themselves and to make the conclusions publicly available.

One other important point has not, in my opinion, received adequate attention at the conference. The growing economic integration of the world economy has been gradually increasing the salience of collective goods—"public goods"—with international dimensions (and, of course, collective "bads" that require international cooperation to mitigate). The traditional rationale for government is to provide collective goods that cannot be, or will not be, provided with decentralized decision making by private-sector agents. An obvious extension of this rationale, which has conventionally been applied to nations in isolation, leads to the conclusion that international institutions will have to play enhanced roles in catalyzing the requisite supply of international collective goods.[3]

The need for better data on the functioning of the world economy is a prototypical example of an international collective-goods problem. National statistical agencies, if they make decentralized noncooperative decisions, will find their individual efforts eroded by the growing importance of cross-border transactions of all types. Conceptual standardization across nations, joint design of surveys and of regular data collection procedures, the preparation of international compilations of comparable statistics—these activities, and others associated with them, become increasingly essential for correct analysis, even of an individual economy.

A significant illustration of the lack of international standardization in statistics was brought out in Ellen Meade's paper. The major countries do not follow comparable procedures when estimating price deflators for computers and other electronic office equipment. Indeed, they do not even place production, exports, and imports of such equipment in comparable categories. We know from recent investigations of the computer prices used in U.S. national income and trade data that this issue can substantially influence analytical conclusions. The lack of internationally comparable data is a serious handicap.

It is not difficult to find other examples of international collective-goods problems in available statistics. I conjecture that many others could be cited in connection with current-account transactions, for goods trade and, perhaps

---

3. I have elaborated on this general theme elsewhere, in *Money and Monetary Policy in Interdependent Nations* (Washington, D.C.: The Brookings Institution, 1980) and *International Financial Intermediation* (Washington, D.C.: The Brookings Institution, 1987).

even more prevalent, for statistics on services and investment income. I know that examples can readily be found in the data on banking assets and liabilities and on securities transactions.

I mentioned earlier the need for improvement in the published international compilations of data on capital flows and asset stocks. The point has a more general applicability. Over time, governments and analysts will have to rely still more heavily on the compilations of data assembled and published by international organizations such as the IMF, World Bank, BIS, and OECD. We should be able to look to these organizations for intellectual and administrative leadership on the data issues. Rather than waiting for their marching orders from national governments, the staffs of the international organizations should be initiating suggestions for data improvements and doing what they can to promote evolutionary progress.

Someone at the conference mentioned to me an example of possible leadership that struck me as constructive. Suppose the IMF staff were to include in *International Financial Statistics* some of the purchasing power parity indexes that have emerged from the ICP program?[4] This ready availability of the indexes could help to promote a wider understanding of country comparison issues (and would probably reach many more individuals than could be reached by circulation of the data on computer diskettes, as Robert Summers suggested).

Several times at the conference I found myself asking whether the economics profession is better off than it was a decade ago with respect to the data issues we have been discussing. On the whole, I am coming away from the conference with an upbeat impression. Lots of evidence about improvement has emerged at the conference. The national statistics for the United States have progressed in a variety of ways. The Maskus and Walter papers, those identifying many remaining problems, recorded significant improvements in the trade data. Jack Triplett observed that the Maskus view might not be optimistic enough. The Alterman paper documents many improvements in the data for prices and cost of trade. Just think of how much better off we are today, in being able to use the BLS trade-price indexes, than we were when we were forced to use only the unit-value data! Whichard's paper shows that the data for cross-border service transactions are substantially improved. The ICP project has continued to make progress. A panel to review international economic statistics was appointed in 1989 under the auspices of the National Academy of Sciences. The Council of Economic Advisers under Michael Boskin's leadership has established a working group on statistics.

One can also cite evidence that intergovernmental cooperation on statistics has made progress. The collaboration between Canada and the United States on the trade data has gone very far. Jack Bame indicates that intergovernmen-

---

4. IMF would not, of course, endorse the estimates as correct, but merely publish them and refer readers to ICP sources for further details and discussion.

tal consultations on services data are making headway. BIS and IMF have substantially expanded and strengthened their compilations of the data on cross-border banking. The IMF staff's recent report on the global discrepancy in current accounts is a valuable document.[5] Among other contributions, its appendixes contain informative compilations of the international banking data and the associated flows of interest payments and receipts. I have been told that there are even signs of a new innovative and aggressive spirit at IMF's Bureau of Statistics.

Notwithstanding all the progress, much remains to be done. On the first day of the conference, I started to make a list of important gaps in the data. But during the course of our discussions on this second day, I gave up the task as too lengthy and difficult. If an analyst is inclined to be discouraged about the quality and availability of data, there are ample stimuli! Richard Marston did not have his puzzle about the BLS price series resolved. Catherine Mann rightly remains dissatisfied with the data on the terms of trade between manufacturing and primary commodities. No one is comfortable with the measures we have for the stocks of physical capital, in particular the comparability of the measures across countries. The large statistical discrepancies in the national balance of payments accounts of the United States and several other major countries are flashing neon advertisements of what we do not know. One can get still worse headaches thinking about the statistical discrepancies in world accounting identities (on the order of $40 billion per year for trade and some $90 billion for services and investment income).

Are enough resources allocated to the collection, evaluation, and publication of data? Should governments and international organizations allocate still more to remedy the gaps in the data? I have not thought systematically about this question, but will nonetheless venture my prejudices.

It is probably true, I conjecture, that it is more difficult to identify the benefits of public expenditure on collection and publication of data than it is to identify the benefits of most other types of public expenditure. It is true that we need to guard against collecting data that are not beneficial and not much used. Robert Lipsey, Samuel Pizer, and others at the conference noted correctly that the collection of international trade data by state would probably be an example; such data could easily pander to the worst instincts of state mercantilism. The National Trade Data Bank could be a low-priority use of resources; I am poorly informed about this effort, but inclined to be skeptical about it. Robert Baldwin spoke eloquently about the excessive disaggregated detail that characterizes the trade data of the United States and many other countries. The old Mae West axiom, "Too much of a good thing can be wonderful!" is not an appropriate motto for statistical agencies.

Better data collection by itself, moreover, is not enough. We should bear in

5. International Monetary Fund, *Report on the World Current Account Discrepancy* (Washington, D.C., September 1989).

mind the wise comments of Alan Deardorff and Koichi Hamada that we need better theory, too—and better interaction between the theorists and the empirical researchers. Nor does the economics profession always utilize well the data it does have. The ICP data, for example, does not receive widespread use despite what appears to be a professional consensus about its importance.

Nonetheless, on balance is is my prejudice that data problems do tend to get short shrift in this world. Not only do economists pay inadequate attention, but governments tend to skimp on the budgetary resources that support statistics collection and publication. Conjure up in your mind the waste and abuse in the defense budget, or in subsidies to the Rural Electrification Administration or sugar growers, and on and on. Any waste or excess in statistical programs seems very small indeed in relation to these other misallocations. Given the gaps in the data and given the difficulty of identifying the diffused benefits associated with high quality data, therefore, my prejudice is that societies ought to be wiling to allocate modestly larger amounts of resources to the collection, improvement, and evaluation of statistics. This prejudice of mine is probably shared by many of those who attended this conference. (I say probably, because this theme was only implicit in most of the discussion.)

The preceding general thought leads me to raise the specific issue of whether the public sector in the United States is currently giving adequate attention and budgetary support to economic statistics. This is a question with delicate political aspects, but too important to leave unmentioned at this conference.

Attention and leadership from the executive branch of the U.S. government is crucial for a vigorous and effective national statistical program. For most of the last decade, I have felt rather discouraged about the incumbent administration's attitudes. I did not feel similarly discouraged in the 1960s and 1970s. In the 1960s as I remember them, the Office of Statistical Standards in the Bureau of the Budget had substantial clout. There was strong support for efforts such as the Bernstein Review Committee on the balance of payments statistics. The administration gave explicit backing to efforts to improve data. This favorable climate seems to me to have waned during the 1980s. In recent years, scrutiny of statistical programs by the Office of Management and Budget has primarily emphasized the costs and burdens, not the potential benefits. Some statistical efforts have been starved for budget resources. Long delays have occurred in the release of some data (e.g., the 1984 survey of portfolio assets held in the United States by foreign residents). In the midst of this relatively unfavorable climate in the 1980s, the staffs of the statistical agencies themselves have been doing fine work with their limited resources. From my perspective, many individuals in agencies such as the Bureau of Economic Analysis, the Bureau of Labor Statistics, and the Bureau of the Census deserve high praise.

Have things changed for the better in 1989? Some hopeful signs can be gleaned from statements by officials in the Bush administration. I am thinking in particular of the emphasis Michael Boskin has placed on the working group on statistics that he chairs and of references to the Cabinet Council report that it is hoped will shortly be approved by the President. Perhaps OMB will no longer pay such exclusive attention to the "burdens" of statistical reporting.

What about the role of the Congress in supporting statistical programs? If things have not gone well in the 1980s, one cannot blame the Congress as much as the executive branch. But there is ample blame for Congress, too. Most Congressmen cannot seem to focus on the statistical programs either in good or bad times. And Congress at times has managed to make things worse than they would otherwise be (recall the unfortunate practice, now abandoned, of requiring that the data for imports c.i.f. be emphasized in the monthly trade release several days prior to the release of the f.o.b. data). The attention given in the Congress to the statistical programs reminds me of an old Asian proverb: When the elephants fight, the grass gets trampled; when the elephants make love, the grass also gets trampled. I am unsure what could be done to improve Congressional awareness of the statistical programs and their importance. One idea I heard mentioned plaintively at the conference is a revival of the role played in earlier times by the Joint Economic Committee.

In any event, we need more active leadership and a more far-sighted perspective on statistical issues, especially from the executive but also from the legislative branch of the U.S. government. The international collective-goods aspects of statistical issues also require better leadership from the U.S. government. The international institutions should show more initiative themselves but cannot make good progress without complementary leadership from the major countries' governments.

All of us here no doubt welcome the improved rhetoric from the Bush administration about the U.S. statistical programs. We want to believe what we have heard in the recent statements. But the proof has to come in actions that are strongly supportive of improvement efforts by the agencies that have to do the work. Getting the rhetoric right is not enough.

Contributors

William Alterman
Division of International Prices
Bureau of Labor Statistics
Building BC, Room 3302
U.S. Department of Labor
600 E Street, NW
Washington, DC 20212

Bernard Ascher
Service Industry Affairs
Office of the U.S. Trade Representative
600 17th Street, NW, Room 407
Washington, DC 20508

Robert E. Baldwin
Social Science Building
Department of Economics
University of Wisconsin
1180 Observatory Drive, Room 6462
Madison, WI 53706

Jack Bame
Bureau of Statistics
International Monetary Fund
700 19th Street, NW
Washington, DC 20431

Betty L. Barker
International Investment Division
   (BE-50)
Bureau of Economic Analysis
U.S. Department of Commerce
14th and Constitution, NW
Washington, DC 20230

Ralph C. Bryant
The Brookings Institution
1775 Masachusetts Avenue, NW
Washington, DC 20036

Alan Chung
Department of Economics
University of British Columbia
997–1873 East Mall
Vancouver, BC V6T 1Y2
Canada

Alan V. Deardorff
Institute of Public Policy Studies
440 Lorch Hall
University of Michigan
Ann Arbor, MI 48109–1220

Barry Eichengreen
Department of Economics
University of California
787 Evans Hall
Berkeley, CA 94720

Edward M. Graham
Institute for International Economics
11 DuPont Circle, NW
Washington, DC 20036

Harry Grubert
Office of Tax Analysis
U.S. Treasury Department
15th and Pennsylvania Avenue, NW
Room 5121, Main Treasury
Washington, DC 20220

Richard D. Haas
Economic Research Department
International Monetary Fund
19th and H Streets, NW
Washington, DC 20431

John F. Helliwell
Department of Economics
University of British Columbia
997–1873 East Mall
Vancouver, BC V6T 1W5
Canada

Bernard M. Hoekman
General Agreement on Tariffs and Trade
Centre William Rappard
154 rue de Lausanne
1211 Geneva 21, Switzerland

Peter Hooper
Division of International Finance
Stop 42
Board of Governors of the Federal
   Reserve System
Washington, DC 20551

David J. Klock
U.S. Treasury Department
15th and Pennsylvania Avenue, N.W.
Room 5450, Main Treasury
Washington, DC 20220

Irving B. Kravis
Department of Economics
McNeil Building
University of Pennsylvania
3718 Locust Walk
Philadelphia, PA 19104–6797

Robert Z. Lawrence
The Brookings Institution
1775 Massachusetts Avenue, NW
Washington, DC 20036

Edward E. Leamer
Department of Economics, EC-01
University of California
405 Hilgard Avenue
Los Angeles, CA 90024–1447

Robert E. Lipsey
National Bureau of Economic Research
269 Mercer Street, 8th floor
New York, NY 10003

Catherine L. Mann
Division of International Finance
Stop 23
Board of Governors of the Federal
   Reserve System
Washington, DC 20551

Richard C. Marston
Department of Finance
Wharton School of Management
University of Pennsylvania
2300 Steinberg-Dietrich Hall
Philadelphia, PA 19104–6367

Keith E. Maskus
Department of Economics
University of Colorado
Campus Box 256
Boulder, CO 80309–0256

Ellen E. Meade
Division of International Finance
Stop 42
Board of Governors of the Federal
   Reserve System
Washington, DC 20551

Lawrence Mishel
Economic Policy Institute
1730 Rhode Island Avenue, NW
Suite 812
Washington, DC 20036

Linda Molinari
Customer Services, ISMD Division
LEGENT Corporation
8615 Westwood Center Drive
Vienna, VA 22182–2218

John Mutti
Department of Economics
Grinnell College
P.O. Box 805A-6
Grinnell, IA 50112–0806

Samuel Pizer
Bureau of Statistics
International Monetary Fund
700 19th Street, NW
Washington, DC 20431

J. David Richardson
Department of Economics
Maxwell School of Citizenship and
    Public Affairs
Syracuse University
Syracuse, NY 13244

Lois E. Stekler
Division of International Finance
Stop 42
Board of Governors of the Federal
    Reserve System
Washington, DC 20551

Robert M. Stern
Institute of Public Policy Studies
440 Lorch Hall
The University of Michigan
611 Tappan Street
Ann Arbor, MI 48109–1220

Guy V. G. Stevens
Division of International Finance
Stop 42
Board of Governors of the Federal
    Reserve System
Washington, DC 20551

Bruce C. Walter
Foreign Trade Division
Bureau of the Census
Federal Office Building, No. 3,
    Room 2003
Washington, DC 20233

Obie G. Whichard
International Investment Division
    (BE-50)
Bureau of Economic Analysis
U.S. Department of Commerce
14th and Constitution, NW
Washington, DC 20230

Author Index

Aanestad, James M., 232
Abramovitz, Moses, 390nn5,6
Adams, F. Gerard, 246
Ahmad, Sultan, 451
Allen, R. G. D., 115n6
Alterman, William, 128nn11
Angermann, Oswald, 164
Ascher, Bernard, 210n10, 217n17, 218n20, 248n8
Auerbach, Alan, 298, 300, 316n18

Baily, Martin Neil, 65, 359, 368, 377, 392, 410
Baldwin, Robert E., 20, 112, 145n2
Barro, Robert J., 399n18
Baumol, William, 21, 27, 37, 240n4, 390
Beckerman, Wilfred, 452
Bergsten, C. Fred, 335n23
Bhagwati, Jagdish, 206n3, 219, 238, 453, 456n19
Blades, D., 391n9
Blomstrom, Magnus, 335n23
Boadway, Robin, 298
Bombach, G., 438n3
Boskin, Michael, 293
Bowen, H. P. 19, 20n1, 470n2
Branson, W. H., 20
Brecher, R. A., 20n1
Bruce, Neil, 298
Bruno, M., 399
Bryant, Ralph C., 479n3
Bushe, Dennis M., 149n4, 160n7, 161
Business International, 273

Cartwright, David W., 62, 166
Catron, Brian, 114n5
Caves, Richard E., 338n29, 340n32, 344–45
Chan, Kenneth, 241
Chenery, H., 20, 391n8
Choudri, E. U., 20
Chung, Alan, 391n8, 392n13, 395n16, 399, 433
Clague, C. K., 28n10, 40n16, 453
Cole, Rosanne, 1, 62–64
Congressional Economic Leadership Institute, 325n8, 327
Corbo, Vittorio, 339, 340n32
Courtney, W. H., 328n12, 340
Crouhy, Michael, 166
Crouhy-Veyrac, Liliane, 166
CTC Reporter, 271
Cutler, Frederick, 210n9
Czinkota, Michael R., 325, 347n44

Davidson, R., 403, 405
Deardorff, A. V., 19, 43
De Leeuw, Frank, 11
De Long, J. B., 21, 390
Denison, Edward F., 65, 359, 378, 381n1, 382
Dewald, William G., 329
Dollar, D., 21, 27, 37, 389n2
Dornbusch, Rudiger, 112, 145n2
Dreschler, L., 238n1, 248n8, 441, 449
Duchin, Faye, 246
Dulberger, Ellen, 62–64
Dunning, John H., 323n2, 344
Dutka, Anna, 247

489

Subject Index